Critics, Compilers, and Commentators

Critics, Compilers, and Commentators

An Introduction to Roman Philology, 200 BCE–800 CE

JAMES E. G. ZETZEL

OXFORD UNIVERSITY PRESS

OXFORD
UNIVERSITY PRESS

Oxford University Press is a department of the University of Oxford. It furthers the University's objective of excellence in research, scholarship, and education by publishing worldwide. Oxford is a registered trade mark of Oxford University Press in the UK and certain other countries.

Published in the United States of America by Oxford University Press
198 Madison Avenue, New York, NY 10016, United States of America.

Library of Congress Cataloging-in-Publication Data
Names: Zetzel, James E. G., author.
Title: Critics, compilers, and commentators : an introduction to Roman philology, 200 BCE–800 CE / James E. G. Zetzel.
Description: New York : Oxford University Press, 2018. |
Includes bibliographical references and index.
Identifiers: LCCN 2017049788 (print) | LCCN 2017056725 (ebook) |
ISBN 9780199701513 (updf) | ISBN 9780190878887 (epub) | ISBN 9780195380514 (cloth : alk. paper) | ISBN 9780195380521 (pbk. : alk. paper)
Subjects: LCSH: Latin language—Study and teaching—Rome—History. | Latin language—Study and teaching—Rome—Bibliography. | Classical philology—Study and teaching—Rome—History. | Rome—Intellectual life.
Classification: LCC PA2043 (ebook) | LCC PA2043 .Z48 2017 (print) |
DDC 470.71/037—dc23
LC record available at https://lccn.loc.gov/2017049788

1 3 5 7 9 8 6 4 2

Paperback printed by Webcom, Inc., Canada
Hardback printed by Bridgeport National Bindery, Inc., United States of America

For Katharina

quod spiro et placeo, si placeo, tuum est

A cloud of critics, of compilers, of commentators darkened the face of learning, and the decline of genius was soon followed by the corruption of taste.

Edward Gibbon

Preface

When it was first suggested to me ten years ago that I write a book on Roman scholarship to complement Eleanor Dickey's *Ancient Greek Scholarship*, I naively thought that (since I have been studying these texts off and on since 1970 and since I had an excellent model) it would not be that difficult to renew my acquaintance with familiar material and set it out in a comparable manner. I was wrong. I rapidly discovered not only that the shape of Roman scholarship and the difficulties needing explanation required a different presentation from Dickey's, but also that the field has changed so radically since about 1980 that my previous familiarity was of very little use. The length of time it has taken to produce this volume is at least in part because I had a great deal to (re)learn, and after ten years I certainly do not think that I have produced the last word or anything resembling a complete account of Roman philology. That is partly because of my own limitations, but partly (I hope, in large part) because scholarship about ancient scholarship is now so vigorous and so prolific. I have read and learned much more than I thought possible, but every day there is more, and I hope the reader will remember that what I offer here is a report on others' work in progress. To be precise: I hope to have included all appropriate references up to 2016, and the last additions to the bibliography were made in November 2017. I also do not aim at anything like a complete bibliography: I cite editions and translations of texts as completely as I can, but I have limited secondary literature to major treatments and works that may be useful to those wanting to understand what these texts are. I have tried to be relatively expansive in discussing areas and texts that I believe important, unfamiliar, or difficult to grasp, and fairly succinct with material that is uncomplicated. I will repeat these reminders of the limitations of this book from time to time: they are very real.

When I published my dissertation on Roman textual criticism in 1981, using many of the texts discussed in this volume, scholarship about Roman scholarship was largely quiescent: study of the grammarians flourished in the second half of the nineteenth century and the first years of the twentieth, but study of grammars themselves subsided after Karl Barwick's great book on Remmius Palaemon in 1922; editions of glossaries ended in the 1930s; serious editions of ancient commentaries largely stopped with Paul Wessner's edition of the Juvenal scholia in 1931 and any desire to work on them was put to rest by Eduard

Fraenkel's review of the Harvard Servius in 1947. The debt of all students of Roman scholarship to Wessner and Barwick—and indeed to the whole school of Friedrich Ritschl and his academic descendants—is immense. Beginning in the early 1980s, however, the subject came to life in new and different ways and has continued to flourish. And while it would be redundant to recite here the names of the many scholars whose recent work will be cited often below, I cannot offer a list of acknowledgments without expressing my huge debt to the published work of six scholars in particular, without which this book, and the field, would be immeasurably poorer: Marc Baratin's work on syntax in the grammarians and on grammarians' ideas about language in general; Mario De Nonno's many articles on the manuscripts and the organization of Roman scholarship; Carlotta Dionisotti's studies of the creation and history of glossaries; Louis Holtz's explorations of Donatus and his commentators; Robert Kaster's investigations of the social and intellectual world of ancient scholarship; and Vivien Law's revelations of the complicated history of early medieval grammar. I have gone back repeatedly to their work, for which my admiration only increases with prolonged acquaintance. I am lucky to have been able to learn from them.

I have, over the past few years, incurred other, more personal and immediate debts. I am grateful to those generous scholars who have sent me copies of their work; I can not name them all, but I am particularly grateful to Michael Herren and Rolando Ferri for instruction in areas unfamiliar to me, and to Tommaso Mari and Anna Reinikka for giving me copies of their dissertations, excellent editions of grammatical texts which I hope will see print very soon. I am grateful also for having had the chance to present parts of this work to audiences at the Universities of Edinburgh, Oxford, and Pisa, as well as to the Seminar in Classical Civilizations at Columbia.

Four institutions have also made it possible to complete this book. First is Oxford University Press in the person of Stefan Vranka, who has put up with delays and uncertainties, and who was willing to ransom this project from the former American Philological Association which had originally commissioned it; I greatly appreciate his confidence. Second is the Columbia University Library, in particular the Interlibrary Loan Office, which has supplied countless books and articles that were otherwise not readily available. Third is the Stanwood Cockey Lodge Foundation of Columbia University, which awarded me a generous subvention towards the cost of publication. And finally, the Wissenschaftskolleg zu Berlin, where I have spent wonderful months as the spouse of a Fellow while revising and completing this book, and whose librarians have been as generous and helpful as anyone who knows that remarkable institution would expect.

I have had more than a little help from my friends. Bob Kaster and Gareth Williams firmly but gently pointed out confusions and errors in an earlier draft of Part I, as they have done for much of what I have written for a great many years. Alessandro Garcea and Bob Kaster (again!) read the completed manuscript for Oxford University Press and offered detailed and helpful suggestions. Readers of this book may not recognize how much they owe to such generous learning; I do. Many errors, I am sure, remain, but they are all mine.

Finally, the dedication of this book expresses my debt and devotion to Katharina Volk: she has read it, lived with it, and improved it almost as much as she has improved my life.

November 20, 2017

Contents

Abbreviations

AH	*Anecdota Helvetica* (*Grammatici Latini* Vol. 8), ed. H. Hagen (Leipzig, 1870) [www.hathitrust.org]
BNP	Brill's New Pauly (referenceworks.brillonline.com/browse/brill-s-new-pauly)
CGL	*Corpus Grammaticorum Latinorum* (kaali.linguist.jussieu.fr/CGL/index.jsp)
CGlL	*Corpus Glossariorum Latinorum*, 7 vols., edited by G. Goetz [with others] (Leipzig, 1888–1923) [vols. 1–6 www.hathitrust.org]
CLA	E. A. Lowe, *Codices Latini Antiquiores* (Oxford, 1934–71)
EV	*Enciclopedia virgiliana* (Rome, 1984–91)
FRHist	*The Fragments of the Roman Historians*, ed. T. J. Cornell [with others] (Oxford, 2013)
GD	Grammatici disiecti (http://gradis.hypotheses.org/)
GL	H. Keil, ed., *Grammatici Latini*, 7 vols. (Leipzig 1857–80) [www.hathitrust.org]
GlL	*Glossaria Latina*, 5 vols., edited by W. M. Lindsay [with others] (Paris, 1926–31)
GRF	H. Funaioli, ed., *Grammaticae Romanae Fragmenta* (Leipzig, 1907) [www.hathitrust.org]
GRFM	A. Mazzarino, ed., *Grammaticae romanae fragmenta aetatis Caesareae* (Turin, 1955)
HLL	*Handbuch der lateinischen Literatur der Antike* Vol. 1 (ed. R. Herzog and P. L. Schmidt); Vol. 4 (ed. K. Sallmann); Vol. 5 (ed. R. Herzog) (Munich, 1989–2002)
KfH	B. Bischoff, *Katalog der festländischen Handschriften der neunten Jahrhunderts (mit Ausnahme der wisigotischen)* (Wiesbaden, 1998–2014)
LDAB	Leuven Database of Ancient Books (www.trismegistos.org/ldab/)
LG	*Lexicon Grammaticorum: Who's Who in the History of World Linguistics*, ed. H. Stammerjohann (ed. 2, Tübingen, 2009)
MDZ	Münchener DigitalizierungsZentrum, Bayerische Staatsbibliothek (http://www.digitale-sammlungen.de/)

PIR[2]	E. Groag, A. Stein, et al., eds., *Prosopographia Imperii Romani saec. I. II. III.* (Berlin, 1933–2015)
PL	J. P. Migne, *Patrologiae cursus completus: series Latina* (Paris, 1844–1902) [patristica.net/latina (and elsewhere)]
PLRE	A. H. M. Jones, J. R. Martindale, and J. Morris, eds., *The Prosopography of the Later Roman Empire* (Cambridge, 1971–92)
RE	G. Wissowa et al., *Paulys Realencyclopädie der classischen Altertumswissenschaft* (Stuttgart, 1893–1978)
RLAC	T. Klauser et al., *Reallexikon für Antike und Christentum* (Stuttgart, 1950–)
RLM	C. [K.] Halm, ed., *Rhetores Latini Minores* (Leipzig, 1863) [www.hathitrust.org]
S–H	M. Schanz, *Geschichte der Römischen Literatur*, revised by C. Hosius (vols. 1–2, ed. 4; vols. 3, ed. 3; vol. 4.1, ed. 2; vol. 4.2, ed. 1; Munich 1914–35)
Teuffel	W. Kroll and F. Skutsch, eds., *W. S. Teuffels Geschichte der römischen Literatur* (vol. 1, ed. 6; vol. 2, ed. 7; vol. 3, ed. 6; Leipzig, 1913–20) [www.hathitrust.org]
T&T	L. D. Reynolds, ed., *Texts and Transmission: A Survey of the Latin Classics* (Oxford, 1983)

Unless otherwise noted, all quotations from grammatical fragments are cited from *GRF* and *GRFM*; and with a few exceptions where more modern editions are significantly different (notably Caesius Bassus, Charisius, and Marius Victorinus), for ease of reference all quotations from extant grammarians are cited from *GL* even when newer and better editions are available (and listed in Part II). All references to manuscripts use a brief form of identification; fuller information is given in the List of Works Cited. Unless otherwise noted, all translations are my own.

Part I: A Short History of Roman Scholarship

1

The Face of Learning

1. SCHOLARSHIP AND PHILOLOGY

To define the content of this book is not easy: the texts that are its subject do not all belong to the same kind or genre, and it is by no means clear that the word "text" can even usefully describe some of the writings I am treating. At the same time, however, every work to be discussed falls under one broad rubric: they all aim to explain something about Latin texts or the Latin language; they are all, in some sense, aids to readers. No one ancient or modern term fits all these works: Eleanor Dickey, in her book on the comparable Greek materials, decided on "scholarship"; but as she recognized, the ancient activities that would fall under a modern definition of that word extend well beyond engagement with words and texts. The closest term is "philology": the set of disciplines and interests involved in preserving and explaining texts, in this case, texts written in Latin. It has been succinctly defined by Sheldon Pollock as "the discipline of making sense of texts."[1]

Pollock's definition is not the only one, although it may be the briefest. The work that is in some ways the ancestor of this book, August Gräfenhan's four-volume *Geschichte der klassischen Philologie im Alterthum*, published between 1843 and 1850, begins with a daunting definition of philology (1843–50: 1.2):

> Man kann daher sagen, dass jedes Raisonnement über einen Gedanken, über seine Wahrheit oder Unwahrheit, über die Richtigkeit oder Unrichtigkeit seiner sprachlichen Form, über seine autorische Aechtheit oder Unächtheit u.s.w. ein philologischer Akt zu nennen sei.

> Thus one can say that every act of reasoning about a thought, about its truth or falsehood, about the correctness or incorrectness of its verbal form, about its authorial genuineness or misattribution, etc. should be called a philological act.

1. Dickey (2007: 7); Pollock (2015: 22). See also Zetzel (2015) for an attempt to define the role of philology in Rome.

He goes on to divide philology into four parts, which he labels Grammar, Exegesis, Criticism, and Erudition.

Although Gräfenhan's work is still valuable, his idea of philology is not what is employed here: it is a tool not so much for studying texts as for studying everything that is embedded in them, in an attempt to explain the entire mental life of a people. As a result, his four subdivisions of philology rise up from morphology and syntax, through commentary and criticism (itself moving up a ladder from textual criticism to Higher Criticism) to reach the highest level, erudition (which incorporates the study of writings about religion, law, geography, and history), inexorably leading the student towards a broader understanding of civilization and culture. This ambitious understanding of philology as *Kultur* is very much of its time; and while it is theoretically not unreasonable, it is, and always has been, unmanageable in practice. Philology in Gräfenhan's sense would comprise not only the basic aids to reading and interpreting Latin literature, but, in addition to all the branches of written erudition, it would, for most scholars, now include most of Latin literature itself—a literature marked by its self-referential intertextuality and by the prevalence of implicit commentary on or revision of earlier literature. In that sense, to write a history of Roman philology would demand writing a history of Roman literature as well as of Roman culture. Those are certainly worthwhile projects, but they are not mine: there is quite enough philological writing in a narrower sense—works that explicitly attempt to explain the Latin language or particular Latin texts, and works that describe and illuminate the activities involved in that kind of explanation—for more than one book. And the anatomy of philology underlying this book is, for the most part, formal rather than theoretical: my goal is to explain the frequently unfamiliar texts that embody specifically philological activity, not the ideas about language that they reveal.

A large and austere body of such scholarship about language and literature in Latin survives, largely in the shape it was given in late antiquity. The seven volumes of Heinrich Keil's *Grammatici Latini*; the bulky commentaries on Virgil transmitted under the names of Servius and Tiberius Claudius Donatus; the numerous smaller commentaries on Virgil, Horace, Lucan, Persius, Juvenal, Cicero, and others, not to mention the many commentaries on the grammar of Aelius Donatus composed between the fifth and ninth centuries; the two large corpora of glossaries edited by Goetz and Lindsay, respectively; the dictionaries of Festus and Nonius Marcellus and the encyclopedia of Isidore of Seville—all these, and more, appear to most students of the classical Roman world as an unwieldy and forbidding class of texts defined by being even more unappealing than they are useful. At the same time, however, all students of Latin literature, particularly of republican and Augustan literature, recognize how much we benefit from the survival of such works. Most of what we have of early Latin literature is preserved by later Roman philological scholarship: most of the fragments of Varro come from the dictionary of Nonius Marcellus; large numbers of quotations from early epic and drama come from the longer form of Servius' commentary on Virgil. To take what is perhaps an extreme example, the eighth-century grammatical texts of Malsachanus and *Anonymus ad Cuimnanum* include quotations from early Latin poetry that are otherwise unknown. They may have come from a fuller text of the grammarian Diomedes than we have—or they may derive from a source of which we otherwise know nothing.[2] Beyond the preservation of important remains of Latin literature, moreover, the philological tradition provides much of what we know about how the Romans thought about their own language, both its origins and its structure. What is more, the commentaries of Servius and others not only are valuable guides to how Romans read Virgil, but offer useful assistance to modern readers as well.

While we are all indebted to these texts for a surprising amount of information about Roman intellectual culture, few modern scholars spend much time on them: for the most part we use them indirectly, at one or two removes. As primary sources for the Roman world, however, they need to be understood, if not enjoyed. The main goal of this book is to provide an introduction to these materials: to identify them—who the authors are, what texts survive—and to assist students of Roman antiquity and its reception in finding and using them. To that end, this book falls into two parts: the first is a history and description of Roman philology and our sources for it; the second is a bio-bibliographical guide to the surviving texts, divided crudely into three formal categories: grammars, commentaries, and lexica. Indices and a general bibliography will, I hope, make a somewhat unwieldy structure reasonably accessible.

2. THE FORMS OF LEARNING

The types of text described in the previous paragraphs need further definition. By *grammar* I mean works that explain all or part of the morphology and/or syntax of the Latin language, as their authors understood it, including such topics as metrics and orthography. Such texts range from brief introductions to the parts of speech or the standard paradigms of various classes of nouns and verbs, to treatises on particular problems, such as how to know when to use "b" and when to use "v"—a real difficulty for some Latin speakers in late antiquity—to comprehensive grammars, of which the most expansive is the huge *Ars* of Priscian, composed in Constantinople in the sixth century CE (and preserved, all or in part, in more than five hundred manuscripts).

By *commentary* I mean works written to explain a particular text, following the order of that text; these again range in size and scope from the comprehensive commentary on Virgil by Servius, to the much earlier, strictly historical commentary on Cicero's speeches by Asconius, to rhetorical or allegorical or mythological commentaries, to simple exegesis and grammatical explanation. As they vary in scope, moreover, so they vary in form: some ancient commentaries (Tiberius Claudius Donatus' commentary on the *Aeneid*, for instance) seem to survive

2. The source of these quotations is much discussed and still uncertain; for a very good discussion, see Taeger (1991) and 13.33 below.

in their original shape, while others (such as Aelius Donatus' commentary on Terence) have been seriously abridged and badly distorted in the process of transmission. Some exist as independent texts, others in a much-reduced form as marginal scholia. As a result, it is often hard to define just what it is we have, and how the extant texts relate to what must once have existed.

Lexica—both dictionaries in the modern sense and encyclopedias with some broader form of organization—are the third basic form, lists of words or names, sometimes divided by subject, sometimes simply alphabetical, that offer explanations of words, objects, places, or events. These range from the small scale of the *glossaries*, lists of words accompanied by a short definition or synonym, to the large-scale encyclopedias of Festus (*De verborum significatu*), Nonius Marcellus (*De compendiosa doctrina*), and Isidore (*Etymologiae*), which contain quotations, references to previous scholars, and extensive discussions of meaning or historical context.

There is a fourth category, which might be described as "works of antiquarian erudition" (or more bluntly as "none of the above"; not as all-encompassing as the erudition described by Gräfenhan) and which overlaps with the others: works such as Aulus Gellius' *Noctes Atticae*, Martianus Capella's *Marriage of Mercury and Philology*, Macrobius' *Saturnalia*, and a few others contain learned scholarly discussions which are themselves meant as works of literature rather than as handbooks, commentaries, grammars, or other guides to reading. I have uneasily included most of these under the categories to which they are most relevant: the *Saturnalia* with commentaries on Virgil, Martianus with grammars. Aulus Gellius fits nowhere and everywhere; and since the *Noctes Atticae* is not simply a source or example of Roman philology but a major work of Latin literature that is readily accessible, I have not included Gellius among the grammarians, but have given some bibliography in the footnotes to my discussion of him in Chapter 5.

The borders of this book are as amorphous as some of my categories. As indicated above, defining precisely any aspect of this topic is difficult, and that very difficulty is part of the subject and part of the history of Roman philology. One aspect is the apparently simple issue of defining a text and attaching it to a particular author. For certain texts in each of the areas described above, this is as straightforward as for a modern book protected by copyright: the *Ars minor* and *Ars maior* that are transmitted under the name of Aelius Donatus were recognized as coherent and stable texts, much as they are in modern editions, from the fourth century on; the author is well known as *grammaticus urbis Romae* in the 350s and as the teacher of St. Jerome. But as his text of grammar became the canonical teaching textbook for some centuries, it was revised by individual teachers and amassed around itself a large number of exegetical works, some of which can easily be distinguished as commentaries on Donatus' text, but others, such as the grammar of Malsachanus, attain a shape and order that mark them as independent works. There are relatively few manuscripts of unadulterated Donatus: many of them interweave passages from other sources to supplement Donatus' brief and highly analytic accounts of grammar. What is more, many of the late antique grammatical texts we now read as independent works in separate editions were preserved not alone, but in groups: it was customary to combine a school grammar with a treatise on orthography or one on metrics, an analytic grammar like that of Donatus with a set of paradigms like the *Catholica* of Probus. These texts exist *both* as independent and coherent works, as they appear in Keil's edition, *and* as parts of larger collections: the reception, at least up to the fifteenth century and the invention of printing, is in fact part of the text. This story is part of the topic of my final chapter: the survival and reception of philological writings as independent texts and as parts of a larger whole.

What is true of the texts of grammar is even more true for commentaries: modern editions often mix together the marginalia of several different manuscripts as if they were fragmented parts of a shattered original. The problem of the two versions of Servius (the so-called Vulgate and the extended text known as Servius Auctus, Servius Danielis, or DS) is well known, but the problem of reconstructing an original—or determining if there ever was a single original, or how close it was to what now survives—is even more apparent in the commentaries on Horace or Persius or Lucan. The same applies to dictionaries: the great and fragmentary third-century *De verborum significatu* of Pompeius Festus is partly preserved only in the ninth-century abridgment of Paul the Deacon, and is itself the abridgment of the first-century BCE encyclopedia of Verrius Flaccus. All these texts were not merely read, but used—annotated, altered, and revised over centuries. In writing the history of Roman philology, one must write backward as well as forward, retracing the paths the text has taken back to its sources in antiquity, while also following the path of scholarship from its origins to its fullest development in the fourth and fifth centuries CE. Explaining Roman scholarship requires discussing not merely authors and texts, but also specific manuscripts that preserve and adapt ancient material. Many of these books are now readily accessible in digitized form, and my index of manuscripts identifies their homes on the Internet as well as the libraries in which the physical objects reside.

3. GRAMMARIANS AND GRAMMARS

"Grammar" can be defined from two directions, either in terms of the content and theory of grammar as a discipline, or in terms of how it is practiced and performed in the real world. For the most part, I am concerned more with the second aspect than the first, but it is also true that, in the post-Aristotelian world, elaborate theories of the nature and content of grammar were developed. Grammar was articulated as a set of "parts" or "duties" (*officia*)—the things that a grammarian was supposed to know and teach, including correct reading and pronunciation as well as the understanding and evaluation of literary texts. In various accounts grammar was also given "tools" that specified the areas of grammatical, logical, or historical expertise that the grammarian was supposed to control. Several competing anatomies of "grammar" are attested, but their effect on either the writing or teaching of the grammarian is unclear at best: they are attempts at theoretical definition, marking out the place of grammar in the institutional structures of human knowledge—the apparently endless turf wars between philosophy, rhetoric, and grammar that affected ancient intellectual life as much as they do modern universities. And although there will be some mention below of such definitions in Roman grammatical writings, they have very little to do with grammar as written or as practiced.[3]

For the purposes of this book, a functional definition is more helpful: "grammar" consists of what might be taught or written about by a grammarian. Grammar, from the latter half of the first century CE, was not merely a regular practice in Rome, but an authorized one: *grammatici* such as Donatus, *grammaticus urbis Romae*, and Priscian, described in some manuscripts as *grammaticus Caesariensis doctor urbis Romae Constantinopolitanae*, received a stipend from the government to provide tuition on the Latin language and literature, just as professors of rhetoric such as Quintilian provided the next, higher level of instruction. But if the definition of "grammar" is what grammarians did, it should also be remembered that *grammatici* were not the only people doing it, nor, although Quintilian (1.4.2) defines the work of the grammarian as falling into two parts, *recte loquendi scientia* and *poetarum enarratio* (the knowledge of proper speech and the explanation of the poets), was the writing of grammars or commentaries the only form of philological activity.

There was, to begin with simple chronology, philological activity in Rome before there were professional grammarians, and (as will be seen in Chapter 2) the work of the *grammaticus* and the philological writing during the Republic of which we know anything were quite separate. From our earliest knowledge, from the beginning of the second century BCE, the study of texts and the improvement of (some) texts was a regular activity of the more intellectually active members of the Roman upper classes; the most famous of the early practitioners of non-professional philology is Marcus Terentius Varro, general, satirist, philosopher, antiquarian, and man of letters, some of the books of whose treatise *De lingua Latina* survive (and will be discussed at some length below). As with other areas of intellectual endeavor, notably the study of law and of religion, the study of language was the province of men of letters, not professional teachers, and these fields were only gradually differentiated from one another and defined professionally.

Nor did philological activity ever cease to be part of the equipment of the learned élite. In the high empire, a figure such as Aulus Gellius reveals a wide acquaintance with problems of grammar, diction, style, and texts; in late antiquity Macrobius and Martianus Capella stand out as erudite amateurs. Romans like these not only discoursed on language and literature, but some of them actively worked to preserve it: signatures in manuscripts (*subscriptiones*), often copied along with the texts they accompanied, attest to the efforts not only of

3. For a clear discussion of these theoretical articulations, see Blank (2000), including some very helpful charts.

grammarians like Servius, but of military officers, consuls, and other men of eminence. Philology in the Roman world was not just the province of philologists, and many of the most interesting and important texts of Roman scholarship were composed not for students or teachers, but for lettered people in general. The correct interpretation (and pronunciation and reading) of texts was part of the mental apparatus and intellectual activity of people of culture and social standing. Writing about books, language, and literature; antiquarian studies involving words and texts at least as much as ruins and buildings; and all the verbal arts and cultural equipment necessary for participation in a world in which the proper use of language was a prerequisite for success and distinction in the public forum—these were not professional activities of scholars alone but normal parts of cultivated society.

Just as grammar is not the province of the *grammaticus* alone, moreover, so too the forms of grammatical scholarship, even the most traditional and academic of them, were not limited in subject or context to what we might think of as grammar or philology. The earliest known Roman commentaries (to be discussed in Chapter 2) are not devoted to literary texts, but to legal and religious works. Indeed, in sheer bulk, legal commentary, culminating in the third-century CE commentary on the Edict in eighty-three books (from which more than 1,600 quotations survive) by the jurist Ulpian, rivals in size and scope the remains of literary commentary. There are also rhetorical commentaries, not just on literary texts (such as that of Tiberius Donatus on the *Aeneid*), but also on texts that themselves deal with rhetorical theory, such as Grillius' commentary on Cicero's *De inventione*. The forms of scholarship were fungible and flexible; a text does not need to be literary to need explanation.

Within this broad range of engagement with the study of texts, however, the hard core of basic explanations of language remains central: the large number of works designed to teach people Latin, or to help them with fairly elementary interpretation of texts, attests to the constant need for instruction in the basics. Even elementary texts, however, show a certain amount of variety: the *ars grammatica* and the commentary can be either descriptive ("This is what people have written as correct Latin") or normative ("This is what correct Latin is, and what you should write or say yourself"). In school grammars, the normative clearly prevails: their primary audience is boys of about ten years old, who may or may not (particularly in the fourth century CE or later, the period from which most such extant texts survive) be native speakers of Latin. Commentaries too, again largely from late antiquity in their extant form, necessarily straddle the divide between the descriptive and the normative in a complex negotation between the social position of the (humble) grammarian and the public world to which his teaching provided access. It is striking, however, that many works of grammar were not written by professional grammarians; indeed, some of the most interesting and important such texts (those of Charisius and Diomedes in particular) were written by men whose native language was Greek. Not surprisingly, such works show a greater clarity in explaining some of the peculiarities of

Latin; perhaps equally unsurprising, at least in hindsight, is that these books were greatly valued by other non-Latin speakers in the West, notably the Irish.

4. LIMITS

The historical narrative that follows this chapter begins with fragmentary evidence derived from later sources; the end of my story is crowded with a large number of texts that slide gradually from the Roman world of late antiquity into the Christian worlds of Celts, Visigoths, Vandals, and Franks in the early Middle Ages, the Carolingian period, and beyond. While the beginning is lost in obscurity, there is no clear end. In contrast to the tradition of Greek scholarship, which reaches a sudden and violent end in 1453, the tradition of Roman philology has no sharp conclusion, just as the frontier between Roman culture and the cultures of the early Middle Ages has no wall. In some sense, Roman philology was active and productive until Donatus' grammatical texts ceased to be a staple of European education, some time after the Renaissance, and one could just as easily conclude this account in the time of Alcuin and Charlemagne or extend it to Lorenzo Valla's *Elegantiae*. It is traditional to end histories of ancient scholarship with Priscian and Cassiodorus in the sixth century: Priscian, because his vast grammar is the last (and perhaps most original) great treatment of Latin grammar written within a Roman empire; Cassiodorus, because his *Institutes* are the first major instructional text to incorporate the tradition of Roman education and scholarship into a Christian context. One can also, quite legitimately, extend this story to Isidore of Seville, writing in Visigothic Spain in the seventh century, but relying in his *Etymologiae* on the same texts and methods as his Roman predecessors.

One particular stretching of my chronological framework, however, deserves mention. The tradition of Roman grammar, particularly in the form of commentaries on Donatus, remained active and creative until at least the ninth century, and it would be unreasonable not to give some attention to the development of that tradition. In terms of commentaries on literary texts, moreover, there is no point in trying to distinguish commentaries written in late antiquity from those written in the early Middle Ages (again, roughly up to the ninth century): the form in which ancient commentary survives is frequently in the shape of scholia organized in the ninth century, and one cannot talk about one end of the tradition without talking about the other. In that case, however, I have given relatively scant attention to any commentary that does not show independent knowledge of the ancient world: the annotated manuscripts of Horace or Terence are far too many and too repetitive to try to list; they are of interest to students of medieval education, not students of ancient philology. I have said a few words about such high medieval texts and have given some references to other works that say more.

Even before the sixth century, however, the nature of Roman philology had changed significantly, with Augustine and Jerome. The present volume will deal with commentaries on secular texts and with the traditions of secular education—in some cases, pursuing them well beyond the time of Priscian; it will not deal with the great commentaries of the church fathers on the Bible nor, except in passing, with the Christian education that developed in parallel (and in competition) with the school of the *grammaticus*. Christians—and even Servius was presumably a Christian—commenting on the Latin classics belong here; but the traditions of biblical exegesis are very different, and have very different sources, from the traditions of the Roman schoolroom. The only biblical commentary to be mentioned in this book, very briefly, is Cassiodorus' commentary on the Psalms, and that only because he confronted directly the relationship between the two worlds of Christian and secular exegesis. Even within the secular world, moreover, the focus of this book is limited. As noted above, "commentary" can be applied to many different kinds of text, but the ones on which I will concentrate are literary rather than concerned with such specialized areas as law and rhetoric. For thorough guides to those fields, the reader is encouraged to turn elsewhere. The need for exegetical commentary is shared, but the content being explained and the languages of explanation are very different from one another.

Although the narrative in Part I of this book is (more or less) chronological, it should be stressed again that any account of ancient scholarship runs both forward and backward. That we can only view the ancient world from the perspective of the present is a truism, but in dealing with ancient scholarship it is much more than that. The presence of a piece of ancient lore, or a grammatical observation, in the margins of a Carolingian manuscript reflects a long tradition of study and writing, and the very preservation of what we know about how ancient readers looked at texts often depends on what more recent readers thought important enough to mention or copy. The history that follows is fragmentary and uncertain, and that uncertainty is a part of the history itself.

5. HOW TO USE THIS BOOK

As noted above, this book is divided into two parts; the first, narrative part is itself divided roughly in two, one being a very brief history of Roman philology up to (again, roughly) the beginning of the third century CE—the period for which our evidence is largely fragmentary—the other an account of the surviving late antique texts categorized by form (dictionaries, commentaries, grammars). The final chapter of Part I considers the afterlife of Roman philology in the early Middle Ages, partly in formal terms (the organization of the manuscripts that preserve these texts), partly in terms of geography and social context.

Part II is biographical and bibliographical: under the same three broad rubrics (dictionaries, commentaries, grammars) I have listed all the texts that belong to these categories. In the case of grammars, they are arranged in alphabetical order by author—with a very large section for "anonymous" at the end—while in the case of dictionaries and commentaries, they are listed under the name of the author or the author being explained, in chronological order. Later grammatical texts, those written between the seventh and ninth centuries, are grouped together in a separate list of which a large part is again occupied by "anonymous." For authors whose work belongs in more than one category, one entry (to which cross-references are made) contains the major bibliography, while smaller entries discuss particular works that do not fit the primary category. Thus the major entry for "Macrobius" is under "Commentaries: Virgil," concerning the *Saturnalia*, his most famous work; lesser entries will be found under "Commentaries: Cicero" for his commentary on the *Somnium Scipionis* (which was far more widely read in the Middle Ages than at present) and under "Grammarians: Macrobius" for his work on the comparison of the Greek and Latin verb. The bibliography is deliberately as well as inevitably selective: I have been generous in listing modern editions and translations, but I have aimed at listing only the secondary scholarship that is broadly useful in understanding the identity, character, and importance of the various texts. In some cases there is a great deal; in others there is very little. I have also given references to treatments of particular authors or texts in standard works of reference: these are not always recent, but they provide a quick and reliable source of information and serve as a benchmark against which to measure more narrowly focused scholarship.

To some extent, this organization is repetitive, but it also reflects my sense that to be used and understood, this material must be approached from a number of different directions: from the history of the discipline looking forward (Chapters 2–5); from the forms in which information was conveyed (Chapters 6–8); from the history in which the material was preserved (Chapter 9); and from a bibliographical perspective, in order to help readers find and use it (Chapters 10–13). To make the material more accessible, I have tried to indicate, in the indices and list of works cited, where texts, manuscripts, or older secondary works are available online.

I end with a reminder of limitations. The goals of this book are limited, and I have excluded not only some areas of ancient scholarship that others might include, but also some modern approaches that are beyond my ken. For the former, in discussing commentaries, I have defined the term narrowly: it would be possible to add material about the ancient biographies of poets and other forms of *accessus* (introductions), and I have done so on some occasions where there is genuinely early material (as in the biographies of Virgil and Horace), but much of what survives either exists as part of the commentaries I do discuss or (the *accessus* in particular) is a later medieval creation. Other ancient secondary works the primary intention of which is to help readers—geographical and mythological handbooks—are also excluded, unless (as in the case of the *narrationes* of Ovid's *Metamorphoses*) they actually take the form of commentaries. As far as modern approaches are concerned, mine is largely an external account of philology, not an internal one. It is not about the history of ancient linguistic theory or hermeneutics; it is about the texts and books from which we learn about such things: what they are, where they are to be found, and what the contexts are of their production and preservation.

Finally: if I were to claim to have read with equal attention all the works, ancient, medieval, and modern, that are cited in this book it would strain anyone's credulity, including my own. At one time or another I have read, or at least turned every page of, every ancient text discussed; for texts later than Isidore, I have at least looked at, and read parts of, every text that has been printed, and I have looked at manuscripts (digitized) of some that have not. As far as the secondary scholarship is concerned, I have tried to look at every edition and translation of every text, although a few have escaped me. I have also looked at some point at almost every book or article that is included in the bibliography, although I would not claim, in some cases, to have done more than skim and sample. I note also that while every secondary work (other than reference works and unpublished dissertations and a few other books which I note that I have not seen) cited anywhere in the book is included in the List of Works Cited, many works cited on specific points in the notes to Part I do not reappear in the bibliographies of Part II.

2

The Origins of Roman Grammar

1. "GRAMMAR" AND *GRAMMATICI* IN THE ROMAN REPUBLIC

Our knowledge of the origins of most areas of cultural life at Rome is scanty, and grammar is no exception. Two reasons for this stand out: one is that, in common with other areas of writing (including poetry), early writing about language ("grammar" broadly defined) is preserved only in scraps, quotations by later grammarians, and passing remarks by other authors; the other is that, again in common with other disciplines (including law and rhetoric), the shaping of grammar as a genuine *ars*—the explicit awareness of the goals and methods of the subject, a set of rules and procedures both for its teaching and for its practice—did not even begin to take shape until the late Republic.[1] As noted in the previous chapter, "grammar" and "grammarian" have two sets of meanings, one narrow and one—the one that matches the larger purposes of this book—broad. In the technical sense, a *grammaticus* is a teacher of Latin to children, and grammar is what he teaches, the material that eventually (in the first century CE and later) becomes the core of a textbook, the *ars grammatica*: above all, the parts of speech and their correct inflection. In the broader sense, grammar comprises all sorts of written works about all aspects of Latin: its sounds and spelling, the meaning and etymology of words, their proper formation and use (including certain aspects of rhetorical and poetic diction), prosody, metrics, and syntax. In order to avoid ambiguity, wherever possible the word "grammarian" will be used strictly as equivalent to *grammaticus*—the schoolteacher—and "philology" or "scholarship" will be used for the broader realms of language study.

1. Barwick (1922) wanted to trace the Roman *ars grammatica* back to a putative Stoic *tekhnê* in the mid-second century, but few scholars still accept his reconstruction; for a succinct history of the question, see Baratin (2000), and see below, Chapter 8. On the general patterns of intellectual rationalization in the first century BCE, see in general Moatti (2015), Rawson (1985), and Wallace-Hadrill (2008).

The fact that grammar as an *ars* did not yet exist does not at all mean that there were not writings of a sort that would later become recognized as "grammar": there were quite a few *grammatici* in Rome long before there was an *ars grammatica*. In the second century BCE, there were grammarians who taught children (and Suetonius stretches this back as far as Livius Andronicus in the third century) and there were also philologists who wrote about language. The two categories remain distinct for centuries, although the role of the *grammaticus* as a writer as well as teacher of grammar becomes much more significant in the early Empire.

Given the amorphousness of these categories and the real risk of anachronism, it is entirely proper that the principal (and invaluable) collection of evidence and fragments, Funaioli's *Grammaticae Romanae Fragmenta*, includes whatever materials Funaioli could find not just about grammar in the narrow sense, but about language, libraries, and books in general: to take a narrower definition would inevitably define the early material in terms of the later professionalism of the grammarian.[2] Only gradually do signs appear of the forms of scholarship that later became standard: the *ars grammatica*, concentrating on the parts of speech; works on *Latinitas*, discussing proper morphology and diction; the commentary on a literary text; and treatises on specialized areas of grammatical importance, including orthography and metrics. These are the forms that remain constant and productive until the Middle Ages (and beyond); they represent what, for the most part, Roman grammatical scholarship means to us. But the continuity of those forms depends on both a social and an intellectual construction of grammar and the grammarian that simply did not exist for a very long time.

If Funaioli's *grammatica* is a broad and ill-defined category (with more than 500 pages of evidence and fragments), it includes within it material taken from the one source that actually provides a narrative framework and chronology for the early history of Roman grammar, Suetonius' short treatise *De grammaticis et rhetoribus*, a small part of his larger collection of lives of men illustrious in various fields of human endeavor.[3] The main body of *DGR* (the introduction will be discussed shortly) consists of a list, with brief biographies, of nineteen *grammatici*, starting from the otherwise unknown Sevius Nicanor (c. 5), whose *floruit* is probably to be placed at the end of the second century BCE, and progressing as far as Q. Remmius Palaemon and M. Valerius Probus in the first century CE. Suetonius' list is invaluable, but his criterion for inclusion is narrow: the men he describes were *professores*, people who offered instruction in grammar. His narrative describes the gradual rise of the grammarian in status over the two centuries he

2. On Funaioli's work, its problems, and the principles appropriate for such a collection, see Damaggio (2011).

3. On *DGR*, I rely heavily on Kaster (1995) even when it is not explicitly cited; see also Gianotti (2010) with more recent bibliography. I refer to Suetonius' work as *De grammaticis et rhetoribus* (*DGR*), but am concerned only with the section on grammarians; the section on rhetoricians which follows is very incomplete and not germane to this discussion.

covers: as grammar itself became institutionalized as a stage of Roman upper-class education, the teaching of grammar moved from the household to the school as the *grammaticus* moved from a position of social dependency to one of great importance, and often wealth and influence. This corresponds to the importance of the subject: the ability to speak proper Latin was a requirement in a young man's training for public life (and rhetoric), and that became ever more crucial as the Roman *imperium* (and its upper class) extended further from the confines of Rome itself.[4]

Because *grammatici* were concerned with elementary education only, it is no surprise that relatively few of the men in Suetonius' list have any significant presence in Funaioli's collection of grammatical texts. Of the fifteen who were active before or during the reign of Augustus, there are no fragments surviving of Sevius Nicanor (c. 5), M. Pompilius Andronicus (c. 8), Curtius Nicia (c. 14), Pompeius Lenaeus (c. 15), Q. Caecilius Epirota (c. 16), or Scribonius Aphroditus (c. 19); six more are represented by five or fewer fragments.[5] Some of these figures (notably Caecilius Epirota) are much more important than the lack of verbatim fragments would suggest, but in general these men were not of high social standing or public visibility,[6] and it was their teaching rather than their writing that interested Suetonius, to such an extent that he does not even mention major works by grammarians, such as Verrius Flaccus' *De verborum significatu* or the *Ars grammatica* of Remmius Palaemon. On the other side, of the twelve figures with the greatest number of fragments in Funaioli's collection, only two, Aurelius Opillus and Verrius Flaccus, are actually classified as *grammatici* by Suetonius.

Even though the institutional structure of education was weak, however, that does not mean that there was a lack of interest in tasks that eventually found their way to the classroom of the *grammaticus*. Although there is relatively little overlap between the *grammatici* listed by Suetonius and the remnants of philological writing collected by Funaioli, a great many people, some of them very well known, did write about language: Accius the tragic poet, Lucilius the satirist, Aelius Stilo the philosopher and logographer[7]—the last two definitely also *equites*—and in the later Republic, in addition to Varro himself, Julius Caesar and

4. On the social importance of the grammarian and of correct speech, see above all Kaster (1988, 1995).

5. Bibliography on all fragmentary republican writers on grammar, together with links to the relevant pages of *GRF*, will be found in *GD*.

6. Cf. Christes (1979).

7. Aelius Stilo is named by Suetonius (*DGR* 3.1–2) as the most important figure in the early development of grammatical writing, not as a grammarian in the narrow sense of the word. Stilo is little known except through references to his work in Varro, but he was a figure of great importance, as a speechwriter for at least one of the Metelli and as a teacher of both Varro and Cicero. His Stoicism and grammatical interests overlapped in a work *De proloquiis*; see further 3.6 and 8.2 below. For testimonia and fragments of Stilo, see *GRF* 51–76; *ORF* #74; further bibliography and discussion in Kaster (1995: 68–70).

Nigidius Figulus, not to mention Cicero, who is missing from the collection of grammatical fragments only because his extensive writings on language and literature are not fragmentary. That many men of considerable standing wrote about philology is important, if unsurprising: an interest in words, in language, and in literature is a fairly constant element in the life of the Roman upper classes. Latin was too important to be left to the professionals.

About what the *grammaticus* did in the period before the formalization of the *ars grammatica* itself, we know something from Quintilian and Varro as well as from Suetonius.[8] His basic job was to teach his pupils to read, both in terms of basic literacy (although that was really the job of the *paedagogus* or other truly elementary teacher before a child ever reached the *grammaticus*) and in terms of understanding. For the most part, as far as we can tell, before the proper textbook, the *ars*, was available, the essential vehicle for grammatical instruction was the classroom reading and analysis of poetic texts. As to what this involved, we learn the essentials from the description of the grammarian's task given by Quintilian at the beginning of his account of grammar. For him, the *professio* of the grammarian falls into two parts: *recte loquendi scientia* and *poetarum enarratio* (1.4.2).[9] The knowledge of proper speech, he says, means learning to write as well as to read. *Enarratio* of the poets is more complex (1.4.3):

> nam . . . enarrationem praecedit emendata lectio et mixtum his omnibus iudicium est: quo quidem ita severe sunt usi veteres grammatici ut non versus modo censoria quadam virgula notare et libros qui falso viderentur inscripti tamquam subditos summovere familia permiserint sibi, sed auctores alios in ordinem redegerint, alios omnino exemerint numero.
>
> Before the explanation of a text comes corrected reading, and with all these is blended judgment. The early grammarians were so severe in this that they allowed themselves not only, like censors, to put a black mark against individual verses and to expel from the family, as if changelings, books that appeared to have false attributions, but they also arranged some authors in ranks and threw others entirely out of the service.

The first part of this is treated more fully in a fragment of Varro preserved by the fourth-century grammarian Diomedes (*GL* 1.426.21 = F 236 Funaioli):[10]

8. There is a useful discussion of the various definitions of "grammar" before and by Varro in Collart (1954a: 51–6); Seppänen (2014) is too technical in general, and believes Suetonius too much.

9. The interpretation of poetry as a defining task of the grammarian is much older than Quintilian (cf. Cicero, *De or.* 1.187 and *Div.* 1.34 with Collart 1954: 12), and ultimately stems from the Alexandrian model of grammatical scholarship based on the elucidation of Homer. For a fuller discussion of Quintilian's account of grammar, see 8.2 below.

10. On this, see also 3.5 below; for Diomedes, see 12.18 below.

> Grammaticae officia, ut adserit Varro, constant in partibus quattuor, lectione enarratione emendatione iudicio. lectio est . . . varia cuiusque scripti enuntiatio serviens dignitati personarum exprimensque animi habitum cuiusque. enarratio est obscurorum sensuum quaestionumve explanatio. . . . emendatio est . . . recorrectio errorum qui per scripturam dictionemve fiunt. iudicium est . . . aestimatio qua poema ceteraque scripta perpendimus.

> The duties of grammar, according to Varro, fall into four parts, "reading," "explanation," "correction," and "judgment." "Reading" is . . . the modulated speaking of every text, paying attention to the standing of characters and expressing the mental state of each one. "Explanation" is the elucidation of unclear thoughts or content. . . . "Correction" is . . . the removal of errors made in writing or speech. "Judgment" is . . . the valuation we give to poems and other written texts.

Quintilian's wording ascribes to *veteres grammatici* alone the severe practices of *iudicium* (a topic to which I will return in the next section), but the close correspondence between his account of grammar and Varro's shows that the whole description refers to early (i.e., republican) Roman education. Quintilian makes an implicit contrast between early and modern *grammatici*; the main difference, I suspect, is that the early teachers taught from poetic texts only, while Quintilian's contemporaries now had Palaemon's *Ars grammatica* to work from. The concentration on elucidating texts rather than inculcating grammatical rules in the abstract is characteristic not only of the grammarians described by Quintilian and Varro, but of other philologists as well; it is certainly true that we have precious little sign of grammatical *ars* before Varro.[11]

The four duties of the grammarian are given by Varro and Quintilian in different orders, but Quintilian's (also found in Dositheus, *GL* 7.376.3) is the more logical. Reading comes first, then correction, then explanation, and finally judgment.[12] Quintilian's account makes it clear that these are not (except perhaps the last) very elevated tasks: young students were taught to write a text down from dictation and to read it correctly (that is the sense of Quintilian's observation that *recte loquendi scientia* also includes learning to write properly); the teacher would correct both their copies and their reading; following that would come the explanation of the content of the text,[13] and finally (although, as Quintilian says, it is inevitably mixed with the other parts of the lesson) the teacher would lead his

11. The one exception being a vague reference in *Ad Herennium*: see 3.5 below.

12. One of the scholia on Dionysius Thrax (Bekker, *Anecdota* 2.736–7, cited by Collart 1954: 54–5) places them in yet another order, with *diorthotikon* before *anagnostikon*.

13. Quintilian 1.4.4 also refers to this as *historia*; in the fragment of Varro *quaestiones* refers to the practice of posing questions (Greek *zêtêmata*) about the subject matter (mythology, natural history, etc.) of texts.

students towards some assessment of the merits and failings of the work being studied.[14]

2. A GREEK SCHOLAR IN ROME

Suetonius' *De grammaticis* is important not just for the lives of the grammarians themselves but because he prefaces the biographies with an account of the origins of philology at Rome. After dismissing the importance of the early poets Livius Andronicus and Ennius, who by tradition were schoolmasters who "did nothing more than translate and explain Greek texts or perform their own Latin compositions" (1.2), Suetonius records what he believes to be the precise moment when *grammatica* reached Rome, when Crates of Mallos came as an ambassador from Pergamum, probably in 167.[15] While in Rome, Crates broke his leg in a drain on the Palatine hill; and while his leg was mending, he gave lectures (*plurimas acroasis*), presumably on his various areas of expertise, which included philology. The result, according to Suetonius, was that some of his audience were inspired to imitate him (2.2):

> hactenus tamen imitati, ut carmina parum adhuc divulgata vel defunctorum amicorum vel si quorum aliorum probassent diligentius retractarent ac legendo commentandoque etiam ceteris nota facerent; ut C. Octavius Lampadio Naevi *Punicum bellum*, quod uno volumine et continenti scriptura expositum divisit in septem libros; ut postea Q. Vargunteius *Annales* Enni, quos certis diebus in magna frequentia pronuntiabat; ut Laelius Archelaus Vettiusque Philocomus Lucili *Saturas* familiaris sui, quas legisse se apud Archelaum Pompeius Lenaeus, apud Philocomum Valerius Cato praedicant.
>
> Their imitation amounted to this: that they carefully studied poetry that was not yet widely known, written either by deceased friends or by other people whose work they approved of, and by giving readings and commenting they made them known to others. That is what C. Octavius Lampadio did with the *Punic War* of Naevius, which he divided into seven books, it having previously been set out as one single continuous book roll. That is what Q. Vargunteius did later with Ennius' *Annals*, which he read on set days before a large crowd. And that is what Laelius Archelaus and Vettius Philocomus did with the *Satires*

14. It should be emphasized (and will be repeated) that the four duties of the grammarian are not in my view sophisticated methods of criticism but the routine, daily work of the classroom, helping small children learn to read and understand Latin. The elevation of these definitions of *grammatica* to a theoretical framework for the entire study of language (including the *ars grammatica*) stems from Usener's influential and inventive article "Ein altes Lehrgebäude der Philologie" (Usener 1913: 265–314, originally published 1892), too often taken as fact.

15. The chronology is vexed: Suetonius says that he came soon after Ennius' death (169), but that he was an ambassador from Attalus, who became king only a decade later. An embassy from Eumenes II of Pergamum is otherwise attested for 167, and one from Attalus II in 156; the former date is preferable. For details, see Kaster (1995: 59–60).

> of their friend Lucilius; Pompeius Lenaeus claims to have read them under Archelaus' guidance, and Valerius Cato under that of Philocomus.

Suetonius' account is not very satisfying, because it is hard to see how these activities constitute the origins of *grammatica*.[16] The authenticity of Lampadio's division of Naevius' poem into seven is attested by a fragment of Santra, a younger contemporary of Varro, but Suetonius' other two examples amount to no more than public readings of Ennius and Lucilius, and since Lucilius was alive until near the end of the second century, whatever Archelaus and Philocomus did is likely to have taken place a good fifty years after Crates had thrown away his crutches and gone home.[17]

Despite the difficulties posed by Suetonius' account, Crates' visit and lectures are presumably real enough, and what Suetonius says about the attention paid to the works of Naevius, Ennius, and Lucilius is plausible. The emphasis Suetonius gives to the public reading and explanation of texts as the origin of *grammatica* is consistent with what Varro and Quintilian say about *enarratio poetarum*; what we cannot tell is whether Suetonius describes Crates' effect on Romans in this way because that is what happened or because he anachronistically treated Lampadio and the others as if they were grammarians in the mold of later discussions of *grammatica*.

But whatever Lampadio produced (and there is even less evidence in Suetonius about the other figures), there is no justification for thinking that it was anything like a modern critical edition of Roman literary texts, and even less reason to think that textual criticism was a regular occupation of Roman philologists and *grammatici*. Quintilian's account of grammatical *iudicium*, quoted above, indicates that, at least to him, the use of critical *notae* to censure verses was a part of teaching; *emendatio* was one of the grammarian's four basic tasks, again an occupation of the classroom. That is not to say that people—grammarians as well as their students and other interested readers—did not correct the texts they read; but Quintilian's account makes it educational, not scholarly.

The most significant evidence for scholarly intervention in texts is unfortunately an extremely difficult short passage known as *Anecdoton Parisinum* or *Fragmentum de notis* that survives in a manuscript from the late eighth century, was discovered by Mommsen in the 1840s, and probably derives ultimately from a work of Suetonius. It is entitled *Notae XXI quae versibus apponi consuerunt* ("21 signs that used to be placed next to verses") and is followed by a second list of *Notae Simplices* that ends by describing itself as being *de notis Probianis*. The

16. The vagueness has allowed modern scholars to create very different images of Crates' influence. The brief account of Collart (1954: 7–13) is old, but suitably circumspect.

17. On Lampadio, see Santra F 5: *quod volumen unum nos lectitavimus et postea invenimus septemfariam divisum*. It would be beyond the bounds of coincidence to imagine that anything other than Lampadio's division of Naevius is referred to.

first list is the more informative; it gives the twenty-one signs and then explains the use, and in some cases the users, of each, ascribing their use in general to Valerius Probus at the end of the first century CE and to several earlier scholars (*GL* 7.534.4–6):[18]

> His solis in adnotationibus Ennii Lucilii et historicorum usi sunt †uarrus hennius haelius aequae† et postremo Probus, qui illas in Virgilio et Horatio et Lucretio apposuit, ut Homero Aristarchus.
>
> These are the only *notae* used in the text of Ennius, Lucilius and the *historici* by [3–4 names] and most recently by Probus, who placed them in texts of Virgil, Horace, and Lucretius, the way Aristarchus did with Homer.

The names are frustratingly corrupt, although they almost certainly include Varro and Aelius Stilo. But while the use of critical signs described in this fragment certainly involved careful reading of the text, most of the signs indicate not comparison of manuscripts, but rhetorical and aesthetic judgments of appropriateness. In the case of Aristarchus and the Homeric text there is good reason to believe in serious critical comparison of manuscripts and versions, but even there, much of Aristarchus' critical activity involved matters of appropriateness rather than authenticity.

More than anything else, however, the activity of commenting on a text by putting *notae* in the margin, even if keyed to fuller discussion in a separate commentary (as may well be the case), is an indication of great textual conservatism: leaving the text alone but marking it up in the margins shows that whatever the "editor" believed was wrong with it was not altered, merely marked as dubious. In their intention and effect, the *notae* are the exact opposite of a modern critical apparatus. Whoever lurks behind the corrupt names in the *Anecdoton Parisinum* took the text they found and added marks that explained what they thought of it. There is no indication whatsoever that anyone in this period compared manuscripts or attempted to construct a text.

Whatever "editing" Lampadio (or Stilo or Varro, for that matter) did, it was not textual criticism as we understand it. What Quintilian said the older *grammatici* practiced was a form of censorial activity: placing *notae* against verses of dubious merit just as the censors placed *notae* against the names of people of dubious morals. We have some slight evidence for the discussion of textual problems in the Roman Republic, but none at all for the explicit comparison of readings found in different manuscripts or, indeed, of awareness of the existence of alternative readings of any text. When Cicero describes to his friend Paetus (*Fam.* 9.16.4) the

18. For further discussion of this list, with bibliography, see 4.3 and 10.4.6a below. I give the text as Keil prints it, although in fact it is more corrupt than that: the manuscript reads *hennii lucii* for *Ennii Lucilii* and the first hand reads *uarros*, corrected to *uarrus*. The meaning of *historici* is unclear, although it obviously ought to refer to dramatic texts. For this manuscript (Paris, Lat. 7530) see Holtz (1975); it will be referred to frequently.

skill of the grammarian Ser. Clodius as being able to say "this line isn't by Plautus, this one is" on the basis of his familiarity with Plautine style, it shows very clearly that the *iudicium* exercised by critics was the product of their own judgment and knowledge, not of archival research.[19]

All this is definitely not meant to suggest that people, including grammarians and others interested in literature, paid no attention to the quality of the texts they read or that they did not organize the copying (and public recitation) of both earlier and contemporary literature. Lampadio's Naevius must have been an editorial improvement, and various people did in some sense "edit" various texts. But our sources give no clear description of what that editing actually meant. *Emendatio* is the word that is most frequently used for editorial activity, and, as seen above, its primary meaning in the context of the work of the *grammaticus* is closer to "proofreading" than to editing.

Aspects of Suetonius' story about Crates other than chronology also make it suspect. When Suetonius introduces Crates' name, he describes him as *Aristarchi aequalis*, and the names of these two contemporaries are frequently linked in the Roman scholarly tradition.[20] Crates was the head, and perhaps creator, of the library of Pergamum; a Stoic, he was renowned in particular for his allegorical interpretations of Homer and his development of the concept of linguistic anomaly, with which he is often identified.[21] Aristarchus, the great Homeric critic, is much better known now, but at least some of his Homeric criticism seems to have been written in reply to Crates.[22] As Crates is the preeminent representative of Stoicism and Pergamene criticism, so Aristarchus stands for Alexandrian criticism: for careful attention to diction and grammar, for defense of analogy as a principle of inflectional morphology, for the use of the critical signs in editing texts—although, as noted above, it is never exactly clear what "editing" means in this context.[23]

Given the fact that Crates and Aristarchus are emblematic of what appeared to the ancients themselves to be the single greatest methodological division among grammarians and philologists, what is most perplexing about Suetonius' tale is that the work Romans undertake, apparently under the influence of the

19. All known variant readings and comments about texts from the republican period are collected by Zetzel (1981: 19–23). See also Zetzel (1973, 1980, 1981) for detailed discussion of the evidence for Roman textual criticism and the meaning of *emendatio*.

20. E.g., Varro, *LL* 8.68, 9.1; Gellius, *NA* 2.25.4. On Crates' scholarship in relation to that of Aristarchus, still useful is Pfeiffer (1968: 238–45).

21. As in Gellius 2.25.4, *duo Graeci grammatici illustres, Aristarchus et Crates, summa ope ille ἀναλογίαν, hic ἀνωμαλίαν defensitavit*. For the conflict of analogy and anomaly, see Chapter 3; on Crates, in addition to Pfeiffer (1968), there are collections of his fragments in Mette (1936) and (1952) and more recently Broggiato (2001). Further bibliography in Dickey (2007: 6).

22. Cf. Pfeiffer (1968: 239–40).

23. For further bibliography on Aristarchus, see Dickey (2007: 4–5).

Pergamene Crates, looks much more Alexandrian in inspiration. Thus, the one specific action Suetonius describes as resulting from Crates' visit, the division of Naevius' epic into books, is like the Alexandrian division of the Homeric poems—not the sort of thing that Pergamene scholars did.[24] Another problem is that the texts Crates' Roman disciples are said to have edited—Naevius' *Bellum Punicum*, Ennius' *Annales*, Lucilius' *Saturae*—include no works of drama, the literary texts we know that early Roman philologists studied most carefully. This has no bearing on Alexandrian or Pergamene inspiration, but it is another way in which Suetonius' narrative does not seem to fit the historical circumstances.

But if Suetonius' story seems at odds with its circumstances, it fits very neatly into a pattern of stories (some ancient, some modern) about the origins of various aspects of culture in Rome: a learned Greek comes to Rome, Romans are inspired to take up Greek approaches, and Romans then apply Greek methods to Roman materials. Thus Crates brings textual philology—what he and others had used in the study of early Greek poetry—to the Romans, who immediately start editing the remains of early poetry and developing the linguistic and technical skills to explain difficult texts. The same pattern shapes the story of the Philosophers' Embassy of 155 BCE: the Athenians needed Roman assistance in a border dispute, and to impress the Romans they sent the heads of three philosophical schools, the Stoic Diogenes of Babylon, the Peripatetic Critolaus, and the Academic Carneades. Diogenes is sometimes credited with inspiring the Romans to take up grammar—he was, after all, the author of a *Tekhnê peri phônês* (treatise on speech)—and the electric effect of Carneades' two opposing speeches on justice sparked a serious interest in ethical and political philosophy.[25] Roman literature itself is said to begin with the arrival of the Tarentine Greek Livius Andronicus in Rome, and the arrival of Parthenius in the 60s is sometimes said to have brought Alexandrian poetics to Catullus and his contemporaries.

Tales of this sort are historical constructions, not facts; some of them (like the stories of Crates and Carneades) are ancient, some of them (Diogenes of Babylon and Parthenius) are modern inferences.[26] They all reflect the enduring belief that no Roman could have had an original idea without a Greek whispering it in his ear. Crates did come to Rome and no doubt he was listened to; but it is very improbable that the Romans had never thought about language or texts before his arrival.

24. On the Homeric book divisions (the origins of which are disputed), see Pfeiffer (1968: 115–16).

25. Diogenes' influence (on which see further 8.2 below) was largely invented by Barwick (1922), but Carneades' influence is stressed by Cicero; see Zetzel (1996).

26. Collart (1954a: 8–9) gives a useful list of philosophical and grammatical Greek visitors.

3. LAW AND LETTERS

In fact, we know that the Romans had thought about philology at least a generation before Crates arrived. The earliest known edition of a Latin text, accompanied by the earliest commentary, was the work of Sex. Aelius Catus Paetus, the consul of 198 BCE. His book was called *Tripertita*, and the text in question was the Twelve Tables. Once we set aside the tidy appeal of the Crates legend, that should not be at all surprising: the early laws and hymns were much older than the literary endeavors of Livius Andronicus and his successors and clearly also required considerable assistance for the reader to understand them at all. What is more, aside from Horace's tale about his teacher Orbilius beating Livius Andronicus into his brain (*Epist*. 2.1.69–71), the only text that we *know* was studied in schools in the early first century BCE was the Twelve Tables, which Cicero reports (*Leg*. 2.59) he was made to chant as a boy as a *carmen necessarium*, an essential text.

Equally significant is the evidence of quotations and fragments. Not only do a great many early glosses, definitions, and etymologies concern legal and religious texts (and perhaps no distinction should be made between the two), but some of the most intelligent *philological* comments from the second and first centuries BCE are by lawyers, not grammarians. Along with the definitions of legal terms, there are some very careful analyses of syntax and meaning: thus there was a discussion (reported by Gellius, *NA* 17.7) that began with the great second-century jurists M' Manilius and P. Mucius Scaevola, extended through Q. Scaevola Pontifex (consul in 95) and continued to Nigidius Figulus at the end of the Republic, over the precise meaning of the future perfect *subruptum erit* in the Lex Atinia.[27] What is most suggestive about the history of this problem is that it begins as a legal issue but ends as a grammatical one: Nigidius in his *Commentarii grammatici* (F 8) used it as the basis of a careful explanation of the difference in meaning between independent forms of *sum* and their combination with participles in periphrastic verbs.[28]

Interpretation of documents, often in terms of sense or syntax, was a crucial issue for the jurists. Q. Mucius declared (*D*. 50.17.73.3) that unintelligible parts of a will should be ignored; Ser. Sulpicius Rufus, Cicero's friend and contemporary, discussed the ambiguous gender of *filiis* in a will (*D*. 50.16.122), and from the context it appears that the issue had also concerned Q. Mucius. Sulpicius also

27. The Lex Atinia (republican, but of uncertain date) forbade usucaption of anything that had been stolen, described as *quod subruptum erit*. The debate was whether "shall have been stolen" included objects stolen before the date of the law itself. For a discussion of the legal issues, see Watson (1968: 24–9) and Frier (1985: 158–63). Taylor (1974 and frequently thereafter) is wrong to call Varro the first person to recognize the future perfect; there were quite a few people ahead of him.

28. A similar discussion of the meaning of *erit* in such contexts appears at *D*. 50.16.123 in Pomponius' commentary on Q. Mucius. A related issue of retroactivity seems to be the subject of a dinner conversation and correspondence between Cicero and his young legal friend Trebatius, *Fam*. 7.22.

considered the problem of double negatives in the Twelve Tables (*D*. 50.16.237), and both his pupil Alfenus Varus (a friend of Caesar) and the Augustan jurist Antistius Labeo had trouble interpreting the meaning of *cum* in various testamentary contexts (*D*. 33.2.40, 33.7.5). An argument about the meaning of *supellectilis* that involves Sulpicius Rufus, Labeo, and Aelius Tubero (a pupil of Sulpicius' pupil Ofillius) ultimately moves from etymology to precise contents to the issue of whether a person's choice of terminology should be interpreted in terms of general linguistic norms or individual intention (*D*. 33.10.7). The duration and intensity of grammatical discussion among lawyers is remarkable. It began before anyone had even heard of Crates, and it continued for centuries; the issues discussed were still alive in the *Digest*, compiled in the sixth century CE. There is nothing remotely comparable in Greek grammatical writing.[29]

There is, then, a much better story than Suetonius' fable about Crates to explain the origins of Roman philology, one that emphasizes legal texts over literary and Roman models over Greek. The two are not entirely separate, of course, and each has an element of truth: it is possible that Crates, or someone similar, turned Roman attention away from old laws towards newer poetry; other influences, particularly philosophy and rhetoric, will be discussed later. But the effect on Roman scholarship of its origins in jurisprudence was not small or temporary, and it affected not only writing about grammar, as described above, but the way in which Roman editors and commentators dealt with literary texts themselves.

We do not know how Aelius Catus presented the text of the Twelve Tables or what sort of thing he said in his commentary: there is only one fragment, preserved by Cicero (*Leg*. 2.59), and it reveals only that Aelius said that he did not understand the word *lessum* in the Twelve Tables. But one feature of his text of the laws can safely be assumed: whatever it was, Aelius believed that he was transcribing unaltered the authentic words of the fifth-century code. Whatever work he did was done in his commentary, not in the text.

Aelius and other early writers who discuss language were concerned with laws and religious ritual texts such as hymns and prayers, and the most salient characteristic of these archaic texts is that they are unalterable. That is true by definition: statute law can be changed only by subsequent legislative action. Strict verbal formalism, moreover, was an important feature of Roman religious ritual and of archaic legal procedure: any error in language required the repetition of the ritual or the failure of a claim under the *legis actio* procedure in use until (at least) the second century. Thus even if a text of this kind was linguistically incomprehensible or legally obsolete, it could not in fact be altered—but it could be explained. Like later lawyers, Aelius presumably attempted to explain the Twelve Tables, already more than two hundred years old when he wrote, and to adapt the ancient law to current circumstance. Legal fiction, allegory, reinterpretation: these are

29. So far as I know, no Greek scholar ever commented on the meaning of a law; the only relevant passage I know is Lysias 10, on whether words in Solon's laws should be interpreted narrowly or broadly.

the methods of legal and religious exegetes. They perform close verbal analysis, attempting to determine the (useful) meanings of words and phrases; they study syntax and structure very closely. But they do not change the text.

Literary texts are not so sacrosanct: philologists are not legally barred from removing obvious errors. But the evidence discussed above about the editing of texts during the Republic reveals clear limits on what could or should be changed: the use of critical signs to mark textual problems means that alterations might be desired, but they were not made. In that respect, there is very little substantive difference between how a legal text was interpreted and how a poem was studied. Although much is uncertain about Alexandrian scholarship, it is evident that critics like Zenodotus or Aristarchus were far more interventionist than their Roman successors, who largely confined their editorial suggestions to commentaries and separate monographs. Roman textual scholarship began, and remained, deeply conservative.

4. EARLY ROMAN PHILOLOGY

What then did the early Roman philologists do? Most of what has been said so far has emphasized what they did *not* do: they were not schoolteachers; they did not make Alexandrian critical editions of texts; they did not write *artes grammaticae*. All the same, the five hundred pages of Funaioli's collection contain much writing and many names. One area of work was exegesis, even if it did not mean making editions. The extant fragments show that there were commentaries on, or other writings about, various early authors. Varro (*LL* 7.39; F 105–6) refers to *commentarii*—which need not mean commentaries in the modern sense—on Naevius by otherwise unknown men named Cornelius and Vergilius; Antonius Gnipho and Pompilius Andronicus, both in Suetonius' list (c. 7–8), wrote about Ennius; various people, some of them unnamed but including the grammarian Curtius Nicia (c. 14), wrote about Lucilius.[30] In a less literary vein, both Aelius Stilo and an otherwise unknown (and thus undatable) Sabidius wrote about the *carmina Saliaria*, and Aelius Stilo as well as some unidentified glossators wrote about the Twelve Tables.[31]

Some of the writings we know about correspond to what Quintilian says about the older grammarians' concern with authenticity and with making ranked lists of authors. Thus Aulus Gellius provides us (3.3.1) with an important list of the scholars who wrote *indices* in which genuine plays of Plautus were distinguished from those Gellius describes as *ambiguae*: Aelius Stilo, Volcacius Sedigitus, Ser. Clodius, Aurelius Opillus, Accius, L. Manilius—a very distinguished group, only one of whom (Opillus) is among Suetonius' *grammatici*, while Aelius Stilo was

30. Aulus Gellius (2.24.4) refers to *quidam scriptores* about Lucilius, and the spurious opening lines of Horace, *Serm.* 1.10 refer to Valerius Cato's work on him. On the taste for Lucilius and its place in the history of philology at the end of the Republic, see 4.1 below.

31. On early commentary on the Twelve Tables, see also Frier (1985: 158–9). On Stilo see further below.

an *eques*, a Stoic, and a polymath, and his son-in-law Ser. Clodius was also an *eques*, while Accius was the last great tragic poet of the Republic. By the last third of the second century, indeed, Roman poets were comparing the merits and establishing the chronology of earlier writers: Porcius Licinus wrote about Roman literary history in verse, famously dating the arrival of the Muse in Rome to the Second Punic War (F 1), and including an account of Terence's relationship to the younger Scipio, Laelius, and Philus (F 4); Volcacius Sedigitus wrote a book *De poetis*. Both Lucilius and Accius expressed their literary views: the former commented on both earlier and contemporary poetry (including Accius, F 29), and the latter notoriously attempted to establish a chronology for early Roman poetry that dated the arrival of Livius Andronicus more than a generation later than anyone else.[32]

A great many fragments, however, also deal with topics other than textual and literary exegesis. The vast majority are explanations of the meaning of individual words, largely through etymology, sometimes as straightforward definitions, and occasionally as *differentiae*, distinctions between the meanings of two words in the same semantic field. As preserved, much of this material is not linked to the interpretation of a particular text, and much of it is not even ascribed to a particular author: there are quite a few references to *glossematorum scriptores, glossae veterum, glossae antiquitatum, qui glossemata interpretati*, or *qui glossas scripserunt*,[33] and Quintilian (1.8.15) explicitly includes the explanation of *glossemata* (itself glossed as *voces minus usitatas*) as a significant part of the work of a *grammaticus*.[34]

Many fragments concern the alphabet and orthography: not just Accius' well-known attempt to use single and double vowels to express short and long quantity (F 24), but also the problem of when to use <u>ei</u> instead of long <u>i</u> (discussed, among others, by Lucilius F 10–10d, Stilo F 49), the genitive of nouns ending in *-ius* (Lucilius F 10a), the use of double rather than single consonants (Ennius T 2, in Festus), and the use of Greek consonants (Accius F 26). And in addition to the legal–philological discussions referred to above, there are other interdisciplinary approaches to language, ranging from the rhetorical and stylistic concerns of Lucilius (esp. F 47–9), to Opillus' glossing (F 17) of *soloecismus* as *stribligo* (a term otherwise unknown) and his careful analysis (F 28) of the different meanings of the same word (e.g., *sapiens*) treated as noun or as participle, to Aelius Stilo's having written a treatise *de proloquiis* (logical axioms) in a Stoic vein (T 19).[35]

32. There is a very large bibliography; see, for instance, Mattingly (1957) and Welsh (2011a).

33. Funaioli (*GRF* pp. 111–13) collects the references to anonymous writers of glosses (who are not included in *GD*); the descriptions given here are found in Festus 166.13L (F 6); Charisius 315.25B (F 2); Charisius 297.24B (F 1); Varro, *LL* 7.34 (F 4); and Varro *LL* 7.10 (F 8), respectively.

34. The interest in glosses is sometimes ascribed to Alexandrian influence (e.g., Collart 1954a: 14), but one suspects that people learn to make word lists without being told to do so.

35. For the fragment of Stilo *De proloquiis*, see also Garbarino (2003: 73–4).

Another frustratingly obscure figure is the grammarian Q. Cosconius, of whom four fragments survive: one is from a work on law, *Actiones*; one contains biographical information about Terence; one is about Italian towns named for companions and relatives of Aeneas; and in the fourth he is cited by Varro as the source for the idea that there were roughly 1,000 original word roots (*primigenia*).[36] In the later second century, from which most of this material comes, grammar was not fenced off from other disciplines of language, above all rhetoric, philosophy, and law. Greek models and predecessors were in some areas clearly used and recognized, but they were also actively adapted to Roman language and purposes.

How representative the extant fragments are of the real interests of early students of language and literature we do not know. If we did not have Suetonius' life of Terence and Gellius' chapter about the early history of the text of Plautus (*NA* 3.3), we would have very little sense that either poet was the object of much study. Even though Horace tells us that the poetry of Livius Andronicus was beaten into him by the *grammaticus* Orbilius, there is no other evidence at all of grammatical study of Livius. The second-century scholar about whom we are best informed is Aelius Stilo, and the variety of his interests may be more indicative than the fragments of any other author. Born probably around 150, he lived until about 90 BCE, long enough to teach both Cicero and Varro. A politically conservative *eques* from Lanuvium, he went into exile with Metellus Numidicus in 100 BCE (and presumably came back with him two years later) and wrote speeches for one of the Metelli, for Servilius Caepio, for C. Aurelius Cotta, and for Q. Pompeius Rufus.[37] He is also praised extravagantly for his learning in Roman antiquities and early Latin texts, and the fragments bear that out: in addition to putting critical *notae* in some text (if the emendation is correct),[38] he wrote an explanation of the *carmina Saliaria* (F 1–3) and of the Twelve Tables (F 6, 13, 36, 41); he pronounced on which of the plays attributed to Plautus were genuine (F 4); he interpreted a passage of Ennius as a self-description (F 51); and he offered etymologies and explanations of a great many old and obscure words, some of which can be identified as coming from the Twelve Tables or Plautus, and many of which concern religious or legal terminology. He sometimes gave Greek etymologies for Roman words (e.g., F 28, possibly F 21)—although Varro criticized him (F 12, cf. Varro F 130 = Gellius 1.18.1, from *Ant. Rer. Div.* 14) for his frequent preference for Latin etymologies over Greek ones.[39] He is also

36. On Cosconius, see Norden (1895); the fragments are collected in *GRF* 108–10. He is unlikely (*pace* Norden) to be identical with the Cosconius mentioned by Cicero in *Brutus* 242, who was almost certainly younger than Varro. On the *primigenia*, see 3.3 below.

37. Cf. Cicero, *Brutus* 205–7. On Stilo, see also 2.1 above. For his general reputation, see the testimonia collected by Funaioli, *GRF* 51–3; see also Teuffel 1 §148; S–H 1 §76a; *HLL* 1 §192.

38. On the list of critical signs, see 2.2 above.

39. On Aeolism in general (the derivation, in one way or another, of Latin from Greek), see now Gitner (2015) and De Paolis (2015) with reference to earlier discussions.

reported to have said that if the Muses spoke Latin, they would speak *Plautino sermone* (Quintil. 10.1.99).

The Roman element in Stilo and the other early philological fragments is significant. Greek influence there doubtless was, but little is visible before Varro himself. Romans were concerned with their own past and their own language. They sought to explain how the language they spoke differed from the language they inherited, through etymology and glossing and through noting changes of phonology and orthography. They tried to establish the chronology and authenticity of their own literature. Roman scholarship is sometimes similar to Greek in its interests, if later, and it would be surprising if there were no connections. But we should acknowledge the importance of legal scholarship in the shaping of Roman philology, and it is not before Varro that we can clearly see a conscious attempt to blend Roman antiquarianism with Greek grammatical and philosophical theory in creating a distinctively Roman philology.

3

Word and World: Varro and His Contemporaries

1. VARRO THE POLYMATH

When M. Terentius Varro (116–27 BCE) was born, Roman scholarship was rudimentary and largely exegetical; by the time he died, the discipline of grammar was flourishing both as a form of teaching and as an arena for scholarly research and debate. In part, the transformation of both scholarship and education was the effect of growing Roman literary sophistication and increasing familiarity with Greek literature and scholarship; but in part, it stemmed from Varro himself. Varro is the first Roman philologist of whom any significant, continuous piece of scholarly writing survives: books 5–10 (out of 25) of *De lingua Latina*, written between 45 and 43 BCE. But Varro's writings on language, literature, and grammar extended far beyond that and are represented by hundreds of fragments from more than fifteen works on philological topics ranging from his earliest datable work, *De antiquitate litterarum* (dedicated to Accius, who died c. 84 BCE), to studies of various aspects of the Latin language, the authenticity of the plays of Plautus, the origins of drama, the chronology of early Roman literature; and then what appears to have been one of his last works, the nine-volume *Disciplinae*, of which the first book, *De grammatica*, may well have been the first attempt to define and organize the study of Latin and a model for the later tradition of the *ars grammatica*.[1]

Although it at times discusses issues of grammatical interest, *De lingua Latina* was not itself an *ars grammatica*. In many ways, it was (and to some extent even in its fragmentary form still is) a repository and compendium of Varro's scholarly interests, insofar as they concerned language and literature. Varro was in his early seventies when he wrote it; it looks back to his *Antiquitates* (his huge and now lost antiquarian work on early Rome), to particular works on specific topics of literary

1. For titles, editions, and bibliography see 12.43 below. *De lingua Latina* is discussed in detail later in this chapter.

history or grammar, and to the work, principally on etymology, of his teachers and predecessors.

The surviving books of *De lingua Latina* focus on two issues, etymology and inflection, and the bulk of the following discussion will necessarily concentrate on those. But it could well be claimed that Varro's single greatest contribution to Roman philology was not as a grammarian, but as a student of texts and of literary history and possibly as an editor. Of this last area, however, we have only indirect evidence: neither in any of Varro's surviving writings nor in the later scholarly tradition is a single manuscript or emendation ever ascribed to him, but his name (although the text is corrupt) almost certainly appeared in the list of Romans who made use of critical signs found in the *Anecdoton Parisinum*.[2] The intensity of his study of earlier literature, however, is evident: he had opinions on the authenticity of earlier plays; he studied chronology; he was interested in poetic vocabulary (see below on *De lingua Latina* Book 7) and he transmitted (if he did not invent) information about the lives and epitaphs of earlier poets. In general, it is likely (though unprovable) that much of what we know about the literature of the third and second centuries is owed, directly or indirectly, to Varro's research.

Much the most detailed evidence about Varro's research methods is provided by Aulus Gellius in *Noctes Atticae* 3.3, drawing primarily on Book 1 of Varro's *De comoediis Plautinis*.[3] Varro's concern here is authenticity, and he claimed undisputed authenticity for only twenty-one plays out of the 130 or so which were attributed to Plautus. Gellius describes these genuine plays as *fabulae Varronianae*, and they are clearly the plays that still survive. But Varro's choice of plays, remarkably, did not reflect his own *iudicium* but that of his predecessors: the twenty-one were the only plays which all earlier critics (of whom Gellius names six) believed genuine works of Plautus.[4] Varro's selection is extremely conservative: he himself thought that other plays were genuine, particularly the *Boeotia*. He made that judgment on the basis of style, and Gellius concurs with his approach and claims other plays for Plautus on the same basis.[5] Indeed, Ser. Clodius, one of the six critics Varro mentioned, seems to have made authentications on the same grounds: Cicero tells us that he could state firmly that a verse was or was not

2. On this text, see 2.2 above. See also Zetzel (1981: 19–23) for the very slight evidence for Varro's discussions of textual problems.

3. Given Gellius' habit of turning his sources into narratives and dialogues of discovery, it is by no means certain that the entire chapter comes from Varro, particularly the quotation from the *Boeotia* (3.3.5) and the concluding biographical fictions about Naevius (3.3.15). But Varro's name, with or without the title of his book, appears frequently enough (3.3.3, 4, 9, 10, 14) that it seems reasonable to accept the material as largely Varronian, as does Funaioli, *GRF* 220–2, Varro F 88.

4. On the earlier critics, see 2.4 above.

5. On the *Boeotia*, note also *LL* 6.89, where Varro ascribes it to either Plautus or Aquilius (Turnebus' emendation for F's *alii*). The authenticity of *Nervolaria* is claimed by Favorinus in Gellius' dialogue (3.3.6), that of *Fretum* by Gellius himself (3.3.7–8).

by Plautus *quod tritas auris haberet notandis generibus poetarum et consuetudine legendi* (*Fam.* 9.16.4: "because he had ears honed by identifying poetic genres and by the habit of reading").

From what Gellius tells us, Varro's work seems to have included several lists: not just the undisputed plays, but also *ambiguae* and non-Plautine plays—again, based on the work of earlier scholars, including Accius, whom Varro in fact quoted as denying the authenticity of the *Boeotia*. Varro also sought to explain at least some of the confusion by the desperate expedient of claiming that some of the plays were written not by Plautus but by an otherwise unknown comic dramatist Plautius. What is more, Varro perpetuated biographical fallacies, certainly in Plautus' case by claiming that he wrote several plays while impoverished and working in a mill, and probably in Naevius' case as well, that he wrote two plays while imprisoned for his attacks on the nobility.

Varro himself was probably not so credulous as these stories would make him; but the conservatism of his method—gathering and collating the ideas of earlier scholars—inevitably involved suspension of disbelief and abdication of judgment. The same is probably true of other material about the earlier poets that he transmitted, above all the epitaphs of Naevius, Plautus, and Pacuvius included in book 1 of *De poetis* (F 57, 59, 62 = Gellius 1.24) and allegedly written by the poets themselves.[6]

Varro's work in literary history relied in part on his own research and in part on that of his predecessors. We know in the case of Plautus that questions of authenticity were discussed as early as Volcacius Sedigitus and Aelius Stilo in the second century, and there were commentaries (generally undatable) on Ennius and Naevius. Varro's own study of poetic vocabulary in *De lingua Latina* Book 7 shows that he used glossaries (possibly his own, but possibly compiled by earlier scholars): the last section (7.50–71) of the discussion of words concerning places and objects is a list of twenty-two words, the first quotation for all but four of which comes from Plautus, cited by title without Plautus' name; in the comparable section (7.80–108) about words for time, citations almost all are introduced with only the author's name and no title, from a wide range of dramatic authors.[7] Varro was not the first person to try to explain odd words in earlier poetry.

The same is true of Varro's work on literary chronology, although here his research seems more credible and perhaps original. Above all, he was interested (as in the *Antiquitates*) in the origins of Roman customs and in the chronology of cultural development. In *De scaenicis originibus*, he reported on the origins of the Ludi Saeculares (F 70), presumably connecting *ludi* with the origins of drama, as in Livy 7.7 and Horace's *Ars poetica*. In *De poetis* Varro seems to have worked hard on the disputed subject of poetic chronology: Accius, as noted above, had developed a late chronology for the early playwrights, placing the arrival of Livius Andronicus in Rome at the end of the third century—well after the date Varro

6. See Dahlmann (1963a: 65–100).

7. See Piras (2015) on Varro's sources and methods in *LL* 7.

adopted for Livius' first play in 240. During the first century, particularly in the 50s and 40s, a better chronology for early Rome was developed and became generally accepted: after Nepos' *Chronicle*—which dated the foundation of Rome, following Polybius, to 751/0 BCE—Cicero's friend Atticus in his *Liber annalis* set out the chronology which became standard, including not only political and military events but also important literary milestones. In this, he almost certainly relied on Varro, not only for the dating of the foundation of Rome to 753 but for literary chronology as well: Varro fixed the date of Livius' first play to 240 BCE (F 55, relating it both to Roman history and to the history of Greek drama) as well as setting out the chronology of Naevius (F 56) and Ennius (F 61) and refuting Accius' later chronology.[8]

2. *DE LINGUA LATINA*

None of Varro's works on literary history survives in more than a few fragments, but a substantial piece of *De lingua Latina* does, and most of the remainder of this chapter will concern this work. We know something about the date and circumstances of its composition: it was dedicated to Cicero, and written between 45 and 43 BCE.[9] In the context of Varro's literary production, it follows the *Antiquitates rerum divinarum* (probably completed in 47 or 46); in all probability, it also follows the *De sermone Latino*, a work which, although very fragmentary, seems to have contained material more like that to be found in (later) *artes grammaticae* than does *De lingua Latina* itself.[10]

8. On Varronian literary chronology, there is a useful discussion by Douglas in his commentary on Cicero, *Brutus* 72. The bibliography on the problem is large and of mixed quality. On Atticus and Nepos, see now *FRHist* 1.344–53, 395–401, with fragments and commentary in subsequent volumes. Of earlier bibliography, the most memorable discussion is that of Münzer (2012: 279–329; originally published 1905). It is hard to tell how much Varro relied on predecessors other than Accius (with whom he clearly disagreed). Only Porcius Licinus and Volcacius Sedigitus definitely wrote literary history, but the Suetonian life of Terence relies on other early material. Aurelius Opillus' *Pinax* and the nine books of his *Musae* as well as Ateius Praetextatus' *Pinakes* probably contained some literary history; what Ateius' *An amaverit Didun Aeneas* was, we can only guess.

9. The chronology is fairly clear: when Cicero dedicated the second version of the *Academica* to Varro in July 45, he had not yet received a dedication from Varro (which Varro seems to have promised as early as 47), and it is very unlikely that Varro dedicated a work to Cicero after the latter's death on 7 December 43. Books 2–4 apparently had a separate dedication to Varro's former quaestor Septumius, but the whole work is later referred to as having been dedicated to Cicero.

10. On *De sermone Latino* and Varro's more properly grammatical work, see 3.5 below. *De sermone Latino* was dedicated to a Marcellus, and more than one person is possible. I suspect, however, that it was the same as the title character of his *Logistoricus Marcellus*, i.e., M. Marcellus, cos. 51, who was murdered in 45.

What survives of *LL* is only six books (5–10), several quite damaged, of the original twenty-five. Fortunately, Varro repeatedly described the organization of the whole: after an introductory book (1), the remaining twenty-four books were divided into three sections, each of which was in turn divided in half. In Books 2–7, Varro considered the origin of words; in Books 8–13, their inflection; and in Books 14–25 the ways in which words are linked together.[11] The first half of each division was concerned with determining whether the task at hand was theoretically possible, the second half with practical discussion of specifics. Thus, the lost Books 2–4 were about the possibility of etymology: Books 2 and 3 for and against, Book 4 a synthesis of the arguments. The next three books, which do survive, offer discussions of specific etymologies concerning, respectively, words to do with space and things in space (5), time and actions in time (6), and words created by poets (7). Books 8–10, which also survive, are about inflection (*declinatio*): against analogy (8), in favor of it (9), and a synthesis describing the process and limits of what Varro calls *declinatio naturalis* (10). The next three books (11–13) presumably offered specific examples of the use and limits of analogy in particular types of inflection. The final twelve books concerned what we would call syntax; but whether he divided this into two halves, giving each a theoretical section (14–16, 20–2) and a practical one (17–19, 23–5), or devoted six consecutive books each to theory (14–19) and practice (20–5), we cannot tell.

Varro's work is frustrating and his goals elusive. That is in part because we possess a relatively small portion of the work, including neither the beginning nor the end; but it is in part because modern critics often try to impose their own preconceptions on a work that rarely fits them. As Wolfram Ax has rightly noted, some scholars accuse Varro of "total linguistic incompetence and dishonesty" while others make him into a linguistic genius.[12] Neither position is right: the first depends on assuming that he meant to represent Greek sources slavishly, the second on assuming, because almost nothing earlier than *De lingua Latina* survives of Latin grammatical writing, that everything new in Varro is original with him. But in fact, as will become clear, even the basic category of "linguistic" is highly questionable.

The most immediately striking feature of *LL* is Varro's constant attempt to categorize and divide up his subject, a characteristic visible in most of his major works; as he remarks after introducing his four place/time categories, "That's why pretty much everything can be divided into four parts" (*quare fit, ut ideo fere omnia sint quadripertita*, 5.12).[13] Thus, the etymologies of Books 5–6 are divided into the

11. The clearest statement is at 8.1: . . . *cuius prima pars, quemadmodum vocabula rebus essent imposita, secunda, quo pacto de his declinata in discrimina ierint, tertia, ut ea inter se ratione coniuncta sententiam efferant* ("the first part is how words were imposed on things; the second, how words inflected from these came to be distinguished; the third, how when linked logically to one another they express a thought").

12. Ax (1996: 115).

13. See Tarver (1997) and Volk (2017) with reference to earlier discussions.

four categories noted above ("In this book I will talk about words for places and things in them, in the second about words for times and things taking place in them"; *in hoc libro dicam de vocabulis locorum et quae in his sunt, in secundo de temporum et quae in his fiunt*, 5.10); the same subdivisions are also used in the following book on words employed by poets. Similarly, at 8.44 in his discussion of analogy, he declares that "words are naturally divided into four groups: those with case, those with tense, those with neither, and those with both" (. . . *dividitur oratio secundum naturam in quattuor partis: in eam quae habet casus et quae habet <tempora et quae habet> neutrum et in qua est utrumque*; so also at 10.17 and 9.31, where he says that these categories were devised by the Greeks). The first of these divisions (between place and time) corresponds roughly to the distinction between nouns and verbs. The second can be mapped onto the standard (later) division of the eight *partes orationis*: nouns (which in ancient grammar includes adjectives) and pronouns have cases; verbs have tenses; participles have both; and adverbs, conjunctions, prepositions, and interjections have neither. But neither of Varro's divisions—nor quite a few of his frequent categorizations—matches anything found elsewhere in Roman grammatical writings, even though it is often clear that he is aware of the more familiar categories.[14]

De lingua Latina, however, was not about grammar or for elementary students and their teachers, but about the history and shaping of the language itself: what the Latin language is, where it comes from, and how to use it properly. Thus, instead of beginning by identifying the parts of speech and discussing their forms or, as many later grammars do, defining such terms as "letter" and "syllable," Varro starts from etymology, the origins of words (2–7), proceeds to show how those fundamental elements of the language develop inflections and derivatives (8–13), and follows that by considering how words are linked together (14–25): *impositio, declinatio, coniunctio*. From vocabulary to paradigm to syntax, Varro's goal is to build up the living language through its history. And unlike a grammarian, the linguistic historian has no one "correct" form of the language.

The two parts of *LL* of which some portion survives deal with issues the backgrounds of which are very different. In discussing etymology (5–7) Varro drew, at times explicitly, on a long tradition of Roman study, culminating in the work of his own teacher Aelius Stilo; in discussing paradigms and inflection (8–10), he was dealing with a subject very little addressed in what we have of earlier Roman philology, but of considerable interest in his own day.[15] In both

14. As, for example, the standard division between noun (*vocabulum* [8.11] or *nominatus* [8.45] in Varro's terminology) and verb (*verbum* [8.11] or *verbum temporale* [9.95]). For much fuller information, see Schad (2007) s.vv.

15. There are three known earlier works which discussed inflection, all probably recent when Varro wrote *LL*. Antonius Gnipho wrote a work *De Latino sermone* in two books, and at least one fragment (cited without book title) shows that he discussed inflection and analogy (F 4; see Kaster 1995 on Suetonius *DGR* 7), possibly in the 60s. Staberius Eros' *De proportione* (*GRF* 106; cf. Kaster 1995 on Suetonius *DGR* 13) was clearly concerned with analogy and probably written no later than the 50s; only

extant portions, however, Varro was clearly combining his own construction of the Latin language and its history with Greek techniques, both philosophical and philological. Varro repeatedly, and at important junctures, draws attention to his knowledge of Greek philosophy and philology, often together: at 5.9 he cites in tandem the Alexandrian grammarian Aristophanes and the second head of the Stoic school Cleanthes; at 6.2 he balances two Stoics, Chrysippus and Antipater, against two Alexandrian grammarians, Aristophanes and Apollodorus; and at 9.1 he contrasts Crates' misunderstanding of both Chrysippus and Aristarchus with his own comprehension of both.

As far as Varro was concerned (and indeed this applies to much of the Roman grammatical tradition), there were two principal Greek varieties of grammatical learning. Discussions of the meanings and morphology of words came from Alexandria, as a by-product of the editing and exegesis of the texts of early Greek poetry and resulting eventually, in the second century, in the *Tekhnê* of Dionysius Thrax, a pupil of Aristarchus. Analysis of syntax, on the other hand, was a distinctly philosophical area of expertise, arising from Stoic attempts to define the relationship between language and the real world and between *logos* and *lexis* (reason and its expression), and to classify the truth-value of various types of proposition.[16] Both extant portions of *De lingua Latina* owe something to Stoic preoccupations, on the one hand, with the Stoics' desire to use etymology to explain the world through recovering primordial signifiers that matched the objects they signified, and on the other, with their resistance to overly regularized language, which obstructed or distorted precisely that original relationship between language and world. Presumably the final and longest section of *De lingua Latina* was also related to Stoic concerns, in this case with the logical structure of sentences as statements about the world. But although Varro's work reflects Stoic interests, it is itself not a particularly philosophical work: philosophy may have given him structures to work with and questions to ask, but the result is

one fragment survives. Much more remains of Julius Caesar's *De analogia* (*GRF* 143–57; Garcea 2012) written probably in 54, which will be discussed below.

16. This is a simplification of an extraordinarily complex subject, the development of grammatical theory in relationship to philosophy in Greek. Since my subject is Roman philology, not Greek, and since it is virtually impossible to identify particular Greek sources for most Roman philological texts (or methods), I am assuming a general knowledge of Greek philosophical and grammatical thought on the part of Roman scholars, but (unless there is strong reason to believe otherwise) not dogmatic adherence to a particular approach and certainly not slavish translation of a particular source. For an excellent account of the philosophical underpinnings of Greek and Roman philology, see Atherton and Blank (2013), with extensive and useful bibliography. A briefer and simpler, but sometimes superficial account of Varro's work and its Stoic background is Law (2003: 38–49—but see also the comments of Ax 2003). Luhtala (2005) is a vigorous but not altogether convincing attempt to minimize philosophical influences on grammatical theory prior to Apollonius Dyscolus.

largely independent, continuing the approaches developed in the second century through the study of early Roman texts and the interpretation of early Roman law.

3. MAKING WORDS: *IMPOSITIO* AND *DECLINATIO*

Varro distinguishes, at least in theory, two stages in the creation of the stock of Latin words: creation of basic semantic units by one or more name-givers who attached words to things (*impositio*) and the extension of those original words by inflection and derivation, both of which fall under the broad rubric of *declinatio*. The two overlap to a limited extent, as does Varro's treatment of them, but he keeps them largely distinct.[17] Within the category of *impositio*, Varro immediately makes further refinements: as he states in the opening paragraph of Book 5, *In his ad te scribam, a quibus rebus vocabula imposita sint in lingua Latina, et ea quae sunt in consuetudine apud <populum et ea quae inveniuntur apud> poetas* (5.1: "In what follows I will write to you [Cicero, to whom the book is addressed] about the things from which words were imposed in Latin, both those which are in general use and those which are found in the poets").[18] We are to be aware of several important oppositions: *vocabula* and the *res* from which namers derived them; past imposition and present use; and common language and poetic diction. The last distinction governs the division between Books 5–6 on one side and Book 7 on the other, but the other two are pervasive: on the one hand, the original posited connection between words and things explains the imposers' view of the nature of the world; and on the other hand, the connection between past and present allows us to understand relationships that have been obscured over time.[19]

The processes of linguistic change, as Varro says, are difficult to follow: words change their meaning, many forms no longer show their relationship to other words (hence it is often useful to start from oblique cases), words are altered through the passage of time and through manipulations of words or syllables[20]—and besides, the original *impositio* was not always done correctly: *nec quae [sc. impositio] extat sine mendo omnis imposita, nec quae recte est imposita, cuncta manet* (5.3: "not every original naming was done without error, nor does every

17. *Impositio* merges with *declinatio voluntaria*, which includes both derivational morphology and naming, e.g., of slaves (8.22) or objects (10.51–3). See further below.

18. The added phrase is A. Spengel's supplement; something of the kind is clearly necessary.

19. We are, of course, missing the theoretical discussion of etymology/*impositio* that occupied Books 2–4. Varro describes the debate as between arguments for and against both the status of etymology as an *ars* and its utility (7.109); the parallel between this and the extant debate on analogy in Books 8–10 suggests that Book 2 at least was based on an empiricist or Epicurean attack on etymology, not on a debate among philologists. On this, see Blank (2005).

20. The modes of alteration (*demptio, adiectio, traiectio, commutatio*, applied to either words or syllables) are very old, and derive from the Greek philosophical tradition—if not from any one particular school. On the modes, see Desbordes (1983) and Ax (1987).

correct original naming still survive").[21] The belief in an original "natural" relationship between signifier and signified, with the concomitant belief that one or more individuals applied the correct names to things, is fundamentally Stoic, and perhaps part of Varro's philosophical adherence to the Stoic-inclined Old Academy of Antiochus.[22] But in Books 5–7, at least, Varro writes as a historian rather than a philosopher. He did not aim at a single tidy solution to the origin of language and meaning, particularly in dealing with a city whose origins were as complex as those of Rome. Put very simply, not all words in Latin were originally Latin, and neither Rome nor its language was a unified construction: they were created by many people over a long period,[23] and even though the original *impositio* may have been based on nature (cf. 6.3, 8.10), it was a nature that spoke many languages.

According to Varro's famous (and textually difficult) anatomy of the varieties of etymology, there are four degrees of explanation. The simplest is the one that any fool can do, recognizing an obvious compound: *quis enim non videt unde "argentifodae" et "viocurus"?* (5.7). The next level is that of *antiqua grammatica*, the deciphering of poetic words. These two are straighforward—and Varro himself devotes Book 7 to the latter. But the third and fourth levels are increasingly complex. The third level is that of the philosophers, who explain the significance of common words such as *oppidum* or *via*. Varro links Levels 2 and 3 when he notes *non solum ad Aristophanis lucernam, sed etiam ad Cleanthis lucubravi* (5.9: "I have studied not just by Aristophanes' lamp, but by Cleanthes' as well"): Aristophanes the grammarian is emblematic of those who study the language of poets, while Cleanthes is an example of philosophical understanding. The fourth level is the most problematic, *ubi est aditus ad initia regis* (5.8).[24] The wording and the meaning of the phrase are hard to pin down; but whether the *initia* here refer to mystery initiation in an elaborate metaphor or merely to the origin of words, it is the king that matters. Varro here leaps over the philosophers, moving from Level 2 to Level 4: why should he limit himself to the words invented by Ennius or Livius Andronicus and neglect those of king Latinus and Romulus? In other words, it was, as the first account of Level 4 suggests, the function of kings to invent words, and they did so long before poets did.

21. This recognition of incorrect *impositio* appears also at 8.7–8 and 10.16.

22. On the philosophical background to Varronian etymology, see above all Blank (2008). For an overview of the etymologies themselves, see Coleman (2001).

23. Varro's belief (which he does not state in so many words) is parallel to the ideas of Cato about the Roman constitution, as reported by Cicero, *De re publica* 2.1.

24. The manuscript (F) here reads *aditus* <u>*et*</u> *initia regis*, which makes little sense. The normal solution has been to emend *aditus* to *adytum* (the i/y distinction is not textually significant) and to see this as a metaphor from mystery religions; for the alternative adopted here, emending *et* to *ad*, see Schröter (1963). The long discussion of Lazzerini (2017) reviews other attempts to interpret the passage before offering her own unlikely interpretation.

But as noted above, Latin has messy origins, and Varro is perfectly willing to accept uncertainty, and even multiple origins for the same word. Thus, in the discussion of words for "place" that begins with *terra* (so named, according to Aelius Stilo, *quod teritur*, 5.21), we are told that the word *iter* is derived from *tero* too—but not much later (5.35) we learn that *iter* is so called from *itus*, in other words ultimately from the verb *ire*, which clearly has nothing to do with *terra*. Again, within the discussion of *terra*, Varro says that a boundary is called *terminus* either because the boundary path was most trodden (*teritur*) or—since some Latin towns use *terimen* rather than *terminus*—it is the same as Greek *termôn: Pote vel illinc: Evander enim, qui venit in Palatium, e Graecia Arcas* (5.21: "And it could be from there: Evander, who settled on the Palatine, was a Greek from Arcadia").[25]

Certain words exercise Varro a great deal: Aelius Stilo's view that the rabbit was named *lepus* because it was light-footed (*levipes*) is rejected by Varro in favor of deriving it from the word *leporis* used by the Siculi; the Siculi, who were Aeolic Greeks, had lived in Rome, according to *annales veteres nostri*, and had both taken the word with them to Sicily and left it behind in Rome.[26] In Varro's account, a word can have the same etymology in two languages and can have two etymologies within a single language. But then, Italy (and Rome itself) had been inhabited by multiple *gentes* over time, and words themselves, since at some level they reflect the underlying *res* or *natura*, sometimes are not the result of a single language, but of the truth. Some words are *nostra*, others are *aliena* (5.10), and in a few cases, they can change origins. Thus with the name of the river Tiber: *Tiberis quod caput extra Latium, si inde nomen quoque exfluit in linguam nostram, nihil <ad> ἐτυμολόγον Latinum* (5.29: "Since the source of the Tiber is outside Latium, if its name also flowed from that source into our language, that has nothing to do with its Latin etymology"); but like the Volturnus, which comes from Samnium but flows to Latium, it is now a *Latinum vocabulum*, and we even have a god Tiberinus. The Etruscans, however, claim that it was first named Thebris after an Etruscan *regulus*, while others claim that its original Latin name was Albula (although it was presumably still "Thebris" in Etruria?) and was then changed to Tiberinus after a Latin king (5.30). The development of language also mirrors cultural development: the name for vegetables (*holera*, from *olla*, "pot") is later than that for cheese (*caseus*) because cooking came later than eating raw food; there is a similar progression in the names of the varieties of cooked meats (5.108–9).

Impositio took time, came from many sources, made mistakes, and underwent alteration over time as population or political control changed or as civilization progressed, and it is no accident that one of the most important metaphors that

25. Evander as the bearer of Aeolic dialect to Rome also appears in F 295 (from Johannes Lydus), from the earlier *De origine linguae Latinae*. Varro's view of the multiple origins of Latin (from Gallic, Sabine, Greek, and Etruscan) is likewise reported by Lydus (F 296). On this, see Norden (1895: viii–ix) and Gitner (2015). Pascucci (1979) contains a useful collection of evidence.

26. Discussed more than once: *LL* 5.101; *ARD* 14 F 89; *RR* 3.12.6.

Varro uses to describe the origins of language is a biological one, from trees. He says that he will follow the history of words across his own divisions, because trees extend their *radices* across property lines (5.13).[27] Some divine names have *radices* in both Sabine and Latin (5.74), and the Greek source of the word *lepesta*, a kind of wine vessel, has sent roots into both Sabine and Roman territory (5.123). Words, like plants, can be either fertile or sterile (8.9), and some of them have many offshoots (*propagines*). Words are living things, anchored in soil, but often spreading widely and changing their nature: as Varro says, you don't have to see its roots to recognize a pear tree from its branches (7.4).

Even though Varro mentions Greek models, both philosophical and philological, at the outset of his account of etymology, the content of his etymological books shows little attention to either. The organization he employs is very much his own, and in many sections of Books 5–7 the content is drawn from his own prior researches into Roman antiquities; completeness of categorization is discarded in favor of his own interests and knowledge, about Rome, its institutions, and its literature.[28] When, after discussing the general vocabulary for earth and water (5.21–30), he turns to the particulars of the world itself, his geography starts from the division between Asia and Europe, and Europe swiftly turns into the local geography of Italy (5.31–2); that, in turn, becomes a set of definitions of the varieties of *ager* in Roman law, and before long he is giving an account of the geography of the city of Rome, focusing on the hills (5.41–3), the shrines of the Argei (45–54), and the urban tribes (55–6). So too, his account of time in Book 6 includes a detailed account of the Roman religious calendar (6.12–32) and a set of observations on a group of public documents, arranged in descending order of rank: a censorial *tabula* (6.86–7) is followed by consular *commentaria* (6.88–9) and the quaestorian *commentarium anquisitionis* (6.90–5).[29] In addition to using the results of his own antiquarian researches, he also relied on Roman models, particularly Aelius Stilo: although Varro criticized him for his etymology of *lepus*, he cites his teacher for the etymologies of the two words he discusses first (after *locus* itself) under the rubric of place, *caelum* and *terra* (5.18, 21), and when he discusses Jupiter and Juno as manifestations of sky and earth, Aelius' discussion of *Deus Fidius* is not far behind (5.66). It is possible that Varro draws attention to Stilo in these passages because it was Stilo's organization that he followed.

But if Stilo and archaic Roman texts, both laws and poems, play a large part in the surviving books on *impositio*, they feature very little in the surviving books on *declinatio*. That is partly because Books 8–10 are concerned with the theory of inflection rather than its practice, and citations of particular Roman texts or sources are relatively sparse. Instead—and in this respect the lost theoretical

27. On this topic, I am indebted to an unpublished paper by A. Gitner, "Latin's Creeping Roots: Varro on Latin across Space and Time" (American Philological Association, Annual Meeting, 2014).

28. See Volk (2017).

29. His use of earlier glossaries for the account of poetic words has been noted above.

books on etymology were probably similar—they show considerable indebtedness to the Greek philosophical and philological background. Varro shapes Books 8–9 as a debate between proponents of anomaly (the belief that language does and should have a great deal of irregularity, reflecting both popular habit and the unruliness of nature itself) and analogy (the corresponding belief that language, particularly morphology, is governed by *ratio*).[30] The speaker of Book 8 takes an extreme position: not only does analogy not govern inflectional morphology, but there is no such thing as analogy at all. The speaker of Book 9 is less sweeping in the defense of analogy than the speaker of Book 8 is in attacking it, since the analogist position recognizes that analogy does not apply everywhere, but he offers a point-by-point rebuttal, arguing that analogy is not only dominant, but necessary, in the organization of inflection. It was long thought that these books represented a genuine debate among Greek grammarians—normally thought to be Pergamene (anti-analogist) and Alexandrian (analogist)—and that a conflict between analogism and anomalism was a dominant feature of Roman grammatical thought in Varro's day. Now, however, it appears that the debate, if there ever was one, was philosophical rather than grammatical: the anti-analogist represents an empiricist attack on grammatical *tekhnê*, comparable (and related) to the much broader assault on *tekhnê* given by Sextus Empiricus.[31] The goal of such an argument is not to show that no such thing as grammar exists, but that language, like every other form of intellectual skill, is ruled by *consuetudo*, not by *ars*, and that anyone can speak comprehensibly by simple observation, without detailed study and without requiring a broad principle of analogical word formation. That was not a problem for grammarians: Crates the Pergamene Stoic and Aristarchus the Alexandrian philologist may have differed on the role of analogy and how to determine where or how to recognize (or employ) it, but their differences are those of degree, not of kind. For philosophers, it mattered whether grammar, or any other such area of study, was a *tekhnê* or an *empeiria*, the product of *ars* or *consuetudo*; for a practicing philologist, it was relatively unimportant.[32]

While the philosophical background to the discussion of analogy and anomaly clearly mattered to Varro, the issue that concerns him in Books 8–10 is at heart

30. On the meaning and use of the word *analogia* in the Latin grammarians, see Schironi (2007). Although the debate form recalls Academic disputations *in utramque partem*, Varro's addition of a third book resolving the debate eliminates the Academic goal of suspension of judgment.

31. On this I follow Blank (2005). Earlier valuable contributions to the topic include Fehling (1956–7) and Ax (1995, 1996). Fehling's article is extremely important (and largely began the modern study of Varro's grammatical works) but highly schematic; he forces the history of Latin grammar (particularly works on Latinity) into a single pattern, which his version of Varro simultaneously follows, misunderstands, and alters.

32. On the philosophical issue of technicity, Blank (1998: xvii–xl) has a lucid and valuable explanation; see also Atherton (1996) on the nature of grammatical knowledge and the idea of "correctness."

practical rather than theoretical. How do we form words, and how do we recognize and comprehend the words used by other people? If every single form of every word were the result of an act of *impositio*, then it would be impossible to recognize the relationships either of forms in a paradigm or among derivationally related words: as Varro says, if instead of *lego* and *legi* for the first-person singular of the present and perfect, respectively, we used, for example, *Priamus* and *Hecuba*, then we could not recognize the fundamental paradigmatic relationship between the forms (8.3).[33] The system of language—any language, not just Latin (*in sermones non solum Latinos, sed omnium hominum*, 8.3)—requires a balance between the number of *primigenia*, basic roots which are the result of *impositio*, and the number of forms derived from each of those roots.[34] That derivation is called *declinatio* (generally translated as "inflection" to avoid importing the distinction that Varro does not himself make between declension and conjugation in modern grammatical terminology), and *declinatio* is in turn divided into two varieties, *declinatio naturalis* and *declinatio voluntaria* (8.21–3). The former of these is close to the modern category of inflection, the latter to derivation; but in fact there is no fixed border between *impositio* and *declinatio voluntaria* or between *declinatio voluntaria* and *declinatio naturalis*.[35] In some cases, of course, the categories are distinct: the declension of regular nouns and the conjugation of regular verbs are instances of *declinatio naturalis*, arising *a communi consensu* (7.21), and they exist because of their utility: *propter eorum qui dicunt usum declinati casus, uti is qui de altero diceret, distinguere posset, cum vocaret, cum daret, cum accusaret, sic alia eiusdem <modi> discrimina, quae nos et Graecos ad declinandum duxerunt* (7.16: "Cases were inflected for the utility of speakers, so that someone talking about someone else could tell when he was calling, when he was giving, when he was accusing, and other distinctions of the same sort which have led us and the Greeks to the practice of declension").[36] Some derivatives are equally clearly instances of *declinatio voluntaria*: Varro's famous example is that of

33. Varro clearly chooses Priam and Hecuba as his examples ("what's he to Hecuba?") because they were husband and wife, and therefore in a sense paradigmatically related; but we only know that from knowing the story, not because the forms of their names make the relationship clear.

34. Varro (6.36) cites Cosconius for the estimate of 1,000 *primigenia*, and he calculates that each root could produce 500 forms by *declinatio*, to be multiplied tenfold if compounding by prefix is added (6.38). Belardi (1985: 225–32) discusses Varro's ideas about finite and infinite elements of language in the context of the history of linguistic thought. On Cosconius, see 2.4 above.

35. Modern historians of linguistics sometimes pluck from its context the distinction between the two kinds of *declinatio* and use it to turn Varro into a precursor of modern linguistic distinctions between inflectional and derivational morphology; so Taylor (1974) and frequently thereafter, and Law (2003: 47–9). Recent discussions of Varro as a linguist are frequently unhistorical and are rarely cited here; see further below.

36. So also 8.5, *impositicia nomina esse voluerunt quam paucissima, quo citius ediscere possent, declinata quam plurima, quo facilius omnes quibus ad usum opus esset dicerent.*

three men buying slaves at Ephesus, who might name them "Artemas" after the seller's name, "Ion" from the region, or "Ephesius" from the city (8.21).

The slave names are Varro's own example of *declinatio voluntaria*, and he uses the verb *declinat* to describe the process of naming. At the same time, however, when he distinguishes these derived names from their own case-forms (e.g., *Ionis* as genitive of *Ion*), he refers to them not as derivatives, but as imposed, *impositis nominibus* (8.22). In discussing the derivation of adjectives from places (e.g., *Romanus* from *Roma*), Varro argues that we should not expect analogical formations: *quod in consuetudine vehementer natat, quod declinantes imperite rebus nomina imponunt, a quibus cum accepit consuetudo, turbulenta necesse est dicere* (10.16: "Because [this kind of formation] is in usage completely at sea [swimming], because people making derivatives impose names on things inexpertly; and when usage takes them over, you have to say it's a rough sea at that"). And while within the realm of *declinatio* modern categories make a clear distinction between inflection and derivation, Varro does not: for him (8.23), some voluntary *declinatio* involves *natura*, while some natural *declinatio* involves *voluntas*. The division between the two is not clear: Varro treats the iterative and interrogative forms *scriptito* (10.33) and *scribone* (10.31) as if they were part of the paradigm of *scribo*, just as he treats the derivation of *homunculus* from *homo* as exactly comparable to the creation of the plural *homines* (8.14)—not to mention the fact that he sees *strenuus* as a derivative of *strenuitas* (8.15) rather than the reverse.

Varro's discussion of analogy and anomaly, in fact, contains a number of elements which show that, for him, the boundaries between purely linguistic phenomena and the larger world of which they are a part are very permeable: the act of *impositio* itself is somehow meant to connect word and world; both the anti-analogist in Book 8 and the analogist in Book 9 argue in favor of their respective positions by using (even the anti-analogist) the analogy of nature; and the kind of anomaly that Chrysippus reportedly believed in was based not on the lack of pattern among words, but on the lack of pattern in the relationships between words and things (9.1). What is more, the connection between word and world extends to the organization of paradigms, an area in which modern historians of linguistics have placed great stress on the originality—and modernity—of Varro's explanation purely on the basis of morphology without consideration of semantics. But that is to take Varro's account of paradigms entirely out of context.

In Book 10 of *De lingua Latina*, having set out in the previous two books the positions against and in favor of analogy, Varro attempts to define with some precision the possible uses and limitations of analogy in *declinatio*. He does this in four steps, which he describes as follows: *quid sit simile ac dissimile, quid ratio quam appellant λόγον, quid pro portione quod dicunt ἀνὰ λόγον, quid consuetudo* (10.2: "what 'likeness' and 'unlikeness' are; what 'reckoning' is, which [the Greeks] call *logos*; what 'in proportion' is, which they call 'analogous'; what 'habit' is").[37]

37. My translation is awkward, but unavoidably so. The later explanation of *ratio* (10.35–6, but missing a considerable amount of text before 10.35) shows that it means

The first topic, on likeness and unlikeness, is long and detailed (10.3–34): how can one argue that one word should be inflected *like* another without knowing what *like* means? The issue had been discussed by the Alexandrian grammarians, and the number of categories (*discrimina*) deemed necessary to establish likeness had ranged up to seventy-one (10.10).[38] Varro reduces them to two, *e quis unum positum in verborum materia, alterum ut in materiae figura, quae ex declinatione fit* (10.11: "of which one is based on the *materia* of words, the other in the shape of the *materia* which is created by *declinatio*"). Kent translates *materia* as "substance" and in his note identifies it with "the form which is the starting point for inflection," and Taylor, with remarkable anachronism, as "morphological substance" (with *materiae figura* becoming "phonological configuration").[39] But while *materia* clearly has something to do with the form of the word, it also has to do with what it represents: Varro more than once refers to the problem of words that occur only in the plural such as *scopae*, "broom" or *bigae*, "chariot" (cf. 8.7, 10.24): they are plural because they refer to compound objects, and that is part of the original naming. In other words, the original reflects not just a morpheme, but an object. And although it is in the analogist's argument in 9 rather than Varro's own presentation in 10, the first two items in the list of requirements before analogy can be invoked (or its absence criticized) are very relevant: *In quo animadvertito natura quadruplicem esse formam, ad quam in declinando accommodari debeant verba: quod debeat subesse res quae designetur, et ut sit ea res in usu* . . . (9.36: "In which you should observe that there are naturally four parts [to establishing analogy]: there has to be something being referred to [a *semainomenon*], and it has to be something in use . . .").[40] In other words, referentiality is essential to language, even to the most formal elements of its inflection. At the very end of his explanation of analogical proportion, in making a transition to the explanation of *consuetudo* (his final topic in Book 10), Varro offers a caution about the limits of analogy, which must be *duplex* (*in rebus et in vocibus*) in order to work (10.72).

both "relationship," i.e., between the nominative and dative of *amor*, and "ratio," in the mathematical analogy used to set up paradigms in 10.43, where *logoe* is used for the proportions 1:2::2:4. I use "reckoning" because it can be both logical and mathematical. The use of the phrase *pro portione* as if it were a nominative *proportio* is not without its own problems; for a good discussion, see Schad (2007) s.v. On the terminology of analogy in general, see Schironi (2007); for the meaning of *consuetudo*, see further below.

38. Although Varro does not report it here, Aristophanes of Byzantium had five *rationes* and Aristarchus had six; cf. Charisius 149.22–50.2B, the beginning of the chapter *De analogia, ut ait Romanus*.

39. Taylor (1996: 108–9), quoting Taylor (1974: 99). Lomanto (2001: 178–86) rightly criticized Taylor and finds the origin of Varro's *materia* and *figura* in Aristotle's *hylê* and *morphê*. That is clearly part of the story, but Varro blends it with his emphasis on the relationship between language and the material world.

40. The requirement of *usus* is repeated in the recapitulation of requirements for analogy at 10.83–4 (the last chapters before the text breaks off).

To these two must be added a third requirement: *Quas ad loquendum ut perducas accedere debet usus: alia enim ratio qua facias vestimentum, alia quemadmodum utare vestimento* (10.72: "For this to be a part of speaking you need to add use, because the pattern for making clothes is different from the pattern of wearing them"). Tidy charts are all very well, and analogy as a system (*ratio* as both logic and mathematics) has a degree of elegance, but a chart on the page is not the same as what comes out of people's mouths.

Even the tidy grids that Varro describes for paradigms, following Greek models, have Varronian idiosyncrasies built in:[41] in the first place, he believes that the nominative singular represents *voluntas*, being the form originally imposed, while declension represents *natura, quo decurritur sine doctrina* (10.51), and that one can begin constructing a paradigm from either nature or *voluntas*; that, since some paradigms are defective (owing, sometimes, to the flaws of the original *impositio*), it is best to start inflecting from a form other than the imposed one; and since Latin has a sixth case (ablative) unknown to the Greeks, we do best to start declining Latin words from the form that only exists in Latin (10.62). One of the oddest things about Varro's discussion of inflection is that many of the most striking linguistic elements in it—aside from the fact that very few of them, in all likelihood, were new—are tangential to his main purpose. He is interested in figuring out the logic of inflection and describing the grids in which to compose paradigms; he is interested in the nature of similarity and difference. But his main interest is in the principles that govern not language itself, but our use of it. *Voluntaria declinatio refertur ad consuetudinem, naturalis ad rationem* ("voluntary inflection is related to custom, natural inflection to reason"), he says at one point (10.15). While most students of *De lingua Latina* have dwelt on voluntary and natural declension, what is much more important to Varro himself is the other pairing, *consuetudo* and *ratio*: far more than analogy and anomaly, they define the central problem of the work.

4. THE SOURCES OF SPEECH: *RATIO* AND *CONSUETUDO*

From the point of view of an extreme anomalist, analogy is the opponent of *consuetudo*; from the opposite point of view, anomaly is the opponent of *ratio*. Each proponent, of course, argues that his side takes the best of both; both sides agree that it is not possible to have a workable language without the combination. Each of the words is used polemically, and each therefore has more than one meaning. *Ratio*, from an anomalist point of view, either does not exist at all

41. Taylor repeatedly calls the use of the grid original to Varro, but Varro himself is clear that he borrowed it: for the second (mathematical) grid, he refers to *ab Aristarcho grammatici* (10.42); when he describes the first grid (nominal paradigms) he uses the phrase *ordines deriguntur bini*, in which the simple indicative suggests that he is describing something that already exists, not that he is giving instructions for building it from scratch. The source for it may well be in Greek mathematics: see Garcea (2008b). Duso (2006) on philosophical origins is less convincing.

because language is not completely systematic and logical, or it represents the mindless application of rules to a living system; from an analogist point of view, it is the logical process, at times mathematical, by which we can naturally develop paradigms that enable us to communicate with one another. *Consuetudo*, from this point of view, is an acceptance of error, inconsistency, and slovenly speech that obstructs comprehension; for an anomalist, *consuetudo* is language as it is spoken, including as much paradigmatic rigidity as people need, and as much variety and individuality as they want. To find a balance, one needs to decide whose *ratio* and whose *consuetudo* should be followed.[42]

From the point of view of the anomalist, the goal of all speech is utility, and it reaches that goal through being *aperta et brevis* (8.26): since all long and obscure speeches arouse the audience's hatred for the orator, it is obviously useful for him to be quick and clear. And the way to be clear is to follow *consuetudo,* which accepts many usages with no fuss: who cares if the genitive of *Hercules* is *Herculi* or *Herculis*? So we don't need analogy to tell us which one is right, so long as *consuetudo* admits both (8.26). Although the anti-analogist case moves from this position to say that consequently there is no need for analogy at all, the position itself, that habitual practice cannot be ignored, is perfectly acceptable to the analogist as well; Aristarchus is cited as saying that one should follow likeness only so far, *quoad patiatur consuetudo* (9.1). Indeed, the analogist speaker points out that *consuetudo* and analogy are closely linked, because analogy is itself a kind of *consuetudo*, just as is anomaly. Both are necessary and inseparable, like *corpus* and *anima* (9.2–3).

There are any number of moves in this game, clearly, but in any form of it, *consuetudo* constitutes the boundary of *ratio*. But what *consuetudo*, and whose? The anti-analogist has an unexpected and significant starting point: his argument about brevity and clarity concerns not language as such, but oratory, and as Varro's argument develops over the course of the next two books, it becomes clear that he considers the issue of acceptability in actual use at least as important as the abstract and theoretical workings of *ratio* or analogy. The arguments of the analogist speaker in Book 9 demonstrate that even the fanatical analogist is brought up short by *consuetudo*, and therefore splits analogy itself three ways, depending on who is speaking. Analogy, he says (9.4–6), is not universal: it does not apply to all words; even when it is theoretically correct, it is not always used; and it is not used in the same way by different people. It is this last point that is significant, and which he elaborates: *Alia enim populi universi, alia singulorum, et de ieis non eadem oratoris et poetae, quod eorum non idem ius* (9.5: "Some words belong to the people as a whole, others belong to individuals; and among those the same words do not belong to the orator and the poet, because they do not have

42. On *consuetudo* in Varro, see Baratin (2008) and Garcea (2012: 103–9), with copious bibliography. I discuss the language of *natura, ratio,* and *consuetudo* in Zetzel (forthcoming).

the same rights").[43] The entire people should use analogy in all possible cases, and should correct itself *si perperam est consuetus* ("if it has bad habits"); but the orator should not: . . . *cum orator non debeat in omnibus uti, quod sine offensione non potest facere, cum poeta transilire lineas impune possit* (". . . since the orator should not follow [analogy] in everything: he can't do it without causing offense, while the poet can leap over boundaries with impunity"). There's not much to be done about poets, who will use language as they wish; but the orator is constrained, not by what is correct, but by what can be said without offending his audience. At the end of his pro-analogy argument, the same point is repeated, that as a whole (*universi*) we should follow analogy, but individuals should do so only when it would not offend *consensus communis, quod, ut dixi, aliud debet praestare populus, aliud e populo singuli homines* (9.114: "which, as I said, the people should provide in one way, individual members of the populace in another"), since individuals do not all have the same *ius*; he again introduces the distinction between orators and poets, although this time he suggests that poets have the freedom to follow analogy, not to ignore it (9.115).

In summing up his introduction to the topic, the analogist offers a remarkable simile, comparing the relationship of the people as a whole to the individual speaker with that of the helmsman to the crew of a ship: *ut rationi optemperare debet gubernator, gubernatori unus quisque in navi, sic populus rationi, nos singuli populo* (9.6: "Just as the helmsman should obey *ratio* and each individual in the ship obey the helmsman, so the people should obey *ratio* and each of us obey the people"). Not only is the *populus* equated to the single helmsman and the individual speaker to the collective crew, but the *ratio* of steering a ship is equated to the *ratio* (analogy) which governs word formation and thus language. While the people at large (i.e., the Latin language as a construct) should correct improper usage, the speaker, whose task is less to improve the Latin of his audience than to gain their approval, should follow *consuetudo*, even if incorrect.

Another version of the same argument is made in the frustratingly incomplete last section of Book 10, on *consuetudo* itself. Varro reminds us of the distinction he made (10.72, quoted above) between theoretical *ratio* and actual usage, and proceeds to offer first two, and then three definitions of analogy to correspond to different people's *usus loquendi*. The first is simple: *analogia est verborum similium declinatio similis* (10.74: "analogy is the similar inflection of similar words"); this is the theoretical form of analogy. To make the second definition, he adds the phrase *non repugnante consuetudine communi* ("as long as custom doesn't object"). And he then divides the second definition into two classes of language users, by adding *ex quadam parte* to define poetic analogy. The three definitions so created apply to three groups: respectively, the *populus, omnes singuli*, and poets. The third group,

43. Kent expands *alia* to "words and forms," which is more precise than Varro: the antecedent of *alia* is *verborum*. Note that Varro is describing words as a kind of property (*ius*); there is similar language used of the ownership of words in the discussion of etymology.

the poets, are always seen as exceptional in Varro's account, and he clearly feels a degree of annoyance (see, for instance, 5.9) at the way in which they mess up his account of language and its history by making up words; hence, I suspect, his attempt to limit their rights of variation by adding "to a certain degree," suggesting that poets really have no excuse for not conforming to analogy more closely than individual speakers. In the other two categories, Varro's visualizations of group and individuals are more generalized than in the analogist argument at 9.5: rather than the audience and speaker in a *contio*, here he speaks of the *populus* as a whole and every individual within it, not just orators. Analogy, within the limits where it is applicable at all, is binding on the people as a whole, who represent the collective, personified form of the Latin language itself, even though every individual user of the language has to be wary of following the strictures of analogy too closely: *consensus communis*, although it may be wrong, governs our individual behavior. But should we define "Latin" as the form of the language that follows the abstract rules, or as the *consensus communis* that may violate them? That is not a question the extant text answers.

5. *CONSENSUS* IN CONTEXT

Varro wrote a great deal about Latin, but because so little of it survives outside *De lingua Latina* it is not easy to put his ideas into the broader context, both synchronic and diachronic, of Roman thought about language and about Latin. In fact, however, the peculiar tensions between analogy and *consuetudo* or *consensus* in *De lingua Latina* make much more sense when seen in such a framework. For while Varro's work contains many ideas that fit quite comfortably within the framework of language science or language instruction, he is, as has been emphasized before, never unaware of the real world which underlies and provides a framework for the uses—and the correctness—of the language he describes.

De lingua Latina is not a grammar, and as such it stands apart from most of the texts about Latin to be discussed in this volume. But even within *De lingua Latina*, Varro uses language that seems to show his awareness of formal grammar. In talking about the first two parts of the work, he compares *impositio* to a *fons* and *declinatio* to the river coming from it, in terms both of quantity and relative time: *Ad illud genus, quod prius, historia opus est: nisi discendo enim aliter id non pervenit ad nos; ad reliquum genus, quod posterius, ars: ad quam opus est paucis praeceptis, quae sunt brevia* (8.5–6: "For the part that comes first, you need historical investigation: it doesn't reach us except by study. For the other part that comes later, you need *ars*, and for that you need a few, short pieces of instruction"). The pairing of *historia* and *ars* seems to correspond (in reverse order) to Quintilian's division of grammar into *recte loquendi scientia* and *poetarum enarratio* (1.4.2) or the division of the late fourth-century grammar of Diomedes between *exegetice* and *horistice*, which he further elaborates into the full definition of grammar: *tota autem grammatica consistit praecipue intellectu poetarum et scriptorum et historiarum prompta expositione et in recte loquendi scribendique ratione* (*GL* 1.426.16–20: "Grammar taken as a whole consists above all in the understanding and explanation of poets and writers and historians and in the rule of correct speaking and writing").[44]

Despite the similarity of Varro's division between *historia* and *ars* to those found in the later tradition, however, the context is very different. What Quintilian, Diomedes, and others are talking about is the bipartite division of the job of the working *grammaticus* in the classroom: on the one hand the use of literary texts to improve students' knowledge both of Latin and of the content of the books they read, and on the other hand instruction in the technical rules of Latin grammar. What Varro is talking about has nothing to do with learning Latin. He is describing the tools for learning how Latin became Latin: *historia* is not the explanation of texts, but the discovery of the history of words, and *ars* is not the whole range of grammatical rules, but the system of inflection.

If we look at Varro's writings about language outside the *De lingua Latina* itself, what he talks about clearly overlaps with the later grammatical tradition. Indeed, Varro wrote about grammar itself in some detail in at least two works, *De sermone Latino* in five books, probably written before *De lingua Latina*, and the first book (*De grammatica*) of the nine-book *Disciplinae* which he wrote at the end of his life. *De grammatica* itself may have been (or incorporated) the first Latin *ars grammatica*.[45] Sixteen definite fragments survive of *De sermone Latino* (F 33–48), enough to show that it included heterogeneous materials ranging from orthography to literary history to metrics; the organization of the work is very unclear, but the last book clearly included a discussion (or at least a list) of the characteristics of Roman comic poets.[46] Among the Varronian fragments about language that cannot be assigned to a particular work too, there is a wide range of subject matter, covering many of the areas that came within the purview of later grammarians (and surviving, largely, because Varro was quoted by them)—orthography, the parts of speech, morphology, prosody, and more—but it should not be forgotten that a great many fragments (129 of 461 collected by Funaioli) are etymologies or definitions of words and names. The study of language, for Varro, included what we (retrospectively) think of as grammar; it was not limited to it.

44. The division between studying texts and teaching grammar is a common one (e.g., *Explanationes in Donatum* I, *GL* 4.486.16, Marius Victorinus 65.15M, and [Asper] *GL* 5.547.7). Although Barwick's reconstruction of the divisions of grammar goes beyond the evidence, his collection of material is still useful; see Barwick (1922: 215–24).

45. Not enough fragments directly attributable to *De grammatica* survive (only one) to make that claim defensible, but if (and it is a big if) the *Ars breviata* now recognized as the work of Augustine is related to Varro's work, it becomes much more plausible. On the *Ars breviata*, see 12.8 below.

46. See Welsh (2011b), who makes a strong case for tracing part of Evanthius' account of early Roman drama to Book 5 of *De sermone Latino*.

Later grammarians, particularly Marius Victorinus and Diomedes, preserve some of Varro's definitions of grammar and its parts.[47] The most famous one (F 236), discussed in the previous chapter, identifies the four *officia* of grammar as *lectio, emendatio, enarratio,* and *iudicium*—clearly a description of the *grammatica* of the schoolroom, and of that part of the teacher's task which concerned the explanation of literary texts: reading aloud, the correction of the student's transcription of what the teacher dictated, the explanation of what the text means, and some kind of judgment of the merits of the passage. Marius Victorinus, who quotes Varro's definition of grammar near the beginning of his *ars*, confirms this interpretation of the *officia* (65.18M = F 234):

> Ut Varroni placet, ars grammatica, quae a nobis litteratura dicitur, scientia est <eorum> quae a poetis historicis oratoribusque dicuntur ex parte maiore. eius praecipua officia sunt quattuor, ut ipsi placet, scribere legere intellegere probare.
>
> Varro's opinion is that grammar (which I call *litteratura*) is the knowledge of what is said by poets, historians, and orators, for the most part. Its particular duties are four, as he believes: writing, reading, understanding, and approving.

This account shows Varro defining grammar in terms of only one of the two standard elements, the interpretation of earlier literature; Diomedes, as quoted above (2.1), used very similar language, although he went on to describe the technical part of grammar, as Victorinus does not. Victorinus moves directly from his definition to list the *officia* of the grammarian as *scribere legere intellegere probare*—closely comparable to, although in a different order from, the list of *lectio emendatio enarratio iudicium* which Diomedes explicitly ascribes to Varro (*lectio* ~ *legere; emendatio* ~ *scribere; enarratio* ~ *intellegere; iudicium* ~ *probare*). What is most significant about these descriptions of *grammatica* is that they focus on the grammarian's job, the daily procedure of the classroom teacher in guiding his pupils through their first reading of literary texts.[48] What Varro does not mention is the content of grammatical instruction, the technical rules that make up the *ars grammatica*.

47. These passages are discussed most recently by Seppänen (2014: 131–5), who assumes (in my view, wrongly) that they describe philological rather than classroom activities and that they have important philosophical implications. Delvigo (1990: 104–6) also discusses the lists of the four *officia* in both Greek and Roman grammatical writing, but does not explore the differences in context and meaning. Dammer (2001: 184–207) disputes the authenticity of the fragments attested only in Diomedes, without good reason: the quotation by Marius Victorinus guarantees at least that the two grammarians had a shared source that they thought was Varro, and Diomedes cannot be accused (as Dammer does) of inventing the attribution.

48. Damaggio (2011: 33) rightly notes that Diomedes' list is from the point of view of the grammarian as teacher, while Marius Victorinus' list describes the skills to be acquired by the student.

Varro clearly knew that instruction in proper grammar was an essential element in the teaching of Latin; but when he wrote, was there in fact a written textbook, an *ars grammatica*, available in Latin? The paragraph in Diomedes that immediately follows his discussion of Varro's four *officia* is not explicitly ascribed to Varro, but given the context it is almost certainly his:[49]

> Grammaticae initia ab elementis surgunt, elementa figurantur in litteras, litterae in syllabas coguntur, syllabis comprehenditur dictio, dictiones coguntur in partes orationis, partibus orationis consummatur oratio, oratione virtus ornatur, virtus ad evitanda vitia exercetur.

> The beginnings of grammar arise from sounds, sounds are given shape as letters, letters are organized into syllables, syllables make up the word, words are organized into parts of speech, speech is the sum of its parts, through speech virtue is enhanced, and virtue is employed in the avoidance of vices.

Until the very end (to be discussed shortly), this is quite like the table of contents of a typical *ars grammatica*: in Donatus, for instance, the opening chapters of Book 1 are *De voce, De littera, De syllaba*, followed by an excursion into quantities and accents; Book 2 opens with *De partibus orationis*, followed by chapters on each of the eight parts of speech. While Varro's *grammaticae officia* describe the work of the classroom (and *enarratio poetarum*), this extraordinarily rhetorical sentence is a description of the other part of grammar, *recte loquendi scientia*, as represented in the *ars*. It is also possible, although by no means certain, that something resembling what we have in later grammatical texts already existed in Varro's time.

Early in the first century BCE, probably in the late 80s or early 70s, the anonymous author of the *Rhetorica ad Herennium* provides the first indication of written grammar in Rome. In defining *Latinitas*, the first of the two elements of *elegantia* (itself the first element of *elocutio*), Rhetor (as I will call him) offers the following (4.17):

> Latinitas est, quae sermonem purum conservat, ab omni vitio remotum. Vitia in sermone, quo minus is Latinus sit, duo possunt esse: soloecismus et barbarismus. Soloecismus est, cum in verbis pluribus consequens verbum superiori non adcommodatur. Barbarismus est, cum verbis al<iquid> vitiose effertur. Haec qua ratione vitare possumus, in arte grammatica dilucide dicemus.

> *Latinitas* is what keeps speech pure and protected from any flaw. Flaws of speech—making it less Latin—are two, solecism and barbarism. Solecism is when in a group of words the later word is not concordant with the earlier one. Barbarism is when something in [individual] words is brought out flawed. How we can avoid these, I will speak of expressly in my *ars grammatica*.

49. Diomedes 426.32–7.2 = F 237; Dammer (2001) is predictably skeptical. On the use of *elementum* as a unit of sound, see Schad (2007) s.v.

Proper Latinity is the avoidance of errors in speech, which come in two forms, barbarism (an error within a single word) and solecism (an error involving more than one word). But Rhetor breaks off his discussion and instead refers the reader ahead to an as-yet-unwritten *ars grammatica*. If he ever wrote it, we do not know; it is not unknown even for modern scholars to avoid a subject by deferring discussion to an imaginary future. But Rhetor's tactic here is notable as the first clear sign of a boundary dispute that greatly affected the shape of grammatical writing for centuries: is correctness of speech one of the virtues of style for an orator, or does it belong in the grammarian's classroom?

The boundary dispute over *Latinitas* (and about barbarism and solecism in particular) is not just a turf war between professors in different departments (although it is that too): it has to do with the relationship between the classroom and the world. The invaluable Diomedes again preserves a Varronian definition, this time of *Latinitas* itself.[50] *Latinitas* (which Diomedes—whose native language was almost certainly Greek—defines as *incorrupte loquendi observatio secundum Romanam linguam*, "maintaining uncorrupted speech in accordance with the Roman language") has, according to Varro (*ut adserit Varro*), four elements: *natura, analogia, consuetudo*, and *auctoritas. Natura* is the tralatitious and unchanging element of language: why we say *scribo* rather than *scrimbo* is a function of nature, not the product of analogy (*non analogiae virtute sed naturae ipsius constitutione*). Next is analogy, which is the organization (*ordinatio*) of the language *secundum technicos*; it separates barbarous speech from educated speech the way silver is separated from lead (*neque aliter barbaram linguam ab erudita quam argentum a plumbo dissociat*). Then comes *consuetudo: non ratione analogiae sed viribus par est, ideo solum recepta, quod multorum consensione convaluit, ita tamen ut illi artis ratio non accedat sed indulgeat. nam ea e medio loquendi usu placita adsumere consuevit* ("*Consuetudo* is a match for *analogia* not in its rationality but in its strength, and it is accepted only because it has grown strong through the agreement of many people. But that acceptance comes not with the approval of rational grammar but with its acquiescence, since *ratio* has gotten used to incorporating from common usage things that have gained approval"). Finally *auctoritas*, which is both last and least, words accepted from the *veteres* in the absence of any other

50. Diomedes 439.15–30 = F 268; almost the same text, but leaving out Varro's name and referring to *Latinus sermo* rather than *Latinitas*, appears in Charisius 62.14–3.9B. On this passage (and the unanswerable questions of its source and accuracy), see the recent discussion of Garcea (2012: 31–3). Fehling (1956–7: 222–35) discusses the Latin texts on the criteria for *Latinitas* in great detail, but he distorts the evidence in pursuit of a single, reconstructible source for all such texts; on these criteria the most useful study is still Siebenborn (1976). On the corresponding definition in Quintilian 1.6.1, see 8.2 below. Dammer (2001) is, as ever, skeptical about authenticity; Schenkeveld (1996) believes that it comes from the Elder Pliny rather than Varro. Pliny may indeed be an intermediate source, but it is almost certainly Varro's words that he transmits.

argument, the last hope of desperation.[51] The first and last elements of this series, *natura* and *auctoritas*, are, respectively, inevitable and undesirable; the two middle ones, described as a pair of gladiators (*par*), fight it out over every non-analogic piece of popular linguistic habit. Habit, Varro admits, is the stronger force, but it gets its way only if there is general approval—in which case the grammarians just have to grin and bear it.

The struggle between *consuetudo* and *analogia* in the determination of *Latinitas* puts the relationship between analogy and anomaly in the construction of language as discussed in *De lingua Latina* into a broader and more complicated context. As discussed above, *De lingua Latina* is distinctly interested in the relationship not only between the individual speaker of the language and the community of Latin speakers, but quite particularly in the relationship between speaker and community that is embodied in public oratory: the speaker must tailor his linguistic habits to fit the *consensus* of his audience in order to be effective. We are again, as with the issue of barbarism and solecism, standing on the boundary between grammar and rhetoric. For Varro (more than for any other writer on Latin that we know), grammar is indeed an *ars*, but it is not therefore divorced from its function in the real world. Varro's definition of grammar cited above deserves repetition (F 237):

> Grammaticae initia ab elementis surgunt, elementa figurantur in litteras, litterae in syllabas coguntur, syllabis comprehenditur dictio, dictiones coguntur in partes orationis, partibus orationis consummatur oratio, oratione virtus ornatur, virtus ad evitanda vitia exercetur.

> The beginnings of grammar arise from sounds, sounds are given shape as letters, letters are organized into syllables, the word is composed of syllables, words are organized into parts of speech, speech is the sum of its parts, through speech virtue is enhanced, and virtue is employed in the avoidance of vices.

The last two elements in this series are both like and unlike Donatus' later organization of the *ars grammatica*, which begins with introductory sections on sounds, letters, and words, progresses through the parts of speech, and ends with discussion of *vitia et virtutes orationis*, barbarism and solecism followed by the figures of speech.[52] Varro too talks of virtue and vice, but with a difference. In a description of the order of topics in grammar, we would expect to find *oratio virtutibus ornatur*, that speech (particularly oratory) is enhanced by the use of figures of speech. What we get instead is *oratione virtus ornatur*, a statement that *oratio* is an enhancement of virtue, and that virtue in turn helps us to avoid vice.[53] Assuming

51. According to the text in Diomedes, *auctoritas* is what people resort to *quem ad modum ad ancoram* ("like an anchor"); in Charisius, there is an *ara sacra* ("holy altar") instead of an anchor.

52. On the place of barbarism and solecism in the *ars grammatica*, see below, 8.4c.

53. Dammer (2001: 185n.) would in fact like to emend it to *oratio virtute ornatur*.

that this is Varro's wording, the moral turn has precursors in the Elder Cato's definition of the orator as *vir bonus dicendi peritus* and in the worries over the problem of immoral rhetoric expressed in the preface to Cicero's *De inventione* and elsewhere.

6. WORD AND WORLD

That grammar leads to an ethical life is a stretch, and while I believe that the language of this fragment is authentic, doubt is not unreasonable. More broadly considered, this sentence can be seen as one more element in Varro's insistence on the relationship between the word and the world. Language is a representation of reality; but language is also shaped by the exigencies of the real world and in turn can shape the behavior of those who use (and hear) it. At least as far as the relationship between *analogia* and *consuetudo* in shaping Latinity is concerned, Varro was not the only writer in the late Republic to consider the issue; and in this respect (as of course in others) by far the most significant of his contemporaries was Julius Caesar.

In the early months of (probably) 54 BCE, Caesar wrote a two-book work *De analogia* which, like *De lingua Latina* itself ten years later, was dedicated to the greatest of all orators, Cicero. Varro clearly knew *De analogia*, and even though Caesar's work is represented by only thirty-two definite fragments and we have only the theoretical half of Varro's discussion of analogy, comparisons are possible: although they apparently disagreed significantly in some details and in their general approach to the conflict of analogy and *consuetudo*, there are many areas of overlap. Clear parallels between *De analogia* and *De lingua Latina* include the important question of the similarities necessary for analogical rules to obtain (F 9 Garcea ~ *LL* 10.11–21);[54] the use of the ablative as the starting point for declension (F 12 Garcea ~ *LL* 10.62); the derivation of adjectives derived from place names (F 8 Garcea ~ LL 8.35); and the declension of Greek loanwords (F 27 Garcea ~ LL 8.72, 10.70).[55] Other fragments of Caesar have parallels in fragments of Varro's other grammatical works, and in several cases Varro and Caesar are cited together by the quoting source.[56] Both men were seeking to define "correct" Latin in a way that produces a consistent and comprehensible language without disregarding either history or contemporary usage.

54. Garcea (2012: 167–79) gives a full discussion of the whole issue.

55. On all these topics, Garcea's commentary is illuminating; I am greatly indebted to it.

56. Quoted together: F 3 Garcea + Varro F 2 (the alphabet); F 5 Garcea + Varro F 269 (*sonus medius*; in fact, the fragment of Caesar is cited by Varro, who is cited by Cornutus, who is cited by Cassiodorus); F7 Garcea + Varro F 273 (*lac* or *lact*); F 24 Garcea + Varro T26 (oblique cases of fourth declension). Note also the discussions of *semivocales* (F 6 Garcea ~ Varro F 1) and of natural and grammatical gender and number (F 10–11 Garcea; for Varro, see Garcea 184–6, 194–8).

That both Caesar and Varro had oratory as well as grammar in mind is clear: Varro's references to comprehensibility and popular taste have been cited above, and the fragments of the preface to *De analogia* (F 1–2 Garcea) point in the same direction. One (F 2) is the famous injunction to avoid unfamiliar words as if they were a reef (*tamquam scopulum, sic fugias inauditum atque insolens verbum*); the other is the dedication to Cicero, in which Caesar elevates the study of common language to be at least as important as rhetorical *copia*. The dedication to Cicero is very pointed and has long been recognized as a response to Cicero's emphasis in *De oratore* on *ornatus* rather than *Latinitas* as the essence of proper style.[57]

According to Cicero, *Latinitas* was a prerequisite for elegant speech, not an element of it; grammatical language was the first of the four elements of style in Cicero as in Theophrastus (who seems to have created the list), but Cicero viewed it as the least important in rhetorical theory rather than the most important as it had been for Theophrastus.[58] That would seem to have been the view of the author of *Ad Herennium* as well, since he relegates the subject of *Latinitas* to his unwritten *ars grammatica*. But both Caesar and Varro, in writing about the shape of language, seem to consider it much more important to the orator than did Cicero; and perhaps Varro's dedication to Cicero, like Caesar's, was more barbed than it looks at first sight.

Cicero is of course interested in the Latin language and the proper use of it, but within the vast responsibilities that he places on the orator (both in training and in action), it plays a very small part. To oversimplify: Cicero is interested in the place of oratory in the world, Varro in the relationship of language to the world. Where Cicero, in discussing the use of archaism in public speaking, is generally dismissive and (something Varro clearly did not agree with) makes poetic language the only part of earlier Latin that is useful to the orator, Varro seems to give to the language itself the kind of sweep and breadth that Cicero gives the orator. And it is, finally, worth looking briefly once more not so much at the argument of *De lingua Latina* as at its scope, and in particular at its inclusion of just those areas that Cicero gives the orator: philosophy, rhetoric, and law.

Less than a quarter of *De lingua Latina* survives, and interpreting the larger patterns of the work is necessarily speculative. Most frustrating is the almost complete loss of the portion of *De lingua Latina* (Books 14–25) that dealt with combinations of words, *coniunctio*. Syntax—of which Varro's *coniunctio* is a translation—is not a significant part of Roman grammatical teaching until Priscian,

57. The most important passage is *De oratore* 3.37, Crassus' enumeration of the virtues of style, in which it is suggested that *Latinitas* should be no problem, and in fact belongs to the grammarian rather than the rhetorician. On the relationship of *De analogia* to *De oratore* (and to Cicero's equally pointed response to Caesar in *Brutus*), see in particular Hendrickson (1906), the extensive discussion of Garcea (2012: 49–113), and Volk and Zetzel (2015).

58. On this background, see Garcea (2012: 49–53).

in the sixth century, deployed the Greek work on syntax of Herodianus and Apollonius Dyscolus to explain Latin syntax. Much of this syntactical treatment is philosophical, and indeed one of the origins of grammar in the Greek tradition lies in Stoic dialectic. Only one substantial fragment (F 28 from Book 24) of Varro's treatment of *coniunctio* survives, and it shows Varro considering types of condition and syllogism in a philosophical vein, dealing with sentences in terms of their truth-value, in a Stoic manner. There is precedent for this in the Roman tradition, of course, in the (lost) work of Aelius Stilo on logical axioms (*proloquia*). At the same time, however, much of the little there is about syntax in the Latin grammarians between Varro and Priscian is tied to the problem of solecism, incorrect combinations of words. Varro describes his topic in Books 14–25 in terms of words, and he may well, in part at least, have dealt with combinations of words in terms of the rhetorical category of solecism—just as his discussion of correctness in paradigms is in effect an analysis of barbarism, errors in a single word.[59] The combination of philosophy, grammar, and rhetoric should not be surprising. In the extant portion of *De lingua Latina*, as we have seen, Chrysippus and Crates on one side and Aristophanes and Aristarchus on the other are used not simply as sources and models, but also as emblems for Varro's desire to combine disparate materials and approaches into a single structure. But there is one further element in the mix that needs to be brought in: law.

In part, of course, law and grammar were linked from the outset, from Sextus Aelius to Aelius Stilo: commentary on the Twelve Tables is both etymological and legal. But Varro goes beyond simple discussion of the meaning of legal terms, and legal language is often used to describe linguistic relationships. Thus, Varro invokes property law to describe the origin of words, and uses the legal term *societas* to describe the ancient and honorable company of words (5.13). He uses *ius* for the right of various people to use words differently (9.5). He compares lost etymologies to runaway slaves, with honorable mention of the jurists Mucius and Brutus (5.5).[60]

Varro also pays close attention to legal language and legal sources. He offers a detailed discussion of the physical size of *actus*, the term in property law for the rustic praedial servitude permitting one person to drive his animals across another's land (5.34). While much earlier grammatical writing seems to have been concerned with explaining poetry and the interpretation of a few important legal and religious texts, Varro not only offers extensive citations from early poetry, but also makes massive use of fairly obscure religious documents (the list of the shrines of the Argei and the religious calendar) and gives extended quotations from legal texts including not just the traditional Twelve Tables, but the censor's records, the consular *commentaria* and the quaestor's *commentarium anquisitionis* in Book 6, and the *lex praediorum urbanorum* at 5.27. Varro's definition of Latin is

59. On syntax and solecism, see above all Baratin (1989). The recent speculations of Taylor (2015) about the structure of *LL* 14–25 are no more than that.

60. I am again indebted to the unpublished paper of Gitner (above, n. 27).

broad, far broader than any earlier text of which we know or any later one which we possess, with the possible exception of the great dictionary of Verrius Flaccus a generation later.

Legal thinking plays another role in providing not only texts, but methods. Taylor has rightly drawn attention to Varro's ability to identify distinctive features that allow us to recognize "similarity" in paradigms;[61] but reasoning like this would be familiar to him from law even more than from Alexandrian grammar. In particular, it was (and is) a feature of legal reasoning to draw analogies, to construct from the particulars of specific cases a more generalizable pattern of distinctions; this was done, notably, by the great jurist Q. Mucius, whom Varro cites.[62] So too, although Varro's mathematical ratios among verb tenses allowed him to discuss the future perfect indicative, he did not discover the future perfect nor was he the first to discuss it: as mentioned in the previous chapter, it was a topic of legal debate from the middle of the second century down to the grammatical writings of Varro's contemporary Nigidius Figulus (F 8).[63] Law is an institution in which language actually matters.

To see Varro as a follower of Greek theorists or to see him as a purely linguistic thinker in *De lingua Latina* is to ignore or diminish important aspects of his work. For Varro, the Latin language is not some abstraction, but part of the real world. Words are supposed to reflect the things to which they refer; words only exist if their objects both exist and are in current use; and speech is an ethical construction as well as a linguistic one. The language as used has real effects, whether in public speaking or in legal writing; so too the real users of language have effects on it, through *consuetudo* and the reactions of audience to speaker. The intermixture of the study of language with the study of institutions is constant in Varro, and indeed in what we can infer about most of the earlier writers on Latin. After Varro, that is not so clear.

61. Taylor (1996: 21–3).

62. Cf. Frier (1985: 163–71).

63. See 2.3 above. As Nigidius died in 45, his discussion must have preceded that in *De lingua Latina*. On the history of the future perfect in the grammarians, see Serbat (1978) and Rosellini (2006). The polymathic Nigidius' *Commentarii grammatici* ran to at least twenty-nine books, and Gellius (who cites him in eighteen of the twenty books of *Noctes Atticae*) ranks him second only to Varro in learning. The fragments are unfortunately too few and too various to say much about him: like Aelius Stilo and Varro, he shows some signs of Stoicism; like them, he is very much interested in etymology; and like them, he is well aware of early Roman legal and religious texts. He also considers orthography, pronunciation, derivation, and more. The standard edition of the fragments is still that of Swoboda (1889); the grammatical fragments (placed between Caesar and Varro) are in *GRF* 158–79. For an excellent discussion, see Garcea (forthcoming).

4

Past and Present: From Caecilius Epirota to Valerius Probus

1. MODERNISTS AND ANTIQUARIANS

At the beginning of Horace, *Satires* 1.10, one group of manuscripts preserves eight verses clearly not by Horace which cast some light on the world of the *grammatici* in the late Republic.[1] The lines contrast two men, Valerius Cato and an unnamed *grammaticorum equitum doctissimus* (240.8H), who is often, but not convincingly, identified with Horace's teacher Orbilius.[2] The opening of the fragment is a criticism of the satirist Lucilius:

> Lucili, quam sis mendosus, teste Catone
> defensore tuo pervincam, qui male factos
> emendare parat versus . . .

> Lucilius, how full of faults you are I will prove on the evidence of your defender, Cato, who is preparing to correct badly written lines . . .

and that is obviously the reason it was inserted before Horace's first line:

> Nempe incomposito dixi pede currere versus
> Lucili . . .

> So I said that Lucilius' verses run on unpolished feet . . .

The fragment then goes on to compare Cato favorably with the unnamed grammarian, who attempts to beat his pupils into preferring *antiqui poetae*, despite

1. I follow here the text and translation of Hollis (2007) #240. Still very useful is Fraenkel (1964: 2.199–208, originally published 1933).

2. That Orbilius was fairly certainly not an *eques* seems a decisive objection; see Kaster (1995: 128–9). Hollis is not entirely convinced.

the fact that these poets are now—almost certainly some time in the last years of the Republic—the object of general *fastidium*. Just what Cato is trying to do to Lucilius is not at all clear: the earlier poet is *mendosus*, and so Cato attempts *emendatio*, but that could mean either that Cato is trying to improve the actual poetry of Lucilius, eliminating its flaws, or that he is trying to improve on the poetry of Lucilius by writing satire without the stylistic failures that Horace criticizes both in this poem and in *Satires* 1.4. The latter interpretation seems to me more likely, but in either case the poem makes a set of linked contrasts: between Cato and the *grammaticus* and between their educational methods; between Lucilius and the *antiqui poetae*; and between critical refinement and uncritical adulation of the literary past.

At least some of these contrasts have a broader presence in the philological world of the late Republic. P. Valerius Cato was born in the 90s and was both a poet and a *grammaticus* recognized by Suetonius (*DGR* 11); although not one word of his poetry survives, we know of two titles—a *Lydia* and a *Diana* (also called *Dictynna*)—and they clearly belong to the milieu of Catullus. Suetonius obligingly quotes poetry about Cato, written by Cinna, Ticida, and Bibaculus, as well as an anonymous pair of verses:

> Cato grammaticus, Latina siren,
> qui solus legit ac facit poetas.

Cato the grammarian, Latin siren, who alone chooses/reads and makes poets.

The papyrus fragment of Cornelius Gallus (Hollis 2007, #145) confirms Cato's role as a critic: Gallus links him with Horace's friend Viscus as someone whose literary judgment is to be respected.

Two aspects of Cato are significant here. One is that he combines the writing of poetry with the study of poetry as a *grammaticus*; the other is that he is both a new poet and an admirer of Lucilius. Indeed, what we know about Cato and Lucilius takes us back to Suetonius' story about the beginning of Roman philology: among other effects, Crates' lectures in Rome brought about not only the study of earlier Roman literature, Naevius in particular, but also the study (or possibly only public recitation) of more recent texts: Lucilius, according to Suetonius, was recited by his friends Laelius Archelaus and Vettius Philocomus, and Valerius Cato boasted of having studied Lucilius with Philocomus himself.

As early as the second century BCE, in fact, one can distinguish among the different generations of poets in terms of who was studied or taught, and how. By far the most important texts to students of Latin grammar and literature in the second century were early legal and religious writings; the only poet whose language and text we know were seriously studied was Plautus, and the most significant work on Plautus, other than explanatory glosses on obsolete words, concerned the establishment of the authenticity of the plays and the chronology of archaic literature. But by the end of the second century, some different emphases appear, above all an interest in poetry, particularly on the part of poets themselves. Thus Accius was not only a prolific dramatist but the author of *Didascalica* and *Pragmatica*, both apparently concerned with dramatic history: his chronology of early drama annoyed Cicero by placing Livius Andronicus much too late, but it was still read; and as an old man he received the dedication of a book *De antiquitate litterarum* from the young Varro.

Accius seems—although much is uncertain—to have kept, on the whole, his poetry separate from his criticism: his discussions of poetic history and of orthography were apparently written in prose and were certainly not performed in his tragedies. Lucilius, in this respect, was quite different: he wrote nothing that we know of other than his thirty books of Satires, and within that collection, in Book 9, he included not only a significant discussion of orthography and pronunciation, but an explanation of the difference between *poema* and *poesis*. And while Accius' work was important to Varro and the chronologists of the late Republic, Lucilius was important to the poets and the grammarians.

It is not hard to see why both Lucilius' learning and his choice of a less grandiose and more personal voice in his Satires appealed to the generation of Valerius Cato and (slightly younger) Catullus. The pseudo-Horatian verses assert a contrast between Lucilius and the *antiqui*, and whatever Valerius Cato was doing in "emending" Lucilius, it seems to have involved both scholarly and poetic engagement. The poem of Horace to which the verses are prefixed, moreover, shows that more than one poet in the late Republic tried to write Lucilian satire (*Hoc erat, experto frustra Varrone Atacino/atque quibusdam aliis, melius quod scribere possem, Sat* 1.10.46–7: "It was this that, after the unsuccessful attempts of Varro Atacinus and a few others, I might be able to write better"), and it seems likely that a reference in Gellius to *quidam commentariorum in Lucilium scriptores* (*NA* 2.24.4; *GRF* p. 412) concerns commentaries written in just this period, although we cannot be certain. Indeed, aside from Varro's work on Plautus, Lucilius is the *only* early poet we know to have been commented on in the last generation of the Republic.

From a post-Augustan perspective, we do not generally think of Lucilius as a modern writer, but the switch from Plautus and the Twelve Tables to Lucilius as a subject of paramount scholarly interest is an important one, and it may well be an early sign of the much more drastic shift that took place in the Augustan age. A juxtaposition of two figures in Suetonius' *De grammaticis* marks the transition—although, as ever, Suetonius says very little about the writings of the men he discusses. The first is Q. Caecilius Epirota (*DGR* 16), born probably in the late 60s BCE, and thus a generation younger than Valerius Cato. A freedman of Atticus and friend of Cornelius Gallus, he opened a school after Gallus' death and was the first to teach about Virgil and other new poets.[3] Immediately following him in Suetonius is M. Verrius Flaccus (*DGR* 17), also a freedman and probably born in

3. For information on Caecilius, see Kaster (1995) ad loc. On the pairing of Caecilius and Verrius, see also Gianotti (2010: 347–8).

the 50s, who was hired by Augustus to teach his grandsons, and who lived into the reign of Tiberius. One of Verrius' innovations as a teacher, according to Suetonius, was his practice of having students compete against one another and awarding a book prize to the winner—often, says Suetonius, *liber aliquis antiquus* (17.1). The contrast between Caecilius' taste for the new and Verrius' taste for the old is fortuitous, but not inaccurate. Verrius was in fact an antiquarian, and he is surrounded in Suetonius by modernists: Caecilius on one side, L. Crassicius Pansa (*DGR* 18), the commentator on Cinna's *Zmyrna*, and C. Iulius Hyginus (*DGR* 20), the commentator on Cinna's *Propempticon Pollionis*, on the other.[4]

We know a great deal about Verrius Flaccus, and a certain amount about Iulius Hyginus; Caecilius Epirota and Crassicius Pansa are much less distinct figures. Verrius was clearly a polymath as well as a teacher of grammar; his works included not only a tract on orthography, letters apparently on grammatical subjects, a book *De obscuris Catonis*, and various antiquarian studies (*Res memoratu dignae; Res Etruscae*), but two works that are far more substantially extant: the *Fasti Praenestini*, of which significant epigraphic fragments survive, and which were at least based on his work, and the great *De verborum significatu* in many books, a portion of Pompeius Festus' third-century abridgment of which survives, as well as two fragments quoted by Aulus Gellius (*NA* 5.17, 5.18) from Book 4.

We cannot judge from the surviving portion of Festus—indeed, we probably could not judge from an entire text of Festus, should one ever be found—exactly what Verrius' interests were: it is fairly certain that virtually everything now found in Festus (and the bulk of what is in Paul the Deacon's abridgment of Festus) was originally in Verrius' dictionary, but we have no way of knowing about the types of material that did *not* interest Festus. Nevertheless, the abridgment is substantial enough, and reveals enough about Verrius' working methods and sources, that we can be sure that Verrius had a limited interest in the kinds of text that interested his contemporaries Caecilius, Crassicius, and Hyginus: not only are his contemporaries Horace and Ovid never cited, but there are not many references to Virgil or Lucretius, only three to Catullus, none at all to any of the other neoterics.[5] The recent writers he does cite, repeatedly, are antiquarians and students of archaic language—Aelius Gallus, Antistius Labeo, Ateius Capito, Messalla the augur, Sinnius Capito, Varro. Much of what remains of any of these writers is still available only because of Verrius' interest.[6] He cared about the language of law and religion, about proverbs, about topography; he was not a student of modern poetry. And the fact that in one of his not infrequent snipings at

4. Scribonius Aphrodisius (*DGR* 19) is not attested outside this chapter of Suetonius, which reports that he attacked Verrius, both his person and his book on orthography. As Funaioli notes (525), we have no idea about his philological beliefs or activities.

5. For Verrius' taste in literature, see Reitzenstein (1887: 20).

6. The relevant fragments are all to be found in *GRF*; they should be supplemented by the attempts (not always convincing) of more recent scholars (particularly Strezelecki 1932 and Bona 1964) to assign particular groups of lemmata in Festus to specific sources.

Verrius, Festus says that he has eliminated from his abridgment *intermortua iam et sepulta verba* (242.31–2 Lindsay) suggests—to judge from some of what he apparently did not consider to be dead and buried words—that the archaism of the complete *De verborum significatu* was even more pronounced than that of Festus' abridgment.[7]

Verrius' interests mirror those of many of his contemporaries, and certainly those of the previous generation: such fragments as survive of scholarly writers contemporary with or slightly younger than Varro are largely etymological, morphological, or orthographic. Works on legal language are common; the most important was Aelius Gallus' dictionary *De significatu verborum quae ad ius civile pertinent* (Funaioli 545–54), of which only one fragment comes from Servius Auctus, while all the rest are found in Festus or the *Digest*. So too Cloatius Verus' *Verba a Graecis tracta* (468–70) and *Ordinata Graeca* (470–1) dealt with Greek sources for Roman words or customs, while Sinnius Capito (457–66), along with grammatical *Epistulae* (F 1–2) and a work on syllables (F 3), made a comment on the meaning of *nec* in the Twelve Tables (F 8) and collected a set of proverbs—again, now known through Festus. The form learning took seems frequently to have been a treatise on a specific topic (e.g., Messalla Corvinus' book on the letter s̱) or a set of letters, epistolary essays on diverse philological topics—not just Sinnius Capito, but Valgius Rufus' *De rebus per epistulam quaesitis* and Verrius' own *Epistulae*.

It would be wrong to see Verrius as a throwback, a misplaced relic of the Varronian age. The kinds of historical and antiquarian topics that interested him as well as Varro and others never went out of fashion: Hyginus' freedman Modestus (*DGR* 20; *GRFM* 9–23) may have written about the *Georgics* (although this may be another Modestus, and Mazzarino [*GRFM* 19] is rightly dubious), but he also continues the interest in antiquarian research (a work *De feriis* is attested in Macrobius) and in morphology and etymology; the emperor Claudius' attempts to improve the alphabet are well known. Verrius' historical antiquarianism was absorbed into the traditions of writing about Roman cult and customs, exemplified not least in his older contemporary Livy; his interest in antique words and phrases finds its successors in the long string of discussions of peculiar Latinity, often anomalous archaisms, that stretches from Pliny the Elder to Caper, Romanus, and Nonius Marcellus and is reflected in the medieval collections of *differentiae* and *synonyma*.[8] But it is also perfectly clear that from the time of Augustus at least until the reign of Nero, there was a real change of direction, one represented by the figures already mentioned (Caecilius, Crassicius, Hyginus), preceded to some degree by Valerius Cato and continued by Cornutus and Asconius later in the first century. There are significant differences among these figures, to be sure, but they share a lack of interest in exploring early language and an active interest in

7. On Festus' attitude towards Verrius, see Reitzenstein (1887: 7–17). For a fuller description of the surviving text with bibliography, see 6.1 and 10.1 below.

8. On antiquarian lexicography and treatises *De Latinitate*, see 5.3 below.

discussing modern literature. And that change of direction required a significant change of approach.

Although in some ways the change made by Caecilius—being the first to address the poetry of Virgil and other recent poets—appears the most drastic, it is one we know very little about. Much more significant is the choice of subjects of Crassicius and then of Hyginus. Both of them presumably taught about recent poetry, but they both also wrote commentaries on the poetry of Cinna: Crassicius on the laborious *Smyrna* (see Catullus 95) and Hyginus on the *Propempticon Pollionis*. No fragments of Crassicius' commentary survive,[9] but there are two from Hyginus' commentary (both cited by Charisius [134.12, 134.17B], for Hyginus' use of the forms *iteris* and *itiner*)—which in turn reveal, as Hollis points out, that Hyginus was not the first person to explicate the poem.[10] And for two generations after Crassicius and Hyginus, there is no sign whatsoever of any scholarly interest in any text earlier than Cicero and Cinna.

2. PHILOLOGY IN A NEW KEY

Studying and writing about recent literature is not the same as writing about texts from the distant past. There are relatively few problems in identifying words or forms; there are relatively few problems of authenticity or chronology; there are relatively few difficult textual problems. None of these areas of philological study vanished, but they became much less central. The questions a reader of Plautus or the *Carmen Saliare* needs answered are simply different from those that concern a reader of Cicero or Horace; what is more, on the instructional level, learning Latin based on Cicero is more regular and more predictable than learning Latin based on Ennius or the Twelve Tables. By and large, after the generation of Cicero and Caesar, the written language (if not, perhaps, the spoken language) was relatively stable, and remained so for centuries, particularly in comparison with the rapid changes in Latin between archaic and classical times: Cicero will have had much more trouble reading the Twelve Tables (as he did in school) than Boethius will have had reading Cicero.

In the same way that Latin gained stability, so too the early years of the Empire gave shape and form to the ways in which scholars and teachers wrote and taught about language and literature: it is in the half-century between the death of Augustus and the death of Nero that what became the canonical issues and forms of philological scholarship took shape—with the important qualification that while similar questions and texts definitely existed in some form at least a century earlier than that, they are largely no longer accessible to us. Equally

9. The extent of the survival of other grammatical works by Crassicius Pansa is the object of considerable speculation, especially by Barwick (1922: 167–91), who traced a whole tradition of grammatical scholarship back to Pansa; his reconstruction is no longer generally accepted.

10. Hollis (2007: 25) on Cinna fr. 4–5.

clearly, however, with the exception of some works of Varro, these earlier attempts at scholarship seem not to have been very widely known later in antiquity either.

We know a surprising amount about philology in the period between Augustus and Nero, and not merely from the largely unsatisfactory accounts of Suetonius in *DGR*. Not only do substantial portions of continuous writing survive, but the interest manifested in texts and scholarship by Aulus Gellius in the second century preserves anecdotes and arguments going back to the Augustan period; not coincidentally, as second-century scholarship formed the basis for the late-antique commentaries on classical authors that we still possess, the same scholars are sometimes cited in Servius and Servius Auctus as well as in Charisius' *Ars grammatica*. The surviving texts, moreover, offering an interesting and important range of approaches, were all probably written during the reign of Nero: the commentary on Cicero's speeches by Asconius written in the 50s; the treatise on metrics by Caesius Bassus dedicated to Nero; some extended quotations from the *Ars grammatica* of Remmius Palaemon; and excerpts from the treatise on orthography by Annaeus Cornutus, the friend and teacher of Persius and Lucan. When one adds to this the extensive fragments from the Elder Pliny's work on *Dubius sermo* (written c. 67) and the fewer but still valuable fragments of Virgilian exegesis by Hyginus and Cornutus, it is possible to see at least the outlines of philological practice and interests in the early Empire. The general tendency discussed above, to relinquish antiquarian interest in the early language and literature of Rome in favor of the study of recent texts and contemporary Latin, is everywhere evident. The problem was how to study them, and what to say about them.

Like Alexandrian philology, Roman philology had its origins in antiquarian study; unlike their Greek models and counterparts, however, Roman scholars started not with Homeric poetry but with legal and religious texts—far more difficult and obscure than Homer, and far less amenable to educational purposes. When the focus of scholarship and education changed, first to the early poets, then to the writers of the late second century, then—with Caecilius Epirota, Crassicius, and Hyginus—to contemporary and near contemporary texts, there grew to be a fundamental inconcinnity between the antiquarian and historical tools of philology and the literary and contemporary texts to which they were applied.[11]

There is not enough of Crassicius or Caecilius to say anything, but something remains of Hyginus.[12] In addition to his commentary on Cinna's *Propempticon*

11. The fundamentally different approach to exegesis necessary in dealing with relatively recent texts was already recognized by Madvig (1828: 57–60) in his discussion of Asconius and Ps.-Asconius.

12. Discussions of Hyginus' Virgilian fragments in Zetzel (1981: 31–6) and Timpanaro (1986: 51–67, 2001: 13–23). For broader discussion of Hyginus, see Kaster (1995) on *DGR* 20; for bibliography and discussion of Hyginus' historical works, see *FRHist* 1: 474–81; see also Teuffel 2 §262. It should be noted that while *GRF* prints the fragments from the book on Virgil and most of the fragments of *De italicis urbibus, FRHist* prints only the more historical fragments. Other works ascribed to Hyginus, notably the *Fabulae* and

Pollionis, Hyginus wrote a work about Virgil—probably not a commentary—in at least four books and a work about Italian cities, fragments of both of which survive, in addition to other works largely on Roman religion and history (and a treatise on agriculture). What is notable about the nine fragments about Virgil is that most of them concern either Virgil's use of religious language (*bidens* F 3; the *lituus* F 5; the augural term *praepes* F 6; the *limus* F 11) or anachronism and historical error (*portus Velinos* F 7; the presence or absence of Theseus in the underworld F 8; *Aeacides* F 9; the chronology of Latinus F 10). The sole remaining fragment (F 4) is Hyginus' assertion that Virgil at *G.* 2.246–7 (*at sapor indicium faciet manifestus et ora/tristia temptantum sensu torquebit amaro*: "the clear flavor will give evidence and will twist the unhappy mouths of those trying it with its bitter sensation") wrote *sensus amaror* ("the bitterness of the sensation"), using a Lucretian word, rather than the possibly tautologous *sensu amaro*. That Hyginus' interest is largely antiquarian rather than philological is borne out by the seven fragments of his work on Italian cities, all of which concern origins, and all of which are preserved in the tradition of Virgilian commentary. In that light, it is worth revisiting the fragments of his work on Cinna: it may be no accident that they concern Pollio's itinerary, not Cinna's poetry. In other words, what is most striking about what is left of Hyginus is not that he was interested in modern poetry, but that he treated it as the vehicle for antiquarian study. In important ways, although he was a friend of Ovid, his fragments make him seem more like Verrius Flaccus and the older tradition of scholarship than he is unlike them.

It is perhaps unfair to characterize Hyginus this way: there is at least a strong possibility, given the provenance of the fragments, that the interests he evinces were in fact more significant for Gellius, Servius, and Macrobius who quote him than they were for Hyginus himself; nor is his approach that different from much modern scholarship on Virgil. That being said, however, the fragments have a significantly different character from what remains of the comments on Virgil of Cornutus, writing a generation or so later.[13] The seventeen fragments (20–36 *GRFM*) are far more focused on the text of Virgil himself; some elucidation of references, a famous observation (F 29) on Virgil's invention of the golden bough and the custom of cutting a lock of hair from someone dying, and some very precise comments on Virgilian diction: explanations of *in medio* (F 20) or *commissa* (F 32), perplexity at the language of *comes infelicis Vlixi* (F 27) and at the hysteron proteron of *iamque faces et saxa uolant* (F 24), and above all objections to Virgil's use of inadequate or vulgar diction, such as *inlaudati* and *vexasse* (F 22) or *infixit* (F 24) or *dixerat ille aliquid* (F 34) or *membra* (F 36). It is, quite simply, close reading—perhaps more literal or rhetorical than a modern reader might practice

De astronomia, are not by him, and a recent attempt to assign the biographies normally attributed to Cornelius Nepos to Hyginus is not at all convincing.

13. For bibliography on Cornutus, see 12.16 below. Fragments are cited from *GRFM*.

(and Gellius too criticized Cornutus for inapposite judgments), but deliberately choosing to examine the language of the poem in its own context.

More important, Cornutus looks very much of a piece with contemporaries whose work we can examine in more detail, most significantly the commentary on Cicero's speeches of Q. Asconius Pedianus.[14] Composed (at least the commentary on *Pro Scauro*) in the mid-50s, what now survives consists of commentary (*enarratio* is the term used in the manuscripts) on six speeches: *In Pisonem* (delivered in 55 BCE), *Pro Scauro* (54), *Pro Milone* (52), *Pro Cornelio* I and II (65), and *In toga candida* (64). The commentary is neither complete nor in its original order: internal cross-references to non-extant sections show that it was almost certainly chronological (and hence we possibly have two sections of the commentary in reverse order),[15] and may have included commentary on all the speeches, or at least all that he knew.

Asconius' interests were strictly historical: he explains people, events, chronology, legal and topographical matters, and any other references that he can identify; he is also concerned with sorting out possible inconsistencies and historical problems. Thus, in the commentary on *Pro Cornelio*, he not only explains a discrepancy in Cicero's account of the elder Scipio's part in permitting (or encouraging) separate seating for senators, but also points out that in Cicero's narrative of the first secession of the plebs and the origin of the tribunate, the verb *restituerunt* is wrong—as this was the origin of the tribunate, not its restoration—and should have been *constituerunt*. That is the sole textual or grammatical annotation in the surviving portion of the commentary.

What is most striking about the work, other than Asconius' great care in citing evidence and sources and his apparently quite precise references (by line from beginning or end) to the passages he is discussing, is his awareness of his audience. Repeatedly, he reminds his sons (to whom the work is addressed) of what he expects them to know, or not to know: *confido vos intellegere* (18.12); *credo vos quaerere* (19.25). This appears most explicitly in his discussion of the phrase *postulante nescio quo* at *Mil.* 14. After explaining the procedure for dividing a *sententia*, he goes on (38.25–39.13):

> Forsitan nunc hoc quoque velitis scire, qui fuerit qui id postulaverit. Quod non fere adicitur: non enim ei qui hoc postulat oratione longa utendum ac ne consurgendum quidem utique est. . . . Sed ego, ut curiosius aetati vestrae satisfaciam, Acta enim totius illius temporis persecutus sum. . . .

> And now, perhaps, you would also like to know who made this demand. That's usually not included: someone making this demand didn't need to use a long speech, and he didn't really even need to stand up. . . . But to be more

14. For bibliography on Asconius, see 11.2.1 below. I cite the text of the commentary from Stangl (1912) and the other fragments from *GRFM*.

15. Thus, there is a note on *Pis.* 23 (16.22–3, *iam supra dictum est*) that seems to be referring back to *Pro Cornelio* and *In toga candida*; see Stangl (1912) ad loc.

> inquisitive in satisfying your young minds, I have gone through the *Acta* from that whole period. . .

Asconius tells of his discovery that the *Acta* reported a speech of T. Munatius and quoted a section of it that included the fact that "Divide" had been said by Fufius. He then reminds his sons that they should remember Fufius' role in the trial of Clodius in 61.

In comparison with what we know about earlier commentaries, Asconius takes a very different direction and writes, apparently, in a very different style. In the first place, he has no interest in explaining Cicero's language unless it has a bearing on historical interpretation: there are no glosses, and the only clearly stylistic discussion in the commentary (on *Scaur.* 2, 26.1–16) was rightly excised by Madvig as obviously spurious.[16] There is a clear comparison to be made with what was needed to understand Cicero in late antiquity: the commentator known as Ps.-Asconius (transmitted with the genuine article, but a product of the fifth century) also includes some historical elucidation, but has much more grammar and much more explanation of language. His audience had different needs. In the second place, Asconius' commentary is very informal: it is addressed to his sons (a clear indication that he was not a professional grammarian), it imitates the manner of conversation by repeated direct address, and it regularly uses the first person (*diximus, significavi*). It is hard to imagine that a work of the size the full commentary must have been was really meant for his children alone; the style is a gesture of informality and an indication of the type of audience aimed at. The young, as represented by his children, could read Cicero's Latin: it was very much like their own. What they needed was the historical and constitutional background to a world which had, over the past century, become very distant.

We know frustratingly little about the rest of Asconius' work: he wrote a biography of Sallust and a work *Contra obtrectatores Vergilii* in which he transmitted Asinius Gallus' claim to be the child of the Fourth Eclogue and reported Virgil's famous statement that it was easier to steal Hercules' club than a line from Homer; he was interested, as with Cicero, in the chronology and events of the lives of his subjects. If we had more of what his predecessors had written, Asconius might appear less novel, but one has the sense of original research and an innovative choice of subject. He is trying to establish a history, and at times a chronology, of the literature of the first century BCE: a modernization, in style and in interests, of the work of a Varro or an Accius.

The other scholar of the Neronian age whose work survives in any quantity is very different, and even more than Asconius creates a new kind of scholarship. We possess something like half of the treatise on metrics which Caesius Bassus dedicated to Nero.[17] Caesius was himself a lyric poet, addressed by Persius in his sixth satire; of his poetry, other than examples in *De metris*, a single

16. Madvig (1828: 78–81). On Ps.-Asconius, see 11.2.3 below.
17. For details of the surviving text(s), see 12.9 below.

quotation—oddly enough, a hexameter rather than a lyric meter—from Book 2 of his *Lyrica* is supplied by Priscian. Caesius' work on meter is the first of its kind in Latin—the first of a long tradition of metrical writing, which will be discussed further below. That is not to say that nothing was written about meter before Caesius: Varro certainly had an interest in it, and some discussion of quantities, accentuation, and prosody is found in a great many grammatical texts. But to the best of our knowledge, Varro never wrote a coherent and unified discussion of meter, nor did anyone else before Caesius.[18] The transmitted portion of Caesius' text begins in the middle of a discussion of the Sotadean meter, progresses from there to the Archebulean, Hipponactean, Phalaecean hendecasyllable and on, including the Galliambic and Saturnian before concluding with a discussion of the remaining meters used by Horace.

Caesius' account is designed to explain the metrical patterns used by relatively recent Roman poets: with the exception of the paragraphs on the Saturnian, his earliest examples come from Laevius and the bulk of his quotations are from Catullus, Horace, and Virgil. In every case, including the Saturnian, he traces the meter back to Greek sources, often explaining the name of a Greek meter, sometimes as a misnomer: thus the Phalaecean *qui . . . ut plerique, a cultore suo, non inventore, nomen accepit* (20.9–10 Morelli). But while emphasizing Greek sources, he is equally determined not to use Greek examples; to illustrate Archilochus' use of a "Saturnian" meter, he invents a Latin line, *quem non rationis egentem vicit Archimedes* (33.7) which presumably echoes Virgil (*Aen.* 8.299), *non te rationis egentem*.[19] At the end of his book, in announcing a forthcoming work on the meters of melic poets and tragic choruses, he apologizes for the necessity he foresees of using Greek examples, *quod ne faceremus in hoc libro elaboravimus* (44.8).

Caesius' basic metrical theory (of which his text is the first extant example in either Greek or Latin) is what is known as derivationist: that is to say, he believes that all meters are derived from two fundamental forms, the dactylic hexameter and the iambic trimeter.[20] In the concluding section of his work, after analyzing various Horatian meters, he notes that even if he has not managed to explain them all, other types can be understood with reference to the ones he has discussed, *cum omnia metra varientur aut adiectione aut detractione aut concinnatione aut permutatione* (32.15–16): by adding or removing syllables from any given verse

18. On Varro and the tradition of metrical writing, see above all D'Alessandro (2012). Barwick's assumption (1922: 176) that metrical examples using the name "Pansa" must have come from a work by Crassicius Pansa is very doubtful.

19. One might guess that the final words in the invented verse about Archimedes are (if sense is to be expected in metrical examples) drawn from Livy 24.34, the description of Archimedes' defense of Syracuse.

20. The other major theory is that of "prototypes," which derived all meters from an original set of metrical feet, usually eight or nine. For discussion of the two metrical theories, see 8.4b below.

form, or by combining elements from different forms, or by transposing syllables or words, every type of lyric meter can be seen as a variation based on the two fundamental meters.[21] Accordingly, his method of explaining complex meters is to show their derivation by taking verses, or parts of verses, by earlier poets (and sometimes his own) and then altering them to make other meters. Thus, in explaining the first line of the Alcaic stanza (*vides ut alta stet nive candidum*) (37.15–8.18), he shows that the first part of the line is taken from an iambic trimeter such as *vides ut alta genibus haerebo tuis* while the second part is taken from half of a dactylic pentameter with one syllable removed: *stet nive candidum* is an abridged form of *stet nive candidulum*; similarly, one can derive *Maecenas atavis edite regibus* from the pentameter *Maecenas atavis edite remigibus*.

Examples like these recur throughout the tradition of metrical writing, and it is hard to tell how much of Caesius' work is original. He was unquestionably drawing on a tradition of Greek metrical writing, but the language that he uses of his own work (repeatedly speaking of his own discovery of examples, using *repperi* or *inveni*) and the fact that he prides himself on his method of illustrating verse-forms in Latin through the combination or alteration of real as well as invented examples strongly suggest that his treatise on meter was in fact the first of its kind in Latin. In the conclusion, he compares his method of combining and composing metrical shapes to the *Stomachion* of Archimedes, the set of fourteen *lamellae* he enjoyed playing with as a boy that could be put together as a square or as many other figures, *aliter atque aliter modo galeam, modo sicam, alias columnam, alias navem figurat et innumerabiles efficit species* (43.21–2).[22] And while Caesius may of course be exaggerating the personal element in his work, it gives the impression of being very much his own. As a practicing poet, he created the first guide to the writing of Latin poetry in a modern vein, Greek measures adapted to Latin words.

3. PALAEMON, PROBUS, AND PLINY

Whether or not it was deliberate or simply a matter of chronology and chance, the final two figures in Suetonius' *De grammaticis*, Q. Remmius Palaemon and M. Valerius Probus, offer a striking contrast. Both were men of great scholarship and acclaim, but their lives and approaches to grammar, as Suetonius presents them, were diametrically opposed. Palaemon (*DGR* 23), whose active teaching career extended from the reign of Tiberius to that of Nero and whose pupils included the satirist Persius and (probably) the rhetorician Quintilian, is the only grammarian mentioned in Quintilian's account of grammar (1.4.20); in the second century, he remained for Juvenal (6.452, 7.215–27) the paradigmatic grammarian. An ex-slave, he was famous in his lifetime: on the positive side, for his success as

21. On the fourfold system of explanation, see above, Ch. 3 n.20.

22. Caesius does not name the *Stomachion* (on which see esp. Netz et al. 2004); for a lengthy discussion of its relevance here, see Morelli ad loc. The image is taken over by Apthonius/Asmonius, *GL* 6.100.23–1.4; it also occurs in the explanation of how a cento is composed in the preface to Ausonius' *Cento nuptialis*.

a teacher and speaker and for the wealth he acquired from his skill; on the negative, for his sheer arrogance (calling Varro a pig, claiming that *litterae* were born and would die with him and that Virgil himself had predicted Palaemon's existence), his vulgar extravagance and pleasure in his own fame, and the sexual excess that led both Tiberius and Claudius to proclaim that he should not be left as an instructor in charge of *pueri* and *iuvenes*.[23] Probus (*DGR* 24), in contrast, was a provincial ex-soldier; a man who spent his life in the study of old texts and old manuscripts; someone who did not formally teach but allowed a few *sectatores* to read texts with him after lunch. He had no interest in fame or publicity; indeed, the writings he circulated in his lifetime were few and on his death he left behind *non mediocrem silvam observationum sermonis antiqui* ("a good-sized quantity of observations on ancient language").[24]

Suetonius mentions some of Probus' writings, and between his short biography and the *Anecdoton Parisinum* (probably also by Suetonius) we gain a sharper sense of his areas of interest and expertise.[25] According to the biography, Probus learned in Beirut to study the *antiqui*, as they were not scorned there as they were in Rome. He then devoted himself (presumably in Rome, although Suetonius never says so; see Kaster 1995: 254) to gather many *exemplaria: multaque exemplaria contracta emendare ac distinguere et adnotare curavit, soli huic nec ulli praeterea grammaticae parti deditus* ("He made an effort to correct, punctuate, and place annotations in the many copies he had collected; he was devoted to this part of grammar alone, and to no other besides"). According to the *Anecdoton*, Probus used critical signs in manuscripts of Virgil, Horace, and Lucretius; in specific, he is said to have used the asterisk, like Aristarchus, to mark passages where lines that appeared more than once *did* belong, and similarly the asterisk with an obelus to mark those places where repeated lines did not belong.[26] He also seems to have followed Aristarchus in using the *diplê aperistikton* (the *diplê* without dots

23. On Palaemon's life, see Kaster's commentary on Suetonius (1995: 228–42).

24. For bibliography on Probus, see 12.36.1 below.

25. On the *Anecdoton* (*GL* 7.533–6), see also 2.2 above and 7.4.6a below. The most careful discussion of its relevance to Probus is that of Jocelyn (1984–5); see also the comments of Delvigo (1990: 83–6) and Kaster (1995: 246–7).

26. The meaning of the text is not altogether clear to me. On the asterisk, it says that Aristarchus (followed by Probus and our *antiqui*) used it *ad eos* [sc. *versus*], *qui in hoc puta loco positi erant, cum aliis* [?sc. *locis*; another possibility (suggested to me by R. Kaster) is to emend to *alias*] *non recte ponerentur* (534.18–19: "on those [lines] which were put [e.g.] in this spot, when in others they were not rightly placed"); in the parallel text in Isidore, *Etym.* 1.21.2 the wording is *in his quae omissa sunt, ut inlucescant per eam notam, quae deesse videntur* ("on those that were omitted, so that through this *nota* it should become clear what seemed to be missing"). On the *asteriscus cum obelo* the fragment notes that Aristarchus and Probus used it *in his versibus, qui non suo loco positi erant* (535.1–2: "on those verses which were placed where they did not belong"), and Isidore's wording is the same (1.21.7). I take it that the two signs are correlative.

[>]) to mark a number of features, including anachronism and rhetorical display.[27] Further evidence comes from Servius' commentary on Virgil: there are five places (and one more in the Verona scholia) where *adnotatio* by Probus is referred to, and in two of them (on *Aen.* 1.21 and 10.444) the use of specific critical marks—not those referred to in the *Anecdoton*—is mentioned.[28]

That Probus commented on texts—whether in particular manuscripts or in some other location—is certain; and that he was interested in making observations about the correct wording of those texts is equally clear. And yet that interest needs to be placed in context. Aistermann ascribes some 125 fragments to Valerius Probus, and while his numbering involves some duplication and not all the ascriptions are altogether secure, fewer than half the fragments, fifty-one to be precise, involve annotation or comment on particular texts; and of those fifty-one, only thirteen concern either the wording of the text or the use of critical signs.[29] Ancients and moderns alike have seen Probus as the Roman equivalent to Aristarchus, and that is unfortunate—not to mention the fact that just what Aristarchus did to Homer is not exactly clear either. Even more unfortunate is that he has been taken as the author of "critical editions" that were either like our own or the ancestors of the manuscripts we use. Much modern scholarship on Probus concerns his alleged work as a textual critic, but in fact, and in context, it seems relatively unimportant and is in any case unknowable.[30]

If the modern emphasis on Probus as an editor of texts is a red herring, there are several more interesting and slightly more answerable questions

27. In full: *nunc ea quae praeter consuetudinem tam vitae nostrae quam ipsius poetae apud eum invenirentur adnotans, nunc proprias ipsius figuras, interdum ea in quibus copiosus est, rursus quae semel apud eum ponerentur* (535.12–15: "putting a *nota* now to mark things which were found contrary to the custom of our lives or that of the poet himself, now figures that were particularly his, sometimes places where he is wordy, and again things that appeared in his work only once"). The precise meaning of this too is obscure to me.

28. The first of these passages simply describes the verses as *adpuncti* by Probus (with the remarkable annotation *hi duo si eximantur, nihilo minus sensus integer erit*); the second says that Probus used the *alogus* to criticize the phrase *aequore iusso*. The *alogus* is named (but not pictured) in one of the three lists of signs in the Paris fragment; Isidore defines it as *alogus nota [quae] ad mendas adhibetur* (1.21.27). It is not otherwise associated with Probus.

29. Aistermann (1910) divides the fragments into two groups: those with Probus' name are given Arabic numbers, those which Aistermann believes to be by Probus but do not have his name are given Roman numbers; I am considering only the former group. It should be noted that Aistermann's edition of the fragments is an addition (numbering pages with Roman numbers) at the back of his dissertation, which originally did not contain the fragments.

30. Delvigo (1990: 101–10) has a valuable discussion of what Aristarchus did and what "Aristarchus" meant in Rome.

raised by Suetonius' biography. What, in the first place, is meant by *veteres* or *antiqui*, the texts he says that Probus brought back from oblivion to Rome? He was clearly interested in genuinely early authors: Aulus Gellius, for instance (6.7.3, 6.9.11–12), cites his discussions of passages and words in Plautus, Aelius Tubero, and Valerius Antias, but a far greater number of fragments shows him at work on Virgil and Terence—although that may be because the remaining ancient commentaries on those authors are more learned and extensive than for most. One comment of his survives on the text of Sallust, and the *Anecdoton* states that he studied Horace and Lucretius—although not a single piece of other evidence for that survives. Terence is by any definition an *antiquus*; but Terence was one of the few pre-Ciceronian authors who was closely studied and discussed from the first century BCE until late antiquity, largely because of the clarity and purity (*puri sermonis amator* according to Caesar, F 1.2 Courtney) of his language. The others, particularly Horace and Virgil, are texts of great interest in the Neronian period and it is very hard to think of them as *veteres* at all.

On the other hand, even though the late republican and Augustan classics were studied and admired in the Neronian age, it is equally clear that such a positive appraisal was scarcely universal.

> "Arma virum," nonne hoc spumosum et cortice pingui
> ut ramale vetus vegrandi subere coctum?

> "Arms and the man"—isn't that foamy and thick-barked like an old branch dried out on a big old cork tree?

sputtered Persius' decadent interlocutor in the first Satire (96–7): the *Aeneid* was old hat, crude and unpolished in comparison with the elegance and lubriciousness of modern verse—to be linked to Accius and Pacuvius. And although this is satire, it has an object: the kind of overly precious and rhetorical post-Ovidian poetry (such as Iulius Montanus, Cornelius Severus, or Albinovanus Pedo) that is not well attested now but in the court and environs of Nero provided a more pleasing alternative to classicism. In the same way, Seneca derided Cicero for his long-windedness (what we would call periodic style) and lack of point and polish. As time went on, however, Seneca too went out of fashion, and just as Seneca rejected Ciceronianism, so later in the century Quintilian attacked Senecanism; and Quintilian and Probus were contemporaries. The "old" writers were not archaic writers, but in comparison with writers of the Neronian age and later (and Lucan, Statius, and Juvenal are later referred to as *neoterici*), they were in fact old. The only truly misleading aspect of Suetonius' account is the claim that these writers were forgotten in Rome. They were not.

The other major issues raised by Suetonius' biography are intertwined: what was the *pars* of grammar to which, according to Suetonius, Probus was devoted, and what was the nature of his writing? Hermann Usener long ago, emphasizing Probus' work on texts, said that it was *emendatio*, one of the four *officia* of grammar (along with *lectio, enarratio*, and *iudicium*) described by Varro.[31] Marc Baratin has argued, I think rightly, that we are to think of the "parts" of grammar as the two identified by Quintilian: *recte loquendi scientia* and *poetarum enarratio* (1.4.1). Probus, very clearly, concentrated on the second: what he wrote about language emerged from his study of texts. Nor was that writing limited to annotation or commentary, although that was clearly important. Against Suetonius' rather dismissive phrase about his writings, *nimis pauca et exigua de quibusdam minutis quaestiunculis edidit* (24.4: "His circulated writings were few and small, about some tiny little problems"), we may set what we know from other sources. Gellius' mention of *multos . . . commentationum libros* (*NA* 15.30.4 = T 25 Aistermann) is not very helpful, but he also mentions a work apparently on codes (*de occulta litterarum significatione*, 17.9.5 = T 27), and, more philologically, there are references to works on *consuetudo* (as discussed above, the linguistic opponent of *ratio*), about problems of gender, about unusual forms of the perfect tense, about the Greek genitive, and, most striking, a work *de temporum conexione* (Servius on *Aen.* 7.421 = T 28, F 116) to do with combinations of verbal tenses. The evidence surrounding Probus' work on the syntax of the Latin verb is not altogether easy to assess, but it seems likely that Probus was, in fact, one of the very rare grammarians to talk about syntax at all; in this, it also seems probable, his approach goes back to Varro himself.[32]

If Probus, then, can be taken to represent the tradition of particularity and complexity in grammar, the tradition of close reading of texts, what of his mirror-image in *De grammaticis*, Remmius Palaemon? Suetonius, typically, mentions his teaching, his poetry, and his extravagant and disreputable habits, but says not a word about his grammatical writings. And yet Palaemon's *Ars grammatica* was probably the single most influential work of its kind ever written in Rome. He was the great systematizer, the representative of Alexandrian grammar, the teacher who established the shape of Latin grammatical instruction for centuries. The detailed organization and contents of Palaemon's *Ars* are harder to know. Four substantial fragments attached to his name survive, on adverbs, prepositions, conjunctions, and interjections (F 5–8), but a great deal more of the grammatical lore preserved by Charisius and other related sources almost certainly derives from him—something that both indicates his importance and makes it very hard to determine what is genuinely his and what has been altered over the course of the tradition.[33] As in the later tradition, the eight parts of speech provided the

31. Usener (1913: 282–3).

32. On this subject, see Baratin (1989: 186–201).

33. The most important reconstruction of Palaemon's grammar is that of Barwick (1922, esp. 111–67, 186–91). Barwick's work is a brilliant example of *Quellenforschung*, but is not always credible, particularly in the precision of its details. On the other hand, his general picture of Palaemon's *Ars* is plausible (although the presence of syntax and metrics is very dubious), and the similarities between it and the contents of the grammar presented in Quintilian 1.4–8 (although Quintilian has massively changed order and emphasis to fit his concentration on the relevance of grammar to rhetoric) support the

core of his exposition, and Palaemon recognized those that became standard and is perhaps responsible for their becoming canonical. He divided nouns into four declensions (omitting the fifth) and verbs into the four conjugations that we still use. His discussions were carefully analytic,[34] and there is no sign that any earlier grammar was nearly so detailed or so precise; there is also no sign that his was not the grammar—or at least one of very few grammars—that became the basis for the later tradition. The contrasts between Palaemon and Probus are stark and obvious: between the general and the particular, between rule and exception. Where Probus seems to have relied on Varronian ideas about syntax (although that is uncertain), Palaemon called Varro a pig. And yet, if one looks at their views on the authorities for good Latin and the texts worth discussing, they are not far apart. In those sections of the *ars* tradition that can plausibly be assigned to Palaemon, examples are drawn almost exclusively from Cicero, Sallust, Terence, Virgil, and Horace:[35] his grammar was more narrowly based on classical literary Latin than was Probus', but for the most part it is their methods rather than their reading that differ.

The contrast between Palaemon and Probus is genuine; more than that, it is good to think with. It looks ahead to the formation of the two most important traditions of scholarship, the grammar and the commentary; it displays the different approaches of systematization and particularity; it also shows the continuing centrality of the major classical writers to all later scholars, no matter what their linguistic or stylistic orientation. But if Palaemon and Probus represent two approaches, they leave aside a third of almost equal importance, the tradition of close attention to individual words and forms, leading on one side to the lexicographical tradition, on another to the taste for the different, the obscure, and the archaic (often in works *De Latinitate*, to be discussed in Chapter 5). In the context of first-century philology, that tradition can be represented, albeit somewhat schematically, by the work written by the Elder Pliny during a period

reconstruction. It is also clear, however, that Palaemon was not followed slavishly by the later tradition: in particular, his distinctive terminology (*ordo* for declension and conjugation; *incusativus* for the more common *accusativus*, *qualitas* for *modus*, *finitivus* for *indicativus*, *infinitus* for *infinitivus*, *subiunctivus* for *coniunctivus*, *instans* for *praesens*) was largely abandoned. See also 8.2 below.

34. For a discussion of his (and others') presentations of the adverb, see 8.5 below.

35. See Barwick (1922: 188–91). Given the nature of the tradition, it is not surprising that, particularly in Charisius, examples from earlier authors and quotations from later sources such as Pliny and Romanus also appear (often both at once) in sections that are largely derived from Palaemon; nor, indeed, is it surprising that Palaemon's distinctive terminology is also replaced from time to time by more standard equivalents. As will become clear below, virtually all grammatical works ascribed to an author who wrote before the fifth century, with the exception of Donatus' *Artes*, have been modified to a greater or lesser degree.

of circumspect silence at the end of Nero's reign (66–8), the eight-book *Dubius sermo*.[36]

More than 100 fragments of *Dubius sermo* survive, and a great deal more material has been attributed to Pliny's work by modern scholars. The firmly attributed fragments are very brief, and the vast majority of them are cited by Iulius Romanus (in Charisius) from a single book, Book 6, of Pliny's work. His subject, very clearly, was words about which there was some doubt; the fragments show that the doubts could concern the gender, spelling, or inflection of a word. How the work was organized is unclear: Book 6 is concerned with the morphology of nouns, and to some scholars it has seemed that the arrangement was neither alphabetical nor by declension, but by case-forms. That must remain in doubt; what is clear is that his choice of authorities is far wider and less orthodox than any of the other figures discussed in this chapter. Like some of his slightly earlier contemporaries, Pliny was aware of, and cites with some approval, the usage of modern writers (e.g., Catullus F 89, Bibaculus F 90, Maecenas F 45, Cornelius Severus F 9, Aemilius Macer F 32); indeed, as with Palaemon and Probus, his favorite author was Virgil. On the other hand, he was also well acquainted with Varro and earlier Roman literature: Ennius, Pacuvius, Terence, the autobiography of Rutilius Rufus and much more.[37] In a number of passages, moreover, he seems to elevate *consuetudo* over *ratio* in the choice of forms—although it is not always clear that he is making a choice rather than simply setting out alternatives that may both be acceptable.[38] In one fragment (F 95), Servius, in discussing Virgil's use of both *taureus* and *taurinus* as derivatives of *taurus*, quotes Pliny as rejecting rules about this: *derivationes firmas non habent regulas, sed exeunt prout auctoribus placet* ("Derivations don't have strict rules, but their endings are the authors' choice") and elsewhere Pliny can be seen to prefer euphony to strict

36. There are three relatively modern editions of the fragments of *Dubius sermo*: by Beck (1894); by Mazzarino (*GRFM*); and by Della Casa (1969). Beck is highly speculative in his attribution of fragments, and with some hesitation, I rely primarily on Mazzarino. Some other important attempts at interpretation (and discovery of other fragments) include Bölte (1888); Barwick (1922: 206–15); Mazzarino (1948–9); Schenkeveld (1996, 1998).

37. Given the fact that so high a proportion of the fragments comes from a single book of *Dubius sermo* and is cited by a single source (Romanus/Charisius), it is difficult to be certain about Pliny's overall literary tastes. The author most frequently cited in the fragments as a whole is Virgil, followed by Varro; on the other hand, in the fragments of Book 6 Virgil is cited only once. That might lead one to suspect that Romanus (or an intervening source, such as Caper) simply was not interested in Virgilian quotations and eliminated them. Pliny may have been more of an admirer of Augustan literature than we are able to see.

38. E.g., F 37, on the perennial problem of the genitive of names ending –ius, *Plinius quoque dubii sermonis V<I> adicit <esse quid>em rationem per duo "i" scribendi, sed multa iam consuetudine superari* ("Pliny in book 6 of *Dubius sermo* adds that there is some logic in writing them with two 'i's, but that many things are now overcome by custom").

analogy as well as giving much more leeway to authors and to *consuetudo* than one might expect. One of the few characteristics that Palaemon and Probus seem to share is a certain dogmatism, a sense of their own right(eous)ness. Pliny, like the title of his work, is refreshingly uncertain; the general impression conveyed by the fragments is that Pliny gives heed to both change and choice. It is not that he rejects the older forms, but that he tends to acquiesce in, if not to welcome, linguistic change. Pliny's work appears to have been very influential, and it may be that his openness to archaism, which seems to have been much greater than that of Palaemon and even Probus, made him appealing in the archaizing world of the Antonine age.

5

Finding the Right Word

1. TEACHER AND PUPIL

It was probably in 139 CE that the great orator M. Cornelius Fronto wrote to his pupil Marcus Aurelius (then aged eighteen, but already a member of the Senate), outlining what van den Hout aptly calls "his teaching programme," and displaying an attitude to literature and the nature of rhetorical style that is widely reflected in the philological writing of the second and early third centuries.[1] The letter is written as an amplification of comments that Fronto had apparently made orally to Marcus about some *scripta* that Marcus had read aloud to him (*Ad M. Caes.* 4.3.4); Marcus had seemed relatively uninterested when Fronto changed a syllable, and Fronto now wishes to reinforce the paramount importance of precision in the choice of words. In the carefully constructed letter, Fronto begins with a broad statement about the importance of diligence in all the *artes*, but points out that, as opposed to some other skills where lack of expertise can sometimes be concealed, *in verbis vero eligendis conlocandisque* there is no place to hide (4.3.1). After conceding that most of the older writers were not careful in this regard, he identifies those who were: of prose writers Cato and Sallust, and a long list of poets beginning with Plautus and Ennius and ending with writers whose vocabulary shone in particular kinds of diction (4.3.2). The glaring omission in this list is one to which Fronto then himself draws attention: what about Cicero? According to Fronto, he was a wonderful stylist in all respects other than one aspect of his diction: he had no interest in *insperata atque inopinata verba*, the kind that take a great deal of care to discover and that the reader would not miss if they were not there; they surprise. Marcus, it appears, deserves praise for at least trying to find the right word; but, alas, it might be better to stick to common language if you can't get the rare word right. Marcus looks not learned, but *semidoctus* (4.3.3). And Fronto goes on to give a stunning and nitpicking analyis of the distinctions

1. *Ad M. Caesarem* 4.3; for the quotation and evidence for the chronology, see van den Hout (1999: 150) ad loc.

to be made among the compounds of *lavo* and *lino* (4.3.5) before returning to his discussion of Marcus' homework.

The young Marcus, despite Fronto's occasional flattery, was just not very interested in Fronto's kind of rhetoric: he dutifully read the archaic texts that Fronto recommended, he was polite and even affectionate to his teacher. Even when Marcus was only eighteen, however, his teacher was perhaps not unaware that philosophy rather than rhetoric was his favorite subject. But Fronto persisted: he criticizes Cicero for gaining his effects by repeating the same word rather than varying, for seeking comprehensibility—which to Fronto means that his writing seems *volgatius et ieiunius* (*Ad Ant. Imp.* 3.1.1). In the same vein, more emphatically and brilliantly, he criticizes Seneca and Lucan for repetitiveness and lack of invention (*De orationibus* 2–6). Again and again, throughout the correspondence, Fronto returns to his main point: the precise choice of words matters. Long after Marcus has grown up and Fronto has grown old (in the collection of letters called *De eloquentia*, probably written after 161), Fronto is reminding Marcus of the good old days when he used his spare time to make word lists of synonyms and rare words (*De eloq*. 2.19); he expresses his strong dislike of *solitis et usitatis verbis* (*Ad M. Caes*. 3.14.1). The good orator, he reminds Marcus (*Ad Ant. Imp.* 1.2.7), is distinguished from the mediocre one by his choice not just of good words, but of better ones; those words, moreover, do not fall from the sky into our open mouths, but we must know their *regiones . . . et saltus* and go hunting for them (*De eloq*. 2.3).

The general tendency represented by Fronto's stylistic precepts and lists of recommended readings is well known and abundantly clear: just as Hadrian himself preferred archaic writers to classical ones, so too the writers of the second century—Fronto, Gellius, Apuleius—share a delight in resurrecting and imitating the literature of the middle Republic. Plautus comes into his own; so do any number of writers represented now only in fragments—and we would have neither Plautus nor the fragments had not a taste for the archaic persisted for decades, probably into the next century. The preciosity and archaism (or pseudo-archaism) of second-century style is visible on every page of Apuleius and Fronto (less so with Gellius, to whom we will return shortly); equally important is the underlying belief that style is in essence a matter of vocabulary, not of syntax or rhetorical figures. Everything hinges on the choice of the right word. And the same effect—concentration on the word rather than the thought—is as visible in grammatical writing as in literature. We need not try to assign cause and effect; but several aspects of the archaizing world need further exploration.[2]

2. After long neglect, there has been growing interest in Fronto, Gellius, and second-century style (in Greek as well as Latin); but these are topics that go well beyond the scope of this book. Holford-Strevens (2005) and the essays in Holford-Strevens and Vardi (2004) give an ample introduction and bibliography focusing on Gellius; among other recent studies, see particularly Howley (2017). See also S–H 3 §607–9, *HLL* 4 §408 (Sallmann).

2. WHAT IS A CLASSIC?

Fronto's taste for the odd and unfamiliar is extreme, even for his own time. In the first book of Aulus Gellius' *Noctes Atticae*, there is a famous and telling anecdote (1.10). Favorinus the philosopher (one of Gellius' favorite protagonists for his stories) encounters an *adulescens* who is spouting *voces nimis priscas et ignotas* ("excessively antique and unfamiliar words") in everyday conversation, and Favorinus criticizes him vehemently: men of old like Coruncanius and the triplet Horatii spoke the language of their own day, not the language of the Sicani or Pelasgi, but this hapless youth is talking as if to Evander's mother, in unintelligible words; if he wants to be unintelligible, he should just shut up. But the young man admires antiquity: *vive ergo moribus praeteritis, loquere verbis praesentibus* ("So live with the morals of the past, but talk in the words of the present"). And remember too Caesar's famous statement in *De analogia: tamquam scopulum, sic fugias inauditum atque insolens verbum* ("You should avoid the unheard and unusual word as if it were a reef").[3] *Inauditum atque insolens verbum* is a pejorative equivalent for precisely what Fronto praises, *insperata atque inopinata verba*: at least in this anecdote (as in a parallel one at 11.7), Gellius favors clarity over pyrotechnic displays of archaism.

That is not to say that Gellius is not an archaist, nor that he is sloppy about researching old words: stories in Gellius repeatedly involve the careful and considered selection of words, the study and understanding of archaic texts like Plautus and Ennius, the rejection of modern stylistic vices. Indeed, the rejection of Senecan style is one of the few things that might be agreed on by Fronto and Gellius on one side and Quintilian on the other. But the search for the ideal word was itself not unproblematic. One issue was the matter of authenticity: although earlier writers (including Quintilian and Valerius Probus) sometimes looked at early manuscripts to determine orthography, Fronto and Gellius bear witness to a more serious interest in autograph manuscripts and texts produced by reputable authorities. Many of those of which we know were probably not genuine, but the desire for authenticity is real, and shows an attention to the editing and transmission of texts that is rarely visible in Latin before the second century.[4]

The other issue is one of definition: if the *veteres* are the ones to be sought out for their strange and wonderful language, who are they? When does "old" begin? In this area, too, there is a real divergence between Fronto and Gellius. While both of them revere genuinely early authors like Plautus and Cato, they mark the division between old and new quite differently: for Fronto, Sallust barely counts, and only because he is an imitator of Cato, but Cicero and Virgil fail the acid text of diction, while for Gellius, Cicero and Virgil are not only classics, but *old* classics. Fronto's comments on Cicero (cited above) are clearly derogatory, but

3. On *De analogia*, see 3.6 above.

4. I have dealt (perhaps too dogmatically) with the problem of manuscripts and textual criticism in the second century elsewhere; cf. Zetzel (1973, 1981: 55–74).

more striking is the complete absence of Virgil: there is not a single quotation, not a single mention of his name.[5]

Gellius, by contrast, attempts to moderate the more extreme stylistic views of archaists like Fronto. How does one turn a classical writer into an archaic one? A good example of the technique is shown by Gellius' comments on two of Hyginus' assessments of Virgilian style.[6] One is his preference for reading *sensus amaror* at G. 2.246. Hyginus had said, at least according to Gellius, that *sapor . . . sensu torquebit amaro* was tautological; and besides, he had found *sensus amaror* in a manuscript from Virgil's own house. Gellius in his anecdote has Favorinus defend this (1.21), not because of the documentary evidence or the stylistic judgment, but because *amaror* had been used previously by Lucretius (4.223). The other involves Hyginus' criticism of Virgil for using the augural word *praepes* for Daedalus' flight (*Aen*. 6.15; Gellius 7.6). Gellius rebuts this criticism vigorously by citing precedents: before Virgil, the same usage appears in Matius' translation of the *Iliad* and twice in Ennius. In other words, Virgil is one of the *veteres* because he borrows vocabulary from earlier writers: he is as learned in his own archaism as are Gellius and his friends, and hence is as valuable as earlier writers for word-hunters. The same is true for Cicero: in a manuscript allegedly coming from Cicero's amanuensis Tiro, Gellius found readings that provided authentic Ciceronian archaisms (1.7, 13.21.15–24).

The taste for archaism in literary circles and the retroactive re-categorizing of classical writers as archaic are not, strictly speaking, philological problems, but they both involved the use of philological techniques and materials and probably had an effect on philological activities. The attempt to archaize the classics is not unique to Gellius: we have fragments of a collection of *singularia* in Cicero and Cato by one Statilius Maximus, and his name, not fortuitously, turns up in a note in a manuscript of Cicero: Statilius claims to have corrected the text against several old copies of Cicero, including Tiro's.[7] The search for manuscripts, particularly those attached to trustworthy and scholarly names, certainly sparked an awareness of the mutability of texts and the need for precisely the kind of linguistic analysis of variant readings that was responsible for the development of Alexandrian philology in the first place. Earlier scholars, from Hyginus to Probus, had paid some attention to manuscripts (although it is Gellius [and, for Probus, Suetonius] who tells us that) and had discussed particular texts; but it is not really until after Probus, in the period of Fronto and Gellius, that close exegetical and stylistic commentary began to flourish.[8] Similarly, earlier scholars, notably Pliny,

5. So, rightly, Marshall (1997: 3). The only quotations of Virgil by "Fronto" in van den Hout's index are in fact from one of Gellius' anecdotes and are Gellius, not Fronto.

6. On Hyginus, see 4.2 above.

7. On Statilius, see Teuffel 3 §374.2; Zetzel (1973, 1974); Pecere (1982). Uría Varela (2012) gives an interesting but highly speculative interpretation of Statilius' work on *singularia*.

8. See 5.4 below, on Asper, Acro, and other commentators of this period.

had discussed oddities and uncertainties of language, but it is not until the second century that the collection of desirable linguistic nuggets becomes, at least so far as we can see from our sources, the central preoccupation of grammarians.

3. THE RISE AND FALL OF LATINITY

A focus on words was not something new in Roman grammatical thought, even with Pliny. As shown above (Chapter 2), the original focus of Roman philology was on elucidating the vocabulary of early Roman legal and religious texts; glossaries and dictionaries are well attested from a fairly early date, and they persist as an independent tradition from (merely to use the limits of this volume) the second century BCE to the ninth century CE. But while all word collections of any magnitude offer evidence for the attestation of words, there is a significant difference between those that focus, broadly speaking, on semantics and those that focus on morphology. The former are what we would define as dictionaries; the latter are, in ancient parlance, works about Latinity, and they are as important to rhetoric as they are to grammar.[9]

In this connection, it is worth going back to origins.[10] The *Rhetorica ad Herennium* in the 80s contains the earliest reference to *Latinitas* (4.17), which he considers an element of *elegantia*, itself an important stylistic virtue. Rhetor explains *Latinitas* as *quae sermonem purum conservat, ab omni vitio remotum. Vitia in sermone, quo minus is Latinus sit, duo possunt esse: soloecismus et barbarismus* ("that which keeps language pure and remote from every flaw. There can be two flaws in speech that keep it from being Latin: solecism and barbarism"). What Rhetor describes as *Latinitas*, Cicero calls *sermo Latinus*[11] and explicitly credits Theophrastus with the four virtues of style of which *Latinitas* (*Hellenismos* for Theophrastus) is the first (*Orat.* 79; the others are clarity, decorum, and *ornatus*). In either language, the term arises in the context of rhetorical theory, but lies on the boundary between grammar and rhetoric: for Rhetor, Latinity is a virtue of oratorical style, but a subject to be taught by a grammarian. Works on correct Latinity began early: we know of a work in two books *De sermone Latino* by Antonius Gnipho (*DGR* 7 = *GRF* 99), and (probably before he wrote *De lingua Latina*) Varro composed a work of the same title in five books.

Latinitas and *sermo Latinus* are alternative expressions for the same thing, correctness in speech, defined, apparently, as the avoidance of mistakes—the wrong ending, the wrong gender, the wrong case after a preposition, lack of agreement between noun and adjective; the kinds of mistake we still correct in Latin 101. Varro's work on *sermo Latinus* was presumably different from his work on *lingua Latina*; but it is only a guess to suggest that perhaps *sermo* was primarily

9. On the term *Latinitas*, see Desbordes (2007: 91–105). There has been recent discussion (largely unhistorical) about the relationship between *Latinitas* and the modern notion of "standard language": for a review of the subject, see Clackson (2015).

10. See also the previous discussion of this issue at 3.5 above.

11. Cf. also *De or.* 3.47, where it is simply the adverb *Latine*.

concerned with the language as spoken and written (and perhaps the relationship between the two), while *lingua* (as we know from the extant text) was about its origins and development. The fragments of Varro's work *De sermone Latino* (F 33–48) are not enough to reconstruct its structure, but they are enough to know that he was more concerned with the form of words than their meanings: *aeditumus* or *aedituus* (34), *mutue* or *mutuo* (43), *Cretes* or *Cretenses* (33).[12] But the determination of correctness is not always straightforward, and the grounds for identifying correct Latinity included not only analogy, but custom, usage, and precedent as well.[13] When Varro stated his preference for *aeditumus* over *aedituus*, he rejected the latter as *recenti novitate fictum* and praised the former as *antiqua origine incorruptum*.

To the extent that we can judge from fragments and reconstructions, early work on Latinity involved attempts to determine the importance (and limits) of regularity in paradigms and to offer ideas about the shaping of a literary Latin that was neither excessively rigid nor filled with the morphological disorder of the archaic language. What *Latinitas* actually meant was contested: Caesar's *De analogia* was apparently a somewhat barbed response to Cicero's assumption that *Latinitas* was uncontroversial enough not to need detailed discussion; it seems to have included fairly detailed discussions of both orthography and morphology, probably divided by parts of speech.[14] Other works, fragmentary or reconstructed, appear to have combined articulation of general rules of inflection with extensive exploration of potential anomalies.

In modern discussions, works on Latinity can seem somewhat amorphous—or rather, to take many definite but mutually incompatible shapes—for a simple reason: not one survives complete, and as far as we can see they became extinct by the middle of the third century. They flourished, apparently, in two periods: one is the time of Varro and Caesar, as part of a debate about how Latin should look, where Latinity seems to be very much a part of grammar; the other is the second and early third centuries, when Latinity is much more a part of rhetorical style. The only major work of this kind that falls between these two periods is the Elder Pliny's *Dubius sermo*, discussed at the end of Chapter 4. That work does not seem, so far as one can tell from definite fragments, to have been at all interested in rhetoric;[15] on the other hand, Pliny's book was mined in the following century

12. On *De sermone Latino* see also 3.5 above.

13. On the criteria for correctness, see above all Siebenborn (1976); there is a very valuable discussion also (with particular reference to Servius' commentary on Virgil) by Uhl (1998). See also Zetzel (forthcoming).

14. For the reconstruction of *De analogia*, see Garcea (2012), and 3.6 above.

15. Fragments 121–4 Mazzarino (= 124, 125, 127, 128 Della Casa) concern barbarism and solecism or figures and *vitia orationis*; all come from commentaries on Donatus. Mazzarino assigns them to *Dubius sermo* and Della Casa to the poorly attested *Studiosi libri*, but in any case they do not reveal an interest in rhetoric greater than is found some grammars.

in works with a much more clearly rhetorical orientation, above all Flavius Caper's large treatise *De Latinitate* and Iulius Romanus' *Aphormai* ("starting-points"; "first attempts"), a work which is itself the most important source for our knowledge of Pliny's book.

Caper is hard to discuss: what survives directly of his work are two meager texts (one on orthography, one *De verbis dubiis*) which are probably based on—and probably at some remove from—his original large compilation. On the other hand, his work clearly underlies a great deal of later grammatical writing on questions of proper Latinity, and many quotations survive.[16] Caper is quoted by Romanus; his *De Latinitate* is almost certainly one of the three sources of the complicated chapter of Charisius' *De extremitatibus nominum et diversis quaestionibus* (I 15; 61.14–143.25B: "On the terminations of nouns and assorted problems"); and his work lies behind parts of Books 5 and 8 of Priscian's *Ars* and the anonymous treatise *De dubiis nominibus* (*GL* 5.571–94; see 12.46.5 below). One of the striking features of his discussion of nouns—which, given our sources, is the only part of Caper's work that we know much about—is that it is arranged not by declensions but by the ending of the nominative singular. He was concerned, like most authors writing *De Latinitate*, to use the traditional tools of analysis, primarily *ratio/analogia* and *consuetudo*, to determine which of two or more possible declensions, genders, or meanings was correct. He seems to have been considerably less archaizing than some of his contemporaries: although he is (through the surviving works that made use of his) an important source for fragments of republican Roman poetry, he is also our major source for the fragments of the early imperial poet Cornelius Severus.[17]

Our only extended extracts from any treatise on Latinity, however, come not from Caper's work but from Romanus, who provides our best entry into the philological world of the archaist age. What we know of Romanus, who wrote early in the third century, comes from a single source, Charisius' fourth-century *Ars grammatica*, a work which contains apparently verbatim or near-verbatim extracts of some length from Romanus and other sources, including Palaemon.[18] What Charisius gives us from Romanus are two long extracts, one on nominal morphology (149.22–87.6B) under the chapter title *De analogia, ut ait Romanus* (1.17) and one on adverbs (246.18–89.17) as a part of Charisius' larger chapter

16. Edited by G. Keil (1889)—not the same as the editor of *Grammatici Latini*.

17. I suspect that we know less about the work of Caper in particular than the industrious Quellenforschung of Bölte (1888), Barwick (1922: 191–215), Strzelecki (1936), and others would suggest: he was certainly important, but his name became representative of the genre, and the reconstruction of very specific lines of descent and influence is less convincing than it once appeared. In particular, Strzelecki's view that Book 3 of Nonius Marcellus was based on Caper was decisively refuted by White (1980: 140–91). For more on Caper, see 12.10 below.

18. On Romanus, see Froehde (1892); Della Casa (1978); Schenkeveld (2004); Welsh (2010). See also Teuffel 3 §379.3, S–H 3 §603, *HLL* 5 §439.1 (Schmidt).

on the topic (2.13); there are shorter extracts in the chapters on conjunctions, prepositions, and interjections.[19] Aside from introductions to his various subjects, Romanus' work consisted of alphabetized (by first letter only) lists of words and phrases, divided up into the parts of speech. The longest and generally the most interesting excerpt is the chapter on adverbs. It begins with an extended and self-consciously clever rhetorical introduction blending consideration of the place of the adverb in the system of parts of speech with discussion of particular forms and examples (246.18–52.31);[20] the list follows, extending for more than thirty pages, from *aliter* to *vehementer*. Each entry is illustrated by at least one quotation, some of remarkable obscurity and most taken from republican or Augustan texts, and although Romanus cites Fronto (256.8, 267.6, 287.26, 288.17), Suetonius (260.23), and Hadrian (271.10, 287.1), he never mentions Neronian or Flavian literature. The entries include not only standard adverbial forms of adjectives and independent adverbs such as *heri* (260.11), but nominal phrases and constructions that can be understood adverbially. Thus there are entries for *dedita opera* (256.16) with a quotation from Naevius and a reluctant admission that one might consider this a noun phrase (*declinari ut nomen potest*), for *in mundo* (261.17) with several illustrations, and for the genitive of price *quanti* (279.20). What is more, questions of spelling or meaning (the difference between *setius* and *serius*, 283.19) are interspersed with issues of form and attestation, along with occasional grammatical observations on broader classes of adverbs (e.g., *localibus adverbiis*, 263.31) tucked into the same alphabetical arrangement.

Romanus' work clearly falls under the rubric of *De Latinitate*, and as such does not fit easily into the familiar categories of grammar and dictionary. Like Pliny in *Dubius sermo*, he arranges his work by parts of speech, reflecting the organization of a grammar; but like Pliny, he also reflects the organization of a lexicon, in that the entries are arranged alphabetically. Some of the entries in the list of adverbs concern the formation of adverbs; some of them attempt to distinguish between alternative adverbs from the same stem (e.g., *alias* and *aliter*); most of them cite authorities, who range from Cato and Ennius to Terence, Cicero, and Virgil to Fronto and Marcus Aurelius, either for the proper form of an adverb or for its existence at all, occasionally noting scholarly debates about problematic issues. In some ways, Romanus' technique combines the worst of both grammar and dictionary. By listing words alphabetically under the crude rubrics of "noun" or "interjection" or "adverb" (we have no idea how he handled verbs) rather than, as some kinds of glossaries and grammars do, distinguishing between problems of meaning and problems of form, he forces the reader to scroll through a great deal of irrelevant material in search of an answer to what might be a very specific question. The mixture of two methods, moreover, means that Romanus' work

19. There is also clearly some use of Romanus in the long and strange chapter 1.15, but its origins are very uncertain and much debated. See, among major discussions, Bölte (1888); Barwick (1922); Schenkeveld (1996, 1998). See also *HLL* 5 §493.2 (Schmidt).

20. See Schenkeveld (2004) for detailed commentary and analysis.

is not as useful as it might be for someone who simply wants to improve his or her Latin vocabulary—or to look up the meaning and usage of a word of whose precise grammatical shape the reader is uncertain. This mixture of grammatical and lexical organization is not in itself unusual: the tension that always exists in discussions of morphology, going back to Varro, between *ratio* and *consuetudo* almost inevitably involves such a combination, because the argument for *ratio* is based on the invocation of a regular paradigm, while the argument for *consuetudo* or *auctoritas* requires the citation of examples.

Who, moreover, was the reader for whom this strange book was designed? Inserted into a formal grammar and combined with more "grammatical" discussions as it appears in Charisius, it serves the useful purpose of adding concrete examples to abstract theory.[21] But on its own, it is bewildering. The organization, both the use of the alphabet and the explanation of the meaning of entries through the use of illustrative quotation, strongly suggests that it was designed not for the exposition of grammar, but for looking up words and learning their pedigrees. And the fact that such a large proportion of the quotations is from archaic or archaizing texts (including Virgil and Cicero, in this case) shows that it was meant to help students or readers find just the word they needed in a speech or rhetorical exercise. "Fronto says to collect synonyms": Romanus has lots of them. "He says to collect *singularia*, words that appear only once": after Pliny, one of Romanus' most frequently cited sources is Statilius Maximus' work on *singularia* in Cicero and Cato. "I need a striking adverb in this sentence": look no further. Grammar has become a search for the right word, and it has become a tool to help aspiring speakers avoid doing their own reading.

Romanus, moreover, is himself not unlike the reader I imagine, because he too did not do his own research, but borrowed heavily from other scholars. By far the most frequently cited source in Romanus' work is Pliny's *Dubius sermo*. But Romanus refers only to Book 6, and only in the chapter on analogy in nouns. Either Pliny never talked about the adverb—which is untrue—or Romanus only used, or had access to, one-eighth of the whole.[22] The latter alternative is also suggested by his use of other sources, particularly the second-century commentary on Terence of Helenius Acro. With only three exceptions, all the citations of Acro concern the *Adelphoe*; those three come from the *Eunuchus*. If Acro commented on the rest of Terence (very likely), Romanus did not read him.[23] But what is most important about Romanus' working methods is not the limited nature of his reading but the variety of his sources. Romanus clearly relies on other scholars, some of whom worked in very different formats: he makes use of earlier word lists, such

21. For a fuller analysis of this combination in Charisius, see 8.6 below.

22. On Romanus' use of sources, see Schenkeveld (2004: 39–42) and Welsh (2010).

23. Romanus' quotations from Acro are collected and discussed by Wessner (1905: 16–18). Schmidt believes that Acro commented only on these plays, but it is far more likely, given Romanus' methods, that the selection is due to Romanus rather than to Acro himself.

as that of Statilius Maximus; he draws on grammars such as that of Scaurus and quasi-grammatical works like Pliny or Caper and notes their comments on specific passages of earlier authors; he takes material from commentaries on Terence, Virgil, and Horace. And probably he did just a little of his own reading for himself.

4. GRAMMARIANS AT WORK

Fronto, the teacher of emperors and the greatest orator of his day, is not a good indication of what was going on in the real world of philology and grammar; and as we have seen in the previous section, works like that of Romanus, while not written by or for people at Fronto's cultural level, were probably composed in order to enable lesser mortals to aspire to the linguistic expertise and rhetorical skill that were required for social or political advancement in the Rome of the Antonines. But what of the traditional work of the *grammaticus*? Clearly it went on: then, as now, there was a never-ending supply of ten-year-olds needing grammatical instruction, and presumably there was a corresponding set of teachers, explaining grammar and poetry and writing textbooks.

It is not surprising that we hear little of these teachers: after Suetonius, very few people took an interest in the ubiquitous elementary teacher, and not until the fourth century do *grammatici* appear again to achieve some of the fame and importance that were claimed by a Verrius Flaccus or Remmius Palaemon. What is more, our best and most vivid picture of literary and grammatical study in the Antonine Age is the set of vignettes presented by Aulus Gellius in the *Noctes Atticae*, but while that is an invaluable source, it is not altogether objective. Gellius gives us a portrait of a society fascinated by problems of correct language and engaged in research about an earlier (and perhaps therefore purer and more valuable) stage in Roman language and literature. His stories display men of taste and learning (and, not coincidentally, wealth and power) discussing with scholars and students the proper use of words and texts. But in these stories, very few of the professionals come off very well, and young and know-it-all *adulescentes* too are invariably crushed because of the limits of their knowledge: they need to be put in their place by a Favorinus, Herodes Atticus, or Sulpicius Apollinaris.[24]

It is the last of these heroic figures who is most important in this context, because he was in fact a *grammaticus* and Gellius' own teacher, and he appears in a speaking role in several important chapters about proper language in the *Noctes Atticae*.[25] One of these, near the end of Gellius' book (18.4), is particularly

24. The typical *adulescens* is the young man dissected by Favorinus in *NA* 1.10, discussed above; on the treatment of *grammatici*, see Kaster (1988: 50–60), Vardi (2001), and Holford-Strevens (2005: 172–4). The basic rule seems to be that unnamed *grammatici* are treated rudely (e.g., 4.1, 6.17, 8.10, 14.5, 15.9, 18.9, 19.10, 20.10), while named ones are not.

25. Other than the anecdotes in Gellius, what we have of Sulpicius' writings are verse synopses of Plautus and Terence and an epigram about Virgil (possibly by a different Sulpicius) preserved in the manuscripts of the first two and the biographical tradition

striking. The story presents Gellius as an *adulescentulus* in search of a more advanced teacher, witnessing an encounter between Sulpicius Apollinaris and a *iactator* who claims to be the World's Greatest Expert on Sallust. Sulpicius, whom Gellius describes as toying with the fool in the manner of Socrates with the sophists (18.4.1), asks a question about the difference between *stolidior* and *vanior* in a passage of Sallust (*Hist* 4.1M). The fool, of course, is compelled to recognize his folly: he runs away, and Sulpicius is left to answer his own question with intelligence and learning.

Gellius admires Sulpicius: he describes him as *hominem memoriae nostrae doctissimum* (13.18.2), *vir in memoria nostra praeter alios doctus* (18.4.1), *virum eleganti scientia ornatum* (16.5.5), and *virum praestanti litterarum scientia* (4.17.11). More than once, he reports anecdotes from the time when he was Sulpicius' student (7.6.12; 13.18.3); he also has stories from later on, when they were apparently friends and encountered one another, for instance, in the library of the *domus Tiberiana* (13.20.1). For Gellius, and perhaps in real life, Sulpicius was clearly not like other grammarians; he stands out not only in the subtlety of his linguistic learning and his familiarity with legal and religious terminology as well as literary texts—and his use of antiquarian knowledge to elucidate literary texts—but also in his extremely high social standing and his correspondence and conversations with Erucius Clarus, *praefectus urbi* and twice consul, a man himself of great erudition as well as power.[26]

Sulpicius was not an ordinary grammarian, and from none of Gellius' anecdotes does one have the remotest sense that he ever taught little boys how to decline *domus*.[27] Gellian grammar operates on a higher plane: not basic education, but the elegant erudition that was supposed to inform the language of men of standing and accomplishment. But the kinds of philological questions that appear in the *Noctes Atticae* are in fact part of the larger pattern described earlier in this chapter: a philology that is concerned primarily with words; that looks back to early models; that worries about the correctness of literary texts and their precise meanings in order to avoid the solecisms that would expose the speaker as a person lacking refinement.

Two other grammarians of the Hadrianic period named by Gellius stand out as significant and in some ways representative figures: L. Caesellius Vindex and Q. Terentius Scaurus. Both men receive Gellius' praise, Scaurus as *divi Hadriani temporibus grammaticus vel nobilissimus* (11.15.3) and Caesellius (less

about the last. On Sulpicius, see Teuffel 3 §357, S–H 3 §597, *HLL* 4 §436 (Schmidt); on his role in Gellius see Kaster (1988: 58–60); Holford-Strevens (2005: 83–6). Mantelli (2015) has a new discussion of Sulpicius, with commentary on the comic synopses and all the relevant chapters of Gellius.

26. On Erucius, cf. *PIR*² E96. He died in 146, in his second term as consul, and is referred to by Pliny and Fronto as well as Gellius.

27. Schmidt (*HLL* 4: 231) rightly refers to "eine gewisse Distanz zur üblichen professionellen Produktion."

enthusiastically) as *grammatico . . . hautquaquam inerudito* (18.11.1) and *homo minime malus* (3.16.11); but that does not prevent him from criticizing them, as indeed he criticizes Sulpicius himself at his first appearance (2.16), when Sulpicius is offering a criticism (with which Gellius disagrees) of Caesellius Vindex. The praise of Scaurus—the only place Scaurus is mentioned by Gellius—occurs when he too is wrongly criticizing Caesellius. These passages, and the work of Caesellius in general, deserve a little more attention.[28]

One clearly important work by Caesellius Vindex, his *Commentarii lectionum antiquarum*, is cited by Gellius; it was also used by Iulius Romanus. The latter's quotations reveal that the *lectiones antiquae* were organized not by the author being discussed, but as a dictionary organized into books. But Caesellius' work seems to have been unlike most other alphabetized grammatical works, as it was not (like Romanus') divided by grammatical category, but in fact included all sorts of observations—on passages of Virgil, on the sound made by a trumpeter taking his horn out of his mouth (*but*: see Charisius 312.23B),[29] on the declension of *acer* (second or third?), and on the interpretation of the name *Morta* in Livius Andronicus. Caesellius, particularly as reported by Gellius, was nothing if not opinionated. In a comment severely criticized by Gellius as *turpe erratum* (6.2.1), Caesellius had attempted to show that Ennius (*Ann.* 381–3V) had used *cor* as a masculine noun; but Gellius, looking up the passage in question, found that Caesellius had quoted only two lines of a three-line sentence, and that *cor* was in fact neuter. Elsewhere (18.11), Gellius disagrees with Caesellius' expressed dislike of coinages in *-escere* made by the early poet Furius in his *Annales*.

The two most interesting reports of Caesellius' views, however, juxtapose him with Sulpicius Apollinaris (2.16) in one case and with both Sulpicius and Scaurus (11.15) in the other. The first of these concerns *Aeneid* 6.760–6, in which Aeneas in the underworld sees his future son Silvius, who is described first as *tua postuma proles* and then as being born *tibi longaevo*. The obvious meanings of *postumus* and *longaevus* are incompatible: Silvius was born either when Aeneas was old or after he had died, but not both. The solution offered by Caesellius is to make *postumus* mean *postremo loco*—Aeneas' last son, rather than his posthumous son. To this, Sulpicius objected (*inter cetera, in quis Caesellium reprehendit*, 2.16.8), saying instead that *longaevus* really meant *immortalis*. Gellius' comment (2.16.10) is that Sulpicius' solution was clever (*hoc sane Apollinaris argute*), but wrong: long life is

28. On Caesellius and Scaurus, see Teuffel 3 §352; on Caesellius, see S–H 3 §593, *HLL* 4 §434 (Schmidt). His writing on orthography is also excerpted by Cassiodorus (see 12.11 below), and the *Commentarii* are cited by Priscian as *in Stromateo*. Taifakos (1983) argues unconvincingly that the *Commentarii* (cited by Gellius) is a separate work from the dictionary (or *Stromateus*); he does, however, show that the relationship between book-divisions and alphabetic divisions is very uncertain.

29. Vitale (1977: 249) wrongly thinks it should be *bat* rather than *but*. Her article (one of few modern treatments of Caesellius) is largely a paraphrase of the fragments.

one thing, perpetuity or immortality quite another. At the same time, Caesellius' solution, according to Gellius, had no precedent.[30]

What is significant about this discussion, at least in Gellius' report, is that it is treated exclusively as a question of semantics, not as a question of some importance for the (mythical) history of early Rome. The other passage, involving both Scaurus and Sulpicius, is equally fixed on the meaning of words, in this case the suffix *-bundus*. Here Caesellius, explaining the word *amorabunda* in a passage of Laberius,[31] had said that it was equivalent to *amans*, as *ludibunda* is equivalent to *ludens* (11.15.1–2). Scaurus, in his book *De Caesellii erroribus*, objected, saying that *-bundus* forms indicated not the real performance of the action of the verb but imitation of it: *Nam "ludibunda" . . . ea dicitur, quae ludentem . . . agit aut simulat* (11.15.3: "A woman is called *ludibunda* if she acts or pretends to be playing").[32] This, to Gellius, is nonsense: *Non est enim dubium, quin haec genere ipso dumtaxat idem significent, quod ea demonstrant, a quibus producuntur* (11.15.4: "There is no doubt that these words by their very nature sometimes mean the same thing, because they represent the words from which they are derived"); it leaves the real question of what the suffix means unanswered. As an alternative (which he does not in fact reject), he cites Sulpicius, who believed that *-bundus* indicated *vim et copiam et quasi abundantiam rei, cuius id verbum esset* (11.15.8: "the meaning and richness and something like an abundance of the thing represented by the word")—and that it was derived from *abunde*.

Discussions of this kind, with learned consideration of sources, scholarship, and at times manuscript variants, are typical of Gellius' stories about language. What is worth noting here is not the method, but the simple fact that not one, but two major grammarians (and we will have more to say about Scaurus shortly) took the time to attack the same work, Caesellius' *Lectiones antiquae*. It is not easy to tell why Caesellius' book aroused such indignation (and it may be no more than *odium philologicum* and one-upmanship); Gellius, at least, finds some of Caesellius' discussions perfectly plausible, even though he disagrees with others. Perhaps it was sloppiness on Caesellius' part, as in his discussion of the gender of *cor* in Ennius; perhaps it was that his solutions admitted a certain fuzziness in language (*postumus* has two meanings, while conversely *ludens* and *ludibundus* mean the same thing) which was not acceptable in an age when using words in their precise meaning was a matter of not just stylistic, but almost moral significance. What is apparent is that Caesellius was not alone: his contemporary Velius Longus wrote (in addition to his still extant treatise on orthography and a no longer extant commentary on the *Aeneid*) a work *De usu antiquae lectionis*;

30. What Gellius does not make clear is that the alternative (Silvius as posthumous) is attested as early as Cato, according to D. Hal. 1.70; see Norden on *Aen.* 6.763–5. There is in fact no other use of *postumus* = *postremus*; cf. *TLL* 10.2.220.75 s.v. *posterus*. On this passage see also Mantelli (2008).

31. Laberius fr. 35 Panayotakis; for discussion see his commentary.

32. Tempesti (1977: 179–84) denies (for no clear reason) that there was such a book.

we have already referred to Statilius Maximus' work on *singularia* in Cicero and Cato; and Festus' great and partially surviving abridgment of Verrius Flaccus, *De verborum significatione*, also belongs in this period.[33]

In fact, works written in this period under the broad rubric of "grammar" tend to fall into two particular categories: on the one hand, treatises designed to help the reader get words right—the right meaning, the right spelling, the right gender—and on the other hand, commentaries. Although there were certainly commentaries written in the first century, the impression that they give is that they were selective and specialized (as in the case of Asconius), and we do not know of very many. Few of the commentaries of which we know from the second or early third century survive, but they were clearly numerous: Scaurus wrote on Horace and Virgil; Velius Longus on Virgil; Sulpicius Apollinaris (if his work was in fact a commentary) on Terence and Virgil; Arruntius Celsus on Terence and Virgil; Aemilius Asper on Terence, Virgil, and Sallust; Helenius Acro on Terence and Horace; Porphyrio on Horace. And to judge from the remains, they were all exegetical, concentrating on language, sources, and style.[34]

Nothing substantial survives of any of these commentaries in any form that could confidently be said to reflect the original: the version that exists of the commentary of Porphyrio on Horace is in fact the product of a fifth-century revision, and the relationship of the extant Ps.-Acro on Horace to the original work of Helenius Acro is even more distant.[35] The vast bulk of what we know about the second- and early third-century commentators comes from citations in Servius and the Verona scholia on Virgil, from Donatus on Terence, and from the later versions of the commentaries on Horace. But it may be some indication of their interests that the commentaries of Arruntius Celsus and Helenius Acro and Scaurus are cited by Romanus too. The collector of words found them worth studying, at least in part: he quotes from commentaries of Celsus on only the *Phormio* of Terence and *Aeneid* Book 11, and of Acro on Terence's *Eunuchus* and *Adelphoe*; he cites only Book 10 of Scaurus' commentary on Horace, on the *Ars Poetica*, and of Asper only his commentary on Sallust's *Histories*. Two things are worth emphasizing from this list: one is that we know far more about commentaries on texts where later commentaries are extant, which should encourage caution about assuming that there was actually so clear a preference for canonical authors in the second century; the other is the overlapping of the concerns of different types of grammatical writing. A *grammaticus* like Caesellius includes in his alphabetical lexicon of ancient oddities discussions, apparently in some cases quite detailed, of the interpretation of literary texts of a kind one might expect in a commentary; and Romanus not only collects grammatical oddities in a similar way, but actually

33. On Verrius and Festus, see 4.1 above and 6.1 below. On Velius, see 8.4a and 12.44 below.

34. For bibliography on Aemilius Asper and on the various texts attached to the name Asper, see 12.5 below. For commentaries in general, see Chapter 7.

35. On Porphyrio and Ps.-Acro, see 7.3c and 11.4 below.

relies on commentaries to find or explain some of what interests him. But the focus, on both sides, is on the interpretation of words, and that is something that still endures in the extant traditions.

One second-century figure remains to be considered, the complex and enigmatic grammarian Terentius Scaurus, respected by Gellius, quoted by Romanus, and a constant presence in the later grammatical tradition. His one fully extant work, *De orthographia*, is unique in the tradition of orthographic writing in applying Varronian categories (addition, subtraction, permutation, alteration) to describe the varieties of error in spelling; the peculiarity of this is evident if one contrasts his book with the contemporary treatise of Velius Longus, who is far more interested in the problem that remains central to the tradition of orthographic writing, viz. the difficulties of representing certain sounds in writing.[36] But Scaurus was much more famous for his *Ars grammatica*—the only influential work of its kind of which we know written during the two centuries between Palaemon in the first century and Sacerdos at the end of the third—of which several not altogether consistent representations survive.[37]

Scaurus' work was clearly important. He was frequently cited by later grammarians, apparently in preference to Palaemon in many cases, and his *Ars* was almost certainly one of the major models for the later surviving grammars. At least, it clearly included the elements that became standard in the fourth century: preliminary discussion of topics such as *vox, littera*, and *syllaba* led to the word and the parts of speech. The discussion of the latter, beginning with the noun and generally ending with the interjection, remained the core of the *ars*; what followed the parts of speech was less fixed and could include either the quasi-rhetorical *vitia et virtutes orationis* (particularly barbarism and solecism), as in Donatus, or meter, as may be the case with Scaurus himself. Reconstruction is difficult, but it is almost certain that Scaurus included a discussion of *idiomata*, differences between constructions in Latin and Greek, and that unlike Varro's (almost entirely lost) discussion of syntax, Scaurus, as was suitable for someone of his generation, found the locus of difference (and of error, in terms of solecism) not in the organization of groups of words, but in the individual word. That is something that remains central to the grammatical tradition, with very few exceptions, until Priscian in the sixth century.[38]

36. On these orthographic works, see 8.4a below.

37. On the problems of Scaurus' *Ars*, see 8.5 and 12.39 below. The only other *ars grammatica* from the second century of which we have any knowledge at all is that of Censorinus, but it is referred to only twice, both vague mentions in the sixth century (cf. Schmidt in *HLL* 4 §441). It should be noted that Tempesti (1977), otherwise a useful collection of evidence about Scaurus, asserts more or less a priori that the *ars grammatica* attested in late antiquity was written by someone else of the same name. There are indeed problems; but that is not a good solution.

38. On the importance of Scaurus in the development (or rather disappearance) of syntax in Latin grammatical writing, see above all Baratin (1989), particularly pp. 99–101

5. CODA

By the early third century at the latest, the major forms of philological writing had almost certainly taken the shapes in which they are familiar to us from the mass of extant texts from the fourth and fifth centuries. The *ars grammatica*, the commentary, and the lexicon had all established the basic rules and forms of their genres and the basic issues that concerned the grammarian and his students. They cared about morphology, semantics, the use of literary models by the authors studied (and by the students studying them), and in fact about what authors were suitable for study. These emphases took shape, and changed, in the long period between Varro and the third century; however, they were crucially informed by the stylistic concerns of the end of the period: correct morphology, the choice of the right word, and knowledge of early literature (although the content of each of these elements was clearly variable).

There are other reasons for ending my historical survey here, with the period so firmly criticized by Gibbon in the passage from which my epigraph and title are taken. One is that Gibbon is to a certain extent right about the fossilization that took place: although there are clearly differences in interpretation and explanation among the grammarians, there were few innovations in scholarly form after the second century, at least until Priscian in the sixth. Another is that the nature of our evidence changes: as should have become clear, there are very few extensive philological texts from before the fourth century, and I have accordingly tried to extract a narrative from fragments. After the beginning of the fourth century, narrative becomes nearly impossible: there are too many texts, and their relative chronology is too uncertain. And, finally, what becomes important when we approach the vast bulk of extant grammatical writing is less the history than the form of scholarship. Grammar, commentary, and dictionary become recognizable genres, worth examining in their own right, not least because they have remained dominant forms of scholarly writing in the classical tradition ever since. The history we will encounter too is on a different scale: the gradual change from teaching Romans about their own language to teaching non-Latin speakers how to read Latin. The geography as well as the ethnography of Latin philology contribute a great deal to understanding what these texts are and why we have them at all; but before looking at that (in Chapter 9), it is important to examine in some detail the genres of philology in late antiquity.

(classification of conjunctions) and 343–64 (*idiomata* and *Latinitas*). Baratin's work is necessarily speculative, but is largely convincing.

6

Dictionaries, Glossaries, Encyclopedias

In turning from a narrative account of Roman philology to a consideration of the forms in which it is preserved, lists of words are a good place to begin. As discussed in the previous chapter, the word itself was central to the study of language in the second and early third centuries CE. The choice of correct and apposite vocabulary and forms was essential to good writing; as a result commentaries and studies of particular authors seem to have focused on diction, and even grammatical works (such as those of Caper and Romanus) arranged their material in alphabetical lists. The boundaries between what we would call "dictionary" and what we would call "grammar" were permeable and often very indistinct, and that kind of formal uncertainty remained a feature of philological writing for centuries. Grammars include lists of various types of words (synonyms, idiomatic constructions); glossaries include lists of grammatical forms that look suspiciously like paradigms. Glossaries also overlap with commentaries: a list of words, even partly alphabetized, that follows the order of a literary text owes its origin to commentary, or at least to marginal or interlinear annotation; and by the same token such a list is most useful to someone reading the text from which the glossary was drawn.

Even so, however, the forms of scholarly writing remained fundamentally different from one another, particularly in terms of structure and goals. Commentaries are geared to the reading of specific texts, and follow their order. Grammars offer an orderly presentation of the structure and morphology of language, most frequently (in the Roman tradition) concentrating on the parts of speech, their inflection, and questions of usage. Dictionaries provide explanations of specific words, whether drawn from one text or many, from colloquial language or literary, in the order of the alphabet or in an order determined by subject or by audience. In some respects (as the preceding definition demonstrates) the dictionary is the most amorphous and elusive of the three fundamental forms of philological scholarship: the genre ranges from simple lists of words drawn from a particular text—much as we or our students may make lists of words that we needed to look up—to large and ambitious works like Verrius Flaccus' *De verborum significatu* or the *Etymologiae* of Isidore of Seville in the seventh century or the *Liber glossarum* produced, probably for Charlemagne, late in the eighth.

Most glossographic texts are simply lists, untitled and anonymous. They exist in astonishing profusion and in a variety of shapes and sizes. The present chapter begins with two lexica with firm identities and ends with the complex figure of Isidore of Seville. In the middle comes the difficult and often obscure realm of the glossaries: elements of extant glossaries are clearly ancient, but their history and chronology are very uncertain. Some ninth-century manuscripts contain glossaries compiled in England in the seventh century (and including Old English glosses); some of them, in turn, are based on sources as early as the first century CE. Thus, despite their obscurity (and however difficult they are to find and read), medieval glossaries are a necessary element in any account of Roman scholarship.

1. VERRIUS–FESTUS–PAULUS

Under the reign of Augustus, M. Verrius Flaccus compiled a vast dictionary (at least four books for A, at least five for P) entitled *De verborum significatu*. It was by no means the first Roman dictionary; as we have seen (Chapter 2), a great deal of the earliest Roman scholarship was dedicated to explanations of the obscure and difficult language of early legal and religious texts and consisted of *glossae*. Much philological writing of the first century BCE seems to consist of such lists as well, again particularly explaining the archaic language of law and religion: thus we find L. Cincius, *De verbis priscis* (*GRF* 372–4), Santra, *De antiquitate verborum* (*GRF* 384–6), and Aelius Gallus, *De significatione verborum quae ad ius civile pertinent* (*GRF* 545–53), works that are in large part known because they were exploited and cited by Varro or Verrius.

Verrius' encyclopedia was too big to survive; indeed, there are only two verbatim fragments, both preserved by Aulus Gellius (5.17, 5.18 = F 3, 4 *GRF*). It was also left unfinished: within the entries under each letter of the alphabet, there was an alphabetized section (generally to two letters) and a section arranged by source. In other words, Verrius alphabetized his dictionary, but then continued to accumulate materials from further reading that were never included in the alphabetical ordering.[1] We know of the format of the dictionary from the abridgment (in only twenty books) of Verrius' work made by Pompeius Festus in the late second century CE; that work was itself heavily abridged in the eighth century by Paul the Deacon and dedicated to Charlemagne. Of these three closely related works, only Paul's survives complete; of Festus' twenty-book version our knowledge depends on one incomplete and seriously damaged manuscript.

Even reading Festus, to say nothing of interpreting what he says, is not easy. When it was discovered in the Renaissance, the Codex Farnesianus (F) of Festus had already lost everything up to the letter M and what was left had been damaged

1. The organization was first identified by Müller (1880, originally published 1839). There is a brief and lucid summary of the issues in North (2007: 60–3); see also Pieroni (2004: 22–6). For further bibliography on Festus, see 10.1 below.

by fire; as a result, much of the outer column of many pages is missing. Further loss and damage ensued after F was discovered, and so even F must in parts be reconstructed from renaissance copies made before the latest stages of loss. We have portions of Festus beginning with M and ending with V; but even within that range, much is fragmentary.

Beyond the problems of physical loss and damage, moreover, abridgment itself by definition entails leaving a great deal out. We can see how severely Paulus abridged the dictionary by comparing his text with the corresponding portions of Festus that survive: Paulus has omitted almost all the quotations, most of the detailed discussions of words or names, and a great many lemmata completely. Thus, to take a sample, in the relatively well-preserved portion of Festus including the lemmata from *Suopte* (408.4L) to *Strebula* (410.34L), Paulus preserves only two of ten entries entire (*Suopte* and *Strues*) and rewrites but preserves one (*Strutheum*); he completely eliminated *Suillum genus* and *Sus Minervam*; in the other five entries, he omits quotations from Plautus and Livius Andronicus (*Struices*), from Cato and the Twelve Tables (*Struere*), and a long debate, including a citation from Ateius Philologus, about the significance of *Stroppus*, including local lore from Falerii and Tusculum. In *Strenam* he leaves out a few details and changes tenses referring to religious custom from present to past, and in the damaged entry *Strebula* he eliminates at least two quotations from Plautus. Apart from the severe abridgment of Paulus, some other remains of Festus exist, preserved in medieval glossaries, but they are very hard to identify or use: Lindsay made excessively optimistic reconstructions based on this material in his second edition of Festus in *Glossaria Latina* (1930); but much of his work is misguided and there has yet to be a careful publication of the relevant material.[2]

A second difficulty is that both Festus and Paulus seem to have inserted themselves, at least to a limited degree, into the texts they were excerpting. As noted in Chapter 4, Festus several times offers derogatory comments about Verrius and sometimes argues with his interpretations; even though interested in archaic Roman literature himself, he sneers at Verrius' inclusion of truly useless early words. Furthermore, while Verrius himself quotes no authors later than Virgil, somebody included references to Lucan, Martial, and Ovid; and in the last case (not to mention *Romans* cited at 32.16L) it is fairly clear that it was Paulus. In addition to his abridgments, moreover, Paulus skews the nature of the quotations that had been in Festus and presumably Verrius: while he keeps some poetic quotations, he is not interested in including the names of the antiquarian writers of the first century BCE whom Festus cites frequently and from whom he derived at least some of his knowledge of earlier texts.[3]

2. On Lindsay's methods, see Dionisotti (1996); Woods (2007: 128–35).

3. For Festus' critiques of Verrius, see most recently Lhommé (2007); for Paulus' changes from Festus, see Pieroni (2004: 19–21), Woods (2007), North (2008), and Lhommé (2011). Paulus is also responsible for a commentary on Donatus' *Ars minor* (see 13.21 below). Chiesa (2000) has a valuable collection of essays on Paulus.

The ten entries discussed above give some idea of Verrius' interests: religion, law, archaic literature, and local custom, including the discussion of words from many Italic dialects as well as from Gallic and Punic. A fuller sample would also display Verrius' great interest in explaining the meaning of words found in texts of the third and second centuries BCE (and the differences from usage in his own day) and the large number of entries that concern Roman history and topography or the calendar, the last not at all surprising in the author of the Fasti Praenestini.[4] Nor does this sample give anything like an adequate sense of the range of Verrius' sources: he certainly used Varro extensively, but there are also parts derived from other grammarians and antiquarians—Santra, Granius, Cincius, Aurelius Opillus, Aelius Stilo, and Aelius Gallus.[5] Whether deliberately or not, Verrius' work was an Augustan summary of, and a capstone to, the traditions of republican antiquarianism, and as such it became a major source for later writers.

2. NONIUS MARCELLUS AND FULGENTIUS

The manuscripts of Nonius Marcellus' *De compendiosa doctrina* describe the author as *Peripateticus Tubursicensis*; the existence of an inscription from Thubursicum Numidarum (*CIL* 8.4878 = *ILS* 2943; Khamissa in northeast Algeria, some 250 km west of Carthage) dated to (probably) 324 CE and commemorating the restoration of a *platea* and baths by one Nonius Marcellus Herculius confirms his place of origin and is not inconsistent with what can be inferred from the text: that he was not a professional grammarian but a person of some standing and wealth, and that he belongs somewhere in the period between Aulus Gellius and Apuleius (whom he cites) and Priscian (who cites him). Keyser would date him early in this period, Deufert relatively late.[6] Most scholars compromise on the middle, some time in the fourth century. The honorand of the inscription is presumably not the author of *De compendiosa doctrina*, but a relative. *Peripateticus* in the title has rightly been compared to *Platonicus philosophus* in the titles of the manuscript of Apuleius' *Metamorphoses*.[7]

Nonius is the only author discussed in this book who has had a periodical (*Studi Noniani*) devoted to him.[8] That is an indication not of his literary

4. Verrius' interests in topography, history, and religion clearly reflect Augustan preoccupations; cf. Glinister (2007). On the Fasti Praenestini, see Suetonius *DGR* 17.3 with Kaster (1995) ad loc.

5. On Verrius' use of Aelius Gallus in particular, see Moreau (2007). For a list of his sources, see *CGlL* 1.9–10. Strzelecki (1932) (cf. also Pieroni 2004: 26–30) showed that in general the authors quoted by Verrius were cited in a fixed order that is neither chronological nor alphabetical; the method is in some ways comparable to that of Nonius Marcellus (on whom see below).

6. See Keyser (1994); Deufert (2001).

7. Mantero (1975) is a detailed discussion of the heading in the manuscripts, dwelling at great length on *Peripateticus* and Nonius' African context.

8. For details, see 10.2 below.

merits, but of his extraordinary importance for our knowledge of many republican authors. The text is, unlike that of Festus, remarkably well preserved; unfortunately Nonius is also unlike Festus in being excruciatingly dull. His work consists almost exclusively of lists of words accompanied by brief definitions and illustrative quotations, without any of the scholarly argumentation and marshaling of evidence that appear in Festus' longer articles. It is a dictionary of twenty books (the same size as Festus and as Isidore's *Etymologiae*) articulated by topic: the first twelve books treat various lexical and grammatical categories (e.g., *De proprietate sermonum*, Book 1; *De varia significatione sermonum*, Book 4; *De mutata declinatione*, Book 8), and the last eight such topics as words for ships (Book 13), for colors (Book 17), and for food and drink (Book 18). Book 16, *De genere calciamentorum*, is lost. Unsurprisingly, the books vary greatly in size; the manuscript tradition (followed by modern editors) divides the whole work into three roughly equal sections: Books 1–3, 4, and 5–20. Books 2–4, the three longest books, are arranged alphabetically; it is not clear whether Nonius himself or an editor was responsible for the alphabetization, but since the archetype of the extant manuscripts must have been fairly early, it was done, if not by Nonius, then quite soon after the work was written.

Virgil is the author most often cited by Nonius, and he stands as a great authority for linguistic legitimacy in *De compendiosa doctrina*, particularly in Book 6, *De inpropriis*; Varro is the author next most frequently quoted. Almost all Nonius' non-Virgilian quotations are from early authors: he is our single best source for Roman drama in the Republic as well as for the *Menippean Satires* of Varro and quite a few other early works. What is perhaps most curious about *De compendiosa doctrina* is that, as Lindsay discovered, Nonius compiled the dictionary by copying words and quotations from forty-one collections of excerpts that were written in the order of the texts from which they were drawn; he consulted those collections in the same order for each book and, assuming that he is responsible for the alphabetization, for each alphabetic section of Books 2–4.[9] This astonishing predictability is not perfect—he did allow himself occasionally to group words by association—but it is close enough that Lindsay's Law, as it is known, permits editors of fragments of lost works to know the relative order in the lost text of at least some of the quotations that survive in Nonius. He had, in White's words, "a cumbersome, mechanical regularity linked with a limited intelligence"; his work is "a peculiar mixture of the mechanical with the slapdash."[10]

9. For the reconstruction of the lists, see Lindsay (1901); Cadoni (1987) raises some important questions about the application of Lindsay's Law to the alphabetical books, but his examples of problems do not all inspire confidence. A recent refinement is made by Welsh (2012), who supplies references to earlier scholarship on the lists. The qualifications made by Strzelecki (1932–3) do not seriously affect Lindsay's Law, but the relationship between Nonius' glossaries and other parts of the grammatical tradition is clearly more complicated than Lindsay chose to see.

10. White (1980); quotations from 145 and 193.

To link the diligent and mechanical Nonius to the strange and exotic Fabius Planciades Fulgentius is perhaps unfair to both of them, but they have several things in common. Above all, geography: they both wrote in North Africa, Fulgentius rather later (probably in the early sixth century), but they are both among the few writers to cite their fellow North African Apuleius, and they both have a distinct interest in the vocabulary of republican Rome. What is more, Fulgentius uses Nonius (as well as Martianus Capella), and the later glossaries make use of both of them.

But Fulgentius' dictionary, *Expositio sermonum antiquorum*, is completely unlike that of Nonius. For one thing, it is short: only sixty-two entries, a few of them covering more than one word. And if, like Nonius, Fulgentius cites recondite sources, there is this large difference: while Nonius' sources are completely genuine, Fulgentius' are not. Fulgentius does cite some genuine texts: Virgil, Lucan, and Apuleius each receive accurate quotations, and Plautus is quoted no fewer than eighteen times—except that more than half the attributions are to the wrong play or to lost plays, and even the correct citations are often inaccurate. Famously, he quotes Petronius in this and in his other works—but not a single quotation comes from an extant part of the *Satyricon*, and one (in Fulgentius' *Mythologiae*) actually comes from Statius. Beyond that there are a great many quotations from lost texts (Pacuvius, Naevius, and Fenestella, for instance), some of which give one pause: Cornelius Tacitus' *Liber facetiarum* is itself clearly a joke on the gloomy historian, and the comic poet Flaccus Tibullus looks like a cross between Horace and Tibullus. And that does not include ten highly suspicious Greek sources: one would very much like to be able to read Demosthenes' *Pro Philippo*. Even some of Fulgentius' words are apparently made up.[11]

Fulgentius, thankfully, stands outside the mainstream of Latin lexicography, just as his other works seem eccentric (to use no stronger word) in comparison to less imaginative works on mythology, world history, or Virgil.[12] His language is gaudy as well as abstract; he plays linguistic games not only in his dictionary but in the lipogrammatism of his world history; he has an immense appetite for allegorical interpretation. Fulgentius is no grammarian (indeed he expresses disdain for them at *Virg*. 86.4–6H), but he knows how to use grammarians' tools; he is, in his inventiveness, more like the bogus mythological handbooks of the Hellenistic world or the *Historia Augusta*.[13] And a fictional dictionary is much more enjoyable to read than Nonius ever was.

11. On Fulgentius' citations, see esp. Wessner (1899: 135–9) and Ciaffi (1963: 43–97). More credulous is Baldwin (1988)—although not nearly so credulous as Pennisi (1963), who believes every word of Fulgentius. For further bibliography, see 12.23 below.

12. Fulgentius is in some ways comparable to, but by no means as entertaining or learned as, Virgilius Maro Grammaticus two centuries later in Ireland (see 9.4 and 13.30 below).

13. On Fulgentius as quasi-grammarian, see Hays (2002a). On the bogus lore of Ptolemy Chennus and others, see Cameron (2004).

3. GLOSSARIES

The word *glossa* has more than one meaning. In its original Greek grammatical usage, it refers to dialectal variations of form or meaning; this use is taken over into Latin, in which *glossa* can mean an odd or unusual word, one that needs explanation. From that, it is a short step to defining the *glossa* as the explanation itself as well as (or rather than) the word being explained, and hence *glossarium* rapidly comes to be used for any list of words with definitions or explanations, not merely the list of words that need such definition or explanation.[14]

The collection of *glossae* can be traced in Rome back to the second century BCE, if not before.[15] Quintilian (1.1.35, 1.8.15) includes the learning of lists of *glossae* among elementary exercises for beginning students of grammar. Papyri of glossaries exist, and a great many manuscripts of all periods contain such word lists. Some glossaries are personal and appear in only a single manuscript or papyrus; others seem to have been widely used, and often extended or combined with other useful lists; some seem to preserve their identity, more or less, through many copies and generations of copying.

A list of words can have many forms and origins; it can be derived from one source or many, arranged by subject or in alphabetical order. Even alphabetical lists can take different forms: modern practice aims at complete alphabetization, from the first letter of a word to the last, but ancient and medieval equivalents almost never do that; many are alphabetized by first letter only (generally referred to by the designation A–), or by two letters (AB–), or by three or four (ABC–; ABCD–).[16] It is generally assumed that glossaries develop from the simple to the complex both in contents and in alphabetization: word lists begin by following the order of a single text rather than the alphabet, and then become progressively broader in contents (covering more than one source-text) and more articulated in structure, arranged thematically, as in Nonius Marcellus or Isidore's *Etymologiae*, or alphabetically. It is also clear that alphabetization generally starts from A– and becomes more refined: no sane person would take a fully alphabetized list and reduce it again to alphabetization by one or two letters.

Word lists following text order are often referred to as *glossae collectae*, and although most important glossaries are more complex than that, some still survive, and indeed Nonius' *De compendiosa doctrina* is in large part still a collection of such lists divided by subject and, for a few books, by alphabet. There are

14. It should be noted that medievalists often refer to a set of marginal notes in manuscripts as a gloss. That usage is confusing and will not be employed in this book: *a gloss*, for my purposes, is a definition or explanation of a single word, and *to gloss* is to provide such an explanation. What medievalists call a gloss is what I refer to as scholia.

15. See 2.4 above; also Goetz, *CGlL* 1: 1–12 and Holtz (1996).

16. On the development of alphabetization, see Daly (1967); on the varieties of alphabetization in Latin glossaries, see Dionisotti (1996). My discussion of glossaries is throughout heavily indebted to Dionisotti's work; her individual articles are cited for specific debts as appropriate below. For details of specific glossaries, see 10.4 below.

many sets of Virgilian glosses still extant: the one in the glossary known as *Arma* has been broken up alphabetically, but within each letter of the alphabet it still follows the order of the text beginning, as does Servius, with the *Aeneid*, followed by *Eclogues* and *Georgics*. But the combination of sets of *glossae collectae* drawn from authors is not the only way that glossaries are put together: not only are they drawn from non-literary texts, but they are very frequently merged with other glossaries which may come from much more complex sources than a simple word list. As mentioned previously, glossaries besides that of Paulus included material ultimately drawn from Festus, and it is also clear that quite different types of glossary might be put together in the same manuscript and then, perhaps, combined into a single large dictionary the sources of which are no longer identifiable.

In a narrow sense, it is common to use "Latin glossaries" to refer to the glossaries printed in Georg Goetz's *Corpus Glossariorum Latinorum* (*CGlL*) and Wallace Lindsay's *Glossaria Latina* (*GlL*), but there are many more Latin glossaries than that, even aside from the fact that both collections omit entirely some major classes of glossary described below. Late antique and medieval manuscripts contain hundreds of word lists of one sort or another, many of them unpublished (and many of them unknown, at least to me); Goetz lists some 566 manuscripts used in *CGlL*, some containing more than one glossary, and at least fifty more glossaries that he chose not to include, while many of the texts he did publish are only excerpts or specimens of much longer glossaries.[17] Not all glossaries need detailed discussion; my intention here is to describe the main varieties of glossary and the glossographic texts most likely to contain ancient (or late antique) material.

The various glossaries that exist or have been reconstructed overlap with one another in ways that suggest that they all had a tendency to draw on more than one source. That is not surprising: in a manuscript culture, each owner or scribe made collections of glosses and definitions that suited himself or herself; some aspire to serious alphabetization, others do not. In general, it can be said that glossaries work outward from word lists based on a single text, sometimes following the order of the text, or from lists of words concerning a single subject; such lists only become useful to a wider audience (outside the classroom where they were composed) when they are alphabetized and combined with other lists; and the ultimate result of these combinations is a set of medieval dictionaries beyond the scope of this volume, beginning with Papias' *Elementarium* in the eleventh century and continuing with the comparable and later works of Osbern, Hugutio, and others.[18]

17. *CGlL* 1: 287–308. The count is my own and may not be absolutely accurate. Note that "specimen" in this context means a coherent and continuous portion of a text (e.g., all the entries under the letter G), while "excerpt" means a discontinuous selection picked by the editor and therefore not necessarily representative of the whole set of glosses. For the contents of the glossary collections, see 10.4.1 below.

18. A useful introduction to the later dictionaries (and to the techniques of medieval lexicography) is in Weijers (1989).

Why do these collections matter, and why does their (pre)history matter? In some cases, of course, it makes no difference at all to us how a dictionary was put together; but in other cases, it matters a great deal. Individual words on their own may be helpful to students of the history of language or of the artefacts and customs that particular words imply or describe; but if one wants to know just when those artefacts were used or what books were being read at various places and times, how they were being studied, and how they circulated, the simpler and more transparent glossaries are of immense value. Some of the glossaries have a great deal of Greek in them, and indeed there are large Greek–Latin and Latin–Greek dictionaries; others have words of Old High German, Anglo-Saxon, or Old Irish. One important and still unpublished glossary (*Expositio notarum*, discussed below) shows links between the stenography of the early Roman empire and the vocabulary lists studied in seventh-century England, and in fact there are many lists that consist of symbols with their explanations rather than lists of words with definitions or synonyms: the *Notae Tironianae, Notae iuris*, and critical signs are glossaries just as much as the dictionaries, and they take us into areas of Roman scholarship and education that are often ignored except by specialists.

Lists of words are omnipresent, and not just in the grammarian's classroom. That (and its successor, the monastic school and library) is the home of the central body of glossaries that make up the bulk of the two collections of Goetz and Lindsay, but in fact the range of glossaries in the broad sense is much wider than that. At the high end, if one can call it that, are the lists known as *Synonyma* and *Differentiae*, the first grouping words of similar or overlapping meaning, the second offering pairs of words that should be distinguished from one another. Many such texts are found independently, but they also turn up embedded in larger grammatical works: the so-called *Differentiae Frontonis* are included in the manuscript of Charisius. They clearly stem from the schoolroom: they were used most evidently in the school of rhetoric to improve and refine the vocabulary of budding declaimers, but some comments in grammatical texts suggest that students at the lower level too were expected to know lists of synonyms to which the grammarians merely allude.[19] Next to them are glossaries proper: lists of words with definitions, sometimes amplified with quotations or other comments, designed to help students read the literary texts on the syllabus and, as with *synonyma* and *differentiae*, to increase their vocabulary. The third category of glossaries is a wide one, a diverse group of texts intended to aid in language acquisition and translation, whether Greek to Latin or Latin to Greek. This includes not only bilingual dictionaries, but also the *hermeneumata*, which may include not only word lists, but also simple readings and conversation exercises. It also includes what are called *idiomata: idiomata generis* are lists of words that are equivalent in meaning in Greek and Latin but are of different genders, and

19. Thus Sacerdos *GL* 6.455.8, Probus, *Instituta Artium GL* 4.120.6, and Dositheus *GL* 7.398.6 all seem to cite a list of synonyms beginning with *terra–tellus*, also alluded to by Augustine, *CD* 4.10. On this, see Brugnoli (1955a: 9–11).

idiomata casuum list constructions of nouns that take different cases in Greek and Latin. These lists are sometimes independent glossaries, sometimes part of grammars. The fourth and final division of glossaries, for our purposes, consists of lists of signs and symbols: the various kinds of *notae* of most importance to jurists, editors, and shorthand writers. To one side, the grammarian encounters the rhetor, to the other the *notarius*. But on all sides, there are lists.

a) *Synonyma* and *Differentiae*

Synonyma and *differentiae* are closely related: indeed, the same groups of words might appear in both, with the important difference that in a collection of *synonyma* the similarities of meaning would be emphasized—that one word could be substituted for another, as a primitive form of Roget's Thesaurus—while in a collection of *differentiae* the finer distinctions of meaning among near-synonyms would be pointed out. Both types are clearly designed for *writing* Latin more than for reading texts: the collection of such lists is one of the tasks of the aspiring stylist, as Fronto reminds Marcus (*De eloquentia* 2.19).[20] Cicero in the *Topica* discusses the importance of the type of definition he calls *de eodem et altero* (87) as a philosophical element of rhetoric, and Quintilian instructs his readers that while philosophers claim to be the ones to make fine distinctions among the meanings of words, it is in fact the province of the orator above all to use language correctly (1 *Pr.* 16–17).[21]

The preface to the pseudo-Isidoran collection of *differentiae* known as *Inter aptum et utile* traces *differentiae* back to the elder Cato, in the fragments of whose speeches fine distinctions of this kind are indeed found.[22] Indeed the *differentia*, because it makes fine distinctions, becomes in late antiquity itself classified as a kind of definition, and hence the property of the grammarian as well as the philosopher. Collections of *differentiae* and synonyms circulated widely in the Middle Ages, and the origin of the extant collections—clearly altered and added to over the years—probably goes back to the second century if not before: Romanus in his discussion of the adverb *mutuo* refers (Charis. 266.20B) to *illi qui de differentiis scribunt*. Flavius Caper may be the ultimate source for much of what we have; the extant treatises ascribed to Caper and to Agroecius with the title *De orthographia* are in fact collections of *differentiae* (see 8.4a below).

20. See 5.1 above.

21. See Brugnoli (1955a: 7–9). On the history of *differentiae*, see Beck (1883: 4–24) and Magallón García (1996). On the origins of the extant collections, see Codoñer (1985).

22. Sets of *differentiae* (like synonyms and glossaries) are generally referred to by their first entry, sometimes abbreviated; thus this one is often named simply *Inter aptum*. On its authenticity, see 10.3.2 below: it is an alphabetized version of a set of *differentiae* that is probably by Isidore himself. The identity of the Cato in question has been doubted; Brugnoli (1955a: 13–16) identified him as Valerius Cato, but see already Beck (1883: 4–5), who quotes the relevant fragments of the Censor's speeches.

Parts of some of the lists of *differentiae* are clearly ancient and belong to the territory of the *grammaticus*: they are sometimes found in various versions of *ars grammatica*, and they are used in commentaries on classical authors. But while such lists begin as aids to making fine distinctions of meaning, they increasingly, as in the texts ascribed to Caper and Agroecius, include distinctions of spelling and pronunciation, aiming at an audience whose knowledge of Latin is far more rudimentary. Such distinctions are to be found, rarely, in the *differentiae* used by Servius in his commentary on Virgil; by the later fifth century, as teachers' expectations of students' knowledge of Latin diminished, elementary distinctions increase notably.[23] Every medieval collection, whatever its origin, includes a great deal of relatively late orthographic and phonetic material. Even so, they often carry false ascriptions to famous writers of antiquity: the sets of *differentiae* known as *Inter aptum* and *Inter polliceri* are regularly ascribed to Isidore; a variation on the latter known as *Inter abundare* is ascribed to Cicero. The collection *Inter gnatum* is said to come from Remmius Palaemon as filtered through Suetonius, while *Inter austrum* is in one manuscript (Montpellier 306, foll. 60r–69r) ascribed to Valerius Probus and in another it appears anonymously as Part 4 of the collection known as the *Appendix Probi*.[24]

The collection of synonyms is just as ancient a habit. Well before Fronto advised Marcus to use his spare time to collect *synonyma* and *singularia*, Quintilian (9.3.45–6) discussed their use in rhetorical prose under the rubric of *geminatio* (criticized by Caecilius, he reports, as *pleonasmos*). Although somewhat less attention has been paid to collections of *synonyma* than to *differentiae*, they seem equally widespread, and at least some of the elements in these collections are probably late antique, if not older. Many of the lists are titled *Synonyma Ciceronis*: synonyms are important in rhetoric, and Cicero was after all the greatest of all orators. Indeed, both Servius and Isidore quote lines from the speeches against Catiline as examples of synonymy.[25] *Synonyma Ciceronis* are sometimes prefaced by a pseudepigraphic letter of Cicero to one Veterius;[26] one of the more common collections begins with *Orator actor defensor patronus causidicus disertus eloquens facundus ingeniosus*, and the lemmata following *Orator* are *Promptus, Splendidus,*

23. On *differentiae* in Servius, see Stok (2008, 2012b); on the increasing prevalence of orthographic and phonetic *differentiae* in commentaries, see also Jakobi (1996: 102–3); Diederich (1999: 120); Uhl (1998: 525–36).

24. For more details on these collections, see 10.4.2 below. I draw here particularly on Brugnoli (1955a), augmented by Uhlfelder (1954: 1–33) and Codoñer (1985). For the *Appendix Probi*, see 12.36.4 below; Montpellier 306 is an important anthology of texts, including a version of the Hermeneumata; see 9.4 below.

25. Thus *abiit, excessit, evasit, erumpit* from *Cat.* 2.1 described as *exaggeratio ex synonymis* by Servius on *Aen.* 2.128 and *nihil agis, nihil moliris, nihil cogitas* from *Cat.* 1.8 as an example of *synonymia* by Isidore 2.21.6. See Goetz (1923: 80), Gatti (1993: 12).

26. The letter is printed by Goetz (1923: 78–9) and Brugnoli (1955a: 28) and (1961: 285).

Magnificus, Acer, Valens, Consideratus, Callidus, Capitalis, Subtilis, Politus, Facetus, and *Lepos*.[27] Goetz distinguishes two forms of this collection, one with the pseudepigraphic letter and one without; a second collection has roughly the same elements, but is alphabetized and alters the conclusion of the letter and the name of the addressee (from Veterius to Veturius).

There are several others, including one beginning *Amor ardor* that was (wrongly) included in his edition of Charisius by Barwick (412.19–49.31B), one beginning *Arba humus*, and one beginning *Accusat lacescit*.[28] In a sense, the *synonyma* lie formally between *differentiae*, which contain only a few near-synonyms (or words phonetically similar) under each lemma, and glosses proper, which may contain one or two synonyms as a definition but also include other types of identifying words or names. The *synonyma* tend to be (as the example given above suggests) relatively long lists, and their origin, as was suggested above, is rhetorical. How many ways can you say "orator" without repeating yourself?

b) Latin Glossaries

Glossaries in the narrow sense of the term are sets of Latin explanations (usually a word or a brief phrase or definition) of Latin words; major examples are collected in *CGlL* 4–5 and in *GlL*, but there are many more. Glossaries are generally identified by their first lemma (*Abba, Arma, Abstrusa, Ab oris*; some of the manuscripts themselves give such names, as in Leiden, BPL 67F of *Abavus*), by the location of the (major) manuscript (the Corpus and Épinal Glossaries), or by a title or author given in (some of) the manuscripts (Placidus and the *Liber Glossarum*, also known as *Glossarium Ansileubi*). A great many glossaries remain unpublished and largely unknown, including some that provide important evidence for the history of the form.[29]

Glossaries were not created out of whole cloth every time one was written: they are, in the form in which we generally can see them, compilations from other glossaries, sometimes perhaps mixed with the results of the individual scribe's or scholar's reading, but sometimes entirely tralatitious. They overlap a great deal, something visible in different ways: in some cases, a whole set of entries will appear more or less identically in two glossaries, indicating a common source in a third glossary; in others, multiple glosses essentially for the same word point to multiple sources; in yet others, it is perfectly possible that the same words in, say, Virgil or the Psalms caused the same difficulties in understanding for different people.

27. I take this list from BL, Harley 5792 (late eighth century), fol. 260r; it is in at least eight other manuscripts. To the best of my knowledge, this set of *synonyma* has not been published.

28. For bibliographical details, see 10.4.3 below.

29. Thus the glossaries known as *Amoenum* and *Aptet* discussed by Dionisotti (1996: 225–7); see 10.4.4c(iii) below.

As a small example of how some of these texts work, I take the glosses on the adjective *celsus* "lofty" that appear in some of the larger glossaries. In *Abstrusa* (*CGlL* 4.31.50–2) we find the sequence:

> Celsus excelsus
> Celsa sublimia vel alta
> Celsus altus excelsus.

In *Abba* (*CGlL* 4.217.18–19), there is *Celsa excelsa sublimis / Celsus altus*; in *Affatim* (*CGlL* 4.494.26–7) there is *Celsus excelsus / Celsus sublimis altus* and in the *Glossae Vergilianae* (*CGlL* 4.433.36–7) *Celsa alta excelsa / Celsis in puppibus altis in navibus*—except that in *Abstrusa* the main manuscript actually reads *Caelius excelsus / Celsa sublima vel alta / Celsus altus excelsus*,[30] in *Affatim* the manuscript reads *Caelius excesus / Census sublimis altus*, and in the *Glossae Vergilianae* it reads *suppibus* for *puppibus*.

Several aspects of this set of glosses are worth mentioning. First is the sheer repetitiveness: does the same glossary need to have both *Celsus excelsus* and *Celsus altus excelsus*? In some glossaries, some of the redundancies occur because they include what amount to paradigms with different forms of the same word; but when the same form receives the same gloss twice, the reason is likely to be the combination of different glossaries. That is the second point: both *Abstrusa* and *Affatim* read *caelius* for *celsus*; and in fact *Abstrusa* appears from other evidence to be one of the major sources of *Affatim*. A third point is that some glossaries cite (whether accurately or not) the forms of words found in the texts from which they draw their entries, while others regularize them to nominative singular for nouns and first-person singular for verbs. Thus *Celsa sublimia alta* in *Abstrusa* is neuter plural, while *celsus sublimis altus* in *Affatim* has been regularized to masculine nominative singular.

The presence in the *Glossae Vergilianae* of an entry not for a word, but a phrase (*celsis in puppibus*) drawn from Virgil (*Aen.* 1.183) calls for further comment. In the first place, this glossary, like some others closely based on texts, often takes phrases as lemmata, for example, *Caecae fores occulta ianua et abscondite* (*CGlL* 4.432.26), where *caecae fores* comes from *Aen.* 2.453.[31] More important is the very existence of glossaries based on a single text: there are at least eight manuscripts of this glossary, several other Virgilian glossaries have been printed, and Goetz includes among the miscellaneous glossaries at the end of *CGlL* 5 a Nonius glossary and one on Juvenal.[32] The existence of such author-based glossaries is a key

30. Vatican, Lat. 3321, fol. 21v. I give the corrected text provided by Goetz in the *Thesaurus Glossarum Emendatarum* (*CGlL* 6.197).

31. Neither of these definitions has a parallel in Servius; it is unlikely that they were drawn from a commentary. Another glossary which uses longer phrases as lemmata is the *Expositio Notarum*, on which see 10.4.4f below.

32. *Glossae Vergilianae*, *CGlL* 4.427–70; other sets printed in Hagen (1902: 454–529). Murgia (1975: 26–35) discusses another set of glosses in Paris, Lat. 11308. Nonius glossary from Leiden BPL 67F, *CGlL* 5.637–51 (see also Gatti 2005); Juvenal glossary

to one of the origins of the larger glossaries from which my examples have been cited: word lists based on individual texts were combined into more complex glossaries. In the case of something like *Abavus*, which is highly alphabetized, it is impossible to untangle the sources; but in some cases, the primitive compilation has not yet turned into an alphabetized dictionary, or the alphabetization has not yet progressed beyond the first letter or two. Thus an important glossary which Goetz omitted but Lindsay included, *Arma* (*GlL* 2.1–22; only up to the letter E), has been alphabetized to only one letter (A–), and within each letter the glosses are still drawn from one author at a time, and in the order of the text: one of the sources is Virgil, one Terence, one Prudentius, and a fourth is another glossary, which is attested elsewhere (though unpublished) and which Dionisotti has named (from its first word) *Amoenum*.[33]

Glossaries drawn from single authors are clearly of great importance in the development of larger dictionaries, and Lindsay believed (and frequently stated) that all glossaries took their start in medieval monasteries from *glossae collectae*, lists of words taken from the marginal and interlinear annotations of individual manuscripts of individual texts, in the order of the text. These *glossae collectae* had, as their origin, the ruminations of monastic readers and teachers and had no ancient authority—just medieval readers collecting the thoughts of other medieval readers, and eventually and gradually alphabetizing them.[34] A glossary like *Arma* with its extensive Virgilian glosses in text order is a very clear (and extant) example of exactly what Lindsay was looking for: glosses drawn from the text and margins of a manuscript of an author. The same is true of the earlier dictionary of Nonius, which Lindsay edited, and which was composed from lists of words and quotations, each list in text order. And there is one extremely important glossary which Lindsay knew and discussed, the so-called Leiden Glossary.[35] This text consists of forty-eight lists of glosses with headings identifying (not always very clearly) the source, each one taken in text order from a specific book (many of the books being parts of the Bible, none being classical texts). Michael Lapidge has shown that the basis of this collection was the curriculum of the school of Canterbury in the late seventh century; all

from Paris, Lat. 7730, *CGlL* 5.652–6; for others, see Wessner (1931: xxiii–iv) and Jeudy (1996).

33. On *Arma* and *Amoenum*, see Dionisotti (1996: 225–6).

34. For Lindsay's theory, see (most succinctly) Lindsay (1921b: 1–2) and (1927b: 95–7); it is dissected by Dionisotti (1996: 220–5). That this theory on the one hand led Lindsay to publish with considerable effort a set of texts he believed worthless medieval ruminations and on the other hand contradicted entirely his hope to be able to reconstruct from the glossaries a fuller text of the ancient dictionary of Festus is a peculiarity better left unexplored.

35. Leiden, Voss. Lat. Q 69, foll. 20r–36r, of which a specimen is published in *CGlL* 5.410–25. The manuscript was written at the monastery of St. Gallen c. 800 CE.

or parts of this set of glossaries are found in numerous, largely unpublished, manuscripts.[36]

The Leiden Glossary shows us the first stage, or at least one possible first stage, in the formation of the large glossaries, and there is one more stage visible. Not only do sets of glosses from particular texts tend to congregate, but full-fledged glossaries tend to huddle together under the same covers. Another Leiden manuscript (BPL 67F, mentioned above) contains not just *Abstrusa, Affatim*, and the *Glossae Vergilianae*, but also *Ab absens, Abavus, Arma*, a set of *Synonyma Ciceronis*, and more similar materials (including the *Notae iuris*, discussed in 6.3d below). Bern 258 contains many of the same glossaries, and others including *Amoenum*. Erfurt, Amplonianus 2° 42 (of which more below), contains three glossaries all of which have Anglo-Saxon connections. People who are interested in word lists seem to want to collect them or enlarge them—a process that leads, ideally if not in fact, to a full dictionary of the language.

However, even if we can see in some cases the process of glossary formation, that does not, ultimately, tell us everything. In the case of the Leiden Glossary we know where and when the glosses were collected, and we know that they almost certainly derive from student notes taken at the lectures of Theodore and Hadrian at Canterbury. But although in many cases the scribes and notes are medieval, that reveals little about their origins. The lexicon of Festus is indeed a source for some glossaries, and we cannot be sure that all glossaries derive from extant texts: they are still worth pursuing, as are medieval marginalia themselves (see the next chapter). The Leiden Glossary is closely related to a set of glossaries that contain Anglo-Saxon glosses; they give important insight into the history of English (and of Anglo-Saxon life), but parts of them also include glosses that in fact go back as far as the early Empire.[37]

But although *glossae collectae* are a major source for the extant glossaries, it is not true that the glossaries as a whole are worthless for knowledge of the ancient world. The most significant evidence for both the value of the glossaries and their antiquity has only recently been described and has not yet been published. A manuscript written in central Italy sometime around the year 1000 (Oxford, Bodleian Add. C 144) contains, among other rare texts, a glossary titled *Expositio notarum*. This strange text contains a great many glosses concerning Roman legal and institutional language, and Dionisotti has traced their origin to the *Commentarius notarum Tironianarum*, the collection of shorthand abbreviations that was widely used in the ancient world and is preserved in some very early manuscripts.[38] We

36. See Lapidge (1986); he lists more than twenty-five manuscripts containing all or part of this collection. Another short text—earlier and using classical sources—which may show a glossary emerging from marginalia is the fifth-century *Fragmentum Bobiense de nomine* (*GL* 7.540.20–4.43), on which see Mariotti (1984) and 12.46.4a below.

37. On the Anglo-Saxon glossaries, see 10.4.4d below.

38. Dionisotti (1996: 228–36); see further 6.3d below. On the manuscript as a whole, see now De Nonno (2013).

think of the glossaries as deriving from literary texts, but that is only partially true, and (except for occasional hints they give about lost ancient commentaries and dictionaries) they tell us relatively little about ancient literature and its transmission. Many of the glosses, of course, are from the Bible or other religious texts, but one of the real contributions of the non-religious material is the simple fact of its breadth: not just Latin, but Greek, and not just words, but signs. Those are the other two areas that need exploration here.

c) Latin into Greek, Greek into Latin

The end of the western Empire in 476 ought to mark a firm break between the Greek East and the Latin West, but in fact it does not, even politically: from the middle of the sixth century until the eighth, the (eastern) Empire controlled portions of Italy (and in fact controlled Calabria until the eleventh); and conversely, until at least the reign of Justinian the official language of law, even in the East, remained Latin. Indeed, the two most significant (and massive) Latin texts of the sixth century were written in Constantinople: the *Digest* of Roman law and the *Ars* of Priscian. But after the sixth century, we hear little of Latin in the East until the translations from Latin to Greek made by Maximus Planudes in the thirteenth century. None of the bilingual texts discussed here was preserved in the East; when it was no longer expedient (for commerce, law, or daily life) for a Greek-speaker to know some Latin, the Greeks reverted to their traditional disdain for barbarian tongues. We have fragments of one bilingual dictionary probably written in Constantinople in the sixth century; but like the *Digest* and Priscian, it was preserved in the West.[39]

But if Byzantine Greeks had no interest in Latin, the reverse was not the case: in western Europe (and in North Africa until the Arab conquest), the church's insistence on maintaining Latin as the universal language of religion ensured that Goths, Vandals, Lombards, Celts, and Saxons, as they were won over to Christianity, were also instructed in Latin, and the zealous desire of at least the functionaries of the church to approach more truly to the source of divine inspiration led them to want to get as much Greek as they could. Hebrew was beyond them (although imaginative versions of both Hebrew and Greek appear in manuscripts from Ireland), but some familiarity with two of the three languages of divine scripture might be attainable.

And Latin-speakers had always been interested in Greek. In the first place, there was serious engagement with Greek culture and philosophy, with some ability to read and translate the originals, from the third century BCE at least up to

39. Little will be said here about early glossaries on papyrus from Egypt, which rarely have much connection to the Latin grammatical tradition. The bilingual papyrus glossaries are collected by Kramer (1983, 2001); for discussion, see also Kramer (1996) and Dickey (2012: 4–12). On bilingual grammatical texts (now collected in Scappaticcio 2015), see 12.46.1. On Latin in the Greek world in general, see Rochette (1997); on the teaching of Latin to Greek-speakers, see also Rochette (2015).

the time of Boethius and Cassiodorus in the sixth century CE; what is more, eminent Roman aristocrats (again, Cassiodorus and Boethius come to mind, along with Priscian's patron and Boethius' father-in-law, Symmachus) traveled to, and for a time lived in, Constantinople itself.[40] Secondly, it should not be forgotten that, from the very outset of the Roman scholarly tradition, Latin was sometimes conceived of as a Greek dialect, and the relationship between Latin and Greek was a recognized question for grammarians going back at least to Aelius Stilo. And, of course, Greek remained spoken in parts of southern Italy and Sicily for a very long time. If by the ninth century Latin was in Constantinople a very foreign tongue, Greek was never so far away for readers and speakers of Latin.

However, although Greek was available in some ways in the West, it was not easy and was not, at least after the sixth century, widely available. There were some bilingual texts (mostly biblical) that an intelligent and very hard-working Latin-speaker might use to learn Greek, but instructional aids were not many. The bilingual materials, as Goetz points out, fall into two classes. One group, the so-called *hermeneumata*, seem originally to have been designed for classroom use in low-level language instruction; the nine surviving collections of this material consist of glossaries, both alphabetical and topical, together with varying amounts of both easy bilingual readings and bilingual conversations reproducing, most notably, a day in the life of an elementary student, and various useful phrasebooks, some of them perhaps for travelers. The other group is aimed at more advanced users: grammatical discussions of the differences between Latin and Greek (the so-called *idiomata*) and dictionaries in either direction. It is important for the modern reader using these texts to bear in mind that, in the shape in which they are now extant, they are tools for Latin-speakers to learn Greek, resources for elementary study; at earlier stages of their existence, by contrast, they may have been designed for Greeks to learn Latin, and parts of them may have been for more advanced readers. Neither the conversational Greek of the *hermeneumata* nor the scholarly Greek of the *idiomata* necessarily reflects its original function. Nobody in western Europe wanted to communicate in Greek, either in writing or orally; they wanted to learn to read it.[41]

At the same time as the desire for Greek was intense among some people, actual ability to read the language was very rare. A few people became proficient to some degree; Johannes Scotus Eriugena and Sedulius Scottus, along with Bede, are the most notable.[42] For most readers and scribes, however, knowledge

40. On Latin manuscripts and texts from the East, see 9.4 below.

41. On the bilingual materials in general, see Goetz (1923: 12–59); the division into higher and lower materials at p. 13. I rely largely on Dionisotti (1988) for my understanding of this material; for the *hermeneumata* in particular, see Dionisotti (1982a) and Dickey (2012). For detailed bibliography, see 10.4.5 below.

42. One person who avidly collected Greek, but whose expertise in it remains somewhat unclear, is Martin of Laon (d. 875), whose manuscript of Greek dictionaries and word lists survives as Laon 444. For a recent discussion and detailed description, see Dionisotti (1988: 45–54). For Bede, see Dionisotti (1982b).

of Greek did not extend beyond the alphabet and individual words. The limits of genuine mastery of Greek are reflected in the extant sources: as the demand for whatever resources there were diminished, so too did the supply, and texts that had originally been bilingual lost their Greek, and with it much of their sense. Thus, both the Greek–Latin dictionary of Ps.-Cyrillus and the Latin–Greek dictionary of Ps.-Philoxenus are both attested very sparsely in the ninth century, and they completely disappear from sight thereafter until the Renaissance. Many of the lists of *idiomata* have lost their Greek, and both the *Glossae Servii* and some of the *hermeneumata* transliterate it into near gibberish. A few of the *hermeneumata* are reasonably well attested between the eighth and tenth centuries, but some are unknown until the Renaissance. Quite a few bilingual texts survive, and some grammars, particularly that of Priscian, contain a great deal of Greek. But not many people could read them, and even fewer could understand them.

In some ways, the most useful aids may have been the bilingual *hermeneumata*, because they are so clearly designed for elementary learning and practical vocabulary. The various sets of them differ in content; it seems likely that they all originally had the two sets of glossaries (alphabetical and by topic, the latter known as *capitula*), and most if not all contained the other two elements, conversations and easy readings. How widely they were known, and at what periods, is very unclear; at least one went as far as Britain and became the basis for an Anglo-Saxon dictionary.[43] The reading selections are various in origin: some clearly have a Greek background, but the legal passages were probably in Latin originally, and some of them seem to have been translated back and forth more than once, removing any chance of identifying their origin securely. What is clear is that in antiquity, bilingual education was much more likely to take place in the West than the East, and Latin speakers tended to learn Greek at a much earlier age than Greek speakers learned Latin; but whether these collections were originally monolingual or bilingual has no single answer. Dionisotti points out the striking similarities between the narrative of a student's day in the conversation sections of the *hermeneumata* and Ausonius' versification of his own day in *Ephemeris*; there may be a deliberate reminiscence on the poet's part, or it may be that the daily activities of student and teacher were fairly similar throughout the West.[44]

Attempts have been made to construct the genealogy of the *hermeneumata*, suggesting that the *capitula* in all the collections stem from a single source, but that is unlikely: many of the same topics are treated in the same order, but the words defined under the headings are often quite different. The *colloquia* also seem to fall into two parts, with quite different origins: there is a section on the day of a student, but there is also a section that has more to do with adult life and in which the fictional participants are no longer schoolchildren. Some sections of the *hermeneumata* seem to originate in Greek-speaking areas, but the bilingual collections, as a whole, clearly belong to the West. They give a remarkable

43. See Dionisotti (1982a: 91).

44. Dionisotti (1982a: 123–5).

view into the late antique schoolroom and the teacher's toolkit of instructional devices—word lists, easy readings, conversations—which were clearly widespread and must have existed in more forms than happen to survive. The extant collections seem to have taken shape by the fourth century, including some much older material; how widely they were used in the early Middle Ages is not altogether clear.[45]

The *hermeneumata*, although in their present form they were clearly known and used only by Latin speakers, seem to draw from sources with origins in both linguistic communities; the same is true of the dictionaries. Two large, alphabetical dictionaries survive, the Latin–Greek dictionary that is referred to as Ps.-Philoxenus and the Greek–Latin dictionary known as Ps.-Cyrillus; the author's names were both wrongly assigned in the Renaissance, and the authorship and origin of the two works are unknown.

Ps.-Philoxenus was clearly designed for Greek-speakers who wanted to read Latin, and it is a conglomerate text. A sign of its Greek origin is its alphabetization, which is in the order ABG rather than ABC. Some of its sources have regularized the lemma form to nominative singular for nouns and first-person singular for verbs, while others have kept the form found in the text from which the entry arose. Much of the dictionary has been alphabetized to three letters but there are intrusions and disorders suggesting that at one stage an original (large) dictionary was combined, not altogether successfully, with another fairly substantial work the origins of which are unknown. The fact that it includes vocabulary from Festus and from literary texts (notably Horace), as well as from other sources, suggests that it was not aimed at beginners. It is not at all clear when or why it came to France (where the extant copies were written); it was too demanding for most readers and is not known to have been used between the ninth century and the Renaissance.[46]

The corresponding Greek–Latin dictionary of Ps.-Cyrillus, in its present form, would certainly be useful to Latin speakers who wanted to read Greek, but much of its contents suggest that its original audience (or at least the original audience for considerable parts of it) was in fact Greek as well. Because it is highly alphabetized, its precise sources are not really identifiable. One of them was evidently a (shorter) Greek–Latin dictionary; the presence of some glosses parallel to the Greek lexicon of Hesychius shows that another may have been simply a Greek lexicon to which Latin definitions were added. But a large portion of the dictionary comes from Latin-based sources. Again, one was a dictionary, but a

45. On the *hermeneumata*, see now Dickey (2012: 16–54), with thorough bibliography. Dickey's reconstructed history of the glossaries and colloquia would work for a literary text; it does not take account of the flexibility and variability that make constructing a stemma of sub-literary texts virtually impossible. In that respect, Dionisotti (1982a) offers a more realistic account.

46. On Ps.-Philoxenus, see Goetz (1923: 23–34); Dionisotti (1988: 6–9); and 10.4.5 below.

Latin–Greek dictionary that had been reversed. More important is that a major source was not even a dictionary, but a Latin grammar (which overlaps with some extant grammatical texts, such as Charisius) with Greek glosses. In borrowing from the grammar, the compiler of the dictionary kept some of the Latin grammatical notes (e.g., 2.257.25 *Βια uiolentia uis plurale non habet*) and also included some entries with citations from Latin authors (e.g., 2.242.50 *Αποψις: hic aspectus conspectus prospectus suspectus ut uirgilius lib: VI: quantum ad aetherius caeli suspectus olimpum*): Virgil above all, but also Sallust, Terence, and Cicero. There is enough peculiarity about the dictionary's Latin to suggest that the compiler (or one of the compilers along the way to the present dictionary) did not know Latin, but he (or they) clearly had access to both Greek and Latin sources. Dionisotti suggests that the extant form might have been created in the Byzantine parts of Italy; that would at least explain its mixture of materials and its survival in the West.[47]

One of the most important features of Ps.-Cyrillus, however, is simply the fact that a Latin grammar was one of the more useful sources for a dictionary: bilingual word lists were very much at home in some parts of the Latin grammatical tradition, and one can see them over time moving from grammar to glossary and, at times, from Latin–Greek glossary to Latin–Latin glossary. The earliest bilingual glossary preserved in the West is evidence of this. Two small portions survive of a papyrus codex, or possibly a pair of codices, written in the sixth century, probably in Constantinople. One is the so-called Folium Wallraffianum in Cologne; the other is the Fragmenta Helmstadiensia now in Göttingen. The Folium contains part of an alphabetical Greek–Latin dictionary; the other is part of a Latin–Greek dictionary, arranged alphabetically, but within that, morphologically: what we possess is part of the section on adjectives and nouns ending in *-is* and *-tas*. As Kramer notes, this was a huge work, if the remainder of it was as copious as the small fragments that survive. It was also designed for Latin speakers: at least some knowledge of the language was required to look a word up by its ending as well as its opening letters.[48]

The Latin–Greek glossary of the Fragmenta, organized by ending, is not unique; it is very similar to a text known as *Glossae Nominum* (*CGlL* 2.563–97), a list of nouns alphabetized to two letters (AB–), but in which the words in each alphabetical unit appear in a fixed order of endings, moving from first to second to third declension. The big difference between the Fragmenta and the *Glossae Nominum* is that the latter has no Greek, but it is clearly derived from a glossary that did.[49] What it has instead is some Anglo-Saxon glosses: Greek was no longer the language being studied; Latin was. There are other similar texts of this kind,

47. Dionisotti (1988: 10–15). On Ps.-Cyrillus, see also Goetz (1923: 34–47).

48. See Kramer (1980a, 1980b) for detailed description; see also 10.4.5a below. Dionisotti (1985: 319) believes that the two fragments are more likely to be from the same scriptorium than parts of the same manuscript.

49. On *Glossae nominum*, see Goetz (1923: 41–7) and 10.4.5b(i) below.

and they seem to derive from *idiomata,* a type of text that originated not as a word list, but as part of the Latin grammatical tradition.

A fundamental tool for explaining the Latin language and its particularities, from the earliest times, was comparison with Greek. In part (in Aelius Stilo and Varro, for instance) this involved etymology; but the general sense that Latin was closely related to (if not actually a dialect of) Greek led to the creation of the category of *idiomata.* As Charisius (379.3–5B) defines it at the beginning of the final book of his grammar, *idiomata quae sunt nostri sermonis innumerabilia quidem debent esse. ea enim sunt omnia quae pro nostro more efferimus et non secundum Graecos* ("There ought to be countless *idiomata* in our language. They consist of everything which we say according to our custom and not that of the Greeks"). The most familiar kinds of *idioma,* of which we have many examples, are generally described as *idiomata casuum,* constructions that employ different cases in Greek and Latin, and *idiomata generum,* nouns that mean the same thing but have different genders in Greek and Latin. *Idiomata casuum* appear in several extant grammatical texts (Charisius, Diomedes, Dositheus, and Part 2 of the *Appendix Probi*) without the Greek, which was probably omitted by copyists rather than the grammarians themselves; the Greek is preserved in only one other text, the *idiomata* of the early Beneventan grammatical manuscript, Paris, Lat. 7530.

Idiomata generum appear more widely, and more often with the Greek: as part of the discussion of the noun in the grammar known as *Anonymus Bobiensis* (32–5 De Nonno = *GL* 1.551–5); in the manuscript of Charisius, wrongly attributed to Charisius himself by Barwick (450–63B); in the *idiomata* of Paris, Lat. 7530 (*GL* 1.573–84); and in at least two other collections, in one of which (the *Glossae Servii*) the Greek is transliterated. What marks all these collections is that they are in alphabetized Latin lists divided by gender and ending: Latin masculine ~ Greek feminine, further subdivided by ending (-us; -or; -ex; -ns—with some inconsistencies and breaking down at the end); then Latin masculine ~ Greek neuter; Latin feminine ~ Greek masculine; Latin feminine ~ Greek neuter; Latin neuter ~ Greek masculine; Latin neuter ~ Greek feminine. These lists were clearly created, as they appear in the *Anonymus Bobiensis,* as part of the discussion of nouns in a grammatical context; they then became separate lists of *idiomata,* and finally, as in the Fragmenta, *glossae nominum.* Once they lost their Greek, they survived because they were still useful for other people (Irish, Franks, Goths . . .) who wanted to learn Latin.

d) *Notae*

As mentioned above, Dionisotti has identified an important source for the glossary tradition in the *Expositio notarum,* which offers explanations for words and phrases to be found in the *Commentarii notarum Tironianarum.* Presumably teaching shorthand was not part of the grammarian's job; on the other hand, if one interprets language as a system of signs, abbreviations and shorthand are as much a means of communication as is the regular alphabet. And in fact, Isidore includes sections on no fewer than six different kinds of *notae* in his book on grammar (1.21–6). Three of these are not relevant here, as they do not seem to be attested in any glossary or other list: *notae militares* (1.24) were the marks placed by names in military rosters to indicate survivors or casualties; *notae litterarum* (1.25) are cryptographic codes; and *notae digitorum* (1.26) are non-verbal hand signals. The three that are relevant are described, respectively, as *notae sententiarum* (1.21), *notae vulgares* (1.22), and *notae iuridicae* (1.23). All three are attested elsewhere, and all three seem to have been at least on the periphery of grammatical training.[50]

Notae sententiarum are what we would call "critical signs": those marks that are placed in the margins of literary texts to indicate either textual problems or aesthetic judgments. Isidore lists twenty-six of them, and the two lists found in the *Anecdoton Parisinum* have already been discussed in connection with Varro and Probus. The importance and meaning of these signs is not clear; they include judgments both about the text and about its aesthetic or rhetorical qualities. But whatever their precise meaning, they clearly were at home in the grammarian's library, and perhaps his classroom as well.

Less obviously suitable for the grammarian are the other two, and yet they seem to belong among the varieties of grammatical glossary. The *notae vulgares* are those commonly referred to as *notae Tironianae*. Cicero's freedman Tiro was credited with their invention, or at least with their use, and they seem to have been widely used by suitably titled *notarii*, from at least as early as the first century CE. *Notarii* of this kind took down public and forensic speeches stenographically, according to Isidore (1.22.1), and they were certainly employed in late antiquity: there are many in attendance at the Council of Carthage in 411, some of them public employees, others working for the church. Ausonius writes a poem to his *notarius*; Pompeius, the fifth-century commentator on Donatus, refers to the *notarius* who is taking down his book as he speaks it. The *Expositio notarum* that has been mentioned several times above is a glossary in part based on the Tironian notes, and indeed a massive collection of them survives in a substantial group of ninth- and tenth-century manuscripts.

The final category is *notae iuridicae* (1.23). Isidore gives examples of one- and two-letter combinations intended to speed the copying of legal documents, but he also reports that they are found only *in libris antiquis* (1.23.2) as more recent emperors had, in the interest of clarity and avoidance of ambiguity, forbidden the use of abbreviations. Even if forbidden, however, they certainly survive, and some of them may be quite old. In particular, one list is attributed in the manuscripts (none earlier than the Renaissance) to Valerius Probus, and it seems quite possible that he was responsible for it. Another list, simply headed *Incipiunt notas iuris*, is included in the Beneventan grammatical manuscript Paris, Lat. 7530. A third was dedicated to Charlemagne by Magno, bishop of Sens from 801 to 818. Mommsen printed eight collections in all;

50. For details and bibliography on *notae*, see 10.4.6 below.

the abbreviations in them range from quite technical phrases explicitly drawn (in Probus' list) from the text of laws (e.g., L.I.D.A.C. = *lex Iulia de adulteriis cohercendis*), legal formulae (e.g., A.T.M.D.O. = *aio te mihi dare oportere*), and the praetor's edict (e.g., D.M.F.V.C. = *dolo malo fraudisve causa*) to abbreviations for the forms of conjunctions and relative pronouns of a kind familiar in many medieval manuscripts.

Abbreviations needed explaining by expansion, hence these lists; the explanations too sometimes needed explanation, and hence a glossary like the *Expositio notarum*. I do not know whether any of the glossaries explains the explanations of the *Notae iuris*, but the links between stenography, glossaries, and the grammarian as explainer of all written documents are clear.

4. ISIDORE OF SEVILLE

Including Isidore in this chapter—indeed in this book—presents certain difficulties. In the first place, I have in general not included ecclesiastical writers. That does not mean that there are no Christians (there are many) or no clerics (most of the creators of the glossaries discussed above and many of the commentators discussed below were almost certainly ecclesiastics of some sort, and the same is true of later grammarians like Virgilius Maro); it does mean that writers whose primary orientation is towards religious texts conduct philological activities somewhat differently from those working on secular texts. And to discuss Isidore in any detail would mean linking his work to that of Augustine, Cassiodorus, and possibly Jerome—something that is far beyond my competence. But Isidore, more than any other figure of the late antique church, has always been viewed at least in part within the tradition of Roman scholarship, as a kind of summary, conclusion, and transition to later forms of interpretation. At the same time, it is by no means clear that Isidore should be categorized along with dictionaries and lexicons: the *Etymologiae*, his twenty-book compilation of knowledge, is indeed an encyclopedia, but Isidore is far more widely engaged, both in the *Etymologiae* and in other works, with traditions of ancient learning that extend far beyond grammar and glossaries. And yet, as someone who used lists of words to organize the world, he surely belongs here. It should be noted, however, that my treatment of him is brief and incomplete: he is too large for a book on philology.

As it is, there are three works of Isidore that in some way belong in this chapter, each of which takes a category of glossographic writing and extends and enlarges it to explore a Christian vision of the world. The most familiar of Isidore's works, and one of the most influential books in Europe for centuries, is the *Etymologiae*; it was his last work, left incomplete at his death in 636. At the other end of his career, when he was quite young, he wrote two books of *Differentiae*. Also, at some fairly early (but undatable) point, he composed a work called *Synonyma*. Grammatical categories framed Isidore's writings; indeed, he may well have seemed excessively attuned to secular learning to some of his contemporaries. And yet, perhaps because of his attachment to the secular tradition, he transformed the categories of grammatical writing to accommodate a Christian world.

The two shorter works, *Differentiae* and *Synonyma*, show this very clearly. Although there has been some difficulty in identifying which two sets of *Differentiae* circulating under Isidore's name were actually his, it is now clear that Book 1 was an unalphabetized collection known as *Inter caelum et aethera* (a later, alphabetized version circulated also under his name, but is evidently a revision of the original version)—a fairly traditional set. But Book 2, titled in the manuscripts *Differentiae rerum* or *Differentiae spirituales*, is, as the titles suggest, very different: *Inter deum et dominum* is a set of theological distinctions. Isidore has used a grammatical genre to frame a doctrinal discussion, one that was widely circulated and influential.

Something similar can be said of the *Synonyma*: although it makes use of a grammatical genre, it is in fact a meditative theological work, as its full title makes clear: *Synonymorum de lamentatione animae peccatricis libri duo*. Even less than the *Differentiae* do the *Synonyma* retain the generic form their title would suggest; the two books concern the means of redemption of the sinful soul. In one of the prefaces, Isidore claims that it arose from reading a text called *Synonyma* (some manuscripts explicitly say *Synonyma Ciceronis*); however, the effect of the list of synonyms is less on the content of the work than on its style, which is filled with synonymous phrases and exemplifies the so-called *stilus ysidorianus*, "a style where synonyms and homoeoteleuta are systematically employed and where sentences are broken into short *cola et commata*."[51]

The early and relatively short *Differentiae* and *Synonyma* balance the late and huge encyclopedia of the *Etymologiae*.[52] Isidore's encyclopedia starts with grammar, based largely on Donatus and his commentators, but within his grammatical framework he also includes fuller discussions of the four elements that he finds most important, *analogia, etymologia, glossae*, and *differentiae* (1.28–31), and unlike Donatus, he uses language, particularly etymology, as a means to explain the world. In that sense, he is an heir of Varro. The first books of the *Etymologiae* concern the *trivium* and *quadrivium*, but Isidore gives these sciences very unequal space: grammar has a whole book; rhetoric and dialectic share Book 2; and arithmetic, geometry, music, and astronomy are all stuffed into Book 3. There follow medicine (4), and law and the reckoning of time (both in 5), but thereafter comes what might be called the Christian etymology of the world, starting from the Bible and the church (6), the hierarchy from God down to the congregation of the faithful (7); and after another book on religion and philosophy (8), Isidore essentially begins again, with language.

51. Di Sciacca (2008: 24). My account of the *Synonyma* is based on Di Sciacca's discussion. Law (1995b: 98) describes the *Synonyma* as "a remarkable portrayal of the fate of the soul in a format not unlike Roget's *Thesaurus*."

52. This is (obviously) a very cursory account of a large and complex work; see 10.3 below for more detailed discussions of Isidore.

Thus Book 9 is about languages in general, with some specifics about civic and familial terminology, and Book 10 is simply an alphabetical dictionary, headed *De vocabulis*. The whole second half of the *Etymologiae* then takes us through the material world from humans and animals (11–12) through heaven and earth (13–14), human buildings (15), the physical world including soils, metals, stones, and gems (16), and ending with four books on human activities and creations (17–20). Isidore begins with grammar and treats language, and specifically etymology, as a means of managing and explaining both the universal world of the arts and religion and the particular world of human creativity. Language is both the means and the model for Isidoran explanation: the *Etymologiae* is both a grammar and an encyclopedia of all knowledge, and it can rightly be seen as the end of an ancient (secular) tradition of scholarship and the beginning of a medieval (Christian) one. Along with Cassiodorus' *Institutiones* a century earlier, it is a landmark that should be seen from both directions.[53]

53. On Isidore and Cassiodorus, see Fontaine (1986, reprinted in Fontaine 1988) and Ribémont (2001: 19–38); on Isidore's influence on later medieval encyclopedias, see Ribémont (2001: 193–319).

7

Commentary and Exegesis

As NOTED BEFORE, THE WORK OF THE GRAMMARIAN FALLS INTO two large divisions, which Quintilian (1.4.2) defines as *recte loquendi scientia* and *poetarum enarratio*. The two overlap: reading literary texts (with a teacher's help) encouraged students to acquire a proper sense of language, while the study of grammar aided comprehension of literary texts. We still use literary texts to teach grammar; in the Roman context, it was also important to introduce students to canonical texts, knowledge of which was essential to the nascent mandarins of the imperial bureaucracy. From that point of view, the exegesis of texts reinforced not only knowledge of standard Latin (and in a sense defined it) but also the social order. What that social order was, of course, changed over time—from the Roman *imperium* and social system to a Christian society to (by the end of the eighth century) the system of monastic education fostered by Alcuin and Charlemagne.[1]

Quintilian uses a metaphor from real estate to describe the field of grammar: the grammarian's territory is deep in proportion to its frontage (*plus habet in recessu quam fronte promittit*). *Recte loquendi scientia* (the topic of the next chapter) not only included basic instruction on the parts of speech, but might also incorporate orthography and pronunciation, prosody and metrics, and (overlapping with rhetorical training) discussion of *virtutes et vitia orationis* (tropes and figures; barbarism and solecism). *Enarratio poetarum*, while its fundamental shape consisted of ordered exposition of a literary text in terms of grammar, style, and content, could also be specialized, concentrating on historical or mythological exegesis, allegorical interpretation, or rhetorical analysis.[2] Topics such as meter or prose rhythm seem to fall between the two: while Servius' *De centum metris* is a general introduction to metrics applicable to any poetic text, his brief work *De metris Horatii* is essentially a metrical commentary on one poet. But even setting metrics aside (for Chapter 8), exegesis is a large and varied territory.

1. On the social importance of grammar and the grammarian (which I will not discuss here), see particularly Kaster (1988); Irvine (1994); Chin (2008).

2. For valuable treatments of the grammatical heart of school commentaries, see Jakobi (1996) on Donatus, Uhl (1998) on Servius, and Diederich (1999) on Porphyrio.

1. THE CHOICE OF A TEXT

In discussing a charge of inconsistency in biblical interpretation, Jerome reminded his adversary Rufinus of the kinds of commentary they had read in school (*Adv. Rufin.* 1.16):

> Puto quod puer legeris Aspri in Vergilium et Sallustium commentarios, Vulcatii in orationes Ciceronis, Victorini in dialogos eius, et in Terentii comoedias praeceptoris mei Donati, aeque in Vergilium, et aliorum in alios, Plautum videlicet, Lucretium, Flaccum, Persium atque Lucanum.
>
> I think you read as a boy the commentaries of Asper on Virgil and Sallust, of Vulcatius on Cicero's speeches and of Victorinus on his dialogues, as well as my teacher Donatus on the comedies of Terence and on Virgil; also other people on other texts, i.e., Plautus, Lucretius, Horace, Persius, and Lucan.

This list overlaps considerably with extant commentaries or scholia on Roman authors. No commentary on Sallust survives although he was a regular part of the school curriculum, perhaps because it would have dealt with his major work, the *Historiae*, which now exists only in fragments. Aemilius Asper's commentary on Virgil is lost, but we have extensive quotations from it and a small portion of his treatise on Virgilian grammar.[3] We have parts of commentaries on Cicero's speeches, one of which may be that of Vulcatius, and we have Marius Victorinus' commentary on *De inventione* if not on any dialogues.[4] We have a version of Donatus' commentary on Terence and the dedicatory letter and preface to his commentary on Virgil. We have remains of ancient commentaries on Horace, Persius, and Lucan (as well as Juvenal and Statius, not mentioned by Jerome). But our knowledge of commentaries on Plautus is tenuous, and there is no other evidence at all for any ancient commentary on Lucretius.[5]

Perhaps because *enarratio poetarum* is one of the regularly assigned tasks of the grammarian, perhaps because of Jerome's list, modern *grammatici* tend to think of commentary and exegesis as concerning literary texts alone and as the exclusive province of the grammarian, but neither is true. On the one hand, by no means all the ancient marginalia on literary texts included under the broad rubric of "scholia" are by grammarians: although the bulk of surviving commentary on

3. On Asper, see 5.4, 7.3a, and 12.5. The original Aemilius Asper should not be confused with the later grammatical texts attached to his name.

4. On Cicero commentaries, see 7.3b and 11.2.

5. It is unclear who the Sisenna who seems to have commented on Plautus was; probably not (despite Perutelli 2004: 55–62) the historian of the early first century BCE, but a grammarian of the second century CE; cf. Schmidt in *HLL* 4 §445.1. The true surprise in Jerome's list is Lucretius, who was loathed by both Stoics and Christians and was unlikely ever to have been a standard school text. The only evidence for any exegetical interest is the set of headings preserved in and with the text in the ninth-century manuscripts; see Herren (2012) and Butterfield (2013: 178–202).

literary texts emanated from the mind of some *grammaticus*, the marginalia in the Bembine Terence or the palimpsest of Fronto or the Medicean Virgil are the notes of owners or readers, not teachers (books that grand would have been far beyond the resources of a humble teacher), and the collections of ancient exegesis made in the Carolingian age often depend in part on such personal sets of marginalia, even if a source in the schools is also readily apparent.

On the other hand, literary texts are not the only works in need of explanation, and not only grammatical explanation was needed. Cicero's *De inventione* was studied in rhetorical schools in late antiquity, as his *Topica* was used in the study of dialectic.[6] Macrobius' commentary on the *Somnium Scipionis* does not belong in the ancient classroom at all, but is an introduction to Neoplatonic philosophy in the form of commentary. The commentaries on Germanicus' *Aratea* were meant to explain astronomy, not grammar. Lactantius Placidus' *Narrationes* of Ovid's *Metamorphoses* provide mythological introductions comparable to the potted tales in the *Mythographi Vaticani*. These fall outside the normal classroom, but it should also be remembered that the curriculum of the *grammaticus* was itself fairly narrow: we have the remains of ancient commentaries on Cicero's speeches and the major classical poets taught in schools in antiquity and the early Middle Ages—in other words, on Terence, Virgil, Horace, Persius, Lucan, Statius, and Juvenal—but nothing at all on other writers who certainly could have profited by explanatory comment.[7] Nothing, for instance, on Catullus, Propertius, Tibullus, Ovid's Amatoria, or Seneca; nothing on Caesar or Livy or Pliny or Tacitus or Cicero's letters or a host of other authors whose works survived outside the schools, by luck and chance. Another vast area of exegesis also lies outside the scope of this book: commentaries not only on the Bible, but also on the classicizing Christian poets of late antiquity, such as Arator, Prudentius, or Sedulius. The tradition of biblical exegesis owes something to the tradition of commentary on classical texts, and the commentaries on Christian writers owe as much to the tradition of exegesis on classical poetry as the Christian poets themselves owe to the texts on which those commentaries were written.[8]

By far the largest and most important area of non-literary commentary, however, was reserved for a different profession, that of law. The early importance of the study of legal texts for the development of Roman philology during the Republic has already been mentioned, and while the close link between law and grammar does not seem to have persisted—except insofar as the interpretation of written texts was central to both professions—commentary remained one of the basic

6. On the commentaries on *De inventione*, see 11.2.6 below.

7. It should be noted that (except in the case of Terence and Virgil) there is no explicit evidence that the extant commentaries were composed by *grammatici*; but in the case of Cicero's speeches certainly, and Horace and Lucan probably, there is enough emphasis on grammar in the commentaries to make it seem likely that they were written for students, if not necessarily by grammarians.

8. See particularly Irvine 1994. Also excluded here are other texts of late antiquity that did not receive glossing or commentary before the ninth century.

forms of legal writing. In the earliest period, commentaries on the Twelve Tables were fundamental, going back to Sex. Aelius. While originally such commentaries must have been written to clarify the law itself, later work on the Twelve Tables took on an antiquarian character: the last known is by Gaius, in the second or third century CE, long after the archaic law code had ceased to have practical importance. As the Twelve Tables were superseded by edictal law (starting in the second century BCE), so too commentary followed the text: Antistius Labeo, the pupil of Cicero's and Horace's friend Trebatius, commented on both the Twelve Tables and the Edict; after the text of the Edict was edited by Salvius Iulianus and became tralatitious in the reign of Hadrian, the massive commentaries of Pomponius (about 150 books), Paul (80 books), and Ulpian (83 books) were central to legal writing and jurisprudential thought.[9]

Commentary, in the juristic sense, was far more than simple exegesis of meaning: unlike the work of grammarians, it had ramifications in the real world. The wording of a legal document, whether statute or edict or a civil document such as a will or contract, was unchangeable: that is the whole point of a legal document. On the other hand, wording needs explanation, because laws, wills, and contracts are (now as then) often fairly opaque. At the same time, if one is to apply or enforce a legal document, particularly if it is old or badly written, the text which is unalterable must in fact be interpreted in order to adapt its meaning for current use or to extend its application. The importance of philological interpretation of legal documents as part of advocacy appears as early as Cicero's *De inventione*: the discussion of controversy arising *ex ambiguo* (*Inv.* 2.116–21) involves not only character and intention, but word order and grammar. In a juristic context rather than a rhetorical one, the role of legal commentary goes further: not only simple exegesis of language, but the exploration of extended meaning and implication. Authoritative legal commentary could be used to change the law without actually changing it, to adapt it while simultaneously asserting its permanence and unalterability.

Legal commentary was central to the practical workings of the law. It established at times (philologically or historically) what the words of the base text meant; it also determined what they ought to mean.[10] Thus, for example, in one very minor section of Ulpian's commentary on the portion of the Praetor's Edict dealing with wills, he first explains the proper meaning of *testamentum* as narrowly defined by law while simultaneously extending the word from valid wills to invalid ones for the purposes of praetorian jurisdiction: *Testamentum . . . proprie*

9. On legal commentaries in general, see particularly Schulz (1946: 183–223) and Wieacker (2006: 40–2). It should be clear that I offer here nothing more than a reminder of the importance of legal literature to the study of Roman philology.

10. There is some similarity in this to the opposition between *scriptum* and *sententia* common in rhetorical theory, but legal argument typically involves the general interpretation of a statute or a legal term, while the rhetorical argument usually turns on the will (both volition and testament) of a particular individual or document.

illud dicitur, quod iure perfectum est: sed abusive testamenta ea quoque appellamus, quae falsa sunt vel iniusta vel irrita vel rupta: itemque imperfecta solemus testamenta dicere ("*Testamentum* in its narrow meaning is a legally complete document, but we improperly also call *testamenta* documents that are forged or illegal or ineffective or broken. We even call *testamenta* documents that have not been completed"). Commentary is then used to enlarge the definition even further to include other relevant documents: *Ad causam autem testamenti pertinere videtur id quodcumque quasi ad testamentum factum sit, in quacumque materia fuerit scriptum, quod contineat supremam voluntatem; et tam principales quam secundae tabulae edicto continentur* ("For cases involving inheritance, any document seems relevant that was created as if in the place of a will, whatever material it was written on, if it contains someone's last wishes; both the primary documents and secondary additions are covered by the edict").[11] By the end, the narrow language of the law describing one of the most formal Roman legal documents has been interpreted by commentary to mean anything that reveals the intention of the testator.

In many ways, legal commentary is very different from literary commentary: its sheer expansiveness, its concentration on the effective (rather than just the verbal) significance of the text, and its status as performative speech rather than simple interpretation mark it off from the grammarian's task of explaining the literal meaning, and only much less often the significance, of an author's words. At the same time, however, the two have remarkable similarities: both are highly conservative in that they interpret the text rather than changing it; both at times claim to reveal what the text should have said had it been more carefully expressed; and thus both attempt to mediate between the original expression and current use. In legal terms, that can be seen in Ulpian's distinction between the strict meaning of *testamentum* in the Edict and "our" use of the word (*proprie dicitur; appellamus*); in a literary context, it is the method that underlies Servius' constant distinctions between what Virgil was entitled to do with grammar and rhetorical figures in his poetry, and what we (i.e., his young pupils) can say ourselves.[12] Legal commentary, much more explicitly than literary commentary, reveals the fundamental strain in the work of exegesis: it simultaneously establishes a fixed authority (statute or edict; a canonical author) and undercuts it; it interprets a past text while also adapting it to present needs.

The same is true of many varieties of commentary: rhetorical commentaries extend the meaning and usefulness of *De inventione*; biblical commentaries have doctrinal as well as exegetical goals. And there is yet one more area of commentary where this is quite explicit, the long series of commentaries on the grammars of Donatus. These will be discussed later, but it is worth mentioning them here: Donatus' succinct texts were simply not intelligible to later generations of students, particularly those whose native language was not Latin, without the

11. *D.* 29.3.2.1–2 = Ulpian fr. 1221 Lenel (1889); cf. also Lenel (1883: 289–90) (*Edictum perpetuum* T. XXVI §166).

12. On this, see above all Kaster (1980a, 1988: 172–95).

explanations and expansions of the commentators. Bare copies of Donatus are relatively uncommon; his work is generally accompanied by one or more of the many texts that filled in what he had thought self-explanatory but which no longer was.

2. THE PLACE OF COMMENTARY

While the role of commentary in its various contexts, literary, legal, and otherwise, is fairly straightforward, its history is not. The issue is partly formal and codicological: ancient manuscripts, whether papyrus rolls or codices, were in general not designed to include commentary. In papyrus rolls, the book is arranged in columns of text without much space between them; in codices, there is often more room in the margins, but not before the fifth century is there any sign of books being organized with wide enough margins to hold more than occasional notes.[13] That does not mean that marginalia were not added; they were. It does mean that full-fledged commentaries were not composed with the goal of appearing on the same page as the texts they were intended to explain. That is clear from even a cursory glance at a representative ancient codex, even one with a great many notes such as the Verona Virgil, and at a representative medieval manuscript of Virgil in which the text itself is either surrounded on three or four sides by commentary which encloses and dwarfs the words of the author, or text and commentary appear in two columns side by side—with the column of commentary considerably wider than the column of text. Medieval books were designed to display text and exegesis together; ancient books generally were not, and those marginalia which are present in surviving codices from late antiquity seem (although the sample is too small to be certain) to have been reader's notes, often added much later than the original copying of the manuscript. They are not the formal presentation of a preexisting commentary.

The physical constraints on the placement of commentary have corresponding effects on the forms of exegesis. In the first place, if explanations were not

13. Lowe's discussion of the earliest manuscripts (1972: 1.187–202) makes it clear that prose texts were usually written in two columns (which leaves little room for commentary) and that there was a preference for a square written area, which again is not likely to leave much room in the margins. (As many ancient books have suffered repeated trimming, however, the size of the margin is not always clear.) By the fifth century that was no longer entirely true: the margins of the Verona Virgil, for instance, were clearly meant to be big enough to hold quite a lot of commentary, as in fact they do (see Daintree and Geymonat in *EV* s.v. *scholia non Serviana*). But there is not a single instance of a Latin manuscript that (as is the case in some Greek manuscripts) was equipped with scholia before being bound, nor is there any evidence of the activity of anyone other than intelligent readers who were wealthy enough to own or commission a manuscript with wide margins; see also McNamee (1997). Holtz (1995) is a careful discussion of the physical relationship of text and commentary from late antiquity through the Middle Ages. Gatti (2014: 15–25) is a valuable if overly rigid review of the subject, including both Greek and Latin materials.

physically tied to the text, there was less need to comment on every line: early commentaries tend to contain a series of observations rather than a full explanation of the text. The lack of physical connection also means that there is no compelling reason for the commentator to proceed in the order of the text: it is no accident that the earliest explications of Virgil are not what we would call commentaries at all, but *libri de Vergilio*: that is true of Hyginus, of Asconius, of Cornutus, and in all probability of Valerius Probus as well. To judge from the fragments, such works were sometimes thematic rather than broadly exegetical: the surviving comments of Hyginus, for instance, concern matters of religious and historical detail, and there is no reason to believe that he included all the topics that a modern commentator would include, nor that he even examined every passage that might have matched his interests. Commentary begins as monographic, not exegetical—but that is a perfectly normal meaning for the Latin word *commentarius*.

The disconnection of commentary and text, however, poses a practical problem: how does one link the two if they do not appear on the same page? Modern commentators generally employ standardized line or section numbers to which commentary can be keyed; the ancient system was much less efficient. The earliest extant Latin commentary, Asconius on Cicero's speeches, uses a rudimentary system of numbering. Thus, on *Pro Milone*, the first note is headed *Vers. a primo L* (50 lines from the beginning) and refers to a sentence in what is now numbered §3. The next note is to line 200 from the beginning, in §12, and the next two notes, each headed *Paulo post*, concern §13 and §14. Finally, towards the end of the commentary, there is a heading *Vers. a novis. CLX* (160 lines from the end) referring to §95. The surviving text of Asconius does not provide such helpful headings everywhere; some are probably lost. In the commentary on *In Pisonem*, the numbering from the beginning of the speech reaches *Cir. ver. a primo DCCC*, 800 lines from the beginning, at §35; and after two notes *Cir. medium*, we start the countdown at 900 lines from the end referring to §52.[14]

All this is fairly laborious: counting back 900 lines to find the passage on which Asconius was commenting would be tedious in a modern book that includes line or section numbers, and even if there was a standard length of line, it would be agonizing in a papyrus roll. The other method of connecting commentary to text was to use lemmata, quotations from the text being explained. In contrast to the very short lemmata that are often found in commentaries closely aligned to the text, Asconius' quotations are long: if you had a reasonable memory of the text being explained, you would not need to look at more than he quoted, without going back to the text of Cicero.

These two features—the lack of need to follow the text closely and the use of extended lemmata to introduce commentary—merge in a third characteristic: selectivity. In part, for Asconius, that is the result of his specialized focus on

14. In fact, the manuscripts read DCCC; an extra C was added by Buecheler to match the actual amount remaining.

historical exegesis: not every fact needs explaining. But in the commentary on *In Pisonem*, for instance, there are some gaps of more than ten (modern) chapters that go without any comment, and Asconius rarely comments on two chapters in a row, much less on more than one point in the same chapter. That is not the result of the transmission, but reflects the fact that early Roman commentators did not feel the need to talk about everything.

Early commentary, then, was an independent text, selective in its focus. How then does one get to the more familiar extant forms of ancient exegesis, commentaries like Servius on Virgil or the *scholia vetera* on Juvenal? We do not know, for instance, how the commentary on Virgil of Aemilius Asper (probably late second century) was organized, or how it was attached to the text of Virgil: it was clearly extensive and exegetical, talking about both language and content, but all that we have of it comes from Servius and the Verona Scholia, and they are unlikely to have preserved Asper's words exactly, let alone his lemmata. There was almost certainly no one pattern of transmission, just as there was not one single type of commentary at any given period.

For the transition from late antiquity to the Carolingian period, we are on somewhat firmer ground. There is a pattern that seems to apply fairly often, visible in the case of Donatus' commentary on Terence: the original (and probably huge) commentary was abridged into margins in late antiquity, presumably by readers, some of whom may have been teachers or students, who incorporated those notes that seemed useful in the space that was available. Sometime later, probably in the late eighth century, at least two of those sets of marginalia were recombined and rewritten into the commentary that we have: it includes many notes that derive from (but are probably not identical to) the commentary of Donatus, and it also includes notes made by other readers or exegetical comments inserted by whoever recombined the ancient marginalia.[15] The process can be glimpsed in two ways in the case of Donatus: in late antiquity, part of a set of excerpts from Donatus exists among the notes written in the margins of the Bembine Terence, showing the process of marginal abridgment in action; and at the end of the extant Donatus, in the commentary on *Phormio*, there is a section where the two sets of marginalia have not been combined, but still exist separately (printed in parallel columns in Wessner's edition).[16]

But that is not the end of the process nor the only way in which it occurred. Some commentaries continued to exist as full, continuous texts from antiquity to the Carolingian period and beyond: Asconius and Ps.-Asconius on Cicero are one clear example, but it is also true of Servius and Tiberius Donatus on Virgil and other texts as well. In some cases, ancient marginalia were copied into the margins of medieval books: the ninth-century codex Pithoeanus (Montpellier 125, Wessner's P) of Juvenal is our major source for the *scholia vetera*, and that these

15. A clear and useful hypothetical account of what goes into the margins of a manuscript (based entirely on late antique Greek papyri) is McNamee (2010).

16. For details, see 11.1.1 below.

scholia are indeed old is shown by the existence of one leaf of an ancient manuscript of Juvenal (Vatican, Lat. 5750), written in the fourth century and supplied with marginalia probably in the sixth century, that overlap significantly with the ninth-century version. Here, quite clearly, ancient marginalia formed the basis for the marginal scholia written in the Carolingian period. This story, however, continues: there is a fragment of a manuscript with marginal scholia (Fragmenta Aroviensia = Q) that is virtually identical in text and even the placement of notes to P; but there is another ninth-century manuscript (St. Gallen 870 = S) that contains the same notes written as a continuous text, with no text of Juvenal. There are also other Carolingian commentaries that are related to, but not identical to the *scholia vetera*: they contain some ancient material, but it is combined with clearly medieval annotation. And finally, there is the mysterious group of annotations included by Giorgio Valla in his 1486 edition of Juvenal ascribed to a "Probus": again, not the same commentary as the *scholia vetera*, but—even though attested only in a printed edition—also containing similar ancient material.[17] There is no one pattern for the survival of ancient commentaries. For Persius, we have various sets of marginalia in medieval manuscripts, together with a continuous commentary reconstituted in the eighth or ninth century, but it is impossible to determine a single direction for the flow of these notes.[18] So too, commentaries on Lucan (yet to be sorted out in any definitive way) exist in both marginal and continuous forms. In the case of popular authors who were read and studied in late antiquity and the Carolingian period, the form in which annotation was presented changed often and rapidly, depending on the needs of the scribe and his expected audience.

Much of the history of these commentaries is based on the reconstruction of lost texts, and it is worth offering, very briefly, some idea of the kinds of evidence that reveal something about the shape and form of lost manuscripts:

a) Lemmata: The quotations used to introduce annotation often reveal something of the history of a text. In general, marginal commentaries need short lemmata or none at all, just using *signes de renvoi* to link margin and text, while independent commentaries need much fuller quotations. The presence of long lemmata in marginal scholia suggests that they have passed through an independent stage. Lemmata that either disagree textually with the note they introduce, or simply use the wrong part of the line (as is often the case, for instance, in the Juvenal scholia), generally show that the commentary has had a marginal stage (often without lemmata) and been mis-adapted to a new home.
b) Glosses: Commentaries that contain very short (one or two word) glosses or explanations, often introduced by *id est* (abbreviated *.i.*) or *scilicet*

17. On the various forms of the Juvenal scholia, Wessner (1931: vi–xxxii) is still the best introduction. Further discussion and bibliography at 11.10 below.

18. See Zetzel (2005) and 11.7 below.

(abbreviated *s*) have generally been compiled from marginal scholia, including the glosses that would, in most cases, have been written between the lines of the text. Independent commentaries usually have longer notes, not simple glosses.

c) Doublets: While any late antique or medieval commentary that is not a completely original composition—and there are very few of those—may originally have included more than one explanation of the same thing, possibly drawn from different sources, the presence of two notes on the same thing that offer the *same* explanation suggests that the commentary has been compiled from two manuscripts, almost certainly two sets of marginal scholia that have in turn drawn on the same source. Notes introduced by *aliter* are also generally the product of Carolingian (or later) compilation of multiple sources.

d) Displaced notes: How one writes scholia in the margins of a book does not have a fixed pattern, nor does how one copies scholia out of the margins of a book. Some manuscripts of scholia give notes following the order of the text from the top margin of the page, down both sides equally, and ending in the bottom margin. Others go down one margin in order, and then down the other side. Some put the longest notes in the top and bottom margin, where there is more room. A manuscript that contains notes on a set of lines followed by another set of notes on the same lines is a sign that one of its sources had marginal scholia rather than continuous commentary. Disordering of notes that stems from the physical arrangement of a model is one of the clearest indications of change of form.

Such indications of the history of a commentary are not always—indeed, are hardly ever—consistent; what that shows, in turn, is that the manuscripts we have are evidence of much more active copying and circulation than the surviving copies reveal. Almost every ancient commentary has a complex tradition; they cannot be explained by a single template.

With few exceptions, what we possess of ancient commentary on classical authors cannot safely be described as the genuine, original form in which it left the pen of its author or ancient scribe. Commentaries are practical books, valued by readers as aids to comprehension of a text: they are not valued for their *ipsissima verba*, and can be rewritten—abridged, expanded, revised—to fit the needs of the immediate audience. Sometimes ancient annotations are preserved fairly accurately: a substantial portion of the commentary on Statius ascribed to Lactantius Placidus still retains the rhythmical clausulae of a commentator who wrote no later than the fourth century.[19] On the other hand, the remainder of that same commentary clearly comes from a different, and probably later, source. The history of Donatus' commentary on Terence has been briefly described above, and that of the commentaries of Porphyrio and Acro on Horace will be described in

19. For bibliography, see 11.9 below.

more detail below: none of these works is what the author originally wrote. In almost no case are the form and the words in which we read ancient commentaries now—in printed books, in orderly pages—the same as they were in antiquity: commentary, at least up to the time of printing, is always a work in progress.

3. THREE HISTORIES

To give a more concrete idea of the history of commentary from antiquity to the Carolingian period, it may be useful to look at three of the most complex and best-attested traditions of authors who were constantly and widely read: Virgil, Cicero, and Horace. I choose these three because among them, they display almost all the characteristics and varieties of ancient commentary, in both form and transmission.

a) Virgil

The beginnings of interpretation of Virgil have been discussed above. The tradition of commentary, if Suetonius can be trusted, starts with Caecilius Epirota's oral exposition in the late first century BCE; both Aulus Gellius and the fourth/fifth-century commentaries cite a string of subsequent scholarly studies, starting from the palace librarian Hyginus to Asconius and Cornutus in the mid-first century CE to Valerius Probus at the end of the century to Scaurus and Aemilius Asper in the second century as well as others who are less clearly identifiable or datable: Nisus, Cornelius, Carminius, Urbanus, ending with the one about whom we know a great deal, but not quite enough, Aelius Donatus in the middle of the fourth century CE. Cameron has also argued that there was at least one extensive mythological commentary on Virgil, possibly by Scaurus and/or the slightly earlier commentator Modestus.[20] And there can be no question that a great deal was written about Virgil: we know some authors' names from the later tradition, but there will have been many whose ideas survive anonymously in Servius and his successors—or whose ideas have perished beyond recovery. Virgil was not just a classic, but was *the* author read in the school of the *grammaticus*: and everyone with literary pretensions, from graffiti writers to Trimalchio and other people aspiring to elevate their social standing to the aristocracy of the late empire to the grammarian and schoolboy, had to have something to say about him.

The text that stands at the center of the Virgilian commentary tradition is Servius, but "Servius" is not easy to define. A successor (perhaps not immediate) of Donatus, who was *grammaticus urbis Romae* in the middle of the fourth

20. Cameron (2004: 184–216). There are many accounts of ancient Virgilian criticism; Ribbeck (1866: 114–200) is still valuable (more for the evidence than for his interpretation), Stok (2012a: 464–9) is brief and to the point, and *HLL* 4 §445.2 (Schmidt) is a very succinct account of the names about whom we know almost nothing. Timpanaro (1986, 2001) gives extensive discussions of the Virgilian commentators before Servius, focusing on textual comments; see also Zetzel (2002, reviewing Timpanaro 2001). For further bibliography, see 11.3 below.

century, Servius probably wrote his large commentary on Virgil early in the fifth century. That commentary (in the order *Aeneid–Eclogues–Georgics*) was designed for school use, although probably for teachers more than for students; the general emphasis is on using the text as a peg on which to hang instruction in grammar and style. Servius' explanations are relatively simple and straightforward; they are filled with information (on history, religion, literature, myth, grammar, style, and rhetoric), but they do not attempt to stuff young ears with excessive antiquarian learning. There are relatively few quotations of recondite sources, relatively few citations by name of earlier scholars, and relatively little presentation of multiple interpretations. As a result, the commentary was extremely popular and is transmitted in a great many manuscripts as well as influencing the content of the marginal annotations of a great many more.

But that repeated "relatively" requires expansion: relative to what? Among the many manuscripts of Servius' commentary exist a few that reveal a wider world of exegesis, a much larger commentary of which Servius' text forms the core, but is here expanded to include just those kinds of information that Servius himself spared his pupils but are hugely important for modern students of Virgil and Roman culture: quotations from early poets; obscure information about cults; the history of Virgilian interpretation; and more. Servius became a commentary surrounded by another shell of commentary, not well preserved but clearly resting on a much wider range of sources and knowledge than Servius himself supplies. By convention, the shorter Servius is known as the Vulgate (or simply as Servius); the longer one, after its first editor Pierre Daniel, is known as Servius Danielis or Servius Auctus or (as will be used here and is common in modern scholarship) DS. It is the relationship between these two—and between the additions of DS and other late antique commentaries—that is the central problem in understanding the tradition of Virgilian scholarship.

Much of what has been (and still is) written about this question is polemical and not particularly enlightening.[21] A few things seem generally to be agreed: that the DS additions very frequently fill out Servius' relatively unscholarly notes; that DS shows a degree of stylistic unity in itself which is different from Servius' style; that DS was drawn from a commentary that discussed Virgil in the order *Eclogues–Georgics–Aeneid*; and that the person who added DS material to Servius' commentary was not the same person as the author(s) of most of the material itself. What all this points to is that the major source of DS material was a commentary related to, or possibly the same as, Servius' own main source; and given the relationship between Servius and Donatus—not just as grammarians in Rome in relatively close succession, but considering Servius' role as the earliest commentator on Donatus' *Ars maior*—it seems almost certain that the source (or at least a major source) of both Servius and DS was the commentary on Virgil of Aelius Donatus himself. The larger form of Servius thus supplements the shorter

21. A fair and clear summary of the relationship between Servius and Donatus in Stok (2012a).

commentary with material from Servius' source that Servius himself had chosen to omit. The fact that Macrobius' *Saturnalia*, written later than Servius' commentary but long before the compilation of DS, has passages close to DS also suggests that Donatus was the common source of all three.

But while a close relationship between DS and Donatus is very likely, no absolute precision is possible. We are definitely not entitled to assume that everything in DS came from Donatus; the hand of the compiler is too visible for that. It is equally clear (more below) that more of Donatus survives in medieval marginalia and glossaries than is found in DS. It is thus also not possible to accept (as has sometimes been done) the misleading equation "Donatus = Servius + DS": even if Donatus was the principal source of DS, there was clearly material in Donatus that DS omitted, and material in DS that did not come from Donatus. But it is equally wrong to use the fact that the DS notes are not identical to Donatus' commentary and that material from Donatus exists elsewhere than in DS as a pretext for rejecting the reasonable conclusion that DS used Donatus, Servius used Donatus, and therefore that we have from DS and Servius *together* some idea of what sorts of material Donatus' commentary contained. What seems to have happened is that, probably in Ireland (or, less likely, in an Irish foundation on the continent) and probably in the seventh or eighth century, someone made a concerted effort to expand his copy of Servius with a set of notes taken directly or indirectly from Donatus' commentary. He made a number of changes to Servius, mostly fairly minor (e.g., altering *diximus* to *dictum est* throughout); he tried to blend his new notes with the old; he attempted to create a reasonably consistent style. He did not always succeed in his endeavors, but on the whole he did not do badly. But what emerged in the full DS + Servius is not Servius and is certainly not Donatus: it is an original scholarly compilation that reflects both sources, Servius obviously a great deal more than Donatus.

The previous paragraphs gloss over a great many questions about particulars, of interest only to those wanting to immerse themselves in the problems of late antique scholarship. The question of DS matters for several reasons, of which the most important, very clearly, is the evaluation of the material contained in DS notes about Roman literature, Roman antiquities, and Roman scholarship: How reliable is it? What paths did it take to reach the margins of Servius' commentary? Are these simply random notes—as is true, to some extent, of other marginalia in ancient manuscripts such as the Bembine Terence—or are they largely drawn from a single, coherent, scholarly source? Less important but closely related is the significance of this problem for our understanding of the nature and quality of scholarship in late antiquity. Did a grammarian like Servius simply take over Donatus' commentary and dumb it down for his students? Was a fuller and better commentary (Donatus') available beside Servius for centuries, and if so, why did it disappear while Servius survived? And, of course, Donatus is a figure of some importance in the history of ancient scholarship, the author of a commentary (preserved in a very imperfect fashion) on Terence and of the Latin grammar that was standard, and commented on beginning with Servius himself, for centuries. Knowing more about his methods and his abilities is valuable in itself.

Aside from DS, there is important evidence about Donatus' methods. Together with his biography of Virgil (based on Suetonius, and evidently the main source for the other brief lives of the poet), one manuscript transmits a letter from Donatus to one L. Munatius, designed to accompany his commentary.[22] In that letter, the grammarian describes his methods: he has excerpted from many sources, aiming at brevity, but has not said much himself, wishing instead to preserve the words of his authorities: *agnosce igitur saepe in hoc munere conlati<v>o sinceram vocem priscae auctoritatis* ("recognize frequently in this assembled offering the authentic voice of ancient authority").[23] What Donatus says here matches the material in DS: quotations from earlier scholars reproduced in a variorum commentary, keeping himself and his own ideas in the background. Some scholars have used Servius' criticisms of Donatus, of which there are a number in Servius' commentary, to suggest first, that Donatus was not that good a scholar and second, that therefore he was unlikely to have been the model or primary source for such a good scholar as Servius. That is doubly wrong: to judge from the letter and from DS, a great deal of Donatus' work was in fact excerpts from earlier scholarship, and therefore the quality of Donatus' mind (which from his grammars seems pretty good) is not at issue in the value of what he preserves; what is more, to judge the quality of Donatus' work from the relatively few places where Servius criticizes him is to condemn what is good about a book because it also has some errors.[24]

The fact that Donatus wrote a variorum commentary makes it very difficult to be certain about the relationship between his (lost) work and the (extant) Virgilian commentaries: if he was as reticent as he suggests in the letter to Munatius, then most of what later writers might borrow would not be Donatus' words, but those of earlier scholars whose words he appropriated. Furthermore, reconstructing Donatus is almost impossible for another reason: as with his commentary on Terence, which was rapidly excerpted into the margins of copies of Terence, so one might expect that the fairly large and self-standing commentary on Virgil would rapidly have been excerpted into margins. The effect of such excerpting, moreover, is both to simplify and shorten individual notes and to introduce the very real possibility of misunderstanding and error. As with almost all

22. It should be noted that the letter and introduction no longer accompany a text of any form of Servius; their provenance and history are also problematic.

23. Accepting Stok's emendation; Brugnoli and Stok (1997: 15).

24. Criticism of Donatus' scholarship goes back to Ribbeck (1866: 178–86) (*quae restant vituperatione multo saepius quam laude digna*), echoing down to Timpanaro (1986: 148–59; 2001: 115–17). Servius' criticisms seem tendentious, suggesting deliberate carping. The relationship may be similar to Festus' sniping at Verrius Flaccus: in neither case did a desire to establish intellectual independence from an author's major source stop that author from using that source exclusively or almost exclusively.

grammatical writings from late antiquity, stability of text is not to be expected. Even if we could reconstruct a "Donatus" from the later tradition, our "Donatus" would not be Donatus' "Donatus."

In a certain sense, then, Donatus' commentary on Virgil, while real and reflected in the later tradition, is also an imaginary reconstruction: because it was a variorum commentary, it is very easy to imagine that it contained everything worth preserving, or at any rate everything that was preserved, of earlier Virgilian scholarship; and if we believe that, then it goes almost without saying that any sign of genuine early imperial scholarship in the commentary tradition must have come from Donatus. The reasoning is both speculative and circular; but as long as we recognize that "Donatus" is a plausible fiction rather than a real and concrete thing, it does not matter much. "Donatus" is simply shorthand for the scholarly traditions about Virgil.[25]

One reason for believing in an encyclopedic Donatus, however, is that so much does in fact come from him. There is a great deal of scholarship on Virgil that is not in Servius or DS, but which probably derives from Donatus. One such source is the so-called Virgil of Tours, Bern 165, which has corrections and marginalia in no fewer than six different hands, some of which clearly had access to the tradition of Donatus (11.3.7c). Much more important, and much earlier, are the annotations in the Codex Veronensis of Virgil, a palimpsest preserved in the Biblioteca Capitolare in Verona (11.3.3). The manuscript is badly damaged and preserves only a portion of the original annotation. What is there, however, is extremely learned, including both quotations from pre-Virgilian poetry—including part of a missing line of Catullus 64—and citations by name from earlier scholars. There is clear overlap between the Verona scholia and DS, leading some to suspect that Donatus was the source of both.

That is possible, but it is just as likely that the overlaps reflect earlier scholarship that Donatus and the Verona scholiast drew on independently. Comparison of the Servian commentaries with the Verona scholia shows that (the real) Donatus, although authoritative, was not alone: in the fourth century and later, those elements of earlier Virgilian scholarship that grammarians or other learned readers found valuable were collected, recopied, turned into larger commentaries (as in the case of Donatus' variorum commentary)—or excerpted into margins. In other words, we cannot expect, in the tradition of Virgilian commentary or in any other similar tradition, to find a uniform and unified line of descent from antiquity to us. We see what survived; but behind the survivors lie more scholars, more interested readers, and more manuscripts in more places than we can possibly know. In that respect, it is worth mentioning another ancient Virgilian manuscript, the Codex Mediceus: at the end of the *Eclogues*, it contains a subscription by Turcius Rufius Apronianus Asterius, who corrected the text (and wrote a poem about it) while attending the games as consul in 494 CE. The poem is written in

25. For a suitably (perhaps excessively) skeptical view of the Donatus question, see Daintree (1990).

the same hand as a collection of marginal scholia on the *Eclogues*, and both were almost certainly copied, together, into the Codex Mediceus, probably sometime in the early sixth century.[26] Not surprisingly, there seems to be some overlap between the issues the Medicean scholiast thought worthy of comment and the commentaries of Servius and DS. There was, quite simply, a substantial amount of Virgilian exegesis available in late antiquity, certainly in Rome and probably elsewhere as well. The precise relationship among the extant collections cannot be determined, and the pervasive dogmatism of modern scholarship (in support of one reconstruction or another) is simply unjustified. We do not know, and never will: too much is lost—and too much survives.

Only slightly less complicated (and less well understood) is the set of commentaries on the *Eclogues* and *Georgics* known loosely as the Bern Scholia (11.3.4).[27] This exists in multiple forms: the fuller version is the *Scholia Bernensia* proper, a commentary found in the margins of the text of the *Eclogues* and *Georgics* in a ninth-century manuscript from Fleury (B);[28] three later and lesser manuscripts supply what has been lost by damage to the Fleury manuscript.[29] The other form is found as an independent commentary (without a text of Virgil) in three manuscripts of the ninth century, one of which (Paris, Lat. 11308, s. ix) is also the sole source for Donatus' dedicatory letter to L. Munatius; in all of these there are two commentaries in sequence on the *Eclogues* (known as *Explanatio* I and II) followed by a commentary on *Georgics* 1.1–2.91 known as *Brevis expositio*;[30] in a fourth manuscript (Leiden, BPL 135, s. xi) it extends to the end of *Georgics* 2.

Even cursory examination of these texts—the three commentaries on the *Eclogues* and two on the *Georgics*—makes it very clear that they overlap and are related to one another, but (as often seems the case with the Servian corpus too) it is not always possible to define the relationships precisely. Where do they come from, and who wrote them? The manuscripts supply a few, not always

26. See Ihm (1890). On subscriptions, see 9.1 below.

27. For my account of the Bern Scholia I rely heavily on Daintree and Geymonat in *EV* s.v. *scholia non Serviana*.

28. Bern 172 contains *Eclogues* and *Georgics* (with Bern Scholia), and *Aeneid* 1–5 (with some notes that are possibly from DS); the second half of the same manuscript, containing *Aeneid* 6–12 with DS in the margins, is Paris, Lat. 7929 (F, for editors of Servius). The index of manuscripts gives details about fuller descriptions and facsimiles of these manuscripts (and of all others cited in this book).

29. Bern 167 (= C); Bern 165 (= D); Leiden, Voss. Lat. F 79 (= V). The scribe of Bern 167 copied only the contents of the left-hand margin of B; it also contains DS on the later portions of the *Aeneid*, with the same peculiarity (Murgia 1975: 10–14). Bern 165 is the Virgil of Tours, on which see above. At least some of these notes are apparently also to be found in a great many other manuscripts of Virgil.

30. The other two manuscripts are Paris, Lat. 7960 and Florence, Laur. 45.14 (from Tours; for a description see Murgia 1975: 83–4). For description of Paris, Lat. 11308 see Murgia (1975: 26–35).

helpful, answers. In the first place, the title at the end of *Explanatio* I ascribes it to one Junius Filargirius; the similar title at the end of *Explanatio* II adds *Valentiniano*, a dedication, but not (unless it has lost something) to any emperor of that name. More important is the note after the *Eclogues* in the *Scholia Bernensia*: *Haec omnia de commentariis Romanorum congregavi, id est Titi Galli et Gaudentii et maxime Iunilii Flagrii Mediolanensis. Iunilius Flagrius Valentiano Mediolani*. Each of these three commentators, moreover, is cited as an authority for specific notes within the commentary; sometimes more than one of them is cited in the same note, although Gallus is cited only in the commentary on *Georgics* 1.

Most modern authorities consider that the name of the principal authority cited is in fact Junius Filargirius, and that he was a grammarian working in Milan. Of the other two, nothing else is known.[31] Although the *Explanatio* (in both versions) is attributed in the manuscripts to Filargirius, it does not seem likely—given the overlaps between the two versions—that it is his alone, and that it was then combined with commentaries by the other two at a later stage: it seems far more likely, although unprovable, that all the versions of this collection descend from a single commentary composed from the work of all three in late antiquity. Notes attributed in the scholia to Filargirius and to Gaudentius appear to draw on Servius, thus placing their work after the first quarter of the fifth century.[32] What we have, however, must be later than that. In the first place, it is Christian: all three versions of the commentary on the *Eclogues* (4.6) identify *virgo* as Maria; the *progenies* in *Schol. Bern.* is *Saloninus vel Augustus vel Christus vel Marcellus, Octaviae filius*. Some idea of where and when the collection was compiled comes from the presence of glosses in Old Irish, and on *Ecl.* 3.90 *Expl.* I has the note *De Maevio vero nihil reperi, ut Adamnanus ait*. Even though it has become usual to identify this *Adamnanus* with the abbot of Iona who died in 704, there is no particular reason for that, but it is certainly an Irish name. Both the DS tradition and the tradition of the Bern scholia passed through Irish hands, probably in Ireland, but perhaps in an Irish foundation on the continent. We cannot tell.[33]

The manuscripts of the Bern scholia show that, as far as commentary on the *Eclogues* and *Georgics* is concerned, we have every reason to believe that there was, in the early Middle Ages, considerable interplay between the Servian tradition and that of Iuni{li}us and his friends. The manuscript tradition of DS on the *Eclogues* and *Georgics* is itself very poor, and it is not at all easy to tell the commentaries apart. Servius himself, to be sure, is a much more sober commentator than the author(s) of the Bern collection, which offers allegorical readings

31. For information about these three, see most conveniently Kaster (1988) #60, 222, 223.

32. On the Bern Scholia as a form of Servius *auctus*, see Cadili (2008).

33. See Daintree (1999) for a review of the evidence for Virgil in Ireland.

wherever possible.[34] It is perhaps cheering to find, in *Schol. Bern.* on *Ecl.* 1.39–40 not only that Tityrus stands for Virgil, but that the pine trees stand for Rome, the fountains for senators, and *arbusta* for *scholastici*. But beyond the imagination it reveals, it shows all too clearly that these commentaries, as they now exist, were produced and reshaped over several centuries. The most substantial work of composing large-scale commentaries on Virgil was performed in the fourth and fifth centuries—but except for the Verona scholia, we only see the results as they filtered down to the Carolingian age.

From what we can see, then, the three bodies of commentary represented by the Servian corpus, the Bern sylloge, and the Verona scholia seem to be the best representatives of the major lines of Virgilian criticism in antiquity. In each case, there are problems with the kind of representation they give us—the blurring between Donatus, Servius, and the extended Servius; the multiple versions and layers and the peculiar Irish additions to the Bern collection; the sheer fragmentariness and difficulty of reading the Verona scholia—but in combination, they give a sense that there was a strong tradition of exegesis of Virgil, one that focused on grammar and explanation of names, words, myths, and places; one that, for the most part, limited its explanatory horizon to one word, or at most one sentence, at a time. This tradition can in some cases be traced back to Virgil's lifetime, or at least to the reign of Augustus. It becomes more concerned over time with line-by-line exegesis than with elucidation of myth or religion or history. And it begins to take real shape as a tool created by, and for, the grammarian and his pupils by the early second century at the latest.

But this picture of the Virgilian exegetical tradition needs to be framed and somewhat modified: these three corpora are not the only representatives of the tradition they represent. One important text that is considerably earlier is the so-called *Grammatica Vergiliana* of Aemilius Asper (12.5), composed probably late in the second century. Although the authenticity of this text was questioned in the nineteenth century, it is almost certainly genuine. What survives consists of ten columns of the lower script of a palimpsest, probably written in the fourth century, now damaged and difficult to read, but having an unmistakable running header saying *Vergilius Aspri*. It contains a very fragmentary section on the preposition, then one headed *De interiectionibus*, followed immediately by a long section *De casibus*. The last extant, and very fragmentary, section is headed *De generalibus et specialibus*. Under each of these headings, Asper lists various usages and departures from what might be considered "standard" Latin: under prepositions, he discusses the different meanings of *pro*, each illustrated by a quotation from Virgil; under interjections, what survives is a discussion of *heu*: examples of usage, followed by the remark *Deinde attendendus etiam usus ille interiectionum, quod, quae sunt severiores, has in carmine graviore usurpat, ut e et heu, at a, quod est*

34. On the different types of historical/allegorical interpretation available in late antiquity, Stok (2014) provides an illuminating discussion of commentary on the Sixth *Eclogue*.

humilius, tantum in bu[colicis . . . (534.5–7H: "We should pay attention to the use of interjections: more solemn ones like *e* and *heu* are used in the more serious poem, while the more lowly *a* only appears in the <*Eclogues*>"). This is followed by appropriate quotations from the *Eclogues*. Under the much bigger rubric *De casibus*, Asper goes through passages where (in his interpretation, at any rate) one case is used for another: nominative for accusative, accusative for nominative, nominative for vocative, and on, through accusative for dative. That in turn is followed by a paragraph (or perhaps more; there is a gap) on variable declensions; then on *singularia tantum* declined as plural and the reverse, leading eventually to figures such as the *schema alcmanicum* (named in Greek) and a final paragraph on Virgil's use of numbers, from three to a thousand. The final extant sections are on *genus* and *species*, instances of Virgil's use of one for the other, and on some verbal constructions.

Several things are striking about this text. One is that it is meant as a sequel to Asper's commentary: in discussing the *schema alcmanicum* (which he defines as *ubi proposito singulari adsumitur non suo loco plurale*; in modern usage, cases in which a plural verb separates two singular subjects), he notes *quod genus et ab Homero usurpatum in commentariis pluribus exemplis struimus* (537.25: "This variety of schema is used by Homer too and I have illustrated it with many examples in my commentaries"); and indeed, as Tomsin points out, there are comments attributed explicitly to Asper in DS and the Verona Scholia that are very similar in content and method to the examples given in the grammatical palimpsest.[35] Another is the singularly close and precise attention to Virgilian usage, with his repeated instructions *attendendum* and *adnotandum*: these are very clearly addressed to students. And finally, it is worth observing that Asper seems to assimilate the discussion of Virgilian usage to the formal structure of an *ars grammatica*: the early part of the extant text is about the parts of speech, and after that, introducing the section *De casibus*, he moves from the parts of speech to their accidents (534.12: *Qui autem partes orationis explicare voluerunt, ea, quae his accidunt, ut* . . . where the text breaks off); the discussion of the accidents is itself followed—at what distance we do not know—by a discussion of tropes and figures. In both respects, Asper's organization is comparable to that of the *Ars maior* of Donatus.

Although our impression of Asper's approach is clearly skewed by the existence of this text, it seems likely that his main interests were, in fact, grammar and style. So too Servius and the other commentaries discussed above: they devote at least as much attention to explanation of Virgil's language as they do to the content of the poems. That is definitely not true, however, of the other important Virgilian commentaries. Ps.-Probus' commentary on *Eclogues* and *Georgics* (11.3.5), in its extant form compiled no earlier than the fifth century, begins with a life of the poet and an introduction to pastoral poetry, but the vast majority of the notes elucidate names, generally mythical. As it stands, the text shows clear signs of more

35. Tomsin (1952: 25–8), following Ribbeck (1866: 135–6).

than one source: not only are the longer notes supplemented by comments that clearly derive from marginal glosses, but at the end of each book of the *Georgics* there is a supplementary set of notes, occasionally disagreeing with notes in the body of the text. The most striking note in Ps.-Probus is the huge and learned discussion of cosmology attached to *Ecl.* 6.31, beginning ominously with *Hactenus breviter* and going on for nearly thirteen pages (331.29–44.18) in Hagen's edition. There are some notes in Ps.-Probus related to comments in Servius or in the Verona scholia, but it appears to have independent sources as well, and it illustrates once more the complexity and the breadth of the tradition of Virgilian exegesis in late antiquity.

The school tradition, not surprisingly, dominates in this material: *enarratio poetarum* prevails. But Virgil was also too important to be left to the grammarians: he was the cultural property of everyone who read Latin. Of the second-century work (presumably) on Virgilian rhetoric, Florus' *Vergilius orator an poeta*, we have only the preface; on the other hand, we possess almost the whole vast *Interpretationes Vergilianae* composed by Tiberius Claudius Donatus (not the Aelius Donatus on whose work Servius leaned) in the fifth century.[36] This Donatus, indeed, is proud of not being a grammarian. His work is addressed to his son: *Cum adverterem nihil magistros discipulis conferre quod sapiat, scriptores autem commentariorum non docendi studio, sed memoriae suae causa quaedam favorabili stilo, multa tamen involuta reliquisse, haec fili carissime, tui causa conscripsi* . . . (1.1.5–9: "When I observed that teachers were giving their pupils nothing intelligent and that writers of commentaries, less eager to teach than to be memorable, said some things elegantly but left a great deal confused, I wrote this book for you, dearest boy"). Not to be read alone, he goes on to say, but to supplement the stuff his kid is being fed by the schools; from Ti. Donatus' point of view, Virgil is the perfect rhetorician, setting up everything properly in the plot to enhance the character of Aeneas, and the *Aeneid* is itself a great textbook of rhetoric—and indeed of life: *Quo fit ut Vergiliani carminis lector rhetoricis praeceptis instrui possit et omnia vivendi agendique officia reperire* (1.6.15-17: "The result is that someone who reads Virgil's poem can be equipped with the precepts of rhetoric and find all the obligations of life and performance").[37] That, after more than 1,250 pages, he was able to say to his son that his work was written rapidly and selectively because of his increasing age, and then that, should he survive, he intended to produce a Virgilian encyclopedia discussing all the characters of the *Aeneid* and (2.643.1–4) *oppidorum insularumque rationem et regionum, montium, camporum, fontium*

36. There are gaps in the surviving text in the commentary on books 4, 7, 8, and 12, and the very end is missing (the gap in the printed editions at 6.1–157 has now been filled; see Marshall 1993). My account of the remaining works in the Virgilian tradition is brief, as they offer no great problems of identification or transmission; for bibliography, see 11.3 below.

37. A brief but sympathetic appraisal is in Marshall (1997: 5–7), who speaks of his "moral urgency."

vel fluminum, templorum ac fanorum, herbarum quin etiam et lignorum vocabula et cetera his similia ("an account of towns and islands and the names of regions, mountains, fields, springs and streams, temples and shrines, and even plants and kinds of wood and other similar things") is a terrifying thought. Needless to say, that proposed work does not survive and was probably never written.

In his view that Virgil was too important to be left to the grammarians, of course, Ti. Donatus was right—and he was not alone. Not only was Virgil used as a text for the next level of education (as by Florus and Ti. Donatus),[38] he was regarded in some respects as a source for all knowledge. The clearest example of this is given by the *Saturnalia* of Macrobius, written after 430 CE. In it, Roman aristocrats and men of learning (overlapping categories) devote the eve and the first three days of the holiday to discussing Virgil: his religious and philosophical erudition, his rhetorical skill, his Greek learning, his knowledge of earlier Latin literature, his style, and more. The young Servius is one of the participants in the dialogue—an anachronism in the dramatic setting of (probably) December 383, allusively acknowledged in Macrobius' preface—and it is not surprising to find considerable overlaps between the scholarly content of the *Saturnalia* and the commentaries of both Servius and DS.[39] The *Saturnalia* takes its content from a number of learned sources—Aulus Gellius, Plutarch, the commentary of Donatus, and more—and places it in the context not of the school, but of elevated aristocratic conversation; it should be seen as a product and reflection of the same milieu that produced the beautiful and expensive manuscripts of Virgil, Livy, Cicero, and others in the same period. In each of Macrobius' three works (his now fragmentary comparison of the Greek and Latin verb, his Neoplatonic commentary on Cicero's *Dream of Scipio*, and the *Saturnalia*, written in that order) he uses the grammatical and scholarly tradition, respects it, and attempts to write works that take their topics beyond the limited horizon of the schoolroom.

Macrobius' view of Virgil as the embodiment of the learning that was conveyed through a literary education—the source of all cultural knowledge—is not unique to him. Within the frame of rhetoric, Tiberius Donatus has something of the same idea; Macrobius' contemporary, the grammarian Phocas, is comparable to him in his reverence for the Virgilian text as representative of learning and cultivation.[40]

38. The uses of Virgil sometimes went beyond straightforward *enarratio poetarum* to much more active engagement with the text. The Codex Salmasianus contains within the anthology collected in Vandal Africa in the early 530s not only a dozen Virgilian centos (*Anth. Lat.* 7–18R), but also several rhetorical exercises in verse on Virgilian themes: a long letter of Dido to Aeneas (83R); fifteen lines on the theme *Nec tibi diva parens* (255R); and a poem by Coronatus (223R; on his grammatical work see 12.17) on *Vivo equidem vitamque extrema per omnia duco*.

39. On the anachronism, see *Sat.* 1.1.5, with Kaster (2011a) ad loc. The best general introduction to Macrobius and the *Saturnalia* is now Kaster (2011a: xi–lii); for further bibliography, see 11.3.2 below.

40. See Kaster (2011a: xxi).

One other work on Virgil of (probably) the early sixth century deserves to be mentioned. Fabius Planciades Fulgentius composed an *Expositio Virgilianae continentiae*, a work that interprets all of Virgil's works as hermetic and allegorical, with the *Aeneid* in particular as a reflection simultaneously of the stages of education, the stages of human life, and the philosophical underpinnings of human existence.[41] What is more, Fulgentius has an authority for this interpretation: the work is conceived as a dialogue between the author and the shade of Virgil himself, who explains, for instance, the opening line of the poem to Fulgentius as follows (89.16–25 Helm):

> Nam ut tuis saturantius aliquid adhuc satisfaciamus ingeniis, trifarius in vita humana gradus est, primum habere, deinde regere quod habeas, tertium vero ornare quod regis. Ergo tres gradus istos in uno versu nostro considera positos, id est: "arma", "virum" et "primus": "arma," id est virtus, pertinet ad substantiam corporalem, "virum," id est sapientia, pertinet ad substantiam sensualem, "primus," vero, id est princeps, pertinet ad substantiam censualem, quo sit ordo huiusmodi: habere, regere, ornare.

> To provide something more satisfying to your mind, there are three steps in human life. The first is to have it; the second is to control what you have, the third is to adorn what you control. So consider these three steps as they are placed in one verse of mine, that is: *arma*, *virum*, and *primus*. *Arma*, in other words *virtus*, applies to our physical being; *virum*, in other words *sapientia*, applies to our sensory being; and *primus*, in other words *princeps*, applies to our intellectual and critical being. Thus the order is as follows: to have, to control, to enhance.

Virgil as the source of interpretation of his own text makes literal the approach of the grammatical tradition, to interpret a text from the author's own usage (originally applied to Homer); it also embodies the late antique perception of Virgil as the source of all knowledge. This is not the place to offer an account of the traditions of Virgil in the Middle Ages as magus, as oracle, and as the source of all wisdom and all knowledge and a proto-Christian, but it is worth at least mentioning the strangest manifestation of that tradition, the Irish grammarian who gives himself the name Virgilius Maro sometime in the seventh century and presents the poet, his characters, and his commentators all as equivalent, and real, sources of knowledge of Latin.[42]

41. For bibliography on Fulgentius, see 12.23 below; his *Expositio sermonum antiquorum* is discussed in 6.2 above. He is not the same person as the bishop Fulgentius of Ruspe.

42. For a collection of readings in the later Virgilian tradition, see Ziolkowski and Putnam (2008); the classic study of Virgil's medieval afterlife remains Comparetti (1997, originally published 1872). For Virgilius Maro, see 9.4 and 13.30 below.

b) Cicero

The scholarly tradition surrounding Cicero is not as gaudy as the collection of eccentrics that attached itself to Virgil, but it is nonetheless worth exploring.[43] Cicero, like Virgil, was a school author from the earliest times; Cicero, like Virgil, received commentary beginning not long after his death; and the various works of Cicero, like those of Virgil, could be seen from different perspectives and used for different purposes. The Ciceronian tradition is much scrappier than the Virgilian tradition, but again, it gives some indication of the varieties of exegesis in antiquity and late antiquity.

In the Virgilian tradition, the *Eclogues* and *Georgics* seem to have attracted a different kind of attention from the *Aeneid*—more allegorical, more Christian, more Irish—and in a less exotic way, the different parts of the Ciceronian corpus were treated differently. Three kinds of works received exegesis in antiquity (at least, to the extent of our knowledge): the speeches were discussed both in grammatical and rhetorical education;[44] the rhetorical works, particularly *De inventione* and *Topica*, were discussed in rhetorical and perhaps philosophical education; and the *Somnium Scipionis* was a philosophical text, a primer of Neoplatonism. All these are very different kinds of work, intended for different audiences. Even within the tradition of commentary on Cicero's speeches, however, one has some sense of the varieties of exegesis that were needed and were available at different periods, as well as seeing, on a smaller scale, exactly the same kind of identity crises that beset the tradition of Virgilian commentary.

For commentaries on Cicero's speeches, we possess much more from a much earlier date than is the case for Virgil. The surviving portion of the commentary of Asconius (first century CE) is the earliest significant piece of Roman exegesis; as discussed earlier, his comments are almost exclusively historical and what survives was originally part of a complete commentary on Cicero's speeches in chronological order. The next surviving commentary had its origin a century or so later: the Bobbio scholia (which survive in a damaged form quite difficult to read, as the lower script of a palimpsest) emphasize history, like Asconius, but add to that a strong interest in matters of rhetoric and diction. Again, like Asconius, the Bobbio scholia seem originally to have been a complete commentary on all the speeches in chronological order.[45] The surviving text of Asconius seems to be authentic, aside from scribal errors and damage in transmission; the Bobbio scholia,

43. For bibliography on Ciceronian commentaries, see 11.2 below.

44. Cicero was one of the authors of the so-called *quadriga* (Cicero, Sallust, Terence, Virgil) used in elementary education and enshrined in the *Exempla elocutionum* of Arusianus Messius (12.4). The huge number of quotations in the grammarians shows how fond they were of the speeches.

45. This is not the place for, and there is no satisfactory answer to, the question of what "all the speeches" means. Suffice it to say that both Asconius and the Bobbio scholiast appear to have written commentaries on all the speeches they knew and had texts of—but that "all" may be different for the two of them.

on the other hand, exist in what is probably a fourth-century revision, possibly by one Vulcatius, of the second-century original. In both cases, however, the extant form is a selection: neither the five speeches in Asconius nor the twelve in the Bobbio palimpsest are in chronological order; each has been manipulated, either by chance or deliberately, to provide only a part of what must originally have been massive works.

The pattern of selection and reorganization in these cases, moreover, extends well beyond antiquity. Asconius survives only in humanistic manuscripts, and his work survives together with a quite different commentary, now known as Ps.-Asconius: a late antique commentary on the first half of the *Verrines* (to 2.2.35) that is largely exegetical and grammatical. Conversely, there is a piece of the same commentary represented by the Bobbio scholia surviving in a different context, a set of notes, again on the *Verrines* (2.1.45–62) preserved as part of the so-called *Scholia Gronoviana* which survive in somewhat different forms in two manuscripts of the ninth and tenth centuries now in Leiden. The combination and separation of commentaries is similar to the Virgilian tradition, in which texts of the Bern sylloge appear in the same manuscripts as the DS commentary on the *Aeneid*. Collections of commentary, like collections of texts on grammatical subjects (on which see 9.4 below) come into being as a result of the interests and needs of readers. In the case of the Bobbio scholia, unless commentary on the *Verrines* has disappeared from the palimpsest—by no means impossible—the rather odd collection of a dozen speeches must have had some rationale we can no longer discern; conversely, the addition of commentary on the *Verrines* to Asconius' collection of five speeches points to someone's desire to include the *Verrines* in whatever context the archetype of the rest of the manuscript was created.

The collection of the Bobbio scholia is likely to remain opaque: it almost seems as if this set of speeches, including four from the *Post reditum* collection interrupted by *Pro Milone*, and with chronological order consistently violated, was chosen to avoid the most popular texts. To judge from the index to *Grammatici Latini* (not perfectly accurate, but generally reliable), only five of the speeches in this collection are ever quoted by a grammarian, and of these only *Pro Sestio* and *Pro Milone* have any breadth of citation, while *Pro Sulla* and *Pro Flacco* appear only in Arusianus Messius, and *Pro Plancio* only there and in Priscian. These were not standard texts in the grammarian's classroom.

What was standard in the classroom, however, was the *Verrines*, along with the *Catilinarians*, the *Caesarianae*, and the *Philippics*, the significant groups (other than *Post reditum*) of related speeches; and if we look at what are clearly somewhat later collections of commentary, they are the speeches that predominate. The *Verrines* are discussed not only by Ps.-Asconius and the Gronovian scholia, but in fact by three different commentators in the Gronovian collection and by the collection represented by the Cluny and Ambrosian manuscripts as well, not to mention five marginal notes in the Vatican palimpsest of the *Verrines*. The Caesarian and Catilinarian orations appear in the Gronovian and the Cluny/

Ambrosian collection. But the shifts and combinations in these traditions, particularly in the Gronovian manuscripts and the Cluny/Ambrosian collection, are themselves indicative of the ways in which ancient commentary survived or was lost.

Of these two sets of notes, the Cluny collection is easier to comprehend. Two manuscripts, London, BL Add. 47678 (formerly Holkham Hall 387, a ninth-century manuscript originally from Cluny) and Milan, Ambros. C 29 inf. of the tenth or eleventh century, contain marginal scholia to Cicero; the speeches included are *In Catilinam* 1–4, *Pro Marcello, Pro Ligario, Pro rege Deiotaro,* and *Verrines* 2.2, clearly a set of ancient school texts. Identical notes appear in some places in the two manuscripts, while each also contains notes not found in the other. In other words, we have two sets of notes drawn from a single exegetical commentary, itself probably compiled no later than the sixth century. The notes now exist as marginalia; whether the shared model was marginal scholia or a continuous commentary we cannot tell.

The Cluny/Ambrosian scholia reveal what is in fact a regular occurrence in the transmission of commentaries (and in fact other grammatical and lexicographical texts as well): they are not stable, but change in accordance with the needs or interests of the scribes and users of the manuscripts. What gets copied is what is wanted, not necessarily everything that is available. That leads to problems of definition and reconstruction: the Ambrosian scholia, as they now exist, are a text in themselves, and so are the Cluny scholia, but they are, when taken together, witnesses to a larger collection from which both scribes drew and which is now largely lost. The same process of excerpting (from the scribes' point of view) and reconstruction of a lost original (from our point of view) takes place with the *Scholia Gronoviana*, but here it is far more complicated and in some respects insoluble.

The main witness to this commentary is Leiden, Voss. Lat. Q 130, a manuscript written at Tours probably in the second quarter of the ninth century, containing portions of a continuous commentary on a group of speeches of Cicero.[46] As it now stands, it contains commentary on parts of the *Verrines* followed by notes on *In Catilinam* 2, 3, and 4; *Pro Ligario, Pro Marcello,* and *Pro rege Deiotaro; Pro Sex. Roscio; De Imperio Cn. Pompei*; and *Pro Milone*. But another Leiden manuscript, Voss. Lat. O 88, written at the end of the ninth century, includes in a glossary a set of words from Cicero's speeches with explanations drawn from the Gronovian scholia. The order in Voss. Lat. O 88 is different—the *Verrines* come at the end rather than the beginning—and the contents show that the collection once included *Pro Caelio* between *Pro Milone* and the beginning of the *Verrines*.

In its origins, the commentary on Cicero's speeches represented by the Leiden manuscripts was a large and complex text: it had arguments for each speech and fairly extensive notes, with an emphasis on historical background and on rhetoric

46. I note that in Stangl's edition (and all earlier discussions I have seen) the shelf number is given as VLQ 138. I use the number in the Leiden website.

and argument. It included three of the four most familiar sets of Ciceronian speeches (*Catilinarians*, *Caesarians*, and *Verrines*, but not *Philippics*, at least in what we now have), and it ranged over Cicero's entire career. The order of the speeches is not chronological, but Goetz's suggestion (1891: 432) that it moved from easier to harder does not seem very likely either. It may reflect simply what was available at Tours in this period.

What now survives in Voss. Lat. Q 130 has some distinct peculiarities. In the first place, the commentaries on the shorter speeches (setting aside the *Verrines* for the moment) have gaps: the text of *In Cat.* 2 begins with §11, and is also missing §18–23; *In Cat.* 3.2–14 is missing, and so too *Marc.* 2–20, *Deiot.* 10–32, *Rosc.* 20–34, *Imp. Cn. Pomp.* 1–3; the commentary on *Mil.* breaks off after §1. Gaps themselves are not surprising, and they are found in many medieval representatives of ancient commentaries. In this case, however, every one of these gaps comes at the transition between one leaf of the manuscript and the next. That would make perfect sense if the manuscript itself had lost pages, but it has not: the text, written by one scribe, is complete. What that suggests is that VLQ 130 is an exact copy of an earlier manuscript that was missing pages.

When we turn to the pages containing the *Verrines*, the situation is even more peculiar. The commentary is clearly not complete: while there is commentary on the *Divinatio* (with a gap at page-end between §8 and §71) and on parts of *Verr.* 1 and 2.1, it comes to an abrupt end at the end of a page in the middle of 2.1.62. It is also far less orderly than my summary suggests: there are gaps, pages out of order, and one passage on which there are two quite different sets of comments, clearly by different authors. Stangl analyzed it further: he believed that there were the remains of three different commentaries in the Gronovian scholia on the *Verrines*.[47] To his division, I have added notes about the gaps within the commentary that match the end of one folio and the beginning of another (similar to those in the other speeches, discussed above):

Pages	Content	Page-end gaps	Author
foll. 1–10	*Div.* 3–73, *Verr.* 1.1–21	beginning; loss of *Div.* 8–71; end	Gronovianus B
foll. 11–16	*Verr.* 2.1.1–5; 2.1.45–62	beginning; end	Gronovianus A
foll. 17–18	*Verr.* 1.16–30	beginning; end	Gronovianus C
foll. 19–20	*Verr.* 1.30–45	beginning; loss of 1.33–8; end	Gronovianus B

In Stangl's view, foll. 1–10 and 19–20 were by the same person, Gronovianus B, and in his edition he rearranged the pages so that the two were continuous—with, of course, a page-end gap between the end of fol. 10 (*Verr.* 1.21) and the beginning of fol. 19 (*Verr.* 1.30). He saw the intervening pages (foll. 11–18) as

47. See Stangl (1884); for further bibliography see 11.2.5 below.

fragments of two different commentaries (Gron. A and Gron. C) that had been sandwiched between the two parts of Gron. B. As in the commentary on the other speeches, it would appear from the gaps and the tidy divisions between sections, matching the page breaks, that this part of the manuscript had had the same kind of origin as the other part, an exact copy of a manuscript from which pages had been lost—except in this case, two chunks of extraneous matter had been stuffed into one of the gaps. We get a picture of a damaged manuscript, broken off near the end of the first *Verrine*, which some helpful soul had tried to fix by adding commentary from another manuscript, but putting the additions in the wrong place.

That part of the story may be right: the fact that there are two very different commentaries on *Verr.* 1.16–21 might have been caused by an addition that was neat at the end—Gron. C ends where the second part of Gron. B takes up—but messy at the beginning. But of course it is made even messier by the presence of six leaves of commentary on *Verr.* 2.1 in the middle of a commentary on *Verr.* 1, and becomes still odder when one looks at the section of the text that Stangl assigned to Gron. A. There are two problems: one is the fact that the commentary on 2.1.45–62 is closely related to the Bobbio scholia (and is printed with them by Hildebrandt) while the commentary on 2.1.1–5 is a grammatical commentary very much like Ps.-Asconius. Given the habits of this manuscript, moreover, one would expect that the gap between 2.1.5 and 2.1.45 would match the end of a page; but this is the one place in the whole collection of Gronovian scholia where there is no physical sign of a gap—the two parts, by two different authors, are continuous, in the middle of a page, with no sign of a break.

All this is confusing to say the least, but the complexity of this manuscript provides important evidence about the history of these texts—from the one manuscript Voss. Lat. Q 130 we can infer the earlier existence of three or perhaps four different commentaries on the *Verrines* which had been amalgamated at least twice: the two parts of Gron. A must have come together from different sources and been copied as a unit before they were combined into a single manuscript with the other two commentaries on the *Verrines*; and that manuscript in turn must have been damaged through severe loss of pages before it was again copied as a single text. Commentaries on Cicero's speeches could be divided up, combined, and recombined in accordance with their availability and the interest of the compiler. Most of the medieval commentaries in both the *Scholia Cluniacensia* and the *Scholia Gronoviana* were derived (possibly at some remove) from late-antique manuscripts, themselves derived (again, possibly at some remove) from at least three ancient commentaries of different sorts, like the three partially extant commentaries of Asconius (historical), the Bobbio scholia (historical and rhetorical), and Ps.-Asconius (exegetical); but it is fairly clear that these are only types and possible sources, as notes and commentaries of different types flowed from one set of notes to another, from one margin to another. What we perceive is only what survives, and that is only a small fragment of what must once have existed.

In the case of commentaries on a school text, for use in fairly elementary education, most of the annotation is directed to what one might think of as its obvious purpose, to help the novice read a text for the first time: necessary information about names, facts, words, and grammar (not necessarily in that order). But that is very clearly not the only aim of the commentator: one could imagine, for instance, that Asconius' purpose in his commentary on Cicero was less to teach his sons about Cicero than to use Cicero to teach his sons about the history of the late Republic; similarly, it is quite clear that (to pick an egregious case) Ps.-Probus' note on *Ecl.* 6.31 has very little to do with Virgil, and is instead an exposition of cosmology tied loosely to the text of the *Eclogues*. And while the medieval commentaries on Cicero's speeches, unlike the ancient ones, are fairly elementary in their annotations, the commentaries on other works of Cicero, notably *De inventione, Topica*, and *Somnium Scipionis*, show a broader range of interests.

In the case of *De inventione* two commentaries survive: the fourth-century exposition by Marius Victorinus on the whole text, and the incomplete (probably through damage) commentary of Grillius on *Inv.* 1.1–22, probably written in the fifth century. *De inventione* was the simplest of Cicero's writings on rhetoric and oratory and the most amenable to being used as an instructional text. But Cicero's text was certainly not enough for the instructional needs of the late-antique classroom. Both Victorinus and Grillius wrote commentaries intended to supplement rather than explain Cicero's treatise, using it as the base for more elaborate expositions of rhetorical theory; in Victorinus' case, it is philosophical as well as rhetorical. It is indicative that both texts begin by treating Cicero's preface itself as an example of rhetorical prose and offer a rhetorical analysis of it before proceeding to explain the contents of the treatise itself.

The same is true, in fact, of Boethius' commentary on Cicero's *Topica*. The work is not complete: six books survive, taking the commentary through §76 of Cicero's work, but the end of Book 6 and the one further book that must have followed are lost—or were possibly never completed. Boethius' commentary and the accompanying further work *De differentiis topicis* were his last works on logic, completed early in the sixth century. In addition to explaining *De inventione*, Marius Victorinus had also started to comment on the *Topica*; according to Boethius' account in his preface, Victorinus wrote four books but did not get very far.[48] Like the commentaries on *De inventione*, moreover, Boethius' commentary uses Cicero's text as a vehicle for expounding his own theory of topics, further elaborated in his companion work.[49] Nor is Boethius' commentary

48. Boethius, pp. 270–1 Orelli–Baiter (pp. 21–2 Stump); Marius Victorinus reached the end of *Top.* 23.

49. *Topos* (*locus*) has a very technical meaning in rhetorical theory, which Cicero defines (*Topica* 8) as follows: *Itaque licet definire locum esse argumenti sedem, argumentum autem rationem quae rei dubiae faciat fidem* ("Therefore we may define a Place as the location of an argument, and an argument as a reasoning that lends belief to a doubtful issue"; transl. Reinhardt). On Boethius' elaboration of the theory, see the brief and lucid account of Reinhardt (2003: 29–35).

set out in lemmatized form: instead, his own extended essay contains numerous paraphrases and quotations from Cicero. The *Topica* itself was widely read from the Carolingian period on, and there are a great many manuscripts. Of the fifty-two manuscripts earlier than the fourteenth century listed by Reinhardt, twenty-one also contain Boethius' commentary and another contains excerpts from it; of those twenty-one, six interweave the commentary with Cicero's text, section by section. That makes perfect sense: in certain respects, Boethius' commentary, designed to be read independently of the text of Cicero, lends itself to a structure not so different from that employed by Asconius at the very beginning of the tradition.[50]

The final text of Cicero on which ancient commentary survives is the *Somnium Scipionis*. There are two commentaries: one is a brief work by Favonius Eulogius, probably writing in Africa at the end of the fourth century or the beginning of the fifth, which consists of two essays, the first on the numbers from one to nine, the second on the music of the spheres. The work is attached (fairly loosely) to Cicero's text—but only to two sentences of it. The longer and more famous work is by Macrobius, a commentary in two books that was extremely popular in the Middle Ages. It too is only loosely attached to Cicero (although more closely than Favonius), but again, Macrobius uses Cicero as a vehicle for an essay on philosophy. His goal is to lead his readers upward to the spirituality of Neoplatonism; he does so in considerable detail that has very little resemblance to anything Cicero actually said. In that respect, his *Saturnalia* seems much closer to being an explanation of Virgil's text than the *Commentary* is of Cicero's.

c) Horace

Horace was a school author to a lesser extent than Virgil and Cicero. He is not one of Arusianus' *quadriga*; Donatus did not write a commentary on his poetry; the grammarians quote Virgil roughly eight times more often than they quote Horace, and there are more citations from the *Georgics* alone than from all of Horace's works. And yet he was obviously read and studied with considerable care, and the interpretive tradition, if we cannot trace it back to Horace's lifetime as we can in the case of Virgil, certainly begins no later than the middle of the first century CE.

The two oldest and most important extant commentaries on Horace go under the names of Pomponius Porphyrio and Helenius Acro. What is transmitted under the name of Porphyrio is clearly based on what the real Porphyrio wrote in the early third century, but it has been both abridged and interpolated a great deal. The commentary to which Acro's name was attached in the fifteenth century, however, has nothing at all to do with what the real Acro wrote sometime around 200 CE; it is, indeed, not a single commentary but an amalgam of at least two, put together in late antiquity. Neither Porphyrio nor Ps.-Acro, in the form in which we have them, is a product of the high empire: they are works of the fifth

50. On the form of Boethius' commentary, see Reinhardt (2003: 84–5); on the manuscripts, Reinhardt (2003: 73–7). The Orelli–Baiter edition leaves the relationship between Boethius' commentary and the interspersed text of the *Topica* very unclear.

century at the earliest, and although they represent an older tradition, they do not reflect it completely or accurately.

As far as genuine, ancient commentary on Horace is concerned, our information is not large, but it is clear that the central concern of Horatian exegesis (as it survives) was not the explanation of grammar. Instead, from a fairly early stage, readers of Horace required help in two different areas: meter and content. I have discussed above (4.2) the work that marks the beginning of metrical analysis of Horace, the treatise of Caesius Bassus written in the reign of Nero; Caesius, a lyric poet himself, wrote to explain meter not just for readers but for those attempting to write poetry themselves; and it would appear from what remains that Horace was an author to be emulated. The tradition of writing about Horatian meter goes on for centuries: the grammarian Servius, in addition to explaining Virgil, wrote two short works on meter, one of them devoted specifically to the meters of Horatian lyric.[51] Knowledge of how to scan Horace was just as essential to students reading him as to students studying verse composition.

Students (and would-be poets) probably needed help in Horatian metrics somewhat sooner than they needed help with the content of the poetry, but that too was not easy. The extant late-antique commentaries drew on a tradition of exegesis that went back at least to the first century and is attested not much later than the work of Caesius. Porphyrio cites (on *Serm.* 2.3.83) an explanation by one Claranus of the link between the island Anticyra and the plant hellebore, and one of the lives of Horace transmitted in some manuscripts of Ps.-Acro names a Modestus as someone who commented on Horace. We know from Martial (10.21.1–2) that Claranus and Modestus were grammarians and Martial's contemporaries—although we know little more about them.[52] Porphyrio also twice refers to people who have written about characters in Horace (*qui de personis Horatianis scripserunt; Serm.* 1.3.21, 90–1) who explained who Maenius and Evander were. We cannot date those writers (if the plural is not simply exaggeration), but they are probably also relatively early: it does not take long (witness

51. On Servius, see 11.3.1 and 12.40 below. Other late antique texts specifically on Horatian meter include Atilius Fortunatianus *De metris Horatianis*, the short text appended to Apthonius and probably by him, and the anonymous *De epodo octosyllabo* (12.46.8c[iv]). Horatian meter is also discussed in the last part of Apthonius' larger treatise and in the *Ars* of Diomedes. A version of Servius' treatise is also prefixed to the text of the *Odes* in Paris, Lat. 7900A, of which more shortly.

52. Claranus is also mentioned as a grammarian by Ausonius (*Ep.* 13) together with Scaurus and Asper (see *GRFM* 342). There are two grammarians named Modestus: Iulius Modestus the pupil of Hyginus (and thus early first century) and Aufidius Modestus in the late first and early second centuries. Almost certainly it was Aufidius, not Iulius, who commented on Horace; he may also be the Modestus who wrote about Virgil, although that is much less certain. Mazzarino (*GRFM* 9–12) gives a sensible review of the evidence.

Asconius on Cicero) for knowledge of historical facts and persons to fade, particularly in the minds of schoolchildren.

Interest in grammar proper, as in other traditions, begins later. One commentary, by the Hadrianic grammarian Q. Terentius Scaurus, is known to have been written before the genuine work of Helenius Acro. As a grammarian, Scaurus is well known and some of his writings still (in some form) survive.[53] His commentary on Horace was not so lucky and is directly attested by only two quotations in Charisius, referring to Scaurus "in book ten of his commentaries on the *Ars poetica*" (263.11, 272.27B). The idea that even a wordy commentator could take ten books to cover a poem of fewer than five hundred lines is scarcely credible, but a commentary devoting one book to each book of Horace could very well have the *Ars poetica* as book 10; in all probability, Scaurus wrote a substantial commentary on the complete works of Horace. The two comments surviving in Charisius concern the adverb *impariter* (which Scaurus believed Horace made up) and the use of *primus* for *in primis*, with the comment *non qui ante omnes, sed ante quem nemo est . . . quo genere plures primi accipi possunt* ("not the person who comes before everyone, but the one before whom there is nobody. . . . In that category there can be more than one person considered 'first'"). Both are grammatical comments; we have no idea how much Scaurus had to say about any other aspect of Horace. And while Scaurus' work was probably used by the later commentaries, we cannot identify anything specific.[54]

After Scaurus comes the genuine Helenius Acro. He too is quoted by Charisius, but his commentary on Terence, not his commentary on Horace. To that, in fact, we have only a single reference: Porphyrio on *Serm.* 1.8.2 says: *Memini me legere apud Helenium Acronem* [*helenum cronem* in the manuscripts] *Saganam nomine fuisse Horati temporibus Pompei sagam senatoris, qui a triumviris proscriptus est* ("I remember reading in Helenius Acro that Sagana was the name of a witch belonging to the senator Pompeius, a contemporary of Horace, who was proscribed by the triumvirs"). The language seems odd, because it suggests that Porphyrio was relying on his memory of a book no longer at hand. That may be disingenuous: most commentary is tralatitious, and if Porphyrio really did not draw on Acro except from memory, then he is fairly unusual.

The commentary of Porphyrio differs from other late antique commentaries on Latin authors both in its diction and in its relative lack of interest in grammatical exegesis. The condition in which we have received it, however, makes the genuine Porphyrio's characteristics somewhat harder to discern. The extant text survives in two relatively early (ninth–tenth centuries) manuscripts and then nothing until several copies made in the Renaissance. It is preserved as a continuous commentary (written as an independent text, not in the margins of a copy of Horace), but it was not always in that form. At some point, it was written as

53. On Scaurus, see 5.4 above and 8.5 and 12.39 below.

54. Although Servius on *Aen* 1.1 (*PRIMVS non ante quem nemo, sed post quem nullus*) almost looks like a reply.

a marginal commentary; indeed, the presence of a note (on *Sat.* 1.9.52) which refers to the marks for division of speakers in the manuscript in which the commentary itself was written has led many scholars to believe that the real Porphyrio put his commentary in the margins of a text of Horace. That is unlikely: when Porphyrio wrote, in the early third century, books were generally written in scrolls, which leave no room for a full commentary in the margins; even codices did not do so regularly until the fifth century. The person who wrote that note was writing in late antiquity.[55]

Porphyrio's commentary on Horace, whatever its original form, was a work of considerable learning. It has little if anything to say about meter and not a lot about grammar; on the other hand, it has a great deal about rhetoric and a considerable amount about historical events and background. Porphyrio liked to use the technical terminology of rhetoric in Greek; he also liked to display his wider knowledge of Greek whenever possible, sometimes supplying Greek glosses for Latin words or quoting proverbs or Homeric tags in Greek. He was equally (or more) learned in Latin: there are citations not only of Virgil and writers in the satiric tradition (Lucilius and Persius, but not Juvenal), but also of some recondite and archaic works: Ennius, Varro's *Menippean Satires*, Pacuvius, and the writer of *fabulae togatae* Atta along with a fairly wide knowledge of Plautus. What Porphyrio did not do—but some apparent interpolations do—is offer the sort of simplistic paraphrases and elementary grammatical observations found in the work of lesser and later commentators. In that respect, his work is clearly consistent with the interests of the archaist age; the process of transmission has eroded the archaism and Greek, adding instead more notes on word order and elementary glosses, but the nature of the original can still be perceived.

Over the centuries, the commentary of "Porphyrio" expanded, contracted, and was revised by more than one person. In the first place, the extant version often has lemmata that do not agree with the text accepted in the commentary itself. Secondly, a great deal of the commentary has been lost: Wessner gives a list of nearly forty places where there is no commentary on a sequence of ten or more lines of Horace, all in book 2 of the *Satires*, the *Epistles*, and the *Ars poetica*, suggesting that at some stage the second half of the manuscript was damaged or unreadable.[56] And third—a major topic of Wessner's and Kalinina's dissertations—there are some fairly consistent types of alteration, both simplifications and interpolations, that have taken place over time. Kalinina has also recognized a striking feature of Porphyrio's language: the rhetorical terminology used in the commentary on the *Ars poetica* is significantly different from that used in the rest of the commentary. That means one of two things: either the commentary we know as Porphyrio in fact incorporates a commentary on the *Ars* by someone else, or (more likely) the work of the real Porphyrio reached the compiler of the

55. On the problem of margins, see 7.2 above; Kalinina (2007: 19) discusses the history of the question and rightly doubts the idea of a marginal original.

56. Wessner (1893: 185); see also Kalinina (2007: 46).

extant version (whether in late antiquity or the eighth century) through more than one channel.

One of the reasons that Wessner and Kalinina have been able to define and in some cases correct the modifications that have been made over time to the original commentary of Pomponius Porphyrio is that it was used, at various stages, in the composition of other commentaries, and in particular the commentaries edited by Keller under the single name of Ps.-Acro. That name is misleading in more than one way: not only does it suggest a relationship that does not exist with the lost commentary of Helenius Acro, but it also implies that there is a single, coherent commentary being edited. Unfortunately, that is not true, and it is very difficult to sort out the layers and combinations of the texts that Keller has put together.[57] As is so often the case with the preservation of ancient commentaries, what now exists in fact is several sets of annotations that were created or compiled no earlier than about 800 CE. One of these sets (to be discussed below), known as Φ, is clearly a Carolingian product; two others are what has come, in modern editions, to be defined as Ps.-Acro. In brief, Ps.-Acro is made up of two commentaries: one, known as A, is represented in a single manuscript, Paris, Lat. 7900A, which contains a commentary on Horace's lyric poetry (with a few gaps) in the margins of a text of Horace; the other, known as §, is found in slightly varying forms in a number of manuscripts, and is a commentary on all of Horace's poetry.

Neither of these late antique commentaries survives intact. If A ever continued to comment on the hexameter poetry, there is no sign of it. What exists is a largely exegetical commentary: for the most part, it offers an introductory exposition of each poem (although some are lost), followed by explanations, sometimes accurate, of names and allusions. Thus, on *Odes* 1.6 to Agrippa, the note on the first line explains:

> Dicit Agrippae: navales seu terrestres victoriae tuae scribentur a Vario perfecto oratore; ceterum ingenium suum inpar metrorum ludo deditum laudes bellicas canere.

> He addresses Agrippa: your victories by land and sea will be written about by Varius, an outstanding orator; furthermore, his own talent, devoted to poetic games, is unequal to singing praise of your exploits in war.

That Varius was an orator is wrong, and clearly a guess (whether by A or his source we cannot tell); in the note on line 8, the commentator is well aware that Varius had written a *Thyestes*. Furthermore, the somewhat contorted word order of *ingenium . . . deditum* is also typical of A. In further notes on the same poem, he offers reasonable explanations of words and phrases (e.g., 1.6.2 *Maeonio*, 6.6 *cedere nescii*, 6.19 *vacui*), and he gives a double explanation of *duplices* at 6.7 as referring both to the length of time and back-tracking of Odysseus' travels

57. For what follows (on the composition and history of the text of Ps.-Acro), I am dependent almost entirely on Noske (1969); see also Longobardi (2014a and 2014b).

and to his reputation as *dolosus*. A also borrows from the original commentary of Porphyrio (and thus is useful for correcting the text of the extant version of Porphyrio). On the other hand, A's range of quotation is fairly narrow: by far the most frequently cited is Virgil; that he also cites Lucan and Statius shows that he was not writing any earlier than the beginning of the fifth century—something also clear from his equating the Scythians to the Huns at 2.11.1 and from the fact that he sometimes borrows from Servius' commentary on Virgil.

The commentary in A, in general, is not elementary, although if one uses Keller's edition without careful attention to what is preserved in which manuscript, that is not altogether clear. Immediately after the note in A on Odysseus' duplicity, there is a much more elementary note:

> Ordo est: nec conamur dicere duplices cursus Vlixei per mare, nec conamur dicere saevam domum Pelopis, dum pudor et Musa potens lyrae vetat deterere laudes egregii Caesaris et tuas culpa ingenii.

This note is not found in A, nor are the many other *ordo*-scholia found in the rest of the manuscript tradition of Ps.-Acro: notes of this form—in which the words of the text are simply rearranged to make the grammar clearer—are typical of later commentaries and are frequent in ninth-century texts such as the *Commentum Cornuti* on Persius. So too elementary glosses on single words: their presence in A is very limited, but they are extremely common in the rest of the tradition.

The *ordo*-scholia on the *Odes* are not found in A; the reason that Keller prints them together is that the manuscripts in which they are found constitute the bulk of the tradition of Ps.-Acro, those which also contain commentary on Horace's hexameter poetry. But the relationship between this more complete commentary on Horace, which is called Γ′ by Keller and § by Noske, and the commentary in A, is a very peculiar one. In the first place, the § tradition contains virtually every note on the *Odes* that is found in A, supplemented by additional fairly elementary notes such as glosses and *ordo*-scholia, with the important difference that while A continues through all the lyric poetry (missing a section in *Epodes* 15–17), § ceases to follow it at the end of *Odes* 4.2 and most of the § tradition from that point on offers a different commentary from A: more elementary, and consistent with the commentary offered by § on the hexameter poetry. One branch of the § tradition (N), however, continues to contain A material to the end of the A commentary, although towards the end it includes two sets of notes, one from A and one from §.[58]

58. It is not easy to understand the peculiarities of the N tradition, which moves from following A (with all other § manuscripts) up to *Odes* 4.2, then follows A (against all other § manuscripts) until *Epod.* 14.16 and from *Epod.* 16.33 through the *Carmen Saeculare*, but which on *Epod.* 15.1–16.32 goes back to agreeing with §. One might conjecture that this may have something to do with damage to the manuscript of A: for Keller, the text ended at *Epod.* 15.1, but subsequently a missing leaf of A (now Hamburg 53b) was

The relationships among these commentaries are not altogether clear, but the process that Noske has deciphered, although it seems unlikely, must be somewhere near the truth. In late antiquity, two commentaries on Horace were created, A, whose methods have been briefly described above, in the early fifth century, and the slightly later §, a much larger commentary on all of Horace which included both some fairly learned antiquarian lore (with references to archaic literature) and some very elementary grammatical material. The date is made clear by a note on *Serm.* 1.5.97, concerning the town name Bari: *Civitas est, quae Atbaris dicitur hodieque, ut dixit grammaticus Theotistus*. Theoctistus was the teacher of Priscian; hence this note is not likely to have been written before about 500 CE.

Each of these commentaries survived, in some form, until the Carolingian period, but not in perfect condition: A was damaged, probably abbreviated, and extended by metrical annotations inconsistent with the original commentary, while § somewhere along the way lost the opening of the commentary (up to *Odes* 4.2) and experienced damage to the last part of the commentary, on the *Epistles*. The first problem was solved by adding from A what was missing at the beginning; the N branch of the tradition, as noted above, subsequently added more from A. In its latter portions, where the source manuscript may have been physically damaged—or where the scribe of the source had become tired—the compiler of what is now the complete § collection added other material: some of it came from the now-extant form of Porphyrio, while some of it was drawn from the Carolingian compilation Φ.

The history of the ancient and medieval commentaries is in many ways typical of the story that can be told about the commentary tradition on many Latin poets, particularly the more complicated traditions such as those on Persius, Lucan, and Juvenal, with the important difference that while all these traditions, at least in the Carolingian period, go back and forth between margins and continuous commentary, and are constantly reshaped and recombined, abridged and expanded, in different manuscripts and (presumably) different monasteries, the tradition of commentary on Horace is considerably more complicated both because Horace was more widely read in antiquity, and earlier than poets such as Lucan, Juvenal, and Statius, who came into favor only at the end of the fourth century, and (not unrelated) because there actually were serious commentaries on Horace written in antiquity—not just beginning in the late fourth century, but going back as far as the reign of Nero. This creates an extraordinarily complex and peculiar history, which is not yet entirely clear. First, the third-century commentary of Pomponius Porphyrio made use of the earlier commentary of Helenius Acro; the commentary of Porphyrio in turn was used by the author of the A version of Ps.-Acro. Over time Porphyrio's work was itself significantly altered, as described above, and emerged in the form in which we now have it. In all likelihood, the main work of alteration took place (like so much other grammatical simplification

discovered containing the commentary on *Epod.* 16.32–17.66. A description, transcript, and text in Noske 1969: xxxii–vii.

and explanation) in the early fifth century. Not much later than that, the revised Porphyrio was itself used by the author of the § version of Ps.-Acro (who once, on *AP* 120, quotes the extant form of Porphyrio under the designation *commentator*). Even later, in the reconstruction of § in the ninth century, the compiler borrowed the first section of the A commentary, made extended use of the extant Porphyrio, and filled out his commentary through the use of Carolingian sources. It is a constant process: as each commentary is simplified for the needs of a less literate audience, it is borrowed by a commentator in the other tradition. The only thing missing is anything at all of the commentary apparently at the base of this tradition, the one actually written by Helenius Acro.

Does anything ancient survive this long set of transformations and permutations? Certainly it does, although to be used with care, in the commentary of Porphyrio and in the two commentaries combined as Ps.-Acro—more in the A version than in the § version. But beyond those two collections, antiquity becomes less visible and more distorted. The Φ commentary, mentioned above, is represented by a host of manuscripts written in the tenth century and later; they have been edited, in parts, by Botschuyver, who believed that it was put together in or near Metz in the early seventh century; his argument is entertaining, but wrong.[59] The various forms of scholia on Horace found in medieval manuscripts are all in fact medieval, and while one or more of them may come from the scholarly milieu of Heiric and Remigius of Auxerre in the late ninth or early tenth century, no certainty is possible. There is nothing ancient in any of them that does not come from the extant version of Porphyrio or from other familiar sources of Carolingian scholarship, such as Servius and Isidore.

This account can end with a famous ghost. The sixteenth-century scholar Jacobus Cruquius attributed some of the scholia in his edition of Horace to a manuscript source; in fact, his notes were conflated from a wide variety of sources, some of them related to the extant traditions, others copied from printed editions.[60] Cruquius' attribution gained credibility because of his citation of at least one genuine reading in the text of Horace from a manuscript (*Blandinius vetustissimus*) subsequently destroyed by fire, but there is no reason to attribute any particular authority to his commentary.

4. WHOSE COMMENTARY?

What emerges, I hope, from a survey of these specific traditions of commentary is the variety of approaches and the variety of forms in which commentary and annotation survive. What is unusual about Virgil, Cicero, and Horace, of course, is that they were among the most widely read of classical authors. Virgil is pervasive, the single author most frequently quoted in grammatical texts, the single secular

59. See Botschuyver (1939).

60. For a succinct explanation of Cruquius' souces and methods, see Wessner (1908: 179–80). For bibliography on the medieval commentaries in general, see 11.4 below.

author most educated people knew best—and thought they had something to say about. Cicero is illustrative because of the range of his works and the educational levels at which he was read: from elementary grammar through the rhetorician's school to logic and Neoplatonism. Horace was studied both for his meter and his content, admired and imitated in both antiquity and the Middle Ages. But although no other authors individually receive all the same kinds of exposition, all the kinds of exposition are applied to them as well: continuous, specialized explanation, as with the *Narrationes* of Ovid's *Metamorphoses*; grammatical and rhetorical explanations, as in the commentaries on Terence and Persius; exegesis of historical or mythological detail, as in the scholia to Statius and Juvenal.

What is not always so clear about ancient commentaries, however, is where they come from and in what contexts they were meant to be read. Most of what we have—of the commentaries, at least, on Juvenal and Persius, Terence and Horace, Lucan and Statius—survived as marginalia, not as continuous commentary: we possess, by and large, what teachers in the eighth and ninth centuries put together from what they found in margins of manuscripts written in the fifth and sixth centuries, and those marginal notes were not necessarily put there by teachers or scholars, simply by readers excerpting from longer explanations or jotting down thoughts of their own. The fact that an extant commentary concentrates on grammar does not mean that it was originally a schoolbook; the fact that it concentrates on history or mythology does not mean that it was not one. And in fact, all these areas of exegesis were the province of the *grammaticus*, subsumed under the rubric of *enarratio poetarum*. Some few commentaries, as they now survive, can be located in place and time, but not many: we must read these texts backward from the ninth century, trying to see through them what ancient students thought.

8

Grammars and Grammarians

DICTIONARIES COULD BE WRITTEN BY *GRAMMATICI*, SUCH AS Verrius Flaccus; commentaries generally were. In neither area, however, were these forms of writing the sole province of the *grammaticus*, and the same is true of the writing of grammar itself. The *ars grammatica*, as a genre, was of course largely for educational use, either by students or by their teachers; but it should be remembered, in contemplating the large and unruly body of material described in this chapter, that many of these texts, including some formal *artes grammaticae*, were not written by professional grammarians: Charisius probably was not one, Macrobius definitely was not—just as, in earlier periods, learned non-*grammatici* like Aelius Stilo, Varro, and Cornutus did not feel inhibited by their amateur status from writing some very technical books about Latin.[1]

But just as grammar could be written by non-grammarians, so too the kind of book that could be written about grammar was not limited to the *ars* narrowly defined. Quintilian's definition is still relevant: grammar consists of teaching both proper language and the understanding of literary texts. That goes beyond commentary in the narrow sense: there are explanations of orthography, of prosody and meter, and of rhetorical figures both within the framework of formal grammars and outside them. Just because a given grammar book does not talk about everything germane does not mean that its author conceived of "grammar" as limited to the contents of a single book—any more than that is true of a modern writer or scholar. The grammatical writings we possess, most of them composed between the fourth and the sixth centuries CE, vary in content, approach, and audience: there was a standard goal (to teach students to read and write good Latin) but there was no standard curriculum throughout the Latin-speaking world—and our texts range geographically from Constantinople to Africa, Gaul, and Spain, not to mention (somewhat later) Ireland—and no Committee on Instruction to

1. Some scholars (e.g., Ax 2011a = 2011b: 2–17) use *ars grammatica* in two senses: one is the book (as I use it), the other is the broader study of grammar including whatever the *grammaticus* taught and was expected to know. I use "grammar" for the latter meaning.

approve or reject a syllabus or textbook.[2] "Grammar" is what the teacher (or student) makes it.

1. *GRAMMATICI LATINI*

There are good reasons, however, for thinking of "grammar" as limited to the *ars grammatica*. One is our own institutional position: we *do* have committees on instruction, state boards of education, and standard textbooks. A more important reason is the nature both of the tradition in antiquity—highly tralatitious—and of the publishing history of these texts in modern times. Heinrich Keil, who between 1855 and 1880 oversaw and largely edited the seven volumes of *Grammatici Latini*, was not the first to do so: he was inspired (and sometimes took his information from) the earlier collections of Putschen and Lindemann.[3] Keil grouped his material by content and audience rather than by date.[4] The first three volumes contain the most elaborate works, designed for scholars and teachers rather than for students, the grammars of Charisius and Diomedes (Vol. 1) and of Priscian (Vols. 2–3, edited by Martin Hertz), together with lesser but related texts. Volume 4 contains the major school texts of the fourth and early fifth centuries—the *Catholica* and *Instituta artium* ascribed to Probus and the two *Artes* of Donatus, together with the most substantial early commentaries on Donatus; Volume 5 contains the lesser and later commentaries on Donatus and works on the parts of speech. Volume 6 has texts on metrics and Volume 7 texts on orthography, together with a group of texts that are eccentric or difficult to classify, including the bilingual grammar (Latin, with partial Greek translation) of Dositheus, the excerpts of earlier grammars made by Audax, and the *Exempla elocutionum* of Arusianus Messius.

Keil's editions of many texts are no longer satisfactory: he took over collations of manuscripts from earlier editors and was at times not aware of the best evidence. Even so, his skill and judgment as an editor remain impressive and his introductions are still essential reading. Equally important, the way in which he organized his collection is still (although I will not follow the same order) a valid articulation of the corpus of late antique Latin grammar, and *Grammatici Latini* remains a constant point of reference.[5]

2. For the absence of normative structures in education, see Kaster (1983b) and (on rhetoric, but applicable to grammar) Reinhardt and Winterbottom (2006: xxiv–vi).

3. Putschen (1605); Lindemann (1831–40). These are the most important broad collections, but Keil also borrowed heavily from Eichenfeld and Endlicher (1836–7), which contains the grammatical contents of Naples, Lat. 1 and 2 (then Vienna, Lat. 17 and 16). Keil's is by far the fullest collection.

4. On Keil and the *Grammatici Latini*, see Desbordes (2007: 235–50).

5. The valuable online version of *GL* (*CGL*) itemizes 103 different texts in Keil's collection (thirty-one of them anonymous), of which forty are presented in an edition more recent than Keil's. But of the most important (and bulky) authors, very few have been edited since Keil: for Priscian's *Institutiones*, Diomedes, and the major works ascribed to Probus, *GL* remains the last (indeed the only) critical edition. The eighth

Obsolescence aside, however, Keil's collection has significant limitations. One problem is that, even in seven fat volumes, *GL* is not remotely complete. Some new texts have been discovered: perhaps the most important is the so-called *Ars Pseudo-Scauri* to be discussed later. Keil also defined "grammar" fairly narrowly: Lindemann, for instance, had included texts of Festus and Isidore. Chronologically, in one direction, Keil left out the beginning of the story: Varro is not there, nor are the fragments of grammarians earlier than the full texts Keil prints. In the opposite direction, Keil barely indicates, without adequate documentation, some areas of the post-sixth-century tradition, particularly the long series of commentaries on Donatus that begins with Servius and lasts until the ninth century and beyond. Indeed, he gives only the most meager of excerpts from some commentaries, and others he omits completely. Hagen in his supplement (*AH*) did something to remedy this, but Hagen was not so good an editor as Keil, and there are many texts still unpublished and probably some still unidentified.

Incompleteness, obsolescence, and a third problem: Keil, like most editors, wanted to believe in the fixity of the texts he edited, but for grammars or commentaries, that should not be taken for granted. Different and possibly fuller versions of some texts in *GL* circulated in late antiquity and the early Middle Ages: of Scaurus, of Charisius, of Diomedes, of the commentaries of Servius and Pompeius on Donatus. Donatus himself was one of the most canonical of all grammarians and the object of commentary from the fifth century on. Over the centuries, however, Donatus' name was attached to several different forms of the text: a Christianized version, a version in which the *Ars minor* and *Ars maior* Book 2 appeared together before *Ars maior* Books 1 and 3, and other forms of revision.[6] Keil gives little indication of any of that. Only because of Louis Holtz's monumental labors on Donatus can we glimpse his *Ars* as a living and changing tradition, whose reception is an important part of the text itself.[7] To identify a grammatical text by the author's name printed by Keil is conventional rather than strictly accurate: the tradition was not concerned with reproducing itself precisely, but it would merely be distracting always to refer to "Scaurus" rather than Scaurus. Within the tradition, there is much greater respect for the *names* of important grammarians—Palaemon, Scaurus, Sacerdos, Probus—than for the precise words these men actually wrote. For the most part, the idea that we can firmly connect a specific set of words to a specific scholar is a chimera; on the

volume in *GL* is *Anecdota Helvetica*, a supplement produced by Hermann Hagen in 1870, collecting a congeries of texts from Swiss libraries (Zurich, Bern, and Einsiedeln); they are generally later and often the products of Anglo-Saxon and Irish scriptoria, either in Britain or in insular monastic foundations of the seventh and eighth centuries on the Continent.

6. On the versions of Donatus, see Holtz (1981) and 9.4 below.

7. The same is to some extent true for Priscian, but not until the ninth century and later; on the diffusion of Priscian, see the useful brief analysis of Holtz (2009).

other hand, that we can identify texts associated with them in a less rigorous fashion—fuzzy authorship—is perfectly reasonable.[8]

There is another side to this, however. For us, as for Keil, it is reassuring to see individual works as unities—with clear external boundaries, even if the contents may be a little dodgy. But for many readers and writers of grammatical texts, that is not true: the people who commissioned and copied manuscripts were interested in learning Latin, not in a particular grammarian. As a result, many manuscripts pick and choose. "Here is a good introduction to spelling, here is one to meter, here is one to the parts of speech: let's take one thing from one book, another from another, cutting and pasting as we go." Any student of Roman scholarship needs to remember that grammatical manuscripts are frequently eclectic anthologies in which the contents matter more than the source.[9]

2. ORIGINS OF THE *ARS*

Despite the flexibility of the concept of "grammar," at its center remains the basic text, the *ars grammatica*. Much has been written about the origin and sources of the Roman *ars*, but any history of it is necessarily speculative. In part, the uncertainties are the result of our ignorance on the Greek side rather than the Roman: the extant grammar attached to the name of Dionysius Thrax, the second-century BCE pupil of Aristarchus, is largely inauthentic, and Stoic grammatical theory, generally accepted as being of great importance in Rome, is attested only in much later sources.[10] What is more, our earliest sources for Greek grammar other than a few papryri are, in general, Roman grammatical writings; that makes the reconstruction of the sources for Roman grammar more than a little circular. A full account of these hypothetical origins in no-longer-extant texts is in any case not relevant here. Some bibliography will be found in the footnotes; what follows is merely a sketch of the issues and possibilities.[11]

We have already seen that in the first century BCE, in the work of Varro, Caesar, and others, there were genuine attempts to clarify and explain the Latin language, largely concentrating on its vocabulary and morphology. Varro in *De lingua Latina* explicitly acknowledged his debts to both sides of the Greek grammatical tradition: on the one hand, the Alexandrians (notably Aristarchus), whose main interest was in developing standards for determining the correct texts of Homer

8. On problems of authorship and identity, see 8.5 below.

9. Again, see more fully 9.4 and Chapter 13 below.

10. A brief summary of modern views of the origins of Greek grammar in Law (2003: 55–7); a much fuller and well-documented account is given by Pagani (2011). On (Ps.?)-Dionysius, see the collection of papers in Law and Sluiter (1995); the strongest argument against authenticity was made by Di Benedetto (1958), and a great deal has been written about the issue since then. On grammar and philosophy, see now Atherton and Blank (2013).

11. Some bibliography on the internal history of grammar will also be found at the beginning of Chapter 12, but I do not pretend to completeness.

and other early authors, and on the other hand, the Stoics (notably Diogenes of Babylon and Crates of Mallos), who were far more concerned with logic and with questions concerning the relationship between language and the real world. Varro himself worked in both directions: the verbal study of etymology and inflection combined with an interest in syntax, broadly defined. At the very least, *De lingua Latina* included some discussion of the structure of complex sentences and the uses of conjunctions and prepositions.[12]

But *De lingua Latina* was not an *ars grammatica*: it was a learned work designed for other men of letters, not a book designed to introduce students to the formal study of their language. Other than the forecast of his own future writing made by the author of *Ad Herennium*, in fact, there is no sign of a formal *ars grammatica* until the first century CE. That does not mean that none existed: as noted in Chapter 2, the first century BCE is the period in which the formalization of *ars* seems to have taken place in other areas of intellectual life, and that is probably true for grammar as well. Part of that formalization is the result of internal developments in Roman culture, but part of it, quite clearly, was prompted by Greek models and the influx of Greek scholars into Rome. In the case of grammar, we know of important work in this period in Greek, by Greeks either in Rome or closely associated with Rome, from the beginning of the first century BCE—Posidonius, Tyrannio the Elder, and at the end of the century Tryphon.[13] But the only possible contemporary Latin equivalent is Varro's late—and lost—*De Grammatica*.

The name most associated with the Latin *ars grammatica*, however, is not Varro in the late Republic but Q. Remmius Palaemon in the early Empire. Certainly, both for contemporaries and later readers, Palaemon often seems to stand for grammar itself.[14] That his work was the first of its kind is very unlikely. Many of Palaemon's categories (when we can discover them) correspond to those in the grammar preserved under the name of Dionysius Thrax, and Alexandrian grammar must have played an important role in shaping Roman grammar. At the same time, however, the shape taken by the Roman *ars grammatica*—a preliminary set of sections discussing sounds, letters, syllables, and other basic concepts, followed by the central section on the parts of speech, followed in turn by some discussion of the virtues and vices of speech—was traced by Karl Barwick to Stoic grammatical writing, and in particular to the work of Diogenes of Babylon in the middle of the second century BCE. That is no longer generally accepted; and indeed the various modern accounts that give credit for the creation of Roman grammar to the inspirational use of a single Greek model (whether Crates, Diogenes, Tryphon, Tyrannio, or someone else) are all serious oversimplifications. Roman grammar was shaped in Rome, but its changing shape was clearly influenced by a

12. See above, Chapter 3; see esp. Baratin (1989: 202–52).

13. See, for instance, Usener (1913: 265–314); Siebenborn (1976: 32–5); Baratin (1989: 17–60).

14. On Palaemon see also 4.3 above.

steady stream of Greeks that flowed from Athens and Alexandria to Rome; Roman scholars both revised Latin models and—at least until the sixth century—profited from Greek ones.[15]

Palaemon may have been important in the grammatical tradition because of effective expression or self-promotion, at which he was clearly skilled. But he also flourished at a moment when the structure of grammatical teaching at Rome underwent a major shift: Vespasian established salaried positions for grammarians and rhetoricians in Rome, and it would be surprising if the public recognition of grammatical teaching did not encourage grammarians to look for an instructional model to use, if not follow slavishly. Palaemon's *Ars* seems to have been the work that most successfully filled that need. And although it is clear that not all later *artes grammaticae* were written by professional grammarians, it is equally clear that the form of education by the *grammaticus* and the dominant form of writing about grammar became very closely linked: there is little, if anything, in the grammatical tradition after Palaemon that does not show signs of being shaped by the *ars* as it came to be defined in the first century.[16]

What was in that *ars*? We get a good early view of the subject from Quintilian, who in a long discussion in Book 1 of the *Institutio oratoria* (1.4–9) explains what he thinks his incoming students of rhetoric should already have learned from their *grammaticus*.[17] The rhetorician does not follow precisely the arrangement of any extant grammar, and he unsurprisingly stresses those elements of grammar that are most important for the budding orator. Chapter 1.4 contains the basics: beginning from definitions of the content and tasks of grammar, he turns first to

15. Attempts to find specific foundational moments and sources of Greek influence on Roman grammatical writing are generally based on the a priori assumption that Romans only learn from Greeks; there is very little real evidence. Stoic grammar is important, but when, how, and for whom? Modern scholars from Barwick (1922) to Taylor (1986), Law (2003), and Luhtala (2002, 2010) have proposed fairly rigid schemes of Greek influence. Luhtala is, I think, right to argue that Stoic definitions did not take root in Greek grammar until Apollonius Dyscolus in the second century CE, and in Rome only beginning in the late third century; this fits with the argument of Matthaios (2005). On the other hand, she assumes a teleological model (moving towards philosophical grammar) and blurs the distinction between the broad and narrow definitions of grammar. On the equivocal Latin evidence for the Stoic *Tekhnê peri phônês*, see Schenkeveld (1990: 101–3).

16. So, rightly, Ax (see next note). Caution is necessary in this area, and it is important to remember that the *ars grammatica* was less standardized than modern accounts assume; see esp. Baratin (1994). Latin grammars in antiquity no more contained exactly the same things than do modern Latin textbooks and reference grammars.

17. On Quintilian's grammar, see above all Ax (2011a in English = 2011b: 2–17 in German); for the most part, I agree with his analysis in all but very minor ways, and his commentary on 1.4–8 (2011b) is invaluable. Luhtala (2010: 215–18) discusses this passage of Quintilian, but forgets that he is talking about what a student should learn from his *grammaticus*, not what he might find in an *ars grammatica*. Also useful are von Fritz (1949) and Desbordes (1995).

the *elementa*, then to syllables (although he barely mentions the topic at 1.4.17, noting that he will take it up under the rubric of *orthographia* [in 1.7]).[18] Then comes a section on the parts of speech, warning his charges about the importance of learning paradigms.[19] Chapter 5 focuses more on the elements of grammar particularly important for the orator, offering instruction on the *vitia orationis* that are to be avoided in writing and in speech:[20] he discusses barbarism (5.5–33) and solecism (5.34–51), but eschews discussion of *schemata*, because he is, after all, not writing a grammar: *neque enim artem grammaticam componere adgressi sumus, sed cum in ordinem incurreret, inhonoratam transire noluimus* (5.54: "I am not undertaking to write an *ars grammatica*, but since the subject has come up, I am reluctant to leave it unmentioned").[21] Instead, he provides a brief discussion of categories of words in terms of propriety in writing and speech: native, foreign, and regional (5.55–64), with particular emphasis on the thorny problem of the inflection of Greek names; simple and compound (5.65–70); *propria* and *translata* (5.71–2).

Chapters 4–5 contain the tasks of grammar and the grammarian, introduced by the appropriate definitions; chapters 6–7 are introduced by Quintilian's list of the grammarian's tools, the criteria by which to judge linguistic correctness, in this case *ratio, vetustas, auctoritas*, and *consuetudo* (1.6.1).[22] *Vetustas* and *auctoritas* are relatively simple: the first is simply the justification of words by their antiquity, the second is justification by their use by particular *auctores*—in this case, as Quintilian is training orators, meaning historians and orators rather than poets. *Ratio* (subdivided into a major section, *analogia*, and a minor one, *etymologia*) and *consuetudo* are opposed here, as almost always, and Quintilian gives a long and cautionary discussion of analogy (6.3–27) and a shorter and rather skeptical one of etymology (6.28–38) before examining the other criteria and then returning to his preferred one, *consuetudo*, at the end. In the parallel chapter (7) he moves from the rules for speaking, *loquendi regula*, to those for writing, *quod Graeci orthographian vocant* (7.1), again emphasizing *consuetudo*. In the final two chapters (8–9), he first discusses *lectio, enarratio*, and how the *grammaticus* should train his students, and finally (9) their transition from the

18. He in fact discusses syllables in several different passages; see Ax (2011b: 120).

19. On the parts of speech, see the detailed discussion of Ax (2011b: 120–34).

20. Ax (2011b:148–9) takes the discussion of *virtutes et vitia* to be a reflection of the tripartite grammar as found above all in Donatus. It is, however, not at all clear that the inclusion of rhetorical elements is as essential as he (following Barwick) believes; see in particular Baratin and Desbordes (1986).

21. Quintilian's full discussion of *schemata* is to be found in 9.3.

22. Ax (2011b: 230) rightly equates 1.6–7 with treatises *De Latinitate*, a topic in which grammar clearly overlaps with rhetoric (see 5.3 above). On the lists of criteria, see above all Siebenborn (1976: 53–163). On the structure of Quintilian's list and its relationship to Varro, see Lomanto (1994); Grebe (2000) adds nothing useful. On the entire chapter, Ax (2011b) offers detailed and valuable explanations.

grammarian to the rhetorician by means of elementary rhetorical exercises such as the *chria*.

Some aspects of Quintilian's grammar clearly diverge from standard grammars: there is the rhetorician's heavy emphasis on oral as well as written competence, and his use of the oratorical stylistic virtues (*oratio . . . emendata, . . . dilucida . . . ornata*, 1.5.1) to introduce the topic of barbarism sounds more like Cicero than like Donatus.[23] Nor is it inconvenient for the teacher of rhetoric to have the grammarian introduce elementary rhetorical exercises—leaving the rhetorician more time for the much more interesting *suasoriae* and *controversiae*. At the same time, however, his use of the standard grammarian's division between tasks and tools to articulate the two major divisions of his account; his awareness, in announcing his postponement of the discussion of syllables, that the topic did have a specific place in the grammatical curriculum; and his occasional patronizing comments about teachers of grammar all show that he is writing both in and against a well-recognized format. That format, moreover, is quite close to the patterns we find in the major grammars of the fourth to sixth centuries.[24] Quintilian's order in 1.4–5 is (marking the major divisions as [a] [b] [c])

a) De grammatica; De elementis; De syllaba,
b) De partibus orationis (followed by the individual parts of speech),[25]

23. For comparisons with Cicero, see Ax (2011b: 149–50), although what he would see as a relatively early rhetoricization of grammar I would prefer to see as the result of Quintilian's being a rhetorician rather than a grammarian. This was not necessarily a standard part of grammatical training in the first century.

24. Ax (2011a, 2011b) argues that the close similarities between Quintilian's account of the *ars* and that of Donatus and other later grammars show that the *ars* took a fixed shape by the first century CE and that there was little change thereafter; he thinks it likely (as do I) that Palaemon's *Ars* set the pattern. On the other hand, it is clear (see esp. Baratin and Desbordes 1986 and Baratin 1994) that the shape is not so rigid as Ax suggests and (see Luhtala 2002, 2010) that within the shape of the *ars* there were considerable changes in doctrine and content. For a summary of similarities between Quintilian and other grammars, see Jeep (1893: v–vii). Jeep's thorough account (1893: 103–294) of the elements of standard grammar and collection of parallel passages remains extremely useful. On Quintilian's linguistics, see Law (2003: 60–5).

25. The *partes orationis* are problematic in several respects, but the details are not relevant here. The origin, identity, and number of the so-called parts of speech (*merê tou logou* in Stoic terminology more accurately meant "elements of discourse") is a long and vexed subject. The most useful recent account is that of Matthaios (2005) (with reference to his earlier discussions), which shows beyond much doubt that the system of eight parts of speech was developed by Aristarchus and owed relatively little (compared to what some modern accounts have suggested) to Stoic ideas of syntax. But the problem was discussed by grammarians in antiquity themselves: see Swiggers and Wouters (2010). For their history in Latin grammatical writing, see, as ever, Jeep (1893); also the summary of Holtz (1981: 64–9). There are many more discussions. Until Priscian, the normal order of the parts of speech is noun, pronoun, verb, adverb, participle (with some

c) De barbarismo; De soloecismo; De schematibus.

In the *Instituta artium* of Probus in the fourth century, the order is

a) De voce; De arte; De litteris; De syllabis,
b) De partibus orationis (followed by the individual parts of speech).

In the *Ars maior* of Donatus, the canonical grammar for the early Middle Ages, the order is

a) De voce; De littera; De syllaba; De pedibus; De tonis; De posituris,
b) De partibus orationis (followed by the individual parts of speech),
c) De barbarismo; De soloecismo; De ceteris vitiis; De metaplasmo; De schematibus; De tropis.

Not all are like this: few have a full discussion of the virtues and vices of speech; some include metrics; some focus almost exclusively on the parts of speech, and even in Donatus and Probus there are differences in emphasis. Donatus in the first part of his *Ars* has sections about metrical feet, word accent, and punctuation between the syllable and the word; Probus (who devotes a large amount of space to paradigms) says nothing about *vitia et virtutes*. The opening of Diomedes' grammar at the end of the fourth century reflects on the possibilities, almost all of which can be exemplified in an extant text (*GL* 1.300.3–6):[26]

> Artis grammaticae auctores exordium scribendi varium diversumque sumpserunt. quidam enim ab ipsa arte coeperunt, alii ab elementis vel a litteris, multi a casibus, plerique a partibus orationis, non nulli a voce, pauci a nominum declinatione; nos vero ab ipsa oratione auspicemur.
>
> People who write an *ars grammatica* start from various and divergent points. Some begin from *ars* itself, others from *elementa* or *litterae*, many start from the cases, many from the *partes orationis*, some from *vox*, a few from declension of nouns. I will begin from *oratio* itself.

Similarly, the bilingual fifth-century grammar of Dositheus begins with the statement (*GL* 7.376.3–7.4):[27]

> Ars grammatica est scientia emendati sermonis in loquendo et scribendo poematumque ac lectionis prudens praeceptum. grammaticus est qui uniuscuiusque rei vim ac proprietatem potest explanare loquela. artis grammaticae officium constat partibus quattuor, lectione emendatione enarratione iudicio. lectio est varia cuiusque scripti pronuntiatio serviens dignitati personarum exprimensque habitum animi cuiusque. emendatio

variation in the last three indeclinables). Priscian reverts to the standard Greek order of noun, verb, participle, pronoun . . .; see 8.8 below.

26. On Diomedes' definition of grammar, see Luhtala (2010: 214–15, 218–20).

27. On Dositheus' definition, see Bonnet (2005) ad loc. I give the Latin only.

> est recorrectio errorum, qui per scriptum dictionemve fiunt. enarratio est obscurorum sensuum quaestionumque narratio. iudicium est quo poemata ceteraque scripta perpendimus et discernimus. artis grammaticae initia ab elementis surgunt, elementa figurantur in litteras, litterae coguntur in syllabas, syllabis comprehenditur dictio, dictiones coguntur in partes orationis, oratio in virtutes ac vitia descendit.
>
> The *ars grammatica* is knowledge of correct language in speaking and writing and careful instruction in the reading of poetry.[28] The grammarian is a person who can explain in speech the meaning and the proper use of every word. The task of the *ars grammatica* has four parts: *lectio, emendatio, enarratio*, and *iudicium*. *Lectio* is the modulated pronunciation of every kind of writing, paying attention to the status of characters and expressing the mental characteristics of each person. *Emendatio* is the correction of mistakes made in writing or aloud. *Enarratio* is the explanation of puzzling statements and of *quaestiones*. *Iudicium* is that by which we assess and distinguish among poems and other writings. The beginnings of *ars grammatica* start from the *elementa*, the *elementa* are figured as *litterae*, *litterae* are herded together into *syllabae*, from *syllabae* comes *dictio*, *dictiones* are herded into the *partes orationis*, and *oratio* ends with *virtutes* and *vitia*.

Dositheus here combines several things that are also in Quintilian: a) the two basic elements of grammatical instruction, namely, proper speech and the explanation of poets; b) the four tasks of the grammarian, namely *lectio, emendatio, enarratio,* and *iudicium*; and c) the order of presentation of grammar itself, from *elementa* to *litterae* (a step blurred in Quintilian) to *syllabae* to *dictio* to the *partes orationis* to *virtutes et vitia*. This last explains the regular order of instruction: we begin from the smallest element (whether sound or symbol), move to the next level, the syllable, and then to the word. Once we have reached the word, we deal with types of word, the *partes orationis*, and then move on to the correct and incorrect use of words both alone (barbarism) and in context (solecism).

Although there are very significant differences in choice of material, focus, and emphasis, there is much in common among texts of grammar; the basic content was already there, and generally accepted, in the first century.[29] That Quintilian was drawing on only one *ars* is unlikely: he knew Palaemon's work (but his one reference at 1.4.20 makes it seem as if Palaemon was not his primary source), but he also knew the general practices of *grammatici*. He was himself a teacher and a man of wide reading: his account of grammar, like his account of rhetoric itself, is the distillation of his years in the classroom. He had no need to look it up and certainly no need to depend on a single source.

28. Or "poems and reading" (Dickey 2016b: 214).

29. A version of the sequence already appears in a simile in Manilius 2.755–64, where it runs from letter to syllable to word before moving off (as some grammars do too) in the poetic direction of feet and *carmina*.

3. VARIETIES OF GRAMMAR

The general structure of the major grammatical texts from the fourth to the sixth centuries is fairly constant: the center is occupied by the eight parts of speech, with some discussion of smaller elements in front (letters and syllables, with a range of other options, including prosody and accentuation), and sometimes something else to follow (virtues and vices or metrics). But not all grammars do everything, and they vary a great deal in size and purpose. Donatus, at least in retrospect, is the canonical grammarian: unlike any other grammar (at least until the ninth century), his work became the object of commentary (see further below). Furthermore, his two grammars are helpul examples of two styles and audiences for grammatical writing. The *Ars maior* in three books is the one summarized above: it is rigorously analytic, setting out information clearly and concisely. In the chapter on pronouns, for instance (*Ars maior* 2.11, starting *GL* 4.379.23), the definition ("A pronoun is a part of speech . . .") is followed by a list of six accidents (quality, gender, number, figure, person, case).[30] That in turn is followed by a division of *qualitas* into definite (e.g,. *ego*) and indefinite (e.g., *quis, quae, quod*). This broad division is in turn qualified by a section on pronouns that are *minus quam finita: praepositiva*, such as *hic; subiunctiva*, such as *is*; those related to *gens*, numerical order, number. More subdivisions and qualifications follow.

Only after Donatus has exhausted the subdivisions of *qualitas* does he turn to the next accident, gender. And here, the analysis is understandably much briefer: "Just about all the possible genders of nouns apply to pronouns: masculine, such as *quis*; feminine, such as *quae*; neuter, such as *quod*; common, such as *qualis, talis*; of all three genders, such as *ego, tu*." End of subject. Each of the other four accidents follows. At the very end comes a paragraph defining the distinctions between pronouns and articles (the latter are, given that Latin has no article corresponding to the Greek, unsurprisingly the same as some of the pronouns, such as *hic*, when used to modify nouns). And we then proceed to the verb, which has seven accidents and takes rather longer to expound. The didactic structure is one shared by other *artes* and was clearly inspired (at whatever remove) by Greek models: it is constructed, as Holtz describes it (1981: 49–57), pyramidally, and its fundamental method is division and definition.

But while Donatus' exposition is logical and lucid, it is not exactly for beginners; that is the function of the *Ars minor*. This little booklet discusses only the parts of speech (no syllables or metrics yet), and it does so in catechistic form (*GL* 4.357.2–11):

> Pronomen quid est? pars orationis, quae pro nomine posita tantundem paene significat personamque interdum recipit.

30. On the varieties of definition used in the various grammars, see Luhtala (2002, 2010: 224–37). On the use of *accidens/accidit*, see Holtz (1981: 68–9) and Schad (2007) s.v. The term is derived from Stoic terminology (*sumbebêkos/sumbainei*) indicating the non-essential qualities of a word or concept. For its history and use, see Vitale (1982) and Garcea (2009). On Donatus' chapter on pronouns, see Holtz (1981: 125–35).

Pronomini quot accidunt? sex.

Quae? qualitas, genus, numerus, figura, persona, casus.

Qualitas pronominum in quo est? bipertita est: aut enim finita sunt pronomina aut infinita.

Quae sunt finita? quae recipiunt personas, ut ego, tu, ille.

Quae sunt infinita? quae non recipiunt personas, ut quis quae quod.

Genera pronominum quae sunt? eadem fere quae et nominum: masculinum, ut quis; femininum, ut quae; neutrum, ut quod; commune, ut qualis, talis; trium generum, ut ego, tu.

Numeri pronominum quot sunt? duo.

Qui? singularis, ut hic; pluralis, ut hi.

Figurae pronominum quot sunt? . . .

What is a pronoun? A part of speech which, when used in place of a noun, means pretty much the same thing and sometimes indicates a *persona*.

How may accidents do pronouns have? Six.

What are they? Quality, gender, number, form, person, case.

In what does the quality of pronouns consist? It is bipartite: pronouns are either finite or infinite.

What are finite pronouns? Those that indicate *personae*, such as *ego*, *tu*, or *ille*.

What are infinite pronouns? Those that do not indicate *personae*, such as *quis quae quod*.

What are the genders of pronouns? Pretty much the same as of nouns: masculine, such as *quis*; feminine, such as *quae*; neuter, such as *quod*; common, such as *qualis* or *talis*; of three genders, such as *ego* or *tu*.

How many numbers of pronouns are there? Two.

What are they? Singular, such as *hic*, plural, such as *hi*.

How many forms of pronouns are there? . . .

Eventually, the catechism gives out in favor of paradigms, which go on for some distance. It is no accident that the discussion of the pronoun in the *Ars minor* is in fact longer than that in the *Ars maior*. Admittedly, the pronoun is difficult for the ten-year-old, but after memorizing this (and that is presumably what the student was supposed to do), the austerity of the more advanced text would be less daunting.

The distinction between texts for elementary and more advanced students that appears in Donatus is not always so sharp, but broadly speaking there appear to be three sorts of grammatical texts, which sometimes overlap.[31] At the center is

31. By this I mean general grammars, not works that are specialized either in form (commentaries on Donatus) or topic (metrics, orthography), which will be discussed separately below. For details on all the authors named here, see Chapter 12 below.

what Karl Barwick christened the *Schulgrammatik*.[32] All such texts are basically analytic in method and generally cover the equivalent of Books 1–2 of the *Ars maior*. Two important writers earlier than the fourth century belong in this category, Scaurus (second century) and Sacerdos (late third century). From the fourth century, in addition to Donatus himself, one can include the *Instituta artium* of Probus, the *Ars* of Victorinus, the (fragmentary) *Ars* of Marius Victorinus, the recently discovered (and even more recently named) *Ars Pseudo-Scauri,* and the so-called *Ars breviata* of Augustine; later are the bilingual grammar of Dositheus, what is now called the *Ars de nomine et verbo* of Consentius, part of what was originally a full grammar (early fifth century), the grammar of the *Anonymus Bobiensis* (fifth century?), and the *Excerpta* of Audax (fifth century?).

As the existence of the *Ars minor* shows, however, these were not always suitable for beginners—and true beginners became much more common as Latin became less likely to be someone's native language.[33] Some of the texts listed above include many more paradigms than Donatus, in order to suit the needs of their authors' classrooms; but other books, named *regulae* texts by Vivien Law, were made to fit more elementary needs.[34] The earliest of these may be Book 2 of Sacerdos' *Artes grammaticae*, a text all but identical to the *Catholica* of Probus; the other extant ones are from the fifth and sixth centuries: Phocas, *Ars de nomine et verbo*; Priscian, *Institutio de nomine et pronomine et verbo*; Eutyches, *Ars de verbo*; Anonymous, *De nomine et pronomine*; Ps.-Augustine, *Regulae*; Ps.-Palaemon, *Ars*. The method of such texts, in general, is to take one form in the paradigm and use that one to derive the rest. For the noun (generally the longest treatment), Ps.-Augustine (apparently following Caper) uses the nominative singular, while Ps.-Palaemon uses the ablative singular.[35] The analysis of verbs is conducted slightly differently, but the goal is the same: to teach paradigms to those whose Latin morphology is shaky. Ps.-Augustine deals with all eight parts of speech; other texts are less thorough: Ps.-Palaemon deals with six (omitting the indeclinable preposition and interjection); Phocas and Consentius with noun and verb alone.

32. Barwick (1922: 3–111) is the fundamental reconstruction, clearly right in its general principles, if not always believable in its details; for a good account of Barwick's argument, see Lammert (1931: 43–8). It should be noted that in modern scholarship *Schulgrammatik* is used to mean two quite different things: for Barwick, it included both fairly elementary grammars and the advanced texts such as Charisius, but more recently others, such as Law (2003: 65–80) and Luhtala (2010), distinguish an elementary *Schulgrammatik* from the more advanced texts, as do I.

33. It should, however, be recognized that *none* of these texts is designed for the completely Latinless: they presume the ability to understand at least some instruction, oral as well as written. On this, see Herren (1981) in connection with Latin in Ireland.

34. See Law (1997: 54–69, 2000).

35. In this he is following, although probably not aware of, Varro in *De lingua Latina*. Our use of the genitive singular is unusual in antiquity; even Donatus (*GL* 4.378.3) starts from the ablative, which is considerably more common; cf. Jeep (1893: 160–73).

There is a third category: if there are books for elementary and more advanced students, there are also books for teachers, the ones experienced instructors know to conceal from their students. These are large works, aiming to give a much more thorough and sometimes less normative view of grammar; the major texts in question are the *Artes* of Charisius and Diomedes in the fourth century and Priscian in the sixth. Such works offer a greater number of examples and quotations and a wider range of them than do the school grammars: the vast majority of quotations in Donatus are from Virgil, and the same is true for others, while Charisius and Priscian (Diomedes somewhat less so) are major sources for our knowledge of republican literature. They are also (another aspect of the same thing) all reliant in parts not just on other grammars, but also on treatises *De Latinitate* (see 5.3 above). At the same time, they are often much less prescriptive, even about the nature of grammar itself, than the school grammars: they admit more variety in inflection, they are interested in the changes in Latin over time, and—alone among the *ars* texts—these three offer some account of syntax. For Priscian, heavily influenced by the second-century CE Greek grammarians Apollonius Dyscolus and Herodianus, syntax (Books 17–18) is a large part of his book; for Charisius and Diomedes, it is only a few pages, but they show more sophistication on the subject than anyone else in the Roman grammatical tradition.[36]

4. AROUND THE *ARS*

a) Mastering the Basics: Orthography

Learning proper grammar, or even learning the kind of correctness of language represented by works *de Latinitate*, is not the first task of the budding Latinist (whether native speaker or not): spelling comes first, and in some contexts (e.g., the grammar of Marius Victorinus) spelling is considered as part of learning the alphabet.[37] But works on orthography, of which there are quite a few, occupy an uncertain position in the structure of education: very elementary in one sense, but in another closely related to issues of correct and incorrect Latinity. *Orthographia* (proper spelling) and *orthoepeia* (proper speech) border one another and at times, notably in the *De orthographia* of Velius Longus in the early second century, quite clearly overlap. Although in Greek grammatical writing "orthography" is limited to exploring the ambiguities of representing sounds that have no one obvious graphic representation, in Latin it is considerably broader. Not only can it deal with problems that are strictly orthographic, such as the various representations of the phoneme /k/ as c, k, or q or of the so-called *sonus medius* (as in the choice

36. Baratin (1989) is essential; on the decline of syntax, see also Chapter 5 above. The so-called *fragmentum Donatianum* (12.19 below) is also relevant here, but not enough survives for us to know what shape the complete work took.

37. For a very thorough review of orthographic texts and their contexts with much bibliography, see De Paolis (2010); see also *RE* s.v. *Orthographie B. lateinisch* (Strzelecki). I have not seen L. Chambon, *Les traités orthographiques latins (IIème–VIIIème siècles p.-C.). Historique, traduction, commentaire* (Diss. Lyon, 2008), cited by Biville (2011: 121 n.3).

between writing *maximus* or *maxumus*), or of the presence and representation of aspirates, but it spreads to discussion of the assimilation of prefixes, words with alternate spellings and pronunciations (*arcesso* or *accerso*), and, eventually, to changes in the spelling and pronunciation of Latin over time. Some of these topics appear in works on Latinity, such as Caesar's *De analogia*; others, increasingly over time, are more like lists of *differentiae*. Even Velius, early in the tradition, reveals that some people distinguished in meaning as well as form between *actarios* and *actuarios* (*GL* 7.74.10–11) and between *aspergo* (verb) and *aspargo* (noun) (75.7–9) as well as having difficulty seeing (or hearing) the difference between *aquam* and *acuam* (75.10–11).

In one form or another, works on orthography are attested before we know securely of any *ars grammatica*. Verrius Flaccus wrote a work on the subject, Velius in the early second century was able to draw on another orthographic work (by Nisus, who also commented on Virgil), and the tradition remains active at least until the ninth century: the latest text included by Keil is in fact a work on orthography by Albinus, the name used by Alcuin. Many general grammars touch on spelling, generally under the rubric *De litteris*; thus Charisius 5–6B deals with the orthographic problems of c/k/q as well as some of the uses of letters as abbreviation; Cledonius (*GL* 5.28) deals with the former problem; Dositheus (*GL* 7.11–21) says a little more, but is more concerned with the question of what letters can appear together with which others. Diomedes (*GL* 1.421–6) also talks about the uses of single letters, as well as about the problem of assimilation of prefixes. Priscian includes quite a lot of instruction in spelling (and meter) under *De litteris*, as does Iulianus of Toledo in seventh-century Visigothic Spain (113–26MY). Others, such as the austere Donatus, simply categorize the letters themselves (vowel, semivowel, mute, liquid) and stay entirely away from questions of orthography; his commentator Servius makes up for it a little (*GL* 4.421–3). At the other extreme, Marius Victorinus (70–86M) includes a full discussion of orthography after his chapter *De litteris*. In general, when orthography is included in a larger grammar, the topic is fairly narrowly defined; in this, Marius Victorinus is a clear exception, and he marks his own discussion as being unusual and digressive. The problems of representing sounds and of the relationship of the alphabet to the sounds that need to be represented—the *sonus medius*, /k/, the representation of semivowels (when do you write -ii-, when just -i̲-)—appear regularly, and they are clearly troublesome to ten-year-olds.

The many treatises solely interested in orthography are obviously more expansive, and although they have a great deal in common, they take different tacks. The two earliest complete orthographic treatises are almost contemporary (early to mid-second century) but seem to be entirely independent of one another. Velius Longus starts from the discussion of letters, paying particular attention to the vowels, and only then moves on to spelling itself (*GL* 7.47.18–53.24). There he begins from a topic to which he frequently returns, the relationship between spelling and pronunciation (54.1–5.26); but he spends the most time on familiar topics such as the representation of the sound of long i̲; the *sonus medius*; the spelling of words in which consonantal u is followed by vocalic u (*equus* or *equos*); the phonetic and orthographic effect of combining prepositions and other words (*adcelerare* or *accelerare*); and the various uses of k, q, and c. Unlike some other orthographic writers, he does not say much about the letter h and the presence or absence of aspiration. Scaurus treats the subject very differently; he begins by describing the four ways in which errors of orthography occur—*adiectio, detractio, immutatio*, and *adnexio* (adding or subtracting letters; transposing them; and misdividing syllables)—and the three means of correcting those errors: *historia, originatio* (glossed by the Greek *etymologia*), and *proportio* (glossed by *analogia*). These categories are very familiar, although nowhere else are they connected to orthography; almost certainly, Scaurus took them from Varro, who is one of the few sources he cites by name.[38] After establishing the varieties of error, Scaurus then (like Velius and some others) goes through the relationships and possible combinations of the individual letters (*GL* 7.13.1–18.11), and devotes the remainder of the book to anatomizing various orthographic mistakes in accordance with his four initial categories of error (18.12–29.2).

Velius and Scaurus are the most substantive treatises on orthography; the later tradition is less thoughtful. These later texts also come in groups, one assembled by Agroecius in fifth-century Gaul, one by Cassiodorus at Vivarium in the sixth century. Agroecius' *Ars de orthographia* (written between 434 and 450) presents itself as a supplement to the work of Caper which the dedicatory letter reports had been sent to him by Eucherius, to whom his own book is addressed. He describes it as *de orthographia et de proprietate ac differentia sermonum*, and indeed in the manuscripts it is generally accompanied by two works attributed to Caper, one entitled *Orthographia Capri*, the other *Caper de verbis dubiis*. The first is in fact a set of *differentiae*: some are distinctions of meaning, such as the first entry which distinguishes between *quo* and *ubi* (*GL* 7.92.2), others offer distinctions of pronunciation, for example, between *sevi* and *servi* (93.1), and others note correct morphology, for example, *non est sorbo, sed sorbeo, nec sorbsi, sed sorbui* (94.9). The author occasionally provides his mnemonics in verse: *pauperies damnum est, paupertas condicio ipsa* (99.13: "*pauperies* is the loss of property, *paupertas* is the state of being poor"). The work *De verbis dubiis* provides a similar set of distinctions, occasionally overlapping with *Orthographia*, but much more succinct and grouped alphabetically. Neither work was written by the second-century

38. The fourfold division is rarely found elsewhere in connection with orthography, but (recognizing that *adnexio* is in Scaurus a substitute for *transmutatio* = *metathesis*) is a regular tool for the analysis of both barbarism and metaplasm (cf. Quintilian 1.5.6, Charisius 350.7B, and elsewhere) whose antecedents go back to Plato (*Cratylus* 294b) and Aristotle (*Poet.* 1458a34ff), and which was used in physics and metaphysics as well as in the analysis of language; see, e.g., Desbordes (1983); Baratin (1989: 82–4). Its earliest appearance in Latin is in connection with paronomasia at *Rhet. Her.* 4.29. *Historia* is more problematic: it is distinct from *originatio*, and must be equivalent to *auctoritas* or *consuetudo*, i.e., traditional usage. On this, see Biddau (2008: 73).

scholar Flavius Caper, but some entries may derive from his *De Latinitate*. Agroecius bills his own work as a supplement to "Caper," and like those works is less an orthography than a set of *differentiae* beginning with the spelling of his own name (Agroecius, not Agricius, *GL* 7.114.7–8) and including orthographic distinctions (*abitum/habitum*), differences of meaning (*poculum/potio*), and a few syntactical instructions (*memini me facere*, not *memini me fecisse*). It uses more literary examples than "Caper" but is otherwise very similar.

The other collection of works on orthography is larger, more ambitious, and more deliberate. In order to assist the monks at Vivarium in their Latin, Cassiodorus in his old age collected texts of grammar and spelling to accompany his *Institutes*, and the spelling collection comprises twelve sets of excerpts.[39] Of these, the source of the first (*GL* 7.147.24–54.11) is given as *De enuntiatione vel orthographia* of Annaeus Cornutus; it appears to be a set of excerpts rather than an independent work, but it may well derive from the first-century scholar. There follows a short set of excerpts from Velius Longus, a longer one from the otherwise unknown Curtius Valerianus, and then one from the equally unknown Papirianus.[40] All these excerpts consist of discussions of problematic letters of the alphabet accompanied by longer or shorter sets of admonitions, often *differentiae*, about specific words. Cassiodorus then divides into four sets the advice of Martyrius (sixth century?) concerning the letters b and v; that is followed by a set drawn from Eutyches' *De adspiratione*; two from Caesellius Vindex (the second identified as "Caecilius Vindex") and a final set from Cassiodorus' contemporary Priscian. It can be seen from the sequence of orthographic texts from "Caper" onward that orthography tends rapidly towards becoming lists of proper and improper spellings, some of which are of interest for what they reveal about the changing pronunciation of Latin over time, but very few of which have much concern with any broader issues than individual words and sounds. The end of the series of orthographic texts comes with Bede and Albinus (Alcuin), each of which is simply an alphabetical list of correct spellings and *differentiae*: orthography has become lexicography.

One last area that might be considered orthographical should be mentioned here, however briefly.[41] Discussions of the alphabet, such as are found in the earlier orthographic writers and some of the grammarians' chapters *de litteris*, often include explanation of the use of individual letters as abbreviations, for example, A. for Aulus. The explanation of abbreviations and *notae* in general belonged in part to grammatical education—and Julius Paris' *Epitome* of Valerius Maximus ends with a short treatise *De praenominibus*, which clearly fell under

39. Keil conveniently collects the references in the *Institutes* to the orthographic collection, *GL* 7.210–16. For more on Cassiodorus, see 12.11 below.

40. This may the same person as Q. Papirius, a fragment of whose work *De orthographia* is printed by Keil at GL 7.216.8–14, and may also be the same as the Paperinus cited by various Irish grammarians. See 12.32 below.

41. See also 6.3d above and 10.4.6 below.

the purview of the grammarian—and in part to more specialized fields. We have already had occasion to mention the *Anecdoton Parisinum*, discussing the critical signs used in their textual work by Aristarchus, Probus, and others; Keil also included in *Grammatici Latini* seven lists of *Notae* edited for him by Mommsen. Most of them are quite explicitly legal abbreviations, but the first, ascribed in the manuscript to Valerius Probus, begins with *praenomina* before proceeding, through *a.u.c.* and *s.p.q.r.*, to specifically legal terminology. As in other areas, the task of the grammarian was not always well defined: just as it merged imperceptibly with that of the rhetorician, it was also linked to the technical education designed to prepare students for a practical career in law or business.

b) Towards Poetry: Meter and Prosody

Like proper spelling, the understanding of correct prosody and poetic meter is an essential part of knowing how to read or write Latin; like orthography, these subjects can either be incorporated in the *ars* or treated independently. Sacerdos and Diomedes include discussions of meter, and the table of contents of Charisius' *Ars* shows that he once did; Donatus and Priscian do not (although Donatus includes a chapter *De pedibus* after the discussion of the syllable). Like orthography, the discussion of meter remained important well beyond antiquity: anyone writing Latin (as a second language in particular) needs to know spelling; anyone writing Latin poetry in the classical manner needs to know meter. The tradition continues long past the scope of this volume; it includes Aldhelm, Bede, and Alcuin, and continues until the Renaissance and beyond.[42] But like orthography, metrics is not a part of the core of the *ars grammatica*, which remained focused on the parts of speech and their proper inflection.[43] Metrics, more than most parts of grammar, occupies an unusual position: works about meter and prosody are relevant both to the teaching of proper Latin and to *enarratio poetarum*. On the one hand, one needs to know at least prosody in order to pronounce Latin—prose or poetry—correctly (and at a more advanced level, a knowledge of metrics is needed in order to write poetry oneself); on the other hand, the student reading Latin poetry needs to know something about the meters in which that poetry was written.[44] The interest in verse composition should not be minimized. Caesius

42. For work on prosody after the early Middle Ages, see the valuable collection of material in Leonhardt (1989b).

43. In this connection, it is worth noting that in Martianus Capella, *grammatica* is told not to talk about meter because it is part of music, and that Martianus in fact wrote a treatise on metrics (as yet unpublished; but see De Nonno 1990a and 2014) separate from *De nuptiis Mercuriae et Philologiae*. See 12.27.2 below.

44. On metrical writings in general, see also De Nonno (1990c: 618–26, 1990d, including a substantial discussion of unmetrical quotations in the grammarians). De Nonno (2014) discusses the most important brief treatises on metrics. I note here that J. Luque Moreno and others have produced under the general rubric *Scriptores latini de re metrica: concordantiae, indices* (18 vols., Granada, 1987–2002) a set of concordances limited to those portions of grammatical texts that concern prosody and meter and those

Bassus in his concluding paragraph refers to the pleasure of recognizing meters: *et multa ipsi nova excogitare possimus* (6.271.25–6). Even three or four centuries later, the anonymous text known as *De ultimis syllabis ad Caelestinum* makes it clear that prosody is being explained for students to use, not merely to learn.[45]

The origins of Latin metrical writing—like the origins of Latin grammatical writing—are not altogether clear. Varro certainly wrote about dramatic meters in *De sermone Latino* and about meter in general (probably in other works) but little survives; the only person earlier than Varro cited in connection with meter is Lucilius (fr. 32, 36 Funaioli = 1294, 1209 Marx).[46] Other than Caesius Bassus (discussed above), the earliest writings on metrics are by Terentianus Maurus (late second century or early third) and Sacerdos (late third century).

Introductions to meter that were composed as independent texts sometimes begin, like normal grammars, with a discussion of letters and syllables, but then move not to grammatical morphology but to metrical analysis. Thus, the long poem of Terentianus has a first book on letters and a second on syllables; the third and longest on meters does not begin until line 1300. The same is true of the large fourth-century metrical handbooks of Atilius Fortunatianus and Apthonius (Asmonius): they similarly start from the basics (letters, syllables), and then progress through discussion of feet to the discussion of particular meters; so too the short *De metris* of Mallius Theodorus. But other handbooks are simply explanations of various meters. Some are (or were, when complete) repertories of all meters, according to either derivationist theory, such as that of Caesius, or according to prototypical theory, like Servius *De centum metris*, a relatively unadorned list of the various meters to be derived from the eight fundamental metrical feet.[47] Others are devoted to the meters of particular authors: the difficult scansion of Roman comedy attracted attention in late antiquity, with the odd and probably unfinished treatise of Rufinus from the fifth century and the more sober

words that might be useful to students of prosody and meter. They are accordingly of limited value to anyone else, and I have not included them in the bibliographies in Part II.

45. See De Nonno (1990b: 229–31) and 12.46.6 below.

46. For a careful and detailed reconstruction of what can be known about Varro's writings on meter, see D'Alessandro (2012: 147–82 in particular on the fragments of *De sermone Latino* quoted by Rufinus); more briefly, see also Leonhardt (1989a: 49–50).

47. Derivationist analysis bases all meters on iambic senarius and dactylic hexameter, explaining variations through the processes of addition, subtraction, substitution, and transposition; prototypical analysis bases all meters on the combinations of eight (sometimes nine) fundamental metrical feet, admitting also the existence of the so-called *asynarteta* (translated by Sacerdos as *inconvenientia*, *GL* 6.545.16), complex juxtapositions of two metrical patterns in the same verse. Caesius and Terentianus are the two most thoroughgoing derivationists, while later texts often have some amalgamation of the two. The most thoroughgoing prototypicalist is Servius in *De centum metris*. The clearest and best treatments are those of Leonhardt (1989a) and D'Alessandro (2012: 25–51). See also 4.2 above on Caesius.

and careful work of Priscian *De metris fabularum Terentii et aliorum comicorum* from the sixth. Horatian lyric was of earlier and more insistent interest: not only does the work of Caesius end with a discussion of Horatian meters, but the much longer work of Atilius Fortunatianus also ends with a discussion of Horatian metrics, and Servius too wrote a brief work *De metris Horatii*—not to mention the short and anonymous fragment *De metris Horatii* transmitted with the works of Caesius and Atilius.

In most grammars, there is a chapter *De syllabis*; in general, its purpose is to teach how to determine syllabic length, and in general, the authors assume optimistically that students can distinguish a naturally long vowel from a naturally short one. But while that assumption may have been true in the classical period, it became less and less so. By the fifth century, if not earlier, a high proportion of students would not have been native speakers of Latin. Even by the third century, Latin pronunciation had changed significantly: unstressed syllables tended to be seen as short and stressed ones as long, even though that was, historically, not necessarily the case. This tendency begins early (apparent in the shortening of final -o̱ by the first century CE), and Donatus in the middle of the fourth century classed as a barbarism the pronunciation of *deos* with long -e̱- and short -o̱-.

Thus, one of the most significant alterations of the grammarian's curriculum (no later than the middle of the fourth century) was the addition of prosody: it was necessary to teach students very basic methods for identifying a long or short vowel if the quantity is unknown. Final syllables offered a starting point, both because it was often easier (because of double consonants) to recognize a long syllable in earlier positions and because it was possible to instruct students in the regular quantities of inflectional endings. Discussions of this kind are found in Diomedes and in Martianus Capella's book on grammar, but they more frequently appear as short independent texts, often given the title *De finalibus* or *De ultimis syllabis*; of these Servius' short treatise *De finalibus* (*GL* 4.449–55) is possibly the earliest. Such works offer either an explanation of quantity limited to final syllables or a more elaborate discussion of how to determine syllabic length in any syllable.[48] These texts reveal the necessity for very elementary instruction about pronunciation and they offer often lengthy explanations of how to determine where a syllable begins and ends in order to determine its quantity, at times with a note of resignation: thus "Metrorius"

48. The two fundamental treatments of texts *de finalibus* (on which I draw here) are De Nonno (1990b) and Leonhardt (1989b: 24–71); also useful are Corazza (2003) and (2011). Texts of this sort are sometimes independent, sometimes connected to the tradition of Donatus and his commentators; they include Servius *De finalibus*, Anonymous *De ultimis syllabis ad Caelestinum*, and the interlocking set of texts known variously as "Metrorius" *De finalibus*, Maximus Victorinus *De ratione metrorum*, and *Ad Basilium amicum Sergii* (on all of which see 12.17, 12.40.2, 12.46.4, 6, and 7 below). See also Diomedes, *GL* 1.492.15–4.2 and Martianus Capella 3 §278–88. For a detailed account of the grammarians' treatment of the syllable, see Scialuga 1993.

ends his general account of syllabic length by saying:[49] *Nam quod ad naturam* [sc. *syllabarum*] *pertinet, licet artis praecepta deficiant, primas syllabas solis confirmamus exemplis, medias in latino sermone accentu probamus, ultimas arte colligimus* (*GL* 6.231.1–3: "As far as the quantity of syllables is concerned, if the *ars* is useless, we can determine the quantity of the first syllables of words only from examples, we can find the quantity of medial syllables in Latin by the word-accent, and we learn the quantity of final syllables from the grammar book"), after which he proceeds to discuss the quantity of final syllables by part of speech. At the same time, however, some of these texts show that they had a higher aim, to help students both to write proper metrical poetry and to speak aloud in classical Latin pronunciation rather than the speech of their own day. Discussion of prosody, moreover, is in some cases linked to discussions of prose rhythm: Servius explicitly described his *De finalibus* as a sequel to a discussion of classical prose rhythm written by (or at least attributed to) Donatus, although no such text survives.[50] And that provides a clear link (both in ancient grammatical writing and in this book) to a third para-grammatical theme, the relationship between grammar and rhetoric.

c) Towards Rhetoric: Tropes, Figures, and Elementary Exercises

Where does grammar end and rhetoric begin? Institutionally, the two are continuous: the student ambitious for a public career would move from the instruction of the *grammaticus* to that of the *rhetor* at about the age of seventeen. Quintilian, moreover, makes it clear (2.1) that the frontier between the two, although it might be clearly mapped out in theory, was in fact much less evident on the ground: some grammarians included a lot of the elementary rhetorical exercises, and some rhetoricians were perfectly happy to concede the territory and stick to the higher levels of rhetorical practice.[51] Even Quintilian himself suggests (1.9.1–3) that he would be just as happy if the end of the course of grammar included some instruction in elementary rhetorical exercises such as the *chria* (telling an anecdote), and in fact a short section on the *chria* is embedded among the chapters on prosody and meter that appear in the manuscript between the text of Caesius Bassus and the *Donatiani fragmentum*.[52] That location is consonant with the explanations of prosody discussed above: proper knowledge of quantities is a prerequisite for writing poetry—or for constructing one's clausulae correctly in writing prose for oral delivery.

49. The same sentence (or one very like it) is found elsewhere in texts on prosody.

50. On this, see the discussion of Leonhardt (1989b: 38–56). This lost work of Donatus remains hypothetical at best.

51. On the "border dispute" (Reinhardt and Winterbottom 2006: xxx) see Reinhardt and Winterbottom (2006: 35–7). That there was in fact considerable overlap is shown, for example, by Suetonius, *DGR* 4.4–6, 25.4. There is a useful review of discussions of rhetoric in Roman grammatical texts (up to the ninth century) in Knappe (1996).

52. On the order of texts in the sole manuscript of Caesius, see 12.9 below.

There are two other ways in which one should consider grammar and rhetoric together in addition to the sequential and overlapping progress the student makes from one to the other. One is that the two disciplines, as educational enterprises, exhibit a parallel structure. In rhetoric, there are essentially two varieties of surviving text: one is the *ars rhetorica*—as represented by the *Rhetorica ad Herennium* or Quintilian—and the other is the practical workbook of exercises—the *progymnasmata*. Quintilian, whose treatment is much more expansive than the norm, includes a discussion of these exercises in Book 2, but for the most part they are preserved only in Greek versions; the only Latin text, Priscian's *Praeexercitamina*, is a translation of the *Progymnasmata* ascribed to Hermogenes.[53] The progymnasmata were of immense importance in the schools of rhetoric and the practice of oratory: a set of generally a dozen types of preparation for the courtroom, ranging from narrative and fable to practice in praise and blame, commonplaces, and various types of argument.[54]

The texts of grammar do not divide so neatly as do *progymnasmata* and *ars rhetorica*, but there is clearly a similar kind of distinction between the *ars grammatica*, which is essentially a work used as an instructional tool by the teacher, not directly by the student, and the actual exercises of the classroom. These are most clearly represented by the *Partitiones* of Priscian, with their relentless discussion of every grammatical or metrical topic provoked, however tangentially, by the first lines of each book of the *Aeneid* (the only Latin example of an exercise more widely known in Greek). In some sense, however, this kind of elementary instruction is also the job of the texts of *regulae* and *catholica* (paradigms and morphology) and *differentiae* (precise distinctions between words of similar meaning) or a work like the *Exempla elocutionum* of Arusianus Messius.[55]

Works like that of Arusianus, however, or the anonymous *Carmen de figuris* that may be addressed to him, or indeed a number of treatises on tropes and figures, stand on the border between grammar and rhetoric in a different way. Tropes and figures, in particular, belong to rhetoric; but they are also incorporated in grammarians' discussions of *vitia et virtutes orationis*. That is the topic of the third book of Donatus' *Ars maior*:[56] he starts with barbarism and solecism

53. It is indicative of the uncertainty of the frontier that the *Praeexercitamina* are printed both among the grammars and among rhetorical texts (*GL* 3.430–40 = *RLM* 551–60).

54. For the progymnasmata, see particularly Quintilian 2.4 with the commentary of Reinhardt and Winterbottom (2006: 74–119); a useful brief account also in Frazel (2009: 23–33).

55. On *regulae* and similar texts, see 8.3 above. My analysis of varieties of texts there takes a different approach, but it is important to recognize that there was no strict division among types of grammatical textbook and no fixed barrier between what was elementary and what was advanced.

56. See esp. Holtz (1981: 136–216). For a discussion of the figures as treated by the grammarians, see also Torzi (2000: 37–58).

(3.1, 3.2), then has a chapter *De ceteris vitiis*, with brief illustrations of the ten other kinds of error in Latinity. The second half of the book moves to *virtutes*. *Metaplasmus* (3.4) is the alteration of a word *metri ornatusve causa*. *Schemata lexeos* (figures, 3.5) are seventeen in number, each illustrated. And the thirteen *tropi* (3.6) fill the longest chapter in the book.[57]

In a certain sense, it is clear that barbarism and solecism at least belong in a grammarian's classroom: they are the common forms of simple mistake (in single words and in the connections between words, respectively) against which students need to be warned. But there are several striking features about this discussion, as indeed about most discussions of *vitia et virtutes*: both virtues and vices are illustrated from the works of the poets, particularly Virgil, and the "virtues" are really grammatical or prosodical variations that are permitted to poets—but not to students. The discussion of virtues and vices is in fact a basic introduction to poetic style, on the differences between strict grammar and literary expression. In that respect, the last part of Donatus' *Ars* could be seen to lead seamlessly into the other half of the grammarian's job, *enarratio poetarum*.

In another sense, however, book 3 of Donatus clearly leads not to poetry but to rhetoric. In the introduction to the discussion of *schemata* in 3.5, he distinguishes between two sorts of figure: *Schemata lexeos sunt et dianoeas, sed schemata dianoeas ad oratores pertinent, ad grammaticos lexeos* (*GL* 4.397.5–6: "There are figures of speech and figures of thought, but figures of thought belong to rhetoricians and figures of speech belong to grammarians"). In this case, the frontier between grammar and rhetoric is well marked and patrolled. At the beginning of the tradition, Quintilian makes a similar division: as noted above, in his discussion of the grammarian's role he includes an extended treatment of barbarism and solecism, but breaks off when he gets to *schemata*: it is not until books 8 and 9 that he treats the tropes and figures, under the heading of *ornatus*. Even if those features are found in poetry, they belong to rhetoric.[58]

What is clear about such material, in general, is that while it clearly fell (at least some of it) under the grammarian's purview, it was not an essential part of the *ars* itself any more than was metrics. In this regard, Barwick's influential argument about the Greek model for the Roman *ars* is wrong: he believed that the study of linguistic correctness was a part of the Stoic *Tekhnê peri phônês*, and was transferred, as the study of virtues and vices, to the Roman *ars* as an essential

57. The ten other *vitia* (3.3) are *acyrologia* (wrong word), *cacemphaton* (obscenity), *pleonasmos* (words unnecessary for meaning), *perissologia* (meaningless verbosity), *macrologia* (longwindedness), *tautologia* (just what it looks like), *eclipsis* (leaving out a necessary word), *tapinosis* (humble words for lofty subjects), *cacosyntheton* (poor composition of phrases), and *amphibolia* (ambiguity). If I were to list all thirty figures and tropes, I would be guilty of *macrologia*.

58. Note also that at the beginning of his discussion (8.6.1–3) Quintilian reports with relief that he is ignoring the quarrels among grammarians and philosophers about the organization and number of the tropes. Disputed territory is always dangerous.

element in grammar. In fact, although most of the full grammars (Sacerdos, Charisius, and Diomedes, but not Priscian) do have some discussion of correct language, Donatus' grammar is the only one that seems to follow the structure emphasized by Barwick.[59] Good Latin can in fact mean two quite different things, and the tension between them is exemplified by the fact that examples from Virgil are used to illustrate both good and bad usage. Proper Latinity is either (in terms of grammar) the absence of error or (in terms of rhetoric) the presence of enhancement (*ornatus*). As early as the first century BCE, it is clear that the nature of *Latinitas* was disputed: Cicero, speaking as an orator, found it a very minor part of the analysis of good style, something that should be assumed of every educated speaker of the language, while Caesar, in replying in his *De analogia* to Cicero's scorn for mere *Latinitas* in *De oratore*, demonstrated just how complicated it was to recognize "good" Latin.[60]

There are other ways in which grammar and rhetoric meet or overlap, although generally not within the *ars grammatica* itself. Above all, commentary on literary texts generally includes observations about either the tropes and figures (as with Servius, mentioned above) or about the rhetorical composition and effect of particular scenes and speeches, or even whole poems. In the same way, there are also commentaries on texts studied in the rhetorical schools, and while the commentaries on Cicero's *De inventione* are themselves textbooks of rhetoric and pay little attention to Cicero's grammar, commentaries on his speeches—equally the object of the rhetorician's attention—include a great deal of discussion of language as well as of rhetoric. Both we and the Roman educational system separate the two areas, but one should also recognize that they are adjacent and that at times the line between them is not so sharp as one might think.[61]

59. Barwick (1922: 89–107). For correctives, see particularly Baratin and Desbordes (1986) and Baratin (1994). The notion of "correctness" is a very complex one; an important discussion, in relationship to syntax, in Baratin (1989: 259–364).

60. On this, see 3.6 above.

61. For the practical goals of a book like this, however, it is necessary to draw the line somewhere. In this case, it is between the collections of Keil and Halm: I have given bibliography and descriptions of works included in *GL* (the most rhetorical of them being Arusianus Messius' *Exempla elocutionum* and Priscian's *Praeexercitamina*), but not of the works on tropes, figures, and *schemata* in *RLM*. However, it may be useful to list the works printed by Halm that seem most relevant to the discussions of the same subject in the grammarians. In specific: P. Rutilius Lupus, *Schemata lexeos* (*RLM* 3–21 = Barabino 1967 = Brooks 1970); Aquila Romanus, *De figuris sententiarum et elocutionis liber* (*RLM* 23–37 = Elice 2007); Iulius Romanus, *De figuris sententiarum et elocutionis liber* (*RLM* 38–47); [Iulius Romanus], *De schematis lexeos, De schematis dianoeas* (*RLM* 48–62); Anon., *Carmen de figuris vel schematibus* (*RLM* 63–70 = D'Angelo 2001); Anon., *Schemata dianoeas* (*RLM* 71–7); Beda, *Liber de schematibus et tropis* (*RLM* 607–18; for further bibliography, see 13.4 below). Iulius Romanus should not be confused with the grammarian Iulius Romanus excerpted by Charisius. Desbordes (1996: 239–88) supplies a valuable list and bibliography of rhetorical texts, both Greek and Latin.

5. LOST GRAMMARS AND PSEUDONYMOUS TEXTS

Although I have already listed a great many texts—by no means all—it is important to recognize not only that they represent, iceberg-like, a vast array of grammatical works sunken (almost) without trace but also that the extant works are not always what they claim to be. A good example of this is provided by a text at the later end of one branch of the grammatical tradition, Audax's book entitled *De Scauri et Palladii libris excerpta per interrogationem et responsionem* (*GL* 7.320–62). Audax's work is a relatively traditional *Schulgrammatik* with some variations: after the definitions of *ars* and grammar, it adds chapters *De lectione* and *De Latinitate* before *De voce*, and between that and *De litteris* come three short paragraphs *De definitione, De oratione*, and *De distinctione* as well as some rather longer sections on accentuation and metrics between the syllable and the noun. Then come the eight parts of speech, followed by three further chapters, *Recapitulatio de accentibus, De barbarismo*, and *De soloecismo*.

The text of Audax seems complete, but it has suffered some loss in the middle: the chapter on the participle breaks off after a few lines, in the middle of a sentence, at *GL* 7.349.8. And, strangely enough, everything after that lacuna, except for the last two chapters, is quite close to the corresponding chapters of Probus, *Instituta artium*. At the same time, most of what comes before the lacuna is equally close to the grammar of Victorinus, although some of the sections are in a different order.[62] It is generally assumed that since the models we can identify change at the break in the text, the break is between Audax's use of what he calls Scaurus and of what he calls Palladius who are, from our point of view, in fact Victorinus and Probus.

The relationship between Scaurus, Victorinus, and Audax is complex and difficult to determine, but the problem is illustrative of the confusion often found in the transmission of grammatical works. For while the name "Scaurus" clearly refers to the second-century grammarian Terentius Scaurus whose work on orthography we possess independently, it is not clear that *any* of the versions of his grammar in the manuscripts accurately reflects what he actually wrote. The simpler problem is the relationship between Victorinus and Scaurus. In the first place, Victorinus is clearly not the same as what Audax defined as Scaurus: even though they are almost identical in places, each has material not in the other and the text of Victorinus as we have it is badly disarranged and itself comes from more than one source (in a part not found in Audax, Victorinus refers to Donatus for material on pronouns that he omits). Thus, Audax cannot have been excerpting from the text of Victorinus that we have, and thus our "Victorinus" and Audax's "Scaurus" are not identical: each is an independent excerpt from some original, which may have been by the real Scaurus—except that, while both Audax

62. The last two chapters of Audax, on barbarism and solecism (the latter not printed by Keil), are very similar to a text on the same subject in Basel F III 15d ascribed to *Victo* but not otherwise attested. For details on Victorinus, see 12.45.1 below.

and Victorinus use identical question-and-answer form, Scaurus' original *Ars* was clearly not such a catechism. That leads to the conclusion that the question-and-answer version of Scaurus used by both Audax and Victorinus preserves an intervening stage: from the genuine Scaurus to the catechistic Scaurus to the two representations of it that now exist in Victorinus and Audax.

But there is another element to the problem. In 1987, Vivien Law published a report of an anonymous text found on foll. 52–62 of Munich, Clm 6281, a ninth-century grammatical manuscript. It is a brief *ars grammatica*, consisting of a set of introductory sections (*De arte, De uoce, De litteris, De syllabis, De dictione*, and *De locutione*) followed by the parts of speech. Because of similarities between this text and quotations from Scaurus in other grammarians, and (more important) because four quotations attributed to Scaurus in the fifth-century *Explanationes in Donatum* (and some in Diomedes) are virtually identical to the text in Clm 6281, Law argued that this text was in fact by Scaurus, probably a shorter form of his large, very influential grammar.[63] But while the author of the *Explanationes* clearly thought the book he was quoting was by Scaurus, it is not: in particular, there are significant differences between the definitions of parts of speech in the Munich text and the definitions quoted from (the genuine) Scaurus by Diomedes. There are also further apparent differences in grammatical doctrine, which suggest that the Munich text in its present form was probably composed in the fourth century.[64]

But if not Scaurus, what? Anna Reinikka, who has studied and now edited the Munich text, gives it the title *Ars Pseudo-Scauri*: at some point, the text that is now anonymous must have had the name of Scaurus attached to it, the name by which the later commentator on Donatus knows it. And while parts of it certainly do not derive from Scaurus, there are enough similarities between it and the Scaurus of Audax/Victorinus to make it likely that there is a Scaurus somewhere in the background: whoever composed this text used Scaurus in part, but revised his grammar in some respects. Thus, material deriving from the Hadrianic *Ars grammatica* of Terentius Scaurus had within a few centuries been recycled into perhaps three forms (the *Ars Pseudo-Scauri*, a putative catechistic form used by Audax, and Victorinus), two of which still bore his name although they are not, and were never meant to be, accurate reproductions of the original text.

Something similar may well have happened to Audax's second source. This Palladius is not otherwise known (nor can the Probus of the *Instituta artium* be identified with any other Probus); but Audax's Palladius is not nearly so close to Probus as Audax's Scaurus is to Victorinus, and so there is no reason to assume that the text we know as the *Instituta artium* was "really" written by Palladius.[65]

63. Law (1987).

64. The authenticity of all late-antique representations of Scaurus' grammar was questioned (before the discovery of the Munich text) without serious argument by Tempesti (1977). The authenticity of the Munich text was first questioned by Reinikka (2008); she has now made a full edition, commentary and translation in Reinikka (2013).

65. For details, see 12.31 below.

A terminus post quem for our version of *IA* is provided by the reference (*GL* 4.119.26) to the Baths of Diocletian, completed in 305. Furthermore, the *IA* as we have it is only the first of two books: references ahead show that there was, or was intended to be, a second book, dealing above all with sounds and meters, and there is also a prospective reference to a section *de orthographia*. So we are again left with several possibilities: (a) "Palladius" wrote a full grammar early in the fourth century, which Audax excerpted and from which Probus borrowed extensively; (b) "Palladius" wrote only about the parts of speech, which Audax excerpted and which Probus supplemented (or planned to supplement) under his own name; or (c) the text which we know under the name of Probus was in fact written by Palladius and was mislabeled fairly early. Of these, the most likely seems to me (a), but certainty is impossible.[66] Again, there is a situation in which the same text appears under different names, and different versions of a text appear under the same name. Authorship is not the issue; content is.

But we are not done with "Probus." The other large text preserved under that name is the *Catholica*, a detailed set of inflections (a *regulae* grammar) of nouns and a briefer one of verbs, followed by a short discussion of prose rhythm. The *Catholica* declares itself (*GL* 4.3.2) a sequel to *instituta artium*—but clearly not the *Instituta artium* attributed to "Probus." In fact, the *Catholica* is almost word-for-word identical to Book 2 of the *Artes grammaticae* of Sacerdos, written in the third century; so much so, that the damaged opening of Sacerdos' book can reliably be supplied from the text of Probus. It is a curious feature of the transmission, moreover, that the manuscript of Sacerdos Books 1–2 (Sacerdos 3 is transmitted separately) and the manuscript of the *Catholica* were originally separate books, both written in the fifth century in northern Italy, probably in the same scriptorium but by different hands, but now bound in a single book in which the text of Probus immediately precedes the text of Sacerdos.[67]

We are not quite done with "Victorinus" either. There are several texts that are ascribed to someone named Victorinus; they are not necessarily by the same author, and some have alternate ascriptions. But among the various Victorini there is one very famous one, the mid-fourth-century grammarian, rhetorician, philosopher, and (eventually) Christian convert and commentator C. Marius Victorinus. An *ars grammatica* exists (*GL* 6.3–173) which the incipit and the explicit of the first book ascribe to Marius Victorinus; but the explicit of Book 4 ascribes the text to one Aelius Festus Apthonius. The surviving text, in fact, is a combination of two different works: the very opening (3.1–31.16) is generally agreed to be by Marius Victorinus; there is then a lacuna, and the remainder of the text is generally ascribed to Apthonius. The subject matter and the style are quite different: Marius Victorinus' work is a teaching grammar, while Apthonius' is a treatise on metrics. So far so good: it is perfectly possible to imagine two

66. Schmidt (in *HLL* 5 §522.4) supports (c), without any real argument; it seems to me the least plausible explanation.

67. On the manuscript (Naples, Lat. 2), see De Nonno (1982: xviii–xxvii).

books, one on grammar and one on metrics, that were copied together, and that somehow most of the first and the beginning of the second were lost, leaving behind the uneasy combination that survives. The fact that Marius Victorinus' name appears in the explicit of Book 1—after the switch to Apthonius—is simply a scribal error: whoever wrote it assumed, not unreasonably, that the beginning and end of Book 1 were parts of the same text.

But when did Victorinus and Apthonius come together in this way, and who is Apthonius? The problem is more complicated than it looks at first sight. In the first place, Rufinus of Antioch, writing on comic meter probably in the later part of the fifth century, quotes (*GL* 6.556.23–7.18) from "Victorinus" a passage from the portion of the text that belongs to Apthonius (78.19–9.6): that suggests that the two had already merged by the fifth century. He also quotes (557.19–8.6) another passage from "Victorinus"/Apthonius (*GL* 6.80.27–1.13) which overlaps with a quotation made by Priscian (*GL* 3.420.2–7), probably a generation after Rufinus, from an author Priscian calls "Asmonius." In other words, the second part of this text circulated both under the name of Victorinus (as we have it) and under the name of Asmonius. What is more, although Rufinus' extended quotations from Victorinus match our text, Priscian's much shorter quotation differs significantly; and while some of the differences are the result of Priscian's adaptation to his own context (something Rufinus never does), some strongly suggest that the text Priscian knew as Asmonius differed from the text we know as Victorinus–Apthonius.

Given the similarity of the names Apthonius and Asmonius, it is likely that one is simply an error for the other; and it is generally believed that, since Priscian quotes from two different works under the name of Asmonius while Apthonius is only attested in the explicit of Victorinus–Apthonius, Asmonius is more likely to be correct, although no certainty is possible. Priscian's other quotation from Asmonius (*GL* 2.516.16) also provides a date: he cites a discussion of the perfect tense of the verb *scindo* from an *ars* addressed to the emperor Constantius (presumably Constantius II), written between 337 and 361 CE. Thus Marius Victorinus wrote an *ars grammatica* and Aelius Festus Asmonius wrote both an *ars grammatica* and a four-book treatise on metrics at roughly the same time, the middle of the fourth century. At some point over the next century, Victorinus' *ars grammatica* and Asmonius' treatise on metrics were somehow merged—not neatly, and therefore presumably because of physical damage to a manuscript containing both of them—with one author's name at the beginning and the other's at the end, while at the same time Asmonius' two works also circulated independently of Marius Victorinus, with some textual differences between the two versions.

One last peculiarity remains. Rufinus' useful habit of collecting verbatim quotations from his sources without making much attempt to avoid duplication means, in this case, that we not only have a passage on metrics quoted from "Victorinus" (556.23–7.18), but also another version of the same material, similar but not identical in wording, quoted from "Firmianus to Probus" (564.7–20). "Firmianus," in this case, can be identified as the Christian writer Lactantius, who also wrote a set of four books of letters to one Probus, including grammatical materials;[68] as Lactantius' career is a generation earlier than that of Marius Victorinus and Asmonius (d. 325), it is clear that he is not dependent on our extant text. As with some of the grammatical works mentioned above, so with these discussions of meter: more than one version of very similar texts circulated under the same name, or under different names. The material was shared, borrowed, shaped, and claimed as their own by several different writers. We are hard put to identify what we would think of as *the* author of any of these texts, but that is because our notions of authorship are not applicable.

Even major works in the grammatical tradition are singularly unstable: Diomedes may have used a fuller version of Charisius; Charisius or his source may have had a Palaemon that was fuller than the original; and some medieval Irish grammarians may have had a version of Diomedes fuller than ours, possibly under the name of Probus. Names and texts are not tied in a firm relationship, and just as works ascribed to a Diomedes or a Scaurus existed in more than one form, so texts tended to gravitate to a famous or comfortable pseudonym: not only are there half a dozen Probuses, but there are also three grammars that are attached, at one time or another, to the name of Asper. Assertions about what a given real individual contributed to the tradition should be made very cautiously.

The view expressed here of the uncertainty of authorship and the variability of texts is not universally accepted. Bölte long ago argued that while pre-fourth-century texts were very much ad hoc creations of teachers (not unlike what I have been describing), after Donatus that was no longer the case: teachers of the later fourth and fifth centuries wanted to preserve the documents of the grammatical past and confined their pedagogical innovations to commenting on Donatus.[69] In fact, that is not true: Audax and Ps.-Scaurus are certainly later than Donatus, and even in the tradition of Donatus commentary, modification of earlier texts was the norm rather than the exception. It is also worth drawing attention to a parallel in another area of technical writing: the works of the classical jurists of the Severan period were abridged, altered, and modified in the fourth and fifth centuries, and it is only with the classicizing revival of the sixth century that any attempt was made to recover the originals, which were then once more excerpted, altered—and destroyed by imperial decree.[70]

6. THE CASE OF CHARISIUS

Perhaps the most intelligible way to explore the issues of form and authenticity is through the grammar of Charisius. Fl. Sosipater Charisius was almost certainly not a professional grammarian; a man of some learning, he addressed his five-book grammar to his son, indicating that his son (and thus presumably Charisius

68. See Schmidt in *HLL* 5 §570.

69. Bölte (1888: 429–32).

70. The classic treatment of the pre-Justinianic transmission of juristic texts is Wieacker (1960).

himself) was not a native speaker of Latin. Almost certainly, Charisius was Greek; and almost certainly, his grammar was written somewhere in the eastern empire in, or not long after, the reign of Julian, whose name appears as an example (54.3–6B).[71] What is most striking about Charisius' work is his use of sources, and the relative clarity with which he identifies them: as he announces in the preface, his work is a digest of the work of other scholars, and he indicates his use of a specific source nearly forty times. Although frequently he simply identifies a source as *alii*, he names three regular sources: Cominianus nine times, Palaemon four times, and Iulius Romanus six times. What is more, when these grammarians are cited by name, they are cited in the same order—Cominianus comes first, Romanus last. Various attempts have been made to try to determine how much of this gathering of authorities was done by Charisius himself, and how much is taken over from the figure Karl Barwick labeled "der Gewährsmann der Charisiusgruppe" (the Authority)—so identified because it is very clear that there is one underlying common source shared by large parts of Charisius, Diomedes, Dositheus, the *Anonymus Bobiensis*, and the *Excerpta Andecavensia*. For some scholars, the Authority is identical to Cominianus—who is, incidentally, otherwise unknown, except that in the Middle Ages Charisius himself is often referred to as Cominianus—while for Barwick (with whom, hesitantly, I am inclined to agree), the passages of Cominianus were added to his main source by Charisius himself.[72] What is generally agreed is that all the passages from Palaemon and most of the chunks of anonymous sources were taken over by Charisius from the Authority, while chunks of Romanus (and maybe Cominianus) were added by Charisius himself. The details of the source criticism are doubtful, and while the question deserves to be reexamined, it is not likely to receive a definitive answer. What does matter is that the same stock of basic material appears in a number of works, not just the four closely related texts mentioned above, but in fact in most, if not all, the major surviving grammars of the fourth and fifth centuries. Sometimes a specific source (often Scaurus or Sacerdos) is named, but the material was available for borrowing and recycling over and over, under many names. Unsurprisingly, it appears to have traveled in two routes: one of very elementary outlines of grammar—and the brief passages of Cominianus show that his book was of that type—and one of more advanced texts, starting from Palaemon and reaching full development in Charisius and Diomedes.

71. On Charisius' origins and status, see most recently Uría Varela (2005) and (2009: 7–11).

72. The fundamental work of source-criticism, although probably wrong in many aspects, is Barwick (1922). The Gewährsmann first appears on p. 3, and Barwick summarizes his argument at 61–5. Despite its problems, it remains one of the very few essential works on the Roman grammatical tradition. For an earlier discussion, see Tolkiehn (1910); for good, fairly recent accounts of the source-problems, see Dionisotti (1984), De Nonno (1992), Bonnet (2000), Schenkeveld (2004: 4–28), and Uría Varela (2009: 11–38); a review of older scholarship by Schmidt in *HLL* 5 §523.2.

Charisius' style of taking over large and cohesive blocks of material from his sources is quite unlike that of his slightly later contemporary Diomedes, whose technique has been compared to mosaic (so Kaster 1988: 148) because of the extent to which he broke his sources into small bits and recombined them. As a result, while it is impossible to know exactly what Diomedes read, Charisius is semi-transparent and allows us at times to see through him to the works of earlier scholars: he may have abridged, but by and large he apparently made very little change in what he kept. Romanus' chapter on adverbs has been discussed before (see 5.3 above), but one can gain useful insight into the way that grammars work in general, and how Charisius in particular organizes his material, by looking at Charisius' larger chapter on adverbs of which Romanus' section is only a part.[73]

The chapter has four sources, clearly marked off from one another. Charisius begins from Cominianus, who obligingly defines the adverb (*adverbium est pars orationis quae adiecta verbo significationem eius implet atque explanat*: "an adverb is the part of speech which, when added to a verb, fills out and clarifies its meaning"), categorizes adverbs as either independent words or derived from something else, lists the three accidents of adverbs (*significatio, figura, comparatio*), identifies twenty-one meanings, two *figurae* (*simplex* and *composita*) and the grades of comparison—and all this in twenty-two lines of text (233.2–23B). The following anonymous discussion is far longer (233.27–41.19) and begins with exactly the same definition (substituting *praeposita* for *adiecta*); it adds one more meaning of the adverb (*personative*, i.e., such words as *mecum* or *tecum*). It then proceeds to a much longer discussion of the derivation of adverbs from nouns (including adjectives), anatomized by the termination of the noun (in the order *a, e, o, er, or, ur, es, is, us, ns, rs, x*; then back to further thoughts on *a* and *o*), followed in turn by a paragraph on the views of other grammarians on the formation of adverbs from parts of speech other than the noun and a final paragraph (the ending of which is marred by a serious lacuna and an incomprehensible half-sentence) on the varieties of local adverbs. All this takes nearly eight pages. The third discussion (241.20–6.17) is described as *longius* (but is not) and the discussion of *significationes* has evidently been abridged significantly. The passage is anonymous, but it refers to Palaemon in the opening paragraph and uses his terminology (examples introduced by *velut*; declensions categorized as *ordines*), so that it is almost certainly a version of Palaemon's *Ars*. It too begins with a definition virtually identical to Cominianus' (the two verbs *implet* and *explet* are reversed, but that is the only difference), offers a brief explanation of the endings of adverbs followed by a much longer (although as noted before, clearly abridged) discussion of the *significationes* (essentially the same as those of the other two, although leaving out the category of *eventus* [e.g., *forte*]) and paragraphs on the relationship between adverbs and prepositions and on other dubious types of adverb.

73. For accounts of the grammarians' treatment of the adverb, see Swiggers and Wouters (2002b) and Uría Varela (2016).

The fourth and final discussion of the adverb is that of Romanus (246.18–89.17), which is three times as long as the other three put together. The elaborate introduction to the list discussed above does not follow the categories of the other sources, but interweaves consideration of the place of the adverb in the system of parts of speech, going back to Stoic theory, with explanation of the *significationes*, of which he gives largely the same categories as the others, but five fewer and much less clearly listed. Also incorporated is some discussion of the endings of adverbs, but at the end of his preface he somewhat mockingly gives up on categorizations in favor of his alphabetical list.

What one sees in Charisius' chapter on the adverb, taken as a whole, is the simultaneous variety and homogeneity of the tradition. The definition of the adverb is virtually the same in four quite different sources that are centuries apart; the list of *significationes* varies in terms of order and grammatical form (Cominianus has abstract nouns for the varieties, the others have gerunds) but is essentially the same, except that Romanus has played with it. Romanus' work, of course, is fundamentally different: it is a text about Latinity, not about grammar, although his introduction and some entries in his list make it clear that while his primary interest is lexical rather than grammatical, he has structured his thoughts largely in terms of the *ars* tradition. It is also evident that Charisius, although apparently taking over the words of others, very clearly gave his composition a shape. Different features of the different texts receive emphasis: the formation of adverbs in the unidentified text, the *significationes* in Palaemon, the list of adverbs in Romanus. And that, of course, makes one wonder whether his claim to copy his sources accurately is actually true.

7. COMMENTING ON GRAMMAR: THE TRADITION OF DONATUS

The fundamental uniformity of the grammatical tradition represented by Charisius, Diomedes, and other texts of the fourth and fifth centuries was revealed by the work of Jeep, Tolkiehn, and Barwick in the late nineteenth and early twentieth centuries: there are differences, not to be minimized, in the way in which, for instance, the morphology of the noun was presented or in the order of the eight parts of speech, but there is also a basic similarity in presentation.[74] That is to say, by the end of the third century, the generation of Sacerdos, there appears to have been a consensus about what a Latin grammar should contain and how it should be presented; indeed, that consensus may go back as far as Scaurus in the reign of Hadrian. That does not mean that all late antique grammars are identical: they are not. But while they vary, for instance, in how they categorize nouns (by gender or declension; by nominative, genitive, or ablative endings; and how many declensions) or exactly what definitions they use, or what elements of grammar they emphasize, there is general agreement on the kinds of material a

74. Jeep (1893); Tolkiehn (1910); Barwick (1922).

grammar should supply, and more or less on the order in which it belongs. What we see in the fourth century, when for the first time there are enough surviving grammatical texts to form a less crude image of the subject, is a sequence of what might be called variations on a theme, from the *Instituta artium* attached to the name of Probus, probably composed (in one of its forms, at any rate) at the beginning of the century and probably in Rome, to the grammars of Marius Victorinus and Donatus and Charisius in mid-century (two from Rome, one possibly from Constantinople) to the grammar of Diomedes, probably at the end of the century and almost certainly (although its precise geography is uncertain) from the Greek East.

To some extent, this central tradition of the *ars grammatica* (at least as represented by extant texts) continues all the way to Priscian and his pupil Eutyches, the sixth-century grammarians in Constantinople: some of the texts, as noted before, place greater emphasis on analytic grammar, others, tempering the wind to the shorn lambs of late antiquity, place greater emphasis on paradigms. But one has a strong sense that a student in a classroom using any one of the extant texts would recognize the system and would experience difficulties created by the level of instruction, not by its content. However, of the authors I have named just now, one stands out as significantly different, both in the style of his presentation and in his effect on the shape of the later grammatical tradition: Donatus.

To single out Donatus as eccentric may seem perverse, given that I have several times referred to his *Ars* (or rather, the four books of his two *Artes*) as the canonical text of Latin grammar in its form and its content. That is true, but only in hindsight. For of all the surviving grammars, none would seem to be more difficult for a struggling student than Donatus' *Ars maior*: it is brief and elegant in its presentation, but it is so abstract and distant from the everyday problems of the beginner that it would require a great deal of hard work from the instructor to make it palatable or even intelligible.[75] That, indeed, is what happened, and what the tradition of grammatical writing and grammatical manuscripts from the fifth to the ninth centuries makes abundantly clear.

Donatus offered his grammar in two shapes:[76] the *Ars maior*, in three books, presented the introductory materials, then the parts of speech, and in a final book the *vitia et virtutes orationis*. The *Ars minor* was almost certainly written after the

75. So, rightly, Luhtala (2010).

76. The perception (and thus the transmission) of the arrangement of Donatus' grammatical work changed over time: almost certainly Donatus himself thought of the four books as a single *Ars* and modern scholars generally think of it (not using original titles) as an *Ars minor* in one book and an *Ars maior* in three. In the manuscript tradition, however, it is often divided into two pairs of two books, with Book 2 of the *Ars maior* given the heading *editio secunda*—because it is the second discussion of the parts of speech—or *partes maiores*. This division is apparent as early as Servius—at least the transmission divides his commentary into two pairs of two books—and pervades the commentary tradition. See Holtz (1981: 500–2).

Ars maior: it is a simplification of Book 2 (parts of speech) done in catechistic form, adding considerably more morphology: in the case of the verb, a full conjugation of *lego*. Even so, and even taking the two works as the two stages of a single curriculum, Donatus' lapidary work leaves much to be desired: he gives one paradigm for each gender of noun rather than dividing them by declensions (whether four or five was disputed, but either way is better than what he gives us); he analyzes nominal morphology by the ending of the ablative singular rather than using the genitive; and his rules for inflection take the student from the ablative singular to the genitive plural in generating the paradigm. So too, he divides verbs into three conjugations, distinguishing them by the last vowel of the second-person singular; and the conjugations, like the nominal declensions are arranged in alphabetical order of the relevant vowel. These are areas in which, by Donatus' time, there was already a choice of approaches: it is not merely that his analysis of declensions and conjugations is different from the one in common use now.[77]

In what looks like fairly fierce competition among grammatical textbooks, Donatus was not initially the bestseller he became; and it was not the bare Donatus that, beginning a half-century after he wrote, became remarkably successful. Despite Jerome's admiration for Donatus (which certainly helped his later reputation), not one of his written works did well on its own or in the form he wrote it.[78] His commentary on Terence has come down to us only in radical abridgment; his commentary on Virgil survived largely through its simplification by Servius in the fifth century; and it was Servius again who made Donatus' grammar the iconic text it became. In a paradoxical way, therefore, it was Donatus' uselessness that made him useful: his admirably austere and brief grammars were, as Servius saw, a perfect vehicle for teacherly elaboration. As a result, the dominant textbook for learning Latin for four centuries was not Donatus alone, but Donatus *auctus: Ars* plus commentary. As Holtz rightly notes, the two basic functions of the classical grammarian, teaching Latin and commenting on texts, became fused: Donatus became the classic on which grammarians wrote commentaries.[79]

Servius very clearly respected Donatus, in grammar as in the interpretation of Virgil, but in neither area did he treat his predecessor as unalterable. Servius' commentary both corrects Donatus and elaborates on him. In discussing syllabic length, where Donatus simply gave the eight circumstances in which syllables are *communes* (either long or short), Servius both numbers the eight to help the student keep track of them and gives examples drawn from Virgil of

77. On the history of nominal declension, Jeep (1893: 164–73) is still useful. Beck (1996) goes into great detail about the unreliability of Donatus' account of the alphabet and syllables. It is very easy to find things wrong with a grammar written in the fourth century; the point is not that he does not satisfy modern requirements, but that his grammar is too difficult for ten-year-olds.

78. For details, see 12.20 below.

79. See Holtz (1981: 95–6). On the fusion of Donatus with other texts and on the early medieval tradition in general, see 9.4 below.

both long and short syllables in each case. In discussing the noun, he appends to Donatus' discussion in the *Ars minor* a description of the five declensions (which he calls *regulae*) distinguished by the genitive ending, and makes an excuse for Donatus: *quae regulae apud Donatum quidem non sunt propter conpendium, tamen tenendae sunt* (*GL* 4.408.37–8: "These declensions are not in Donatus for the sake of brevity, but you need to know them").[80] At times, Servius stays very close to Donatus' exposition, but more often he makes the explanations fuller and clearer. That is true even though the surviving version of Servius' commentary is an abridgment itself.[81]

Servius' commentary on Donatus is the first of a very long line extending into the tenth century, but it was quickly subsumed in and replaced by more elaborate explanations. Cledonius, writing in Constantinople in the fifth century, produced a commentary that is lemmatized: it quotes the *ipsissima verba* of Donatus—and is thus our earliest direct source for the text of Donatus—and comments on them. Cledonius clearly used Servius' commentary, as did the other fifth-century commentators (the two *Explanationes in Donatum*[82] and Pompeius, all of whom had a fuller text of Servius than we do); but while there are parallels between those texts and Cledonius, there is no clear proof of dependency either way. Servius' commentary remained at the center of the later tradition of commentary on Donatus.

Although the grammarians tend to agree on certain features of Latin, and thus their own language is often very similar, the growth of the tradition and its variations are worth examining; the basic explanation of the verb provides a good example. Donatus' definition appears twice, as the opening of the discussion of the verb in both the *Ars minor* (as question and answer) and *Ars maior* Book 2 (*GL* 4.381.14–15):

> Verbum est pars orationis cum tempore et persona sine casu aut agere aliquid aut pati aut neutrum significans.
>
> A verb is a part of speech that has tense and person but not case and signifies either taking some action or experiencing it or neither.

In other grammars that are *not* commentaries on Donatus, the opening definition of the verb varies considerably.[83] Thus, of the major texts, two are very spare:

80. On this passage (and in general on the treatment of it in the commentators on Donatus), see Pugliarello (2009: 57–62).

81. On Servius and his immediate followers, my account is heavily indebted to Holtz (1981: 223–37). For particulars on all these texts, see Chapter 12.

82. Note that *Explanationes* I and *Explanationes* II are not by the same author, although it seems likely that the author of *Expl.* II knew *Expl.* I. See 12.40.6 below.

83. My goal here is to describe differences in definition, not to offer a developmental explanation of those differences. For an attempt at developmental explanation (dealing with the noun rather than the verb), see Luhtala (2002, 2010).

Probus, *IA*, *GL* 4.155.31: Verbum est pars orationis.
Diomedes, *GL* 1.334.1: Verbum est pars orationis praecipua sine casu.

Others are very close, although sometimes differently expressed, but they tend to leave out *neutrum* if they include the ideas of active and passive at all in the initial definition:

Sacerdos, *GL* 6.429.15–16: Verbum est pars orationis cum tempore et persona sine casu, qua quid agatur vel actum agendumve sit indicatur.

Audax (Scaurus), *GL* 7.344.9–10: Verbum quid est? pars orationis cum persona et tempore agentem patientemque significans.

Charisius 209.23–4B: Verbum est pars orationis administrationem rei significans cum tempore et persona numerisque carens casu.

Not coincidentally, the first two of these, which are the closest to Donatus, were written earlier than Donatus, and he must have known and used them. A final pair are later:

Consentius, *GL* 5.365.28–6.1: Verbum est pars orationis factum aliquod habitumve significans cum tempore et persona sine casu. factum quod significatur agentis aut patientis vim continet.

Priscian, *GL* 2.369.1–2: Verbum est pars orationis cum temporibus et modis, sine casu, agendi vel patiendi significativum.

Consentius' grammar, probably written at about the same time as Servius' commentary on Donatus, made use either of Donatus or a common source; what is interesting is the addition of *habitus* (also used by Charisius, but by no other grammatical text) to indicate stative verbs.[84] Priscian in the sixth century, with his far greater interest in syntax, substitutes *modi* for *persona*.

But what, in this definition, needs explanation? Servius in his commentary on the *Ars minor* (*GL* 4.411.14–25) explains the following elements (he adds nothing to this in the commentary on *Ars maior*):

a) that *tempus* and *persona* in a verb are linked: "person" alone is a pronoun, "tense" alone is a participle.
b) that the absence of case is a necessary part of the definition because of the existence of constructions like *da mihi bibere* in which the infinitive, as in Greek, takes the place of a noun.

He says nothing about the second half of the definition, although he has something to say about the same topic under the heading of *genera* of the verb later on. *Explanationes* I (*GL* 4.502.26–3.4) simply expands on Servius: the author adds illustrations and clarifications (e.g., *ut si dicas lego scribo meditor. quando dico lego,*

84. Cf. Schad (2007) s.v. *habitus*.

et tempus est et persona, et casus nullus est ["e.g., *lego, scribo, meditor*. When I say *lego*, there is tense and person, and there is no case"] after the first part of the definition); in addition to discussing *da mihi bibere* he quotes from Terence *iussi ei dare bibere* and gives the Greek model δὸς τὸ πιεῖν. He too says nothing here about the second half of the definition, while that is all that is considered—and not very well—by *Explanationes* II (*GL* 4.548.16–17): *verbum est pars orationis, cum quid agatur vel actum agendumve sit indicamus*. Cledonius, making use of lemmata, is much less coherent and perhaps less helpful. After giving an etymology for *verbum* from *verberato ore* (found elsewhere in many of these texts, but not in this position),[85] he goes on to Donatus' words (*GL* 5.16.4–9):

> Cum tempore] quoniam verba temporibus declinantur et modis, quo modo nomina casibus.
> Sine casu] casu caret, et ideo dixit sine casu, propter graeca verba "est tibi loqui," "est ambulare in foro"; "est" verbum, "ambulare" verbum, et duo verba iungi non debent simul. igitur illi sic utuntur infinitis verbis quasi nominibus.
> Neutrum] nec agere nec pati, ut est curro.

> With tense] because verbs are inflected in tenses and moods, as nouns are in cases.
> Without case] it has no case, and so he said without case, because of Greek verbs *est tibi loqui, est ambulare in foro*: *est* is a verb, *ambulare* is a verb, and two verbs should not be joined together. Thus they use infinitives like nouns.
> Neutral] neither active nor passive, such as *curro*.

Cledonius does not explain the difference between verbs on one side and pronouns and participles on the other as do Servius and *Explanationes* I; while he explains the Greek syntax of the infinitive used as noun he uses different examples (Servius, *Explanationes* I, and Pompeius all use *bibere*, with or without quoting Terence); and he does, unlike Servius, explain the meaning of *neutrum*, although much too briefly.

When one turns from the telegraphic Cledonius—a text that largely stands apart from the rest of the grammatical tradition—to Pompeius, teaching his class in Africa in the latter part of the fifth century, it is a different world. Where Cledonius took 8 lines, Servius 12, and *Expl.* I 13 to explain Donatus' 18 words, it takes Pompeius nearly two full pages. On *sine casu* alone, he spends nearly 30 lines; it takes him fully 15 more to say that he will discuss *neutrum* when he gets to *genera*. His exposition often seems to take the form of conversation with himself (*GL* 5.212.28–34):

> Quid est illud quod dixit "sine casu"? nam ita definivit, "verbum est cum tempore et persona sine casu." quid opus fuit ut diceret "casu caret"? ego enim novi quia casus non accidit verbo. sed quae necessitas eum compulit hoc dicere? propter unam elocutionem. est una elocutio, quae paene imaginem

85. The opening of the first sentence is lost, but probably only a few words.

> habet casus, est tamen in verbo; confitemur quoniam in verbo est, tamen imaginem habet casus, ut est illud apud Terentium. . . .
>
> What's the meaning of his phrase *sine casu*? He gave as his definition *verbum est cum tempore et persona sine casu*. Why did he need to say "it lacks case"? I know that case is not an accident of verbs. What necessity forced him to say this? Because of one turn of phrase. There is one turn of phrase which almost has an image of case, but it is in a verb; we allow that it is in a verb, but still has the image of case, as is the phrase in Terence. . . .

It is not merely that Pompeius is verbose, wordy, and repetitive (and not easy to translate); the maddening quality of his commentary on *Ars maior* comes from the fact that it reflects teaching practices. We know from internal references how the book was composed: it was lectures, taken down by a *notarius* whom Pompeius alludes to in his text,[86] and there are passages that only make sense as a record of an oral performance. It has rightly been said by Louis Holtz that Pompeius' commentary is the only text that actually takes us into the late Roman classroom; but as Kaster has shown, it is the record of instruction not to the ultimate audience of ten-year-olds, but to their teachers. It warns of problems to be avoided, such as poor punctuation: *si male distinguas, potest errare puer* (130.31), and contains instructions, as given from one teacher to another, on how to deal with, or avoid, difficult questions in the classroom.[87]

The tradition of commentary on Donatus offers one very striking feature that does not emerge often in other parts of the grammatical tradition and that is the classroom itself. Donatus himself clearly recognized the difficulty inherent in his smooth and abstract *Ars maior*, and the more elementary text he provided is not in fact a textbook, but a script for use in the classroom: questions (What is a verb?) from the teacher followed by perfect answers (A verb is a part of speech . . .) as given by an obnoxiously precocious student. After Donatus, catechism form is frequently used in the transformation of dry grammar into a lively (well, perhaps not so lively) classroom: thus Audax puts Scaurus and Palladius into question-and-answer form, and the fashion, within the tradition, certainly lasts as long as Alcuin's *Dialogue* in the ninth century (if it is in fact Alcuin's). But the commentators on Donatus do it too, sometimes by making their commentaries into catechisms, but sometimes by conversations with imaginary interlocutors. Even Cledonius once mentions a question asked by Iohannes, a clever student (*GL* 5.14.3–6); Pompeius, as in the quotation above, enlivens his endless explanations by posing questions and answering them himself. And the same motive, I suspect,

86. *GL* 5.141.28: *Puta notarium meum volo vocare Africanum*; cf. Kaster (1988: 157–8). It should be noted that the nature of commentary on Donatus changes drastically in the seventh century: commentaries begin to discuss Donatus' choice of language, as if he were a literary text, rather than using his text as the basis for further grammatical elucidation. On this, see Law (2000: 21–3).

87. Holtz (1981: 236); Kaster (1988: 158–61); De Nonno (2010).

is behind a set of imaginary interruptions to the speaker of *Explanationes* I: five times someone named Filocalus and once more someone named Rusticus ask questions, and the questions are always followed by *et respondit*; in a seventh passage, the questioner is anonymous.[88] One needs to keep students attentive.

8. PRISCIAN

In the wide span of the grammatical tradition, three authors in particular deserve to be singled out: Charisius, Donatus, and Priscian. In a sense, they fall into pairs: Charisius and Donatus are more or less contemporaries, while Priscian wrote nearly two centuries later; Charisius and Priscian are the most learned of the grammarians—those from whose writings we gain the most precise knowledge of the traditions of Roman scholarship which lie behind them—and both men worked in the Greek East, while Donatus was the *grammaticus* in old Rome; Donatus and Priscian are united, at least in retrospect, by being the two grammarians most influential on later European education and the two whose works are preserved in by far the greatest number of manuscripts: more than seven hundred of Priscian, at least three hundred of Donatus.[89] Donatus was dominant, particularly in Irish and English contexts, until the beginning of the ninth century; after Alcuin's rediscovery of Priscian, however, Priscian became more and more influential. The decline of one and the rise of the other provides the (approximate) terminus for this book: there is a visible continuity in the grammatical tradition down to the ninth century, while the rise of speculative grammar in the high Middle Ages lies well beyond its scope.

Donatus and Priscian lend themselves to contrast not just in terms of their later influence. Donatus, in Rome in the mid-fourth century, composed an *ars* that—however much the Roman grammatical tradition owes in general to Greek influences—pays little attention to Greek models or the Greek language: in its austerity, it is an exposition of Latin as an independent language, its own tradition. Priscian, in Constantinople in the sixth century, devoted his major efforts, both in his vast *Ars* and in his shorter works, to adapting Greek techniques and ideas for Latin-speakers.

Whether or not, as Courcelle argued, one should see his work as part of a deliberate recuperation of Greek culture for Ostrogothic Italy led by Q. Aurelius Memmius Symmachus and his son-in-law Boethius in the first quarter of the sixth century, Priscian's work is clearly consistent with such efforts.[90] The three short

88. Filocalus *GL* 4.498.23; 501.31, 502.19, 503.11, 515.30; Rusticus: 499.23; anonymous 514.9. At 4.498.23, Keil reads *interrogatus Filocalus* for *interrogavit*, making the instructor into the interrogator. Cf. Jeep (1893: 36); Tolkiehn (1916: 31). On these interruptions see above all De Nonno (2010).

89. Cf. Holtz (1977a).

90. Courcelle (1969: 322–30); cf. Ballaira (1989: 41–53) and De Nonno (2009: 260–8) for the intellectual context. The question of Priscian's audience(s) is complex: see Baratin (2014).

texts, probably written fairly early in his career, that he dedicated to Symmachus, a distinguished Roman aristocrat visiting Constantinople, are on quite different subjects, but they share a single preoccupation with the use of Greek materials to explain Latin ones, and they are intended to encourage a renewal of scholarly interest among Latin-speakers in Ostrogothic Italy: *Romanorum diligentiam vestrorum ad artes suorum alacriorem reddatis auctorum* (*GL* 3.405.17–18: "Render your Romans' concern for the arts of their authors more eager"). The first, a treatise on the signs used to represent numbers and weights in manuscripts, has no parallel in the Roman grammatical tradition (nor, so far as I know, in the Greek tradition), but its goal is to show Greek sources or parallels (often rather strained) for Roman usage; and here, as in his *Ars*, he shows a close attention to manuscripts and variant readings that is more common in Greek scholarly writing than it is in Roman.[91] The treatise on Terentian meter is intended to show that all the apparent anomalies in Terence's iambics had parallels and sources in Greek metrical practice; in this it has a precursor in Rufinus' incomplete and disorderly collection of material on the same subject, but Priscian's work is both much more organized and draws on a wider range of sources, both Greek and Latin.[92] And the third treatise, the *Praeexercitamina*, is a translation—as the title is also a translation—of the *Progymnasmata* ascribed to Hermogenes, thus adapting to Latin use a set of Greek exercises that might serve either as a final assignment for the students of a grammarian or a first one for students of a rhetorician.

Unlike these three treatises, which were aimed at the West, the two smaller works written after the *Ars*, the *Institutio de nomine et pronomine et verbo*, which refers back to the *Ars*, and the *Partitiones duodecim versuum Aeneidos principalium*, which refers back both to the *Ars* and to the *Institutio*, were almost certainly intended for the use of Greek speakers. The *Institutio* is a simplification of part of the *Ars*, offering a very clear and full account of the inflection of nouns, pronouns, and verbs, obviously intended as instructional materials for beginners in Latin. The *Partitiones* is based on a Greek model, the *epimerismoi* used for teaching young students to read Homer, and is meant to provide a familiar pattern of study for Greek students of elementary Latin: it is a relentless analysis of the first line of each of the twelve books of the *Aeneid*, explaining the meter and taking students, in catechistic form, through the morphology of every word.[93]

The five shorter works of Priscian are clearly bicultural, not surprising for a grammarian from Mauretania teaching Latin in Constantinople, but in many ways original in approach: he links Greek and Latin writings on the same subject, he applies Greek methods to Latin texts, he translates from Greek sources to make them available to non-Greek speakers. All these techniques, and more, are visible in Priscian's masterpiece, the *Ars*, his great and huge grammar completed (or at least circulated) in 526–7.

91. See Zetzel (1981: 202–4).

92. On metrical writings, see 8.4b above.

93. On *epimerismoi* and the *Partitiones*, see Glück (1967: 31–46).

In the dedicatory epistle to Iulianus, *consuli et patricio* (a person not otherwise identifiable), Priscian makes his purpose explicit (*GL* 2.1.1–2.11). Although the Romans have successfully appropriated and in some cases improved on Greek learning, in the area of grammar in particular, they are sadly out of date: Greek grammar has improved greatly in the period since the Romans took it over, but the Romans have not paid attention, and in particular, Roman grammatical writing has remained ignorant of the great work done by Herodianus and Apollonius. These scholars Priscian has now adapted in his work and combined them with the traditional (Latin) work of the Roman grammarians.

Both in the details of his account of grammar and in the broad structure of the work, the combination of Greek and Roman traditions is pervasive. In the first place, it is immediately clear that the *Ars* divides (as in many medieval manuscripts it was divided) into two large parts: the first sixteen books replicate on a huge scale the structure of the first two books of Donatus' *Ars maior* (Book 1 and most of Book 2 follow Donatus Book 1; the remainder of Book 2 through Book 16 treat the parts of speech, although following the Greek order [noun 2–7, verb 8–10, participle 11, pronoun 12–13, preposition 14, adverb and interjection 15, conjunction 16] rather than that of Donatus [noun, pronoun, verb, adverb, participle . . .]), while the last two books, *De constructione*, are based on the *Syntax* of Apollonius Dyscolus. On a smaller scale, Apollonius and Herodianus are cited with some regularity on points of grammar, but they are surrounded with a mass of citations from the Roman grammatical tradition: from Servius' commentary on Donatus and other works in the *ars* tradition, from Caper and other works in the *De Latinitate* tradition, from Nonius Marcellus and the lexicographical tradition. From his own reading and from his sources, Priscian cites immense numbers of Latin examples to illustrate his teachings, from a far wider range of texts than is usual in the Roman tradition: while Virgil and Terence as the leading school authors are the authors most often quoted, there are also quotations from scholarly works, from legal texts, from the histories of Ammianus and the poem on meter by Terentianus Maurus.[94] And to match his Latin examples, there are, very often, parallel Greek ones, drawn again in part from his grammatical sources, but in part from his own reading. Although Priscian's main audience is in the West, he is writing in a bilingual world for bilingual readers. His work, moreover, not only contains a great deal of Greek, but is encyclopedic; in that respect, it has rightly been compared with another work that emerged from Constantinople only a few years later, Justinian's *Digest*.

The very size of Priscian's work makes it hard to manage now; it was also hard to write. It is not surprising that Priscian seems to have inserted some preexisting texts into the *Ars*: the second dedication to Iulianus at the beginning of Book 6 (on nominal inflections) implies that this section had been a separate work, and it has also been suggested that the two books on verbal inflection were also separate. What is more surprising is that, even with its bulk, the work is incomplete: not

94. On Priscian's wide range of sources, see De Nonno (2009: 267–8).

only are there short digressions included that seem like drafts or notes (which Martin Hertz, the editor, called *schedae*), but at the ends of four books (5, 11, 14, 16) there are extra sections, not present in all the manuscripts but almost certainly genuine, which had not yet been incorporated by Priscian into the larger argument. The fact that the last hundred pages of the *Ars* simply list *idiomata* arranged in order of the Greek alphabet merely confirms that Priscian had not finished his book. The *Ars* was a work in progress, and the unevennesses and insertions suggest that the reference to pressure and the need for speed in the dedicatory letter is more than simply conventional. And we know, or can imagine, the source of that pressure: possibly at the beginning of Book 1, after Books 5, 8, and 13, and at the beginning and end of Book 17, a pupil of Priscian's, Theodorus, *memorialis sacri scrinii epistularum et adiutor viri magnifici quaestoris Sacri Palatii*, added a subscription indicating that he wrote the manuscript himself; he dates these notes over a period from 1 October 526 (the beginning, if that note is genuine) to 30 May 527. Was Theodorus in a hurry, nagging his teacher for more of the *Ars* to copy? Like the *Digest*, the *Ars* is a product of the Palace, part of the attempt (which also resulted in Justinian's invasion of Italy) to restore or regain the Latin world now controlled by Goths, Franks, and Vandals.

Priscian's *Ars*, while it was certainly available in (at least) southern Italy and the British Isles fairly rapidly, did not replace Donatus as the basis for grammatical instruction for some three hundred years.[95] The abridged *Institutio* was popular (and was used to extend Donatus); the *Ars* was not. And yet even for the earlier period, it remains hugely important as a symbol and a reminder of the importance of the Greek East for the education of the Latin West, even when the inhabitants of the West could no longer read Greek. Theodorus, who copied Priscian's *Ars*, also copied the logical works of Boethius, and his copy was used to correct the copy of one Martius Novatus Renatus—a descendant of which was preserved in the monastery of Fleury on the Loire.[96] We cannot leave the subject of ancient philology without looking at its contexts and continuation.

95. On the early reception of Priscian, see Holtz (2009).

96. For a text of these subscriptions, see Zetzel (1981: 219–22); on Theodorus' work on Priscian, see also Ballaira (1989: 57–64). See also 9.1 below.

9

Author, Audience, Text

With Priscian and his pupil Eutyches comes the end of the best attested period of Roman philological scholarship. The time from Sacerdos at the end of the third century through Donatus and Servius in the fourth and fifth to Priscian in the sixth is what might be called the "classical" era of Roman philology—comparable to the equally unstable designations of the period from Cicero to Tacitus and Juvenal as "classical" Roman literature and the period from Salvius Iulianus to Ulpian (and slightly later) as the "classical" age of Roman law. In the case of philology, to use the three categories of writing examined in Chapters 6–8, we see the composition not just of the vast majority of extant grammatical writings, but also of the commentaries that underlie the Carolingian scholia on classical authors and of lexica and glossaries (the most noteworthy individual authors are Nonius Marcellus and Fulgentius, but many anonymous glossaries must be roughly contemporary) that were the basis of the later lexicographical tradition.

This concentration of philological writing is not accidental. One explanation is technical: these texts physically survived because of the transition from papyrus and roll to parchment and codex, a more durable and convenient material and shape; earlier works not transcribed in the new format are largely lost.[1] Inevitably, books composed in the age of parchment are much better represented than books composed in the age of papyrus. Our evidence for the copying and correction of books is consistent with this: only one subscription (the term for correctors' signatures in manuscripts, generally attested in much later copies) survives from before the fourth century, while a great many survive from the fifth. That is not because books were not corrected or not signed; it is because texts and subscriptions alike have perished. That problem aside, it still appears, from our limited knowledge,

1. The huge difference between Greek and Roman literature in terms of survival and preservation reflects this: the climate of Egypt preserved great numbers of literary papyri from the period before the parchment codex, while the climate of Latin-speaking areas did not. Almost all the fragments of early Latin literature are quotations; most of the fragments of Greek literature of every period are papyri.

that there was a great deal more, or at least more memorable, philological writing in late antiquity than earlier. Commentaries on authors and word lists existed at least as early as the second century BCE, but they do not seem to have taken the regularized form in which we know them until, probably, the fourth century. Again, physical form plays a role: the existence of wide margins in parchment codices makes marginal commentaries possible. There were important grammars before Sacerdos, but we do not know of very many: by Palaemon in the first century, by Scaurus and a few others under Hadrian. But because our extant texts provide few names of grammatical authorities before Sacerdos, it appears that *writing* grammar was not nearly so common in the first and second centuries as *teaching* it.

There are reasons for this. Written books (as opposed to oral classroom instruction) are composed to fill a need; and by the end of the third century, the need was obvious. Neither the young students nor their teachers in late antiquity were as comfortable with classical Latin as their forebears had been. That can be documented through the introduction of instruction in prosody and treatises *De finalibus*: the pronunciation of Latin had changed by the fourth century. Commentaries start to introduce more grammar rather than concentrating on exegesis of history, fact, or rhetoric. Spelling becomes a problem. Glossaries begin to supply not just subtle distinctions among near synonyms or lists of words on recondite subjects, but basic vocabulary and distinctions among near homonyms. Not surprising: by the fourth century, and very definitely by the fifth, a fair portion of the population will not have been native speakers.

The proliferation of grammars, dictionaries, and commentaries on classical texts, then, is evidence both of a technical change in book production and of a change in audience. And that necessarily also entailed a change in attitude towards the world of Latin literature to which such works gave access. Once it becomes apparent—to teachers, to students, to readers—that Latin now is not the same as Latin then, a sense of historical distance, in some quarters a sense of nostalgia or loss, is inevitable: Cicero and Virgil remain "our" classics, but they are no longer written in "our" language.

A second change, perhaps later, but longer and broader, comes with the changed conditions of learning: while the ancient school system survived and the *grammaticus* persisted until the sixth century and later in the East, in the West formal organization of education—not to mention imperial salaries—became distinctly more precarious, and the transmission of linguistic and cultural knowledge passed to other hands. Some teaching was presumably private, but with the Christianization of the (former) empire, responsibility for education gradually passed to the one enduring institution for which a decent knowledge of Latin (classical or not) was essential—the church. It is a truism, but nevertheless true, that if Latin had not been adopted as the universal language of religion in the former western empire we would have precious little left of Latin literature, not to mention Roman scholarship. What remains to be explored in this last chapter are some of the ways in which the transmission of knowledge was maintained, and how it was transformed. This will not be a history of early medieval culture—that is beyond my knowledge—but a reminder of just a few aspects of how the classical world, and Roman grammatical scholarship in particular, was perceived and preserved.[2] And one must begin with the precondition for the philological study of the Latin classics: copying them.

1. THE CORRECTORS

Sometime in the middle of the fifth century, a Roman official called Rusticius Helpidius Domnulus, *vir clarissimus et spectabilis* and *comes consistorii*, signed his name at the end of his copy of the geographical compendium of Pomponius Mela:[3]

> Pomponii Melae de chorographia libri tres expliciti feliciter.
>
> Fl. Rusticius Helpidius Domnulus v.c. et spc. com. consistor. emendavi Rabennae.

This subscription (like most such surviving notes) is not preserved in its original manuscript. It is found in the ninth-century manuscript Vatican, Lat. 4929, in which the text of Mela is preceded by Julius Paris' epitome of Valerius Maximus and followed by Vibius Sequester's geographical gazeteer to Roman poetry.[4] Domnulus' name does not appear at the end of the text of Vibius, but it does, in slightly different form, at the end of the chapter *De praenominibus* which comes at the end of the text of Paris:

> C. Titi Probi finit epitoma historiarum diversarum exemplorumque Romanorum.
>
> Feliciter emendavi descriptum Rabennae Rusticius Helpidius Domnulus v.c.

The same subscription (with the two sentences reversed) is also found in Bern 366 of Valerius Maximus, copied from the Vatican manuscript in the hand of Lupus of Ferrières. The Vatican manuscript itself was corrected by Heiric of Auxerre and was the source of the corrections to the text of Valerius Maximus made by Lupus; the article by Ludwig Traube in 1891 that drew attention to the relationship between these two manuscripts is a major landmark in the history of palaeography and of medieval philology.[5] The Vatican manuscript is complicated; the three texts

2. For a brief and graceful account of the role of monasteries in the diffusion of Latin texts, see Holtz 2003.

3. For the subscriptions of Domnulus, see Zetzel (1981: 216–17) (where I wrongly dated him to the mid-sixth century). The identity of the man is not altogether certain (and unimportant here), but he is probably the *vir quaestorius* known to Sidonius Apollinaris rather than the representative of Theodosius II at the Council of Ephesus in 449. See Cameron (2011: 476).

4. In each case, the text survives in Vatican, Lat. 4929 alone: all other copies descend from it.

5. On the manuscript see, in addition to Traube (1920: 3–17, originally published 1891); Schnetz (1901); Barlow (1938); Billanovich (1956).

mentioned are preceded by a text of Censorinus and one of the *Querolus*, and while the whole book is written by a single hand, it is likely that these three final texts (Paris, Mela, Vibius) formed a preexisting unit. Also, although the text of Vibius does not have Domnulus' subscription, it is likely that these three rare and similar works were brought together by him. The combination of an epitome of rhetorical exempla, a brief work on geography, and an alphabetized list of names of geographical features in Roman poetry makes a certain amount of sense: it is a compendium of useful knowledge about the Roman world of the long-lost past, probably an aid to the reading of classical Roman literature.

Domnulus is not the only person to leave his mark in a manuscript or on the tradition of a Latin author.[6] Many of these notes mean very little, other than the fact that someone did in fact correct the text. But a few of them are important in giving evidence for two things that are very relevant to the world of Roman philology in late antiquity. One is the simple fact that men of position and standing thought it important to record their interest in correcting manuscripts, that what looks like grammarians' work is in fact the undertaking of wealthy amateurs. The other is that they did not do it alone, but often in collaboration with grammarians or rhetoricians. All this is a token of what can be seen in the more narrowly defined activities of Roman philology (the writing of works on grammar or metrics or the exegesis of texts or the compilation of glossaries): as the educational system became weaker or lost funding, as Latin literacy became something less to be taken for granted in Italy and the West, and as the traditional structure of Italic-Roman society became ever more attenuated (or as its leaders moved to the new Rome, Constantinople), the study of letters became too important to be left to the schools. It was not long before grammar moved into the monasteries, entailing major effects on the form and production of grammatical literature (which is, indeed, the most important topic of this chapter), but the transitional changes in late antiquity were in fact a crucial stage. That is true in two important respects: one is the activity of amateurs, who were neither grammarians nor monks, and the other is the tendency to define the world of education and learning in such a way that it easily migrated to an ecclesiastical context.

Domnulus' manuscript of Paris and Pomponius Mela (and possibly Vibius Sequester) exemplifies both tendencies, and while his is the only act of anthologizing that can be directly connected to one of the subscriptions, it does not seem that it was unique. One group of manuscripts of Martial descends from a copy corrected by Torquatus Gennadius, who in his subscription after the prefatory poems of Book 13 gives the year 401 CE as the date of his work.

6. There is a large bibliography on the subscriptions: the earliest important contribution is Jahn (1851); the texts were republished with additions by Zetzel (1981). See also Bloch (1963); Zetzel (1973, 1980); Pecere (1982, 1984, 1986); Cameron (2011: 421–526) with much further bibliography. Zelzer (1995) collects much material about book copying, but does not address the major problems. On subscriptions in grammatical manuscripts in particular, see also De Nonno (2000: 146–9).

This Gennadius is well known: a friend of Claudian and Prefect of Egypt in 392, he seems to have devoted himself to Roman poetry in his retirement. And perhaps not just to Martial: the subscription to Book 13 says *Emendavi ego Torquatus Gennadius cum ceteris Gennadi vatibus. Quirine floreas. lege feliciter.* Although there is a variant text at the end of Book 14 that offers *cum tuis Gennadi vatibus*, that makes little sense. But it is perfectly possible, if a little surprising, that Gennadius had in fact proofread texts of more poetry than just Martial.[7] It is not at all without parallel to find one reader or owner leaving his mark in more than one poet: Asterius does so for Virgil and Sedulius, Mavortius for Horace and Prudentius.[8] In various ways, all these men are trying to collect and shape their heritage.

Many of the subscribers state explicitly that they are correcting their own copy of a text, possibly one that they had had written; some of them claim to have done so on their own. Thus the military officer Julius Tryfonianus Sabinus tells us that at the age of thirty in the year 402 he twice (once in Barcelona, once in Toulouse) read and corrected his copy of Persius. In one of his notes he says *temptavi emendare sine antigrapho meum et adnotavi* ("I have tried to correct my copy without one to check it against, and I have annotated it") and in the other *prout potui sine magistro emendans adnotavi* ("I have corrected and annotated as well as I could without a teacher"). Persius is a difficult author; one wonders whether the annotations Sabinus made in the margins of his copy meant no more than the sea of question marks in mine.[9]

Some of these texts, however, offer a picture somewhat different from the image of the young and bored officer writing in the margins of his manuscript in lonely hours while off duty in Barcelona. Some subscribers worked together with a grammarian or rhetorician: this might be while they were students, as Niceus corrected his Juvenal *Romae apud Servium magistrum* (clearly an elementary student) or as Sallustius corrected his copy of Apuleius in 395, *in foro Martis controversiam declamans oratori Endelechio* ("while declaiming a *controversia* in the forum of Mars to Endelechius the rhetor"). That does not mean that he was proofreading while declaiming (a neat trick), just that he was studying rhetoric under Endelechius (the Forum of Mars is well attested as a

7. For the text of these subscriptions, see Zetzel (1981: 211–13), drawing on Lindsay (1903b). Marrou (1976: 67–8) and Cameron (2011: 431–3) cite the text as *cum tuis Gennadi vatibus* without noting the other version (Fusi 2013 ignores the phrase entirely). That text is, as Cameron observes, corrupt; the version preferred here is not (despite Pecere 1986: 37). One note of caution: these words are preserved in only a single fifteenth-century manuscript; the earlier witness leaves out the relevant portion of the subscription after Book 13 and has lost the last page of the manuscript with the end of Book 14.

8. On these, see Zetzel (1981: 217–19).

9. Cameron (2011: 490) claims that *adnotare* must mean a considerable body of marginal scholia. It certainly could, but it equally clearly need not.

place for holding classes) and had reached the advanced stage of learning to argue *controversiae*.[10]

It is important to recognize, however, that *emendatio*, even conceived as no more than proofreading, was not limited to students correcting a book under the nose of their teachers or to young alumni trying to remember what they had learned in school. Many of these notes give little information about their authors, but in some cases very eminent men are involved: the famous subscriptions in the manuscripts of Livy attest that Nicomachus Flavianus corrected the text while he was *praefectus urbis* for the third time; Turcius Rufius Apronianus Asterius corrected his brother's copy of Virgil in April 494 while he was *consul ordinarius*.[11] And even grandees could bring in teachers to help even though they were long past school age. Thus Vettius Agorius Basilius Mavortius corrects his copy of Horace with the aid of Felix the *orator urbis Romae* at a time when Mavortius describes himself as an ex-consul. It is not his second childhood: we know that Cicero himself regularly practiced the rhetorical progymnasmata with teachers even after he had been consul: orators, like opera singers, need to do exercises regularly to keep fit.[12]

Does the work of these subscribers fit under even the broadest definition of philological scholarship? Not much, and not any more. It used to be thought that every one of these signatures in a manuscript represented an "edition" or "recension" performed in the scholarly method approved by whatever scholar was writing about them. That is obviously not true and was refuted long ago: textual criticism is a modern vice, not a Roman one. On the other hand, to debunk these notes as no more than elementary proofreading (important, but not exactly scholarship) done by earnest students or wealthy men in an idle hour is to throw out more than the bathwater, and it misses the point in two ways: in the first place, checking a manuscript to make sure it was copied accurately is, in a world which has only manuscripts, an extremely important responsibility; and secondly, if a consul or an urban prefect was willing to spend time on such a task, then such people considered it time well spent. Men like Nicomachus or Mavortius could afford to hire experts to do this kind of drudgery (checking references and compiling indices come to mind as modern equivalents, for which some people hire students or professionals). That they chose not to do so is itself significant, and suggests that such people, and the upper-class society of which they were a part, recognized that they shared with the grammarians the job of preserving the past.

10. See Marrou (1976: 65–7).

11. On the chronology of Nicomachus, see Cameron (2011: 498–526); for the texts of these subscriptions see Zetzel (1981: 214–18). There is also the copy of Solinus actually written by the emperor Theodosius, who was known as "the calligrapher" (Zetzel 1981: 215).

12. On Cicero and the *progymnasmata*, see Frazel (2009: 45–9).

Philology in Rome, it is worth repeating, was not a profession. Some of its practitioners were grammarians, and the written contribution of professional *grammatici* looms large in late antiquity. But it was not just the subscribers who were not grammarians: educated people took an interest in such subjects, and they sometimes wrote seriously in ways and on subjects that a professional grammarian, tied to his curriculum and his ten-year-olds, might not do. It is all too easy to pour scorn on the high proportion of fairly elementary grammatical notes in Servius' commentary on Virgil—but that is what he was paid to teach. People not tied to the classroom had more freedom. Charisius was almost certainly not a grammarian but a person of some standing with a serious interest in language. The short (and in later centuries very popular) metrical treatise by Mallius Theodorus was probably written by him as a young man; he then went on to become consul in 399. Among the scholars of the fifth century, Martianus may have been a grammarian, but Macrobius was not, although he knew enough to write not only the learned *Saturnalia* but his Neoplatonic commentary on the *Somnium Scipionis*; he also knew enough about languages to write a learned treatment (surviving only partially) comparing the Greek and Latin verb. And in the sixth century, alongside Priscian there are Boethius and Cassiodorus. As with academics today, some Roman philologists are more deeply versed in the sources than others, some are more original than others: we can respect the intention and the seriousness without claiming that they were great scholars—and without trying to lower their grades when they do not measure up to our definitions of scholarship. And as the institutions of learning (elementary or advanced) became weaker and less broadly available in the Latin-speaking world, it is no surprise that we find gentlemen as well as grammarians taking an active interest in the texts that were their cultural heritage. Until the rise of the narrow professionalism of the modern university, they always did.

What is more, although *emendavi* or whatever other word is used does not necessarily point to anything more than simple proofreading, that does not preclude the possibility that the subscribers did more than that. That is sometimes explicit (Sabinus' *adnotavi*); elsewhere, there are signs in some subscribed texts of other roughly contemporary kinds of editorial intervention. It may not have been done by the same person in the same process, but it was done by somebody similar—these are all expensive manuscripts that lived in wealthy households, not in libraries or schools—in the same period; and that extends the intellectual world of the subscriptions from the simple if demanding task of proofreading towards more substantive philological scholarship.

The evidence for this is of several kinds. In the first place, collation of other manuscripts. Somebody, whether one of the subscribers or not, added variant readings to the text of Livy that came from a source other than the copy from which the text being corrected had itself been copied; the same is true, and still almost visible, in the palimpsest of Fronto.[13] These were not collations in the

13. On these manuscripts, see Zetzel (1980).

modern sense; but they did seek out and report new information to aid in understanding and (just possibly) correcting the text.[14] In the case of both Livy and Fronto, moreover, there is another kind of scholarship, in this case, annotation. These notes—as almost certainly also the case with Sabinus' Persius—are simply personal comments about the text for the benefit of the owner or reader of the manuscript in question, just as *adnotare* is the verb used for writing summaries of paragraphs in the margin. That they are simply reminders, the equivalent of the manicule or *nota bene* in the margins of renaissance printed books, does not diminish their importance: they are no different in origin and perhaps intention from those marginalia now dignified by the name of Verona scholia to Virgil or Bembine scholia to Terence. In a manuscript culture, the distinction between public and private copies is irrelevant, if not non-existent.

The third kind of evidence is more tenuous, but suggests a far greater degree of deliberate intervention than the marginalia and variants found in subscribed manuscripts of Livy or Fronto or Virgil. It is clear, in the case of the manuscript tradition of Martial, that the manuscripts preserving the subscription of Torquatus Gennadius share not only distinctive textual variants but also titles attached to specific poems. While it is impossible to connect textual variants to Gennadius—they may have been in the manuscript he corrected or may have been introduced at a later stage—it has been suggested on linguistic grounds that the titles in this branch of the tradition were composed at about the same time as the subscription itself, and it is by no means implausible to believe that the same person introduced them as well as emending the text in whatever fashion.[15]

What the subscribers did was not nothing. That is itself significant, but equally important is the role they played and the context in which they played it. The idea that the subscriptions are part of a pagan revival or resistance against Christianity has been thoroughly refuted:[16] not only are most of the identifiable subscribers Christians (and later than the date of the "pagan revival" of the 390s), but the texts copied were read and studied by both pagans and Christians alike, mostly the latter. Nor, as discussed above, are the subscriptions evidence of serious philological activity in the anachronistic way they have sometimes been described. But at the same time, the combination of Latin texts and well-to-do correctors *does* reflect a kind of resistance: not to Christianity, but to the degradation of

14. Again, it is important not to use modern definitions of technical terms in order to criticize ancient students for not living up to them. A modern collation requires an exhaustive list of even the most minor variations including nonsense, erasures, and other trivia. Before the nineteenth century and the method of Lachmann, the few scholars who did that are truly remarkable and tend to be singled out for retrospective praise: Lupus of Ferrières, for instance, in the ninth century and Poliziano in the fifteenth. On Poliziano's methods, see Grafton (1991: 47–75); for his subscriptions and comments on manuscripts, see Rizzo (1973: 147–64).

15. Landgraf (1902).

16. See, at great length, Cameron (2011).

knowledge of Latin and perhaps to the large and visible (and powerful) presence of non-native speakers of Latin in Italy and the West. It is an attempt to preserve correct texts (not collating, not performing recension, not editing in the modern understanding of those words, but simply correcting when possible) against the ravages of time, ignorance, and Goths. What is more, the subscriptions *do* reflect the kind of activity that grammarians sometimes did and very definitely the kind of knowledge that grammarians were supposed to impart: one can not correct a text *manu mea solus*, as Paulus Constantinopolitanus says in his manuscript of Lucan, without knowing Latin. The very fact that someone could say that and not be embarrassed by it is the best proof that the subscriptions actually mean something important.

In discussing the subscriptions—indeed, in talking about Roman scholarship at all—it is very difficult to avoid importing anachronistic misconceptions. Cameron, in discussing the subscription of Statilius Maximus in a speech of Cicero—by far the earliest (second century), and the only one to record the use by the emender of a number of specific earlier copies—makes a valid distinction between his work and the work of the later subscribers. They are indeed different: Statilius appears to have done a much more elaborate job of consulting authoritative manuscripts while the later subscribers largely, if not exclusively, simply corrected in a manner much closer to proofreading than to modern ideas of editing. But to speak of Statilius as "a professional scholar" because he also wrote a work on *singularia* in Cicero and to call his work "a serious recension" because he looked at a few manuscripts is wrong.[17] It is not a recension; it is the consultation of several manuscripts, which he almost certainly did not collate the way a modern editor collates manuscripts—letter by letter and word by word.[18] Statilius was a man of letters; so were his contemporaries Gellius and Fronto. They took the study of language and texts seriously. But they were not "professional scholars." They did not have advanced degrees; they did not teach at universities; they were not expected to do research and publish results. Cicero would firmly have rejected the title *philosophus*, but that does not mean that he was not deeply learned in the subject or that what he wrote is not serious philosophy.[19] What the subscribers did to correct texts was indeed not a grand philological project in *our*

17. Quotations from Cameron (2011: 427, 452).

18. At the risk of repetiveness and autobiography—and because not that many students of Latin literature actually study manuscripts—I stress the difference between modern scholarly methods and earlier ones as well as the fact that not every use of a manuscript involves collation or recension. For editorial projects, I have done full and tedious collation of manuscripts, letter by letter, but to describe some grammatical texts for this volume I have looked at photographs and read a few pages of manuscripts without doing any collation at all and have only looked at one manuscript *in situ* (Oxford, Bodleian Add. C. 144) in addition to using digitized images. Some books one reads; others one skims.

19. See Hine (2015: 14–19).

sense, but that does not mean that it is not a significant endeavor, both in what they did and in the very fact that they did it.

2. SUMMING THINGS UP

After copying, collection. Among the subscriptions discussed above are two signs of this. The more tangible one is Domnulus' collection of geographical and rhetorical compendia; Gennadius' Martial, with its puzzling reference to Gennadius' other poets, suggests a poetic collection as well. But as far as the preservation of ancient philology is concerned, it is more important to observe the collection of tools to read the texts rather than the collection of the texts themselves. Domnulus' work perhaps falls into that category, but there are other more important examples.

In 386 or 387, at Cassiciacum, the young Aurelius Augustinus planned a set of works about the *disciplinae*, intending to use them as vehicles for delineating intellectual progress from *corporalia* to *incorporalia*.[20] He seems to have written only two of them, the extant *De musica* in six books and a work on grammar of which there exists a reflection in the short *Ars breviata* preserved under his name. We have no explicit evidence about just what *disciplinae* Augustine meant to include, but it was probably the same set included in *De nuptiis Philologiae et Mercurii*, written by his fellow North African, Martianus Minneus Felix Capella sometime in the fifth century: the triad of verbal arts (grammar, dialectic, rhetoric) and the tetrad of mathematical arts (geometry, arithmetic, astronomy, and music) that are collectively known as the seven liberal arts and which served as the basis for education for centuries.[21]

Martianus' account of the *disciplinae* is set in a strange framework: each of the liberal arts is depicted as a handmaiden introducing herself at the wedding of Mercury and Philology and gives—interspersed with poems and interruptions—a book-long account of her subject/self. While the frame is baroque, the picture within (aside from Martianus' peculiar style) is not: Grammar's potted account of *grammatica* accords closely with what we find in other late antique grammatical texts, and the same seems true (when we can check) for the other six as well. At the end of her book, Grammar is sped along by the gods and not permitted to give an account of metrics, as it might interfere with Music, the coming attraction in the final book; recently a text on that subject apparently by Martianus has been discovered, independent of *De nuptiis*.[22]

Encyclopedic accounts of the liberal arts had been written before. Famous, and almost entirely lost, was Varro's nine-book *Disciplinae*, which included not

20. On Augustine at Cassiciacum, see Brown (1967: 115–27).

21. On the chronology of Martianus Capella, see 12.27 below. The choice of possible dates is not relevant here.

22. See De Nonno (1990a, 2014); the text is not yet published. On metrics see 8.4b above.

only the standard seven, but also medicine and architecture.[23] But Varro's work was fundamentally different from the corresponding work of Martianus: Varro was apparently defining the *artes* for the first time (in Latin, at any rate, and there is no evidence for any earlier comparable Greek work). That may not be true for rhetoric, a subject about which several earlier books existed in Latin; but it is almost certainly true for most, if not all, of the other eight. Martianus, on the other hand, is explaining the familiar and well-established content of each discipline: he is preserving the *artes*, not defining them.

Preservation and compression are the characteristics of a work gathering together brief accounts of each of the *artes*: while Martianus can certainly claim originality in style and presentation, he makes no great effort at originality in content. It is a summary of what is known about the *artes* and of what educated people ought to know about them. Grammar as always takes the lead, as she was to do for centuries: it is grammar, after all, that allows the uninstructed reader to understand the accounts of the remaining six disciplines.[24]

Accounts of particular areas of learning in the fifth and sixth centuries fit the same description: they explain what is known about what educated people ought to know in one field or another. In grammar itself, Priscian's *Ars*, while scarcely brief, is one such work. It is a vast summing up of the Roman grammatical tradition, and as such, as noted in the previous chapter, it stands next to the other great Latin monument of Justinianic Constantinople, the *Corpus iuris civilis* and in particular the *Digest*, Tribonian's immense compilation of the opinions of jurists ranging from Q. Mucius in the first century BCE down to the great classical lawyers of the third century CE. Both works (despite their size) are in fact summaries: they encapsulate the learning of previous centuries with the clear intention of making it useful for present and future generations. Both look back over what was (from at least the authors' point of view) a period of stagnation and decline to an age of greater scholarship; both intend to mark a new beginning but also (from at least our point of view) signal a distinct end. Nothing like them—indeed nothing like the works they updated and replaced—was to be composed in Latin for some centuries. Both are also works of Latin scholarship written in Constantinople, a Greek city which was the center of the Roman empire of which Rome itself was no longer a part. They look west, as did Justinian himself: not long after decreeing the revision of the legal code, he undertook the even larger program of reconquest of those areas of the western Mediterranean

23. For useful introductions to the definition and history of the liberal arts in antiquity, see the articles in *BNP* by J. Christes s.vv. *Artes liberales* and *Encyclios paideia*. See also Bischoff (1966: 273–88) on the Irish afterlife of the liberal arts. The origin of the grouping is obscure; I. Hadot's (2005) theory that the liberal arts as a concept and unit enter Latin thought only after the second century has not met much acceptance, and would not affect my argument here in any case.

24. On the leading role of grammar, see Irvine (1994).

world in which Latin was still spoken, campaigning against the Vandal kingdom in North Africa in 533–4 and against the Ostrogoths in Italy beginning in 535.

But the gaze, at least in the case of Priscian and some of his contemporaries, goes both ways, and the difficult relationship between the Greek-speaking Roman Empire in the East and the semi-Latin Ostrogothic kingdom of Theoderic in Italy provides the context for some of the most interesting works of synthesis and summation in late antiquity. Priscian sums up the Latin grammatical tradition, but at the same time his stress on the importance of Greek grammatical theory and its relevance to the study of Latin grammar brings the history of Roman grammatical writing full circle, back to the apocryphal influence of Crates of Mallos and the genuine influence of Greek grammarians in Rome such as Tyrannio and Tryphon. Who the Iulianus was to whom Priscian dedicated his *Ars* is unknown, but Priscian's three early grammatical treatises were addressed to Symmachus, the great Roman aristocrat whose daughter was married to Boethius and who himself was one of the subscribers to a copy of Macrobius' commentary on the *Somnium Scipionis* together with Macrobius' own grandson, Macrobius Plotinus Eudoxius.[25]

Both Symmachus and Boethius were significant public figures in Ostrogothic Italy, and both had close connections in Constantinople and clearly spent time there; indeed, they were both eventually (525–6) executed by Theoderic because of the king's suspicions of treasonous dealings with the East. Before that, however, Boethius had made a systematic attempt, not unlike Priscian's own *Ars*, to preserve Greek learning for Latin speakers by creating in Latin a library of philosophical texts, both translating from the Greek and supplying introductions and commentaries of his own. It is probably not a coincidence, as was mentioned at the end of Chapter 8, that the surviving collection of these texts goes back to a copy made by the scribe Theodorus sometime before he made his copy of Priscian's *Ars* in Constantinople in 526–7:[26] together with the subscriptions of Martius Novatus Renatus that punctuate the manuscript, there is a first-person note by someone unnamed, saying that he had corrected the text against Renatus' manuscript, which had been written by the scribe Theodorus *qui nunc Palatinus est*—in other words, the anonymous corrector was working after Theodorus had been hired by the government, but Theodorus was not an official when he copied the text of Boethius. Anonymous, presumably in Italy, is working to preserve Boethius' collection that had been written in Italy but copied in Constantinople for a wealthy Roman at some point after Boethius' death.

There is one last contemporary of Boethius to consider, his relative (and successor in office when Boethius was imprisoned and executed) Cassiodorus Senator. After his public career (documented in his *Variae*, a collection of letters he wrote on behalf of his Ostrogothic rulers), after the long sojourn in Constantinople that followed his retirement from office, Cassiodorus settled in

25. On Priscian's connections, see Courcelle (1969: 325–9); Ballaira (1989).

26. See 8.8 above.

the monastery he had founded at Squillace in southern Italy, and lived on and on, writing large amounts of instructional material for his monks and gathering writings that he thought would be useful to them. In the preface to his last work, *De orthographia*, written when he was ninety-three, he first reports that because his monks have reproached him with their inability to write (or read) Latin correctly and thus their inability to study scripture properly, he has collected a set of a dozen excerpts from the orthographical writings of others.[27] And noting that it seems to be time for him to end his life's work, he offers a list of the seven works he has composed for the monks. This begins with his large commentary on the Psalms, continues through the *Institutiones*, an exposition of Romans, a codex *in quo artes Donati cum commentis suis et librum de etymologiis et alium librum Sacerdotis de schematibus* (*GL* 7.144.7–9), two other works of biblical instruction, and finally *De orthographia* itself.

Cassiodorus' second career as a pious Christian and owner of a monastery (*monachi mei* he possessively calls its residents) is itself a large effort of compilation and synthesis with an explicitly educational purpose, but even if some of the material he collected is drawn from the traditional sources of Roman grammatical education, it is gathered in aid of a very different goal: he is not trying to produce civil servants who know classical Latin well, but monks who are to use their training to study scripture. Aside from the codex of Donatus and other grammatical writings, and aside from the extant *De orthographia*, the most apparently traditional part of Cassiodorus' work is the second book of the *Institutiones*, an outline of the seven liberal arts, including both summaries of the disciplines and directions to volumes Cassiodorus had composed as supplements, containing collections of relevant readings. For dialectic in particular, two alternate versions of Cassiodorus' recommendations survive, one promoting the works of Marius Victorinus, the other those of Boethius.[28] Although Cassiodorus presents the liberal arts in a different order and in a slightly different manner from some of his Latin predecessors, it is recognizably part of the same tradition represented earlier by Martianus.[29] But the reason for learning the liberal arts is different, and so is their history. Book 1 of the *Institutiones* is a detailed set of instructions, with extensive reading lists, for the study of the Bible; the *Expositio Psalmorum*—the first biblical text generally read carefully by students—is intimately connected to it. The liberal arts are necessary and significant in two different ways: the more familiar one is that they provide the knowledge that enables the novice to read any text, including the Bible. The other is that, in Cassiodorus' view, the scriptures not only illustrate the use of the liberal arts, but—being of course much older

27. On *De orthographia*, see 8.4a above.

28. There are in fact three versions of *Inst.* 2; on the complicated history, see Mynors (1937), corrected by Van de Vyver (1941) and Courcelle (1942). A lucid summary with some further refinements is in Holtz (1986b).

29. On Cassiodorus' version of the liberal arts and its relationship to the encyclopedic tradition, see Della Corte (1986). See also Irvine (1994: 195–209).

than secular literature and divinely inspired—are the *source* of the liberal arts, particularly of rhetoric and dialectic. Cassiodorus employed his own original set of marginal *notae* in his commentary on the Psalms, borrowing from the practice of literary scholars, but with a different intent: they mark the presence of such things as "rhetoric," "syllogisms," "geometry," and "music" as well as the *idiomata* of the Bible.[30] The liberal arts have gone to church.

3. GOD'S GRAMMAR

God and Latin grammar, in fact, had had an uneasy relationship for a very long time, and it started well before Cassiodorus. At one level, it was obvious that the literary texts of classical Rome, still the basis of grammatical instruction, could only be made Christian by the strenuous exercise of faith and allegory. This affected Virgil more than any other author: his works provided the basis of most elementary grammatical instruction. Some believers looked for Christ in Virgil even before the wholesale takover of the world of texts by monks: even aside from Constantine's famous reading of the Fourth *Eclogue* in the early fourth century, Fulgentius allegorizes all of Virgil in the fifth, and Christ turns up with some regularity in early medieval commentary on the *Eclogues*.[31]

Allegory aside, however, there were fundamental problems in employing classical grammars like Donatus and in using classical texts as literary models: biblical Latin was simply not the same as the language of classical Rome. The tension was the subject of a famous dream reported by Jerome: are you a Christian or a Ciceronian?[32] To bedeck the language of faith and authenticity in the trappings of elegance and rhetoric was of questionable value and could be taken to reveal religious ambivalence. Much more important than the question of what style to use in one's own religious writings and sermons was the Latinity of the Bible itself; that problem received its most memorable expression in Gregory the Great's letter to Leander (Isidore of Seville's elder brother) accompanying the *Moralia in Iob*. After announcing his scorn for *loquendi ars*, Gregory elaborates (*PL* 75.516B):

> Nam sicut huius quoque epistolae tenor enuntiat, non metacismi collisionem fugio, non barbarismi confusionem devito, situs motusque et praepositionum casus servare contemno, quia indignum vehementer existimo, ut verba caelestis oraculi restringam sub regulis Donati. Neque enim haec ab aliis interpretibus in scripturae sacrae auctoritate servata sunt.

30. On Cassiodorus' ideas about the biblical origin of the arts and for a list of his marginal *notae*, see O'Donnell (1979: 157–62). On the source of Cassiodorus' list of rhetorical figures, formerly thought (so Schindel 2002a: 104–11) to be the text preserved in Paris, Lat. 7530 and known as *Anonymus Ecksteinii*, published by Eckstein (1852), see now Grondeux (2013).

31. On Christian exegesis of the Fourth *Eclogue*, see Courcelle (1957).

32. Jerome, *Ep*. 22 (*PL* 22.416–17). For a broader interpretation of the relationship between grammar and Christianity in the fourth century, see Chin (2008).

> As the style of this letter makes clear, I do not avoid the clash of mytacism, I do not shrink from the confusion of barbarism, I have no concern with preserving the placement, order, and cases of prepositions. That is because I strongly believe that it is shameful to restrain the words of the heavenly oracle under the rules of Donatus. And in fact they are not preserved by other interpreters of the text of holy scripture.

It is clear from this passage, however, that while in theory the rules of classical Latin were deemed irrelevant to the Bible, Gregory's own rhetorical attack on them is highly stylized and shows precise awareness, as Holtz has demonstrated, both of Cassiodorus' similar reservations in the *Institutiones* and of the passage of Donatus himself on which Cassiodorus was drawing.[33]

The question of how to reconcile grammar and Christianity was a complicated one: Latin was still required to read the scriptures and participate in religious life, but the Latin taught by Donatus, while theoretically still valid, created difficulties in two areas in particular. One was the problem of grammatical instruction itself: why should a budding Christian be taught to decline *Musa* (Donatus' paradigmatic example for feminine nouns) when he really needed to learn about *ecclesia*? Much more difficult is the issue raised by Cassiodorus and Gregory: biblical Latin does not meet the standards of classical style, and a new rhetoric was clearly necessary; there was a constant pressure to make the unconventional Latin of the Bible respectable, just as there was also strong pressure to celebrate that unconventionality as a sign of Christian difference. But despite Donatus' problems for the pious, his work remained fundamental to all grammatical instruction until the ninth century.[34]

The simpler problem was the question of paradigms. Donatus, as seen in the previous chapter, already posed difficulties for the novice Latinist: his descriptions of Latin inflection were inadequate, and he had not nearly enough paradigms. Those could be, and were, supplied in collections of *regulae* and *catholica*. But very early on, no later probably than the middle of the sixth century, someone began to make paradigms more orthodox. A text ascribed to one Asperius or Asporius provides clear evidence for a Christian version of Donatus'

33. Holtz (1981: 254–5); cf. Donatus 4.392.27–3.4 and Cassiodorus, *Inst.* 45.7–7.11 and 94.18–6.15. Cassiodorus' whole chapter 1.15 *Sub qua cautela relegi debeat caelestis auctoritas* is extremely important for the tension between classical rules and biblical idiom. The complaints of Jerome, Gregory, and others about the irrelevance of classical grammar to Christian students are echoed down to (at least) the Carolingian period, leading to the thoroughly Christianized grammar of Smaragdus; see Law (1997: 140–4) and 13.26 below.

34. Donatus is not the only source—various medieval grammarians at various times and places knew and used a much wider range of material—but his name is virtually synonymous with grammar until the revival of interest in Priscian in the ninth century, and it therefore makes sense to concentrate on his role in the tradition.

Ars minor: where Donatus illustrates genders (MFN + *commune*) by *magister, Musa, scamnum*, and *sacerdos*, Asporius gives *iustus, ecclesia, ieiunium*, and *finis* and *sacerdos; Hierusalem Iordanis Sion* are his specific examples of geographic names, *Michael Petrus Stephanus Esaias Aaron Ezechiel* of personal names, and *angelus apostolus martyr propheta sacerdos rex* of the categories of which they are instances. There are numerous other changes to lists of nouns and verbs, as well as in other illustrations of grammar.[35] A number of other early medieval texts independent of Asporius preserve some portion of this Christian *Ars minor*, but no single model of the whole thing survives, nor is it altogether clear that there was only one: it did not take a genius to substitute Christian examples for secular ones, and the whole later tradition of elementary grammars shows how much they borrowed from one another.[36]

To switch the paradigms from classical to biblical was relatively simple; to adjust the last part of the *Ars*, concerned with the barbarism, solecism, tropes, and figures, took much more effort. Biblical Latin was filled with constructions that paid scant attention to the norms of classical Latin, and the language of the Bible certainly fell short of the standards of Ciceronian or Virgilian Latinity. Furthermore, while Virgilian locutions were regularly used by grammarians to illustrate both vices and virtues of speech, it was distinctly uncomfortable for a pious Christian to find any flaws in God's word. Rhetoric, as well as grammar, needed Christianization.

As is the case with the posited Christian *Ars minor*, the demand for a Christian *Ars maior* Book 3 was met by a text now lost, but very well represented in extant writings of the early Middle Ages. An eighth-century manuscript now in Fulda preserves under the name Isidorus Iunior a treatise on the figures of speech; it was written after the *Etymologiae* of Isidore of Seville (d. 636), but can have been written no later than c. 670, because it was used in the Christianizing grammatical work of Iulianus of Toledo (d. 690), and given that sequence, it was almost certainly written in Visigothic Spain. Isidorus Iunior's work, it is clear, was itself based on an earlier text: as its editor Ulrich Schindel suggests for compelling reasons, the ur-Christian rhetoric was almost certainly composed in Ostrogothic Italy, sometime in the middle of the sixth century.[37] This treatise on figures makes use of Book 3 of Donatus' *Ars maior*, but also adds a range of biblical examples, many of them borrowed from multiple works of Augustine and Jerome. It represents a deliberate attempt to merge secular grammatical

35. On Asporius, see Holtz (1981: 272–83), Law (1982: 35–41); for details and bibliography on grammatical texts later than Isidore of Seville, see Chapter 13 below. The history of *sacerdos* is worth noting: in the earlier grammars, it is in fact the name of the grammarian Sacerdos, but by the fifth century it is reinterpreted as the common noun.

36. As Law herself rightly notes (1982: 71): "The distinction between a revised version of an old work and a new compilation based on that old work is difficult to draw and usually arbitrary."

37. On Isidorus Iunior, see 13.15 below.

teaching with biblical illustrations; not, in the manner of Cassiodorus, claiming that the Bible was the source of the rhetorical figures, but trying to synthesize classical and biblical examples. The influence of this treatise extended beyond Spain: Bede's *De schematibus et tropis*, written in Northumbria in the early eighth century, takes Donatus' list of figures of speech and tropes in *Ars maior* Book 3 as its backbone, but the content is much more heavily indebted to Isidorus Iunior and to Cassiodorus' *Expositio Psalmorum*. And where Isidorus Iunior adds biblical examples to the secular ones in Donatus, Bede employs exclusively the former, creating a truly Christianized rhetoric. The tradition of Christianizing Donatus continued, at least down to Smaragdus, the most thoroughly Christianizing of the Carolingian grammarians; to pursue it further would go well beyond the bounds of this book.

4. TRAVELS AND TRANSFORMATIONS

The account of Christianizing grammar given above refers to books written in a variety of locations: Cassiodorus and the anonymous Christian rhetoric in Ostrogothic Italy; Fulgentius in Vandal Africa; Isidore of Seville, Isidorus Iunior, and Iulianus of Toledo in Visigothic Spain; the mysterious Asporius in Southern France or Ireland; and Bede in Northumbria. To understand the survival of Roman scholarship and the nature of what survives, geography matters a great deal. In this respect, the tradition of Roman scholarship—and hence the nature of the surviving texts—is significantly different from the tradition of Greek scholarship. In the Greek tradition, the broad geographical spread of education and scholarship, incorporating in antiquity Alexandria and Pergamum, Athens and even Rome, progressively narrowed: the loss of the western empire (and the loss of Greek in what remained) and the Arab conquests of the seventh century significantly reduced the domain of Greek scholarship as well as of Greek power, while the gradual reduction of the area under Byzantine control to little more than Constantinople itself had, among other effects, the result that the traditions through which we learn about Greek scholarship pass through an extremely narrow corridor of transmission: by and large, except for some texts from Nicaea or Thessalonica, what we possess is what was known in a single city.

In the case of Roman scholarship, the progression is the opposite. From the city of Rome, the importance of being able to speak and understand Latin, and to read and remember major texts of classical Latin literature, spread to encompass at one time or another in late antiquity and the early Middle Ages not only all of western Europe, but the imperial bureaucracy of the eastern empire as well. It should not be forgotten (and has already been said above) that the largest and greatest works written in Latin in the sixth century (Priscian's grammar and Justinian's legal code) were written in Constantinople; so too, some of the most interesting grammatical writing before Priscian, including the works of Charisius, Diomedes, and Dositheus, was composed in Latin by and for Greek-speakers. But while these texts are of crucial importance for our knowledge of the Roman grammatical tradition, the great bulk of scholarly writing took place in the West, and all of what survives, except for a few relatively unimportant papyri, was copied and preserved there.

The geography of grammatical writing and the geography of the preservation of grammatical texts overlap, but are significantly different. Grammar of some kind was studied everywhere Latin was needed; not all of it was preserved and, more important, Latin was not taught in every location continuously: not in the Byzantine world after the sixth century, not in Africa or Spain after the Arab conquests, not in various parts of northern Europe before their reconversion to Christianity through the missionary activities of Irish and English monks, the former founding the monasteries of Luxeuil in France c. 590 and Bobbio in Italy in 614, the latter founding Fulda in Germany in 744. The active production of grammatical scholarship is, not surprisingly, consistent with political and linguistic changes: while Rome itself was a major locus of both teaching and scholarship until the early fifth century, it seems to fade from prominence, replaced by Constantinople (if that is where Charisius and/or Diomedes worked) in one direction and the capitals of Ostrogothic Italy (the Virgilian commentator Philargyrius in Milan) and Vandal North Africa (Martianus Capella, Fulgentius, and Pompeius probably in Carthage) in the other.

Grammatical writings of the fifth and sixth century come from a wide variety of locations: Priscian's pupil Eutyches was still writing in Constantinople in the later sixth century; Consentius and Agroecius wrote in Gaul. But one direction, through North Africa, seems to have been particularly productive. In addition to the extant texts mentioned above we have hints of a much wider grammatical culture in the late fifth or early sixth century in Africa: we possess the dedicatory letter and a few paragraphs of a treatise on prosody written by Coronatus, who may have been a grammarian, in North Africa and dedicated to another possible grammarian, Luxorius (or Lūxurius). Poems by both of them are preserved in the collection made in the early 530s in North Africa and now found in the so-called Latin Anthology, in the eighth-century Codex Salmasianus.[38] From Africa, to Spain: in the seventh century, Isidore of Seville made use of Pompeius' commentary on Donatus, and Isidorus Iunior knew the same rhetorical texts that were available to Cassiodorus and Pompeius.[39] From Spain, some texts (including a version of Donatus and some of the work of Iulianus of Toledo at the end of the seventh century) seem to have traveled to France; but they were also rapidly known in Ireland. And paradoxically it is Ireland—the one area of transmission of Latin texts that was never under Roman control—that plays a crucial role in the preservation of the tradition of Roman scholarship.

Very few texts of classical literature can be shown to have been in Ireland at any time, but a credible estimate places no fewer than eighteen different works of grammatical scholarship there in the seventh and eighth centuries, on

38. On Coronatus, see 12.17 below.

39. See Schindel (2002b).

the basis of which a vast and complicated grammatical literature was produced, either in Ireland or by Irish monks on the continent, between the sixth and eighth centuries.[40] Indeed, Ireland is the location of the most striking and ingenious grammatical compositions of the early Middle Ages. Precise origins of such works are disputed: whether they are Irish or continental, and in some cases Irish or English, is not always clear, but the presence of distinctively Irish elements in many such texts is indisputable. The sequence of major texts begins with Asporius, whose geography is uncertain but whose primary influence is certainly in Ireland; it progresses through the anonymous *Ad Cuimnanum* and *Ars Ambrosiana* (both probably written at Bobbio in the seventh century), the grammarian Virgilius Maro (almost certainly in Ireland), Malsachanus (whose very name, not to mention his location, is disputed) and the multiform text known as the *Ars Ambianensis*, to Murethach, who came from Ireland to France in the early ninth century, and beyond. Nor are Irish productions limited to grammars, although that is what I will concentrate on here: the most important traditions of Virgilian scholarship, the larger form of Servius and the Filargyrian Sylloge, may well have been compiled and transmitted in Ireland itself.

For the transmission of grammar, however, it is probably not manuscripts present or written in Ireland that matter so much as manuscripts copied or preserved at the great Irish foundation of St. Columbanus at Bobbio, near Milan; and what is striking is that many, if not most, of the texts preserved there survive in no other source. Thus, the first two books of the grammar of Sacerdos survive only in one section of Naples, Lat. 2, a composite collection (four manuscripts bound together) of grammatical texts preserved at Bobbio; another section of the same manuscript contains, among other texts, the *Anonymus ad Caelestinum* on prosody and the grammar of the *Anonymus Bobiensis*.[41] The most important manuscript of Charisius was preserved there; so was a large collection of works on meter and orthography taken from Bobbio to Milan in 1493, copied, and—as often happened to manuscripts in the Renaissance—promptly lost. Velius Longus, Adamantius Martyrius, Caesius Bassus, Terentianus Maurus, and more were preserved in a single copy stored, and probably written, at Bobbio.[42]

40. On grammars in Ireland, see Herren (1981) and Hofman (2000). I will not attempt to explain, much less join, the debate over what texts the Irish knew, and where and when they knew them: it is extremely difficult to separate works actually written in Ireland from those written in Irish centers on the continent (Luxeuil, Bobbio, and St. Gallen in particular), and in some cases hard to tell Anglo-Saxon works from Irish ones. Extreme anti- and pro-Irish positions are equally untenable, and a certain degree of fuzziness is inevitable and indeed, in such a political issue, desirable. Useful and moderate guides to the conflict include Herren (1981); O Cróinín (1993); Szerwiniack (2003). On grammars written by the Irish, focusing on the eighth- to ninth-century texts, see also Holtz (1977d).

41. On this manuscript, see particularly De Nonno (1982: xviii–xxvii).

42. On the Bobbio manuscripts, see particularly Ferrari (1970) and Morelli (1989 and 2011–12); see also the entries for specific authors below.

But if there is a distinct group of texts that survive in unique or almost unique copies preserved in Bobbio (and smaller numbers of similarly rare texts that come from other locations), what is most striking about the tradition of more widely known grammatical texts in the early Middle Ages is that they very frequently form parts of anthologies, and that equally frequently these texts are excerpted, rearranged, recombined, and reshaped to fit the needs of a particular community at a particular time. Most such manuscripts were written in the Carolingian period, between the late eighth century and the end of the ninth, but they draw together the grammatical traditions of the previous five hundred years, from Donatus at one end to works by Alcuin and other Carolingian grammarians at the other. Grammatical centos of this kind are found in several varieties: some collect texts on particular areas of study such as orthography or prosody; others focus on Donatus and supplement his work with that of commentators or with more elementary texts; others are more elementary than that, while yet others combine grammatical works with literary texts studied in the monastic schools together with grammar.[43]

Some of these texts (e.g., the collection of works on orthography and vocabulary in Bern 330) are simply anthologies, bringing together unaltered (more or less) works on the same or complementary subjects, but most of them involve some degree of excerpting and reshaping. One such important manuscript is the great early Beneventan codex from Monte Cassino (Paris, Lat. 7530, written between 779 and 797), which not only preserves such treasures as the *Anecdoton Parisinum* (discussed above) and the didascalic notice for Varius' *Thyestes*, but also includes sections that are taken from Iulianus of Toledo, Pompeius, Servius, and many others—and in some cases blends them together. It is very likely that the collection should be associated with Paul the Deacon, an important figure at Monte Cassino at the time.[44] A ninth-century manuscript written in Tours (Angers 493) contains some complete short grammatical texts, including the *Regulae* of Ps.-Palaemon, Phocas' *Ars de nomine et verbo*, the *Ars* of Ps.-Asper together with the *Ars* of Asporius, and Alcuin's *Dialogus Franconis et Saxonis de octo partibus orationis* (which may not be by Alcuin). It also contains, moreover, some unique combinations of texts, sets of extracts from earlier grammatical writings: the so-called *Excerpta Andecavensia*; a grammatical compilation made from bits of Priscian, Phocas, Charisius, and others; a metrical compilation taken from Maximus Victorinus and Metrorius. And it also includes a list of verbs, a set of declensions of nouns, and other useful bits of grammatical lore.[45] Montpellier

43. For what follows, I have made use of the treatments of complex medieval grammatical manuscripts in Irvine (1994: 334–404) and De Paolis (2003a, 2003b) and on the descriptions of particular manuscripts in Holtz (1981). De Nonno (2000) is a careful analysis of the structure of late antique grammatical manuscripts, including the Naples manuscripts from Bobbio; there is further bibliography in De Nonno (2013: 63–5).

44. See Holtz (1975). It is by far the most frequently cited manuscript in this book.

45. On Angers 493, see De Paolis (2003a: 32–3) with full bibliography. On the *Excerpta Andecavensia* in particular, see De Nonno (1992).

306, another ninth-century French manuscript, concentrates on spelling and glossaries; again, it includes not only whole texts on orthography—Caper and Agroecius, Alcuin and Bede—but sets of extracts from various other works in order to supplement the basic readings.[46]

Manuscripts such as these were completely straightforward instructional tools to the people who compiled and used them: they were books of grammar. They are less transparent from our point of view because their concern is not to preserve unaltered specific earlier works, but to create something useful. That is one reason it is so difficult to find, or identify, specific works of late antique grammatical scholarship: they may have been specific works from their authors' point of view and even from ours; but for the people who preserved them, it was the content and not the source that mattered.

One final manuscript illustrates the complexity—and the identity problems—of these texts. Bern 207 was written at the great Benedictine monastery of Fleury-sur-Loire in the late eighth century in a continental Irish hand.[47] The manuscript is no longer complete: the first 195 folia survive bound together with two folia from later in the manuscript, and an additional twenty-four folia from the same manuscript (originally foll. 212–35) are now part of Paris, Lat. 7520. Most of Bern 207 consists of two different grammatical collections, one of Donatus and Donatus-related materials (foll. 2–113r) and one with a large component of Insular and early Carolingian materials (foll. 113r–194v + Paris folia); that they were deliberately combined into a single grammatical anthology is shown by the fact that one ends and the other begins on the same folio. It is unclear how long these two parts had traveled together before Bern 207 was written; it is quite possible that they were united by the early eighth century. In any case, the two halves need separate treatment.

Bern 207 begins with a text of Donatus, but as is often the case in grammatical anthologies, it is Donatus with a difference. It starts with the *Ars minor*, but to the chapter on the noun (*GL* 4.356.36) it adds a brief paragraph on the five declensions—one of the most significant gaps in Donatus' grammar—and to the chapter on the verb (362.13) it adds a discussion of impersonal verbs, including the declension of *pudet* and *itur*.[48] In moving on to the *Ars maior*, it omits the opening brief section *De voce*. Within *Ars maior* Book 1 there are also larger changes: a paragraph is added to *De syllaba* (369.15, printed at *AH* xviii) and after that comes a copy of Metrorius, *De finalibus* before the final portion

46. On Montpellier 306, see De Paolis (2003b: 208–10).

47. The manuscript is often discussed; for a detailed description see Holtz (1981: 361–4), on which I rely; see also *AH* xv–xxxi and Munzi (1980–1: 161–4). Law (1982: 100–1) grouped it with several other similar compilations as reflecting the interests of Charlemagne's court; for discussion and more recent bibliography see De Paolis (2003b: 199–203) and Krotz and Gorman (2014: xxxiv–xlvii).

48. The beginning and end of this section are printed at *AH* xviii.

of *Ars maior* Book 1.[49] But what follows the end of Book 1 is Book 3, not Book 2; Book 2 appears only at the end of the first half of the manuscript. Between Book 3 and Book 2, occupying the bulk of this section of the manuscript, is the *Ars grammatica* of Iulianus of Toledo, followed by Servius, *De centum metris*, two poems by Optatianus Porfyrius, and the *De partibus orationis* of Iulianus of Toledo.

All the distinctive qualities of the version of Donatus in Bern 207 (the additions to *Ars minor*, the metrical addenda, and the order of books being the most significant) also appear in other witnesses, in a group of Donatus manuscripts (α) which Holtz designates as Visigothic, coming from Spain.[50] It is thus not surprising that the text of Iulianus of Toledo's grammar, which is really an extended commentary on Donatus, matches precisely the idiosyncrasies of the text of Donatus in Bern 207; the only difference is that Iulianus' *Ars* includes (as chapters 20–5) a discussion of meter sometimes given the separate title *Conlatio de genere metrorum*—which is itself a compilation based closely on Mallius Theodorus' handbook on meter and the metrical portions of Audax. Furthermore, Iulianus' work is, in Bern 207, divided into two different works (*Ars* and *De partibus*), corresponding to the division of the text of Donatus.[51]

But if the first half of Bern 207 has clear Spanish connections, it has been attached to a very different collection. Because this part of the manuscript is less coherent than the first part, and because it is no longer complete, certainty about its sources and structure is impossible. A significant portion of the texts, however, is either British or closely connected to the court of Charlemagne: it contains the *Ars* of Asporius, the oldest of the Irish grammars, discussed above; Bede's treatise *De schematibus et tropis*; Alcuin, *De dialectica*; and two different versions of the grammar of Peter of Pisa, Charlemagne's teacher of Latin grammar. It also contains a version of "Sergius," *Primae explanationes* with Irish glosses, a set of extracts from Isidore put together to form a mini-treatise on the liberal arts, the *Catholica* of Probus, and other short texts; according to the table of contents

49. On Metrorius and other texts on the prosody of final syllables, see 8.4b above and 12.46.7 below. In Bern 207, the version of Metrorius embedded in the text of Donatus omits the opening sections (*GL* 6.229.1–31.3) because they repeat what is found earlier in Donatus himself. Many other manuscripts of Donatus *auctus* could be cited; particularly thorough in its mixing of Donatus with other texts is the so-called *Ars Augiensis* (see 13.36 below) in Karlsruhe 112 foll. 61v–101v, which includes three or four snippets after each section of Donatus. For description, see Holtz (1981: 367–71).

50. On the manuscripts and characteristics of this group, see Holtz (1981: 453–75). On the Spanish origins of Part I of Bern 207, see especially Holtz (1974). Beeson (1924) believed that the whole manuscript had Insular origins, but pan-Insularism was fashionable at that time and there is no reason to follow his hypothesis.

51. In other words, Donatus *Ars minor* + *Ars maior* 1 + 3 is immediately followed by Iulianus, *Ars* (on the same text of Donatus); Iulianus, *De partibus* (on *Ars maior* 2) immediately precedes the corresponding text of Donatus.

on fol. 1, it once contained a text of Priscian, presumably the short and popular *Institutio de nomine*.

Whatever the origins of the collection in Bern 207, it is a good example of what happened to grammars and in grammatical manuscripts in the early Middle Ages. In the first place, compilation and combination: the manuscript was composed from two different collections, each of which is made up of a number of different works. Secondly, the dominance of Donatus: in the first part of Bern 207 are a text of and commentary on Donatus; in the second there are several texts—Peter of Pisa, Bede, "Sergius," Asporius—that are versions of Donatus or commentaries on Donatus. Finally, there are several ways in which Donatus was extended or modified. In this period, both Probus, *Catholica* and the (missing) *Institutio* of Priscian were used as inflectional supplements to Donatus, and in this case, there are also changes to the text of Donatus itself: paragraphs were added within the text to supply extra material on inflection and on prosody, and the books themselves were rearranged to make one grammar out of *Ars minor* + *Ars maior* Books 1 and 3 and a separate one from *Ars maior* Book 2. That is a mark of one tradition of Donatus, but it was also common to combine the two treatments of the parts of speech (*Ars minor* and *Ars maior* Book 2) as an independent work.

Latin grammar was itself not very flexible, but the books in which it was explained were. Donatus was explained; he was rearranged; he was supplemented and adapted. The kinds of adaptation found in manuscripts like Bern 207 are readily comprehensible as adjustments to fit new circumstances. In some cases, however, the adaptations and the circumstances in the seventh and eighth centuries seem from a modern point of view to go far beyond the rational needs of grammatical instruction. A manuscript written at Corbie at the end of the eighth century or the beginning of the ninth (Amiens 426) contains in its first section a collection of short grammatical texts, including some that are clearly Irish in origin. One is a very short commentary on Donatus' *Ars maior* Book 2 on the noun, known by its first words as *Aggressus quidam*; the other, known as *Quae sunt quae*, starts out as a commentary on the opening of the *Ars minor*.[52] *Aggressus quidam* begins by announcing its intention to collect a few materials *ad adulescentem perfectum faciendum in nomine in editione secunda* (1: "to perfect the student in the study of nouns from *Ars maior* 2"); the author then launches into a paragraph on the importance of the number three, including the triad *locus tempus persona* typical of the introductions to Irish grammars (2). And after announcing that Donatus needs to be interpreted first *iuxta historicam doctrinam*, then *in moribus*, and finally *in altioribus rebus* (3), he begins to illustrate this by explaining the word *oratio*, taken from the phrase *nomen est pars orationis*, the opening of Donatus' chapter. The author starts from the categories of *oratio*, word, syllable, and letter found regularly in classical grammars but then adds the additional category, used in dealing with scripture, of *spiritalis intelligentia*: just as grammarians

52. See 13.32, 42 below. These texts are also found in other manuscripts; both are edited by Munzi (2004).

speak of three times or tenses, past, present, and future, so too speech about God has three forms, thanks for what we have received, petition for what we desire, requests for others. As the author goes on, he explains the meaning and sometimes the etymology of each of the major words in Donatus' definition, whether or not it is relevant. He then offers a *differentia* between *genus, gens*, and *generatio* before getting to grammatical gender (using a mixed collection of examples: *sanctus, ecclesia, templum, sacerdos*). And then through *numerus, figura, casus, qualitas*, and *species*, ending (13) with *Simon Petrus* as an example of *cognomen*.

Quae sunt quae is more ambitious, comprising a commentary with digressions on the *Ars minor* followed by small amounts of commentary on parts of *Ars maior* Books 1 and 3 before turning into a set of excerpts from Isidore. Again, of course, it is Christian: although the author leaves *Musa* and the like as illustrations of nouns, he quotes Gregory for an etymology of *sacerdos*, uses *laudate Dominum de caelis, laudate eum in excelsis* to illustrate the agreement of the pronoun with the noun to which it refers (19), and *cum venisset Paulus Romam, accesserunt ad eum omnes Iudaei* to illustrate the subjunctive (22). He tells us that there are three persons of the verb because there are three persons in the trinity (27) and, when the author comes to the chapter *De voce* that begins *Ars maior* Book 1, we learn that the first *vox spiritalis* (i.e., without letters and syllables and the like) was *fiat lux* and the first *vox corporalis* was *ecce nunc os de ossibus meis et reliqua* (38). But what is most striking about this text is that *Quae sunt quae* begins not with the first words of the *Ars minor*, but—after discussing *locus tempus persona* (1)—with the title of the book itself. *Incipiunt* is the author's first lemma, and (again, typical of Irish grammars) he starts explaining the first word by explaining the first letter, I, in the three sacred languages (Hebrew, Greek, Latin) and then, in the manner of Priscian's *Partitiones*, relentlessly parsing the verb: what is its part of speech, what are its accidents, what is its *qualitas*, and on, and on, doing the same thing to almost every word of the title. Donatus' grammar is no longer a text the content of which needs to be expanded by commentary; it is now a text whose every word is itself the object of commentary. Donatus has become literature, grammar's answer to scripture.[53]

The intense piety of Irish monks led them to enfold the sacred languages, the church, and all time within the alphabet and within grammar. One striking characteristic is a continuing interest in the three sacred languages and in particular in the alphabets of those languages; that is evident in the discussion of the initial letter of *Incipiunt* in the opening paragraphs of *Quae sunt quae*. The same manuscript that contains the fullest version of *Quae sunt quae* (Paris, Lat. 13025, written at Corbie in the early ninth century) also contains, within a perfectly normal collection of grammatical writings starting with a text of Donatus, a set of four short tracts on the alphabet (foll. 24v–26v), versions of each of which also appear elsewhere. The first and longest of them, with the title *De litteris Latinis*

53. On the complex attitude to Donatus (and to Donatus' relationship to scripture) in these texts, see Munzi (2011).

quidam sapiens interpretatus est, varies between exegetical and catechistic form, with some letters receiving considerably more attention than others and having more references to Hebrew or to theological allegory. The letter A is among the fullest (but note also I and X), beginning[54]

> A vocalis est. Quibus virgulis conparatur? Ex tribus virgulis. Deinde dicitur triplex sono et figura. Quibus nominibus dicitur A? Ex tribus nominibus: aleph in Hebraeo dicitur, alfa in Graeco dicitur, a in Latino dicitur. Quare prima ex litteris est A? Quia dicitur primus de nominibus hominum <u>A</u>dam, et in <u>a</u>nima et in <u>a</u>ngelo, qui fuit ante saecula, dum animae creatae fuerunt a Deo vivo. . . .
>
> A is a vowel. How many strokes is it composed from? From three strokes. Thus it is said to be triple in sound and shape. By what names is A called? By three names: it is called aleph in Hebrew, alfa in Greek, a in Latin. Why is A the first letter? Because <u>A</u>dam is the first of human names, and in <u>a</u>nima and <u>a</u>ngel, who existed before all time, until souls were created by the living God. . . .

The three strokes of A, we also learn, are emblematic of the trinity, just as the two strokes of B represent the two testaments, the openness of C represents the church, and, eventually, X stands for the cross. Even more inventively, the alphabetic treatise of Sergilius gives the names of the three strokes of the letter A as *abst, ebst, ubst* in Hebrew and *albs, elbs, ulbs* in Greek.[55]

It is not possible to leave the topic of the metamorphoses of classical grammar without mentioning one last case, the bizarre and enigmatic grammarian Virgilius Maro.[56] Two works have come down to us, the *Epitomae* and the *Epistolae* (the first well preserved, the second surviving only in one manuscript), which seem, roughly, to be modeled on the two *Artes* of Donatus. But in terms of content, the resemblance is minimal: Virgilius is, apparently, a brilliant parodist, but whether there is a serious purpose, perhaps theological, under his catalogue of the twelve Latinities (none of which is ours) and the great debate of the grammarians Terrentius and Galbungus about the vocative of *ego*, is completely unclear. He does, however, know Donatus, and knows him well; indeed, he describes Donatus (together with Donatus' brother Don) as one of his teachers—but that category also includes Aeneas and two other Virgils, neither of whom is the poet. Virgilius is quoted by later grammarians, down to the ninth century at least, as a reputable source, and some of what he says bears some resemblance to Latin. On the other hand, there is a kind of similarity between the glossing of Donatus' title in *Quae*

54. I cite the text (with a few typographical changes) from *AH* 302–5, where it is printed from Bern 417 (with fewer errors than in Paris, Lat. 13025, but otherwise identical).

55. Sergilius or Sergius is very similar in character to Virgilius Maro, on whom see the next paragraph; on his alphabet, see Marshall (2010: 225).

56. See 13.30 below for some of the (extensive) bibliography about this strange and wonderful text.

sunt quae and Virgilius' treatment of Aeneas, Virgil, and Donatus as all belonging to the same realm, characters who live and argue in the world of grammar itself.[57]

5. CODA

Between the middle of the sixth century and the end of the eighth, the classical tradition of Roman grammar was stretched if not beyond recognition, at least beyond anything that the original authors intended: a different world, with different beliefs and goals, needed books quite different from the models that were adapted. The approaches taken—whether the Christianization of grammar and the exploration of the mystical meanings of the alphabet or the canonization of Donatus as a classical author to be commented on and the transformation of classical authors into grammarians—are always comprehensible, if at times strange. At the same time, if the grammatical fantasies of the early Middle Ages provided our only evidence for what Donatus (or Servius, or Priscian) actually wrote, then we would be hard put to reconstruct the originals.

But the fantastic constructions of the seventh and eighth centuries, although they are preserved in later manuscripts, clearly went out of fashion, and some grammarians recognized that the texts of classical grammar had a certain integrity of their own. At least one teacher, probably in the early ninth century, complained of textual pollution:[58]

> Artium Donati liber ita a plerisque vitiatus est et corruptus, dum unus quisque pro libitu sui sive ex aliis auctoribus quod ei visum est addidit, sive declinationes aut coniugationes et cetera huius modi inseruit, ut nisi in antiquis codicibus vix purus et integer, ut ab eo est editus, reperiatur.
>
> The book of Donatus' grammars has been so spoiled and corrupted by many people, each one adding what he liked at his own whim or from other sources, or inserting declensions or conjugations and other things of that sort, that it cannot be found in a pure and uncorrupted form, as it came from the author, except in ancient manuscripts.

The boundary between Donatus and the materials used to supplement Donatus had become very unclear. That was not true in late antiquity (with the possible exception of Pompeius at the end of the fifth century), where there is generally no difficulty in distinguishing text from commentary, nor was it true for the most part in the ninth century.

57. It should be noted that Cicero too becomes a character in grammatical writings: as the author of the *Synonyma Ciceronis* (and the dedicatory letter to "Veterius" that accompanies some texts), and as the sponsor of Donatus for membership in the Roman senate in the (probably Irish) mock biography of Donatus ascribed to one Flaccus Rebius, on which see 12.20 below.

58. *GL* 5.325.2–6, the preface to a text known as *Cunabula grammaticae artis*, an elementary parsing grammar preserved in three ninth-century manuscripts and sometimes wrongly attributed to Bede. See Law (1997: 133) and 13.41 below.

The orthographic reforms of Alcuin were only one part of a large change visible in scholarly writings. In grammars, where the evidence is clearest, by the late eighth century there begins to be a distinction between the late antique grammatical texts as independent and coherent works on the one hand, and whatever newer scholars choose to write about them, or about their subjects. The boundary between text and commentary, between past and present, was restored. Commentaries on Donatus begin again to be lemmatized; independent grammars, though dependent on Donatus (or, from the ninth century on, Priscian) are presented as works distinct from classical models. The break in the tradition allows the modern reader as well to distinguish what is ancient from what is not. In certain respects, the Irish (and to a lesser extent, English) grammarians are the last original writers within the living tradition of Latin grammar; Carolingian scholars recognize the distance of the past. The break is not absolute: manuscripts of selections and compilations continued to be made, but they become much less frequent, and manuscripts of specific texts become more common.

The same, to some degree, is true of both dictionaries and commentaries. It is in the eighth and ninth centuries that the compilation of large dictionaries begins: the idiosyncratic shorter lists of words from particular authors or about particular subjects begin to be combined into more orderly and more universal collections, of which the Carolingian *Liber glossarum* is the largest and most ambitious. In the case of commentaries, the difference between the scrappy and irregular notes in the margins of ancient manuscripts and the tidy and rigid columns of text next to, or surrounded by, commentary is immediately apparent. Commentaries are compiled from multiple sets of marginalia; they are codified and organized; they are sometimes given fuller lemmata with subordination of lesser notes beneath a single heading. Signs are used to indicate the beginning of a new note. As with grammars and glossaries, of course, this change is by no means universal: it is, rather, that the orderly and classicizing version of all these forms of writing is rarely found before the late eighth century and becomes ever more dominant thereafter.

The ways in which the various forms of Roman scholarship are preserved are similar, but are not the same. In the case of grammars, we possess a great many of the ancient models as well as the early medieval transformations: we can document the processes of change. That is not true, for the most part, for dictionaries and commentaries: we have in general only scraps of the ancient commentaries in their original form, and must try to see through Carolingian order to the disorder of late antique marginalia, and through that disorder to the presumably coherent works of ancient scholarship that underlie the marginalia. Dictionaries have a little of both characteristics: some ancient texts (such as Nonius) survive more or less intact, while the prehistory of glossaries is still largely unknown.

The ninth century, then, is for many reasons a good place to stop. We need to use the work of Carolingian scholars to uncover the scholarship of antiquity, but what the Carolingians themselves did marks a significant break from the traditions they inherited. And those traditions, I have tried to show, were not themselves static. What remains true throughout, however, is that the philological study of the Latin language and its texts in antiquity and the early Middle Ages constantly responded to the needs of its audiences: from the early desire to understand the even earlier texts of law and religion, to the attempt to shape a comprehensible and useful Latin in the age of Varro and Cicero, to assisting the stylistic demands of rhetoric in the early empire, to the need to teach Latin to the new populations of Latin-speakers in the later empire, to the Christianization of grammar in the early Middle Ages. This sequence could easily be extended to later periods, up to the present day: the desire to understand Latin continually adapts itself to new contexts and new audiences. Learning has more than one face.

Part II: A Bibliographic Guide

THE GUIDE WHICH FOLLOWS IS DIVIDED INTO FOUR PARTS, arranged in different ways. Chapter 10, on dictionaries and similar lists, is arranged chronologically by author, with the anonymous (and largely later) glossaries at the end. Chapter 11, on commentaries, is arranged in chronological order of the author being explained, from Terence to Juvenal (sometimes subdivided by the specific works being explained); commentaries are discussed in order of age or importance. Chapter 12, on ancient grammatical writings, is arranged in alphabetical order, at least in part because the chronology of many of the texts is so uncertain; a large collection of texts is grouped under "anonymous" at the end of the chapter. Chapter 13, on early medieval grammars is arranged in the same way, except that the category of "anonymous" is further subdivided into commentaries on Donatus and other grammatical writings. The amount of detail in the entries is highly variable, partly because many texts have already been discussed, and in those cases little more than a cross-reference is necessary; about other texts, little is known and I have therefore said little. I have also been very sparing in connection with well-studied authors whose major writings extend far beyond their philological activities: Martianus Capella, Cassiodorus, Isidore, Augustine, Bede, Alcuin, and a few others. To give general bibliographies in such cases would be largely irrelevant—and beyond my capacities. My primary goal has been to make unfamiliar texts and authors accessible, and to provide secondary bibliography, when it exists, with an emphasis on recent work (particularly studies that provide more bibliography than I do) and older scholarship of enduring value. In general, my intention has been to be as complete as possible in identifying modern editions and translations (as well as concordances); to list separately brief accounts in works of reference or handbooks that can be used for rapid orientation; and to be far more selective in citing secondary scholarship. I have not been altogether consistent in the structure of entries, as different texts sometimes require different sorts of explanation, but in general I have used the same categories, indicated as follows:

T = Texts and translations. In general, the standard edition (or editions) come first, followed by other translations and editions in chronological order. I have indicated whether a given work includes text, translation, and/or commentary, and noted the language into which translations are made. I have included translations, when I could find them, into languages I can (more or less) read: English, Catalan, French, German, Italian, and Spanish. I have normally not included online texts, because they have no apparatus; instead, in the list of abbreviations and bibliography I have tried to indicate where digital copies of printed editions are available.

I = Indices, lexica, and concordances.

B = Bibliographies. Starting from Wessner (1902), the bibliographical articles in *JAW* included scholia and commentaries as well as grammatical and glossographical materials. The five articles are those of Wessner (1902, 1908, 1921) and Lammert (1931, 1936). These are more than bibliographies, but often provide intelligent critical discussions of major works and a synthesis of current knowledge at the time; I have included references to specific entries below. The two subsequent bibliographical articles (Della Casa 1985 and Pugliarello 1998) are largely lists, and include neither scholia nor glossaries; they are useful rather than valuable, and I have not given specific citations to them. There are also bibliographies both on grammarians in general and on specific authors in CGL; they are uneven in coverage, are not always current, and are simply lists of titles. Bibliographical works (e.g., in *Lustrum*) on particular authors or texts are included where they exist.

R = Reference works and brief accounts or introductions. I have generally put proposographical sources (*RE*, *PLRE*, and the like) first; collections of brief accounts of grammarians (*LG* and *EV* in particular) second; and handbooks (Teuffel, S–H, *HLL*, and Manitius) last. While they overlap, they are very different in orientation (and date); in my own view, Teuffel (the relevant articles generally written by Paul Wessner), while it is often out of date, is for this material the most intelligent and useful of the standard works, while *HLL* (largely written by P. L. Schmidt) is, where it exists, recent, thorough, opinionated, and difficult to read. It should be noted that for reference works arranged in alphabetical order, I have given the name of the author of the entry, and the lemma (e.g., Donatus 3) if necessary to avoid ambiguity, but no volume and page numbers. *RE* Supplements are identified individually.

C = Collective volumes on specific authors or texts, not all of the individual contributions of which are included separately.

S = Secondary scholarship. In chronological order, except that I have grouped together multiple works by the same author. In a very few cases I have divided this section by topic.

10

Dictionaries and Encyclopedias

1. FESTUS

(including Verrius Flaccus, *De verborum significatu*; Pompeius Festus, *De significatione verborum;* and Paulus Diaconus, *Excerpta ex libris Pompei Festi de significatione verborum*)

For the history and methods of this set of texts, see 6.1 above. In brief, Verrius (Augustan) cannot be read directly but only through the abridgment of Festus (second–third century), which is itself fragmentary and needs to be supplemented by Paulus' excerpts from Festus (ninth century).

T: Lindsay (1913); Müller (1880); Pieroni (2004; detailed commentary on the entries for the letter N, 154.19–86.29L). Lindsay's second edition in *GlL* 4 (1930) has no apparatus and makes radical and unsuccessful attempts at reconstruction. A new edition is in progress by the Festus Dictionary Project of University College London.

R: *RE* Pompeius 145 (Helm), Verrius 2 (Dihle); *BNP* Festus 6 (Schmidt), Verrius 1 (Schmidt), Paulus 2.4 (Phillips); *PIR*[2] P607; *LG* (Desbordes–Garcea); Kaster (1995: 190–6); Teuffel 2 §261 (on Verrius); *HLL* 4 §440 (on Festus).

C: Glinister et al. (2007).

S: Reitzenstein (1887); Strzelecki (1932); Bona (1964, 1982); Lhommé (2001, 2011); North (2008).

2. NONIUS MARCELLUS

For description and discussion of *De compendiosa doctrina*, see 6.2 above.

T: Lindsay (1903a); Mazzacane (2014; Books 1–3); Gatti et al. (2014; Books 5–20). For recent work on the manuscript tradition, see Gatti (1996) and Llorente Pinto (1996). The Mazzacane/Gatti edition (with one volume as yet to be published) is not a significant improvement over Lindsay, and the apparatus in particular is repetitive and confusing. It should be noted that Lindsay's text and apparatus are keyed to page and line of Mercier's edition;

modern citations often give a hybrid reference, using Lindsay's page numbers but Mercier's line numbers. The new edition omits line numbers altogether and instead numbers by lemma and sentence (although including both Mercier and Lindsay page numbers in the margin).

B: Wessner (1902: 152–7, 1908: 111–18).

R: *RE* Nonius 38 (Strzelecki); *BNP* Nonius 3.1 (Schmidt); *PLRE* I Marcellus 11; Kaster (1988) #237; Teuffel 3 §404a; S–H 4.1 §826.

C: *Studi Noniani* (1967–97), succeeded by *Prolegomena Noniana* (2000–5) published respectively by Università di Genova, Pubblicazioni dell'Istituto di filologia classica e medievale and Pubblicazioni del Università di Genova: Facoltà di lettere, Dipartimento di archeologia, filologia classica e loro tradizioni.

S: Lindsay (1901); Strzelecki (1932–3, 1936); White (1980); Cadoni (1987); Keyser (1994); Deufert (2001); Chahoud (2007); Llorente Pinto (2009); Gatti (2011); Welsh (2012).

3. ISIDORE OF SEVILLE

Isidore (d. 636), at least in this volume, marks the boundary between ancient and medieval. Of his many works, only three are included here; for fuller discussion, see 6.4 above.

1. *Synonyma*

As Elfassi says (2009: ix), Isidore "a fait d'un exercise grammatical un ouvrage de spiritualité." Little more than the title and aspects of the style reflect the *Synonyma Ciceronis* on which it claims to be modeled.

T: Elfassi (2009).

S: Di Sciacca (2008).

2. *Differentiae*

The first question about Isidore's *differentiae* is which sets are genuine. Isidore's biographer Braulio says that he wrote two; as one might expect, they were written in his youth, if Braulio's apparently chronological arrangement can be trusted. By the eighth century, however, manuscripts attribute three sets of *differentiae* to Isidore, and a fourth one sometimes has his name. The one set that is almost certainly by him is *Inter deum et dominum* (also called *Differentiae rerum* or *Differentiae spirituales*), a set of theological distinctions generally printed as Book 2. What has often been printed as Book 1 is the set of *differentiae* known as *Inter aptum et utile*; but as Codoñer has shown, *Inter aptum et utile* (an alphabetical set of *differentiae* with more than 600 entries) is an expanded and alphabetized version of a thematic, non-alphabetical set, *Inter caelum et aethera*, which she prints as Book 1 in her 1992 edition. The alphabetized version is clearly not by Isidore, but *Inter caelum et aethera* probably is. Both versions of Book 1 are ascribed in their earliest manuscripts (and some others) to "Isidorus Iunior"—the same mysterious figure (13.15) who wrote a work on figures of speech in the generation after

Isidore of Seville and before Iulianus of Toledo. It is not impossible that Isidore Iunior is also the author of at least one version of the *Differentiae*, but given Braulio's attribution of two sets to the real Isidore, it seems unlikely. The last set of *differentiae* to which Isidore's name (sometimes as Iunior) is attached is *Inter polliceri et promittere*, also titled in some manuscripts *De proprietate sermonum*. It is generally agreed that neither Isidore is responsible for this collection, which must remain anonymous.

T: a) *Inter deum et dominum* (not, as Brugnoli 1955a: 133 reports it, *Inter deum et hominem*): *PL* 83: 70–98; Andrés Sanz (2006: 7–112).
b) *Inter aptum et utile*: PL 83: 9–70.
c) *Inter caelum et aethera*: Codoñer (1992: 84–301).
d) *Inter polliceri et promittere*: see 10.4.2a below.

S: Uhlfelder (1954); Brugnoli (1955a: 133–50 and 1964); Codoñer (1984–5, 1986, 1996); Magallón García (1996: 235–61).

3. *Etymologiae sive Origines*

Although in one sense the entire, vast *Etymologiae* falls under the rubric of grammar, in a narrower sense only a few books deal directly with problems of language: the first two, on grammar, rhetoric, and dialectic, and Books 9 and 10, about language and words. The works cited here concern either Isidore in general, the *Etymologiae* as a whole, or the specific books about language.

T: Lindsay (1911); Marshall (1983; Latin text of Book 2 with English translation; this is part of a complete edition of Isidore being published by Les Belles Lettres); Oroz Reta and Marcos Casquero (2000; Latin text with Spanish translation); Canale (2004; Latin text with Italian translation); Barney et al. (2006; English translation); Möller (2008; German translation). Excerpts from Book 1 and 2 are translated and annotated in Copeland and Sluiter (2009: 232–47).

I: Magallón García (1995–2006).

R: *RE* Isidoros 27 (Schmekel and Philipp); *BNP* Isidorus 9 (Schmidt); *RLAC* Isidor 4 (Fontaine); *LG* (Poirol); Teuffel 3 §496; Manitius (1911) §3.

B: Wessner (1921: 148–59); Hillgarth (1983) and (1990).

S: Fontaine (1959–83) and (1988); Amsler (1989); Irvine (1994: 209–43); Ribémont (2001); Kindermann (2005); Henderson (2007); Merrills (2013).

4. GLOSSARIES

For discussion of glossaries, see 6.3 above. The lists of specific types of glossary given here consist of those of which I have seen printed editions, and they are certainly not exhaustive. Much glossographic material is unpublished, and sometimes uncatalogued.

1. Collections

The two major publications of glossaries are *CGlL* (Goetz) and *GlL* (Lindsay). *CGlL* contains (a rough summary; see Dionisotti 1996):

Vol. 1 (the last volume published, long after the rest): *De glossariorum Latinorum origine et fatis* (still the best introduction to the whole range of glossographic material, with a supplementary essay by Paul Wessner).
Vol. 2: Latin–Greek and Greek–Latin dictionaries.
Vol. 3: Hermeneumata and medico-botanical bilingual glossaries.
Vol. 4: Latin glossaries (1), including *Abstrusa/Abolita*, *Abba*, *Abavus*, *Affatim*, and *Asbestos* (plus others).
Vol. 5: Latin glossaries (2), including Placidus, excerpts from *Liber glossarum*, and the glossaries with Anglo-Saxon elements, with all or excerpts of another sixteen shorter glossaries, including *Aa*.
Vol. 6–7: *Thesaurus glossarum emendatarum*.

GlL contains:

Vol. 1: *Liber glossarum* (*Glossarium Ansileubi*). Not complete, but more than in *CGlL*.
Vol. 2: *Arma*, *Abavus*, Ps.-Philoxenus.
Vol. 3: *Abstrusa* and *Abolita*.
Vol. 4: Placidus and Festus.
Vol. 5: *Asbestos/Abba* and *Aa*.

The two collections work on very different principles. Goetz printed what are essentially diplomatic transcripts, not attempting to construct a critical text or to emend; his annotations and emendations are only to be found in the invaluable *Thesaurus glossarum emendatarum*, the essential starting point for anyone wishing to pursue a specific gloss. Lindsay, in contrast, attempted to recombine and emend glossaries in order to reconstruct what he felt were large and complex compilations of late antiquity; as a result, he descended into what one might call a whirlpool of circular arguments from which the study of glossaries has only recently surfaced. *GlL* should be consulted, but it is a hopeless starting point, cannot be trusted, and is never easy to use.

Several things about these collections need to be kept in mind:

1. Both collections define "glossary" very narrowly: neither, for instance, includes *differentiae* and *synonyma*, and they pay little attention to *idiomata*.
2. Most of *GlL* consists of texts also in *CGlL* (except for *Arma* and Lindsay's second edition of Festus) but has rather fewer, in part because Lindsay attempts to reconstruct glossaries, in part because he had treated the Anglo-Saxon glossaries in separate publications.
3. Goetz's texts must be emended to be read at all; Lindsay's texts are often very speculative in their emendations and reconstructions.

4. Goetz was too prone to print excerpts: many of the glossaries especially in *CGlL* 5 are not adequate representations of what the manuscripts contain.
5. With the exception of the *Folium Wallraffianum* and the *Fragmenta Hersfeldensia* in *CGlL* (see below), neither collection includes glossaries on papyrus. For bilingual glossaries, see 10.4.5 below; for Latin glossaries on papyrus, see Scappaticcio (2015).
6. Lindsay's descriptions of the work of Goetz and his colleagues (in *GlL* as in many of the glossographic publications collected in Lindsay 1996) are generally both false and polemical. He began to work on glossaries seriously during the First World War, and his anti-German sentiments affect his scholarship. For "Ritscheliani" (his label for Goetz and his collaborators) one might as well read "Hun."

R: *RE* "Glossographie" (Goetz); *BNP* Glossography II (Schmidt); S–H 4.2 §1119.

B: Wessner (1902: 219–27, 1908: 195–206, 1921: 237–49); Lammert (1931: 95–121).

S: Loewe (1876); Goetz (1923); Lindsay (1996; originally published for the most part between 1915 and 1930) with Lapidge (1996); Dionisotti (1985, 1996); De Nonno (1990c: 603–12).

2. *Differentiae*

Differentiae are lists of distinctions between words (generally pairs) that are alike in meaning, form, or sound; the older ones concern meaning, and their original purpose was almost certainly as an aid to writing Latin, probably rhetorically.

a) *Inter polliceri et promittere* in four versions; i–iii discussed by Brugnoli (1955a: 41–57):
   i) *Inter polliceri et promittere*: *PL* 83.1319–32 (wrongly attributed to Isidore); Uhlfelder (1954: 47–83) under the title *De proprietate sermonum*; see Magallón García (1996: 235–61).
   ii) *Inter metum et timorem* (in some manuscripts with the title *Differentiae Ciceronis*): *AH* 275–90 with additions by Beck (1884: 51–7) from Montpellier 306; also in Filiscus (1518).
   iii) *Inter auxilium et praesidium*: Hand (1848).
   iv) *Inter accidit et contigit* (an alphabetical version of *Inter polliceri* ascribed to Suetonius): Roth (1877: 314–20); see Brugnoli (1955a: 61–94).

b) *Inter gnatum et natum* (ascribed to Palaemon): Roth (1877: 306–14); see Brugnoli (1955a: 97–110).

c) *Inter austrum et ostrum*: Stok (1997: 85–93). This text is preserved anonymously in Naples, Lat. 1, as part 4 of the text known as *Appendix Probi* (*GL* 4.193–204; see 12.36.4), and also preserved in Montpellier 306 where it is attributed to Valerius Probus; many of the entries also appear in an interpolated version of Isidore, *Diff.* Book 1 in Vatican, Lat. 3321. For a full account of the evidence see Stok (1997: 69–81); see also Brugnoli (1955a: 113–18).

d) *Inter ultionem et vindictam*: *GL* 7.519–32; Barwick (1964: 387–403). Preserved in the same manuscript as Charisius (Naples IV A 8) but (contra Barwick) not part of his grammar. A version of the text was used by Bede in *De orthographia*; it was incorrectly ascribed to Fronto by Parrhasius in his edition of 1509. See Brugnoli (1955a: 121–9) and Dionisotti (1982b: 114–19).

e) There is a short but remarkable set of *differentiae* on fol. 68v of Naples, Lat. 2, one of the parts of the manuscript written at Bobbio in the late seventh or early eighth century. It is a shaped text (in the form of a St. Andrew's cross, according to Stok) and is composed of selections drawn from several different kinds of source: it has Virgilian *differentiae* related to those in Servius, a group related to those in the *Appendix Probi* (2c above), and others related to the *differentiae Terentii* (2j below). For extensive discussion, see Stok (1999).

f) *Inter absconditum et absconsum*: Beck (1883: 28–90). In Montpellier 306, ascribed to Cicero; see Brugnoli (1955a: 153–82).

g) *Inter auferre adimere et eripere*: Brugnoli (1955b: 201–16).

h) *Inter servum et famulum et mancipium*: Widmann (1883). A small collection, most of which is found elsewhere; see Beck (1885); Brugnoli (1955a: 182–3).

i) There are *differentiae* in the *Liber Glossarum*; cf. Brugnoli (1955a: 183–5) with earlier references, and see 6.4.4a below.

j) Flobert (1994: 17) also cites two *differentiae*-like collections that do not have the standard *inter* . . . formula: a small set ascribed to Terentius (i.e., Scaurus), printed in *AH* cxxxiii from an Einsiedeln manuscript (see also Brugnoli 1955a: 171–82; part also in Naples, Lat. 2); and Book 5 of Nonius, *De differentia similium significationum* (3.681–718L).

k) There are *differentiae* in Servius' commentary on Virgil; see Stok (2008, 2012b).

l) For the *differentiae* of Isidore of Seville, see 10.3.2 above; for Agroecius, see 12.1 below.

R: *RE* Differentiarum scriptores (Goetz); *BNP* Differentiarum scriptores (Schmidt); S–H 4.2 §1121.

S: Hagen, *AH* cxvii–cxxxiv; Beck (1883); Uhlfelder (1954); Brugnoli (1955a); Codoñer (1985); Della Casa (1992); Flobert (1994); Magallón García (1996); Stok (1997: 27–45, 1999).

3. *Synonyma* (*Synonyma Ciceronis*)

Synonyma are the opposite of *differentiae*: they emphasize similarity of meaning rather than difference. Relatively few sets of *synonyma* have been published, but according to Munk Olsen (1982: 133–5), there are twelve different forms of *synonyma Ciceronis* (with variant forms as well, together with five of *differentiae*

Ciceronis), and his catalogue (340–50) lists five manuscripts of the *synonyma* earlier than the ninth century and thirty-three between the ninth and twelfth centuries (and seven of *diff. Ciceronis*). The attribution to Cicero is very common, although not universal.

a) *Orator actor* (not *Orator auctor* as in Brugnoli 1955a: 27–8): unpublished; see 6.3a above.
b) *Abditum opertum*: ed. W. L. Mahne, *Synonyma ad Lucium Veturium secundum editiones Romanas* (Leiden, 1850) and id., *Synonyma ad Lucium Veturium secundum editionem Parisinum* (Leiden, 1851), reprinted respectively from the Roman edition of 1487 (reprinted in Filiscus 1518) and the Paris edition of 1583 (so Dionisotti 1985: 308n). I have seen only Filiscus.

These are the two main versions; *Abditum* is an alphabetized version of *Orator*. Other pubished sets of various dates include:

Amor ardor: Barwick (1964: 412.19–49.31).
Arba humus: Gatti (1993).
Accusat lacescit: Gatti (1994); see also Jakobi (1999).

The others are unpublished:

Acer intentus.
Abditum absconditum.
Cohibet compescit.
Inanis vanus verbosus.
Vitare declinare.
S: Goetz (1923: 75–86); Brugnoli (1955a: 27–37, 1961); Steinová (2014).

4. Glossaries (Latin–Latin)

Given that so few glossaries have been described or published completely, a full list of what is in *CGlL*, too much of which is in the form of excerpts, would not be useful. Some of the larger or more important texts are:

a) The *Liber glossarum*, also known as *Glossarium Ansileubi*, has a misleading title: it is not a glossary, but a large Carolingian encyclopedia (located by Goetz in Spain c. 700–50; more correctly now assigned to Corbie c. 800 CE) which includes a great many glosses. It is not a primary source for any of them. While it is of great importance for students of the Carolingian world, it has relatively little value as evidence for ancient glossaries.

T: There is no complete edition (but see below); excerpts and lemmata in *CGlL* 5.161–255; *GlL* 1.15–604 (as *Glossarium Ansileubi*).
R: *LG* (Grondeux); Manitius (1911) §13.
B: http://liber-glossarum.linguist.univ-paris-diderot.fr/node/13.

C: Three volumes of articles have recently been published in preparation for an edition of *Liber Glossarum* now in progress: an issue of the journal *Histoire epistémologie langage* 36:1 (2014); Cinato and Grondeux (2015); and Grondeux (2016).

S: Goetz (1923: 104–17); Barbero (1990, 1993); Ganz (1991, 1993); Codoñer (2012); Steinová (2016).

b) *Abstrusa* is a large glossary (*CGlL* 4.3–198; *GlL* 3.1–183) preserved in two forms: the oldest manuscript, Vatican, Lat. 3321 of the mid-eighth century, has a longer form, known as *Abstrusa–Abolita*; some later manuscripts lack the additional sections (of which the first begins with *abolita*). Lindsay in *GlL* separated the two glossaries, but as Dionisotti (1996: 223) points out, there is no sign that *Abolita* ever existed independently before Lindsay created it in 1926. Although both Goetz and Lindsay believed in the importance of *Abstrusa*, it is not a first-order glossary, but a large compilation of other glossaries.

S: Loewe (1876: 143–51); Goetz (1923: 118–25); Dionisotti (1996: 236–8).

c) Leiden, BPL 67F (late eighth/early ninth century) contains twelve glossaries, including the following:

i) *Abavus*, foll. 62r–104v (*CGlL* 4.301–403 = *GlL* 2.29–121) is alphabetized to four letters (ABCD–), which means that it represents a late stage in compilation and its sources cannot be determined. A few of the many manuscripts of this glossary contain a longer form (christened *Abavus maior* by Loewe) which Goetz thought was simply interpolated from other known glossaries; while that is partially true, *Abavus maior* was in fact based on a larger form of *Abavus* than we possess, and it has some important genuine readings. A sample of *Abavus maior* is given at *CGlL* 4.589–99, and a digital image of the first page of *Abavus* is available online at the Leiden website.

S: Loewe (1876: 87–106); Goetz (1923: 129–33, 135–9); Dionisotti (1996: 236).

ii) *Ab absens* (foll. 54r–62r; *CGlL* 4.404–27), *Glossae Vergilianae* (foll. 104v–118r; 4.427–70), and *Affatim* (foll. 1r–54r; 4.471–581) are relatively straightforward. The last appears to be a compilation from *Abstrusa* and the unpublished *Aptet*.

S: Loewe (1876: 106–11); Goetz (1923: 133–5, 139–41); Dionisotti (1996: 227–8).

iii) *Arma* (foll. 119r–28r; *GlL* 2.1–22; omitted by Goetz) is a fragment covering only A–F, with the title *Glossae proprietatum*. It is alphabetized A–; each letter begins with vocabulary from Virgil (in text order, and in the order *Aeneid–Eclogues–Georgics*), followed by glosses from Terence and Lucan, by a section of glosses from an unknown source, beginning

(A342) *Amoenum: iucundum, fertile*, and by glosses from Prudentius. *Amoenum* is also found independently (and complete) in one other manuscript and in related forms in several others. Dionisotti has shown the importance of *Amoenum* and one of its sources, the unpublished *Aptet*—which in turn is an important element in the Amplonian glossaries which have Anglo-Saxon glosses. See (d) immediately below.

iv) Leiden 67F also contains two versions of the *Synonyma* (129r–41v), a version of the *Notae Iuris* (148v–49r), and more; see Steinová (2014) for a fuller account.

S: Dionisotti (1996: 225–7); Steinová (2014).

d) Glossaries containing Anglo-Saxon. The crucial text in this group is the so-called Leiden glossary written at St. Gallen but with contents originating from Canterbury (on which see 6.3b above). Important manuscripts containing Anglo-Saxon that made use of this glossary include the two glossaries in Erfurt, Wissenschaftliche Bibliothek, MS Amplonianus 2° 42 (Amplonianus II = Erfurt; *CGlL* 5.259–337; Amplonianus I [also found in Épinal 72 (2)] = Épinal–Erfurt; *CGlL* 5.337–401) and the Corpus Glossary (Cambridge, Corpus Christi College MS 144; a specimen in *CGlL* 5.401–9). The Épinal manuscript was written in the late seventh century, and all three glossaries share some early sources identified by Dionisotti.

S: Loewe (1876: 111–25); Lindsay (1921a, 1921b; reprinted in Lindsay 1996); Lapidge (1986, 2003); Dionisotti (1996: 238–41). Facsimiles in Bischoff et al. (1988); a sample critical edition of Épinal–Erfurt with commentary in Herren and Sauer (2016).

e) *Glossae Placidi* (*CGlL* 5.3–158; *GlL* 4.12–70). The fullest extant form of this (the origins of which are unknown, and the identification of the author impossible) exists only in manuscripts of the fifteenth century and later; groups of glosses labeled "Placidus" (in various abbreviations and forms) form part of the *Liber glossarum* (a, above) and there are similar identifiable groups in two manuscripts of the ninth or tenth centuries written in Spain. Goetz did not try to reconstruct a single version of this; Lindsay tried and failed.

R: *RE* Placidus (Dahlmann); *BNP* Placidus 2 (Schmidt); Kaster (1988) #123; Teuffel 3 §482.6; S–H 4.2 §1120.

S: Loewe (1876: 151–4); *CGlL* 5.v–xx; Goetz (1923: 59–71); Dionisotti (1996: 212).

f) *Expositio notarum*. This glossary in the early eleventh-century Italian manuscript Oxford, Bodleian Add. C. 144, foll. 114v–32r and as yet unpublished has been described by Dionisotti; it is one of the most important glossaries to be identified since Goetz's time. It is based, in part, on the entries in a collection of *Notae Tironianae* (see below, 10.4.5a) including some nonsense words given for practice in stenographic schools for which the gloss is *latinum non est* (e.g., fol. 116rb *Maximius: latinum non est* and *Nomenculator: latinum non est*); it has glosses also found in Amplonianus II (see d above), and in at least one case that I have noticed (the gloss on *Interregnum*) it has a better reading of one word and a shared error in another. Dionisotti believes that the *Expositio* itself was composed in North Africa in the fifth century; its sources clearly go back at least as far as the first century CE. Until it is published in detail, the early history of the Latin glossaries awaits full explanation.

S: Dionisotti (1996: 228–42); a detailed description of the manuscript in De Nonno (2013).

g) A small ninth-century glossary in Bern A 91(18), foll. 2–7 is printed with useful commentary by Gatti (2001); on its organization and sources see also Jakobi (2009). It should be noted that the previous leaf contains a fragment of a bilingual Greek–Latin glossary (unpublished) and the following leaf contains the opening of the glossary *abscida lucida* (see below, *Hermeneumata* ii).

h) Scappaticcio (2015: 462–3) prints the text of LDAB 5824, an alphabetical Latin glossary with some declensions embedded in it.

i) I have not included here glossaries based on specific authors other than one set of *glossae Vergilianae* mentioned in (c) above. There are also glossaries based on other authors, as well as glossaries drawn from earlier lexicographical sources, particularly Nonius Marcellus and Fulgentius. For a list of manuscripts of the latter, see Wessner (1899: 139–41). For Virgil, Nonius, and others, see 6.3, n.32 above.

5. Bilingual (Greek/Latin) Glossaries

In general:

T: *CGlL* 2 contains the major dictionaries and *idiomata; CGlL* 3 contains the *hermeneumata* and specialized medico–botanical glossaries. The only one of these texts in *GlL* is Ps.-Philoxenus (*GlL* 2.138–291). I have not included the scientific glossaries here. For an introduction to the category as a whole, which is large, diverse, and not altogether easy of access, see particularly Dionisotti (1988, concentrating on medieval evidence) and Dickey (2012: 1–15, with a valuable list of ancient bilingual texts). Papyrus glossaries are collected by Kramer (1983, 2001); Kramer (1996) includes a selection of papyri with bilingual texts (and an introduction to glossaries of this type).

S: Loewe (1876: 180–222); Goetz (1923: 12–59); Bischoff (1967: 246–75); Dionisotti (1982a, 1982b, 1985, 1988); Kramer (1983, 1996, 2001); Dickey (2012); Rochette (2014).

a) **Dictionaries**

i) Latin–Greek (Ps.-Philoxenus): *CGlL* 2.3–212 (transcript), *GlL* 2.138–291 (more speculative, less trustworthy). It survives independently in one ninth-century manuscript (Paris, Lat. 7651) and in combination with other texts in other manuscripts of that period; otherwise it is not known until the Renaissance.

S: Loewe (1876: 180–94); Goetz (1923: 23–4); Dionisotti (1988: 6–9).

ii) Greek–Latin (Ps.-Cyrillus): *CGlL* 2.215–483, in London, BL Harley 5792 fol. 1v–240v, c. 800; another copy in Laon 444, Martin of Laon's Greek collection; the remaining copies are from the fifteenth century or later. It seems likely that at least parts of the lexicon were available in Ireland in the seventh century; see Marshall (2010: 180) with further references.

S: Loewe (1876: 210–17); Goetz (1923: 34–47); Dionisotti (1988: 10–15) on Ps.-Cyrillus in the West and (1988: 45–54) on Martin and Laon 444, with a detailed table of contents.

iii) Greek–Latin fragment (*Folium Wallraffianum*): *CGlL* 2.561–3; better text in Kramer (1983) #4 (LDAB 6279). This is one leaf of a sixth-century papyrus codex from Constantinople; it or a close relative was used in the creation of the glossary *Abavus* or one of its ancestors. It is generally taken to be from the same codex as the *Fragmenta Helmstadiensia* (see *Idiomata* below); it is at least from the same scriptorium.

S: Kramer (1980a); Dionisotti (1988: 9–10).

iv) Greek–Latin glossary (*Glossae Laudunenses*): *CGlL* 2.553–9, in Laon 444, foll. 306r–9r. Its origins are uncertain, except that a Latin–Greek glossary was one of the sources.

S: Dionisotti (1988: 9, 53–4).

v) Hagen (*AH* c–ci) prints a fragment of a Greek–Latin glossary from Bern 83 (s. x), which has an odd theological bent, including explanations of Cybele, metempsychosis, and *hamartigenea*.

vi) The Latin–Greek glossary of P.Sorb. inv. 2069 (LDAB 5438) is printed by Scappaticcio (2015: 467–71). There is full discussion of this early text by Dickey and Ferri (2010) and Dickey (2010).

b) ***Idiomata***

For a description of *idiomata*, see 6.3c above. While originally at least some of these collections were probably intended to help Greek-speakers write correct Latin, their place in the Latin grammatical tradition is very old (possibly Remmius Palaemon): they were meant to clarify Latin grammar for Latin-speakers by comparing and contrasting Greek usage.

S: Dionisotti (1988: 15–17); Baratin (1989: 343–60, 1994: 154–5).

i) *Idiomata generum* (differences of gender between Greek and Latin nouns) exist in several forms:

a) *Idiomata codicis Harleiani* (*CGlL* 2.487–506) is the first of several texts of *idiomata generum* printed by Goetz; it appears in London, BL Harley 5792 immediately after the text of Ps.-Cyrillus, of which these *idiomata* were clearly a source. Like Ps.-Cyrillus, the collection of *idiomata* is also found in Laon 444 and many of the same fifteenth-century manuscripts. The text is arranged in Latin alphabetical lists: Latin masculine ~ Greek feminine, further subdivided by ending (*-us*; *-or*; *-ex*; *-ns*—with some inconsistencies and breaking down at the end); then Latin masculine ~ Greek neuter; Latin feminine ~ Greek masculine; Latin feminine ~ Greek neuter; Latin neuter ~ Greek masculine; Latin neuter ~ Greek feminine. The heading (in short phrases in Latin and Greek) is (in Latin) (487.1–7): *suntquedam/nominaque/latine quidem/masculino genere/efferuntur/grecae autem/feminino*. Similar headings appear before each of the other divisions.

b) *Glossae Servii* (*CGlL* 2.507–36) is a set of *idiomata generum* preserved in a twelfth-century manuscript (London, BL Harley 2773) with some portions also found in one ninth-century manuscript and others in various fifteenth- and sixteenth-century transcripts. The *Glossae Servii* have a bizarre organization: third-declension Latin monosyllables, marked with their genders and giving Greek equivalents (some of which are of the same gender as the Latin), but in alphabetical order; Latin masculine ~ Greek feminine, in alphabetical order with some grouping by declension, but scattered with headings often indicating the wrong declension; Latin masculine ~ Greek neuter similarly set out; and continuing in the same pattern as the Harleian *idiomata*. Aside from the peculiar headings, this collection also has the Greek transliterated (badly) throughout. The attribution to Servius (clearly false) is found in subscriptions in the manuscripts; see 12.40.8 below.

c) *Idiomata nominativa quae per genera efferuntur* (*CGlL* 2.537–48 = Charisius 450.1–63.36B = *GL* 4.573–84) is a text found in Naples IV A 8, the manuscript of Charisius; it is wrongly attributed to Charisius by Barwick. It is in the order Latin masculine ~ Greek feminine; Latin feminine ~ Greek masculine; Latin masculine ~ Greek neuter; Latin neuter ~ Greek masculine; Latin feminine ~ Greek neuter; Latin neuter ~ Greek masculine, with each section in A– alphabetical order. The opening part of the text is also found in Paris, Lat. 7530, foll. 47r–8v, where the list breaks off (from physical damage). The Paris excerpt is edited together with the Naples text by Barwick and Keil, but is printed separately after it by Goetz, *CGlL* 2.549.1–53.43.

S: Holtz (1975: 116); Dionisotti (1982b: 119).

d) There is a set of *idiomata* included in the grammar of the *Anonymus Bobiensis* (12.46.2), 32.1–35.33 De Nonno; it has lost some of the Greek.

e) *Glossae nominum* (*CGlL* 2.563–97) is an alphabetical glossary derived from a set of Latin–Greek *idiomata generum*, but with the Greek omitted. Its striking feature (and what shows its origin as *idiomata*) is that, within the AB– alphabetization, the words appear in a fixed order of endings: *-a*, *-us*, *-um*, *-o*, followed by the other third-declension endings. The earliest witness, Erfurt, Amplonianus 2° 42 of the ninth century, ends at *CGlL* 2.586.26, and the remainder is supplied by later witnesses. It is also equipped with some Anglo-Saxon glosses, as are the other two glossaries (Amplonianus I and II) that precede it in the manuscript. Text also in Loewe (1884: 2–63; only the portion contained in Amplon, 42).

S: Loewe (1876: 126–34); Goetz's introduction in Loewe (1884: iii–xviii); Lindsay (1921a: 80–3; on the Anglo-Saxon glosses); Dionisotti (1988: 18).

f) *Fragmenta Helmstadiensia* (*CGlL* 2.559–61; better text in Kramer 1983 #4 [LDAB 6279]) is a set of sixth-century scraps from a papyrus codex written in Constantinople; it is from the same scriptorium, and possibly the same codex, as the Folium Wallraffianum (5a, iii above). It is not, however, a dictionary but the remains of a set of Latin–Greek *glossae nominum*, covering nouns/adjectives in *–is* and *–tas*.

S: Kramer (1980b).

g) A very small remainder of a set of *idiomata generum* appears in the *Appendix Probi*; see below, *Idiomata casuum* f.

ii) *Idiomata casuum* are not normally found as independent texts, but are embedded in grammars:

a) Charisius 379.1–86.28B is the only part of Book 5 of Charisius as edited by Barwick that is in fact by Charisius; the preface (379.1–81.3; see 6.3c above), in Charisius' manner, offers two definitions of *idiomata*, both describing them as a set of contrasts between Latin and Greek usage. The list that follows (arranged by Latin cases), however, contains no Greek.

b) Diomedes *GL* 1.310.30–20.9, *De consensu verborum cum casibus* is partly based on Charisius (or his source) and partly independent; it too has no Greek. For a careful analysis, see Baratin (1989: 322–42).

c) Dositheus *GL* 7.424.17–6.11 = §62–7 Tolkiehn; again, related to Charisius or his source, and probably not an original part of Dositheus' grammar (and not printed by Bonnet 2005). This section of Dositheus has no Greek, although the following collection of idioms (not *idiomata*) is genuinely bilingual. See Tolkiehn (1913: 111–24), and 12.21 below.

d) An untitled and anonymous text (*GL* 4.566.1–72.10 under the title *De idiomatibus casuum*) preserved in Paris, Lat. 7530, foll. 41r–6r (incipit: *De idiomatibus quae pertinent ad genitivum casum*); it concludes with a fairly elaborate explicit, including *Feliciter Iuliano scolastico sardiano Servii grammatici maximae et antiquae Romae*, which is presumably linked to the ascription to Servius of the *idiomata generum* that follow this set and also appear (more fully) in Charisius; see above, *idiomata generum* c and see 12.40.9 below. Like the other set of *idiomata* in Paris, Lat. 7530, this version has the Greek. This set is fairly closely related to (but in much better condition than) the set in Dositheus; both are closely related to the source used by Bede in *De orthographia*.

S: Tolkiehn (1913: 111–24); Holtz (1975: 116); Dionisotti (1982b: 120), and 12.40.9 below.

e) A very small set is found in *Explanationes in Donatum* II 4.556.8–32; without Greek.

f) Part 2 of the so-called *Appendix Probi* (see 12.36.4 below) consists of the remains of a collection of three types of *idiomata*—*idiomata casuum*, what Barnett calls *idiomata accentuum*, and *idiomata generis*—from which the Greek has been eliminated.

S: Barnett (2006).

g) Augustine, *Ars breviata* 103, the very end of the text. The list is closely related to that in *Explanationes in Donatum* II (e above).

S: Bonnet (2013: xxiv–vi, 88–90).

c) *Hermeneumata*

Nine sets of the so-called *Hermeneumata Pseudo-Dositheana* (so named because one set is found in manuscripts of the grammar of Dositheus) survive; clearly intended at some point for instructional use (in their present form, they seem to be used to teach Latin-speakers Greek, but some parts were originally composed to teach Greek-speakers Latin), they all consist of one or more of four bilingual elements: a set of glossaries by subject (known as *capitula*); an alphabetical glossary; a set of conversations, generally describing a schoolboy's day and/or adult activities such as bathing or dining (*colloquia*); and some bilingual readings, ranging from Aesop to legal texts. To some extent, the similarities among the sets of *capitula* and *colloquia* suggest common origins, and clearly some parts are at least as old as the second century CE; on the other hand, the *hermeneumata* in their present form are the result of combination, borrowing, and reshaping of materials that circulated widely in antiquity as school exercises and are almost certainly the product of late antique schools. In modified form, these texts are now again available for classroom use: see Dickey (2016a).

S: Dionisotti (1982a); Dickey (2012: 1–54); and 6.3c above. My account of the individual texts is based on the fundamental work of Dickey and Dionisotti; full bibliography in Dickey (2012, 2015).

The texts are:

i. *H. Amploniana* (*Hygini H.*): apparently originally had all four elements, although the oldest manuscript contains only glossary and *capitula*.

T: *CGlL* 3.72–94 (glossary and *capitula*); *CGlL* 3.108–16 (*colloquium*); Dickey (2015: 19–37; *colloquium* with introduction, translation, and commentary). The *colloquium* is known as *colloquium Harleianum*.

S: Dionisotti (1985: 327–30, 1988: 27); Dickey (2012: 19, 2015: 7–11).

ii. *H. Montepessulana*: glossary, *capitula, colloquium* (and probably once also contained one reading selection). Material from *H. Montepessulana* is also embedded in a larger glossary (known as *Abscida lucida*) which is printed in two forms in *CGlL* 3.487–531 as *Glossae Bernenses* and *Glossae Vaticanae*. The main witness to the text, Montpellier 306, is an important collection of glossaries also including part of the *Appendix Probi*; see 12.36.4 below.

T: *CGlL* 3.283–343 (all three extant parts); Dickey (2015: 95–107; *colloquium* with introduction, translation, and commentary).

S: Dionisotti (1988: 27, 31); Dickey (2012: 19, 2015: 83–92).

iii. *H. Bruxellensia*: a very fragmentary (and necessarily reconstructed) text, which seems to have contained a glossary and *capitula*.

T: *CGlL* 3.393–421 with Dionisotti (1985: 305–13).

S: Dionisotti (1988: 27–8); Dickey (2012: 19).

iv. *H. Stephani*: a complicated collection, for the text of which editors necessarily rely on an edition (Stephanus 1573) printed from lost manuscripts. It contains two glossaries, a set of *capitula*, two *colloquia* (one also found in *H. Leidensia*), and a number of readings.

T: *CGlL* 3.347–90, 438–87 (and 3.313–18, possibly from the same collection); Dickey (2012: 197–204 and 225–33; *colloquia* with introduction, translation, and commentary).

S: Dionisotti (1985: 313–20, 1988: 28); Dickey (2012: 18–19, 187–94, 219–22).

v. *H. Leidensia*: glossary, *capitula, colloquium*, readings.

T: *CGlL* 3.3–72; Flammini (2004); Dickey (2012: 197–204; *colloquium* with introduction, translation, and commentary).

vi. *H. Monacensia*: glossary, *capitula*, two *colloquia*.

T: *CGlL* 3.119–220; Dickey (2012: 101–30; *colloquia* [edited with *Einsiedlensia*] with introduction, translation, and commentary).

S: Dickey (2012: 59–97).

vii. *H. Einsiedlensia: capitula*, two *colloquia*.

T: *CGlL* 3.223–79; Dickey (2012: 101–30; *colloquia* [edited with *Monacensia*] with introduction, translation, and commentary).

S: Dickey (2012: 59–97).

viii. *H. Vaticana: capitula* only.

T: *CGlL* 3.421–38; Brugnoli and Buonocore (2002, with useful bibliography and apparatus of parallel passages).

S: Dickey (2012: 19).

ix. *H. Celtis: capitula, colloquium* (glossary lost). Discovered by Dionisotti and partially published in Dionisotti (1982a); a full text is being prepared by R. Ferri.

T: Dionisotti (1982a: 97–105; *colloquium* with introduction and commentary); Dickey (2015: 165–91; *colloquium* with translation and commentary).

S: Dionisotti (1982a, 1988); Ferri (2011b); Dickey (2015: 141–61).

x. Papyri: there are fragmentary papyri that are clearly related to the *hermeneumata*.

T: Dickey (2015: 269–99; with translation and commentary).

d) Bilingual Grammars

Other than the translation of (most of) Dositheus into Greek (see 12.21 below), there are a few attempts in the early Middle Ages to produce a Greek or bilingual grammar for Latin-speakers, including the parsing grammar *TI ECTIN DOCTUS* (see 13.51 below) and the start of a Greek translation of Donatus now in Vienna; see Ciccolella (2008: 90–1). In general, see Dionisotti (1988: 21–6) on medieval Greek grammars in the West and Ciccolella (2008) on renaissance ones.

6. *Notae*

Instruction about abbreviations was not a regular part of the grammarian's job (*notae* were the concern of the *notarius*), but they are in fact a form of writing, and enough lists of abbreviations survive to be included here as yet another form of glossary. Many lists of them are included in *GL* (listed below, and edited by

Mommsen) as they were previously included in the collections of Lindenbrog and Putschius; so too the abbreviations for Roman *praenomina* are frequently discussed in grammarians' accounts of the alphabet or the noun. It should be noted, however, that I am concerned here with glossaries, lists of abbreviations that are ancient in origin, and not with the abbreviations themselves. A brief introduction to the subject of Roman abbreviations may be found in Frenz (2010: 17–52); he also supplies an excellent bibliography of discussions of, and lists of, the abbreviations themselves. The three most useful and important works are Capelli (1961), Lindsay (1963), and Traube (1907).

Isidore (*Etym.* 1.21–6) includes six varieties of *notae* in his account of *grammatica*, placing them between punctuation and orthography. The last three varieties—military abbreviations (*notae militares*, 1.24), codes (*notae litterarum*, 1.25), and sign-language (*notae digitorum*, 1.26)—have no equivalent in manuscript *laterculi*, although the section on codes is almost certainly taken from Suetonius, and we know that Valerius Probus wrote a *commentarius de occulta littèrarum significatione in epistularum C. Caesaris scriptura* (cf. Gellius, *NA* 17.9.5). Each of the first three, however, is attested in independent lists.

a) *Notae sententiarum* (Isid. *Etym.* 1.21)

Much more important than Isidore's list is the *Anecdoton Parisinum* that has already been referred to several times. It is found in Paris, Lat. 7530 foll. 28r–9r, and it presumably comes (at some remove) from Suetonius. The modern designation for these *notae* is "critical signs": marks put in the margins of texts indicating a scholar's opinion about the line or passage in question. These range from indications of dubious authenticity to omissions, repetitions, misplaced lines, changes of speaker, or obscurity. Isidore's list of twenty-six signs includes some specifically for biblical criticism, but the original list clearly goes back to Alexandria, with Roman modifications. A third collection, drawn from both earlier collections (and perhaps other sources) is included in the *Liber glossarum*; discussion and edition in Steinová (2016).

T: *GL* 7.533–6.

R: *RE* Kritische Zeichen (Gudeman); *RLAC* Kritische Zeichen (Stein).

S: Fontaine (1959: 75–80); Holtz (1975: 114); Jocelyn (1984–85); Steinová (2016) with copious bibliography. See also 2.2 and 4.3 above.

b) *Notae vulgares* (Isid. *Etym.* 1.22)

Better known as *notae Tironianae*, these shorthand abbreviations were used by *notarii*, and a large collection of them—some 18,000—survives; the most important collection is the codex Cassellanus, used by Schmitz (1893) as the basis of his edition. Whether the history given by Isidore (the first 1,100 invented by Ennius, then extended by Tiro, Vipsanius Philargius and Aquila the freedman of Maecenas, and finally extended to 5,000 by Seneca) is remotely accurate, it is clear that the very large extant collection is an amalgam of more than one set. The *notae* were used in the Carolingian period, and numerous manuscripts have scholia or other notes written in the *notae* (for a list, see D. Ganz 1990: 49–50), most of which have not yet been transcribed (for an example, see Hellmann 2000). As noted before (see 10.4.4f above), a list of *notae Tironianae*, sometimes better than what is preserved in Carolingian manuscripts, lies behind parts of the *Expositio notarum*.

T: Schmitz (1893).

C: P. Ganz (1990).

S: Chatelain (1900); Traube (1920: 254–73); Mentz (1931, 1939, 1941); D. Ganz (1990); Dionisotti (1996: 228–36); Hellman (2000).

c) *Notae iuris* (**Isid.** *Etym.* **1.23**)

Isidore's brief chapter is headed *De notis iuridicis*, and he points out the use of abbreviations such as *SC* for *senatus consultum* in legal texts—and also that *novicii imperatores* had banned their use because of confusion. A century before Isidore, Justinian had indeed, repeatedly and emphatically, forbidden the use of abbreviations in all legal texts and set penalties for anyone selling or using a law book with abbreviations (see *D. Const. Omnem* 8; *C.* 1.17.1.13 [to Tribonian] and 1.17.2.22 [*Ad senatum et omnes populos*]). That makes it clear that the origin of the many collections that include legal abbreviations is earlier than 530, and in fact the oldest of them, the attribution of which to Valerius Probus in the manuscripts is almost certainly correct, gives evidence of a state of Roman law prior to the codification of the edict by Iulianus in the reign of Hadrian. Keil entrusted them to Mommsen to edit; to the best of my knowledge, with the exception of Probus' list (see below), they have not been re-edited since 1860, although they clearly should be, as Mommsen's edition is not without flaws, and new manuscripts have in some cases been discovered since. Codoñer (2015) has recently proposed a possible set of relationships among the various lists.

Like the *Expositio notarum* (10.4.4f above), the collections of abbreviations lie on the border between the study of Latin language and the study of particular kinds of Latin texts. But the explanation of *litterae singulares*, particularly the abbreviations for *praenomina* with which Probus' list begins, is a regular feature of grammatical texts: Lehmann (1929: 14–16), in correcting Mommsen's statement that only in Naples, Lat. 2 (of which he prints the text in a footnote) is there a comparable list of *praenomina*, cites (in chronological order) Scaurus, Velius Longus, Marius Victorinus, Donatus (with additional examples in some manuscripts), Diomedes, *Explanationes in Donatum* II, Consentius, Pompeius, and Priscian, as well as Bede. Neither Mommsen nor Lehmann, so far as I can see, mentions the short tract *De praenominibus*, including some discussion of abbreviations, found at the end of Iulius Paris'

Epitome of Valerius Maximus (587.16–91.13 Kempf) which has a subscription attributing it (or all of Paris?) to C. Titius Probus.

T: Mommsen in *GL* 4.265–352; a list of *notae iuris* in manuscripts in Lindsay 1963: 413–43. On Probus see (i) below.

S: Lehmann (1929); Weiss (1933); Codoñer (2015).

The lists edited by Mommsen for Keil are the following:

i. *M. Valerii Probi de litteris singularibus fragmentum*. This is clearly an extract from a larger text, as it begins *Est etiam . . .* ; Mommsen thought it might be a work of Probus comparable to that on codes mentioned by Gellius. All the abbreviations in this text are by initial letter only; they are divided into four groups: the first, described as *publicae*, include the *praenomina* and a few very familiar abbreviations such as SPQR (and the author points out that there are similar ones peculiar to various groups and occasions, such as the names of *curiae* and tribes, the *fasti*, and the like); the second is headed *Litterae singulares in iure civili de legibus et plebiscitis*; the third *In legis actionibus haec*; the fourth *In edictis perpetuis haec*. Mommsen believed that the original list (which has been modified) was created in the mid-first century. The author makes a distinction between what he is listing, *litterae singulares*, and *notae*, claiming that the former are older than the latter. The text is clearly missing its end, and Mommsen prints at the end of the text of *de litteris singularibus* those entries from the missing portion of the text that can be supplied from the Einsiedeln collection (see below, vii), but in the wrong order; Girard corrects that, and also makes use of another manuscript.

T: *GL* 4.271–6; better in Girard (1937: 212–19).

S: Girard (1907, 1910); Lehmann (1929: 4–6).

ii. *Notae Lugdunenses*. This list is preserved in Leiden, BPL 67F, a collection of glossaries (see 10.4.4c above). Unlike (i), this text is in alphabetical order; it also includes very few, if any, *litterae singulares*. It does include legal terminology, but it also includes the abbreviations for many common words that might turn up in documents or elsewhere (e.g., *deinde, sunt*, and various forms of the relative pronoun) and even for word endings such as *–bus* as well as the familiar tachygraphic abbreviations for *per* and *pro*. It also has mistakes: *LAS* is expanded *lex alia sentencia* instead of *Lex Aelia Sentia*. Mommsen viewed it as a product of the fifth or sixth century, but in fact (see Lehmann 1929: 6–7) it is an amalgam of two lists of uncertain provenance.

T: *GL* 4.277–81, with the MS title (in Leiden, BPL 67F, foll. 148r–49r) *incipiunt glose iure*.

iii. *Notae ex Cod. Reginae* (Vatican, Reg. 1128 and 1462). Composed, according to Mommsen, at roughly the same time as (ii), and similar in content. It lacks any tachygraphic elements and has more imperial nomenclature, including *Divi Fratres* and *nobilissimi Caesaris.*

T: *GL* 4.282–4. Mommsen (1907: 214–16) subsequently found and published a fuller version of the first part of this list (A–F).

iv. *Magnonis laterculus alter* and v. *Notae Lindenbrogianae*. These two lists (and the *Notae Vaticanae*, vi below) are closely related. The first collection was dedicated to Charlemagne by Magno, the Archbishop of Sens (801–18). It consists of two lists that have been melded: under each letter, there are first entries taken from the *Notae Vaticanae* and then entries from another source, which Mommsen designated here as *alter* in the title. The *Notae Lindenbrogianae* were printed by Lindenbrog in 1599 from a manuscript written in Scaliger's hand, from which Mommsen printed the text. The Magno and Lindenbrog collections clearly derive from the same source and overlap to a very large extent, which is why Mommsen edited them in parallel columns. The shared ancestor can have been no older than the fifth century and has many entries that derive from imperial rescripts: that is why a great many possible recipients of rescripts appear in the list in the dative case, e.g., *consulari* while the names of provinces appear in the genitive, e.g., *Africae*. The Magno collection retained more antiquarian entries, e.g., *Prisci Latini, flamen Dialis*, which the Lindenbrog collection omitted; that collection, conversely, has added more Christian language, e.g., *spiritus sanctus*. Lehmann (1929: 6–13) has a detailed discussion of the relationships among these and the next two collections.

T: *GL* 4.288–300.

vi. *Notae Vaticanae*. A single manuscript (Vatican, Reg. 1128) contains a set of legal texts followed by three collections of *notae*. The third Mommsen prints by *praeteritio*, putting it in a long footnote: it is a late and not very useful text. The second is a more corrupt version of (iii) above. The first, which Mommsen does print, is one of the most widely circulated texts of its kind. Mommsen has little use for it: *Ipsae autem notae pessimae sunt et magis ut ab iis caveamus adhibendae, quam ut iis utamur* (303); he draws attention to such marvels as DM (for *dis manibus*) explained as *domus mortui*. He also points out that while most of the other texts were actually derived from, and used for, legal writing, the *Notae Vaticanae* have antiquarian elements and some of the entries derive from Cicero's speeches, e.g., *Lucius Morena* (i.e., *Murena*).

T: *GL* 4.304–14.

vii. *Notae Papianae et Einsidlenses*. So named by Mommsen because the text was included by Papias in his glossary s.v. *notatio*; but his source was

Paris, Lat. 7530 (foll. 148v–154v). Another overlapping list, missing its opening, is found in Einsiedeln MS 326 s. ix/x foll. 1r–10v under the title *Notae Iulii Caesaris*; at the end of the list (10r–10v) are two appendices, one apparently giving equivalents in paces for the letters of the alphabet (A = 50 *passus*; B = 70 . . . Z = *mille*), the other equivalents in miles (maybe). The core of the list, which is drawn from the Vatican list (vi), is supplemented in the Paris manuscript by entries which Mommsen describes as *pleraque pessima . . . et aetatis omnino barbarae* (315); in the Einsiedeln manuscript it is supplemented by glosses drawn from Probus' list (i). Entries shared with the Vatican list are marked by Mommsen with an asterisk; entries taken from Probus are printed in capitals.

T: *GL* 4.316–30.

viii. *Petri Diaconi Notae Litterarum More Vetusto*. Peter the Deacon, a monk and historian at Monte Cassino, dedicated a list of *notae* with an elaborate preface to the Emperor Conrad III (1138–52). Mommsen detected three sources: the Papias list, the Einsiedeln list, and Peter's own additions. Of the last category, Mommsen (332) singles out the wonderful *Fodi sub via XX passus, invenies monumentum laudabile*; there is also the curious sequence *Sine testiculis; Sine viribus; Sine genitalibus; Sine oculis; Sine manibus; Sine pedibus.*[1] The fifteenth-century physician Giovanni Marcanova, whose copy of this text is one of two manuscripts, and whose changes Mommsen described as worse than Peter's, added to these definitions *vel sine testibus, vel sine virtute*, and similar phrases. Mommsen designates with one asterisk entries drawn from the Papias list, with two asterisks those drawn from Einsiedeln.

T: *GL* 4.333–46.

ix. There is another, alphabetic list ascribed to Probus, but it is the creation of Marcanova and Mommsen discusses it (*GL* 4.347–52) but does not print it.

x. Lehmann adds to this collection (aside from later medieval lists) a short collection written by Hartmann Schedel in 1463 which is clearly copied from a list excerpted from Probus (i).

T: Lehmann (1929: 28–9).

1. On the character of Peter, for whom "mentally unbalanced" is one of the kinder descriptions, see for instance Rodgers (1972: xxiii–viii). My quotation is from p. xxiii.

11

Commentaries

EVEN MORE THAN IN THE CASE OF GRAMMARS, IT IS HARD TO find the boundary between ancient and medieval; even more than with grammars, most of what we have of ancient exegesis is filtered through medieval commentators. The scholia to Latin poets (and Cicero) were written into margins in the ninth century and later; and yet in many cases it is perfectly clear that they draw—in some fashion, at some remove—on ancient scholarship. My limits, therefore, are not consistent or absolute: I have tried to include medieval commentaries that seem to be based on ancient sources, but I have not included the commentaries that have no such obvious connection. That means, of course, that much material that seems to me medieval rather than ancient is not included here: twelfth-century commentaries come from a different world from that of someone like Servius or Porphyrio, and it is a world I do not know, although some indications about later commentaries are given below.

There has been much attention given to classical commentaries of late, and several volumes of essays deal, at least in part, with ancient commentaries. Among them are Most (1999); Goulet-Cazé (2000); Gibson and Kraus (2002); Geerlings and Schulze (2002–4); Kraus and Stray (2015). As a general introduction, the long article in *RLAC* s.v. Kommentar (Fladener and Börner-Klein) is also useful.

1. TERENCE

Terence was popular in antiquity and was a standard school text from an early period. Donatus' biography (drawn from Suetonius) provides evidence of discussions of Terence's life and literary merits going back to the second century BCE and including treatments in verse by Porcius Licinus, Volcacius Sedigitus, Cicero, and Julius Caesar; there are detailed didascalic notices composed by the grammarian Sulpicius Apollinaris in the second century CE. As a consequence, there was a great deal written about Terence; but perhaps because of his popularity and ubiquity, all the surviving commentaries are in one way or another textually problematic.

1. Donatus

The great and influential fourth-century grammarian Aelius Donatus wrote, in addition to his grammars (see 12.20 below), a commentary on Terence as well as one on Virgil (on which see 7.3a above and 11.3 below). That the commentary on Terence survives better than the commentary on Virgil says little: what we possess is a compilation, probably made in the late eighth century, of marginalia on Terence from at least two (probably late antique) manuscripts that consisted of excerpts from the original commentary of Donatus, but which certainly did not contain the whole commentary and equally certainly did include some notes from other sources; in that respect, the relationship between the extant commentary and the original is similar to that between the longer Servius' and Donatus' commentary on Virgil. The extant version of Donatus includes a full introduction, including Suetonius' life of Terence and an excerpt from Evanthius (see below), followed by commentary on *Andria, Eunuchus, Adelphoe, Hecyra*, and *Phormio*; the process of excerpting and recombination is demonstrated not only by the large number of doublets (two notes on the same passage that say the same thing in slightly different words) but by the fact that the compiler gave up at *Phormio* 350, and from 350–440 provides two separate sets of notes. For the remainder of that play the notes are fairly brief and may come from only a single source, and there is no commentary at all on *Heautontimoroumenos*. The *Scholia Bembina* (see below) also contain a set of excerpts from Donatus that were almost certainly drawn from a marginal abridgment rather than the full text.

Despite its poor condition (the excerpting and recombination in the early Middle Ages, and the fact that there is no complete manuscript earlier than the Renaissance and only two partial ones before that), the commentary is extremely valuable, particularly for its notes on Terence's Greek models, on characterization, and on style and rhetoric; Barsby (2000) gives a good introduction using illustrations from the commentary on the *Eunuchus*.

T: Wessner (1902–8, vols. 1–2); Karsten (1912–13) is unreliable. Cioffi (2017) is a new edition of the commentary on the *Andria*; one hopes that more will follow. A full text and French translation, with lexicon and thesaurus, at http://hyperdonat.huma-num.fr/.

I: Mountford and Schultz (1930) indexes names and subjects only; it is not always reliable.

R: *T&T* (Reeve).

B: Wessner (1902: 176–82, 1908: 136–43, 1921: 161–76); Lammert (1936: 137–40 on Terence commentaries in general); Marti (1961: 147–53).

S: Zetzel (1975); Jakobi (1996); Barsby (2000); Magallón Garcia (2002); Maltby (2007); Cioffi (2012; on transmission: gives references to many earlier studies); Victor (2013: 353–8). For general bibliography on Donatus, see 12.20 below.

2. Eugraphius

The commentary of Eugraphius (who is otherwise unknown) is a product of late antiquity: it is later than Donatus, but beyond that it is difficult to date or locate. It consists largely of rhetorical analysis of individual scenes and of paraphrase, supplemented by a few grammatical notes. Thus, for instance, the explanation of the second scene of *Eunuchus* (*Eun.* 81; 96.4W) begins with *in hac scena primo controversia est, dein deliberativa. controversia talis est: . . . haec controversia venialem statum continet: confitetur enim se fecisse iniuriam, verum dicit necessitate . . .* The influence of the rhetorical schools is apparent.

Two versions of the text exist (particularly for *Andria*), known as α and β; Wessner showed that β is the earlier form, while α is a Carolingian compilation which both abridges β and supplements it. The supplements are what make the β text (mildly) interesting, as it draws on a list of rhetorical figures (known as *Anonymus Ecksteinii*; cf. Eckstein 1852) related to that used by Cassiodorus in his commentary on the Psalms.[1] It also draws on the *Commentum Brunsianum* (see Jakobi 2007), thus dating it to no earlier than the ninth century.

T: Wessner (1902–8, vol. 3.1).
B: Wessner (1903: 185–7).
R: *RE* (Wessner); *BNP* (Gatti); *PLRE* II; Teuffel 3 §482.3; S–H 4.2 §1117.
S: Wessner (1907).

3. *Scholia Bembina*

The oldest and best manuscript of Terence, the so-called Bembine Terence (Vatican, Lat. 3226) was written (probably) in the fifth century and was equipped with marginal notes in two hands perhaps a century later. These notes are of variable quality and come from multiple sources. The note on *Eun.* 366 cites Donatus, but identifies him as *commentator Vergilii*, which suggests that the authorship of the set of notes on *Phorm.* 1–59 (which come from a version of Donatus) may have been unknown to the scholiast. Other sources cannot be identified, although they may include the commentary of Aemilius Asper.

T: Mountford (1934); Prete (1970) is a photographic facsimile of the manuscript.
S: Zetzel (1975).

4. Evanthius

The short text *De fabula* is included by Donatus as part of his introduction. Evanthius died in Constantinople in 358 according to Jerome, who calls him *eruditissimus grammaticorum*; but nothing else is known of his writings, and

1. It was argued by Schindel (2002a: 104–11) that Cassiodorus drew on the *Anonymus Ecksteinii* himself, but the relationship among these various texts, including Eugraphius and Cassiodorus, has been shown to be much more complex: see Grondeux (2013).

whether the focus on Terence was his or is the result of editing by Donatus is unclear. Most of what he writes is very traditional (and related to comparable Greek tracts connected to the Aristophanes scholia), but it seems likely that he made use of Varro to some extent. *De fabula* is followed by a text titled *De comoedia*, which does not seem to be part of Evanthius' work and is not printed by Cupaiuolo.

T: Wessner (1902–8: 1.13–22); Cupaiuolo (1992; with commentary and Italian translation).

B: Wessner (1903: 182–5).

R: *RE* Euanthius 2 (Wessner); *PLRE* I Euanthius 2; Teuffel 3 §405.4; *HLL* 5 §526.2.

S: Welsh (2011b).

5. Medieval Commentaries

There are a great many manuscripts of Terence, and many of them contain scholia or glosses. Two commentaries seem to be relatively early (that is to say, Carolingian): the *Commentum Brunsianum* is a set of marginal scholia published originally by Bruns (1811) from a manuscript in Halle (now Halle, Marienkirche 65); and the *Commentum Monacense* (Munich, Clm 14420), a continuous commentary not attached to a text of Terence but clearly derived from marginal scholia. The *Commentum Brunsianum*, which is now known from some thirty-seven manuscripts, is probably the most interesting of the medieval commentaries: Jakobi (2007) has shown that it made use of ninth-century Horatian commentaries and the *Ars poetica* itself, as well as Priscian and Orosius. More interesting than what its author has read is what he has not: Donatus' commentary, in any of its forms other than a few notes that were probably found in the margins of other manuscripts. On the other hand, it appears that the author made use of an earlier form of version α of Eugraphius, while the extant form of that text in turn made use of the *Commentum Brunsianum*. It is the *Commentum Brunsianum* that we have to thank for the idea that Calliopius (whose name is found in a subscription to a great many manuscripts of Terence) was the *recitator* of the plays.

The *Commentum Brunsianum* contains material drawn from late antique sources, but there is no sign at all that the commentator had access to any text which we do not have: it is a Carolingian commentary. So too is the *Commentum Monacense*, although it is later than, and makes use of, the *Commentum Brunsianum*. Until very recently, the only printed text of the *Commentum Monacense* was in Schlee (1893), a very unreliable edition in which it was combined with the evidence of four other manuscripts and redistributed into three layers of exegesis, the oldest showing borrowings or explicit citations from works of ancient scholarship (most frequently Servius, Priscian, and the earlier commentaries on Terence); the second and largest layer consists of the introductions to the plays and those marginal scholia which Schlee thought probably derived from ancient material. As he says (Schlee 1893: 43), these notes are of three types: *aut verba explicant, aut sententias circumeunt, aut ad res pertinent*; he also rightly observes that the last of these three, which one might hope would say something about the ancient world, is in fact rare and often worthless. The third layer, of which he prints only a part, is from the eleventh century and is largely taken from Donatus.

Both the *Commentum Brunsianum* and the *Commentum Monacense* are elementary commentaries, clearly designed for (monastic) school use: of Schlee's five manuscripts, only two have anything of interest beyond glosses, and the Munich manuscript itself is not one of those. In general, there is an extensive tradition of commentary on Terence in the Middle Ages, with at least four distinct commentaries in the twelfth century and more later; those lie well beyond the purview of this book, but I include here works that describe them. For a survey (emphasizing post-ninth-century texts), see Riou (1997). For manuscripts containing commentary and glosses, see also Munk Olsen (2009: 107–11).

T: Bruns (1811; *C. Brunsianum*); Schlee (1893; amalgam of five manuscripts, including *C. Monacense*); Schorsch (2011; *C. Monacense* on *An. Heaut. Phorm*; another volume is expected); San Juan Manso (2015; *C. Monacense*, with copious parallels and testimonia).

B: Wessner (1903: 188–91); Friis-Jensen et al. (1997: 245–7).

S: Rand (1909); Riou (1973, 1997); Villa (1984, 2007); Jakobi (2007); Victor (2013: 360–1); San Juan Manso (2013a, 2013b).

6. Glossaries

Both Terentian glossaries and glossaries containing entries drawn from Terence manuscripts and scholia exist. See Marti (1961: 155–6) for a list of those in the major collections.

2. CICERO

Cicero was a school author from a very early stage, possibly in his own lifetime, and the commentary tradition reaches back nearly as far—perhaps originating with his own freedman Tiro. Cicero was studied, moreover, in many contexts at various periods: for grammar, for rhetoric, and for philosophy. See 7.3b above.

ORATIONS

The basic collection of commentaries on the orations is Stangl (1912). Unfortunately, Stangl completed volume 2 only; he never published volume 1, which would have contained the introduction. As a result, information about some of these texts must be pieced together from other sources (not least, Stangl's own earlier articles).

1. Asconius

Much the oldest extant Roman commentary, written in the first century CE and strictly historical in its approach; what survives (in humanistic manuscripts only) contains commentary on *In Pisonem, Pro Scauro, Pro Milone, Pro Cornelio* I and II, and *In toga candida*. They are not now in chronological order, but the original commentary almost certainly was. See 4.2, 7.2, 7.3b above.

T: Clark (1907); Stangl (1912: 11–72); Giarratano (1920); Wessner (1968; *Pro Milone* only); Lewis (2006; with English translation and commentary; a new edition by John Ramsey is in progress).

B: Wessner (1921: 177–80) on Cicero commentaries in general.

R: *RE* Asconius 3 (Wissowa); *BNP* (Kugelmeier); *PIR*[2] A1206; Teuffel 2 §295.1–2; S–H 2 §476; *T&T* (Reeve).

S: B. Marshall (1985).

2. *Scholia Bobiensia*

The continuous commentary known as the Bobbio scholia is part of the lower text of the palimpsest discovered by Angelo Mai in two parts, in Milan (Ambros. E 147 sup.) and the Vatican (Lat. 5750). There is a photographic reproduction of the Vatican portion in Ehrle (1906). The commentary is sometimes ascribed to one Vulcatius, whose commentary on Cicero's orations Jerome says he used in school; that is possible, but quite uncertain. Commentary on parts of twelve speeches survives: *Pro Sulla, In Clodium et Curionem, De rege Alexandrino, Pro Flacco, Cum senatui gratias egit, Cum populo gratias egit, Pro Milone, Pro Sestio, In Vatinium, Pro Plancio, De aere alieno Milonis, Pro Archia*, of which three (*In Clodium et Curionem, De rege Alexandrino, De aere alieno Milonis*) are not otherwise preserved. The extant form of the Bobbio Scholia is probably a fourth-century revision of a second-century commentary on all the speeches in chronological order, emphasizing matters of rhetoric and history. The rhetorical approach is consistent with second-century archaism, while the historical sources (which are very good) are clearly earlier. What survives is a non-chronological selection; another commentary drawn from the same source in the set of scholia on *Verrines* 2.1.45–62 which Stangl prints as *Scholiasta Gronovianus* A (344.9–8.8S) and Hildebrandt includes in his edition of the Bobbio Scholia (Hildebrandt 1907: 1–6, cf. Hildebrandt 1894: 4–8).

Stangl's text is far better than Hildebrandt's; but since Stangl never wrote his prolegomena, Hildebrandt (1894) is the only real introduction. The two men originally planned to edited the text jointly, but had a bitter falling out; the dispute between them in print is neither illuminating nor edifying, but those interested should consult the articles listed here.

T: Hildebrandt (1907); Stangl (1912: 77–179); Wessner (1968; *Pro Milone* only).

B: Wessner (1903: 192–3).

R: *HLL* 5 §526.1.

S: Hildebrandt (1894, 1908); Stangl (1907, 1908a, 1908b).

3. Pseudo-Asconius

Transmitted together with the text of Asconius and long thought to be by him, the late antique commentary on the *Verrines* (breaking off at *Verr.* 2.2.35) was severed from the genuine work of Asconius by Madvig (1828: 57–142), with detailed analysis of the differences. Madvig rightly considered Ps.-Asconius to be post-Servian; Gessner's more specific suggestion that Ps.-Asconius was a pupil of Servius is unnecessary. The commentary is largely exegetical and grammatical.

T: Stangl (1912: 185–264).
R: Teuffel 2 §295.3.
S: Gessner (1888); Stangl (1909).

4. *Scholia Cluniacensia et Recentiora Ambrosiana ac Vaticana*

Under this heading, Stangl (1912), following Orelli and Baiter (1833), grouped three quite different sets of notes; they have in common that they are all marginal scholia.

a) *Scholia Bobiensia recentiora*: These marginal notes are found in a palimpsest copy of *Pro Scauro* (Milan, Ambros. R. 57 sup.) written in the fifth century. The material is historical (possibly deriving at some remove from Asconius) and exegetical.

T: Stangl (1912: 274–6).

b) *Scholia Vaticana*: A set of five marginal notes on the *Verrines* (on 2.3.47, 2.4.7–8, and 2.4.17) that Mai printed from the fifth-century palimpsest of the *Verrines*, Vatican, Reg. 2077. They contain brief and uninteresting exegesis.

T: Stangl (1912: 276).

c) *Scholia Cluniacensia et Ambrosiana*: See 7.3b above.

T: Stangl (1912: 269–73).
R: *T&T* 61–2 (Rouse and Reeve).
S: Peterson (1901: lv–lxii); Clark (1918: 235–40, 310–23).

5. *Scholia Gronoviana*

On the composition of this collection, see 7.3b above.

T: Stangl (1912: 281–351).
S: Stangl (1884); Hildebrandt (1894: 4–7); Goetz (1891).

RHETORICAL AND PHILOSOPHICAL WORKS

6. *De inventione*

Two late antique commentaries on Cicero's early rhetorical treatise survive (together with a small fragment; see below); the earlier, by Marius Victorinus in the mid-fourth century, is complete; the later one (late fifth century?) by Grillius, breaks off in the middle of a note on *Inv.* 1.22. Both commentaries are themselves intended as instructional texts in rhetoric, using Cicero as the base for more elaborate exposition; in Victorinus' case, it is philosophical as well as rhetorical. Both also begin by offering a rhetorical analysis of Cicero's preface before proceeding to explain the contents of the treatise itself.

a) Marius Victorinus: Professor of Rhetoric in Rome, mid-fourth century, author of a grammar and many other works. For general bibliography, see 12.26 below.

T: *RLM* 155–304; Ippolito (2006); Riesenweber (2013). Halm's edition is out of date, and Ippolito's, although a great improvement, is apparently marred by errors of collation and proofreading; see Riesenweber (2009). Excerpts translated in Copeland and Sluiter (2009: 107–24).

S: Riesenweber (2015); Hadot (1971: 73–101).

b) Grillius: Possibly to be identified with someone who wrote a work *ad Vergilium de accentibus* cited by Priscian (*GL* 2.35.24); if so, then probably working in the fifth century.

T: Martin (1927: 1–94); Jakobi (2002). Excerpts only in *RLM* 596–606.

R: *RE* (Münscher); *BNP* (Gatti); *PLRE* I; Kaster (1988) #225; Teuffel 3 §445.7; S–H 4.2 §1122.

S: Jakobi (2005).

c) *Incerti auctoris tractatus de attributis personae et negotio*: This short and late work, transmitted together with Marius Victorinus' commentary, is itself a commentary on *Inv.* 1.34–43.

T: *RLM* 305–10; Riesenweber (2013: 213–20).

S: Riesenweber (2015: 1.454–6).

d) Iulius Victor, *Ars rhetorica*: As Orelli notes, this is a textbook of rhetoric, not a commentary on Cicero, although it is included among them by Orelli and Baiter.

T: Orelli and Baiter (1833: 1.195–267); *RLM* 371–448.

7. *Topica*

a) Marius Victorinus wrote a huge, never completed, and lost commentary on part of Cicero's *Topica*; for reconstruction, see Hadot (1971: 115–40). What does survive is the *Liber de definitionibus*, a treatise on the definition of definition, excerpted (probably by Victorinus himself) from his commentary; it corresponds to *Topica* 26–37.

T: Stangl (1888: 17–48); Pronay (1997; Stangl's text, lightly corrected, with German translation and commentary).

S: Hadot (1971: 163–78). For further bibliography see 12.26 below.

b) The extant commentary of Boethius is extensive but incomplete: it breaks off in Book 6 of the commentary (at *Topica* 76), and a seventh book is lost. Boethius' treatise *De topicis differentiis* is a companion to it.

T: *PL* 64: 1039–174; Orelli and Baiter (1833: 1.269–388); Stump (1988; English translation). Di Maria is apparently preparing a new edition; see Di Maria (2001).

R: *RE* Boethius 3 (Hartmann); *BNP* (Gruber); *PLRE* II Boethius 5; Teuffel 3 §478; S–H 4.2 §1080; Manitius (1911) §1.

S: Reinhardt (2003: 29–35). I offer no general bibliography on Boethius.

c) The short text entitled *De diis et praesensionibus* was presented by Orelli and Baiter (1833: 1.389–95) as a fragment from Book 7 of Boethius' commentary (and apparently accepted as genuine by Reinhardt 2003: 77 n.5), but Stangl (1883) argued that it is a medieval text, possibly as late as the twelfth century. Di Maria (1989) is agnostic.

8. ***Somnium Scipionis***

a) Macrobius, *Commentarii in Somnium Scipionis*: More an introduction to Neoplatonic philosophy (at some length) attached to the concluding portion of Cicero's *De re publica* than a real commentary, Macrobius' work was extremely popular in the Middle Ages and was responsible for the preservation of the *Somnium*.

T: Willis (1970b); Stahl (1952; English translation); Scarpa (1981; text, Italian translation, and commentary); Regali (1983–90; text, Italian translation, and commentary); Armisen-Marchetti (2001–3; text and French translation); Navarro Antolín (2006; Spanish translation); Pégolo and Cardigni (2006; Spanish translation of *Somnium* with excerpts from Macrobius and Favonius); Neri (2007; text, Italian translation, and commentary).

For general bibliography on Macrobius, see 11.3.2 below.

b) Favonius Eulogius, *Disputatio de Somnio Scipionis*: Not a true commentary, but two tracts on numerology loosely attached to the *Somnium*. Favonius is to be identified with Augustine's successor as rhetor in Carthage; the *Disputatio* was written at the end of the fourth or early in the fifth century.

T: Holder (1901); Van Weddingen (1957; text and French translation); Scarpa (1974; text, Italian translation, and commentary); Pégolo and Cardigni (2006; excerpts in Spanish translation); Marcellino (2012; text, Italian translation, and commentary)

R: *RE* Favonius 2 (Wissowa); *BNP* Favonius 2 (Flamant); *PLRE* I Eulogius 3; *RLAC* (Sicherl); S–H 4.2 §1123.

S: Dorfbauer (2011).

For later commentaries and glosses on Cicero, see Munk Olsen (2009: 60–6).

ARATEA

See 11.6 below.

3. VIRGIL

On Virgilian commentaries, see 7.3a above.

Not many modern works discuss ancient and late antique Virgilian commentaries as a whole, but Starr (1995) and Stok (2014) discuss a range of ancient interpretations of *Eclogues* 7 and 6, respectively, and Georgii (1891) is still fundamental for ancient criticism of the *Aeneid*. Ziolkowski and Putnam (2008: 623–824) includes texts and translations of excerpts from the commentary tradition going up to the Renaissance, but most are too brief to be useful. Suringar (1834–5: 2.1–350) and Ribbeck (1866) are still useful guides to the history of Virgilian scholarship; so are Wessner's (1908: 147–65, 1921: 181–212) and Lammert's (1931: 85–92, 1936: 141–50) bibliographical accounts of the whole range of texts. A more recent account of Virgilian commentary from a medieval perspective is Irvine (1994: 118–61). Many of the works cited below in connection with a particular text also deal with the wider tradition.

1. Servius and Servius Auctus

As discussed above (7.3a), there is not complete consensus about the relationship between the two forms of the commentary. It is now generally agreed that the shorter and better-attested form of the text ("Vulgate") is what Servius, grammarian in Rome in the first part of the fifth century, actually wrote. His commentary is designed for the use of other *grammatici* and contains the information that would be most useful in the classroom: grammar, rhetoric, style, meter, and exegesis of fact, fable, geography, and history. The longer version (DS or Servius Auctus) incorporates a great many additions to the Vulgate and was compiled in the seventh century, possibly in Ireland. The compiler has his own personality and editorial principles, but he made use of a source much more learned than the Vulgate; it seems fairly certain that the source was, perhaps at some remove, the commentary of Aelius Donatus. It also now appears from the Spangenberg fragment of DS (Marshall 2000) that our version of DS may itself have been abridged after the collection was compiled; that would explain the fuller detail in the scholia to Statius' *Achilleid* noted by Jakobi (1997: 205–9). The whole compilation, in any case, provides our best window into the ways Virgil was read in late antiquity.

On Servius' grammatical works (genuine and pseudepigraphic), see 12.40 below.

T: Thilo (1881–7) is the only complete edition. The so-called Harvard Servius (Rand et al. 1946 for *Aen.* 1–2; Stocker and Travis 1965 for *Aen.* 3–5) has revived after a half century, and the commentary on *Aen.* 9–12 has just appeared (Murgia and Kaster 2018). Any printed edition of Servius is problematic, and Fraenkel (1964: 2.339–90; review of Rand et al. 1946) is necessary reading. Other partial editions and translations of Servius (all *Aeneid*) include Book 1: Baudou and Clément-Tarantino (2015; with French translation); Book 4: transl. McDonough et al. (2002; Vulgate only); Book 6: Jeunet-Mancy (2012; with French translation); Book 7: Ramires (2003); Book 9: Ramires (1996).

Excerpts from the commentary on Books 1 and 6 translated in Copeland and Sluiter (2009: 127–40). Ramires is said to be preparing an electronic edition of the whole commentary. Note: The bibliography in Bouquet and Méniel (2011) records a translation of Servius on the *Eclogues* by F. Daspet (Gradignan, 2007) and an edition of Servius on the *Eclogues* by M. Bouquet as Habilitation at Lyon 3 (2008). I have not seen either.

I: Mountford and Schultz (1930) includes names and subjects only and is not complete.

B: Wessner (1903: 195–200); Lammert (1931: 73–4). There is a useful survey of recent (1970–96) work on Servius in Uhl (1998: 5–18) and an excellent bibliography in Bouquet and Méniel (2011).

R: *RE* Servius 8 (Wessner); *BNP* Servius 2 (Suerbaum); *PLRE* I; Kaster (1988) #136; *EV* (Brugnoli); *LG* (Petrilli); Teuffel 3 §431; S–H 4.1 835; *T&T* (Marshall).

C: Santini and Stok (2004); Casali and Stok (2008); Bouquet and Méniel (2011); Garcea et al. (2016). Like all collections of this kind, these are uneven, but collectively they give a useful view of recent research.

S: Among the more important or useful works are:

a) Focusing on Servius' text and identity problems: Thomas (1880); Barwick (1911); Marinone (1990: 193–286; originally publ. 1946); Goold (1970); Murgia (1975); Marshall (2000, 2012).
b) On Servius' methods and ideas: Kaster (1978, 1980a, 1988: 169–97); Dietz (1995); Marshall (1997); Fowler (1997); Uhl (1998); Murgia (2003); Pellizzari (2003); Fleischmann (2006); Delvigo (2011, 2012); Holtz (2011); Maltby (2011); Gioseffi (2012a); Stok (2012a). There are also extensive discussions of particular passages of Servius in Timpanaro (1978: 427–567, 1986, 1994: 405–58, 2001).

2. Macrobius, *Saturnalia*

Macrobius Ambrosius Theodosius (known as Theodosius in his own time and Macrobius in modern times) was a public figure of some importance (praetorian prefect in 430 CE), and he was also a scholar in an unusual range of subjects: his earliest work was a comparison between the Greek and Latin verbs (see 12.24 below); that was followed by his Neoplatonic commentary on the Ciceronian *Somnium Scipionis* (see 11.2.8a above)—and his philosophic affiliations are also shown by his grandson's name Plotinus—and that in turn by the work most widely read in modern times, the literary dialogue *Saturnalia*.

Saturnalia is why Macrobius is listed among commentaries on Virgil: in a conversation the dramatic date of which is nearly fifty years before the time of composition, Macrobius brings eminent Roman aristocrats (notably Vettius Agorius Praetextatus, Virius Nicomachus Flavianus, and Quintus Aurelius Symmachus) and some younger men of similar background together with an assortment of scholars, of whom, in the present context, by far the most important is the grammarian Servius, whom Macrobius admits was in fact too young to have taken part in such a gathering. These men gather to celebrate the Saturnalia of (probably) 383 CE by taking part in a learned discussion that goes on for several days (one day apiece in the houses of each of the three great men); and just as Macrobius intends to paint a nostalgic portrait of the Roman aristocracy of the late fourth century, so too do his characters celebrate the greatness of Rome's greatest classical writer, Virgil. In this respect, Macrobius' creation is closely parallel to the dramatic pattern of Cicero's *De re publica*—the work on whose conclusion (the *Somnium*) he had already written a commentary.

The main subject of the *Saturnalia* (determined by the participants, in the fiction of the dialogue, at the end of Book 1) is Virgil; and in particular, Virgil's learning. In a series of discourses in Books 3–6, the various participants discuss in considerable detail and with a great many quotations a number of areas in which Virgil was omniscient: his expertise in Roman religion, his knowledge of Greek literature and early Roman literature, his rhetorical skill, and more. The *Saturnalia*, moreover, is important here not just for the specific content he gives us, but also because there are very significant correspondences between what Macrobius says and what we learn from Servius and DS. Macrobius took his learning, often wholesale, from earlier scholars: Aulus Gellius, Plutarch, and others. He also very clearly used at least one commentary on Virgil, and the overlaps strongly suggest that he was making use of the same commentary that lies behind DS—in other words, Donatus. Some of the strongest evidence about the history of Virgilian learning in the fourth and fifth centuries is provided by comparison between Macrobius and Servius: the *Saturnalia* is included here because it is in parts virtually another commentary on Virgil.

T: Kaster (2011a; text and English translation) and Kaster (2011b; Latin text only) are far superior to earlier editions. Others are Bornecque (1937; text and French translation); Davies (1969; English translation); Willis (1970a); Marinone (1977; text and Italian translation); Guittard (1997; Books 1–3, French translation); Raventós (2003–6; text and Catalan translation); Schönberger (2008; German translation); Mesa Sanz (2009; Spanish translation with notes); Navarro Antolín (2010; Spanish translation).

R: *RE* Macrobius 7 (Wessner); *BNP* Macrobius 1 (Flamant); *PLRE* II Theodosius 20; *RLAC* Macrobius (Bruggissen); *EV* (Marinone); *LG* (Petrilli); Teuffel 3 §444; S–H 4.2 §1092–4; *T&T* (Barker-Benfield and Marshall).

I: Marina Sáez and Mesa Sanz (1997). I have not seen M. C. Granados Fernandez, *Léxico de Macrobio* (8 vols., Madrid, 1980).

B: De Paolis (1986–7); Raventós (2003: 1.53–7) gives a sensible selection of recent bibliography, with emphasis on later reception.

S: a) on Macrobius in general: Cameron (1966); Flamant (1977); Lecompte (2009; on reception).

b) on *Saturnalia*: Kaster (1980b, 2010); Syska (1993); Schmidt (2008); Dorfbauer (2010); Goldlust (2010); Cameron (2011: 231–72).

3. *Scholia Veronensia*

The Verona scholia are, after Servius and DS, the most valuable source for ancient scholarship on Virgil, but they are also the most difficult, as they consist of fifth-century marginal notes in the lower (erased) text of Verona, Biblioteca Capitolare XL (38); not only are the scholia erased and damaged, but the amount of readable text has substantially decreased since the nineteenth-century transcriptions on which Hagen based his edition. To compound difficulties, there is no single adequate edition. Lunelli (2001–3) is, for *Ecl.* and *Geo.*, by far the most careful and accurate version. Baschera (1999) is complete, but lacks any testimonia and, where I have compared it with the other editions, it is not altogether accurate (see also Lunelli 2001: 63–4). One should therefore still use Hagen (1902), a very good edition for its day (with some testimonia), but it is generally worth consulting the two more recent editions for more information.

The only recent scholarship on the Verona scholia consists of two repetitive attempts by Baschera to use the Verona material to help explain the identity of DS. All that can safely be said is that the Verona scholia are extremely learned and cite sources by name; that the material sometimes overlaps with what is to be found in DS; and that the two collections, taken together, reveal (what is clear in any case) a very active scholarly world of Virgilian interpretation in the fourth and fifth centuries.

T: Hagen (1902: 393–450); Baschera (1999); Lunelli (2001–3; *Eclogues* and *Georgics* only).

R: *EV* "Scholia non serviana" (Daintree and Geymonat).

S: Baschera (2000, 2008).

4. Philargyrius, *Brevis expositio, Scholia Bernensia*

T: Cadili (2003b; combined text of *Bern.* and *Br. exp.*, on *Georgics* 1.1–42 only); Hagen (1867; *Bern.*); Hagen (1902: 1–189; Philargyrius, 193–320; *Br. exp.*).

R: *RE* Gaudentius 1 (Funaioli), Iunius 127 (Tolkiehn); *BNP* Gaudentius 6 (Pollmann), Iunius III 2 (Schmidt); *PLRE* II Gallus 2, Gaudentius 10, Philargyrius; Kaster (1988) #60, 222, 223; *EV* "Scholia non serviana" (Daintree and Geymonat); Teuffel 3 §472.9.

S: Barwick (1908); Funaioli (1930); Cadili (2003a, 2008).

5. Ps.-Probus

This fifth-century commentary on the *Eclogues* and *Georgics* is an odd combination of considerable learning (in Greek literature and philosophy) with banal and potted accounts of mythology and historical events. It is preceded by a long and curious *vita*, which (among other things) tries to determine which poems were recited, and which were sung. Some parts of the text seem quite different from others; its origins remain as mysterious as its preservation (only in fifteenth-century manuscripts, which ascribe it to Valerius Probus) is tenuous.

T: Hagen (1902: 323–87)
B: Wessner (1903: 201–4).
R: Teuffel 2 §300.6(5).
S: Gioseffi (1991, 1995, 2007–8, 2011).

6. Tiberius Claudius Donatus

T: Georgii (1905–6); Marshall (1993; commentary on *Aen.* 6.1–157, previously unknown); Copeland and Sluiter (2009: 143–7; English translation of prefatory letter).
R: *RE* Donatus 9 (Wessner); *BNP* Donatus 4 (Pollmann); *PLRE* I Donatus 4; Kaster (1988) #209; *EV* Donato, Tiberio Claudio (Brugnoli); Teuffel 3 §431.5–6; *T&T* (Rouse).
S: Georgii (1893); Wölfflin (1908); Squillante Saccone (1985); Starr (1991, 1992); Gioseffi (2003, 2014); Pirovano (2006); and several articles in Stok (2013).

7. Marginalia

A great many manuscripts have some marginalia and glosses; some of them are ancient, but few are of much importance:

a) P. Ant. I 29 (LDAB 4148; late fourth/early fifth century) contains the end of *Georgics* 2 and the beginning of *Georgics* 3 with a few marginalia and an argument; the latest editor also reports seeing two critical signs. Text and discussion: Scappaticcio (2013: 171–3, 295–7).
b) The Codex Mediceus (Florence, Laur. Plut. 39.1) contains some marginal annotations on the *Eclogues*. Text and discussion: Ihm (1890).
c) Of the medieval annotated manuscripts much the most important is Bern 165 of the first half of the ninth century, with annotations in six different hands, drawing on Servius, Ti. Donatus, and a range of other sources. See Savage (1925). For other medieval commentaries and glosses, see Munk Olsen (2009: 111–21). On the Virgilian *accessus*, see Upson (1943); Irvine (1994: 121–6).
d) Many manuscripts, and the *Anthologia Latina*, contain summaries and arguments; some of them are ancient. See Gioseffi (2012b).

8. Biographies

In general, lives of the poets are not discussed in this volume, but the sheer quantity and antiquity of the lives of Virgil, and the fact that they are well edited, makes them exceptional. Brugnoli and Stok (1997) include some seventeen lives of Virgil. To the extent that their content is ancient, they are all descended, directly or indirectly, from Suetonius' biography as preserved and revised in Donatus' biography. That text is fairly widely attested (Stok 1991) in more than one version; in a single manuscript (Paris, Lat. 11308, ninth century) it is preceded by a dedicatory letter from Donatus to L. Munatius. The transmission of the letter is mysterious; it was written by a different scribe from the *Vita* itself, and the preceding sections of the manuscript contain the commentary of Philargyrius on the *Eclogues* and the *Brevis expositio* on the *Georgics*; it is thus not connected to the transmission of Servius or DS. Of the other lives, most of them fairly brief, that of Phocas (on whom see 12.33 below) is worth noting because of its verse preface.

T: Brugnoli and Stok (1997) is the largest collection; others include Brummer (1912) and Hardie (1966); Ziolkowski and Putnam (2008: 179–403; with English translation and including later biographies); Copeland and Sluiter (2009: 99–103; English translation of letter to Munatius and portions of Donatus' life).
S: Brugnoli and Stok (2006); Stok (2010).

For other Virgilian critics, see 12.5 (Asper) and 12.23 (Fulgentius).

4. HORACE

For discussion of these commentaries, see 7.3c above.

1. Porphyrio

T: Holder (1894); lightly revised with Italian translation but without apparatus in *Enciclopedia Oraziana* 3 (1998): 694–782.
B: Wessner (1902: 205–9).
R: *RE* Pomponius 106 (Helm); *BNP* (Schmidt); *RLAC* Horaz (Schmidt); Teuffel 3 §379.1; S–H 3 §602; *HLL* 4 §446.
S: Wessner (1893); Landgraf (1896); Diederich (1999); Kalinina (2007).

2. Pseudo-Acro

T: Keller (1902–4); lightly revised with Italian translation but without apparatus in *Enciclopedia Oraziana* 3 (1998): 785–925.
B: Wessner (1908: 165–82, 1921: 212–19).
R: *RE* Helenius Acron (Wessner).
S: Noske (1969); Longobardi (2014a, 2014b).

3. Other Scholia

There is no sign that any of the medieval commentaries contains anything ancient that is not otherwise attested. There is also no full inventory and certainly no detailed exploration of the composition of and relationships among the various sets of marginal scholia; there is a list of manuscripts with commentary, with some bibliography, in *Enciclopedia Oraziana* 3 (1998): 177–9 (Villa). For later commentaries and glosses, see Munk Olsen (2009: 68–79); a fuller discussion with copious bibliography is in Ciccone (2016: 23–62).
T: Cruquius (1597); Botschuyver (1935–42).
B: Wessner (1908: 179–80, 1921: 215–17); Friis-Jensen et al. (1997: 232–3).

S: Endt (1906); Botschuyver (1939); Friis-Jensen (1997, 2007).

4. *Vita*

Suetonius' life (or a version of it) is preserved in several manuscripts of Horace and edited (among others) by Rostagni (1964: 109–23) (with commentary); by Klingner in his Teubner edition of Horace; and by Della Corte in *Enciclopedia Oraziana* 1 (1996): 5–6 with Italian translation.

5. OVID

Only two works of Ovid, *Metamorphoses* and *Ibis*, received any commentary in antiquity: he was not, by and large, read in schools, he is rarely quoted by grammarians before the sixth century, and the extant commentaries themselves very definitely do not belong in an educational context. The only signs of early medieval interest in Ovid are two sets of glosses on a small part of the *Metamorphoses* (edited by Gatti 2014: 190–208) and the rather negative argument that pieces of knowledge preserved in various ninth- or tenth-century texts could not have come from any source other than a commentary. That is too speculative to be useful, and Gatti's attempt to recover an ancient commentary is unconvincing. Hexter (1986: 26–41) discusses a set of glosses on *Ars Amatoria* Book 1 that date from the ninth or early tenth century, but they are of interest only because some of them are written in Old Welsh; the annotations on the *Heroides* he edits are medieval, and probably no earlier than the twelfth century, and the *summa memorialis* of Oricus de Capriana on the *Metamorphoses* edited by Munzi (1990) is a product of the thirteenth century. Aside from the two commentaries discussed below, there is virtually no evidence of scholarly interest in Ovid in antiquity. There are many later commentaries and glosses: see Munk Olsen (2009: 88–95).

1. *Metamorphoses*

The summaries of Ovid's *Metamorphoses* known as the *Narrationes* are transmitted both with the text of Ovid and as a separate text (although generally later in this form); they are ascribed to several different authors, most frequently Lactantius Placidus (on the names of the author, see Tarrant [1995: 89–92]; see also 11.9.1 below on the homonymous and equally pseudonymous commentator on Statius). The work is a mythological commentary on the *Metamorphoses* drawn (at whatever remove) from Hellenistic mythographic texts and compiled no later than the third century (so Cameron). The exegetical notes contained in the *Narrationes* have been taken to show that a full exegetical commentary once existed, but that is unlikely; the present version of the text is a product of late antiquity and includes some exegetical comments not in the putative original.

T: Magnus (1914: 625–721), Slater (1927: unpaginated appendix). There is no modern critical edition.

R: *RE* Lactantius 2 (Wessner).

S: Tarrant (1995); Cameron (2004: 3–88); Gatti (2014: 27–85) with thorough citation of earlier scholarship.

2. *Ibis*

That Ovid's most obscure and riddling poem needs commentary is no surprise, and quite a few manuscripts (most of them from the Renaissance, but one from the eleventh century) preserve extensive notes on the last two-thirds of the poem (and much briefer notes on the opening portion). This commentary (an independent text in the earliest manuscript, marginal scholia in the rest) is indeed learned, but some of its learning, particularly its invented quotations from lost poets, is distinctly bogus. On the other hand, there are parallels between some mythological notes and the *Diegeseis* to Callimachus. Various hypotheses about origins have been devised, but there is no real way to pin the whole collection of notes (which vary somewhat from manuscript to manuscript) to a single author and date. It certainly contains early and genuine material, and somewhere behind our collection lurks a scholar of ancient myth and Hellenistic poetry. But there is also a great deal of fraud, and the language of some of the commentary seems medieval rather than ancient. In all probability, like many of the surviving sets of scholia on Latin poets, the text underwent many transformations and reshapings, along with the incorporation of material at different times and from different sources, before emerging as the rather strange document that it is. It should be used with caution and suspicion.

T: La Penna (1959).

S: Gatti (2014: 111–63) with copious earlier bibliography.

6. GERMANICUS

"Scholia to Germanicus" is the customary name for several related astronomical texts that are in fact not commentaries on Germanicus' translation of Aratus' *Phaenomena*, but discussions of the constellations, derived (at some remove) from the *Catasterismoi* ascribed to the Alexandrian scholar Eratosthenes and possibly derived (again, at some remove) from a text actually by Eratosthenes. The tradition of these texts is extraordinarily complex and closely linked to the exegetical tradition on Aratus, in both Greek and Latin; on the Latin side it is clearly connected to the *De Astronomia* transmitted under the name of Hyginus—but neither Hyginus nor the Greek tradition will concern us here.

1. *Scholia Basileensia*

Scholia Basileensia are the oldest form of this material, consisting of forty-four notes inserted into the text of Germanicus; aside from the introduction and two final sections on the planets and the Milky Way, each of the other forty-one notes consists of a mythological account of the origin of a constellation (catasterism)

followed by a list of the stars in that constellation and, for the most part, a picture of it. These scholia (given the siglum α by Dell'Era) are cited by (and are therefore older than) Lactantius in the early fourth century.
T: Breysig (1867: 55–104); Dell'Era (1979b).
R: *HLL* 4 §445.4.

2. *Scholia Sangermanensia*

This was Breysig's name for what is in fact the interpolated version of Aratus Latinus; as printed, it also includes excerpts from Fulgentius, Isidore, and the Elder Pliny that entered the tradition at some stage. It is printed at the foot of the page by Maass, and blended with the *Scholia Strozziana* (see below) by Breysig (and given the siglum β by Dell'Era). It is no earlier than the eighth century, as the Aratus Latinus itself is a product of the seventh.
T: Breysig (1867: 105–232); Maass (1898: 180–297).

3. *Scholia Strozziana*

These are an amalgam of *Basileensia* and *Sangermanensia*, and more (given the siglum γ by Dell'Era); compiled some time between the eighth and the twelfth century.
T: Breysig (1867: 105–232); Dell'Era (1979a).

4. *Scholia Bernensia*

Scholia Bernensia are simply the star-lists of *Basileensia*. Formerly considered a work of Bede, the text is labeled *Beda de signis coeli* by Maass. Dell'Era gives it the siglum θ. It was used by Hrabanus Maurus, *De computo* c. 51, hence earlier than 820.

T: Breysig (1867: 233–8; partial text); Maass (1898: 582–94); Dell'Era (1979c).

5. Scholia on Cicero's *Aratea*

The so-called scholia on Cicero's *Aratea* exist in two versions: one (made into wonderful pictures of the constellations themselves in London, BL Harley 647) consisting entirely of excerpts from Hyginus *De astronomia*, the other adding to that base some excerpts from *Sangermanensia*. There is no modern edition, so far as I know, but see Kauffmann (1888). Versions 1 and 2 were printed in parallel with other texts in aid of reconstructing Ps.-Eratosthenes by Robert (1878); the more recent edition of Eratosthenes (Pàmias i Massana 2013) prints only the Greek.
S: Cameron (2004: 18–24); Dickey (2007: 56–60).

7. PERSIUS

No ancient commentary survives (although Persius is named in Jerome's list of school authors with commentaries), but ancient material, including some otherwise unknown fragments and some (sometimes garbled) reports of Roman customs and history, survives in commentaries the present form of which is Carolingian or later. Like many other such Carolingian commentaries, it was composed from at least two sets of marginalia; as it now exists, in manuscripts of the tenth century and later, it is a deliberately composed commentary, with an extensive system of lemmata and fairly well-articulated notes.

Robathan and Cranz (1976) divide the medieval tradition into five parts, of which three (C, D, E) are from the twelfth century or later and have no direct access to any otherwise unknown ancient material. The earliest form of continuous commentary (Tradition A) is known as *Cornuti Commentum* and was probably composed in western France (Loire valley?) in the ninth century. There are also quite a few sets of marginal scholia (Tradition B), some of which are closely related to the *Commentum* but which generally also contain notes based on the familiar medieval repertory of Isidore, Fulgentius, Solinus, and the like. The only other early commentary is that of Remigius of Auxerre; only a small fragment survives. It is clear that Remigius was heavily dependent on the *Commentum* and had no additional ancient material.

T: Clausen and Zetzel (2004; *Cornuti Commentum*); Zetzel (2005; Remigius and Tradition B); Scholz, Wiener, and Schlegelmilch (2009; *Commentum* and Traditions D and E).

S: Robathan and Cranz (1976); Wiener (2002); Schlegelmilch and Mayer (2004); Zetzel (2005); Munk Olsen (2009: 95–9).

8. LUCAN

No remains of an ancient commentary on Lucan survive: what there is exists in manuscripts of which the earliest is from the very end of the ninth century, and most manuscripts are from s. x–xii. In terms of modern editions, they can be divided into three collections: the *Commenta Bernensia*, edited by Usener (1869); the *Adnotationes super Lucanum*, edited by Endt (1909); and a *Supplementum Adnotationum* edited by Cavajoni (3 vols., 1979–90). The most important predecessor of these editions also deserves mention: in the third volume of his edition of Lucan, C. F. Weber (1831) printed a large collection of scholia drawn from a substantial number of manuscripts, identifying sources fairly carefully with sigla and identifying the manuscripts themselves in an appendix. His sources included the manuscripts used by Cavajoni as well as those used by Endt and Usener, but quite a few others as well. His discussion of the manuscripts is learned, but his edition is eclectic and unreliable, and deciphering his sigla is not a task for the faint-hearted.

Cavajoni's collection is what he calls it, a supplement: it is a collection taken from a group of manuscripts (the most important is Paris, Lat. 7900A, a poetry collection written in northern Italy in the tenth century and including sets of scholia to other authors) that Endt knew and largely dismissed because their notes only partially overlap with the *Adnotationes* themselves and often give a different version of essentially the same note. What Cavajoni prints is simply a set of marginalia: largely exegetical and glossographic, they may contain some ancient material, but surely not very much. It is clear, however, that these manuscripts are a group and overlap with one another a great deal.

The other two texts exist both as marginalia and as continuous text, and in certain respects they overlap with one another. The most important manuscript—the only complete manuscript—of the *Commenta* is Bern 370 of the late ninth or early tenth century. It contains the *Commenta* as a continuous text, without a copy of Lucan. For 1.1–396, however, it is mixed with the *Adnotationes*; and after the end of the *Commenta* the text of the *Adnotationes* continues, again as a continuous text, from 1.397 to 4.824 (omitting, however, 3.65–182) and then from 9.17 to 10.36. On the other hand, Bern 45, of the tenth century, contains the *Commenta* as marginal scholia up to 3.286. There are scattered marginal scholia after that, but according to Usener they are not related to the *Commenta*; according to Hagen in the catalogue of the Bern manuscripts, some of the scholia were written by Pierre Daniel in the sixteenth century. Endt's edition of the *Adnotationes* uses Bern 370 where available, but then relies on the continuous commentary in a twelfth-century manuscript supplemented by various other sets of marginalia. There is also a mysterious commentator named Vacca, whose name is attached to a short life of Lucan printed with the *Adnotationes* and to a number of scholia in later manuscripts.

Werner (1994, 1998) makes the relationships among these collections relatively clear, and rightly shows that the continuous Carolingian commentaries of the *Commenta* and *Adnotationes* were based on sets of marginalia, and that at least some of those marginalia themselves were derived from a variorum commentary composed in late antiquity. Jerome (*Adv. Rufinum* 1.16) lists Lucan among the authors that he and Rufinus had read in school with commentary, but he does not identify an author of the commentary; and as Lucan does not fully enter the school curriculum (or the commentary tradition) until Servius, the ultimate origin of the extant commentaries must remain obscure. There is some genuine ancient material to be found: the most notorious is the set of notes in the *Commenta* about Nero's unpleasant physical characteristics (e.g., on 1.57: *SENTIET AXIS ONVS iocatus est. dicitur enim Nero obeso fuisse corpore.*). Werner demonstrates that none of the editions available gives an adequate representation of the manuscript evidence, and there is certainly not yet an adequate account of the relationships among the commentaries or between continuous commentary and marginal scholia. None of the editions supplies testimonia adequate to illustrating the relationship between Lucan commentary and the popular late antique sources of learning, such as Servius and Isidore, although a few of the essays in Esposito (2004) make a start. Esposito (2011) surveys the early medieval material and tries to imagine what an ancient commentary might have looked like. The later commentaries on Lucan by Anselm of Laon and Arnulf of Orléans are beyond the scope of this volume. For later manuscript commentaries and glosses see Munk Olsen (2009: 83–7).

T: Weber (1831; hodgepodge); Usener (1869; *Commenta Bernensia*); Endt (1909; *Adnotationes super Lucanum*); Cavajoni (1979–90; *Supplementum Adnotationum*).

B: Wessner (1921: 221–8).

R: *RLAC* Lucanus (Schmitz).

C: Esposito (2004).

S: Marti (1950); Werner (1994, 1998); Esposito (2011). Earlier bibliography (including many articles by Endt on particular manuscripts) is supplied by Cavajoni and Werner.

9. STATIUS

Statius is not among the authors with commentaries listed by Jerome (*Adv. Rufinum* 1.16), but there exists nonetheless a substantial commentary on the *Thebaid*, a lesser one on the *Achilleid*, and a short introduction to the *Thebaid*. There is no sign of any ancient or medieval commentary on the *Silvae*.

1. "Lactantius Placidus"

Although the extant text of "Lactantius Placidus" on the *Thebaid* is Carolingian or later, it contains material going back to the sixth century, and possibly the fourth. There are no specifically identifiable earlier sources, and the few places with multiple interpretations need not be early: Statius (so Wessner 1929) did not become popular until the fourth century. A few manuscripts wrongly give the author's name as Lactantius Placidus; that evidently stems from a note on *Theb.* 6.364 the author of which says that he is writing a separate *libellus*—and the subject of the first-person verb is given as Caelius Firmianus Lactantius Placidus. It has long been known that the first half of this name is a mistake, taken from the Christian author of the *Divine Institutes*; it has become evident (see most recently Cameron 2004: 313–16) that the second half is wrong too, although not entirely explicable.

In its present form, the commentary on the *Thebaid* shows signs of a history similar to that of the commentaries on Persius and Juvenal: in the most important manuscript (Munich, Clm 19482, written in the late tenth century) it is a continuous text; in other copies it has been transposed into the margins of a text of Statius. The continuous commentary itself almost certainly derived from a late antique marginal commentary (or commentaries), which in turn may have been excerpted from the assumed work of a single author in the fourth or fifth century. The argument in favor of unitary authorship of at least the bulk of the commentary is the consistency of the use of rhythmical clausulae, and, as Klotz showed, of deliberate choices of word order and vocabulary to create clausulae. There is also evidence for the existence of a continuous ancient commentary in the absence of an argument before Book 1 (there are arguments for the other books) and no notes at all on two passages (10.96–147 and 12.512–615), making it likely that leaves of a continuous text with twenty-six lines to the page were missing at these points. On the other hand, it is clear too (as Klotz also showed) that some notes show no attempt at rhythmical clausulae; and even the most cursory inspection of Sweeney's text shows that some passages have only a few notes derived from glosses, while for others there is extensive commentary. Jakobi (2004a) attempts a more refined separation of layers in the ancient commentary, but his results are not altogether convincing.

If at least a substantial portion of this text derives from a single source, its author has a distinctive personality different from that of most extant ancient commentaries. He uses the first person; he has almost no interest in grammar (and the standard sorts of notes on *ordo* and *sensus* are few and far between); he has a great deal of interest in natural philosophy and theology, including Mithraism. His notes on myth, history, and the like often resemble the notes of Servius, the first Vatican mythographer, and other traditional material.[2] The author was probably not a *grammaticus*, and thus the absence of Statius from Jerome's list may not be accidental. But the author knows the language of school commentaries and his range of reading reflects school curriculum, even if this work was not part of it.

"Lactantius Placidus" was edited badly by Jahnke in 1898, and when Sweeney in his preface (1997: xxxvii) asserts that no other editor has ever made more changes in a Latin text, he may unfortunately be right; but in a text of this kind radical emendation is out of place. Sweeney has regularized and changed the lemmata so much that it is impossible from his edition to reconstruct the history of the text, and the second volume, which was to contain testimonia and indices, remains unpublished. The deficiencies of both editions are discussed without much progress by Santini (2014); the discussion of the identity, date, and place of origin of "Lactantius Placidus" in the same volume by Cardinali (2014) is equally inconclusive.

T: Jahnke (1898: 1–484); Sweeney (1997: 1–659).

B: Wessner (1908: 186–9, 1921: 228–34).

R: *RE* Lactantius 2 (Wessner); *BNP* Lactantius 2 (Schmidt); *PLRE* II Lactantius 5.

S: A. Klotz (1908); Wessner (1929); Van de Woestijne (1950); Sweeney (1969); Brugnoli (1988); Cameron (2004: 313–16); Jakobi (2004a); Wolff (2010); Cardinali (2014); Santini (2014); Kaufmann (2015: 491–4).

2. It is likely that the scholia to Statius draw on Servius, and that the first Vatican mythographer (a compilation composed probably in the tenth century) drew on the scholia to Statius. I have not discussed any of the Vatican mythographers, because they are clearly late and are based entirely on otherwise known ancient material. For the text of the first mythographer, see Kulcsar (1987) and Zorzetti (1995).

2. *Achilleid*

The short commentary on the *Achilleid* that accompanies the commentary on the *Thebaid* in Munich, Clm 19482 and appears in a few other manuscripts is not ancient, but was compiled in the eighth or ninth century from Servius and perhaps other Virgilian materials, incorporating also a number of glosses on individual words. It is possible that the compiler had access to a fuller, or slightly different, version of Servius/DS; it is far less likely that he had access to a full copy of Donatus, as Jakobi suggests.
T: Jahnke (1898: 487–502); Sweeney (1997: 665–91).
S: R. Klotz (1895); Jakobi (1997: 305–9).

3. "Fulgentius"

The short allegorical interpretation of the *Thebaid* preserved with the title *S. Fulgentii episcopi super Thebaiden* in a manuscript of the thirteenth century (Paris, Lat. 3012) and a copy made by Pierre Daniel is definitely not by the bishop Fulgentius of Ruspe and almost certainly not by his contemporary the mythographer Fabius Planciades Fulgentius (12.23 below) but by someone in the twelfth century with a taste for allegory and for the style of Martianus and Fulgentius the mythographer.
T: Helm (1898: 180–6); Sweeney (1997: 697–704).
S: Stock (1971); Hays (2002b); Jakobi (2004b).

4. Later Medieval Commentaries

On later medieval commentaries on the *Thebaid*, see also De Angelis (1997) and Anderson (2009: 2.83–143); for medieval commentaries on the *Achilleid*, see Jeudy and Riou (1974). On *vitae* and *accessus*, see Anderson (2009: 3.1–121). See also Munk Olsen (2009: 103–6).

10. JUVENAL

Juvenal is not an author cited in the grammatical tradition before Servius (early fifth century), and the bulk of the surviving scholia and commentaries come from the ninth century or later. There are two important exceptions to this: the Antinoe papyrus of Juvenal 7.149–98 written probably in the early sixth century and the Bobbio palimpsest (Vatican, Lat. 5750) written perhaps in the fifth. The latter shows that one important group of Carolingian manuscripts descends from an ancient model: the notes are very similar in content, although those in the palimpsest are significantly fuller than those found in the ninth century.

Although there have been attempts to define the sources and date of an ancient commentary on Juvenal underlying the extant scholia, they are generally unsuccessful or at best inconclusive. Some historical notes and some literary quotations have valuable ancient content; some notes seem to use the language of the mid-fifth century, not much earlier than the date of the Bobbio fragment.

But if what we have was put together in the fifth century, it was almost certainly already in the form of marginal scholia in a codex rather than an independent commentary, and in that case it probably had no single primary author but was assembled from the work of many hands.

1. Antinoe Papyrus

The Antinoe papyrus published by Roberts (LDAB 2559) deserves mention, if only because it is one of very few Latin manuscripts to show the use of a critical sign, in this case the *diple obelismene* appearing before and after Juvenal 7.192, probably to mark the verse as doubtful or spurious. But the scholia in the papyrus, in both Latin and Greek, do not progress beyond paraphrase and simple explanations (Latin) or translation and paraphrase (Greek). The only overlap with the *scholia vetustiora* (see below) is a single gloss on a single word, and the notes in general, as the first editor noted, "have little to tell us except about the depth of ineptitude of which fifth-century commentators were capable" (Roberts 1935: 206). There is no reason to believe (as Roberts did) that these notes are the work of a grammarian or even of a single person, although both are possible. They are simply marginalia of little use and less learning.
T: Roberts (1935).

2. *Scholia vetustiora*

The so-called *scholia vetustiora* are found in the margins of the codex Pithoeanus (Montpellier 125 = P); they are also preserved in other Carolingian sources, one of which (St. Gallen 870) presents them as an independent text (not in the margins of a text of Juvenal). Wessner's edition of this collection is still the best edition of any ancient Latin commentary (although not easy to read); it includes the Bobbio scholia, parallel material from other Carolingian commentaries (see below), and some related notes found in the fifteenth-century edition of Giorgio Valla and attributed to a mysterious "Probus."
T: Wessner (1931).

3. Carolingian Commentaries

A great many manuscripts from the ninth to the twelfth century (and indeed later) contain marginal commentaries; the traditional interpretation of the relationship among the various forms, by Wessner and subsequent scholars (notably Sanford and Grazzini) is that there are two Carolingian commentaries, labeled φ and χ, that are based on the work of Heiric and Remigius of Auxerre in the ninth century; and that there is another tradition, represented by the manuscripts LZ, that mixes the tradition of the *scholia vetustiora* with other material. There is also a mysterious Cornutus—clearly connected to the "Cornutus" who wrote a commentary on Persius—who does not appear in sources until somewhat later. It now appears, after von Büren's investigation of

Cambridge, King's College 52, that this is in some respects backward: the new manuscript is an earlier form of L, and its multiple hands show the commentary in the process of formation. At its core is a marginal commentary closely related to the *scholia vetustiora*, to which other notes have been added. The manuscript, moreover, was written in the scriptorium of Hincmar of Reims in the second half of the ninth century, and one of the scribes is almost certainly Heiric of Auxerre himself. That suggests that Heiric is not the author of the φ and χ commentaries, and that the whole tradition needs re-examination. Grazzini has begun an edition of the φ and χ commentaries; it should be noted that no commentary other than the *scholia vetustiora* has any independent access to ancient material.

T: Grazzini (2002; φ and χ commentaries, Satires 1–6 only).

4. Glossaries

Juvenal has an interesting vocabulary, and there are quite a few glossaries.

T: *CGlL* 5.652–6; Jeudy (1996: 277–82; Wolfenbüttel, Gud. Lat. 64); Lendinara (1996: 642–8; London, BL Harley 3286). See also Goetz, *CGlL* 1.382–90.

B: Wessner (1902: 215–19, 1908: 189–94); Lammert (1936: 153–6).

R: *RLAC* Juvenal (Schmidt).

S: Wessner (1929); Sanford (1960); Townend (1972); Munk Olsen (2009: 79–83); Cameron (2010); von Büren (2010).

12

Grammars and Other Forms of Erudition

As has been noted before, I am less concerned with the internal history of linguistic thought in antiquity and the early Middle Ages than with the identification and explanation of the texts themselves. There is a large and learned bibliography on the history of linguistic thought in antiquity, and some (by no means all) of the useful works on the internal history of Latin grammar and the grammatical tradition are:

a) General histories of linguistics: I have not found these altogether reliable or useful and I have rarely referred to them. Exceptions to that are Matthews (1994); the chapters by Baratin, Desbordes, and Codoñer in Auroux and Koerner (2000: 459–83); Law (2003); and Atherton and Blank (2013).
b) Specific studies (to most of which I have referred elsewhere): Barwick (1922); Baratin (1989, 1994, 1995); De Nonno (1990c: 626–46, 2003); Desbordes (1995); Luhtala (2002, 2005).
c) Research tools: Lomanto and Marinone (1990) is an index in three volumes; more practical is the search function in CGL online (see list of websites, below p. 365). Much more valuable for its careful analysis and definitions is the lexicon of Schad (2007).
c) For the earlier history of the study of this material, Wessner (1902: 117–20, 1921: 36–50) is very valuable.

1. AGROECIUS

Agroecius' *Ars de orthographia* was dedicated to Bishop Eucherius of Lyon (whom he addresses as *decus et praesidium meum*; see Munzi 1992: 109), therefore between 434 and 450 CE. He is probably the Agroecius, bishop of Sens, addressed by Sidonius in 470 CE (*Ep.* 5.10); Pintus provides historical and ecclesiastical context. Agroecius is the only grammarian of this period from Gaul other than Consentius, whose treatise on the noun and verb precedes the text of Agroecius in one of the earliest witnesses, Bern 432.

Agroecius' work is a set of *differentiae*; he presents his work as a supplement to the work of Caper (see 12.9 below) which the dedicatory letter reports Eucherius had sent him. Not surprisingly, in a number of manuscripts Agroecius' work is accompanied by the two surviving works ascribed to Caper, *Orthographia* and *De uerbis dubiis*—presumably the same texts to which Agroecius refers. Agroecius' work was used in later grammars and collections of *differentiae* (e.g., Isidore, Bede, and indirectly Alcuin; see Uhlfelder 1954: 21 and 10.4.2 above, on *differentiae* in general).

T: *GL* 7.113–25; Pugliarello (1978). The dedicatory epistle is edited separately by Pintus (2006–7).

R: *RE* Agroecius 3 (Goetz); *BNP* (Gatti); *PLRE* II Agroecius 3; Kaster (1988) #203; Teuffel 3 §457.11; S–H 4.2 §1100.

S: Pintus (2006–7); Holtz (1981: 232–3) and 6.3a above.

Alcuin: See 13.1 below.

2. APTHONIUS (ASMONIUS)

Aelius Festus Apthonius is the name found in the subscription at the end of a treatise on metrics; the opening of the text is lost and it now begins abruptly at *GL* 6.31.17, having been merged with the opening sections of the grammar of Marius Victorinus. The same text is also cited as the work of Asmonius by later sources, and that may well be the correct form of the author's name. For details, see 8.5 above.

Apthonius' work (to give him his traditional name) originally consisted of four books, and probably little is missing at the beginning: it opens with a discussion of vowel quantities and after further consideration of the pronunciation of the letters, moves on to the discussion of syllables—which is where the text of Marius Victorinus had broken off. The first book discusses the basics of poetry: quantities, stress, rhythm, feet, meters, larger metrical structures; the second book is an equally theoretical discussion of the nine prototypical meters. The two final books, described in each title as *pragmaticus*, switch from prototypical metrics to derivationist: on the adaptations of the two fundamental meters, the iambic trimeter and dactylic hexameter (Book 3), and the so-called *asynarteta*, complex juxtapositions of two different meters in the same line with a diaeresis between them (Book 4). Caesius Bassus is clearly one of Apthonius' sources, as are Iuba (an important metrician whose work is now lost, although frequently cited in extant texts) and Terentianus Maurus. He should probably be dated to the latter part of the fourth century, but that is very uncertain. It is very likely that the short treatise on Horatian meters that follows Book 4 is also by the same author. He is not to be confused with the Greek rhetorical writer Aphthonius.

T: *GL* 6.31.17–173.32.

R: *RE* Aphthonios 3 (Goetz); *BNP* Asmonius (Schmidt); *PLRE* I Asmonius; Kaster (1988) #19; *EV* Aftonio (Lomanto); Teuffel 3 §395; *HLL* 5 §525.1.

S: Hadot (1971: 62–8); Nosarti (1992: 96–101).

3. APULEIUS

Three grammatical works are ascribed to an Apuleius; none of them is by the second-century African writer. One is a work *De orthographia* ascribed to L. Caecilius Minutianus Apuleius, consisting of a set of observations on the proper spelling of individual words (largely names) that, in its present form, regularly cites ancient authorities for a given spelling but equally regularly omits the quotations that would have contained the word in question. This text was forged in the Renaissance; it is regularly cited only by Caelius Rhodiginus, but (as there are two citations of it by Giovanni Pontano in 1481) it is too early to have been entirely invented by him. Recently credulity has grown about its possible ancient sources, particularly a lost, very learned commentary on Ovid's *Metamorphoses*. "Apuleius" may have had a few genuine facts about Hellenistic poetry, but it is very doubtful; whoever created this work was learned, but also imaginative. The other works, *De notis aspirationis* and *De diphthongis*, ascribed simply to Apuleius, are clearly meant as a pair. Until recently, there was no evidence for these works before the Renaissance, but twenty years ago a late twelfth-century manuscript was discovered in Reims, and it is now evident that they were written in the eleventh or twelfth century. None of these works is ancient.

T: Osann (1826: 3–13, 87–146) to be supplemented by Biondi (1997).

R: *HLL* 4 §457 (Sallmann); *LG* (Biondi).

S: Jeudy (1976); Biondi (1997, 2001); Hollis (1992); Gatti (2014: 69–78).

4. ARUSIANUS MESSIUS

The heading in the manuscripts of the *Exempla elocutionum* of Arusianus Messius identifies him as *uir clarissimus, orator,* and *comes primi ordinis*; the description of the work in the list of books in Berlin, Diez. B Sant. 66 (which now appears to be a book list from Verona rather than the catalogue of Charlemagne's library; see Villa 1995, and for a text of the list, see Gorman 2000: 260) gives its *incipit* as *Olybrio et Probino Messius*. Olybrius and Probinus were the consuls of 395 CE, and it seems plausible to date Arusianus' work to that year, and to locate him (and it) in Rome, where he clearly taught rhetoric. It is also possible that the anonymous *Carmen de figuris vel schematibus* (*RLM* 63–70 = D'Angelo 2001), addressed to a Messius, is dedicated to Arusianus.

The *Exempla elocutionum* is a handbook of usage, consisting of quotations from the four central school authors (Virgil, Terence, Cicero, and Sallust; it is referred to as the *quadriga Messii* by Cassiodorus, *Inst.* 1.15.7) arranged in rough alphabetical order (first letter only). Thus, for instance, there is a group of four lemmata illustrating the constructions of *incumbo: Incumbo illi rei* illustrated from the *Eclogues, Incumbo illam rem* from Sallust's *Historiae, Incumbo ad illam rem* from two speeches of Cicero, and *Incumbo in illam rem* from two different speeches of Cicero (*GL* 7.478.24–9.5). The list also includes some observations by Arusianus on perplexed usages (e.g., confusion between *ad* and *apud*, 451.18–26). At times, the work reads like an insufficiently digested collection of note cards; if the work was actually equipped with a dedication, we must assume that Arusianus did not aim at perfection. The work survived among the texts found at Bobbio in 1493 by Giorgio Galbiate; as with most of the others, the earliest and most important witness is the copy made then, now Naples IV A 11. See 12.6 and 12.42 below.

T: *GL* 7.449–514; Marmorale (1939); Della Casa (1977); Di Stefano (2011).

R: *RE* Arusianus (Goetz); *PLRE* I Messius; *EV* Arusiano Messio (Maggiuldi); Teuffel 3 §427.4.

S: Pugliarello (2003).

Asmonius: See 12.2 above (Apthonius).

5. ASPER

Three authors and texts need to be distinguished from one another:

1. Aemilius Asper

The first and most important Asper is Aemilius Asper, the grammarian of the late second century. Part of one work by him survives, the *Grammatica Vergiliana*, but there are also fragments of commentaries on Virgil, Terence, and Sallust. See 5.4 and 7.3a above.

T: Hagen in Thilo (1881–7: 3.2.533–40; *Grammatica Vergiliana*); Wessner (1905: 44–50; fragments); Tomsin (1952: 125–43; fragments on Virgil); Buffa (1977; fragments of commentaries on Sallust and Terence).

R: *RE* Aemilius 29 (Goetz); *BNP* Aemilius Asper (Schmidt); *PIR*² A335; *EV* Aspro (Geymonat); Teuffel 3 §374.1; S–H 3 §598; *HLL* 4 §443.

S: Timpanaro (1986: 134–41, 2001: 108–11).

2. Asper, also known as Asper Iunior

The text printed by Keil under the title *Aspri grammatici ars* is a brief and jejune grammar, presumably based on Donatus, but also showing some knowledge of Victorinus; it is so brief and empty that it is hard to have any very firm opinion about its sources, date, or origin. It has sections on *ars*, then on letters, syllables, and (metrical) feet followed by the parts of speech in the order noun, pronoun, verb, adverb, participle, conjunction, preposition, interjection. All examples come from Virgil, but this is certainly not the work of the Virgilian commentator but of someone writing probably in the fifth century. It apparently survives in one manuscript of the eleventh or twelfth century (Keil, *GL* 5.527n.), but otherwise is found only in manuscripts of the fifteenth century, in most of which it accompanies the *Regulae* attributed to Palaemon (see 12.30 below).

T: *GL* 5.547–54.

3. Asperius, also known as Asporius or Asper Minor

These are various names for the same seventh-century text; see 13.3 below.

6. ATILIUS FORTUNATIANUS

Title, date, and identity of the author are all uncertain. Kaster argues from the reference to the praetorship in Atilius' highly rhetorical preface addressed to an unnamed aristocratic young man that it was written no later than the third century. The fact that Servius in the early fifth century adapted the language of Atilius' preface in the preface to his own *De centum metris* (see Morelli 2008) gives at least a relative chronology; the fact that Servius dedicated his *De metris horatianis* to a Fortunatianus does not mean that the two are the same person.

Atilius' work was part of the collection of grammatical works found in Bobbio in 1493; it survives in Naples IV A 11 (foll. 87r–96r), written in 1494 by Giorgio Galbiate, where it is sandwiched between the genuine work of Caesius Bassus (followed by the *Donatiani fragmentum* [see 12.19 below] and some other scraps) and the pseudepigraphic work on Horatian meters also ascribed to Caesius. In the lost Bobbio manuscript, it would appear that Atilius and Caesius were accompanied by a text of Terentianus Maurus, but only the printed edition of that text survives; for a clear description of the Naples manuscript, see Ferrari (1970: 144–50). In the manuscript, Atilius' work is simply called *Ars* in the explicit, as it is titled in Keil's edition. Morelli (2011) labels it *De metris horatianis*, but that is no more than an inference from the preface.

The work itself only reaches the discussion of Horatian meters in its last ten pages. The first part of the work (279.1–83.3) runs rapidly through basics (letters, syllables, feet, rhythm); the second (283.4–94.6) discusses the *metra principalia*, i.e., the prototypical feet (eight in this version, although Atilius then supplies discussion of two more). The discussion of Horatian meter itself (294.7–304.11) is a mixture of prototypical and derivationist metrics, emphasizing that Horatian meters are what Atilius calls *paragoga*—meters that do not fit the prototypical schemes. Like Servius' later work on Horatian meters, Atilius takes them in the order in which they appear in the *Odes*, but he offers much more discussion of their origin and structure.

T: *GL* 6.278–304; Morelli (2011–12: 1.59–100; text with commentary).

R: *RE* Atilius 39 (Consbruch); *PLRE* I Fortunatianus 2; Kaster (1988) #221; Teuffel 3 §405.3; S–H 4.1 §827; *HLL* 5 §525.2.

S: Morelli (2008).

7. AUDAX

One work of Audax is preserved, the title of which is a fair description: *De Scauri et Palladii libris excerpta per interrogationem et responsionem*. What the works of Scaurus and Palladius are, and who Palladius is, are problems discussed in 8.5 above (and see also 12.31, 36, 39, and 45 below). Audax is essentially undatable: Schmidt would like to identify him with the African Audax with whom Augustine corresponded (*Ep.* 260–1), while Holtz (1981: 431) dates him to the sixth century. He is earlier than Iulianus of Toledo, almost certainly earlier than Isidore of Seville, and definitely later than Donatus: not only does he use *Donatus* as an example of a name with a long penult (359.14), but he also seems to have used Donatus' work. Fifth century seems reasonable for both content and method.

T: *GL* 7.320–62.

R: *RE* Audax 2 (Goetz); *PLRE* II Audax 2; Kaster (1988) #190; Teuffel 3 §482.4; S–H 4.2 §1105; *HLL* 5 §522.2, 4.

S: Jeep (1893: 85–9).

8. AUGUSTINUS

The vast majority of the works of Augustine lie beyond the scope of this book, and the same applies to the immense bibliography. What follows concerns only the two works of formal grammar that have been attributed to him; there is no discussion here of other broadly relevant works, such as *De doctrina Christiana* or *De dialectica*.

1. *Regulae*

Regulae is certainly not by Augustine, but because his name was attached to the text, it circulated much more widely than many more important grammatical works. *Regulae* supplies the name for what Vivien Law christened the "*regulae* type" of grammar, "characterised by its insistence on terminations" (Law 1984: 165), teaching students how to derive one form of a word from another, and (in this text) giving fairly extensive paradigms. It is very similar to, but much fuller than, the comparable work ascribed to Palaemon (see 12.30 below): unlike that text, these *Regulae* give frequent citations of authors and much fuller paradigms. The two texts probably have a common model, but neither seems to be derived from the other. Although not by Augustine, *Regulae* includes a collection of African place names (506.22) which suggests its place of origin. It was probably written between the fourth and sixth centuries CE, but no precision is possible. It is generally transmitted either in the company of genuine works of Augustine or as a part of larger collections of grammatical texts.

T: *GL* 5.496–524; Martorelli (2011; with Italian translation and commentary).

2. *Ars breviata*

Until not long ago, it was generally believed that the *Ars pro fratrum mediocritate breviata* was not by Augustine; opinions have changed. Cassiodorus in the sixth century probably knew the *Ars breviata* as Augustine's work. The difficulty is that, according to Augustine himself (*Retract.* 1.6.6) he had lost the work on grammar he wrote at Cassiciacum—but he had also lost the first five books of *De musica*, a text which is extant. In shape, the *Ars breviata* is similar to Donatus' *Ars minor*, but it has some significant differences, and it appears that one of Augustine's main sources was the grammar of Terentius Scaurus; it owes something to Varro indirectly (through Scaurus) and perhaps (given Augustine's wide knowledge of Varro's work) directly. It describes a set of *conexiones* equivalent to the modern use of the present stem, the perfect, and the perfect passive participle as starting points for deriving verb forms (and Oniga argues with some plausibility that this system, if not the term *conexio*, is derived from Varro); in its concern with the relationship between *auctoritas* and *consuetudo*, as in a few other mannerisms, it seems parallel to genuine works of Augustine; and it is one of the few pre-sixth century grammatical texts to use Christian examples and to quote St. Paul. It is clearly an abridgment; when and how it was abridged is unknown.

T: Weber (1861); Bonnet (2013; text with French translation and commentary).

R: *RE* Augustinus 2 (Jülicher); *BNP* (Pollmann) *PLRE* II Augustinus 2; *RLAC* Augustinus (Capelle); Law (1982: 24–5); Kaster (1988) #20; Teuffel 3 §440.6; S–H 4.2 §1170.

S: Barwick (1922: 170–3); Law (1984, 1990); Pizzani (1985); Oniga (2007); Garcea (2015); Munzi (2015). See also Luhtala (2005: 138–50) on Augustine's linguistic theories in general.

Bede: See 13.4 below.

9. CAESIUS BASSUS

Caesius Bassus' *De metris* is one of the earliest surviving grammatical texts, written in the reign of Nero and apparently dedicated to him. Caesius was himself a lyric poet, addressed and so described by the satirist Persius (6.1–6); the surviving portion of the text deals largely with lyric meters (including Catullus, Laevius, and Maecenas as well as Horace), among which are included not only the Sotadean, but the Saturnian as well, interpreted as a Greek meter. Caesius is, like most Roman metricians, a derivationist, explaining all meters in terms of alterations from the two "original" forms, the dactylic hexameter and the iambic senarius. *De metris* is incomplete; what survives is preserved in Naples IV A 11 (= N), the copy made in 1494 of a lost Bobbio codex. It should be noted that Keil (followed by Mazzarino) based the text on copies of N, not on N itself, and hence Morelli's edition is more reliable. For fuller discussion of Caesius, see 4.2 above; for metrical theory, see 8.3b above; for the manuscript, see 12.42 below.

Immediately following the text of Caesius in N (and printed with it in modern editions) is an anonymous set of grammatical chapters (*De positura, De chria, De poemate, De versu, De accentibus*) that for the most part have to do with prosody and meter—although the *chria* is an elementary rhetorical exercise. Those chapters are in turn followed by a grammatical text that claims to be *ars grammatica accepta ex auditorio Donatiani* (on which see 12.19 below), then by the text of Atilius Fortunatianus (12.6 above) and another set of metrical chapters wrongly ascribed in the manuscript to Caesius Bassus.

T: a) Caesius: *GL* 6.255–72 (without fragments); *GRFM* 124–55 (text and fragments); Morelli (2011–12: 1.5–44; text and fragments, with commentary).
b) anonymous excerpts: *GL* 6.273–7, 305–12; Morelli (2011–12: 1.47–55, 103–19).

R: *RE* Caesius 16 (the poet; Skutsch); Caesius 17 (the metrician; Consbruch); Teuffel 2 §304.1–2; S–H 2 §3d85.

S: D'Alessandro (2001–2).

10. CAPER

The second-century scholar Flavius Caper is credited in quotations by later authors (Charisius, Servius, Pompeius, and Priscian) with two works: *De Latinitate* and *De dubiis generibus*. These were greatly influential, although the relationship between the two works is impossible to determine; it is possible that the latter was a subdivision of the former. Priscian cites *De dubiis generibus* as the major source for Book 5 of his *Ars* in discussing nominal gender, and he similarly cites Caper (without a book title) for active and passive verb forms in Book 8 (*GL* 2.171.14, 393.8). In addition to having a significant presence in Priscian, Caper was clearly a major source for Charisius (Bölte 1888 and Barwick 1922 identified particular sections of Charisius I 15 as deriving from him; see 5.3 above), and his work also lies behind the anonymous treatise *De dubiis nominibus* (see 12.46.5 below).

On the other hand, the two short treatises actually transmitted under Caper's name, *De orthographia* and *De verbis dubiis*, are in their present form clearly not his work, although they owe something to him: the idea that there are two grammarians of the same name with the same interests several centuries apart (so Rutella 1977) is implausible at best. These extant works made use of other sources besides the genuine Caper; one of them seems to have discussed *differentiae* in hexameters. The attempt to find more hexameters than now survive has led some scholars (notably Strzelecki) to emend the text extensively; the resulting lines are clumsy and inelegant beyond even the low standard to be expected in a dictionary written in verse. Strzelecki also seriously exaggerates Caper's (at best indirect) presence in Nonius Marcellus; Keil is, as often, more sensible. See 5.3 and 10.2 above.

T: *GL* 7.92.1–107.2 (*De orthographia*); *GL* 7.107.3–12.5 (*De verbis dubiis*); G. Keil (1889) (fragments).

B: Wessner (1921: 98–104).

R: *RE* Caper (Goetz); *BNP* Flavius 2.14 (Schmidt); *PIR*^{2} F231; Teuffel 3 §374.3; S–H 3 §599; *HLL* 4 §438, 492.1.

S: Keil in *GL* 7.85–91; Strzelecki (1936, 1949); Rutella (1977); De Paolis (1995, 2013–14).

11. CASSIODORUS

Flavius Magnus Aurelius Cassiodorus Senator (c. 490–c. 585) spent much of his long life in public service (his *Variae* represent his official correspondence as praetorian prefect for the Ostrogothic king Theoderic). When replaced, he migrated to Constantinople to study theology for about the next twenty years, and then returned to Italy, where he founded the monastery of Vivarium at Squillace in southern Italy. Cassiodorus wrote a great deal, but only a few works are relevant here; the bibliography below is correspondingly brief.

1. *Institutiones*

The two books of the *Institutiones* (Book 1, *I. divinarum litterarum*; Book 2, *I. saecularium litterarum*) were written for the education and guidance of Cassiodorus' monastic community at Vivarium: the first is an introduction to the Bible (with, for the purposes of this book, one very important chapter [1.15, *Sub qua cautela relegi debeat caelestis auctoritas*] on how to read and correct the text of the Bible) and the second an introduction to the seven liberal arts, beginning with grammar and rhetoric. *Inst.* 2.1, on grammar, is based on Donatus, *Ars maior*, with significant additions of paradigms and elementary material; in the introduction to the chapter he states that he is leaving for his monks a copy of Donatus with two commentaries together with a brief *ars* by Augustine; the last is almost certainly to be identified with the extant *Ars breviata* (see 12.8.2 above). In the course of the chapter, however, he announces the preparation of a different codex, this one containing Donatus, a book of his own on orthography and one on etymology, and Sacerdos *De schematibus*. The work on etymology is not otherwise attested; the work on orthography survives: see below.

The *Institutiones* was a work in progress; its origins go back to Cassiodorus' attempt to found a Christian university in Rome (see Marrou 1931), and he continued to work on it for the rest of his life. There is only one version (at least, surviving) of Book 1, but there are apparently three of Book 2, the result of Cassiodorus' own notes and revisions in his lifetime and the revisions made after his death by at least one of his followers. *Inst.* 2.1 on grammar is not a particularly significant text, and very little of it, if anything, is original; it is more significant for the collections of grammatical material it announces, and for the simple (or not so simple) fact that Cassiodorus here explicitly attempted to link the secular liberal arts to the study of the Bible.

T: Mynors (1937); Jones (1946; English translation); Bürsgens (2003; text with German translation); Halporn (2004; English translation); Pronay (2014; German translation with commentary). Chapters on grammar and rhetoric (2.1–2) translated in Copeland and Sluiter (2009: 221–31).

S: Van de Vyver (1941); Courcelle (1942, 1969: 331–60); Holtz (1986b); Halporn (2002); Ferré (2002).

2. *De Orthographia*

In the preface to *De orthographia*, Cassiodorus identifies it as his seventh work (*GL* 7.144.1–18), written when he was ninety-three. After the preface, it consists of twelve sets of excerpts from seven earlier writers on orthography: Cornutus (I; 147.22–54.11), Velius Longus (II; 154.12–5.22), Curtius Valerianus (III; 155.23–8.8), Papirianus (IV; 158.9–66.8), Martyrius (V–VIII; 167.1–99.3; for nomenclature, see 12.28 below), Eutyches (IX; 199.4–202.17), Caesellius Vindex (X–XI; 202.18–7.12, under two names, as Caesellius and as L. Caecilius Vindex), and Priscian (XII; 207.13–9.4). Cassiodorus' work on spelling is intimately connected to the broader instruction he gives in the *Institutiones*: At *Inst.* 1.30.2, he reported having collected a set of works on spelling that is almost identical to the actual contents of *De orthographia* (the relevant excerpts from the *Institutiones* are collected by Keil, *GL* 7.210–16).

Cassiodorus seems to have meant to put his excerpts in chronological order, but in fact they are not: Cornutus is the earliest and Eutyches (a pupil of Priscian) the latest, but Caesellius Vindex is certainly earlier than Martyrius. Of the seven authors cited, Cornutus' work (which Cassiodorus names *De enuntiatione vel orthographia*) is not otherwise attested (see 12.16 below); Velius Longus' *De orthographia* survives (12.44 below), and Cassiodorus has drastically abridged it with some alterations (see Stoppacci 2010: cxxxii–ix). Curtius Valerianus is otherwise unknown and generally undatable, but makes use of second-century sources; there are similarities between some of what is ascribed to Valerianus and what is ascribed to the following author, Papirianus, but there is no clear argument for determining whether either is dependent on the other (see Kaster 1988 #271 and [disagreeing] Stoppacci 2010: cxxxix). As for Papirianus, in this excerpt he cites Cornutus, Velius Longus, and Caesellius Vindex; he is in turn cited several times by Priscian (and at least once Priscian's citation contradicts the excerpt in Cassiodorus). He may be identical to Papirius, of whom Keil prints a short excerpt, and Paperinus, who is cited by various Irish grammarians. See further 12.32 below, and for Martyrius and Priscian, see 12.28 and 12.35 below. The excerpts from Martyrius are followed by a brief excerpt from Eutyches *De aspiratione*; the work is otherwise unknown. Eutyches was a pupil of Priscian, and his work *De verbo* is extant; see 12.22 below. Caesellius Vindex is well known as a grammarian of the reign of Hadrian; it is not clear what work(s) were the source(s) for the two chapters ascribed to him under different names; it is possible that c. 10, which is longer, is genuine, while c. 11, a set of short snippets, is not. The excerpts from Priscian are taken from Book 1 of the *Institutiones*; for detailed comparison, see Stoppacci (2010: clxvii–xxv).

T: *GL* 7.143–210; Stoppacci (2010).

S: Keil, *GL* 7.129–42; Bertini (1986); Stoppacci (2012).

3. *Expositio Psalmorum*

The commentary on the Psalms does not belong here, as it is a commentary on a biblical text. It is worth mentioning briefly, however, because Cassiodorus used a set of marginal signs to indicate to readers, among other things, the use of figures of speech and syllogisms. His intent was to demonstrate that the Bible anticipated classical literature in deploying all the resources of ancient rhetoric

and logic, and to permit the use of the Psalms as a tool for teaching rhetoric. See also 9.3 above.
T: Adriaen (1958).

4. *Commentarius de oratione et de octo partibus eius.*

Almost certainly not by Cassiodorus, and ascribed in the manuscript to Sergius. See 12.40.11 below.

The bibliography on Cassiodorus, from various directions, is not small. Some starting points:
R: *RE* Cassiodorus 4 (Hartmann); *BNP* (Eder); *PLRE* II Cassiodorus 4; *RLAC* (Helm); *LG* (Petrilli); Teuffel 3 §483; S–H 4.2 §1044–54; Manitius (1911) §2.
C: Leanza (1986).
S: Courcelle (1969); O'Donnell (1979); Jenal (2005).

12. CENSORINUS

Following the text of *De die natali* the manuscripts contain (without any titles) a short encyclopedia generally referred to as *Fragmentum Censorini* or (Schmidt) *Anonymi disciplinarum liber*; it includes excerpts on astronomy, geometry, music, and metrics. The author is clearly not Censorinus, but some of the examples used suggest that they were roughly contemporary (*De die natali* is dated to 238 CE); Keil included the sections *De musica* and *De metris* among the shorter texts on meter that conclude *GL* 6. The mythological origins of music the author supplies (e.g., *Rhythmus creditur dictus a Rythmonio, Orphei filio et Idomenae nymphae Ismaricae, ut tradit Nicocrates libro quem composuit de Musio* (*GL* 6.608.10–11 = 108.16–17 Cristante) are entertaining if not enlightening. The metrical theory is largely derivationist in its emphasis on the hexameter and iambic senarius and in its terminology, but it shows some signs of prototypical theory. His astronomy seems to have been taken over by the *Scholia Sangermanensia* on Germanicus (see 11.6 above).

The real Censorinus is credited by Priscian and Cassiodorus with an *ars grammatica* and a work *De accentibus*, neither of which survives; see Sallmann in *HLL* 4 §441.
T: *GL* 6.607–17; Sallmann (1983: 71–86). Portions (chapters 9–11; 12) in Cristante (2012) and (2014), respectively.
R: *RE* Censorinus 7 (Wissowa); *BNP* Censorinus, Fragmentum Censorini (Sallmann); PIR[2] C655; Teuffel 3 §379.4, 6; *HLL* 4 §449.
S: Freyburger (1994).

13. CHARISIUS

Flavius Sosipater Charisius was almost certainly Greek, almost certainly worked in the East, possibly in Constantinople, and almost certainly was not a professional grammarian; his work can be dated with a reasonable amount of confidence to the early 360s. For discussion of Charisius' biography and methods, see 8.6 above. Charisius' *Ars* is large and somewhat disorderly, and that is not the result of just difficulties in transmission. Book 1 contains preliminaries (*de grammatica, de voce, de litteris, de syllabis*) and then launches into a very long discussion of the noun, including a great deal of learned and complex material, some of which derives from Caper and the Elder Pliny. Book 2 then discusses the eight parts of speech, with less space for the noun but an extremely long discussion of adverbs (mostly from Romanus). Book 3 is devoted to the verb and Book 4 to *vitia et virtutes orationis*—although at the (fragmentary) very end there are pieces of a discussion of meter, after which the text becomes problematic. In general, Charisius' work seems to be a standard *ars* that has had large pieces of works on *Latinitas* grafted onto it; its proportions are consequently not very harmonious. Because the sources Charisius excerpted often offer similar accounts of grammar, his *Ars* is also at times quite repetitive. Nevertheless, the very similarity of his sources is an indication of the uniformity of at least one major part of the grammatical tradition, and it is Charisius' apparently mechanical approach to composition that has permitted reconstruction of the earlier history of the Roman *ars grammatica*.

Charisius' *Ars* originally consisted of five books, but there is considerable uncertainty about the actual extent of the surviving text. The only reasonably complete manuscript of Charisius, Naples IV A 8 (= N), is a complex creation that includes other grammatical material, and much of what is printed in Barwick's edition as coming from Book 5 (pp. 387–480), especially the *Differentiae verborum* and the *Synonyma Ciceronis*, is clearly not authentic.[1] On the other hand, N is not our only source, and Holtz (1978) has shown that other medieval grammatical manuscripts probably contain sections of Charisius that are not in N.[2] As with other grammatical texts (e.g., Diomedes), it is almost impossible to decide whether the extant form is an abridgment of a text that was once fuller, or if later works that appear to know more of Charisius than we do were relying instead on his sources.

T: *GL* 1.1–296; Barwick (1964); Uría Varela (2009; Spanish translation of Book 1).

B: Wessner (1902: 157–9, 1921: 121–7); Lammert (1931: 67–71).

1. The continuous text of N breaks off with a discussion of *schemata* followed by the heading *De lectione* (375.10B). Both Keil and Barwick regard as genuine (and from Book 4) two short sections found in two discontinuous leaves that follow, *De saturnio* and *De rythmo et metro* (375.12–8.15B); those sections in turn are followed by a copy of Servius *De centum metris*, and then the heading *Incipit liber V de hidiomatibus* and a section of *idiomata casuum* (379–86B). For a lucid account of the problems, see Dionisotti (1982b: esp. 118–20).

2. In addition to Holtz (1978), see De Nonno (1992) and Schenkeveld (2004: 133–40); it should be noted that Charisius is frequently referred to or cited as "Cominianus" (and even "Flavianus") in the Middle Ages.

R: *RE* Charisios 8 (Goetz); *BNP* Charisius 3 (Gatti); *PLRE* I Charisius 3; Kaster (1988) #200; *LG* (Baratin); Teuffel 3 §419.1–2; S–H 4.1 §833; *HLL* 5 §523.1–2.

S: Bölte (1888); Tolkiehn (1910); Barwick (1922, 1924); Dionisotti (1982b, 1984); Holtz (1978, 1981: 84–5); Schenkeveld (1996, 1998, 2004); Bonnet (2000); Uría Varela (2005); Garcea (2016). For bibliography on Charisius' important source Iulius Romanus, see 5.3 above; see also Wessner (1902: 148–52).

14. CLEDONIUS

Cledonius' commentary on Donatus was written in Constantinople, probably in the mid-fifth century; it is preserved in a single manuscript, Bern 380, written in Italy or southern France in the sixth or seventh century. The manuscript is damaged at the very beginning and breaks off after three lines of *De barbarismo* in Book 3 of *Ars maior*, but originally it included both *Artes*. It is equipped with lemmata and is the earliest commentary on Donatus to have them; but their authenticity is doubtful, as the lemmata often do not match the comment to which they are attached. Even so, Cledonius' lemmata provide the earliest direct evidence for the text of Donatus. The title in the manuscript reads *Ars Cledonii Romani senatoris Constantipolitani grammatici*; a comment (of which the end is unfortunately missing) refers to his class on the *Capitolium* (14.3–6K) with an interrupting student (see above, 8.7). Cledonius made use of more than one source: he clearly employed Servius' commentary on Donatus, and there are close parallels between his words and those of Probus, *Instituta artium* as well as Pompeius and *Explanationes* I.

T: *GL* 5.9–79; Bertsch (1884).

R: *RE* (Goetz); *BNP* (Gatti); *PLRE* II Cledonius 2; Kaster (1988) #31; Teuffel 3 §472.1; S–H 4.2 §1101.

S: Jeep (1893: 40–3); Holtz (1981: 429–31).

15. CONSENTIUS

It can be inferred from Consentius' frequent use of Gallic place names as examples that he was himself from Gaul, possibly from Narbo; he is generally believed to be related to, or identical with, one of the two Consentii (father and son) addressed by Sidonius Apollinaris (*c.* 23 and *epist.* 8.4). Of these, the father is the more likely candidate, which would place Consentius at the very end of the fourth century or early in the fifth. He is described in the manuscripts as *vir clarissimus*, and it seems likely that he was not a professional grammarian.

Two works by Consentius (*De duabus partibus orationis nomine et verbo* and *De barbarismis et metaplasmis*) are transmitted separately, but internal references to no longer extant parts (e.g., verbal paradigms and a discussion of the syllable) make it likely that they were originally parts of the same work, a full *ars grammatica* on the model of Donatus; the anonymous grammar described by Löfstedt (1987; 13.49d below) also cites some no longer extant passages from Consentius. Consentius identifies the parts of speech in the same order as Donatus, and his discussion of the noun and verb tracks that of Donatus throughout, but whether Consentius used Donatus directly is disputed: Barwick (1922: 10–11 and elsewhere) believed they had a common source; others believe that the *Ars maior* was itself Consentius' source. Consentius' treatment is quite different from that of Donatus: he enlarges and elaborates, giving many more samples of declension, using the genitive as well as the ablative to generate plural forms of nouns, and providing for verbs an extended discussion of *genera*; the cross-reference to missing verb paradigms shows that, at least to some extent, he combined elements of *regulae*-texts with the underlying *Schulgrammatik*. It is also evident that Consentius shares an approach to categorizing nouns with one of the sources of Charisius (who may not be Pansa, as Barwick thought, but is probably earlier than Palaemon) and with such texts as Ps.-Augustine's *Regulae*.

De barbarismis et metaplasmis is the only text that links barbarism and metaplasm directly; the usual pattern puts all the *vitia orationis* together (with barbarism and solecism first) followed by all the *virtutes*. Consentius offers a list of metaplasms followed by a comparable list of barbarisms; the text ends with a discussion of scansion based on the principle that metrical irregularities are in fact explicable as metaplasms. The discussion of barbarisms is notable for Consentius' refusal to cite poetic examples (as they are, by definition, metaplasms rather than barbarisms), instead using mistakes from common speech in his own time.

Keil edited the first section of Consentius from three manuscripts; one of them (M = Munich, Clm 14666, s. ix) continues it with *De barbarismis et metaplasmis*, from which Keil edited that section. Another copy of *De barbarismis et metaplasmis* was later discovered in Basel F III 15d (= B; written at Fulda in a very difficult insular hand in late s. viii), and the text was edited from both manuscripts by Niedermann in 1937. A third manuscript (Venice, Marciana Lat. Z. 497, s. xi) has since been discovered and is used by Mari. Niedermann's edition is better than Keil's, but Mari's is better than either.

T: a) *De nomine et verbo: GL* 5.338–85.
b) *De barbarismis et metaplasmis: GL* 5.386–404; Niedermann (1937: 1.1–32.20); Mari (2016a).

B: Wessner (1921: 136–9).

R: *RE* Consentius 3 (Goetz); *BNP* (Gatti); *PLRE* II Consentius 3; Law (1982: 17); Kaster (1988) #203; Teuffel 3 §472.3; S–H 4.2 §1103.

S: Jeep (1893: 68–73); Fögen (1997–8); Maltby (2012); Mari (2016b).

16. CORNUTUS

L. Annaeus Cornutus, the friend and tutor of Persius, author of a Stoic treatise on theology in Greek, and student of Latin grammar and poetry wrote a book on orthography of which we have excerpts and a work about Virgil of which we have fragments.

What survives of *De enuntiatione vel orthographia*, a work addressed to an unidentifiable Aemilius, is a set of excerpts made by Cassiodorus (*GL* 7.147.22–54.11; see 12.11.2 above). They are presumably genuine, but we do not know how many removes they are from the original. What survives is a collection of observations on problems of pronunciation (how do you pronounce final –um? It depends on whether the following word begins with a vowel or a consonant), the alphabet (digamma), and particular orthographic problems: *causa* with one s or two, *vestra* or *vostra, lacrimae* or *lacrumae*, c and q, and more. The only authority regularly cited is Varro, with some frequency; that suggests that at least some of the text is in fact old.

There are only meager fragments left of Cornutus' *Libri de Vergilio*; we know (from Charisius 159.27–9B = F 35) that there were at least ten books and that it was dedicated to Silius Italicus. Whether or not this work was separate from a commentary on Virgil is unclear, and the speculations of Takács (2004) about its Neronian context are just that. On Cornutus' Virgilian criticism, see 4.2 above.

T: *GRFM* 167–209; *GL* 7.147.22–54.11 (*De orthog.* only); Boys-Stones (2018; text and English translation).

R: *RE* Annaeus 5 (Von Arnim); *RE* Suppl 5.995 (Nock); *BNP* Cornutus 4 (Leonhardt); *PIR*² A609; Teuffel 2 §299.2; S–H 2 §451.

S: Reppe (1906); Zetzel (1981: 38–41); Timpanaro (1986: 71–5, 2001: 26–35); Cugusi (2003); Takács (2004); Gourinat (2008).

Note that the name of Cornutus is attached to various medieval commentaries on Persius and Juvenal; see 11.7 and 10 above.

17. CORONATUS

At the very end of St. Paul im Lavanttal, Stiftsbibliothek 2/1 after *Explanationes in Donatum* (see 12.40.6 below), there is an incomplete treatise on the quantity of final syllables (by parts of speech, but the manuscript breaks off after the first sentence of the section on pronouns; for other texts *de finalibus*, see 12.46.7 below) introduced by a dedicatory letter from Coronatus to Luxorius. The dedicatory letter alone is also preserved in two other manuscripts. Both Coronatus and Luxorius (or Luxurius) are known: poems by both of them (a great many by Luxorius, a few by Coronatus) survive in the *Anthologia Latina*; they are among a group of writers in Vandal Africa in the first third of the sixth century, and the portion of the *Anthologia* containing their work was apparently composed c. 532–4. There is a useful introduction to the *Anthologia Latina* and Luxorius in particular in Rosenblum (1960: 25–48); more recent and more succinct in *RLAC* Suppl. I 216–18, s.v. Africa II (litteraturgeschichtlich) (Fontaine et al.). The text itself is an unexceptional work of the *De finalibus* variety.

T: Keil (1868: 4n.; dedicatory letter); Rosenblum (1960: 259; dedicatory letter, with English translation); Cristante (2003: 83; dedicatory letter, with Italian translation and commentary); Corazza (2003: 112–13; text); Corazza (2011: 170–3; dedicatory letter and text); Jakobi (2015; dedicatory letter and text).

R: *RE* (Skutsch); *PLRE* II "in *PLRE* I, wrongly"; Kaster (1988) #204; Teuffel 3 §476.5.

18. DIOMEDES

Like Charisius, Diomedes appears to have been a native speaker of Greek and to have worked somewhere (possibly Constantinople) in the Greek-speaking part of the empire; unlike Charisius, he seems to have been a professional grammarian. Writing in the late fourth century and addressing an otherwise unidentifiable Athanasius, in his preface he describes his work in a baroque style that approaches incomprehensibility in its abstraction (not altogether unlike the Latin of his fellow Greek and contemporary Ammianus).

Diomedes' *Ars* is very different in its structure and content from Donatus' *Ars maior*. In Book 1, he places what he calls *universi sermonis membra* (*GL* 1.299. 14–15): after two short chapters *De arte grammatica* and *De oratione* he introduces the parts of speech, and discusses them in the order noun, pronoun, verb, participle, adverb, preposition, conjunction, interjection. Within this, he not only includes a great many paradigms, but also, under the broad rubric of the verb, gives one of the very few discussions of syntax in the Roman grammatical tradition (388.10–95.10, *De coniunctione temporum*; possibly taken from Valerius Probus, according to Baratin 1989: 186–201); he also has a particularly full discussion of prepositions. Book 2 includes the remainder of a standard three-book grammar: a large set of introductory topics (*De voce, De definitione, De arte, De littera, De grammatica* [again], *De syllaba, De accentibus, De dictione, De pronuntiatione, De discretione, De modulatione*, some of them subdivided) followed by *virtutes* and *vitia orationis*. In this last, his order is again unusual: after *De Latinitate* and a section on styles (or dialects, in Greek), he begins from metaplasm, then figures, then *vitia orationis*, then finally to the broader consideration of *virtutes*, ending with (also unusual) a discussion of prose rhythm. The final book about poetry also has a strange order: after explaining metrical feet he includes a long (and important) section *De poematibus* (482.13–92.13) before discussing prosody (*Catholica de extremitate nominum*, one of the earliest versions of the standard fifth-century and later *De finalibus*, on which see 8.4b above), and then, at last, meters themselves, ending with a list of Horatian meters.

Diomedes' grammar deserves more attention than it has received. It is striking in its organization on the large scale, and equally unusual in terms of its structure on the small scale: while his models and sources for the formal grammar can sometimes be recognized, his method of combining them has been compared to a mosaic (Kaster) or a montage (Holtz). Where Charisius did cut-and-paste with shears on a large scale, combining whole chapters of various sources and often identifying them, Diomedes uses a sharp razor to gather a set of tiny extracts. It is still unclear whether he used Charisius directly or drew on Charisius' own sources. The grammar is also striking for its divergences from the general run of grammars, including particularly his interest in syntax and his access (probably indirect, and through Scaurus) to texts of Varro for which parallels sometimes exist in other texts but without Varro's name.

A copy of Diomedes made for Charlemagne in 780 (according to a poem in one of the manuscripts, *GL* 1.xxix–xxx) was the ancestor of all our manuscripts; that makes it difficult to tell whether (as used to be thought) there was a fuller version of Diomedes circulating in the seventh and eighth centuries to which Malsachanus and the *Anonymus ad Cuimnanum* had access or (as seems the more common opinion today) one of Diomedes' sources was still being used in the early Middle Ages along with Diomedes himself. The idea that a version of Diomedes expanded by extracts from his sources circulated in that period (possibly under the name of "Probus"; so Schmidt) seems a compromise between the other two, but none the worse for that.

T: *GL* 1.299–529.

B: Wessner (1902: 160–4, 1908: 120–4).

R: *RE* Diomedes 14 (Goetz); *BNP* Diomedes 4 (Gatti); *PLRE* I; Kaster (1988) #47; *LG* (Baratin); Teuffel 3 §419.3–4; S–H 4.1 §834; HLL 5 §524.

S: Jeep (1893: 56–68); Barwick (1922: 3–111); Holtz (1981: 82–9); Del Castillo Herrera (1990); Taeger (1991: 39–84); Dammer (2001); D'Alessandro (2001–2).

19. DONATIANUS

The manuscript containing the surviving continuous text of Caesius Bassus and Atilius Fortunatianus (see 12.9 and 12.6 above) also contains between these two texts several small fragments mostly concerning meter (discussed in 12.9 above) and one important grammatical excerpt entitled *Ars grammatica accepta ex auditorio Donatiani*; this heading has led to the text being generally labeled *Donatiani fragmentum*.

The text contains first a discussion of analogy and anomaly, then a discussion of nouns ending with the letter –a. It is strikingly close to, but not identical with, passages from Romanus preserved in Charisius, and the shared origin of both may well be Caper. Donatianus himself cannot be identified, although it is possible (if unlikely) that he is to be identified with Ti. Claudius Maximus Donatianus, the son and addressee of Ti. Claudius Donatus (11.3.6 above).

T: *GL* 6.275–7; Morelli (2011–12: 1.52–5).

R: *RE* Donatianus 3 (Goetz); *PLRE* I Donatianus 6 (identifying him as son of Ti. Claudius Donatus); Kaster (1988) #51 and #208; Teuffel 3 §445.6.

S: Barwick (1922: 207–10).

20. DONATUS

Of virtually no grammarian do we know more than we do about Aelius Donatus. His student Jerome in his *Chronicle* describes Donatus as *insignis* in the year 354 (along with the rhetorician and grammarian Marius Victorinus [12.26 below], to whom a statue was erected in the Forum of Trajan); the manuscripts of his grammar identify him as *grammaticus urbis Romae*, the recipient of an imperial teaching stipend. He wrote not only his grammar, but also commentaries on Terence and Virgil; a sadly abridged version of the commentary on Terence survives (see 11.1.1 above), and it is very likely that much of the set of additions to Servius' commentary on Virgil (DS or Servius Auctus) derives from that of Donatus (see 7.3a and 11.3.1 above). As Holtz emphasizes, Donatus' work, like that of Servius after him, encompassed both the basic functions of the grammarian: to explain texts and to teach Latin grammar.

Unquestionably Donatus' most important surviving work is his grammar, divided into two parts: the *Ars minor*, designed for young students, is an elementary catechism on the parts of speech, while the *Ars maior* is a full treatment of the standard elements of grammar. Whether because of his eminence as a teacher in Rome or because of the succinct clarity of his exposition, Donatus' paired *artes* became the single most important textbook of Latin until at least the Carolingian period (and, arguably, until the eighteenth century), attested in a large number of manuscripts and accompanied by a great many commentaries—at least six before the end of the fifth century and more than twenty-five more before the end of the ninth. Holtz (2005b: 117) aptly compares the tradition of Donatus with commentary to a snowball, accumulating material surrounding the austere presentation of Donatus himself.

Donatus' grammar was not only explained, it was adapted. Most manuscripts of the complete set of four books reverse *Ars maior* Books 1 and 2 in order to juxtapose *Ars minor* and *Ars maior* Book 2 (both of which concern the parts of speech). There was also, quite early, a Christianized version of Donatus, shared by the Spanish and Irish traditions of Donatus, that involved a combination of *Ars minor* and *Ars maior* Book 2, as well as a distinctively Irish version of *Ars maior* Book 2 (called *Partes maiores*), which eventually spread from Ireland to the continent in the ninth century; it is marked by some Hiberno-Latin linguistic features and some interpolations from Consentius.[3] On Donatus' afterlife, see 9.3–4 above and many of the texts listed in Chapter 13; Donatus himself is discussed throughout Chapter 8, but particularly in 8.3 and 8.7. There is a brief summary of Donatus' medieval activities in Ciccolella (2008: 1–20); on his altered appearance as the late medieval/renaissance *Ianua* (which will not concern us here), see Ciccolella (2008: 20–44).

3. On these versions, see particularly Holtz (1981: 301–14) and Law (1982: 30–4), and entries below on specific authors, especially Iulianus of Toledo (13.17), Asporius (13.3), Malsachanus (13.18). On the Christianized alternative to *Ars maior* Book 3 discovered by Schindel (1975), see on Isidorus Iunior (13.15 below).

Donatus seems to have attained a quasi-mythical status among the Irish in particular, as can be seen by his importance as a teacher in Virgilius Maro's writings (see 9.4 above) and by the strange life of Donatus *grammaticus* ascribed to one Flaccus Rebius and modeled, parodically, on the dedicatory letter and preface of Donatus' own commentary on Virgil. It includes, among other things, Donatus' early life as a goatherd and a report that he gained the notice of Cicero the aedile, *a quo toga donatus est, quod erat signum libertatis*. At the death of Aemilius the senator, Cicero put him in the senate in his place. "He died on December 13 and his body was thrown in a ditch where foreigners (or pilgrims? *peregrini*) gathered."[4]

T: *GL* 4.355–402; Holtz (1981: 585–674); Chase (1926; English translation of *Ars minor*). Substantial excerpts from both *Artes* translated in Copeland and Sluiter (2009: 86–99).

R: *RE* Donatus 8 (Wessner); *BNP* Donatus 3 (Gatti); *PLRE* I Donatus 3; Kaster (1988) #52; *LG* (Petrilli); Teuffel 3 §409; S–H 4.1 §832; *HLL* 5 §527.

S: Holtz (1981; with Kaster 1983a); Beck (1996); Holtz (2005b); Ciccolella (2008). Donatus is discussed somewhere in virtually every work on Latin grammar and grammarians; these are works that concentrate on Donatus and his afterlife.

21. DOSITHEUS

Nothing is known directly of Dositheus, but from the surviving text it can reasonably be inferred that he was a grammarian, that he was Greek, and that he probably wrote in the second half of the fourth century. Dositheus' *Ars* is unique in that it is, at least partially, bilingual: while the content of his grammar is very traditional and has close, often verbatim, parallels with Charisius, Diomedes, the *Anonymus Bobiensis*, and other texts, the parallel partial Greek version is by Dositheus himself. As Dickey has shown, the Latin text is stylistically different when it has a Greek translation from when it does not: it has been structured to fit the short-line pattern of bilingual texts. It is thus clear that the choice of what to equip with a Greek translation was made for teaching purposes: it was intended as an elementary Latin text for (adult) Greek-speakers, presumably those bureaucrats and lawyers in the eastern empire who needed to know Latin. In format, it was originally written in two columns (Latin, the language to be learned, on the left, and Greek on the right), although none of the three manuscripts now presents it in that way; of the three editions, Keil places Latin at the top of the page and Greek at the foot, Tolkiehn puts them on facing pages, and Bonnet gives an interlinear Greek/Latin text facing the French translation. Both Keil and Tolkiehn

4. The *vita* is preserved in two manuscripts (Par. Lat. 7730, s. x and Kassel, Philol. 4° 1, s. xi) and printed from Pierre Daniel's apograph of the Paris MS by Hagen, *AH* 8.cclx–lxi. It has attracted much attention recently; see particularly Brugnoli (1989); Munzi (2003–4, 2008); Conte (2005).

(but not Bonnet) print at the end of the text some other grammatical writings that appear entire or partially in the manuscripts, including a set of *idiomata casuum* (no longer bilingual), observations on punctuation, lists of verbs (bilingual), and a handy set of phrases from (or for) the usage of the law courts (mostly bilingual). This last will clearly have been useful to the original students with bureaucratic ambitions. It also corresponds to one of the sets of idioms preserved under the heading *De Latinitate* in the manuscript of Charisius, printed by Barwick (404.1–8.24) but omitted by Keil; that is consonant with the similarity between Dositheus' Latin grammar and the closely related group of grammars of which Charisius is one.

It should be noted that Dositheus is *not* the author of or otherwise connected to the *Hermeneumata Pseudo-Dositheana*: see 10.4.5 above.

T: *GL* 7.376–436; Tolkiehn (1913); Bonnet (2005; with French translation).

R: *RE* Dositheos 8 (Goetz); *BNP* Dositheus 9 (Gatti); *PLRE* I; Kaster (1988) #53; Teuffel 3 §431.7; S–H 4.1 §836.

S: Lenoble et al. (2000); Dickey (2016b).

22. EUTYCHES

A Latin grammarian in Constantinople and a pupil of Priscian, Eutyches therefore worked in the mid-sixth century. His *Ars de verbo* (given the title *Ars de discernendis coniugationibus* by Sedulius Scottus) in 2 books (*De coniugationibus verborum; De finalitatibus*) is preserved in the portion of Naples, Lat. 2 written at Bobbio in the eighth century; it became popular in the ninth century, and was the object of commentaries by both Sedulius Scottus and Remigius of Auxerre. An excerpt of another work by Eutyches, *De aspiratione*, is preserved by Cassiodorus, *De orthographia* (*GL* 7.199–202).

T: *GL* 5.447–88.

R: *RE* Eutyches 6 (Goetz); *BNP* Eutyches 2 (Gatti); *PLRE* II Eutyches 2; Law (1982: 21–2); Kaster (1988) #57; Teuffel 3 §482.1; S–H 4.2 §1116.

For Sedulius and Remigius, see 13.23–4 below.

23. FULGENTIUS

Fabius Planciades Fulgentius (as the manuscripts give his name) wrote in the early sixth century, under the Vandal kingdom in Africa. He has sometimes been identified (again, in some manuscripts) with Fulgentius, Bishop of Ruspe, who died in 546, but they are very unlikely to be the same person. Four genuine works survive written by the non-bishop Fulgentius, together with two works wrongly ascribed to him.

1. *Mitologiae*

A three-book exposition and allegorization of Greek mythology.

2. *Expositio Virgilianae continentiae*

See 7.3a above. This text is an interpretation of the *Aeneid*, in which Virgil himself is cast as the interpreter of his own poem. The *Aeneid* is read simultaneously as an allegory of human life and as an allegory of the education of the student in grammar and rhetoric.

3. *Expositio sermonum antiquorum*

See 6.2 above. *Expositio sermonum antiquorum* is a glossary, with quotations emphasizing archaic and archaizing language, drawn from authors some of whom are familiar, and some of whom seem to be figments of Fulgentius' vivid imagination. It is dedicated to a grammarian, Chalcidius; on chronological grounds he cannot be the translator of Plato's *Timaeus*.

4. *De aetatibus mundi et hominis*

A history of the world (of which about two-thirds survives, and which was not discovered until the seventeenth century) written in a highly rhetorical and declamatory style, with an engaging form of lipogrammatism: one letter of the alphabet, in order, is avoided in each successive chapter.

5. *Super Thebaiden*

A brief commentary on Statius' *Thebaid*; it is not genuine. See 11.9 above.

6. Commentary on Virgil's *Eclogues* and *Georgics*

This Virgilian commentary is attributed to Fulgentius in the sole manuscript that preserves it, Padova, Bibl. Univ. 1084. It is not genuine; it has not been published except for a small excerpt in Ottonello (2008: 438–9), and it was written no earlier than the thirteenth century.

Fulgentius was not a grammarian, but everything he writes is redolent of someone who spent too long in school (see Hays 2002a). His works, particularly the *Expositio Virgilianae continentiae*, deserve to be seen in the tradition of non-academic interpretation, of which Tiberius Claudius Donatus' vast reading of the *Aeneid* is the most notable example. There are also considerable similarities between Fulgentius' glossary and that of Nonius Marcellus, and between his language and that of Martianus Capella, but in each case most readers would agree that Fulgentius is both later and less erudite than his predecessors.

T: Helm (1898; all five works); Wessner (1899; *Expositio sermonum antiquorum*); Pizzani (1968; *Expositio sermonum antiquorum* with Italian translation and commentary); Whitbread (1971; English translation of all five works); Agozzino and Zanlucchi (1972; *Expositio Virgilianae continentiae* with Italian translation and notes); Stokes (1972; *Expositio Virgilianae continentiae* with English translation); Manca (2003a; *De aetatibus* with Italian translation and notes); Wolff (2009; *Expositio Virgilianae Continentiae* and *Super Thebaiden*, with French translation and notes); Wolff and Dain (2013; *Mythologiae* with French translation and notes).

C: Manca (2003b).

R: *RE* Fulgentius 3 (Skutsch); *BNP* Fulgentius 1 (Pollmann); *PLRE* II Fulgentius 3; *RLAC* (Langlois); Teuffel 3 §480; S–H 4.2 §1095–99.

S: Ciaffi (1963); Pennisi (1963); Rauner-Hafner (1978); Baldwin (1988); Hays (2002a, 2003); Wolff (2003, 2008); Ottonello (2008).

24. MACROBIUS (MACROBIUS AMBROSIUS THEODOSIUS)

In addition to his *Saturnalia* (see 11.3.2) and his commentary on the *Dream of Scipio* (see 11.2.8), the learned Macrobius wrote a treatise comparing the Greek and Latin verb (given the title *De differentiis et societatibus Graeci Latinique verbi* by Keil and *De verborum Graeci et Latini differentiis vel societatibus* by De Paolis). The work does not survive complete, but is represented by three sources:

a) Excerpts made in the ninth century by Johannes Scotus Eriugena *ad discendas grecorum verborum regulas* (according to the colophon in the manuscript). Eriugena tried to keep close to the order and wording of the original and, as far as can be seen from comparison with the other versions, was generally successful.
b) A short but important extract in Naples, Lat. 2, containing the dedication *Theodosius Symmacho* and a brief preface explaining that, unlike other peoples who simply gasp and whistle, Greeks and Romans have real, elegant, and closely related languages, which Macrobius will now explain as far as verbs are concerned.
c) An anonymous treatise *De verbo* found together with the anonymous *De nomine et pronomine* and [Probus] *De nomine* in Naples Lat. 1 (see 12.46.4 and 12.36.5 below). It is addressed (in high-flown Ciceronianism) to one Severus and has evidently been adapted to accompany the texts on nouns and pronouns that are found with it in the manuscript: while it is clearly based on Macrobius, it has no interest in Greek verbs but instead aims to explain Latin verbs to Greek speakers. It includes paradigms of Latin verbs that were clearly not part of Macrobius' original work.

Macrobius' treatise seems to have combined fairly elementary instruction with more abstruse lore and an elegant and discursive style. He seems to have made use of the work of Apollonius Dyscolus on the verb, and it is in turn possible (as De Paolis suggests) that Priscian in sixth-century Constantinople may have made use of Macrobius. Since the anonymous *De verbo* is also written for a Greek audience, and since a Symmachus (in this case, Aurelius Memmius Symmachus) both assisted Macrobius' grandson in correcting a text of the *Commentary* and received from Priscian the dedication of three short treatises (see 12.35 below), it seems likely that *De differentiis* circulated and was used in the Greek East before returning to the West, probably in the sixth century.

T: *GL* 5.599–630; 5.631–3; 5.634–55; Passalacqua (1984: 21–60; anonymous *De verbo* only); De Paolis (1990b). Keil and De Paolis omit the paradigms at the end of *De verbo* which Passalacqua includes; Passalacqua does not include the paragraph at the end which Keil has taken from another manuscript source beginning *Exempla barytonorum secundum Macrobium Theodosium*. It appears as fr. 5 of De Paolis.

S: Cameron (1967); Dionisotti (1984, 1988: 19–21); De Paolis (1990a).

For general bibliography on Macrobius, see on the *Saturnalia*, 11.3.2 above.

25. MALLIUS THEODORUS

The author of this short treatise on metrics is generally identified with Fl. Mallius Theodorus, consul in 399 CE, correspondent of Symmachus, recipient of a poem by Claudian, and dedicatee of Augustine's *De beata vita*, written in 386. As none of the references to him in other writers refers to this work, and as none of the manuscripts of this work (which is dedicated to his son) indicates any titulature, it may fairly be assumed that (if indeed it is by the consul of 399) it was written rather earlier: he was born c. 350, began his public career in the late 370s, and the work was probably dedicated to a child still in the clutches of the *grammaticus*. After a short preface (1), it consists of sections on syllables, feet (the opening portion of which is lost), and meter in general (2–4), followed by one section each on the eight prototypical meters Mallius recognizes (dactylic, iambic, trochaic, anapaestic, choriambic, antispastic, ionic a maiore, and ionic a minore) (5–12.4) and a brief and somewhat abrupt conclusion (12.5–7).

The text of Mallius—like many other such texts—was relatively popular in the Carolingian period and is generally found in manuscripts in the company of other works or excerpts on grammar and meter. It is also sometimes itself excerpted and altered: the Carolingian grammatical manuscript Berlin, Diez. B Sant. 66 contains a version of this text that heavily abridges non-hexameter material and adds Christian examples (e.g., from Prudentius), some of which also reappear in Iulianus of Toledo (Bischoff 1973: 33).

T: *GL* 6.585–601, Romanini (2007; with Italian translation); Diaz y Diaz (1996; Spanish translation with notes).

R: *RE* Theodoros 70 (Wessner); *BNP* Theodorus 2.1 (Groß-Albenhausen); *PLRE* I Theodorus 27; Teuffel 3 §442.3; S–H 4.2 §1085.

S: Diaz y Diaz (1982); Romanini's bibliography and introduction are extensive.

26. C. MARIUS VICTORINUS

Marius Victorinus is one of the few writers on grammar about whom we know anything independent of his own writings. He taught rhetoric in Rome in the middle of the fourth century; he is named together with Donatus in Jerome's *Chronicle* for the year 354 CE. He was successful and important enough to have his statue erected in the Forum of Trajan (the site of the rhetorical schools); he is also renowned for having converted to Christianity near the end of his life—but not so near that he could not write some tracts against Arianism, three hymns, and the first Latin commentaries on the epistles of Paul. In his earlier career he had translated and commented on the logical works of Porphyry and Aristotle.

But while his logical works were known and commended by Cassiodorus (in the first version of Book 2 of the *Institutiones*), they were largely replaced by (and incorporated in) the corresponding works of Boethius in the sixth century (which were recommended in Cassiodorus' second version), and no longer survive. Of his secular works three survive: a commentary on *De Inventione* (see 11.2.6 above); *Liber de definitionibus*, probably from his commentary on Cicero's *Topica* (see 11.2.7 above); and the beginning of his *Ars grammatica*, written earlier than the commentary on *De inventione*, which refers to it (238.16 Halm, on 1.30).

The surviving *Ars* is no more than the opening section of what was presumably a full grammar; as it is, it breaks off in the discussion of syllables and never reaches the parts of speech. In the manuscripts, it is followed with no indication of change of source (but with a clear lacuna at the join), by a work on meter which the subscription to the fourth and final book ascribes to Aelius Festus Apthonius (see 12.2 above). In at least one section (*De littera*), Victorinus uses many of the same phrases as his contemporary (and fellow-teacher in Rome) Donatus, but in a quite different order; almost certainly, the two were drawing on the same source (see Holtz 1981: 220–1), who is possibly also the Authority of the Charisius group.

Although not much survives of Marius Victorinus' grammar, its manner and concerns are distinctive and reflect what is known of his interests: the concern with definitions; the extended and idiosyncratic digression (1.4) on orthography; the frequent use of Greek terminology. The use at times of question-and-answer form and the repeated addresses to a second-person plural audience point to its use as a classroom text. It has relatively little in common with other school grammars: it is both more idiosyncratic and more original than many grammatical texts of its time. The long discussion of orthography, moreover, was known in the Renaissance much more widely than the full text of Marius Victorinus/Apthonius; it circulated as *Excerpta de orthographia*, and De Nonno (1988) lists twenty-one manuscripts—compared to the three earlier manuscripts of the complete text.

T: *GL* 6.1–31.16; Mariotti (1967; text and commentary).

R: *RE* Marius 70 (Wessner); *BNP* Marius 2.21 (Markschies); *PLRE* I Victorinus 11; *RLAC* (Drecoll); *LG* (Petrilli); Teuffel 3 §408; S–H 4.1 §828–31; *HLL* 5 §564. Note that many of these also discuss the grammatical writings attributed to Victorinus (12.45 below).

S: Jeep (1893: 83–5); Hadot (1971; 61–72 on *Ars*); Dahlmann (1970); De Nonno (2010).

On the *Excerpta de orthographia* see Keil (1874); De Nonno (1988).

27. MARTIANUS CAPELLA

Martianus Minneus Felix Capella (known as Felix or Felix Capella in his lifetime, but now known as Martianus Capella) was the author of two works of which we know: the large *De nuptiis Philologiae et Mercurii* and a short independent work on Latin metrics, identified by Mario de Nonno in 1990 but not yet published in full. That Martianus wrote in Africa, probably Carthage, is clear, but when he wrote is not: sometime in the fifth century, but whether before or after the Vandal conquest is a matter of dispute. My own inclination is to see him as writing in the 470s or 480s, closer to Fulgentius than to Augustine; for arguments in favor of an early or late fifth-century date, see, respectively, Cameron (1986) and Shanzer (1986: 5–28). Barnish (1986) favors the later date and locates Martianus in Rome rather than Africa.

De nuptiis is a gaudy work written in an astonishing style (not unlike that of Fulgentius). In form it is a Menippean satire, with alternating sections of prose and verse; in substance it is an account of the wedding of Mercury and the (now deified) Philology, in which, after the narrative of courtship and wedding, the seven liberal arts—identified clearly as such for the first time by Martianus and allegorically envisaged as handmaidens of philology—give accounts of themselves: Grammar (Book 3), Dialectic (4), Rhetoric (5), Geometry (6), Arithmetic (7), Astronomy (8), and Music (9). The work is valuable as a guide to knowledge of these fields in (more or less) the fifth century; the accounts themselves of the various disciplines are each heavily reliant on a few sources apiece and show few signs of original thought.

No full account of *De nuptiis* is offered here: it is only because of Book 3 that it is included here at all. After Martianus sets the allegorical scene (§221–8—paragraphs of Martianus are numbered sequentially through all nine books), Grammar gives a description of grammar (§229–31) followed by sections *de littera* (§232–61), *de syllaba* (§262–88, including a discussion of the prosody of final syllables, on which see now Jakobi 2014), and on the parts of speech (§289–325). She has barely gone through the noun and verb before being rudely interrupted in the final paragraph (§326), being warned not to talk about metrics because that belongs to Music.

In fact, metrics is not discussed by Music either, but it is the subject of the separate short treatise discovered by De Nonno (1990a) in Oxford, Bodleian Add. C 144, but not yet published. It is a fairly standard treatise of prototypical metrics, drawing a great deal from Servius, *De centum metris*, but marked by Martianus' own distinctive style, in this case including a dactylic poem in which each line is one syllable longer than the one before. There can be no doubt of its authenticity, as the author speaks of himself as Minneus and quotes verses from his own *De nuptiis*. It was clearly intended to fill in a subject that had somehow been omitted in the earlier work.

The bibliography given below is minimal and includes only editions and translations of the complete work, of Book 3, and (for meter) of Book 9; secondary literature is similarly limited. Discussion of the later commentary tradition on Martianus is beyond the scope of this volume, but there is a very rich set of glosses and commentaries from the ninth century. A good introduction to the medieval material in Teeuwen and O'Sullivan (2011); Italian translation of the commentaries in Ramelli (2006).

T: Willis (1983); Dick (1925/1978); Stahl et al. (1971–7; English translation); Cristante (1987; text of Book 9, with Italian translation and commentary); Diaz y Diaz (1995; Spanish translation of Book 3); Ramelli (2001; text, Italian translation, and notes); Zekl (2005; German translation); Guillaumin (2011; text of Book 9, with French translation and commentary). Copeland and Sluiter (2009: 151–66) give excerpts of Book 3 (grammar) and Book 5 (rhetoric) in Stahl's translation.

B: Wessner (1921: 131–6).

R: *RE* Martianus 2 (Wessner); *BNP* (Krapinger); *PLRE* II Capella; *RLAC* (Aris); *LG* (Casadio); Teuffel 3 §452; S–H 4.2 §1084.

S: Shanzer (1986); Cameron (1986); Barnish (1986); De Nonno (1990a, 2014); Grebe (2005); Jakobi (2014).

28. MARTYRIUS

The titles in the manuscripts of the treatise *De B muta et V vocali* give the author's name as *Adamantius sive Martyrius*; in the manuscripts of Cassiodorus he is variously called *Adamantius Martyrius* or *Martyrius*. As in the preface he refers to his father Adamantius who was also a grammarian, it is reasonable to assume that the name of the author of this treatise is Martyrius; in all probability, he wrote in the sixth century CE, and he may well have been from Sardis.

Martyrius' work is unique in concentrating on a single orthographic problem; the distinction between b and v is indeed problematic and is revealed not only by numerous manuscript errors but by the phonological development of the Romance languages. Martyrius (165.9–6.2) is aware of his originality. His division of the subject also seems original: his discussion of nouns is broken into sections on initial, medial, and final syllables, and each of those categories is divided into open and closed syllables. This might suggest that his organization is dependent not on the orthographic tradition, but on the treatises on prosody *de finalibus* (on which see 8.4b above and 12.46.7 below); he also seems to have employed a bilingual glossary. His discussion of the verb is far briefer and less thoroughly anatomized.

Martyrius' work survives as an independent text in Naples, Lat. IV A 11 (on which see 12.42 below); there is also a copy made by Politian (Munich, Clm 766). The earlier Bobbio manuscript from which the Naples text was copied does not survive. The bulk of Martyrius' work was also preserved by Cassiodorus as sections 5–8 of his *De orthographia* (see 12.11.2 above), with quite a few changes, on which see Stoppacci (2010: cxl–lxv).

T: *GL* 7.165–99 (lower half of the page, beneath the parallel text of Cassiodorus).

R: *RE* Martyrios 23 (Wessner); *BNP* (Gatti); *PLRE* II Adamantius 3, Martyrius 6 (treating father and son as co-authors); Kaster (1988) #95; Teuffel 3 §472.6; S–H 4.2 §1109.

S: Pugliarello (2005); Biville (2011).

29. METRORIUS

The name is attached to some forms of the treatise *De finalibus*, but is almost certainly not genuine. See 12.46.7 below.

30. PALAEMON

The *ars grammatica* of the first-century Remmius Palaemon does not survive, although passages from his work are preserved by Charisius (see 4.3, 8.2, 8.6 above). On the other hand, the *Regulae* under his name is definitely not by him: it is a very elementary text about the six declinable parts of speech (including prepositions, as they are considered subject to declension in that they are followed by one or another case of the noun), guiding the novice Latinist towards finding one form of an inflected word when confronted with another. Its last sentence (*GL* 5.547.2) sends the reader to continue with a full-fledged *ars*. Like the closely related but fuller *Regulae* attached to the name of Augustine (see 12.8 above), this text does not know the now standard declensions of nouns: like Donatus, it begins from the ablative singular, although some renaissance interpolations add the use of the genitive singular. Unlike Ps.-Augustine, Ps.-Palaemon gives very few illustrative quotations and does not give full paradigms. For verbs, the author describes only the present tense.

The text was widely known in the fifteenth century, and it was believed at one time that Pontano, who discovered it in 1460, had actually written it. The subsequent discovery of two earlier medieval manuscripts disposed of that theory, but it was obviously no more composed by Remmius Palaemon in the first century than by Pontano in the fifteenth. Like other works of its type, it is a product of the fifth century or later. The text has three forms: the original text is found in the two medieval manuscripts, while the renaissance witnesses all share a number of interpolations, and one subset of the renaissance manuscripts also abridges the text drastically. The only critical edition is that of Rosellini; she prints the original text on the right-hand page and the altered versions on the left, as well as providing a full and useful commentary. Other texts are sometimes attached to Palaemon's name; these include a metrical text also attributed to Victorinus (see 12.45 below); a set of *differentiae* (see 10.4.2b above); and the medieval Donatus commentary *Aggressus quidam* (see 15.32 below).

T: *GL* 5.533–47; Rosellini (2001; with commentary).
R: *RE* Remmius 4 (Wessner); Teuffel 2 §282.3; S–H 2 §475. All these concern the real Palaemon, but give some notice of the pseudepigrapha.
S: Rosellini (1998, 2000); Holford-Strevens (2003).

31. PALLADIUS

The grammarian Palladius receives no rubric or mention in *L'Année philologique*, and for a good reason: he is a zombie brought to life by P. L. Schmidt in *HLL* 5. The name of Palladius appears only in the title of the grammatical work of Audax, *De Scauri et Palladii libris excerpta per interrogationem et responsionem*. Both sources of Audax are problematic (see 8.5 and 12.7 above and 12.39 below), but it is generally agreed that everything in Audax up to the lacuna at *GL* 7.349.8 can be assigned to Scaurus, and that therefore what follows belongs to Palladius. That consists of six sections:

a) *De coniunctione* (349.9–51.23), closely parallel to Probus, *Instituta artium* 4.143.23–5.37;
b) *De praepositione* (351.24–5.29), closely parallel to Probus, *Instituta artium* 4.147.4–50.26;
c) *De interiectione* (356.1–7.12), closely parallel to Probus, *Instituta artium* 4.146.1–7.1;
d) *Recapitulatio de accentibus* (357.13–61.12), with no parallel in Probus;
e) *De barbarismo* (361.13–2.21), possibly from Victorinus (see 12.45 below);
f) A section *De soloecismo*, not printed by Keil (cf. *GL* 7.315) but again possibly from Victorinus.

From the first three sections, Schmidt concluded that what we now have as Probus, *Instituta artium*, was in fact written by Palladius rather than Probus; and from the fact that in the extant text of Probus, *Instituta artium*, there are a great many references forward (always using either *tractare debe'a'mus* or *tractabimus*) to sections *in metris vel structuris, in metris, in sonis, in metris propter sonos, in orthographia*, and *in accentibus*, he further inferred not just that Probus planned to write another book of his *Instituta*, but that Palladius in fact had written one and that chapters (d)–(f) came from that. Hence, in Schmidt's version of the history of Latin grammatical writing, Probus' *Instituta artium* is now the work of Palladius.

Schmidt's argument has little relationship to the facts. In the first place, each of the three sections (a)–(c) is longer in Palladius than in Probus; indeed, at the end of the section *De praepositione* there is a citation from the elder Pliny (7.355.20) not included in *IA*. Secondly, the three sections are in a different order in the two works. Thus, even in the few sections where they are related, Probus is not identical to Palladius. Finally, the fact that Audax has rewritten both Scaurus and Palladius as question-and-answer catechism means, at the very least, that exact correspondence is not to be expected.

All this does not mean that the *Instituta artium* attributed to a Probus is not related to a comparable work by a Palladius, but it does mean that the two are not the same, nor do we really know which came first. There is a *terminus post quem* of c. 305 CE for Probus, as the text refers to the Baths of Diocletian (4.119.26), but the person who wrote then could be either Probus or Palladius. Palladius may have written two or more books of an *ars grammatica*—but the fact that Probus meant to write another book says nothing about Palladius. What the relationship among these texts shows is precisely what we already knew and might expect: that grammatical texts are tralatitious; that subsequent writers of *artes* borrow from their predecessors, often changing the form and perhaps the wording; and that while some of them retain the name of their model as author, while changing the text, others give a revised text their own name. "Probus," as is universally recognized, is a name that attracts grammatical texts, but it is also (see Dionisotti 1984: 206) a fairly common name in late antiquity; it may even be that men named "Probus" were attracted to grammar because they shared a name with Valerius Probus.

T: (Excerpts in Audax, *GL* 7.349.9–57.12.)

R: *RE* Palladius 4 (Aly); *BNP* Palladius 1.4 (Gatti); Kaster (1988) #242; *HLL* 5 §522.4.

32. PAPIRIUS (PAPIRIANUS, PAPERINUS)

Cassiodorus (see 12.11.2 above) includes excerpts from a work of Papirianus *De orthographia* in his book of the same title; this Papirianus probably wrote in the fifth century. He is possibly the same person as Q. Papirius, a fragment of whose work *De orthographia* is also printed by Keil. Whether or not he is the same person as the Paperinus or Papirinus cited by various Irish grammarians, including Donatus Ortigraphus, Malsachanus, Ps.-Clemens, and the *Ars Bernensis*, is less certain: that work is cited by Politian (who quotes only about 10 percent of what he found in a manuscript from Bobbio) as *De analogia*, and it consists of excerpts from Martianus Capella and Diomedes (with other material the source of which is unidentified) and cannot have been written much before the end of the fifth century, and possibly considerably later.

T: *GL* 7.158.9–65.6 (Papirianus); *GL* 7.216.8–14 (Papirius); *AH* cclii–iii (with a correction by Collignon 1883: 16); Pesenti 1917: 77–85 (Paperinus/Papirinus).

R: *PLRE* I Papirianus 2; Kaster (1988) #244; Teuffel 3 §472.5; S–H 4.2 §1108.

S: Keil (1868: 15n.); Taeger (1978) with earlier bibliography.

33. PHOCAS

Phocas' *Ars de nomine et verbo* is of the *regulae* type, and offers instruction on the two most important parts of speech. His advice on the noun is divided into what he thinks of as the two most important problems, gender and declension. After a brief discussion of monosyllabic nouns, he goes through Latin nouns by ending, assigning them to the proper genders and declensions (he is aware of all five), then discusses Latinized Greek nouns in a similar fashion, concentrating almost exclusively on proper names. In explaining the verb, the problems he emphasizes are the identification of a verb's conjugation (he knows three, with the fourth being either a separate group or described as *tertia producta*) and the formation of the perfect system. His prefaces make it clear that Phocas is not sanguine about the attention span of his students: he has therefore written as briefly as possible, *concinna brevitate*, to diminish the expected boredom of the young. For a discussion of his methods and sources, see Casaceli (1973: 11–23).

The *Ars* was an extremely popular text in the Carolingian period, and it is preserved in no fewer than fifteen witnesses from the eighth and ninth centuries. It received commentaries from Remigius of Auxerre and an unknown "Cornutus" of roughly the same period and location who seems to use (or to adapt) Remigius: for details, see the full account in Jeudy (1974b). The manuscripts describe Phocas as *grammaticus*, and the sole manuscript of his Life of Virgil (Paris, Lat. 8093) describes him as *grammaticus urbis Romae*; there is no reason to doubt this description. That the two genuine works by Phocas are by the same author is revealed by their taste for versifying: six stanzas of Sapphics precede the hexameter life of Virgil, and six elegiac couplets precede the (prose) treatise on the noun and verb. There are also two pseudonymous works, both considerably later: *Orthografia*, according to Sabbadini, between the eleventh and thirteenth centuries, *De aspiratione* in the fifteenth, probably in or near Milan, according to Jeudy (1976).

Phocas' date is disputed. Strzelecki, Casaceli, and Mazhuga favor a date in the early third century because Cassiodorus (*GL* 7.214) and some other late sources place him before Donatus. On the other hand, his life of Virgil apparently uses Donatus' life (denied by those who favor an early date), his citations of Lucan and Juvenal point to a date no earlier than the late fourth century (see Wessner 1929), and his use of *Petrus* (*GL* 5.423.20) as an example of Greek nouns in –os that do not change to –er suggests a relatively late date as well. Casaceli compromises on the late third or early fourth century. A balanced review of the evidence in Kaster; on the whole, a later date seems more likely.

T: a) *Ars de nomine et verbo*: *GL* 5.410–39; Casaceli (1973);
b) (spurious) *De aspiratione*: *GL* 5.439–41; Jeudy (1976: 212–15);
c) (spurious) *Orthografia*: Sabbadini (1900: 537–41);
d) *Vita Vergilii*: see 11.3.8 above.

R: *RE* Phocas (Strzelecki); *BNP* Phocas (Focas) (Schmidt); *PLRE* I Phocas, II Phocas 3; Kaster (1988) #121; Teuffel 3 §472.4; S–H 4.2 §1106.

S: Sabbadini (1900); Jeudy (1974b, 1976); Mazhuga (2003).

34. POMPEIUS

Pompeius' detailed (and unlemmatized) commentary on Donatus' *Ars maior* was written for other teachers to use (see Kaster 1988: 152–68; Zago's objections are unconvincing) and is one of the very few grammatical texts that actually demonstrates classroom technique, complete with much repetition and some local references; and as it clearly is a verbatim (or near verbatim) record of a teacher at work, taken down by a *notarius*, it is pretty much unreadable as a written text: "Pour saisir la valeur de ce course, il faut le lire à haute voix, avec ses redites, ses hésitations, ses à-peu-près, ses vulgarismes, toutes chose choquantes, décourageantes à la fois pour les copistes . . . et pour l'éditeur" (Holtz 1981: 236). The text as printed by Keil, from very few manuscripts, is poorly edited and is missing the opening of the preface, which is found in only two manuscripts and printed by Holtz (1971). Holtz (2005a) promises a new edition.

The history of Pompeius' commentary, as Holtz has reconstructed it, provides an excellent illustration of the transmission of a great many grammatical texts. Written in Africa, it was used in Spain early in the seventh century by Isidore of Seville (in an augmented form: see Fontaine 1959: 192–4) and late in the century by Iulianus of Toledo (in the form known to us). In Italy, it was used at Bobbio by the author of *Anonymus ad Cuimnanum* in the early eighth century (see Bischoff and Löfstedt 1992: 18), while at Monte Cassino, a mixture of Pompeius and Iulianus of Toledo appears in Paris, Lat. 7530, written at the end of that century (cf. Holtz 1975: 133–5). Pompeius' commentary was popular in Insular contexts (both in Northumbria and on the Continent) from the seventh century until the early ninth; it was copied in Northumbria in the eighth century and was at the abbey of Murbach by around 800, before going out of fashion around 825. See also 8.7 above.

T: *GL* 5.95–312; Holtz (1971: 59–60; Preface); Zago (2017; Commentary on *Ars maior* Book 3).

R: *RE* Pompeius 143 (Helm); *BNP* Pompeius 3.1 (Schmidt); *PLRE* II Pompeius 1; Law (1982: 16–17); Kaster (1988) #125; Teuffel 3 §472.2; S–H 4.2 §1102.

S: Jeep (1893: 43–55); Holtz (1971, 2005a); Schindel (1975: 19–33, 101–14); Kaster (1988: 139–68); De Nonno (2010: esp. 178–85); Zago (2010).

35. PRISCIAN

Priscian's place of origin was probably Caesarea in Mauretania (rather than Caesarea in Palestine), but his career as a grammarian was in Constantinople: his teacher, whom he cites, was Theoctistus (Kaster 1988 #149) and his pupils included the grammarian Eutyches (12.22 above) and the scribe Theodorus (*PLRE* II Theodorus 63), whose subscriptions in the manuscripts of Priscian's *Ars* date it with precision to 526–7 CE. Aside from the great *Ars* (the correct title of Priscian's work, not *Institutiones grammaticae*; see most recently and thoroughly De Nonno 2009: 250–9), Priscian's extant works include a panegyric, *De laude Anastasii*, written probably in 503 (see Cameron 1974), and a translation of the geographical poem of Dionysius Periegetes (neither included here) as well as five grammatical works: a group of three short treatises dedicated as a group to Q. Aurelius Memmius Symmachus, certainly written before Symmachus' execution in 526 and possibly (given that his titles are not mentioned) even before his consulate in 485: *De figuris numerorum quos antiquissimi habent codices, De metris fabularum Terentii et aliorum comicorum*, and *Praeexercitamina*. After the *Ars*, there are two further works: *Institutio de nomine, pronomine et verbo* and *Partitiones xii versuum Aeneidos principalium*. There are also pseudepigraphic works (see below). The *Ars* itself was not widely used before the early ninth century, but the *Institutio* (a summary of the forms of the inflected parts of speech, classifying nouns by declension and verbs by conjugation) was widely copied, used, and modified in the early Middle Ages; it was commented on by Remigius and others, and served as a basis for numerous treatises on the declensions, including one copied by Walahfrid Strabo in St. Gallen 878 (see 13.31 below) and one in the form of a dialogue between teacher and student in Oxford, Bodleian Add. C 144 (see Jeudy 1972 and Passalacqua 1993, both including catalogues of manuscripts). Like the *Institutio*, the *Partitiones* was very popular, and its opening paragraphs (known as *prima pagina*) were commented on by Remigius and others, including Walahfrid Strabo (Jeudy 1971). A biography of Priscian found in Bern A 90 (s. xi) is printed by Hagen, *AH* clxviii–ix.

See 8.8 above for further discussion.

T: a) *De figuris numerorum quos antiquissimi habent codices, De metris fabularum Terentii et aliorum comicorum*, and *Praeexercitamina*: *GL* 3.405–40; Passalacqua (1987: 3–49); *RLM* 551–60 (*Praeex*. only); Miller (in Miller et al. 1973: 52–76; English translation of *Praeex*.). Note that Passalacqua's text of *De figuris numerorum* rightly follows the order of the oldest manuscript, Paris, Lat. 7530, while Keil prints the arrangement found in the other manuscripts.

b) *Ars*: *GL* 2.2.1–3.377 (edited by M. Hertz). The Groupe *Ars grammatica* has undertaken a revised text (based on Hertz) and new French translation of the *Ars*. To date: Book 15, *De adverbio* (Baratin et al. 2005); Books 14–16 (Baratin et al. 2013, incorporating Baratin et al. 2005); Book 17 (Baratin et al. 2010). Yanes (2017) and Rosellini (2015) have published a new edition of Book 18 in two parts. The text and German translation of Book 14 by Schönberger (2008) is far less helpful; I have not seen his other translations (Schönberger 2009, 2010a, 2010b: Books 12–13, 16, and 17, respectively). Brief excerpts from the dedicatory letter and Books 1, 2, and 17 are translated by Copeland and Sluiter (2009: 171–85).

c) *Institutio de nomine, pronomine et verbo*, and *Partitiones xii versuum Aeneidos principalium*. *GL* 3.441–515; Passalacqua (1999: 5–41, 45–128). Brief excerpt of *Partitiones* translated by Copeland and Sluiter (2009: 186–9).

I: García Román et al. (1999, 2001, 2003; *Ars* 17–18, 1–16, and *Opera minora*, respectively).

B: Wessner (1908: 129–32, 1921: 142–7).

R: RE Priscianus 1 (Helm); BNP (Schmidt) PLRE II Priscianus 2; LG (Baratin); Law (1982: 20–1, 86–91); Kaster (1988) #126; Teuffel 3 §481; S–H 4.2 §1111–15.

C: Baratin et al. (2009); Martorelli (2014).

S: a) On the *Ars* and on Priscian in general: Jeep (1893: 89–97); Courcelle (1969: 322–30); Passalacqua (1978); Baratin (1989, 2005, 2014); Ballaira (1989); Luhtala (2005, 2009); De Nonno (2009); Ferri (2014).
b) On minor works: *De figuris numerorum*: Garcea (2013) with further bibliography. *Partitiones Duodecim Versuum Aeneidos Principalium*: Glück (1967).

Spurious works:

1. *De accentibus*

Priscian once (3.133.1–2) refers to a work on accents: . . . *nomina, de quibus in libro, qui est de accentibus, latius tractavimus*. That may be why the work *De accentibus* was attached to his name, but it is certainly not his. The work deals to some extent with accents (meaning both stress in words and the physical signs that guide reading, which include long and short marks, rough and smooth breathings, and hyphens as well as accents proper), but it is more a guide to pronunciation. The author's method is to go through each of the parts of speech (in which his order is a mixture of Priscian and Donatus), divided by final syllable, and discussing the quantity of the penultimate syllable (which determines the accent). It uses one of the treatises *De finalibus*, probably Servius', and seems to have one source shared with Isidore and another with Iulianus of Toledo. It may have been written in northern Spain at the very end of the seventh century or the beginning of the eighth, or it may have been written by someone who beat a timely retreat towards the north from the Arab invasion of Spain in the same period.

T: *GL* 3.519–28; Schönberger (2010c; text and German translation); Giammona (2012; text, Italian translation, commentary).

2. *Scalprum Prisciani*

According to Martianus Capella §224, *Grammatica* carries with her a *scalprum* designed to cut away faults of speech (*vitia linguarum*) from infants. That seems to have been the source for the name of *Scalprum Prisciani*, a parsing grammar (see 13.47 below) preserved in five manuscripts of s. xi–xii. Its original title was *Excerptum*; it did not become the *Scalprum Prisciani* until the twelfth century. Its origin is no earlier than the late ninth century.

Unpublished; see Jeudy (1982–3) and *LG* (Jeudy).

3. *Excerptiones de Prisciano*

This set of excerpts, taken from both the *Ars* and the *Institutio* (as well as from some other texts, including Donatus, and supplemented at the end with selections from Isidore), is a basic grammar, compiled in the tenth century. It may have been compiled by Aelfric; it was certainly used by him in the composition of his own Latin grammar in English.

T: Porter (2002; with English translation and source notes).

S: Law (1997: 200–23).

36. PROBUS

The name "Probus" (sometimes "Valerius Probus") is attached to a great many texts, including grammars, commentaries, and glossaries. M. Valerius Probus is a genuinely important figure of the late first century CE, the subject of the last biography in Suetonius, *De grammaticis* (c. 24), but almost everything authentic of that Probus is fragments, while most of the texts that come with the name Probus were written much later. It is perfectly possible that one or more of them was written by someone else named Probus, but we have no way to know that and no real reason to care. Of the texts described here, it should not be assumed that any two are by the same person. For disambiguation, Kaster (1988) #127 gives a convenient list of five grammarians named Probus, with bibliography; of early discussions, see particularly *GL* 4.ix–xxxi and Steup (1871). Pugliarello (2014) summarizes, but adds little.

1. M. Valerius Probus of Berytus

There are many fragments of Valerius Probus, both grammatical observations and quotations from his commentaries on Virgil and Terence. Suetonius (*DGR* 24.4) reports of his writings: *nimis pauca et exigua de quibusdam minutis quaestiunculis edidit; reliquit autem non mediocrem silvam observationum sermonis antiqui*. As a result, there is much discussion but little certainty; a list of works attributed to Valerius Probus is given by Kaster (1995: 267–9). Baratin (1989: 186–201) has advanced persuasive arguments for attributing to Probus the short text on syntax entitled *De coniunctione temporum* (Diomedes *GL* 1.388.11–91.29; see 12.18 above), but certainty is impossible. One text that should be attributed to him is the collection of abbreviations known as *De litteris singularibus* (*GL* 4.271–6; see 10.4.6c[i] above); on Probus in general, see 4.3 above. It is unlikely that the quotations from "Probus" (or "Valerius") found in various early medieval insular grammars should be taken as genuine, but it is not impossible; see Taeger (1991) and 12.18 above.

T: The fragments are collected by Aistermann (1910) and Velaza (2005); the latter has more current bibliography and fuller apparatus, but is far less critical.

B: Wessner (1902: 133–6, 1921: 78–88).

R: *RE* Probus 26 (Helm), Valerius 315 (Hanslik); *BNP* Probus 4 (Schmidt); *PIR*[2] V176; *LG* (Desbordes and Garcea); Teuffel 2 §300.1–4; S–H 2 §477–9. Many of these include discussion of the various later Probuses.

S: Of recent scholarship, note particularly Jocelyn (1984–5); Timpanaro (1986: 77–127, 2001: 37–105); Delvigo (1987, 1990). Kaster (1995: 242–69) supplies balanced discussion and further bibliography.

2. *Catholica*

Probus, *Catholica* (more properly *De catholicis*; see De Nonno 1983b: 388, n.2) is almost identical to Sacerdos Book 2 (see 12.38 below), except that the text in Probus is in much better condition and preserves the opening of the book

(*GL* 4.3.1–6.24), which is missing from the text of Sacerdos. Each text can be supplemented from the other, and there can be little doubt that each represents a modification of the original text of Sacerdos. As a result, *Catholica* can be no earlier than the beginning of the fourth century. *Catholica* is cited under Probus' name by Servius (on *Aen.* 2.15) and must therefore have existed under his name by the early fifth century; it should, however, be noted that Servius several times elsewhere cites from Probus material that is not found in *Catholica*.

Catholica is about inflection. The author begins by summarizing noun declensions, identifying genitives and normal paradigms of each; he then discusses nominal declensions in full, first reminding the reader of the possible nominative endings of each declension and then going through a twenty-five-page list (more than half the whole work) of nominative endings, not divided by declension but in alphabetical order, with nouns ending in –r and –s subdivided into further alphabetical lists of syllables with those final consonants, and matching each ending with the possible genitive endings appropriate to it. After mentioning monosyllables—always treated as a separate category in discussions of nouns—he then briefly divides up nouns and pronouns in terms of the number of distinct case endings they have (indeclinables have only one form, words like *cornu* have two singular forms, *bellum* has three, up to *nullus* and other pronouns which have six). The subsequent treatment of verbs is much briefer: a summary of the conjugations is followed by a list of verbs in terms of the letter which precedes the final –o, then more briefly verbs ending in –or. The last few pages turn to a very different subject, clausulae (*De structura*); the author intends the discussion to complement his treatment of metrical feet in his (lost) first book.

The text is preserved in a fifth-century portion of the composite manuscript Naples, Lat. 2 (on which see De Nonno [1982: xviii–xxxii]; the four sections were not bound together until the Renaissance); it is also partially preserved in Paris, Lat. 7520 (originally part of Bern 207; see 9.4 above). De Nonno (1983b: 389–90) rightly observes that Keil seriously undervalued this witness.

T: *GL* 4.3–43.

R: *RE* Probus 26 (Helm); Kaster (1988) #127; Teuffel 2 §300.6(1).

S: De Nonno (1983b); Simoni (1988).

See also on Sacerdos, 12.38 below.

3. *Instituta artium*

As discussed elsewhere (see 8.5, 12.31 above), it is clear that the *Instituta artium* (*IA*) attached to the name of Probus is closely related to a grammar by one Palladius; in all probability, Probus' work is a slight revision of Palladius'—which we know only from the extracts attributed to him by Audax. Some form of this text—but we cannot really say which—can be dated to roughly 305 CE by a reference to the Baths of Diocletian at *GL* 4.119.26. Internal references that look forward show that there was, or was intended to be, a second book, dealing above all with sounds and meters; there is also a prospective reference to a section *de orthographia*. None of this survives, unless perhaps in parts of the *Appendix Probi*, on which see below. The extant text has a distinctive style, carefully analyzed by Barwick (see below, on *Appendix Probi*): the author repeats certain phrases very frequently and has an almost formulaic structure.

Instituta artium is a basic grammar, comparable in content to the first two books of Donatus, *Ars maior*. After initial sections *De voce* and *De arte* (which includes subsections on analogy and anomaly, and which should probably precede *De voce*) come chapters on letters, syllables, and the parts of speech, followed by the eight parts of speech: what is surprising is that adverb and verb come at the end, after the indeclinables. As usual, the noun requires more than half the entire treatise, and the analysis in *IA* has some similarity to that of Donatus, although far less succinct and far less well organized. Like Donatus, *IA* begins declension from the ablative; like him, he divides nouns by gender rather than declension. But where Donatus has six accidents, *IA* has eight (adding *accentus* and *ordo*, meaning base form, derivative, and diminutive); *IA* divides his explanations of inflection very confusingly, dealing with comparison (by gender and ending) before he gets to the case system. The account of the noun ends with the declension of some specific words, followed by a long set of notes on particular oddities in the usage of authors, each beginning *quaeritur*. Almost certainly, this comes from a treatise on *Latinitas*.

Keil edited the text from two manuscripts: Naples, Lat. 1 and Lindemann's transcript of a manuscript from the Vatican used by Mai, but not found by Keil. It was identified by Lindsay in 1927 as Vatican, Urbinas Lat. 1154, an elegant uncial manuscript written in northern Italy with marginalia in a script very much like that of the marginalia in the palimpsest of Fronto. It seems probable that a new edition is needed. The end of the text in Naples Lat. 1 has a subscription: VTERE FELIX LAPPADI MERCVRI SCRIPTOR CVM PATRONIS GAVDE.

T: *GL* 4.47–192.

R: Teuffel 2 §300.5; *HLL* 5 §522.4.

S: Lindsay (1927a).

4. *Appendix Probi*

Following the text of Probus, *Instituta artium* in Naples, Lat. 1, there is a group of short texts on grammatical subjects. Keil gave this collection the title *Appendix Probi* (the earlier edition of Eichenfeld and Endlicher had called it *Appendix ad Probi artem minorem*). It was evidently (De Nonno 2007) copied in the late seventh or early eighth century (probably at Bobbio, where the manuscript was preserved, but see Lo Monaco 2007) as a single unit together with *Instituta artium*. At times scholars have thought that the *Appendix* was in origin a set of excerpts from the otherwise missing second book of *IA*, but that seems unlikely. The *Appendix* consists of the following:

1. A list of nouns, classified primarily by gender and ablative ending (193.1–6.12);
2. Three short sections on nouns: a list of nominal constructions, organized by case (196.13–7.6; see 10.4.5b[ii]f above); a paragraph on nouns (largely names or Greek borrowings) listed by the length of the penultimate syllable (197.7–14); and a short list of masculine nouns (197.15–18);[5]
3. A list of *orthographica* (197.19–9.17);
4. A list of *differentiae* (199.18–203.34): *Inter austrum et ostrum* (see 10.4.2[c] above);
5. A list of deponent verbs and a very fragmentary discussion of passive and common verbs (203.35–4.6).

Of these five short texts, section 3 has attracted by far the most attention, as it has considerable importance as evidence for the changing pronunciation of late Latin. Of the five, moreover, it is the only portion that does not seem to have any stylistic resemblance to the *Instituta artium* which it follows in the manuscript. Each section of the *Appendix* shows some relationship to standard categories of grammatical writing: the first is *de nomine*, a necessary part of discussions of the parts of speech; the second is (so Barnett 2006) a collection of comparisons of Latin with (omitted) Greek—*idiomata casuum*, what Barnett calls *idiomata accentuum*, and *idiomata generis*; the third, independent of its linguistic importance, is (so Powell 2007) a tract *de orthographia*; the fourth is a set of *differentiae*; and the fifth is part of a treatise *de verbo*. Three of the sections have links with other grammatical texts: section 2 was almost certainly used by *Anonymus ad Cuimnanum* (see 13.33 below) in the early eighth century (at Bobbio?); the first twenty-six items of section 4 appear as a separate text under the name of Valerius Probus in Montpellier 306, a manuscript of glossaries (on which see 9.4 above); and section 5 also appears in the fifth-century grammar of Cledonius (5.56K; 12.14 above). There is more than one possible explanation for these connections, but such varied links suggest that these were not originally a single text, but have merely come together by chance.

T: *GL* 4.193–204; Asperti and Passalacqua (2014), including a DVD with detailed pictures of the manuscript. There are two simultaneous diplomatic transcriptions of section 3 by Asperti (2007) and Powell (2007), and a separate edition of section 4 by Stok (1997).

B: *CGL* has a helpful bibliography of older scholarship; Asperti and Passalacqua (2014) has a huge bibliography.

5. Some scholars divide section 2 into two parts (196.13–7.6 and 197.7–18), thus increasing the numbering of the successive sections by one; so Barwick (1919: 409) and De Nonno (2007: 21), the latter based on the layout of the text in the manuscript. That may be codicologically correct, but the numbering into five sections is traditional and thus is kept here.

R: Teuffel 2 §300.6(3).
C: Lo Monaco and Molinelli (2007); several articles are cited individually here.
S: Barwick (1919); Quirk (2006); Barnett (2006, 2007); De Nonno (2007); Lo Monaco (2007); Passalacqua (2007); Powell (2007, 2011).

5. [Valerius Probus] *De nomine*

This set of extracts about nouns is attributed in the manuscript (Naples, Lat. 1) to Valerius Probus. It probably derives, perhaps at several removes, from the second-century treatise of Flavius Caper, *De Latinitate*, an important source for many later grammatical works, and, through Caper, from the Elder Pliny's *Dubii Sermonis Libri*; it shares some very rare quotations with Charisius 1.15, a chapter derived in part from Caper. In its present form, the fragment is no earlier than the fourth century, and may well have been written by someone named Probus—perhaps, given some similarities, by the same Probus who wrote the *Instituta artium*.
T: *GL* 4.207–16; Passalacqua (1984: 61–74).
R: Teuffel 2 §300.6(2).
S: Beck (1893); Fröhde (1893); Dionisotti (1984).

This text is listed also as 12.46.4d.

6. *De ultimis syllabis*

Not attributed to Probus until the sixteenth century; discussed at 12.46.6 below.
And more: see 11.3.5 on Ps.-Probus' commentary on Virgil and 11.10 on *Probus Vallae* on Juvenal.

37. RUFINUS

Frequently preserved in conjunction with one or more works of Priscian, the text ascribed to Rufinus of Antioch is a very strange thing. The title is given as *Commentarium Rufini V.D. grammatici Antiochensis in metra Terentiana* (with one of the earlier manuscripts expanding *V.D.* to *Viri Disertissimi* and another substituting *V.C.*), and the first part of the text (*GL* 6.554.4–65.8) is indeed a set of excerpts from grammarians and metrical writers about comic meter. But with no break, the manuscripts then continue with a discussion about prose rhythm (565.9–78.8) for which d'Alessandro supplies the title *De compositione et de numeris oratorum*; like the first part, it consists of a set of excerpts, many of them from Cicero, ending abruptly with a quotation from *Ad Herennium*.

The peculiarities of this text are well discussed by d'Alessandro in the preface to his edition, but they remain peculiar. In the first place, the combination of texts on two quite different subjects without indication of a break: there is clearly something wrong. Secondly, the discussion of Terentian meter ends (565.1–6) with a list of authorities (matching the sources quoted in the text) who have believed that Terence, Plautus, and the other early poets wrote in meter, followed (565.7–8) by a couplet by Rufinus:

Haec ego Rufinus collegi mente benigna
discipulisque dedi munera pulchra libens.

No such summary or epigram concludes the discussion of prose rhythm, although it begins with a poem by Rufinus about the subject. Indeed, both halves of the text are interspersed with poems by Rufinus, but unlike the epigram closing the first half, the others are generally introduced by a title in the third person, e.g., *Versus Rufini grammatici de metris Terentii et Plauti et ceterorum* (558.7); *Versus Rufini v.c. litteratoris de numeris et pedibus oratorum* (565.9, 566.6); *De Theophrasto idem Rufinus metro sapphico sic* (567.31). These imply that the text was assembled by a later editor.

The fact that many of Rufinus' verses match in content the excerpts from earlier authorities suggests that what we possess is Rufinus' notes and drafts for a poem or poems on these subjects, circulated by a devoted follower or descendant; but that is no more than speculation. Rufinus' reading is wide, and what he preserves is often unique or otherwise significant: he knows Euanthius, Servius, the commentaries of Asper on Terence and Scaurus and Sisenna on Plautus, and he also cites Terentianus Maurus, Charisius, Diomedes, and Donatus. On the other hand, his excerpting is peculiar: more than once he cites virtually the same text from different authors (e.g., Victorinus [actually Apthonius, see 12.2 above] 556.23–7.13 ~ Lactantius 564.7–20; Diomedes 555.5–10 = Charisius 555.16–21), again suggesting that what survives is not a finished work.

T: *GL* 6.554–78; d'Alessandro (2004, with long introduction); I. Thomson in Miller et al. (1973: 37–51; English translation of poems on prose rhythm).

R: *RE* Suppl. 5 Rufinus 39 (Wessner); *BNP* Rufinus 2.2 (Gatti); *PLRE* I Rufinus 8; Kaster (1988) #130; Teuffel 3 §445.5; S–H 4.2 §1104.

38. SACERDOS

Sacerdos (Marius Plotius Sacerdos correctly in the manuscripts of Book 3, M. Claudius Sacerdos in the manuscript of 1–2) is the author of the earliest extant grammatical treatise, with the title *Artes grammaticae*, in three books; it was clearly, at one or more removes, a source for Charisius and other later writers. The first book contains the theoretical sections on sounds, letters, syllables, words, and metrical quantities and feet, the parts of speech, and the *vitia et virtutes orationis*—the material of the three books of Donatus' *Ars maior*. Book 2 contains *catholica* (basic paradigms of noun and verb) followed by a brief discussion of prose rhythm. The third book is an account of metrics.

Of the three books, only the third (preserved separately from the other two) is complete, if very poorly transmitted; Keil edited it from three ninth-century manuscripts. The first two books are preserved in a portion of Naples, Lat. 2 (foll. 112–39) written in the fifth century; it is badly damaged and now consists of three quaternions numbered III, IV, and VI followed by half of a fourth. Assuming that the original text began at the start of a lost quaternion I (not a necessary assumption, to be sure), we are missing more than half of Book 1 as well as nearly half of Book 2. Part of the gap in Book 2 (the missing fifth quaternion) has been filled: fragments of the manuscript were identified and transcribed by De Nonno (1983b). As has long been recognized, however, another version of Book 2 is preserved as the *Catholica* ascribed to Probus (12.36.2 above); it is clear that neither one is a completely accurate representation of what Sacerdos wrote.

Sacerdos is generally dated to the late third century; the dedication to the third book (the only book opening to survive) records that the first book (*Instituta artis*) was dedicated to Sacerdos' friend Gaianus V.C., the second to Gaianus' father Uranius V.C., and the third to Maximus and Simplicius, none of them otherwise known. The separate dedications suggest that he composed them separately, although the plural *artes* is probably not significant. Orlandi's attempt to identify Sacerdos with a senator named on a block from the Colosseum is doubtful.

T: *GL* 6.427–546; De Nonno (1983b: 401–9; material lost between 475.26 and 476.1).

B: Wessner (1921: 108–15; on Probus as well as Sacerdos);

R: *RE* Plotius 17 (Dahlmann), Sacerdos 3 (Wessner); *BNP* Plotius 2.5 (Schmidt); *PLRE* I Sacerdos 3; Kaster (1988) #132; *LG* (Petrilli); Teuffel 3 §394; S–H 3 §604–5; *HLL* 5 §522.3.

S: De Nonno (1983b); Simoni (1988, 1990); Orlandi (2001).

39. SCAURUS

Q. Terentius Scaurus was, according to Aulus Gellius 11.15.3, *diui Hadriani temporibus grammaticus uel nobilissimus*—a rare accolade from someone who is generally scornful of grammarians. Gellius' praise may well have been deserved; Scaurus' *Ars grammatica* was very influential in the shaping of the later grammatical tradition. One work of his, his treatise *De orthographia*, survives in something like its original form; what survives of his *Ars*, however, is more problematic. Various sources cite him also for comments on the *Aeneid*, on Horace's *Ars poetica* and *Sermones*, and on Plautus' *Pseudolus*, and for criticisms of the grammatical work of Caesellius Vindex. See 5.4 above.

1. *De orthographia*

De orthographia is missing a small part of its opening, but otherwise seems complete. For discussion of Scaurus' methods, see 8.4a above.

2. *Ars grammatica*

Scaurus' most famous and influential work is lost, but has left clear traces in three different sources: the first part of Audax (12.7 above); the grammar of Victorinus (12.45 below); and the grammatical text in Munich, Clm 6281 foll. 52–62 identified as Scaurus by Law (1987). None of these is an accurate representation of the real grammar of Terentius Scaurus, but they all clearly owe a great deal to him. For fuller discussion, see 8.5 above.

3. *Dubia*

Immediately following the text of *De orthographia*, in all the manuscripts, is an excerpt of a text on prepositions (*GL* 7.29.3–33.13), beginning in the middle of a discussion of *cum* and continuing with a detailed discussion of *ab, ad, ex*, and *in*. It ends with an apparently unrelated paragraph on distinctions between long and short vowels (32.21–3.10), and the instruction to the reader to attach this little tract to "the *libellus* you have received from me about new letters" (33.11–13). In one manuscript (Vatican, Pal. Lat. 1741), there is a further short paragraph, clearly not genuine, headed *Terentius Scaurus de ordinatione partium orationis* (33.14–4.5) on the proper order in which to discuss the parts of speech. Another, short version of part of the text on prepositions is also printed by Keil (34.5–5.6) from Paris, Lat. 7520; its interest lies in its final lines—again, irrelevant to what has preceded—on alternate conjugations of verbs ending in *-io* (*veniebam* or *venibam*), which tell us that a book on the subject was addressed by Aufustius the grammarian to Asinius Pollio. Probably none of these scraps is actually by Scaurus, although many people (including Keil) have believed that the first one was his. Biddau omits them all. Whoever wrote the section on prepositions very clearly was drawing on, but was not, Varro.

T: *GL* 7.11–29 (*De orthographia*); Biddau (2008; *De orthographia* with Italian translation and commentary); Reinikka (2013; *Ars Pseudo-Scauri*).

R: *RE* Terentius 70 (Wessner); *BNP* Terentius 3.3 (Schmidt); *PIR*^{2} T92; *LG* (Petrilli); Teuffel 3 §352.2; S–H 3 §594–95; *HLL* 4 §433, *HLL* 5 §522.1–2.

S: Tempesti (1977); Law (1987); Holford-Strevens (2008); Reinikka (2008).

40. SERVIUS (AND "SERGIUS")

THE GENUINE SERVIUS

The name Servius is now most closely associated with his commentary on Virgil, but that is by no means his only surviving work, nor was it the only one that influenced later grammarians. The name itself is problematic, in two respects. For one, it is uncertain whether the fuller names that are (sparsely) attested (Maurus or Marius Servius Honoratus) are correct. More important is that the names "Servius" and "Sergius" are often confused in the grammatical tradition, particularly in connection with the various commentaries on Donatus' *Artes* to which these names are attached. Our knowledge of the real Servius is both extensive and difficult to evaluate. He is a character in Macrobius' *Saturnalia*, probably written in the early 430s, in which Servius is described as in fact having been too young to participate in a conversation the dramatic date of which is December 383. He followed Donatus as a grammarian working in Rome, although he was probably not his immediate successor, but there is in fact no evidence for his having been *grammaticus urbis Romae*. In all probability, Servius' works were composed in the first decades of the fifth century, and he is likely to have died before Macrobius used him as a character in his dialogue.

The connection between Servius and Donatus is not merely that they practiced the same profession in the same place a few decades apart: Servius' major works are dependent on Donatus. That is fairly certainly true of the commentary on Virgil (see 8.3a above) and definitely true of his commentary on Donatus' *Artes*, which was a major source for other commentators on Donatus. There are also three genuine short works on prosody and metrics, to be distinguished from the works (discussed below) ascribed in the manuscripts to "Sergius" or sometimes "Servius" which are not by Servius. For general bibliography on Servius and for discussion of his commentary on Virgil, see 11.3.1 above.

1. *Commentarius in Artem Donati*

The text of Servius' commentary on Donatus printed by Keil is an abridgment: a fuller form of the text was known to Cledonius, Pompeius, Cassiodorus, and the *Explanationes in Donatum*. What survives is preserved in two parts (separated by a short paragraph *De accentibus*) in Paris, Lat. 7530. The first part (*GL* 4.405.2–28.6) covers *Ars minor* and *Ars maior* Book 1, and is found only in Paris, Lat. 7530; the remainder (428.7–48.17), on *Ars maior* Books 2 and 3, is also found in a few other manuscripts (notably Oxford, Bodleian Add. C 144). Each half is preceded by a title identifying the author as Sergius and followed by a title identifying him as Servius; the confusion is not unusual.

T: *GL* 4.405–48.

S: Schindel (1975: 21–33); Holtz (1981: 223–30); Pugliarello (2009).

2. *De finalibus*

This short treatise on the quantities of final syllables (beginning with a general discussion of syllabic quantities) explicitly defines itself as a supplement to Donatus; it is addressed to an unidentifiable Aquilinus. The oldest text is an eighth-century addition to the fifth-century grammatical manuscript Naples, Lat. 2, where it is tucked in at the end of the text of Sacerdos 1–2. It also appears in several ninth-century grammatical manuscripts. For other treatises of this kind, see 8.4b above and 12.46.7 below.

T: *GL* 4.449–55.

3. *Centimeter* (*De centum metris*)

This brief treatise on meter is dedicated to one Albinus, who is generally identified with Caecina Decius Aginatius Albinus, precociously Praefectus Vrbi in 414; as he is described in the dedication as a *praetextatus*, the *Centimeter* must have been written in the first years of the fifth century.[6] Morelli has demonstrated

6. On the chronology, see Kaster (1988: 358); Cameron (2011: 240); Elice (2013: lvi–ix).

the dependence of Servius' preface on that of Atilius Fortunatianus, *De Metris Horatianis* (see 12.6 above).[7] Servius is a prototypicalist: he divides meters into groups based on the eight prototypical meters (followed by a large collection of meters that do not fit the scheme, *dispersa*), which he illustrates by invented examples. There are exactly one hundred meters listed.

Aside from the commentary on Virgil, the *Centimeter* is Servius' most widely attested work. It is found (among other manuscripts) in Naples IV A 8 from Bobbio, where it replaced a missing section of Charisius on metrics; in the early Beneventan collection Paris, Lat. 7530 (in which other works of Servius are also preserved); and in Oxford, Bodleian Add. C 144, which preserves the second half of Servius' commentary on Donatus, among other important and unusual texts.
T: *GL* 4.456–67; Soraci (1988); Elice (2013; text and commentary).
S: Morelli (2008); Elice (2008–9).

4. *De Metris Horatii*

This brief text was first (and apparently last) published by Keil, from Paris, Lat. 7530. It is dedicated to one Fortunatianus, who may be Atilius Fortunatianus, but no certainty is possible.
T: *GL* 4.468–72.

PSEUDEPIGRAPHIC WORKS ("SERGIUS")

In general, see Kaster (1988) #255.

5. *De littera*

A work to which Keil gives the title *De littera, de syllaba, de pedibus, de accentibus, de distinctione* (an accurate description of the contents) has in its oldest manuscript the heading *Incipit de littera commenta Sergii*; it is in fact a commentary on Book 1 of Donatus, *Ars maior.* It is preserved in the eighth-century portion of Naples, Lat. 2, foll. 42–4; the section *De pedibus* is also preserved in Paris, Lat. 7530. Later in the same section of Naples, Lat. 2 there is another text ascribed to Sergius (*GL* 7.537.1–9.15) consisting of a short chapter on the contents of the *ars* (headed *Incipit de arte grammatica Sergii*) and a chapter *De littera* which differs from the first version, although it too is apparently a commentary on Donatus *Ars maior* I.
T: *GL* 4.475–85.

6. *Explanationum in Donatum libri II*

It has been recognized since Jeep that the text printed under the title *Explanationes in Donatum* by Keil is not a single work; in more recent times, it has become clear that Keil's text is seriously misleading as well as incomplete. The only early

7. The dedication of Atilius' work is acephalous, but the similarity of language has led some to the not unreasonable belief that it too was addressed to the same Albinus.

manuscript to preserve the whole text is St. Paul im Lavanttal, Stiftsbibliothek 2/1 (along with a related renaissance manuscript, Oxford, Magdalene College 64), in which it is the last of three major grammatical texts (the other two are Pompeius and the *Anonymus ad Cuimnanum*). Keil divided the work into two books, the first dealing with *Ars minor* and *Ars maior* Book 1, the second with *Ars maior* Books 2 and 3. But Keil omitted a great deal: most important, he chose not to print most of the commentary on *Ars maior* 3, which was only published by Schindel in 1975. He also left out (although he mentioned their existence in the apparatus) various excerpts from other sources included in the commentary on *Ars* 2—some from Metrorius (see 46.7 below), and some from what he prints as *Explanationes* Book 1.

Following De Paolis' investigations, it is now clear that there are two different texts of very different sorts preserved under the title *Explanationes*, and the divisions are not what Keil and Jeep thought. What should now be called *Explanationes* I is a commentary on the *Ars minor* alone (ending at *GL* 4.518.29), written later than Servius' commentary (which the author uses). It is notable less for its grammatical content than because it includes interjections, presumably by students: Filocalus at 498.23, 501.31, 502.19, 503.11, 515.30; Rusticus at 499.24; an anonymous interjection at 514.9. On this, see above all De Nonno (2010: 185–205). Mysteriously, as well as being far more widely attested in the Carolingian period than *Explanationes* II, *Expl*. I survives fragmentarily as the middle script of the *codex ter scriptus* London, BL Add. 17212, sandwiched between the bottom text (Granius Licinianus) and the top one (Syriac version of St. John Chrysostom). The grammatical layer was written probably in the late sixth century, either in Italy or in Africa.

What should now be called *Explanationes* II is a commentary on the entire *Ars maior* largely made up of quotations from earlier sources, which include not only *Explanationes* I, but also the text of Ps.-Scaurus preserved in Munich, Clm 6281 (see 12.39.2 above). Not everything about De Paolis' division is certain, and there is, as he says, as yet no complete and accurate text of *Explanationes* II. It is obviously later than *Explanationes* I, but dating and localization are uncertain. In the manuscript in St. Paul, it is followed by the beginning of a treatise *De finalibus* by the sixth-century African grammarian Coronatus (see 12.17 above), but as that is in a different hand, it tells us little about the origin of the text.

T: *GL* 4.486–565, supplemented by Schindel (1975: 258–79).

S: Jeep (1893: 35–9); Schindel (1975: 34–52); Holtz (1981: 234–6); De Paolis (2000); De Nonno (2010: 185–205).

7. *Primae Explanationes Sergii de prioribus Donati grammatici urbis Romae*

An elementary commentary on the *Ars minor*, preserved in Bern 207 and partially in Karlsruhe 112. The author repeatedly refers ahead (e.g., 145.12, 146.13, 147.32) to a future treatment of the *secunda ars*; he refers to discussion

of verbal modes by *Donatus vel Sergius* or *Sergius* (151.24, 33); and he seems to follow Pompeius' treatment of possessive pronouns (a section which Hagen has apparently omitted with the note *sequitur pronominum XXI enumeratio secundum Pompeium p. 201.30sq.* in the apparatus to 149.35). On the other hand, it is not Christianized like Asporius. It is probably a text of the early sixth century.
T: *AH* 143–58.

8. *Glossae Servii*

A set of *idiomata generum*, attributed to Servius in the manuscript subscriptions. See 10.4.5b(i)b above.

T: *CGlL* 2.507–36.

9. *De idiomatibus quae pertinent ad genetivum casum*

Despite the narrow title given in the sole manuscript (Paris, Lat. 7530), this is in fact a full set of *idiomata casuum* that is the first part of a complex set of texts of which the last, a set of *idiomata generum*, appears more fully in Naples, Lat. IV A 8 and is ascribed to Charisius by Barwick. See further 10.4.5b(ii)d above on these texts.
T: *GL* 4.566.3–72.10.

10. *Ad Basilium Amicum Sergii*

This is a version of the opening portion of the anonymous *De finalibus metrorum* (ascribed to "Metrorius"); see 12.46.7 below.
T: *GL* 6.240.11–2.33.

11. *Commentarium Sergii de oratione et de octo partibus orationis artis secundae Donati*

This text was ascribed to Cassiodorus by Garet, who edited it in the seventeenth century from a manuscript (since lost) from Mont-St-Michel. The title in Garet's manuscript was damaged where the author's name should have been, but it appears from his description that the name began with S, and Law attributed it to the ever-useful Sergius, the name under which it is cited in various early medieval grammars. A second copy of the bulk of this text (*De oratione* and *De nomine*) is preserved in Paris, Lat. 7530, which combined it with extracts from Pompeius and an unidentified source to make a full treatment of the parts of speech; the title given in the Paris manuscript is simply *De partibus orationis artis secundae Donati*—which may be intended as a title for the combined collection of which this text is only the first part. Be that as it may, the only plausible reason for thinking it is by Cassiodorus is that it uses *Anicius* as an example of a proper name

(45.11 Stock); as the connection of Cassiodorus to the Anicii has been much diminished in recent scholarship (see Cameron 2012), that is not a strong argument, although the presence of the name (which does not occur in *Grammatici Latini*) is still striking. Equally curious is the parallel the author makes between *curator: procurator* and *nomen: pronomen*. But the text is not nearly so Christian as one would expect from Cassiodorus: there are two words cited from Paulinus of Nola, and two more from a variant text of Matthew (41.16, 106.4). Whoever wrote it (and "Sergius" is as likely as anyone else), it is a commentary on *Ars maior* Book 2, probably from the late fifth or early sixth century.
T: *PL* 70.1219–40 as Cassiodorus; Stock (2005; text and commentary).
S: Holtz (1975: 135–8); Law (1982: 18–19).

41. SEVERUS

A short metrical text ascribed to Iulius Severus is preserved in Wolfenbüttel, Weiss. 86 foll. 141r–4v. It consists of a list of combinations of metrical feet (beginning with spondee + anapest = antibacchius + iamb) starting with two-syllable feet (spondee, iamb, trochee) and continuing through the eight three-syllable feet. That in turn is followed by a discussion of the ratios between the two halves of the various metrical feet. It is related to (but briefer than, and probably not based on) the account in Diomedes *GL* 1.474–82. The collection of metrical material in the manuscript also includes a Greek (transliterated)–Latin glossary of grammatical and rhetorical terms apparently drawn from Isidore, an anonymous paragraph on the caesura (see 12.46.8e below), and the earliest copy of Mallius Theodorus *De metris*.
T: *GL* 6.641.1–5.24 (with the supplied initial subtitle *De spondeo*).
S: Romanini 2007: cxliii–vi.

42. TERENTIANUS MAURUS

Terentianus' verse treatise on metrics entitled *De litteris, syllabis, et metris* was composed in the late second or early third century. The author speaks of himself as *Maurus* (line 1971); in the preface to Book 2 he addresses his son Bassinus and his son-in-law Novatus; he shows knowledge of the so-called *poetae novelli* of the second century, and his work was in turn used by metrical writers in the fourth century such as Apthonius. The work is divided into the three books indicated by the title: following a preface in glyconics (1–84), Book 1 on letters (85–278) is written in sotadeans; Book 2 on syllables in trochaic septenarii (279–996) and hexameters (997–1299); Book 3 on meters (1300–2981, where the text breaks off) in appropriately various meters. The relationship among the three parts and the chronology of their composition is disputed: Beck may well be right to argue that the three parts were written separately, *De metris* first and *De syllabis* last, and that they were only combined at some later date. It is certainly striking that *De litteris* and *De metris* are heavily used by Apthonius in the fourth century, while

De syllabis is not known until the fifth. Terentianus gives the fullest exposition of derivationist metrical theory, and he has at times been much admired both for his exposition and for his own poetry.

The text of Terentianus was part of the important collection of metrical and grammatical texts discovered at Bobbio in 1493 by Giorgio Galbiate, most of which are otherwise unattested.[8] One group of these texts come from a manuscript (or possibly more than one) that disappeared immediately after it was copied; this includes not only the orthographic treatises of Velius Longus and Martyrius and the small but important grammatical text known as *Donatiani fragmentum*, but some of the most important works on meter: Caesius Bassus, Atilius Fortunatianus, and Terentianus. With the exception of Terentianus, these texts (and more) survive in the copy made by Galbiate, Naples IV A 11, the best source for these texts. Terentianus, however, survives only in the *editio princeps* of 1497. The Bobbio manuscript itself has not been seen since 1493.

T: *GL* 6.325–413; Beck (1993a; *De syllabis* only, with German translation and commentary); Cignolo (2002; with Italian translation and commentary). Selections from *De litteris* and *De syllabis* translated into English in Copeland and Sluiter (2009: 72–81).

I: Beck (1993b).

B: Lammert (1931: 61).

R: *RE* Terentianus 1 (Wessner); *BNP* (Schmidt); Teuffel 3 §373a; S–H 3 §514; *HLL* 4 §493.

S: Polara (1992); Beck (1998).

43. M. TERENTIUS VARRO

Varro (116–27 BCE) is the earliest Roman any of whose writing about language or grammar survives as an independent text, but most of his works are known only from fragments. For discussion of his philological scholarship, see above, Chapter 3; what follows is largely bibliographical and does not pretend to completeness. A letter of Jerome (*Ep*. 33 ed. Hilberg, *ad Paulam*) gives (in parallel with a catalogue of Origen's works) a list of Varro's works, which is our single most important source for Varro's writings. Jerome lists thirty-nine titles, including the number of books in each work (there are some errors in both titles and book counts); he then says that his list includes barely half. From Jerome and from quotations and other sources, we know the titles of seventy-four works by Varro; Ritschl's estimate, which still seems valid, is that these seventy-four works included approximately 620 individual *volumina* (of which, it should be noted, 150 were *Menippean Satires* and another 76 were *Logistorici*). The following works dealt with language and literature;

8. The discoveries at Bobbio have been discussed repeatedly, and in some detail. In particular, see Sabbadini (1967: 1.156–64); Ferrari (1970); and the extensive (and repetitive) discussions of Morelli (1989, 2000, 2011–12: 1.xlvii–clxviii).

some are known only by title, and significant numbers of fragments survive of very few. They are grouped here thematically, as much as possible:

De antiquitate litterarum ad Accium, 2 books?
De origine linguae Latinae ad Pompeium, 3 books
De sermone Latino, 5 books
De similitudine verborum, 3 books
De utilitate sermonis, 4 books
Epitoma linguae Latinae, 9 books
De poematis
De poetis
De actionibus scaenicis, 3 books (Jerome lists both *De scaenicis actionibus* and *De actis scaenicis*; they are probably the same work)
De scaenicis originibus, 3 books; edited also by Cichorius (1888)
De comoediis Plautinis (more than one book)
Quaestiones Plautinae, 5 books
De personis
De compositione saturarum
De bibliothecis, 3 books
De lectionibus
De descriptionibus, 3 books
Περὶ χαρακτήρων, 3 books
De proprietate scriptorum, 3 books

The bibliography given here does not include editions or studies of his non-grammatical works.

T: a) Complete works: Popma (1788); Semi (1965); Traglia (1974; *De lingua Latina, Res rusticae*, grammatical fragments); Salvadore (1999–). Popma's commentary is still sometimes useful; Semi's edition generally is not.

b) *De lingua Latina:*

i) Complete editions: Goetz and Schoell (1910); Kent (1938; with English translation); Marcos Casquero (1990; with Spanish translation). A new edition with commentary is being prepared by W. de Melo. For now, Kent's is the most useful edition.

ii) Individual books: Book 5, Collart (1954b); Book 6, Riganti (1978; text with Italian translation); Flobert (1985; text with French translation); Book 8, Dahlmann (1966); Book 9, Duso (2017); Book 10, Taylor (1996).

c) Grammatical fragments (editions of more than one work): Willmans (1864); *GRF* 179–371; Goetz and Schoell (1910). *Caveat lector*: Of the 461 fragments in Funaioli's collection, only 89 are explicitly cited from a specific work about language or literature, and of those 27 are from the lost portions of *De lingua Latina* itself. Twelve works are represented by five or fewer fragments, and some are known only by title from Jerome's list; 142 of the fragments are incidental comments of a linguistic nature from other specified works; and fully 228—nearly half—are cited with Varro's name alone. Funaioli in *GRF* is rightly conservative in his arrangement of the fragments; Wilmanns' attempt to reconstruct the grammatical works, particularly *De sermone Latino* (of which there are only 12 definite fragments), is a work of ingenuity and imagination, but more speculative than reliable.

B: Wessner (1902: 121–8, 1921: 52–69); Collart (1965); Riposati and Marastoni (1974); D. Butterfield, *Oxford Bibliographies Online*.

I: Salvadore (1995).

R: *RE* Supp. 6 Terentius 84 (Dahlmann); *BNP* Varro 2 (Sallmann); *LG* (Gambarara); Teuffel 1 §164–9; S–H 1 §182–94.

C: Reverdin (1963); Butterfield (2015). *Papers on Grammar* 6 (2001) is devoted to Varro; some articles in it are cited individually below.

S: This is a small selection of recent work and some important earlier scholarship.

a) General works on Varro: Ritschl (1866–79: 3.419–505); Della Corte (1954); Cardauns (2001); Ax (2005b); Volk (2017).
b) Works on *De lingua latina* or Varro's ideas about language: Reitzenstein (1901); Dahlmann (1932); Collart (1954a, 1963, 1978); Fehling (1956–7); Barwick (1957); Schröter (1960, 1963); Traglia (1963); Taylor (1974, 1977); Pisani (1976); Cavazza (1981); Pfaffel (1981); Ax (1995, 1996; both reprinted in Ax 2000); Piras (1998); Coleman (2001); Lomanto (2001); Blank (2005, 2008, 2012); Duso (2006); Baratin (2008); Garcea (2008a, 2008b).
c) Works on Varro as literary historian (particularly *De poetis*): Waszink (1948); Dahlmann (1953, 1963a, 1963b); Sbordone (1974); D'Alessandro (2012); Citroni (2013).

44. VELIUS LONGUS

Velius Longus is cited as an authority by Gellius, *NA* 18.9.4 for a work *de usu antiquae lectionis* in which he seems to have expressed a preference for reading *insece* rather than *inseque* in Ennius (*Ann.* 322 Sk.); he also wrote a commentary on the *Aeneid* which is cited by Servius, Macrobius, and particularly in the Verona scholia. But the only one of Velius' works to survive is *De orthographia*, one of the earliest extant apparently complete grammatical texts. It was probably written in the first third of the second century CE; there is no absolutely conclusive indication of date, and modern estimates have varied by fifty years in either direction. It is in any case roughly contemporary with Scaurus' treatise on orthography (see 12.39), and neither makes use of the other.

Velius does cite some earlier scholars, notably Verrius, Varro, and Nisus, and there is little reason to believe that much of *De orthographia* was original to him. The book was either designed for classroom use or provides a written representation of classroom experience: when Velius writes about the choice between *arcesso* and *accerso* or *forpices* and *forcipes* (problems of *orthoepeia*, not *orthographia*), he says that the difference is easily audible: *proinde ac dixero scribes* (*GL* 7.71.13 = 63.3 Di Napoli). Almost certainly, we hear the voice of a teacher addressing students, and somewhat peremptorily at that.

De orthographia was one of the texts discovered at Bobbio in 1493 by Giorgio Galbiate (see 12.42); it is now found in Naples IV A 11, foll. 1r–13r, and in copies of that manuscript.

T: *GL* 7.46–81; Di Napoli (2011; text, Italian translation, and commentary). A small excerpt also in Cassiodorus, *GL* 7.154.12–5.22.

R: *RE* Velius 10 (Dihle), Orthographie (Strzelecki); *BNP* Velius 3 (Rüpke); *LG* (Desbordes and Garcea); *EV* (Lomanto); Teuffel 3 §352.3; S–H 3 §596; *HLL* 4 §435.

S: Strzelecki (1938); Codoñer (1985: 210–17); De Paolis (2010, 2014).

45. VICTORINUS

1. *Ars Victorini grammatici*

While not quite so common as names like Probus and Sergius, the name Victorinus is attached to several late antique grammatical texts, possibly because of the famous Marius Victorinus. Victorinus, or Maximus Victorinus, may be a real person; but he is not necessarily the same person as Marius Victorinus, nor is he necessarily one person. Keil groups four texts together under the heading *Maximi Victorini qui feruntur libri*, but that is over-confident. The first two texts, *Ars Victorini grammatici* (*GL* 6.187–205) and *Ars Palaemonis de metrica institutione* (206–15) are clearly part of the same grammatical compendium; the first is attributed in the manuscripts to either Victorinus or Palaemon, the second to Palaemon or anonymous (an attribution to Victorinus was added in the sixteenth century). The first half of this combined work deals with the preliminary matter (*De voce* and the like) and the parts of speech; the second half concerns meter, the hexameter in particular. There has clearly been some disturbance to the order of the first half, as *De casibus* appears between *De voce* and *De sententia*, and there are no sections *De nomine* and *De pronomine*. Both Victorinus and portions of Audax are drawn from Scaurus and are often identical except for abridgment and rearrangement of sections (see 8.5, 12.7, and 12.39 above), but the dependence of Victorinus on the common source ends at 6.197.19 and does not resume until the beginning of the section *De metro* at 206.3. The intervening section of Victorinus contains a reference to Donatus (200.24) for material on pronouns (which Victorinus omits), suggesting a degree of revision, stitching, interpolation, or the like not before the last part of the fourth century.

There is also more of Victorinus than appears in *GL* 6. Among the small excerpts of commentaries on Donatus included in *GL* 5, Keil published from Leiden, Voss. Lat. O 37 a paragraph on solecism (5.327.32–8.10); this was subsequently found to be the opening of a text *De soloecismo et barbarismo* in

Basel F III 15d following the text of Consentius *De barbarismis et metaplasmis* (see 12.15 above), with the heading *Victo*. In publishing this text, Niedermann rightly recognized the similarities between this text of Victorinus and the final section of Audax printed by Keil, *De barbarismo* (*GL* 7.361.13–2.21); he further recognized that the section on solecism of his new text of Victorinus was likewise similar to Audax *De soloecismo*—but Keil had not printed that final section of Audax, which survives only in a single manuscript, in part because it is badly damaged and at times not legible, in part (so Keil ad loc.) *neque quidquam quod gravioris momenti esset inesse videbatur*. But what is there, is very much like Audax:

Audax (Munich, Clm 6434)	Victorinus, ed. Niedermann
barbarismus nullo modo excusari potest. si enim per inprudentiam fiat vitium est, si a paetis virtus aelucutionis. et appellatur grece metaplasma. (fol. 108r; *GL* 7.362.19–21)	Barbarismus nullo modo excusari potest. si a nobis per inprudentiam fiat, vitium est; si a poetis vel oratoribus, virtus locutionis et appellatur graece μεταπλασμός. (37.3–5)
[illegible] nam sicut de barbarismo dictum est ita et solacismus, si a nobis fiet per inprudentiam, vitium est; si a peticis vel musitis afectate dicatur, figura elocutionis est quae scemata appellatur. (fol. 111r)	Numquam ergo soloecismus excusari potest. si a nobis per inprudentiam fiat, vitium est; si a poetis vel oratoribus affectate dicatur, figura locutionis est et appelatur graece σχῆμα. (35.16–18)

They end with the same sentence (my second example) attacking poetic misuse of language, although one has orators, the other has musicians. There are other slight differences, but the main significant variation is that in Audax, as is normal, barbarism precedes solecism, while in Victorinus it is the reverse.

T: *GL* 6.187–215 (*Ars*); Niedermann (1937: 32.21–7.5; *De soloecismo et barbarismo*); *GL* 5.327.32–8.10 (opening paragraph of *De soloecismo*).
B: Wessner (1902: 169–71).
R: *PLRE* I; Kaster (1988) #273; *HLL* 5 §522.2.
S: Keil (1872); Jeep (1893: 85–9).

2. Maximus Victorinus, *De ratione metrorum commentarius* (GL 6.216–28) and *De finalibus metrorum* (*GL* 6.229–42)

The second pair of texts grouped under the name of Maximus Victorinus by Keil is very difficult, and Keil's arrangement is also misleading. There is no reason to ascribe them to anyone in particular, and I have therefore treated them as anonymous; see 12.46.7 below.

46. ANONYMOUS GRAMMATICAL TEXTS

A great many grammatical treatises are transmitted with no author's name; some of them are damaged at the beginning and/or end and have thus lost a name through physical loss, while others simply have no author's name attached and are often part of larger strings of unnamed short texts.

1. Papyri

Scappaticcio (2015) offers new texts of the grammatical papyri with commentary, of which the more significant items are the following:

a) P.Lit.Lond. II 184 + P.Mich. VII 429 (= LDAB 5065): three columns, in two papyri now separated but from the same roll, that clearly come from an *ars grammatica*: there are the remains of discussions of *dictio, oratio*, the parts of speech, and semivowels and diphthongs, with a quotation from Virgil. The papyrus itself dates from the late second or early third century, and it has been ascribed to Palaemon, the elder Pliny, and various other candidates, none of whom is likely. The most distinctive thing about it is the author's impatience with the *turba praeceptorum* who keep multiplying parts of speech. That does sound like Pliny, but the text is clearly a grammar, not a work on *Latinitas*. There is also a text and useful commentary in Wouters (1979: 93–108).
b) Various sets of *regulae* texts, some bilingual. The most noteworthy is P. Louvre Inv. E7332 (= LDAB 6148), a fifth- or sixth-century text that declines nouns of the third declension divided by nominative singular ending, and giving the cases in the order Nom. Gen. Dat. Acc. Voc. Abl.

2. *Anonymus Bobiensis*

Naples, Lat. 2 is a manuscript in four parts (of different dates) containing several different grammatical texts. The text known as *Anonymus Bobiensis* or *Excerpta Bobiensia* is found on foll. 142–55, written in northern Italy in the fifth century. It consists of a very brief section *De oratione* (1.1–6 De Nonno), followed by sections *De nomine* (1.7–39.24), *De pronomine* (39.25–46.24), and *De verbo* (47.1–53.30). It has long been recognized that this anonymous text closely resembles (and is at times identical to) the similar expositions in Charisius, Dositheus, and Diomedes. In addition to their general similarity, what all these texts have in common is their frequent use of Greek—indeed, the grammar of Dositheus is bilingual—and their origin in the eastern half of the empire. *Anonymus* was copied in Italy, but we do not know where it was written. Bonnet suggests that it is was intended to provide an aid, more practical than theoretical, for businesspeople who spoke Greek in a Latin-speaking area; he also suggests that it was written in a Latin-speaking area under Greek authority, and proposes Syracuse. That is appealing, but fanciful.

T: *GL* 1.533–65 as *Excerpta ex Charisii arte grammatica*; De Nonno (1982).
R: Teuffel 3 §419.5.
S: De Nonno (1983a); Dionisotti (1984); Bonnet (2006).

3. *Excerpta Andecavensia*

This text comprises a set of forty grammatical chapters on various aspects of the parts of speech, and on other topics (including, it appears, *Latinitas*). The *excerpta* come from more than one source (and some chapters have no obvious parallels), but they show particular affinities with the Charisius group, and apparently with the *Anonymus Bobiensis* in particular. It is preserved in one manuscript written at Tours in the ninth century (Angers, Bibl. Mun. 493; hence the name given to the text) which contains a variety of curious grammatical texts (see De Nonno 1992: 215–19) and in two humanist manuscripts which give the name of the author as Charisius. Not coincidentally, these manuscripts all also provide valuable evidence for the text of Charisius itself. The *Excerpta* were almost certainly composed in late antiquity, probably in the fifth century.
T: De Nonno (1992).

4. *Fragmenta Bobiensia*

Anonymous grammatical fragments from Bobbio divide most easily into three groups.

4a: a single text on a bifolium (f.156/159) in Part III of Naples, Lat. 2 written in the fifth century;

4b–d: Three texts found at the opening of Naples, Lat. 1, written in the seventh and eighth centuries, probably but not necessarily at Bobbio itself;

4e–j: A set of small grammatical and metrical texts included among a larger assortment of grammatical excerpts taken from (or ascribed to) specific authors, in Part II of Naples, Lat. 2, written in the eighth century, probably at Bobbio.

4a. This complex and nameless text consists of a short section on nouns followed by a longer section comprised of notes on classical authors, notably Virgil, Lucan, Horace, Sallust, and Juvenal. It was written, according to A. Campana (cited by Mariotti 1984) by no fewer than six hands, and Mariotti persuasively argues that the text we have is original to this manuscript: in the second part, we see the process of creating a glossary from marginalia and commentaries. The text shows knowledge of notes on Virgil related to, but at times fuller than, those of Servius and DS, and while the primary interest of the excerpts is in words and grammar, there are also antiquarian notes of some interest, including an otherwise unattested fragment of Ennius and two quotations (otherwise known) from the Twelve Tables.

T: *GL* 7.540.20–4.43; Mariotti (1984).

4b. *De nomine et pronomine*. Along with 4c and 4d, *De nomine et pronomine* appears at the opening of Naples, Lat. 1; the first two are written by the same late seventh-century hand, the third by an eighth-century one. In the present state of the manuscript, they are followed by Probus, *Instituta* *artium* and the *Appendix Probi*, but that arrangement is not original. The manuscript (which is a palimpsest) was preserved, and probably written, at Bobbio. *De nomine et pronomine* is missing its opening; it concerns inflection only, emphasizing throughout the form and importance of the ablative singular for declension. Dionisotti has suggested that it is essentially a commentary on Donatus, emphasizing things that Donatus omits; it was also very clearly, if not necessarily composed in the Greek east, at least transmitted there before reaching Bobbio. It concludes with the subscription *Explicit de pronomine feliciter. bono milicho romalco*, and Dionisotti plausibly emends *romalco* to *romaico*, i.e., ῥωμαικῷ (= *grammatico*).

T: *GL* 5.555–66; Passalacqua (1984: 5–19).

S: Dionisotti (1984).

4c. *De Verbo:* see 12.24 above.

4d. [Valeri Probi] *De Nomine:* see 12.36.5 above.

4e. *De propriis nominibus:* A single paragraph on proper names, related to Servius on Donatus, *GL* 4.429.4–14. It appears on fol. 47 of Naples, Lat. 2, and is immediately followed by a very confused list of single-letter abbreviations, printed by Mommsen in *GL* 4.268n.

T: *GL* 7.540.10–19.

4f. *De accentibus:* A paragraph on the rules of Latin accentuation, which appears on fol. 49 immediately before the next excerpt.

T: *GL* 7.539.16–40.9.

4g. *De versibus:* Brief accounts of iambic, trochaic, dactylic, and anapaestic meters, clearly prototypical rather than derivationist and closely related to Apthonius. It is remarkable for the use of (Latin) examples said to come from Greek poets. Found on foll. 49–50, immediately following 4f.

T: *GL* 6.620.1–5.6; Nosarti (1992: 88–95).

4h–j. *De finalibus syllabis, De structuris, De metris:* These three selections are grouped together on foll. 69–70. The first is a brief discussion of the length of final syllables, proceeding through the parts of speech (noun, pronoun, verb, participle, adverb) with a final paragraph on ambiguous initial syllables; all examples are taken from Virgil. The second is a discussion of clausulae of which part is also found in Paris, Lat. 7530 (on which see 8b below), and the third is a very short list of lyric meters.

T: *GL* 6.625.7–6.37; 6.627.1–9.7; 6.629.8–22.

5. *De dubiis nominibus*

This text is a list of nouns, alphabetized by first letter, largely but not exclusively concerned with questions of gender. It is distinctive in its use of illustrative quotations, many of which (including, for instance, those drawn from Aemilius Macer, Asinius Pollio, and Propertius) must have been inherited (as Keil saw) from a learned source such as Caper; Beck prefers to find Pliny's *Dubius sermo*, but one does not exclude the other. The author's own contribution may include another set of examples from Christian sources, including Prudentius, Avitus, Juvencus, the Psalms, and the New Testament. It is clearly quite late, sixth or even possibly early seventh century.

T: *GL* 5.571–94; Glorie (1968: 755–820).
R: Teuffel 3 §495.7; Manitius (1911) §11.
S: Beck (1892, 1893: 26–7); Condorelli (1989–90).

6. *De ultimis syllabis ad Caelestinum*

Neither the author nor the correct title of this somewhat unusual text is known. The plausible title given above was invented by Keil; the sole manuscript (Naples, Lat. 2) introduces the text with a bare *Praefatio*. It occupies foll. 76–95r, the beginning of Part III of the manuscript, written in northern Italy in the fifth century and preserved at Bobbio; it is immediately followed by *De catholicis Probi*. That undoubtedly led Parrhasius in the *editio princeps* of 1504 to assign it to Probus; Putschius in 1605 went further, and labeled it as *M. Valerii Probi grammaticarum institutionum Liber I. Valerius Probus ad Caelestinum* with *De catholicis* accordingly labeled as book 2. The attribution (to any Probus) has no evidence and no justification; all we know about the origins of the work is that it was dedicated to one Caelestinus (also unknown) in a poem of eleven hexameters of no great skill and many dedicatory cliches (beginning *Accipe nostra tuis audacius edita iussis*).

De ultimis syllabis, however, is not a standard text on prosody. Aside from its somewhat affected style, it is addressed, as De Nonno shows, to prospective writers of poetry rather than simply to readers. Although the vast majority of examples are taken from Virgil, there are no fewer than seventeen from Lucan, as well as a few from Plautus, Ennius, Terence, Lucilius, Cicero, Lucretius, Calvus, Sallust, Horace, and Seneca. The number of quotations from Lucan makes it fairly clear that this is a text from the fifth century (rather than the fourth, as Schmidt suggests). De Nonno also points out that the only close parallel to the use of a preface in verse comes in the work of Phocas (see 12.33 above), also probably in the fifth century.

T: *GL* 4.219–64.
R: Teuffel 2 §300.6 (4); *HLL* 5 §522.5.
S: De Nonno (1990b).

7. *De finalibus*

There is an extraordinarily confusing set of overlapping texts on prosody which have not been well served by editors. The core of the work, an exposition of the quantity of the final syllables of words (*De finalibus*), divided by part of speech and subdivided by termination (*GL* 6.231.4–9.18) is found (in a few cases, in altered or damaged form) in some nine manuscripts of the eighth to tenth centuries; in two of them it apears after the chapter *De syllabis* of Donatus, *Ars maior* Book 2; in two others it is inserted elsewhere in the corpus of Donatus, in one (Oxford, Bodl. Add. C 144) bits of it are inserted, along with other excerpts, into the text of Donatus as supplements; in the early Beneventan manuscript Paris, Lat. 7530 it has the incipit *De observatione ultimae syllabae casu singulari omnium partium orationis ac prius de nomine. . . .* This *De finalibus* seems to be a coherent text, albeit one that begins somewhat abruptly, but in addition to its independent appearances, it has been included in larger collections of material useful for prosody; there are four significant further elements in these collections:

a) *Maximus Victorinus de ratione metrorum* (*GL* 6.216.1–28.5): A set of notes on prosody (with more reference to metrical usages than is normal in such texts) followed by a section on final syllables of nouns and verbs only. It ends with a paragraph (227.25–8.5) suggesting a transition to the study of rhetoric. This text has been at times attributed to the more famous Marius Victorinus (see Schmidt in *HLL* 5 §564B3) but in its present form that is impossible: it is a mixture of materials from different sources, and there is no reason to believe that any of them is Marius Victorinus. In the ninth- and tenth-century manuscripts it is almost always followed by *De finalibus* itself, but with an intervening introductory text, which survives under the name of "Metrorius."
b) *Metrorius de ratione metrorum* (*GL* 6.229.1–31.3): A brief text on letters and syllables that connects to the beginning of *De finalibus* without any break. Both the title and the name of the author are questionable: the title because the text is not in fact about meter—but neither is the text of Victorinus which it follows—and the authorship because "Metrorius" is likely to be a misreading of *metrorum* in the title.
c) *De caesuris* (*GL* 6.240.1–10): A very short text which is extraneous to the rest of this collection; its separate origin is clear from the fact that in one manuscript it appears alone, following a text of Caper *De verbis dubiis* and in another it is found twice, once after Victorinus and once at the end of the collection.
d) *Ad Basilium amicum Sergii* (*GL* 6.240.11–2.33): An alternate version of "Metrorius" found as the introduction to *De finalibus* in three important manuscripts (St. Gallen 876, Vatican, Pal. Lat. 1753 [and its copy Valenciennes 397], with the text in slightly different order, and Paris, Lat. 13025, missing a few lines). It is, with the exception of three short paragraphs, virtually identical to "Metrorius"; and of those three paragraphs, the first is virtually identical to the opening paragraph of Servius, *De finalibus* (see 12.40.2 above), which may explain the attribution of this text to "Sergius," while the second is found after the whole Victorinus/Metrorius/*De finalibus*/*De caesuris* collection in the seventh–eighth-century Bobbio grammatical manuscript Naples Lat. 2.[9]

9. That is, at any rate, how Keil describes its location in the apparatus to *GL* 6.240.16; see also Corazza (2003: 97–8).

This is, as noted above, extremely confusing. What seems to have happened is that at some point, no later than the fifth century, a text *De finalibus* was composed to supplement the meager advice on prosody in Donatus. This text was preserved both with Donatus and independently; it was also combined, in a slightly altered form, with various other texts. For the most part, this resulted in the four-part collection, starting with the rag-bag of materials ascribed to "Victorinus," followed in turn by "Metrorius," the slightly altered *De finalibus*, and the stray paragraph *De caesuris*. In another modification, the unaltered *De finalibus* received a different introduction very much like "Metrorius," but with the heading *Ad Basilium amicum Sergii*. All these combinations and changes took place, in all probability, no later than the sixth century.

T: *GL* 6.216.1–42.33; Corazza (2011: 5–64; text [not including *Ad Basilium*] with Italian translation and commentary). Keil's text is based on inadequate manuscript evidence; Corazza's treatment is at times incomprehensible, although she is right to distinguish two versions of the text.

R: Kaster (1988) #239, 274.

S: Morelli (1916); Leonhardt (1989b: 187–8); De Nonno (1990b: 232–3). See also 8.4b above.

8. Anonymous Fragments on Meter and Prosody

a) Berlin fragments: The late eighth-century grammatical manuscript Berlin, Diez. B Sant. 66 contains a large section on metrics (pp. 223–77), including versions of familiar texts such as Servius' *Centimeter* and Mallius Theodorus; smaller excerpts from Diomedes, Marius Victorinus/Apthonius, and Iulianus of Toledo; an apparently unpublished Carolingian commentary on the introduction to the *Centimeter*; and the following short texts (for details, see Bischoff 1973: 17–19):
   i. *De heroo et triametro* (*GL* 6.633.1–4.9): Parts of this are very close to Apthonius, but it includes a quotation (in Greek) from the Homeric *Margites* that is not quoted by Apthonius but is found in Atilius Fortunatianus. Keil wrongly gives the title as *De heroo hexametro* (also giving a wrong transcription of the manuscript title); it clearly comes from a derivationist source.
   ii. *De speciebus hexametri heroici* (*GL* 6.634.10–7.15): The text begins with a list of the thirty-two possible shapes of the dactylic hexameter expressed as variations of the shortest, the Ennian verse (*Dub.* 7 Skutsch) *introducuntur legati Minturnenses*. That is followed by a paragraph on the role of the trochee (as substitute for spondee) at the end of the verse and another on the six possible *vitia* of the hexameter, including a verse misattributed to Horace. Much of this text (to 636.23), with slight variations, is also found in St. Gallen 876 of the late eighth/early ninth century (see 8c below).

iii. *Incipit de heruo* [*sic*] . . . + *Incipit de genere et speciebus*: The first of these texts is very short, the second somewhat longer. As Bischoff (1973: 33) notes, the two go together, and clearly show some similarities with Apthonius. Unpublished.

iv. *Unde oritur elegiacum metrum?*: A very short section (five lines) with no obvious parallels in *GL*, followed by a short section on proper names, an excerpt from the end of Servius, *Centimeter*, and passages taken from Diomedes and Iulianus of Toledo (see Bischoff 1973: 18). Unpublished.

v. *Diximus metrorum species esse iiii: epicam, melicam, comicam, et tragicam*: A short passage of which the beginning and perhaps the end are related to Apthonius, but the middle definitely is not. See Bischoff (1973: 33). Unpublished.

b) Fragments in Paris, Lat. 7530. On the manuscript in general, with detailed table of contents, see Holtz (1975).

i. *Dicimus rhythmum esse* (*GL* 6.631.14–2.12): This is the first metrical fragment in the manuscript, and consists of excerpts from Augustine, *De musica*. See Holtz (1975: 113).

ii. *De observatione ultimae syllabae*. A text of part of *De finalibus metrorum* ascribed in most manuscripts (although not this one) to Metrorius (see 7 above). This text is followed by Servius, *De centum metris*, which in turn is followed by a text *De structuris* also found in one of the Bobbio grammatical collections: see 4i above.

iii. *De iambico metro* (*GL* 6.630.1–1.12).

c) St. Gallen, Stiftsbibliothek 876: Immediately following the explicit of Servius, *De finalibus* at the top of p. 137 the following fragments appear:

i. *De scansione heroyci uersus et specie eorum* (pp. 137–8; *GL* 6.637.16–8.21): This is immediately followed by a portion of the text on the hexameter described in 8a(ii) above (pp. 138–41; *GL* 6.634.11–6.23), in turn followed by

ii. *Recipit iambicus trimeter et tribrachum* (pp. 141–2; *GL* 6.638.23–9.12): A short extract on the trimeter. The title *De iambico trimetro* was supplied by Keil.

iii. *De pentametro. Hic sine ulla dubitatione heroi hexametri suboles est* (pp. 142–3; *GL* 6.639.13–40.11): On the pentameter, citing Victorinus once (in fact, Apthonius *GL* 6.107.10).

iv. *De epodo octosyllabo* (pp. 143–4; *GL* 6.640.12–1.6): A brief discussion of the Archilochean meters of Horace, *Epodes* 1 and 2, based on Apthonius 133–7. This is followed by an excerpt from Diomedes on final syllables (p. 144ff; *GL* 1.492.16).

d) St. Paul im Lavanttal, Stiftsbibliothek 2/1 contains several short texts on final syllables that are part of [Sergius], *Explanationes in Donatum* II (see 40.6 above); they also appear in the closely related fifteenth-century manuscript Oxford, Magdalene College 64.

i. *De syllabis. Litterarum quidem syllabarumque tractatus . . . quia arte corripitur*: This text appears after the section *De litteris* (*GL* 4.522.12). Keil printed the very beginning and end in his apparatus, noting, correctly, that it is essentially the same as the comparable passage in "Metrorius" and *Ad Basilium amicum Sergii* (see 7 above). Text in Corazza (2003: 108–9) and Corazza (2011: 165–8).

ii. *Nomina quae "a" littera terminantur . . . "arbor," "soror," "uxor"*: This text appears before the section *Explanatio pronominis* (*GL* 4.545.19). Keil here omitted two passages: the first is a repetition of *Expl.* I (4.495.24–8.34) on case endings, and the second is this text, on the quantity of the final syllables of nouns (by case, with most space devoted to the nominative singular) with a short and peculiar paragraph at the end on the meaning of *euphonia* and the meaning and declension of *analogia* (the latter garbling Donatus 4.379.14, which describes using analogy, not declining it). Text in Corazza (2003: 110–11) and Corazza (2011: 168–70).

iii. *Hic adscribendum utile iudicamus . . . diptongis quae omnibus patent*: This text is identical to *De finalibus* (see 7 above) except for its opening sentence. It appears at 4.562.25, after the end of the discussion of the parts of speech ending with *De interiectione* and before the discussion of *vitia et virtutes orationis* (which is also omitted by Keil).

iv. For a fourth passage, which appears after the end of *Explanationes*, see 12.17 above.

e) Wolfenbüttel, Herzog August Bibliothek, Weiss. 86, foll. 146v–7r contains a single paragraph beginning "Caesurae versuum sunt quattuor" (*GL* 6.645.25–35) which (as Keil notes) is similar to that attached to "Metrorius" (see 7 above) in some manuscripts. On the manuscript, see 12.41 above.

f) Vienna 2521 (s. xi) contains a pleasant poem of 24 hexameters (*GL* 6.646) explaining the various metrical feet with words of the proper shape. I know nothing of its origin.

g) Oxford, Bodleian Add. C 144 (s. x–xi), contains on foll. 113v–14v, after the *Explanationes in Donatum*, a text to which Corazza gives the title *De primis, mediis, et ultimis syllabis*. It does discuss syllabic length in all positions, emphasizing (on opening syllables) the ways in which we can tell that a syllable is long. It is perhaps worth noting that the last section, on final syllables, is partly written in catechistic form; there is more than one source for this text. Text in Corazza (2003: 114–16) and Corazza (2011: 174–7).

h) Bologna 797, which also contains a damaged copy of the collection *De ratione metrorum*/"Metrorius"/*De finalibus*/*De caesuris* described in 12.46.7 above, preserves on foll. 35v–6v an incomplete copy of a text entitled *De finalibus syllabis omnium partium*; the complete text is found in three humanistic manuscripts. As with the more widespread *De finalibus*, it goes through the endings of words, articulated by part of speech. Text in Corazza (2011: 178–81).

9. For the sake of completeness, I list here the other unattached snippets in *GL*.

a) *GL* 5.325.2–23: What Keil quotes from Leiden, BPL 122 is the *Cunabula grammaticae artis*. See 13.41 below.
b) *GL* 5.325.25–6.23: What Keil describes as *Ex codice Lavantino 24* is in fact two short extracts from the opening of *Anonymus ad Cuimnanum* (1.33–41 and 2.1–20). See 13.33 below.
c) *GL* 5.326.25–30: The excerpt from Paris, Lat. 7570 (s. xi) printed by Keil is on the spelling of *lac* or *lact* (Varro F 273); the text from which it is taken is described in the catalogue as *Anonymi expositio in Donati grammaticam* and by Keil as a commentary on the parts of speech largely drawn from Pompeius, Priscian, and Consentius. The manuscript is apparently not available online, and I have not seen any more of the text than Keil quotes.
d) *GL* 5.327.1–30: Extracts from a commentary on Donatus, *Ars maior* Books 1 and 3 found on foll. 92r–140v of Munich, Clm 14737 (cited by Keil as Emm. G. 121), a tenth-century grammatical miscellany. It is in fact a manuscript of the *Ars Laureshamensis*; see 13.40 below.
e) *GL* 5.328.12–20: A small snippet from a commentary on *Ars maior* Book 3 in what Keil names Paris, Sangermanensis 291. It comes from a set of three leaves added to a manuscript of Hesychius Hierosolymitanus which I cannot identify.
f) *GL* 5.327–8: The anonymous fragment *soloecismus quid est?* which Keil quotes is part of Victorinus as edited by Niedermann (1937); see 12.45 above.

13

Early Medieval Grammars

My original intention was to include only the later (post sixth-century) texts that are found in *GL* and *AH*, simply in order to bring up to date the bibliography for the works classicists would be most likely to encounter. But it rapidly became clear not only that an account of grammar that skips from Priscian to Iulianus of Toledo to Bede to Alcuin to the nameless excerpts in *AH* would be very unsatisfactory, but also that a great many texts that belong with those in *AH* are now much better known and understood than in 1870 and form a fitting sequel to the tradition that ends (in *GL*) with Priscian and Eutyches. Hence this chapter.

Most of the bibliography given below is either editions of texts (where they exist), descriptions of unpublished texts, or studies concentrating on identification and place in the grammatical tradition. Bibliographical citations are uneven, as is my knowledge: I have emphasized the seventh- and eighth-century texts and those that are clearly significant, although I freely admit the subjectivity of that judgment. There is more than I list here; many grammatical manuscripts contain texts that differ in some way from published texts and many manuscripts have yet to be examined carefully. I have included quite a few texts that Hagen did not include (as they are not in Swiss libraries), but while I have tried to track down all the texts mentioned in *AH*, I have discarded some (as too late or too trivial to include), and I could not fully identify some others.

There are good general treatments emphasizing linguistics in the Middle Ages in Vineis (1994) and Law (2003); both go well beyond the limits of this book. For background and context, see especially Riché (1976) and Irvine (1994). For introductions to the available textual material (the works listed below) and the various kinds of grammars, Law's work is the necessary starting point, in particular Law (1982, 1993b, 1995a, with useful lists of manuscripts), together with many of the papers collected in Law (1997), including her bibliography of medieval grammars (Law 1993c, reprinted in Law 1997). That bibliography has been my starting point, and I have tried to include every text she mentions even if I have nothing to add.

TEXTS WITH AUTHORS:

1. ALCUIN

Master of Charlemagne's palace school, abbot of the monastery of St. Martin at Tours, and much else, Alcuin's importance in the Carolingian revival goes far beyond the bounds of this volume. Unfortunately, many more works are attributed to him than can possibly be genuine; Gorman (2002) provides a salutary introduction to the problem. I mention here only the two grammatical works.

1. *De orthographia*

T: *GL* 7.295–312; Marsili (1952); Bruni (1997, with reference to other bibliography).

2. *Dialogus Franconis et Saxonis de octo partibus orationis*

T: *PL* 101: 854–902.
R: *LG* (Jullien and Holtz); Manitius (1911) §42.
S: Irvine (1994: 313–33); Law (1994b: 95–6) for a brief description and bibliography. The *Dialogus* (if genuine) is notable for Alcuin's (very early) use of Priscian's *Ars*; but Gorman (2002: 173) argues that it is spurious.

2. ALDHELM

Aldhelm's two works on meter (*De metris, De pedum regulis*) make up the largest portion of his *Epistola ad Acircium* (probably written 685–95), where they are separated by his hexameter *Enigmata. De metris* is about the hexameter (and thus serves to introduce the *Enigmata*, which also circulated separately), and is considerably indebted to Audax, Donatus, and Victorinus; *De pedum regulis* is about the varieties of metrical foot, and seems to owe something to the pseudonymous *Epistula Sancti Hieronymi de nominibus pedum* (13.44 below) and to Iulianus of Toledo (as well as, apparently, to Phocas, Priscian, and Servius on the *Georgics*).
T: Ehwald (1919: 75–96, 150–201); *De metris* and representative excerpts from *De pedum regulis* are translated with an introduction by N. Wright in Lapidge and Rosier (1985: 183–219).
R: Teuffel 3 §500.2; Manitius (1911) §14.
S: Law (1997: 93–101).

3. ASPORIUS (ALSO KNOWN AS ASPERIUS OR ASPER MINOR)

The *Ars* transmitted under the name of Asporius is a short, heavily Christianized grammar that Holtz describes as a revised and corrected version of Donatus, combining use of the *Ars minor* and *Ars maior* Book 2. It is the oldest of the Insular grammars, cited by Virgilius Maro and the *Anonymus ad Cuimnanum*, and thus cannot be more recent than the early seventh century. Law identifies two versions of this text, one of which makes significantly more use of the (reconstructed) Christian Donatus (see 9.3 above), while the second and more common version returns in parts to the original Donatus. Asporius knows Cassiodorus, *Institutes* Book I (see Holtz 1986b: 289–90), but not Isidore; that is consistent with a date around 600 CE. Law also suggests that it was in fact written in eastern France, as early as the late sixth century, before being transported to Britain.

T: *AH* 39–61.

R: *LG* (Law and Holtz).

S: Löfstedt (1976); Holtz (1981: 272–83); Law (1982: 35–41). For other grammarians named Asper, see 12.5 above.

4. BEDA

The Venerable Bede (672/3–735) wrote several works in the grammatical tradition designed to assist his students:

1. *De arte metrica*

Bede's metrical treatise (GL 7.227–60) is addressed to his student Gutbertus (Cuthbert), *ut, quemadmodum in divinis litteris statutisque ecclesiasticis imbuere studui, ita et in metrica arte, quae divinis non est incognita libris, te solerter instruerem* (260.5–7). He used a wide range of late antique sources including Donatus and his commentators, Servius *De centum metris*, Mallius Theodorus *De metris*, and others. After introductory material on letters, syllabic length, and metrical feet, he concentrates on the hexameter and elegiac couplet, and at the end devotes a little space to other meters *quae magis usui haberi reperimus* (254.12). Of classical poets, he cites Virgil, preferring to use Christian texts. He follows—at some remove, clearly—the derivationist theory of meter, referring to the Phalaecian as a dactylic meter and the Anacreontic as iambic; only the trochaic tetrameter is resolutely described as trochaic. He ends with one brief chapter *De rhythmo* in which he sends interested students to read Servius *De centum metris*, and another on the three types of poem (dramatic, narrative, mixed), before making a transition into his next book.

2. *De schematibus et tropis*

This short text (*RLM* 607–18) is an explanation of the seventeen figures of speech and thirteen tropes that are found in Donatus, *Ars maior* 3.5–6. Donatus provides only the skeleton; the flesh comes largely from the Christianized (and much longer) version produced sometime in the late fifth or early sixth century and best represented now by "Isidorus Iunior" (13.14 below). Bede also made some use of Cassiodorus' *Expositio Psalmorum*. Bede's is a Christianized rhetoric, eliminating classical examples and substituting biblical ones; in this he is a follower of Cassiodorus, but at a more elementary level. It has also become clear (see Franklin 2002) that *De schematibus et tropis* is much more than an elementary textbook of rhetoric for Christians; it is also an ambitious attempt to introduce his students to biblical hermeneutics through figural interpretation.

3. *De orthographia*

Bede's treatise on orthography (*GL* 7.261–94) is separate from the other two books and is transmitted separately from them. It is slightly misnamed: after a single paragraph on the use of single letters as abbreviations, it is an alphabetical list of words (from *ante* to *verbum*) that might cause trouble in meaning, inflection, or orthography, sometimes sliding towards *differentiae*. Virgil is the most frequently cited source, and some other classical authors appear, including (surprisingly) Lucilius and Propertius; the Bible appears in the opening entry but is much less dominant than one might expect.

These three texts used to be considered the work of the young Bede, but recently they have become recognized as more mature compositions. There are also two spurious works: *Cunabula grammaticae artis Donati* (*PL* 90.613–32) is a very elementary commentary on the *Ars minor* (see 13.41 below); *De octo partibus orationis* (*PL* 90.631–42) is equally elementary and very uninspired.

T: *RLM* 607–18 (*De schem.*); *GL* 7.227–94 (*De arte metrica, De orth.*); Tannenhaus (1962 = Miller et al. 1973: 96–122; English translation of *De schem.*); Jones and Kendall (1975; text of all three works); Kendall (1991; *De arte metrica, De schem.* with English translation).
R: Teuffel 3 §500.3; Manitius §4; *LG* (Law and Holtz).
S: Schindel (1968); Holtz (1977c); Dionisotti (1982b); Irvine (1986, 1994: 272–97); Franklin (2000, 2002).

5. BONIFATIUS (VYNFRETH)

Boniface's *Ars grammatica* was written c. 700, while he was still teaching at the monastery of Nhutscelle, before his mission to Germany (716–54) and the foundation of Fulda. The contents are a mixture of Donatus *Ars maior* Book 2 with bits of earlier grammars ranging from Charisius and Diomedes to Virgilius Maro, also adding declensions, conjugations, and lexical lists. It is a more original synthesis than many texts of the period, but was not popular: "an attempt to meet the needs of the eighth century through a medium appropriate in the fifth century" (Law 1982: 80). The dedicatory epistle to one Sigibertus introducing a treatise on the eight parts of speech is printed by Gebauer and Löfstedt as the dedication to Boniface's *Ars*. The *Ars metrica* (properly titled *Caesurae versuum*) consists largely of excerpts from Isidore.

T: Gebauer and Löfstedt (1980: 9–99, 109–13; Dedicatory epistle plus *Ars grammatica* and *Ars metrica*, respectively); Mai (1828–38: 7.475–548; an incomplete text of the *Ars grammatica*).
R: *LG* (Law and Holtz); Teuffel 3 §500.5; Manitius (1911) §15.
S: Law (1979, 1982: 77–80, 1997: 106–11, 169–87); Irvine (1994: 298–305).

6. CLEMENS SCOTTUS

Three grammatical works have been attributed to Clemens, an Irishman who came to France and taught at the palace school during the reign of Louis the Pious in the early ninth century:

1. *Ars grammatica*

The text edited by Tolkiehn (badly: see Barwick 1930) under Clemens' name is not by him; it is an anonymous catechistic *ars* on the parts of speech, with many close parallels to other early medieval *artes*, including *Anonymus ad Cuimnanum*, Malsachanus, Cruindmel, and the *Ars Bernensis*.

2. Donatus Ortigraphus

A late hand in Bern 123 attributes to Clemens the grammatical catena known as Donatus Ortigraphus (see 13.9 below), but although contemporary with Clemens, it is probably not by him.

3. *Pauca de barbarismo collecta de multis*

This collection of material on barbarism, solecism, and figures of speech is parallel to Donatus, *Ars maior* Book 3. If it were certain that a poem with a dedication to the Emperor Lothar (who had been Clemens' pupil in the palace school) actually belonged to this text, then it would seem to be a genuine work of Clemens; but one cannot be certain of that, and according to Mari, *Pauca de barbarismo* more closely resembles the manner of Donatus Ortigraphus.

T: Tolkiehn (1928; *Ars grammatica*); Mari (2017; *Pauca de barbarismo*). I have not seen A. M. Puckett, ed., *Clementis qui dicitur "Ars grammatica"* (Diss. UCLA, 1978).

R: *LG* (Jeudy); *Oxford Dictionary of National Biography* Clemens Scottus (Law); Manitius (1911) §67.

S: Keil (1868: 9–17); Barwick (1930); Löfstedt (1965: 164–5).

7. CRUINDMELUS

The short treatise on meter to which the name of Cruindmelus is attached begins from letters and syllables, rapidly moves to prosody, and then concentrates on explaining the hexameter; at the end, the author makes a brief acknowledgment of the existence of other metrical forms and concludes by telling his readers to consult Servius *De centum metris* if they want to know more. Cruindmelus is heavily dependent on earlier writers: his work overlaps with works of Aldhelm, Bede, and others, and Huemer (vii) rightly calls it a grammatical-metrical cento, expanded only through the more extensive use of quotations from Christian poets.

T: Huemer (1883).

R: Manitius (1911) §82.

S: Keil (1868: 17–18).

8. DICUIL

Although better known for his work on geography and the *computus*, Dicuil (late eighth–early ninth century) wrote a treatise *De primis syllabis*. It is printed as the second half of a treatise by Mico of St. Riquier (see 13.18 below), but its independence was recognized by Strecker (1922) and it was identified as being by Dicuil by Van de Vyver (1935).

T: Manitius (1912: 154.21–177).
R: Manitius (1911) §113.
S: Strecker (1922: 479–87); Van de Vyver (1935).

9. DONATUS ORTIGRAPHUS

The title given in the manuscripts of this grammar is *Eclogae de libris grammaticorum*; it is a catena in question-and-answer form, and each citation is preceded by the author's name (probably taken from an earlier source). The structure follows Donatus: the first part includes sections *de voce, de littera, de syllaba, de accentu,* and *de posituris*, and the second part includes the eight parts of speech. Holtz (1981: 320) suggests that it was designed for teachers rather than pupils. Although it is often considered to be an eighth-century text, the extensive use of Priscian shows that it was written after Alcuin's grammar (whether or not it is by Alcuin), possibly (so Chittenden 1982: xxiii–iv) c. 815. The work itself is anonymous; the traditional attribution comes from the fact that the opening of part 2 (59.4 C), on the parts of speech, begins with the citation of *Donatus ortigraphus*—which is merely the Irish spelling for *artigraphus*, a frequent identification of the grammarian Donatus.

T: Chittenden (1982).
I: CETEDOC (1982b).

10. DYNAMIUS

The Lorsch grammatical anthology Vatican, Pal. Lat. 1746 includes a text ascribed to Dynamius, a complaint about the world and the human condition that is followed by three sets of largely grammatical excerpts, the first of which (a preface on the liberal arts) was drawn from the *Anonymus ad Cuimnanum*. Although the complaint may be by Dynamius, there is little reason to think that anything else in the text printed by Mai under the heading *Dynamius grammaticus Christianus* is by him: it is an anthology of grammatical excerpts making heavy use of Priscian and should not be dated before the early eighth century. The excerpts are heavily focused on the alphabet and prosody with only a brief section at the end on the parts of speech.

T: Mai (1852–1905: 1.2.182–98); to be supplemented by Jeudy (1993).
S: Bischoff (1966: 273–88); Bischoff and Löfstedt (1992: x–xi); Jeudy (1993).

11. ERCHANBERT OF FREISING

Tractatus super Donatum is a ninth-century lemmatized commentary on Donatus (on *Ars minor* and *Ars maior* Books 2 and 1, in that order); it owes a great deal to insular sources, particularly the *Ars Bernensis*.
T: Clausen (1948).
R: Manitius (1911) §76.
S: Law (1993d).

Ermenrich of Elwagen: see below on Godescalc.

12. GODESCALC (GOTTSCHALK) OF ORBAIS

The ninth-century theologian was also the author of two grammatical miscellanies preserved anonymously and without titles in Bern 83, foll. 1r–16v, 63r–74r, surrounding a glossary and an abridged version of Nonius Marcellus, Book 4. They contain a mixture of observations on Latinity drawn from the grammatical tradition (including Priscian, Caper and Agroecius, Servius, Donatus, and Virgilius Maro) with observations on the language of the Bible and other theological texts; the latter category is predominant. Lambot (1932) determined their authorship on the basis of repetitions from Godescalc's securely identified theological works.
T: Lambot (1945: 353–420 and 421–96, respectively); *AH* 172–88 contains a small selection out of order and without attribution. Lambot (1945: 497–503) also prints excerpts from an anonymous grammatical text in Vatican, Reg. Lat. 215 which is very similar to sections of Godescalc together with (504–8) similar excerpts (taken from Dümmler 1899: 536–79) of the letter from Ermenrich of Elwangen written between 850 and 854 to Grimald, abbot of St. Gallen in the mid-ninth century.
R: *LG* (Jolivet); Manitius (1911) §73 on Bern 83, §95 on Godescalc.
S: *AH* xcix–cvi; Lambot (1932). On Ermenrich, see Manitius (1911) §77; Goullet (2009).

[Hieronymus]: see 44 below.

13. HILDERIC OF MONTE CASSINO

Written in the ninth century, Hilderic's *Ars* is a treatment of the parts of speech which owes a great deal to Priscian as well as to Donatus. It is found in a single manuscript from Monte Cassino, and only excerpts have been published.
T: Lentini (1975; excerpts, with full discussion).

14. HRABANUS (RABANUS, RHABANUS) MAURUS

Hrabanus (c. 784–856), abbot of Fulda and then archbishop of Mainz, wrote a great deal, little of it about grammar. The main exception is a work entitled

Excerptio de arte grammatica Prisciani, but the title is in part a misnomer: Hrabanus has a great deal of Priscian (but not the syntax); he also adds to it discussions of meter, prosody, and literary forms drawn from Diomedes, Isidore, and others.

Less germane are three short works: one is a glossary of terms for the body and its parts, most of them with German equivalents (e.g., *Pulmon, lungon* and *Fel id est galla*, but *Cor a cura dictum*) followed by similar short lists of the months and the winds; one is a history of alphabets (*De inventione linguarum*) from Hebrew to German, including runes; the last is a very small fragment of a Latin–German biblical glossary.

T: *PL* 111.613–70 (*Excerptio*); *PL* 112.1375–8 (*Glossae Latino–Barbaricae de partibus humani corporis*); *PL* 112.1379–84 (*De inventione linguarum*) *PL* 112.1383–4 (*Fragmentum glossarii Latino–Theotisci*).

R: *LG* (Holtz); Manitius (1911) §43, esp. 298–9.

15. ISIDORUS IUNIOR

See 9.4 above. The important text *De vitiis et virtutibus orationis* is found in one manuscript, Basel, Universitätsbibliothek F III 15d. In its present form it is later than Isidore but earlier than Iulianus of Toledo, but it is closely based on a text earlier than Cassiodorus.

T: Schindel (1975: 185–241).

S: Schindel (1999, 2002b).

16. ISRAEL SCOTTUS

Versus Israhelis de arte metrica super nomen et verbum belongs to the latter part of the tenth century, beyond the scope of this volume, but this poem on the quantity of final syllables fits into the series of texts *De finalibus*, on which see 8.4b and 12.46.7 above. Israel also wrote a commentary on Donatus' *Ars minor* of which some glosses survive in the manuscripts of Remigius' commentary on the same text.

T: Jeauneau (1985: 22–4) replacing Strecker (1937: 500–2).

R: *LG* (Jeudy).

S: Jeudy (1977); Jeauneau (1985).

17. IULIANUS OF TOLEDO

Iulianus (bishop of Toledo from 680 to 690) was an important theologian and political figure in the Visigothic kingdom of Spain. Two related grammatical works are attributed to him, an *Ars grammatica* and a treatise *De partibus orationis*; taken together, they are a commentary on Donatus, with some distinctive features (see below). The identification of Iulianus as the author of these works has been questioned: they are not included in the catalogue of Iulianus' works made by his successor Felix, relatively few manuscripts of the *Ars* name him as author, and the sole manuscript of *De partibus* is anonymous. Neverthless, the two works were certainly written by the same person (see Munzi 1980–1: 157–9; Holtz

1981: 433). Internal evidence, moreover, shows that the text was written in Spain (Spanish names and a few words; quotations from Eugenius and Isidore); that the *Ars* refers to *Domni Eruigii Regis* (24.376 MY; not in all manuscripts), and *De partibus orationis* to *Egica rex* (171.22 M) suggests that the two works were written in the reigns of Erwig (680–7) and Egica (687–702), respectively. It is theoretically possible that some student or disciple of Iulianus wrote them, but there is no good reason not to trust the titulature of the manuscripts.

Iulianus' *Ars* is a commentary on a version of Donatus in which *Ars minor* is followed by *Ars maior* Books 1 and 3, except that *Ars maior* 1.1 (*De voce*) is omitted. The treatise *De finalibus metrorum* ("Metrorius" or "Maximus Victorinus"; *GL* 6.231.4–9.18; see 12.46.7 above) is inserted between 1.3 and 1.4 to expand on Donatus' rubric of "syllables," and *Ars maior* Book 3 is followed by a metrical treatise closely based on Mallius Theodorus (omitting introductory sections) with some admixture of Audax. The text of Donatus and the order used by Iulianus are part of the "Visigothic" branch of the tradition of Donatus; see Holtz (1981: 453–7). Iulianus' shorter treatise *De partibus orationis* is a commentary on *Ars maior* Book 2, the section of Donatus missing from Iulianus' *Ars*. The most important manuscript of the *Ars* and the only manuscript of *De partibus* is Bern 207, discussed in 9.4 above.

Iulianus' commentaries are lengthy, elementary, and in catechistic form, incorporating material on declension and conjugation into the austere analysis of Donatus. In form they are, like the work of Cledonius, commentaries on Donatus himself; Iulianus makes use of Pompeius and other commentaries, but his focus is firmly on Donatus. He uses quotations from Christian as well as secular sources; Isaiah and the Psalms rub shoulders with Virgil, who is overwhelmingly the most frequent classical source. Quotations from Spanish poets are also to be found, notably Eugenius of Toledo, and the one quotation from Isidore's poetry is consonant with the fairly regular use of Book 1 of Isidore's *Etymologiae*. Iulianus offers an extensive list of every form of metrical foot, which he probably took from a source possibly also used by Aldhelm (Law 1997: 99–100); his work was known and used in Monte Cassino, as reflected in Paris, Lat. 7530 (see Holtz 1975: 101).

T: a) *Ars grammatica*: Maestre Yenes (1973); *GL* 5.317–24 (excerpts); Lindsay (1922; only the section *De vitiis et figuris*, pp. 179–221MY).
b) *De partibus orationis*: Munzi (1980–1); *AH* ccxii–xviii (excerpts).

B: Wessner (1921: 159–61).

R: *LG* (Jeudy); Teuffel 3 §495.6; Manitius 1911 §12.

S: Beeson (1924); Funaioli (1930: 412–43); Holtz (1974, 1981: 260–3); Gómez Heredia (1999); Carracedo Fraga (2005).

18. MALSACHANUS

Two manuscripts of the early ninth century (N = Naples IV A 34; P = Paris, Lat. 13026) contain a set of chapters on the verb and participle; in one of them (N) it is preceded by shorter chapters on the noun and pronoun. According to Löfstedt (1965: 27–9) and Holtz (1981: 296 n.9), these four chapters form part of the same work. N does not give any identification for this text (or these texts); in P it is identified at the end of the text as *congregatio Salcani filii de verbo*. The name *Ars Malsachani* is provided only by a later hand at the beginning of the text in P; this is presumably the same person as "the son of Salcanus" at the end, whose name in Irish was Mac Salcháin. Most scholars adhere to the traditional name Malsachanus; Law insisted on referring to the text as *Congregatio Salcani filii de verbo*.

But disputes over the name are nothing in comparison to the disputes over the text. Whoever Malsachanus was, his name is only securely linked to the sections on the verb and participle. Löfstedt thought that the portions on the noun and pronoun were part of the same text and by the same person; Law believed that the juxtaposition was fortuitous. The noun–pronoun sections, in fact, seem very similar to the comparable sections of the *Ars Ambianensis* (see 13.34 below), another early grammar that exists in multiple forms; Law thought that the sections in N were just another version of the same complex of texts—and not part of the same text as the verb–participle sections of Malsachanus. The *Ars Ambianensis* is so variable in form that it is hard to say what it originally looked like, but the noun–pronoun part of Malsachanus is certainly different from the verb–participle part. Law points out real differences in scale and approach between the two parts, and as she also notes, the noun–pronoun section is structured on Donatus, while the verb–participle section is much more independent. On the other hand, Holtz points out that both texts show a dependence on Priscian's *Institutio de nomine pronomine et verbo*, and that is fairly unusual at this date.

Unlike most later Irish grammatical texts, this (at least the verb–participle section) is not a commentary on Donatus, but an original synthesis; and while the author draws on Donatus, he also makes extensive use of Consentius and knows a number of other ancient grammatical texts either at first hand or indirectly and also uses the *Anonymus ad Cuimnanum* and Virgilius Maro. Law views him as an unoriginal compiler from lost previous compilations, while Löfstedt and Holtz see him as a much more original compiler, using both previous compilations and his own research. In any case, he can be dated from his use of Virgilius and *ad Cuimnanum* to (probably) the early eighth century. But that too is disputed: Law would date him to the eighth century; Löfstedt and Holtz to the seventh.

T: Löfstedt (1965: 173–260).

R: *LG* (Law and Holtz); Manitius (1911) §81.

S: Holtz (1981: 295–300); Law (1981, 1982: 71–4, 90–3). Löfstedt's introduction is a very important contribution to the study of Irish Latin grammars.

19. MICO OF SAINT RIQUIER

There are two works of Mico on prosody, one in verse and one in prose. The poem (*Opus Prosodiacum*) is an alphabetical collection of verses, emphasizing the word that is hard to scan, composed c. 824. Mico made use of the similar (but non-alphabetical) anonymous text in Vatican, Reg. 215; see 13.49b below. His prose

work, *De primis syllabis*, begins as a discussion of prosody of the first syllables of words, but then turns into a list of words with more than one possible pattern of inflection, which in turn gives way to lists of idiomatic usages (e.g., verbs that take the genitive or ablative) and lists of nouns declined only in the singular or plural. There it breaks off, and the work of Dicuil, which is fused with Mico's in the manuscript tradition (see 13.8 above), reverts to being about the quantity of first syllables.
T: Traube (1896: 279–94; verse); Manitius (1912: 126.1–54.20; prose).
R: Manitius (1911) §72, esp. 473–4.
S: Traube (1920: 79–80).

20. MURETHACH (MURIDAC)

Murethach or Muridac (there are several spellings) was Irish in origin, but came to the Continent probably c. 835–40; after teaching at Auxerre, he was then at Metz, where he wrote his grammar (a lemmatized commentary) sometime after 840. His principal source was a lost (Irish) commentary on Donatus that is also the main source for the *Ars Laureshamensis*, the commentary of Sedulius Scottus, and the *Ars Brugensis*. On the chronology, see Holtz (1977b: xxi–xxxv).
T: Holtz (1977b).
S: *LG* (Jeudy); Holtz (1972, 1991).

21. PAULUS DIACONUS

Paul the Deacon (the author also of the epitome of Festus, 10.1 above) created a version of Donatus' *Ars minor* with the title *Ars Donati quam Paulus Diaconus exposuit*, consisting of quotations from Donatus followed by excerpts from other sources, including the so-called Christian *Ars minor* reconstructed by Law (see esp. Law 1993d: 231–8) and a number of sets of paradigms imported from various other sources. The text occupies foll. 27–40 of Vatican, Pal. Lat. 1746 from Lorsch, written in the late eighth century; in all probability (see Law 1994a) it was composed after Paul reached Charlemagne's court in 782.
T: Buffa Giolito (1990; with Italian translation and commentary).
R: Teuffel 3 §500.6; Manitius (1911) §41.
S: *LG* (Holtz); Law (1994a); for further bibliography on Paulus, see 10.1 above.

22. PETER OF PISA

Peter the Deacon, from Pisa, was Charlemagne's teacher of grammar. Two grammatical works by Peter—not printed completely until 2014—survive: one is his *Ars grammatica*, which is closely based on Donatus' *Ars minor*. There are two versions of it: one is found in Bern 207, Bern 522 (apparently the best manuscript), and St. Gallen 876; excerpts from that version were printed by Hagen. The other is the opening text in the grammatical anthology Berlin, Diez. B Sant 66; it was thought by Bischoff (1973: 27–30) that the Bern version was older and the Berlin one a revision. It is clearly more complicated than that, and the distinction between the two versions is not altogether clear, as there are some sets of grammatical excerpts that seem to know both of them. The Berlin version contains some excerpts from Peter's adaptations of Priscian in his other grammatical work, the *Quaestiunculae* (see below), and Krotz and Gorman have suggested that it may have been prepared by one of Peter's students. Whatever the precise history, the Berlin version is more sober than the Bern version: it lacks, for instance, the declension of *honorificabilitudinitas*.

The other text by Peter is the *Quaestiunculae*, adapted excerpts from Jerome's commentary on the book of Daniel followed by more extensive grammatical excerpts from Priscian *Ars* Books 1–16, Diomedes, and Pompeius. This text is found in a remarkable manuscript with the title *Incipit liber de diversis quaestiunculis cum responsionibus suis quem iussit domnus rex Carolus transcribere ex autentico Petri archidiaconi*: it was prepared for Charlemagne (or is possibly itself a copy of Charlemagne's manuscript), copied from the autograph manuscript of Peter, and consists of his work (Brussels II 2572). The sixty-nine *quaestiunculae* on the book of Daniel have long been known; the *quaestiunculae* on grammar were first described by Michael Gorman in 1997. The relationships among the texts to which Peter's name has been attached and even their attribution are not altogether certain; the edition by Krotz and Gorman may now make greater clarity possible.

T: *AH* 159–171 (excerpt from Bern *Ars*); Gorman (2000: 251–9; excerpt from *Quaestiunculae*); Krotz and Gorman (2014) contains all the grammatical texts associated with Peter.

R: Manitius (1911) §66.

S: Bischoff (1973: 27–30); Gorman (1997, 2000); Luhtala (2000); Munzi (2010).

23. REMIGIUS OF AUXERRE

Remigius (c. 841–c. 908) falls outside even the flexible chronological limits of this volume, but his extensive writings are so important for the traditions of classical grammar and commentary that at least some mention of the most relevant works is appropriate; full details in the superb bibliography of Jeudy (1991b), which is the necessary starting point for any serious research. I have seen some, but by no means all, of the editions cited below; I rely in part on Jeudy and on Law (1993c).

In general, on Remigius, see:

B: Jeudy (1991b).

R: *LG* (Jeudy); Manitius (1911) §79; Jeudy (1991a).

C: Iogna-Prat et al. (1991).

1. Commentaries on Authors

Outside the scope of this volume (Chapter 11 in particular) fall almost all Remigius' commentaries on literary texts, for the simple reason that most of the authors he chose to explain are outside my chronological limits: Arator, Boethius'

Consolatio, Disticha Catonis, Martianus Capella, Prudentius, and Sedulius. Of classical authors, Remigius is credited at various times with commentaries on Virgil and Juvenal, but there is no reason to believe that they are genuine (see Jeudy 1991a: 390, 393); that leaves his commentary on Persius, which is genuine, but of which only a very small part survives.

T: Zetzel (2005: 182–92).

2. Grammatical Commentaries

a) Donatus, *Ars minor*: There are in fact two versions of Remigius' commentary on the *Ars minor*. The earlier one, edited by Fox (1902), circulated very widely. The later and longer one, incorporating portions of Israel Scottus and other additions, is unedited.

T: *AH* 202–18 (as *Commentum Einsidlense*); Fox (1902).
S: Jeudy (1977, 1991a: 381–2).

b) Donatus, *Ars maior*: Again, there are two versions. The first, apparently originally intended to go with the earlier commentary on the *Ars minor*, was published from one (incomplete) manuscript by Hagen. It was supplemented for the commentary on *Ars maior* Books 1–2 by Elder from Vatican, Reg. 1560, a major Remigian manuscript which contains his commentaries on Phocas, Donatus *Ars maior*, Bede *De arte metrica* (the end only), Bede *De schematibus et tropis, Disticha Catonis*, and Persius (the opening only). Elder did not notice that the manuscript also included a commentary on *Ars maior* Book 3, which was only published by Coletti in 1985. The second commentary, on *Ars maior* Book 2, is much fuller but remains unpublished.

T: *AH* 219–74 (as *Commentum Einsidlense*; incomplete); Elder (1947; supplement to *AH*); Coletti (1985; commentary on *Ars maior* 3).
S: Jeudy (1975, 1991a: 385–6, 2003).

c) Phocas: *In Phocae Artem de verbo commentum*: Excerpts were edited by Manitius; the whole was edited by Jeudy as her (unpublished) dissertation. Remigius' commentary seems to form part of a larger set of commentaries and glosses on Phocas composed in the ninth century.

T: Manitius (1913a: 73–88; excerpts only).
S: Jeudy (1974b, 1991: 383–4).

d) Priscian, *Institutio de nomine pronomine et verbo*: De Marco edited a commentary that might have been by Remigius, but another version was identified by Jeudy as definitely by Remigius. Excerpts were edited by Huygens, but there is no edition of the whole text.

T: De Marco (1952; probably not Remigius); Huygens (1954; excerpts); Jeudy (1972: 73–9; excerpts).
S: Jeudy (1972, 1991: 382–3).

e) Priscian, *Partitiones*: The opening paragraphs of this text, known as *Prima pagina*, were widely studied, and Remigius wrote a commentary on them which is still unpublished. It is not clear that Remigius ever wrote a fuller commentary on the *Partitiones*.

S: Jeudy (1971, 1991a: 386–7).

f) Eutyches, *Ars de verbo*: The text is known from marginalia and glosses in manuscripts of Eutyches, and is largely unedited.

T: Manitius (1913b; excerpts).

S: Jeudy (1974a, 1978a, 1991a: 384–5).

g) Bede, *De arte metrica* and *De schematibus et tropis*.

T: M. H. King (in the apparatus of Jones and Kendall 1975: 77–171).

S: Jeudy 1991a: 386.

24. SEDULIUS SCOTTUS

The learned Irish scholar wrote in the mid-ninth century (in addition to theology and poetry) a number of grammatical commentaries; that on Donatus, *Ars maior* is closely related to Murethach, the *Ars Laureshamensis*, and the *Ars Brugensis*. The commentary on Priscian is on the dedication and very opening of the *Institutio*, that on Eutyches is on Book 1 only. Löfstedt (1977c: xiii) quotes Sedulius himself (87.10) describing his method in the opening of the commentary on Eutyches: *non omnia explanantes, sed quaedam ex omnibus, quae obstrusa esse videntur, tractantes*. Jeudy (1991a: 384) describes Sedulius' commentary on Eutyches as being in the style of Virgilius Maro.

T: a) *In Donati Artem maiorem*: Brearley (1975; Book 2 only); Löfstedt (1977b).

b) *In Artem Donati de octo partibus orationis* (i.e., *Ars minor*): Löfstedt (1977c: 3–54).

c) *In Priscianum*: Löfstedt (1977c: 57–82).

d) *In Eutychem*: AH 1–38; Löfstedt (1977c: 87–130).

R: *LG* (Jeudy); Manitius (1911) §45.

S: Holtz (1972); Haslam (1988); O Cróinín (1993).

25. SERGI{LI}US

Four different versions of this text on the alphabet appear in four manuscripts, of which Leiden, BPL 135 foll. 71v–75r of the early ninth century is the fullest. Sergi{li}us claims to be a pupil of Virgilius the grammarian, and almost certainly wrote in Ireland in the latter part of the seventh century. Bischoff (1967: 251) considered this text "eine der gelungensten Parodien des Mittelalters."

T: Marshall (2010), a full study of the text; some comments in Munzi (2007: 96 n.4).

26. SMARAGDUS

Smaragdus' commentary (loose enough to be considered as a paraphrase) on *Ars maior* Book 2 was composed c. 805, before Smaragdus became abbot of Saint-Mihiel. It is, as Holtz points out in his preface, the first grammar of the Carolingian period that was written by a monk rather than a public figure (e.g., Peter of Pisa, Paul the Deacon, Alcuin). Smaragdus himself seems to have been from either southern France or Spain, but is very familiar with the insular grammars available in Charlemagne's court (e.g., Alcuin, Clemens). The work consists of fifteen chapters, each preceded by a verse introduction. It is the earliest clearly Christianized commentary on *Ars maior* 2.

T: Löfstedt et al. (1986).
I: CETEDOC (1992a).
R: *LG* (Jeudy); Manitius (1911) §70.
S: Leclercq (1948); Holtz (1981: 438–9, 1986a).

27. TATWINE

Tatwine (Tatuinus) was made Archbishop of Canterbury in 731, near the end of his life (d. 734); cf. Bede, *HE* 5.23. His grammar, an expansion of *Ars maior* Book 2, was presumably written before that, while he was a monk at Breedon in Mercia, probably c. 700.

T: De Marco (1968: 3–93), to be supplemented by Löfstedt (1972a, 1972b).
R: *LG* (Law and Holtz); *Oxford Dictionary of National Biography* (Lapidge); Teuffel 3 §500.4; Manitius (1911) §30.
S: Law (1979, 1982: 64–7, 1997: 105–11). De Marco (1968: 95–141) has a lengthy discussion of Tatwine's sources.

28. URSUS OF BENEVENTUM

Ursus (Bishop of Beneventum from 833) compiled a grammatical compendium based largely on Priscian, *Ars* 1–16 (hence sometimes referred to as *Adbreviatio Prisciani*; the actual title in the manuscript is *Adbreviatio artis grammaticae ex diversis auctoribus ab Vrso composita*), but also making use of Donatus, Pompeius, Virgilius Maro, and other sources. After the adapted excerpts from Priscian, Ursus also included sections on *vitia et virtutes* from other sources. In the sole manuscript, another author (and the scribe notes that he is no longer following Ursus) adds other material of some significance: in the section on vices and virtues he uses both Isidore of Seville (not surprising) and Isidorus Iunior, a fairly unusual text in Italy (see Schindel 2002b: 260 n.17); his other supplements are also notable for their overlap with the earlier Beneventan collection Paris, Lat. 7530, including the didascalic notice for Varius' *Thyestes* and the fragment *De notis*.

T: Morelli (1910; excerpts only).
S: *LG* (Law and Holtz); Holtz (1975); Munzi (2009).

29. USUARD OF SAINT-GERMAIN

Usuard's *Artis grammaticae introductiones* is a very elementary text, consisting largely of paradigms; it was written in the mid-ninth century, according to Casas Homs before Usuard's trip to Spain which began 857/58. Its preservation is more notable than its contents: the most important witness (which contains two versions of the text), Barcelona, Ripoll 46, preserves several sets of annotations (or commentary) on Donatus, including the Visigothic branch of the text of Donatus himself and some material related to the Irish commentary tradition.

T: Casas Homs (1964).

S: *LG* (Law and Holtz); Jeudy (1978b, a much fuller description of the manuscript than Casas Homs); Holtz (1981: 397–9).

30. VIRGILIUS MARO GRAMMATICUS

Virgilius Maro is the oddest (and most interesting) of all grammarians, and his works have been interpreted as parody of grammar, as showing complete ignorance of Latin, and as a mystical and hermetic discussion of wisdom; these are not always mutually exclusive categories, and there is no consensus at all about the significance of his work. Two works survive: the *Epitomae* in five manuscripts and the *Epistolae* which follow the *Epitomae* in only one of them, Naples IV A 34, written at Luxeuil in the early ninth century. Virgilius' two works "correspond approximately to Donatus's *Ars maior* and *Ars minor* respectively" (Law 1982: 42–3), but it is a very distant correspondence. There is a great deal that is bizarre and incredible, most famously the debate between Terrentius and Galbungus about the vocative of *ego*; the identification of Aeneas and Virgilius Assianus as grammatical authorities without any recognition of the better-known people named Aeneas and Virgil; and the twelve Latinities, none of which bears the remotest resemblance to any Latin that we now know. As Holtz rightly observes, "C'est un peu, dans le livre de Virgile, comme si, de la culture scolaire grammaticale latine on connaissait encore la mélodie, mais on avait oublié les paroles" (1981: 316).

In general, it is safe to say that Virgilius worked in the mid-seventh century: he makes use of Isidore's *Etymologiae* (636) and the grammar of Asporius (Asper Minor), and is in turn cited by Aldhelm in a letter written no later than 690 (cf. Law 1982: 48) and parodied by Sergi{li}us, who claims to be his student. Virgilius was widely used by Irish and English grammatical writers (whether writing in Britain or on the Continent) until the early ninth century—but none of them follows his more astonishing contributions. Although Virgilius has at times been identified as French (Virgil of Toulouse), he is clearly Irish; but again, whether in Ireland or on the continent is unanswerable.

T: Huemer (1886); Polara (1979; text and Italian translation); Löfstedt (2003). Law (1995b: 109–15) includes translations of the two most famous sections, the debate on the vocative of *ego* (*Epist.* 2.14–93), and the catalogue of grammarians, including the list of the Twelve Latinities of Virgilius Assianus (*Epit.* 15).

R: *LG* (Polara and Holtz); Teuffel 3 §497.7–9; Manitius (1911) §10; Law (2003: 120).

S: Herren (1979, 1992, 2014); Holtz (1981: 315–18); Law (1982: 42–52, 1995b, 1997: 224–45, incorporating earlier publications); Desbordes (1985); Polara (1993); Löfstedt (2005). This is a small selection from a large bibliography; for more, see Herren (1992: 141 n.1) and more recently Gamberini (2014).

31. WALAHFRID STRABO

The poet, scholar, and Abbot of Reichenau in the first half of the ninth century was (not surprisingly) also interested in grammar, and his versions of *Ars minor* and *Ars maior* Book 2 can be found, written in his own hand, in St. Gallen 878, with alterations, additions, and copies of other grammatical texts included. The same manuscript includes also a collection of alphabets, while a later manuscript (St. Gallen 831) contains Walahfrid's treatise on metrics, consisting of edifying Christian phrases and sentiments illustrating different combinations of feet.

T: The texts in St. Gallen 878 are unpublished; the opening of the metrical treatise is printed by Huemer (1885), but see Bischoff (1967: 45 n.30).

R: Manitius (1911) §44.

S: Bischoff (1967: 34–51); Jeudy (1971).

ANONYMOUS COMMENTARIES ON DONATUS

32. *AGGRESSUS QUIDAM*

This short text (named after its opening words) is a commentary on Donatus, *Ars maior* Book 2 on the noun; it makes use of Asporius, and was probably written in the late seventh or early eighth century. It is found in four manuscripts (Amiens 426, Angers 493, Bern 522, and Naples IV A 34) in conjunction with other texts of insular origin; like many such texts, it is of slightly variable extent. On the Amiens manuscript, see Jeudy (1974b: 78–9) and Holtz (1981: 436–7); on the Bern manuscript (which also contains *Quae sunt quae*), see Law (1982: 92–3) and Munzi (2011).

T: *AH* xxxix–xli (from Bern 522); Munzi (2004: 75–9; with commentary).

33. *ANONYMUS AD CUIMNANUM*

The lemmatized commentary on *Ars maior* Book 2 (the name of the dedicatee, Cuimnanus, is preserved) was written in the first half of the eighth century in an insular milieu, possibly Bobbio or Luxeuil. This text is remarkable for a number of features: its extensive introduction about the place of grammar in the liberal arts (including the assimilation of the eight parts of speech to the eight beatitudes);

the inventiveness of the author; his emotional complaints about the difficulty of Latin and the insufficiencies of Donatus; and the range of his reading. His major sources are Pompeius and Consentius, but the author also knows some surprising texts: the *Appendix Probi* and Martianus Capella as well as Isidore and *Quae sunt quae*. He also seems to share with Malsachanus, Ps.-Clemens, and the anonymous text *De verbo* in Paris, Lat. 7491 (see 13.49c below) a source which has variously been described as *Diomedes plenior*, as a commented version of Diomedes that includes material on which Diomedes himself drew, or as a source of Diomedes which may or may not have included quotations (at some remove) from Valerius Probus himself. In any case he, like Malsachanus, knows some quotations from archaic Roman literature (notably Accius) which are otherwise unknown. Should the source problem ever be solved, we would have a much clearer idea of the patterns of circulation of late antique grammars, but no rapid solution is likely.

The sole complete copy of *ad Cuimnanum* is the middle of three commentaries on Donatus bound together in St. Paul im Lavanttal, Stiftsbibliothek 2/1, where it is surrounded by Pompeius and the *Explanationes* of "Sergius." Excerpts are also found in several other manuscripts, notably the Lorsch anthology Vatican, Pal. Lat. 1746 and the central Italian collection Oxford, Bodleian Add. C 144. See also on 13.35 below.

T: Bischoff and Löfstedt (1992).
I: CETEDOC (1992b).
R: *LG* (Jeudy).
S: Bischoff (1966: 273–88); Holtz (1981: 267–71, 284–94); Law (1982: 87–90); Taeger (1991); Irvine (1994: 280–7, 297–8).

34. *ARS AMBIANENSIS*

The *Ars Ambianensis* is so named because it is found on foll. 48–71 of Amiens 426, a grammatical miscellany written at Corbie in the late eighth or early ninth century; other texts found in the same collection include *Quae sunt quae* and the *Epitomae* of Virgilius Maro (for details, see Holtz 1981: 436–8 and Giammona 2016: xxxv–vi). The *Ars* in Amiens 426 contains discussions of noun, pronoun, and verb (incomplete), but there are at least two other versions of this text: one that is considerably longer and contains sections on the adverb and participle is found in St. Gallen 877; a shorter version found in three other manuscripts contains only the portion on the noun.

Even where all the versions are extant, none is identical to any other. They all reflect a putative original which each has adapted: by additions from Virgilius Maro, by greater or lesser presence of paradigms, by the use of Priscian. The common source made use of the Irish (Christanized) version of Donatus, combining parts of the *Ars minor* and *Ars maior* Book 2, but it organizes the account of the noun on the basis of Priscian's division into declensions rather than Donatus' division into genders. The same text also has more distant relatives: something like it was used by Clemens Scottus, and a version of it preserved in Naples IV

A 34 (the manuscript that contains the complete Virgilius Maro) is linked to the treatise on the verb ascribed to Malsachanus (on that problem, see 13.18 above), but despite Löfstedt, it probably is not by the same author.

It seems likely that, in its "original" form (if there ever was one), the *Ars Ambianensis* dealt with the parts of speech in the manner of Donatus, but adding additional materials. It was probably composed in the late seventh or (more likely) early eighth century. It is a matter of definition, and generally uncertain, whether one should consider these to be versions of the same text or distinct texts; it matters only to someone trying to edit them.

The *Ars Ambianensis* was unpublished until very recently, but Giammona's new edition is not much help either: he prints the three versions of the treatment of the noun separately, does not include any of the material on other parts of speech found in two of the three versions, and describes what he has published with the misleading title *Declinationes nominum*. *Declinationes nominum* (on which see 13.48 below) is a name generally given sets of paradigms frequently attached to the *Ars* of Asporius. *Ars Ambianensis*, however, is not that: although elementary and incomplete, it is (or was) in fact an *ars*.

T: Giammona (2016; partial).
R: *LG* (Law and Holtz).
S: Holtz (1981: 436–8); Law (1982: 67–74); Irvine (1994: 112–15).

35. *ARS AMBROSIANA*

The lemmatized commentary on *Ars maior* Book 2 is preserved in Milan, Ambros. L 22 sup. written in the ninth century; the commentary itself is considerably older than that, possibly pre-700, as it shows no knowledge of either Asporius or Virgilius Maro. It cites instead a number of grammatical texts that appear in the (later) catalogue of the Bobbio library, and it may well have been written there. Both this text and *Anonymus ad Cuimnanum* show a wider knowledge of grammatical literature than does Asporius, who knows (basically) only a version of Donatus. These two texts make use also of the earlier commentaries on Donatus, notably Sergius and Pompeius. Both are also careful to distinguish words of Donatus from their own words (which are in fact often not their own, but are taken from the earlier commentaries). They also employ, and explain, Hiberno-Latin forms, something that continues in later Irish grammars, and their works are filled with false etymologies and explanations of things they no longer understood. The text is in poor condition.

T: Löfstedt (1982).
I: CETEDOC (1982a).
R: *LG* (Jeudy); Manitius (1911) §80.
S: Löfstedt (1980); Law (1982: 93–7).

36. *ARS AUGIENSIS*

Karlsruhe, Aug. 112 foll. 61v–101v contains a grammatical compilation in which small parts of Donatus, *Ars maior* Book 2 are supplemented by small parts of other grammatical texts, including Isidore, Audax, the *Explanationes in Donatum* and others, some of which cannot be identified; Holtz gives a detailed analysis. In the margin at one point is found the name *Vuolfinus* and at another *FINIT DEO GRATIAS VVOLVVINVS*; that has suggested that, somehow, this text has something to do with the Vulfinus mentioned as a grammarian by Theodulf of Orleans (s. ix; see Manitius 1911 §68), but Holtz points out that it is probably the name of the scribe rather than the author. It is unpublished.

S: Keil (1868: 22); Holtz (1981: 367–71).

37. *ARS BERNENSIS*

The *Ars Bernensis* is the surviving portion of what must have been an extremely long grammatical compilation; what survives is *De partibus orationis, De nomine*, and *De pronomine*. It is largely based on *Ars maior* Book 2, with some mixture of *Ars minor*, and it includes a great many citations from other grammatical sources (some, probably, not at first hand), including Priscian, Sacerdos, Charisius, Isidore, Virgilius Maro, and Pompeius. It is similar in some respects to other Insular and Insular-related texts, including *Ars Ambianensis* and Ps.-Clemens; it apparently influenced both the latter and the grammar of Alcuin.

The text was printed by Hagen from Bern 123, foll. 78v–117r (from Fleury, s. ix), and his edition is not altogether satisfactory. There is at least one other witness to the text, the marginal commentary on Donatus found in Barcelona, Ripoll 46, written at Ripoll in Catalonia. There is a partial re-edition of the *Ars Bernensis* (and description of the manuscripts) in Holtz (1992).

T: *AH* 62–142.

R: *LG* (Jeudy); Manitius (1911) §71; Law (1982: 74–7).

S: *AH* lxxxiii–xcvi; Holtz (1981: 434–6, 1992).

38. *ARS BRUGENSIS*

A grammatical compilation close to Murethach and Sedulius Scottus, dating to the second half of the ninth century and preserved in Bruges 537 foll. 19rb–38vb and 41rb–6va. Unpublished.

S: *LG* (Jeudy); Jeudy (1975: 228–9).

39. *ARS EST AB ARTU DICTA*

A commentary on the *Ars minor* found in Berlin, Staatsbibliothek Lat. Fol. 641, foll. 214vb–21ra. The manuscript was written in northern Italy, late ninth or early tenth century; the commentary itself is older. It has close relationships with the early insular texts *Quae sunt quae* (noted also by Munzi 2004: 48) and *Aggressus quidam*, and also with the grammar of Peter of Pisa; the direction of these relationships has not been determined, and the text is largely unpublished.

T: Jeudy (1990: the first two sections [*De partibus orationis* and *De nomine*] and the beginning of *De verbo*).

40. *ARS LAURESHAMENSIS*

This anonymous lemmatized commentary covered all three books of Donatus *Ars maior* in the order 2–1–3 (as is not uncommon), but only one manuscript has all three books: Vatican, Palatinus Lat. 1754, written at Lorsch s. xi. The commentary itself is Irish in origin, written in the ninth century, drawn from the same source as Murethach, Sedulius Scottus, and the *Ars Brugensis*, and related also to one of the commentaries in Barcelona, Ripoll 46 described by Jeudy (1978b).

T: Lofstedt (1977a).
S: *LG* (Jeudy); Holtz (1972).

41. *CUNABULA GRAMMATICAE ARTIS*

A very elementary commentary on the *Ars minor*, preserved in three ninth-century manuscripts of which the most important is Leiden, BPL 122, foll. 97v–109r; the earliest manuscript (Paris, Lat. 7558) lacks the opening section and interrupts the text with sets of declensions following the discussion of the noun and conjugations following the discussion of the verb. The prefatory paragraph of the text (printed at *GL* 5.325.2–23) complains loudly about the corruptions and interpolations of manuscripts of Donatus.

The text was wrongly attributed to Bede and as a consequence it is printed among his works; for discussion of its origins (which are obscure), see Holtz.

T: *PL* 90.613–32 (ascribed to Bede); *GL* 5.325.2–23 (opening paragraph only).
S: Holtz (1981: 389–90 and 449–53).

42. *QUAE SUNT QUAE*

This early text (possibly seventh-century) of insular origins (Ireland or an Irish writer on the continent) is a commentary on Donatus, *Ars minor* with digressions and additions. It starts by glossing the *incipit*, and the commentary on *Ars minor* is followed by a small amount of commentary on *Ars maior* Books 1 and 3; that then turns into a collection of quotations from Isidore. *Quae sunt quae* makes use of Asporius but not Virgilius Maro, and it was in turn used by the *Anonymus ad Cuimnanum*. The manuscripts are familiar carriers of Irish grammar: the longest version is in Paris, Lat. 13025; shorter ones in Amiens 426 and Bern 522.

T: *AH* xli–iii (partial); Munzi (2004: 17–40, with commentary).
S: Law (1982: 85–7); Munzi (2011).

OTHER ANONYMOUS TEXTS

43. *ARS NANCEIANA (SAPIENTIA EX SAPORE)*

The unpublished grammatical florilegium found in Nancy 317 (formerly 356) s. ix and two Munich manuscripts (Clm 6413 and 6415) has in the Nancy manuscript the title *Glosa de partibus orationis*, but is more commonly known from its

first words as *Sapientia ex sapore*. It contains excerpts from a number of sources, including Charisius, Consentius, Pompeius, Priscian, and Virgilius Maro.
T: Collignon (1883) gives a detailed description with a few excerpts.

44. [HIERONYMUS]

A text on the names of metrical feet is preserved in different forms in two ninth-century manuscripts (Paris, Lat. 7520 foll. 69r–v; Munich, Clm 6411 foll. 20v–2v); the Paris manuscript begins *Incipit epistula sancti Hieronimi de nominibus pedum*, while the Munich manuscript simply has *Incipit de pedibus*. Another version is printed in *PL* 82.730–2 as a supplement to Isidore. There is no complete edition.
S: Law (1997: 98–9), discussing it as a source for Aldhelm.

45. ERFURT FLORILEGIUM

Erfurt 8° 8 was written c. 1100, but the grammatical florilegium it contains was probably compiled (from texts as recent as Donatus Ortigraphus and Smaragdus, but also using Priscian) in the ninth century.
T: Jeudy (1983).

46. *DE LITTERIS*

There are many, many short tracts on the alphabet and the meaning of letters: some of them only on the Latin alphabet, others extending to Greek and (often in elaborate fiction) Hebrew; some of them allegorize the pen-strokes required to make a letter (the three strokes of A standing for the trinity), and others discuss shapes as well as meanings. To the best of my knowledge, no extensive list of these small texts exists, but among them are the following:

a) Four texts inserted between the chapters *De syllabis* and *De pedibus* of Donatus' *Ars maior* in Paris, Lat. 13025 from Corbie (early ninth century); see Holtz (1981: 371–4) and Munzi (2007: 39–41) for description of the manuscript.
   i) foll. 24vb–5vb: *A vocalis est* . . . There are three versions of this text. This one is also found in Bern 417 foll. 95–8v[1] from which it was edited by Hagen (see b below); it is preceded by the incipit *De litteris Latinis quidam sapiens interpretatus est*. A second version (without the incipit), edited by Munzi (2007: 123–35), appears in Karlsruhe, Aug. 112 foll. 3v–12v; it is far longer and includes more extensive Christian interpretations, including poems under K and X (see Munzi's commentary for sources). The third version appears in Leiden, BPL 135 foll. 73r–4v (93v–4r at

1. The folia of Bern 417 were misnumbered; what Hagen calls (for this text) foll. 105v–8v are now foll. 95v–8v. See Munzi 2007: 37n.

Munzi 2007: 100 is an error) as the fourth part of "Sergi{li}us"; it is edited by Munzi (2007: 101–4) and Marshall (2010: 227–30).

ii) foll. 25vb–26rb: *Quaeritur enim quis primus litteras Hebreorum Grecorum Latinorum et ceterarum gentium adinvenit.* . . . The same text is found in Bern 417 foll. 94r–5r and Paris, Lat. 1750 foll. 142r–v. Edited by Munzi (2007: 45–7).

iii) foll. 26rb–va: *Item de Hebreis litt(eris). Hebraicarum litterarum formae duae sunt: una antiqua qua Samaritani utuntur, altera posterior quae Iudaei.* . . . It is also found in Bern 417 foll. 95rv. Wrongly attributed to St. Jerome, it is printed in *PL* 30.307C–9A.

iv) fol. 26va–b: *Incipit abcdis Grece cum numero. A alpha pro a* . . . . It too is also in Bern 417 fol. 95. It is apparently unpublished.

b) Hagen, *AH* 302–8 printed three texts *de litteris* from Bern manuscripts. Of these, the first (*A vocalis est* . . .) is listed above, a(i); the third, Bern 417 fol. 98v–9r, is in fact from Martianus Capella §261 (see Munzi 2007: 38). The remaining text is found in Bern 36, fol. 140ra–b (*AH* 305.30–7.18): *A. Simplicitas elementi huius figurae triplicitate linearum ducta* . . .

c) Munzi (2007) prints the following texts (I omit those included in a above):

i) *Genera litterarum diversa sunt* . . . : Munzi (2007: 23–5) from Bern 207, foll. 112r–13r (114r–15r).

ii) *Audivimus multos de initium litterarum* . . . : Munzi (2007: 63–9) from Vatican, Lat. 6018, foll. 51r–4r.

iii) *Littera est aelimentorum vocis articulatim* . . . : Munzi (2007: 83) from Vatican, Lat. 6018, fol. 54r–v (also in Paris, Lat. 2772 fol. 89r).

iv) *Interpretatio litterarum de Hebreo in Latino. A aleph* . . . : Munzi (2007: 86) from Vatican, Lat. 6018, fol. 54v.

v) *Quia video te de scripturis* . . . : Munzi (2007: 89–90) from Vatican, Lat. 6018, fol. 97rv. This is the opening of a much larger text, *Interrogatio de littera et de singulis causis*, in which questions about the alphabet are followed by considerably more questions about the Bible. Its sources and content point to an origin either in Spain or in Verona, probably in the early eighth century; it was apparently popular in the ninth century, but faded from view after that. Text in Everett (2006).

d) *Littera quid est? Pars minima vocis articulatae* . . . : This text (printed in Munzi 2016 from Paris, Lat. 13025) is in reality part of *Interrogatio de grammatica*, a text published previously in Munzi (2000: 377–8); it is apparently also related to *Quae sunt quae* (13.42 above).

e) *Versus de nominibus litterarum seu Versus cuiusdam Scoti de alphabeto*, ed. Glorie (1968: 725–41). See also Manitius (1911) §25.

f) See also Sergi{li}us, 13.25 above, and Walahfrid Strabo, 13.31 above.

g) There are many more overlapping and related such texts; most derive from Isidore, Jerome, and the commentators on Donatus' chapter *De litteris*;

there are, for instance, three such in Berlin, Diez. B Sant. 66 (see Bischoff 1973: 30–3).

47. PARSING GRAMMARS

These are texts of very simple question-and-answer type, substituting for or introducing the similar format of Donatus, *Ars minor*. Law (2000: 29–30) gives a list of fourteen of them (which, as she says, is not complete) from the ninth and tenth centuries; most are very short or fragmentary, and only the following three, to the best of my knowledge, have been printed at all:

a) *Codex quae pars*: an excerpt published in *AH* xxi.
b) *TI ECTIN DOCTUS Quid est doctus*: published by Omont (1881). This short text is a futile attempt at a bilingual parsing grammar; see also Ciccolella (2008: 90–1).
c) *Beatus quid est*: published by Bayless (1993).

For the so-called *Scalprum Prisciani* see 12.35 above.

In general, see Law (2000: 25–32).

48. *DECLINATIONES NOMINUM*

Various versions survive of this text, which is in all but one manuscript attached to Asporius' *Ars*; it consists of paradigms of nouns and lists of them, in various orders and with various contents. No original version can be reconstructed; as Law (1982: 56) notes: "The freedom with which the work was treated means that it is inaccurate to speak of the *Declinationes nominum* as a single text. The original collection of material was reworked to varying degrees, and these versions were themselves reworked or incorporated into other texts." As it uses vocabulary from Aldhelm's *De virginitate*, it may be British rather than Irish, and its original (if there ever was a single original) belongs in the early eighth century. Law intended to edit the text, but never did so.

T: *AH* 61 (a short form, in the apparatus criticus); there is also a version in Paulus (13.21 above) 4.12–10.22.

S: *LG* (Law and Holtz); Law (1982: 56–64, 1997: 104–5).

49. MISCELLANEOUS MINOR TEXTS

a) Four short orthographic treatises, late and elementary, are printed by Hagen, *AH* 291–301.
b) An anonymous metrical text in Vatican, Reg. 215 (described by Chatelain fairly accurately as a *Gradus ad Parnassum*) contains some 220 verses of classical and late antique hexameter poetry, not in any clear order, but indicating after each verse the word the scansion of which was problematic. It is followed by similar excerpts from particular poets. The text was

used by Mico of St. Riquier, and thus dates at latest from the early ninth century.

T: Chatelain (1883).

c) An anonymous and unpublished text *De verbo* is preserved in the tenth century manuscript Paris, Lat. 7491, foll. 89r–114v. It is discussed in connection with the problem of the identity of various grammarians named Probus by Keil (*GL* 4.xx–xxiv) and in connection with the sources of *Anonymus ad Cuimnanum* by Taeger (1991: 43–5). See also Löfstedt (1998).

d) Fragments of an early commentary on Donatus, with similarities to other early Irish grammars, are described (but not published) by Löfstedt (1987). They are now Würzburg, M. P. Misc. F. 28 and come from book bindings.

e) I have not been able to find what Law (1993c) labels *Ars Toletana*, in Toledo, Biblioteca del Cabildo 99–30, foll. 33v–4v.

f) Not a commentary, but perhaps a suitable ending, is a manuscript of Donatus (now National Library of Wales, MS 21553c) written c. 825 in France, possibly in Auxerre or Fleury according to McKitterick (1976), with annotations in several hands. Among them (probably tenth century) is a schoolboy whose grammar clearly needed improvement: *Sadonis iste liber est sua mater dedit illi Magnum onor illa sit qui dedit hunc librum.*

Works Cited

WHEN I BEGAN TO WORK ON THIS BOOK IN 2007, THE TOOLS for research and the resources available were very different: so many of the texts, so much of the manuscript material, and so much of the secondary bibliography are available online in one form or another (digitized images; PDF; searchable texts), that it is far easier to gain access to rare and obscure materials than was true only a few years ago. These resources will continue to change and expand after this book is printed, but it may be useful to include what is inevitably a partial guide to some of these websites. I do not include standard works of reference and bibliographical tools (e.g., JStor, *Année philologique, Brill's New Pauly*, and other databases); what is given here is a selection of materials that I have used, specifically relevant to the study of Roman scholarship and its transmission. It is in no sense (even while I write it) exhaustive.

WEBSITES

1. Texts of Roman Grammars, Dictionaries, or Commentaries

Corpus grammaticorum latinorum: A searchable database of all the texts included in Keil's *Grammatici Latini*, with texts divided into topical sections (e.g., *de littera; partes orationis*). Where more modern editions are available, they have been substituted for Keil. There is also a very useful bibliographical section.
http://kaali.linguist.jussieu.fr/CGL/index.jsp

digilibLT: Digital library of late antique Latin prose texts, including a good number of grammatical and other scholarly texts.
http://digiliblt.lett.unipmn.it/index.php

Grammatici disiecti: A list (with links to texts and bibliography, where available) of all fragmentary grammarians.
http://gradis.hypotheses.org/

Hyperdonat: A project to put ancient commentaries online; so far, only Donatus on Terence and Cassiodorus on the Psalms.
http://hyperdo.nat.huma-num.fr/editions/html/index.html

2. Older Printed Materials

Hathi Trust: Access to out-of-copyright editions and works of scholarship, mostly since c. 1800.
https://www.hathitrust.org/

Münchener DigitalizierungsZentrum (MDZ): An invaluable collection of early printed books (as well as a gateway to the collections of Bayerische Staatsbibliothek).
https://www.digitale-sammlungen.de/

3. Access to Manuscript Materials

a) Gateways

The following sites offer links to multiple websites containing images of manuscripts. There are more than I list here, but I have found these very useful:

Archivalia and Medieval Manuscript Catalogues and Inventories: These two sites contain lists of online lists of manuscripts and manuscript catalogues; very useful.
http://archivalia.hypotheses.org/6505
http://www.utm.edu/staff/bobp/vlibrary/mscatalogs.shtml

DigiPal: A very limited site, focusing on palaeography and in particular on British manuscripts of the eleventh century.
http://www.digipal.eu/

Europeana Regia: More entertaining and more limited than standard bibliographical sites, it does link to copies of Carolingian manuscripts from a number of different libraries.
http://www.europeanaregia.eu/en

Historical Auxiliary Sciences: Codicology: A broad bibliographical site for students of manuscripts. It is aimed at historians, but the catalogues and collections it links to include a much wider range of materials. It ceased adding materials in 2009, but is still useful.
http://www.vl-ghw.uni-muenchen.de/kodikologie_en.html

Marginal scholarship: A small but growing set of links to early medieval annotated manuscripts.
https://www.marginalscholarship.nl/

Mirabile: Digital Archives for Medieval Culture: A very broad site, containing within it useful search tools for finding digitized manuscripts.
http://www.mirabileweb.it/index.aspx

Mittelalter: A medieval studies blog, valuable for long lists of resources, primarily historical, but often useful.
http://mittelalter.hypotheses.org/

New York University, Bobst Library: The page on medieval manuscripts has some obsolete links, but it is a very good starting point.
http://guides.nyu.edu/c.php?g=276597&p=1844931

b) Reconstructed Monastic Libraries

St. Gallen and Reichenau:
http://www.stgallplan.org/en/index_library.html

Lorsch:
http://www.bibliotheca-laureshamensis-digital.de/

c) Large Groups of Libraries (Mostly National)

Austria: http://manuscripta.at

France. There are two sites:

Bibliothèque virtuelle des manuscrits médiévaux (BVMM): sponsored by the Institut de recherche et d'histoire des textes.
http://bvmm.irht.cnrs.fr

Gallica: A frustrating website to use, but it links to the general catalogue of manuscripts in France.
http://gallica.bnf.fr

BVMM and Gallica seem to be complementary websites and do not overlap a great deal. For the Bibliothèque nationale de France, see "individual libraries" below. It is much easier to use than Gallica.

Germany: http://www.manuscripta-mediaevalia.de

Switzerland: http://www.e-codices.unifr.ch/de

d) Some Individual Libraries

Biblioteca Apostolica Vaticana: http://digi.vatlib.it/

Bibliothèque nationale de France: http://archivesetmanuscrits.bnf.fr/

British Library: http://www.bl.uk/manuscripts/

Leiden, Bibliotheek der Rijksuniversiteit: https://socrates.leidenuniv.nl

Munich, Bayerische Staatsbibliothek: https://www.bsb-muenchen.de/sammlungen/handschriften/

List and Index of Manuscripts Cited

1. Papyri

2. Manuscripts

If images are available, the URL or publication is given below the shelf-mark; absence of any such reference means that I have not found any images, not necessarily that there are none.

http://bvmm.irht.cnrs.fr/resultRecherche/resultRecherche.php?COMPOSITION_ID=3449

Barcelona, Arxiu de la Corona d'Arago
MS Ripoll 46 — 354, 358, 359

Basel, Universitätsbibliothek
MS F III 15d (*CLA* 7.847) — 183, 292, 329, 346
http://www.e-codices.unifr.ch/de/searchresult/list/one/ubb/F-III-0015d

Berlin, Staatsbibliothek zu Berlin, Preussischer Kulturbesitz
MS Diez. B Sant 66 (*CLA* 8.1044) — 281, 301, 335, 349, 362
http://digital.staatsbibliothek-berlin.de/werkansicht?PPN=PPN685264297
Bischoff (1973) also provides a full facsimile.

MS Lat. Fol.641 — 358

Bern, Burgerbibliothek
MS A 90 — 310

MS A 91.18 (*KfH* #517) — 240

MS 36 (*KfH* #493) — 361

MS 45 (*KfH* #494) — 272

MS 83 (*KfH* #502) — 241, 345

MS 123 (*KfH* #538) — 343, 358

MS 165 (*KfH* #541) — 135, 136, 266
http://www.e-codices.unifr.ch/de/searchresult/list/one/bbb/0165

MS 167 (*KfH* #542) — 136
http://www.e-codices.unifr.ch/de/searchresult/list/one/bbb/0167

MS 172 (*KfH* #545) (+Paris Lat. 7929) — 136
http://www.e-codices.unifr.ch/de/searchresult/list/one/bbb/0172

MS 207 (*CLA* 7.**568; *KfH* #551a) (+Paris Lat. 7520) — 221–3, 313, 322, 347, 349, 361
http://www.e-codices.unifr.ch/de/searchresult/list/one/bbb/0207

MS 258 (*KfH* #564) — 109
http://www.e-codices.unifr.ch/de/searchresult/list/one/bbb/0258

MS 330 (part of *KfH* #579) — 220
http://www.e-codices.unifr.ch/de/searchresult/list/one/bbb/0330

MS 366 (*KfH* #586) — 203
http://www.e-codices.unifr.ch/de/searchresult/list/one/bbb/0366

MS 370 (*KfH* #587) — 272

MS 380 (*CLA* 7.864; *KfH* #588a) — 291

MS 417 (*KfH* #592) — 225, 360, 361

MS 432 (*KfH* #595) — 279

MS 522 (*KfH* #601) — 349, 355, 359

Bologna, Biblioteca universitaria
MS 797 (*KfH* #649) 337

Bruges, Stadsbibliotheek
MS 537 358

Brussels, Bibliothèque royale
MS II 2572 (*CLA* 10.1553; *KfH* #755) 350
http://uurl.kbr.be/1558120

Cambridge, Corpus Christi College
MS 144 (*CLA* 2.122) 239
https://parker.stanford.edu/parker/actions/manuscript_description_long_display.do?ms_no=144

Cambridge, Kings College
MS 52 (Phillipps 16395) (*KfH* #826) 276–7

Einsiedeln, Stiftsbibliothek
MS 326 (*KfH* #1132) 251
http://www.e-codices.unifr.ch/de/searchresult/list/one/sbe/0326

Épinal, Bibliothèque municipale
MS 72 (2) (*CLA* 6.760) 239
http://www.bmi.agglo-epinal.fr:8084/base_patrimoine/Francais/collection.php?id_col=3&type=glossaire&etat=d

Erfurt, Wissenschaftliche Allgemeinbibliothek
MS Amplonianus 2° 42 (*KfH* #1174) 109, 239, 243

MS 8° 8 360

Florence, Biblioteca Medicea Laurenziana
MS Pl. 39.1 266

MS Pl. 45.14 136

Halle, Marienkirche
MS 65 256

Hamburg, Museum für Kunst und Gewerbe
Cod. 53b in scrin.: *See Paris 7900A*

Karlsruhe, Badische Landesbibliothek
MS Aug. perg. 112 (*KfH* #1642) 222, 322, 357, 360
http://www.stgallplan.org/en/index_library.html

Kassel, Gesamthochschulbibliothek
MS Philol. 4°1 297

Laon, Bibliothèque municipale
MS 444 (*KfH* #2120) 111, 241, 242
http://gallica.bnf.fr/ark:/12148/btv1b84921401

Leiden, Bibliotheek der Rijksuniversiteit
Most images in the Leiden website provide sample pages of manuscripts only.

BPL 67F (*KfH* #2142) 106, 107, 109, 238–9, 249
https://socrates.leidenuniv.nl/R/-?func=dbin-jump-full&object_id=673839

BPL 122 (*KfH* #2151) 338, 359
https://socrates.leidenuniv.nl/R/-?func=dbin-jump-full&object_id=670032

BPL 135 (*KfH* #2156) 136, 352, 360
https://socrates.leidenuniv.nl/R/-?func=dbin-jump-full&object_id=2959063

Voss. Lat. F. 79 (*KfH* #2202): *see also Paris1750* 136
https://socrates.leidenuniv.nl/R/-?func=dbin-jump-full&object_id=678698

Voss. Lat. O. 37 (*KfH* #2247) 328
https://socrates.leidenuniv.nl/R/-?func=dbin-jump-full&object_id=679073

Voss. Lat. O. 88 (*KfH* #2255) 145
https://socrates.leidenuniv.nl/R/-?func=dbin-jump-full&object_id=679387

Voss. Lat. Q. 69 (*KfH* #2222) 108
https://socrates.leidenuniv.nl/R/-?func=dbin-jump-full&object_id=680360

Voss. Lat. Q. 130 (*KfH* #2243) 145–7
https://socrates.leidenuniv.nl/R/-?func=dbin-jump-full&object_id=679793

London, British Library
MS Add. 17212 (*CLA* 2.166) 322

MS Add. 47678 (Holkham Hall 387) (*KfH* #2409) 145

MS Harley 647 270
http://www.bl.uk/manuscripts/FullDisplay.aspx?index=116&ref=Harley_MS_647

MS Harley 2773 242

MS Harley 3286 277

MS Harley 5792 (*CLA* 2.203) 106, 241, 242
http://www.bl.uk/manuscripts/FullDisplay.aspx?ref=Harley_MS_5792&index=486

Milan, Biblioteca Ambrosiana
MS C 29 inf. 145

MS E 147 sup. (*CLA* 3.**28): *see Vatican, Lat.5750*

MS L 22 sup. (*KfH* #2641) 357

MS R. 57 sup. = S. P. 11.66 (*CLA* 3.363) 259

Montpellier, Université Bibliothèque interuniversitaire—Section Médecine
MS H 125 (*KfH* #2829) 128, 276
http://www.calames.abes.fr/pub/#details?id=D01040799

MS H 306 (*KfH* #2857) 105, 220–1, 235, 236, 245, 315
http://www.calames.abes.fr/pub/#details?id=D01041502 (a few images)
http://bvmm.irht.cnrs.fr/resultRecherche/resultRecherche.php?
COMPOSITION_ID=2167 (a few images)

Munich, Bayerische Staatsbibliothek
Clm 766 304
http://daten.digitale-sammlungen.de/~db/0001/bsb00011594/images/index.html

Clm 6281 (*KfH* #3027) 184, 318, 322
http://daten.digitale-sammlungen.de/~db/0001/bsb00013166/images/index.html

Clm 6411 (*KfH* #3078) 360
http://daten.digitale-sammlungen.de/~db/0001/bsb00012886/images/index.html

Clm 6413 359
http://daten.digitale-sammlungen.de/~db/0001/bsb00012884/images/index.html

Clm 6415 (*KfH* #3081) 359
http://daten.digitale-sammlungen.de/~db/0001/bsb00012883/images/index.html

Clm 6434 (*CLA* 9.1285) 329
http://daten.digitale-sammlungen.de/~db/0006/bsb00065411/images/index.html

Clm 14420 (*KfH* #3185) 256
http://daten.digitale-sammlungen.de/~db/0003/bsb00036895/images/index.html

Clm 14666 (*KfH* #3240) 292
http://daten.digitale-sammlungen.de/~db/0008/bsb00082357/images/index.html

Clm 14737 (*KfH* #3255) 338
http://daten.digitale-sammlungen.de/~db/0001/bsb00012921/images/index.html

Clm 19482 273, 275
http://daten.digitale-sammlungen.de/~db/0008/bsb00082348/images/index.html

Nancy, Bibliothèque municipale
MS 317 (356) (*KfH* #3570) 359

Naples, Biblioteca Nazionale
MS Lat. 1 (Vindob. 17) (*CLA* 3.388) 160, 235, 300, 314, 316, 331

MS Lat. 2 (Vindob. 16) (*CLA* 3.394, 397a, 397b, 398) 160, 185, 219, 236, 248, 298, 300, 313, 317, 320, 321, 330, 331–4

MS IV A 8 (*CLA* 3.400) 236, 242, 290, 321, 323

MS IV A 11 282, 283, 285, 304, 325, 328

MS IV A 34 (*KfH* #3573) 347, 354, 355, 356–7

Oxford, Bodleian Library
MS Add. C 144 109, 209, 239, 303, 310, 320, 321, 334, 337, 356

Oxford, Magdalene College
MS 64 322, 336

Padova, Biblioteca Universitaria
MS 1084 299

Paris, Bibliothèque Nationale de France
The first reference is to the online catalogue; the second (if any) is to the digital reproduction of the manuscript.

MS Lat. 1750 (*KfH* #4061) 361
http://archivesetmanuscrits.bnf.fr/ark:/12148/cc59715h
http://gallica.bnf.fr/ark:/12148/btv1b8479009h

MS Lat. 2772 (*KfH* #4225) 361
http://archivesetmanuscrits.bnf.fr/ark:/12148/cc60553c
http://gallica.bnf.fr/ark:/12148/btv1b8572242w

MS Lat. 3012 275
http://archivesetmanuscrits.bnf.fr/ark:/12148/cc608494

MS Lat. 7491 (*KfH* #4444) 356, 363
http://archivesetmanuscrits.bnf.fr/ark:/12148/cc66722p
http://gallica.bnf.fr/ark:/12148/btv1b9078025j

MS Lat. 7520 (*CLA* 5.568); *see Bern 207*
http://archivesetmanuscrits.bnf.fr/ark:/12148/cc66722p
http://gallica.bnf.fr/ark:/12148/btv1b90664807

MS Lat. 7530 (*CLA* 5.569) 22, 115, 116, 214, 220, 242, 244, 247, 251, 309, 310, 320, 321, 323, 332, 334, 336, 347, 353
http://archivesetmanuscrits.bnf.fr/ark:/12148/cc94636q
http://gallica.bnf.fr/ark:/12148/btv1b84900617

MS Lat. 7558 (*KfH* #4473) 359
http://archivesetmanuscrits.bnf.fr/ark:/12148/cc66791w
http://gallica.bnf.fr/ark:/12148/btv1b8585599x

MS Lat. 7570 338
http://archivesetmanuscrits.bnf.fr/ark:/12148/cc66804x

MS Lat. 7651 (*KfH* #4490) 241
http://archivesetmanuscrits.bnf.fr/ark:/12148/cc668951

MS Lat. 7730 (*KfH* #4498) 107–8, 297
http://archivesetmanuscrits.bnf.fr/ark:/12148/cc669778
http://gallica.bnf.fr/ark:/12148/btv1b8478988x

MS Lat. 7900A (*KfH* #4510) +Hamburg 53 150, 153–6, 272
http://archivesetmanuscrits.bnf.fr/ark:/12148/cc67156c

MS Lat. 7929; *see Bern 172*
http://archivesetmanuscrits.bnf.fr/ark:/12148/cc671877
http://gallica.bnf.fr/ark:/12148/btv1b84789952

MS Lat. 7960 (*KfH* #4517) 136
http://archivesetmanuscrits.bnf.fr/ark:/12148/cc67220g
http://gallica.bnf.fr/ark:/12148/btv1b9066486q

MS Lat. 8093 (*KfH* #4529-33) 308
http://archivesetmanuscrits.bnf.fr/ark:/12148/cc673547
http://gallica.bnf.fr/ark:/12148/btv1b85856004

MS Lat. 11308 (*KfH* #4676) 107, 136, 266
http://archivesetmanuscrits.bnf.fr/ark:/12148/cc72921b

MS Lat. 13025 (*KfH* #4861) 224–5, 334, 359, 360, 361
http://archivesetmanuscrits.bnf.fr/ark:/12148/cc74146v
http://gallica.bnf.fr/ark:/12148/btv1b8423831v

MS Lat. 13026 (*KfH* #4863-64) 347
http://archivesetmanuscrits.bnf.fr/ark:/12148/cc741473

St. Gallen, Stiftsbibliothek
MS 831 355
http://www.e-codices.unifr.ch/de/searchresult/list/one/csg/0831

MS 870 (*KfH* #5856) 129, 276
http://www.e-codices.unifr.ch/de/searchresult/list/one/csg/0870

MS 876 (*KfH* #5858) 334, 335, 336, 349
http://www.e-codices.unifr.ch/de/searchresult/list/one/csg/0876

MS 877 (*KfH* #5859-61) 356
http://www.e-codices.unifr.ch/de/searchresult/list/one/csg/0877

MS 878 (*KfH* #5862) 310, 355
http://www.e-codices.unifr.ch/de/searchresult/list/one/csg/0877

St. Paul im Lavanttal, Stiftsbibliothek
MS 2/1 (*CLA* 10.1451-53; *KfH* #5933c) 293, 322, 336, 338, 356

Valenciennes, Bibliothèque municipale
MS 397 334
http://ccfr.bnf.fr/portailccfr/jsp/index_view_direct_anonymous.jsp?record=eadcgm:EADC:D30021377
http://bvmm.irht.cnrs.fr/resultRecherche/resultRecherche.php?COMPOSITION_ID=6373
[both selected images]

Vatican, Biblioteca Apostolica Vaticana
MS Lat. 3226 (*CLA* 1.12) 123, 128, 133, 208, 256
http://digi.vatlib.it/view/MSS_Vat.lat.3226
Prete (1970)

MS Lat. 3321 (*CLA* 1.15; *KfH* #6874a) 107, 235, 238
http://digi.vatlib.it/view/MSS_Vat.lat.3321

MS Lat. 4929 (*KfH* #6899) 203
http://digi.vatlib.it/view/MSS_Vat.lat.4929

MS Lat. 5750 (*CLA* 1.28, 30) 129, 258, 275
Ehrle (1906)

MS. Lat. 6018 (*KfH* #6928) 361
http://digi.vatlib.it/view/MSS_Vat.lat.6018

MS Pal. Lat. 1741 319
http://bibliotheca-laureshamensis-digital.de/bav/bav_pal_lat_1741

MS Pal. Lat 1746 (*CLA* Suppl. 1775; *KfH* #6592) 344, 349, 356
http://bibliotheca-laureshamensis-digital.de/bav/bav_pal_lat_1746

MS Pal. Lat. 1753 (*CLA* Suppl. 1776; *KfH* #6593) 334
http://bibliotheca-laureshamensis-digital.de/bav/bav_pal_lat_1753

MS Pal. Lat. 1754 359
http://bibliotheca-laureshamensis-digital.de/bav/bav_pal_lat_1754

MS Reg. Lat. 215 (*KfH* #6642) 345, 348, 362

MS Reg. Lat 1128 (*KfH* #6765) 249, 250

MS Reg. Lat. 1462 249
http://digi.vatlib.it/view/MSS_Reg.lat.1462

MS Reg. Lat. 1560 351

MS Reg. Lat. 2077 259

MS Urb. Lat. 1154 (*CLA* 1.117) 314
http://digi.vatlib.it/view/MSS_Urb.lat.1154

Venice, Biblioteca Nazionale Marciana
MS Lat. Z. 497 292

Verona, Biblioteca Capitolare
MS XL (38) (*CLA* 4.498) 135, 265

Vienna, Österreichische Nationalbibliothek
MS 2521 337

Wolfenbüttel, Herzog August Bibliothek
MS Guelf. 64 Gud. Lat. (*KfH* #7307) 277
http://diglib.hab.de/?db=mss&list=ms&id=64-gud-lat&catalog

MS Guelf. 86 Weiss. (*CLA* 9.1394; *KfH* #7424a) 324, 337
http://diglib.hab.de/?db=mss&list=ms&id=86-weiss&catalog

Würzburg Universitätsbibliothek
M. P. Misc. F. 28 363

I am unable to find any useful identification of:

Paris, Sangermanensis 291 338
Toledo, Biblioteca del Cabildo 99-30 363

Print and Online

Indications of online availability of books and monographs (not periodicals) are in brackets after the relevant entries.

Adriaen, M., ed. (1958), *Magni Aurelii Cassiodori Expositio Psalmorum* (Turnhout).

Agozzino, T. and F. Zanlucchi, eds. (1972), *Fulgentius: Expositio Vergilianae continentiae* (Padua).

Aistermann, J. (1910), *De M. Valerio Probo Berytio* (Bonn).

Alberto, P. and D. Paniagua, eds. (2012), *Ways of Approaching Knowledge in Late Antiquity and the Early Middle Ages: Schools and Scholarship* (Nordhausen).

Amsler, M. (1989), *Etymology and Grammatical Discourse in Late Antiquity and the Early Middle Ages* (Amsterdam).

Anderson, H. (2009), *The Manuscripts of Statius* (Arlington, VA).

Andrés Sanz, M. A., ed. (2006), *Isidori Hispalensis episcopi Liber differentiarum (II)* (Turnhout).

Armisen-Marchetti, M., ed. (2001–3), *Macrobe: Commentaire au Songe de Scipion* (Paris).

Asperti, S. (2007), "Il testo dell'*Appendix Probi III*." In Lo Monaco and Molinelli 2007: 41–63.

Asperti, S. and M. Passalacqua, eds. (2014), *Appendix Probi (GL IV 193–204)* (Florence).

Atherton, C. (1996), "What Every Grammarian Knows?" *CQ* 46: 239–60.

Atherton, C. and D. Blank (2013), "From Plato to Priscian: Philosophy's Legacy to Grammar." In *The Oxford Handbook of the History of Linguistics*, ed. K. Allan (Oxford): 283–339.

Auroux, S. and E. K. Koerner, eds. (2000), *History of the Language Sciences/Geschichte der Sprachwissenschaften/Histoire des sciences du langage*. 1. Teilband: An International Handbook on the Evolution of the Study of Language from the Beginnings to the Present (Berlin).

Ax, W. (1987), "Quadripertita ratio. Bemerkungen zur Geschichte eines aktuellen Kategoriensystems (adiectio, detractio, transmutatio, immutatio." *Historiographia Linguistica* 13: 191–214 (reprinted in Ax 2000: 190–208).

Ax, W. (1995), "*Disputare in utramque partem*: Zum literarischen Plan und zur dialektischen Methode Varros in *de lingua Latina* 8–10." *RhM* 138: 146–77 (reprinted in Ax 2000: 140–63).

Ax, W. (1996), "Pragmatic Arguments in Morphology: Varro's Defence of Analogy in Book 9 of his *De lingua Latina*." In Swiggers and Wouters 1996: 105–19 (reprinted in Ax 2000: 164–75).

Ax, W. (2000), *Lexis und Logos: Studien zur antiken Grammatik und Rhetorik*, ed. F. Grewing (Stuttgart).

Ax, W. (2003), Review of Law (2003). *Historiographia Linguistica* 30: 448–54.

Ax, W. ed. (2005a), *Lateinische Lehrer Europas: fünfzehn Portraits von Varro bis Erasmus von Rotterdam* (Göttingen).

Ax, W. (2005b), "Marcus Terentius Varro Reatinus." In Ax 2005a: 1–21.

Ax, W. (2011a), "Quintilian's 'Grammar' (*Inst.* 1.4–8) and Its Importance for the History of Roman Grammar." In Matthaios et al. 2011: 331–46.

Ax, W., ed. (2011b), *Quintilians Grammatik (Inst. Orat. 1,4–8): Text, Übersetzung und Kommentar* (Berlin).

Baldwin, B. (1988), "Fulgentius and His Sources." *Traditio* 44: 37–57.

Ballaira, G. (1989), *Prisciano e i suoi amici* (Turin).

Barabino, G., ed. (1967), *P. Rutilii Lupi Schemata dianoeas et lexeos* (Genoa).

Baratin, M. (1989), *La naissance de la syntaxe à Rome* (Paris).

Baratin, M. (1994), "Sur la structure des grammaires antiques." In *Florilegium Historiographiae Linguisticae*, ed. J. de Clercq and P. Desmet (Leuven): 143–57.

Baratin, M. (1995), "Aperçu de la linguistique ancienne: La fin de l'antiquité (3ᵉ–6ᵉ s.)." *LALIES* 15: 139–48.

Baratin, M. (2000), "À l'origine de la tradition artigraphique latine, entre mythe et réalité." In Auroux and Koerner 2000: 459–66.

Baratin, M. (2005), "Priscianus Caesariensis." In Ax 2005b: 247–72.

Baratin, M. (2008), "Usage linguistique et réflexion sur les usagers: Un exemple de croisement entre grammaire et philosophie chez Varron." In Pérez and Griffe 2008: 183–97.

Baratin, M. (2014), "À qui s'adresse Priscien? Pédagogie et bilinguisme dans l'antiquité tardive." In Longobardi et al. 2014: 35–56.

Baratin, M., B. Colombat, and L. Holtz, eds. (2009), *Priscien: Transmission et refondation de la grammaire de l'antiquité aux modernes* (Turnhout).

Baratin, M. and F. Desbordes (1986), "La 'troisième partie' de l'*ars grammatica*." *Historiographia Linguistica* 13: 215–240 (reprinted in Desbordes 2007: 65–90).

Baratin, M. et al. (Groupe *Ars grammatica*) (2005), "Le *De Adverbio* de Priscien." *Histoire, épistémologie, langage* 27(2): 7–91.

Baratin, M. et al. (Groupe *Ars grammatica*), transl. (2010), *Priscien, Grammaire. Livre XVII—Syntaxe, 1* (Paris).

Baratin, M. et al. (Groupe *Ars grammatica*), transl. (2013), *Priscien, Grammaire. Livres XIV, XV, XVI, Les invariables (préposition, adverbe et interjection, conjonction)* (Paris).
Barbero, G. (1990), "Contributi allo studio del Liber Glossarum." *Aevum* 64: 151–74.
Barbero, G. (1993), "Per lo studio delle fonti del Liber Glossarum." *Aevum* 67: 253–78.
Barlow, C. H. (1938), "Codex Vaticanus Latinus 4929." *MAAR* 15: 87–124.
Barnett, F. J. (2006), "The Second Appendix to Probus." *CQ* 56: 257–78.
Barnett, F. J. (2007), "The Sources of the 'Appendix Probi': A New Approach." *CQ* 57: 701–36.
Barney, S., W. J. Lewis, J. A. Beach, and O. Berghof, transl. (2006), *The "Etymologies" of Isidore of Seville* (Cambridge).
Barnish, S. I. B. (1986), "Martianus Capella and Rome in the Late Fifth Century." *Hermes* 114: 98–111.
Barsby, J. (2000), "Donatus on Terence: The Eunuchus Commentary." In *Dramatische Wäldchen: Festschrift für Eckard Lefèvre zum 65. Geburtstag*, ed. E. Stark and G. Vogt-Spira (Hildesheim): 491–513.
Barwick, K. (1908), *De Iunio Filargirio Vergilii Interprete* (Leipzig). [Hathi].
Barwick, K. (1911), "Zur Serviusfrage." *Philologus* 70: 106–45.
Barwick, K. (1919), "Die Sogenannte Appendix Probi." *Hermes* 54: 409–22.
Barwick, K. (1922), *Remmius Palaemon und die römische Ars grammatica* (Leipzig). [Hathi].
Barwick, K. (1924), "Zur Geschichte und Rekonstruktion des Charisius-Textes." *Hermes* 59: 322–55, 420–9.
Barwick, K. (1930), Review of Tolkiehn (1928). *Gnomon* 5: 385–95.
Barwick, K. (1957), "Widmung und Entstehungsgeschichte von Varros De lingua Latina." *Philologus* 101: 298–304.
Barwick, K., ed. (1964), *Charisii Artis grammaticae libri V*, ed. 2 with addenda by F. Kühnert (Leipzig).
Baschera, C., ed. (1999), *Gli scolii Veronesi a Virgilio* (Verona).
Baschera, C. (2000), *Ipotesi d'una relazione tra il Servio danielino e gli scolii Veronesi a Virgilio. Un testimone oculare narra la scoperta del palinsesto di Gaio presso la Biblioteca Capitolare di Verona* (Verona).
Baschera, C. (2008), "Servius Danielinus and *Scholia Veronensia*: Clues to their Relationship." In Casali and Stok 2008: 207–15.
Baudou, A. and S. Clément-Tarantino, eds. (2015), *Servius, À l'école de Virgile: Commentaire à l'Énéide livre I* (Villeneuve d'Ascq).
Bayless, M. (1993), "*Beatus quid est* and the Study of Grammar in Late Ango-Saxon England." In Law 1993a: 67–110.
Beck, J. W. (1883), *Specimen Litterarium de Differentiarum scriptoribus Latinis* (Groningen).
Beck, J. W. (1884), *Sulpicius Apollinaris: adiecta est Appendix dissertationis "De differentiarum scriptoribus Latinis"* (Programma van het Gymnasium te Groningen; Groningen). [Hathi].
Beck, J. W. (1885), "Zu den Differentiae sermonum." *Neue Jahrbücher für Philologie und Paedagogik* 131: 639–43.
Beck, J. W. (1892), "Die Plinianischen Fragmente bei Nonius und dem Anonymus de dubiis nominibus." *Berliner philologische Wochenschrift* 12: 1571–2, 1597–8, 1602–4.
Beck, J. W. (1893), "Studia Gelliana et Pliniana." *Jahrbücher für class. Philol.* Suppl. 19: 1–55.
Beck, J. W. (1894), *C. Plinii Secundi Dubii sermonis librorum VIII reliquiae* (Leipzig). [Hathi].
Beck, J.-W., ed. (1993a), *Terentianus Maurus: De syllabis* (Göttingen).
Beck, J.-W. (1993b), *Concordantia in Terentianum Maurum* (Hildesheim).

Beck, J.-W. (1996), *Zur Zuverlässigkeit lateinischen Grammatik: die 'Ars' des Aelius Donatus* (Stuttgart).
Beck, J.-W. (1998), "Terentianus Maurus: Non paenitendus inter ceteros artis metricae auctor." *ANRW* 2.34.4: 3208–68.
Beeson, C. H. (1924), "The *Ars grammatica* of Julianus of Toledo." In *Miscellanea Francesco Ehrle* [no editor] (Rome) 1: 50–70.
Belardi, W. (1985), *Filosofia grammatica e retorica nel pensiero antico* (Rome).
Bertini, F. (1986), "Il 'De orthographia' di Cassiodoro." In Leanza 1986: 92–104.
Bertsch, H., ed. (1884), *Cledonii Ars grammatica* (Heidelberg).
Biddau, F., ed. (2008), *Q. Terentii Scauri De orthographia* (Hildesheim).
Billanovich, G. (1956), "Dall'antica Ravenna alle biblioteche umanistiche." *Aevum* 30: 319–53.
Biondi, L. (1997), "Mai, Osann e Apuleius grammaticus. Un testis antiquior del *De nota aspirationis* e del *De diphthongis*." *Acme* 50: 65–108.
Biondi, L. (2001), "Apuleius *De nota aspirationis* e *De Diphthongis*: Ricognizioni su modelli strutturali e teorici in due testi medievali sull'ortografia latina." *Acme* 54: 73–111.
Bischoff, B. (1966), *Mittelalterliche Studien*, Vol. 1 (Stuttgart).
Bischoff, B. (1967), *Mittelalterliche Studien*, Vol. 2 (Stuttgart).
Bischoff, B. (1973), *Sammelhandschrift Diez. B Sant. 66: Grammatici Latini et catalogus librorum* (Graz).
Bischoff, B. et al. (1988), *The Épinal, Erfurt, Werden, and Corpus Glossaries* (Copenhagen).
Bischoff, B. and B. Löfstedt, eds. (1992), *Anonymus ad Cuimnanum: Expossitio Latinitatis* (Turnhout).
Biville, F. (2011), "'Quae nusquam nisi in diversis cotidianis glossematibus repperi' (*GL*, VII.167.8–9). Gloses et glossaires bilingues chez Martyrius." In Ferri 2011a: 121–40.
Biville, F., M.-K. Lhommé, and D. Vallat, eds. (2012), *Latin vulgaire—Latin tardif* (Lyon).
Blank, D., transl. (1998), *Sextus Empiricus: Against the Grammarians (Adversus Mathematicos I)* (Oxford).
Blank, D. (2000), "The Organization of Grammar in Ancient Greece." In Auroux and Koerner 2000: 400–17.
Blank, D. (2005), "Varro's Anti-Analogist." In *Language and Learning: Philosophy of Language in the Hellenistic Age*, ed. D. Frede and B. Inwood (Cambridge): 210–38.
Blank, D. (2008), "Varro and the Epistemological Status of Etymology." *Histoire, épistémologie, langage* 30(1): 49–73.
Blank, D. (2012), "Varro and Antiochus." In *The Philosophy of Antiochus*, ed. D. Sedley (Cambridge): 250–89.
Bloch, H. (1963), "The Pagan Revival in the West at the End of the Fourth Century." In *The Conflict between Paganism and Christianity in the Fourth Century*, ed. A. Momigliano (Oxford): 193–218.
Bölte, F. (1888), "Die Quellen von Charisius I 15 und I 17." *Neue Jahrbücher für Philologie und Paedagogik* 137: 401–40.
Bona, F. (1964), *Contributo allo studio della composizione del* De verborum significatu *di Verrio Flacco* (Milan).
Bona, F. (1982), *Opusculum Festinum* (Pavia).
Bonnet, G. (2000), "Charisius et Dosithée, reflets de Cominien." *Revue de Philologie* 74: 7–16.
Bonnet, G., ed. (2005), *Dosithée: Grammaire latine* (Paris).
Bonnet, G. (2006), "La grammaire anonyme de Bobbio: copie ou oeuvre originale?" *RHT* n.s. 1: 73–107.

Bonnet, G., ed. (2013), *Abrégé de la grammaire de Saint Augustin* (Paris).
Bornecque, H., ed. (1937), *Macrobe: Les Saturnales* (Paris).
Botschuyver, H., ed. (1935–42), *Scholia in Horatium*, Vols. 1, 3, 4 [all publ.] (Amsterdam).
Botschuyver, H. (1939), "Quelques remarques sur les scholies parisiennes λφψ d'Horace." *Latomus* 3: 25–51.
Bouquet, M. and B. Méniel, eds. (2011), *Servius et sa réception de l'Antiquité à la Renaissance* (Rennes).
Boys-Stones, G. (2018), *L. Annaeus Cornutus: The Greek Theology, Fragments, and Testimonia* (Atlanta).
Brearley, D., ed. (1975), *Commentum Sedulii Scotti in maiorem Donatum grammaticum* (Toronto).
Breysig, A., ed. (1867), *Germanici Caesaris Aratea cum scholiis* (Berlin). [Hathi].
Broggiato, M. (2001), *Cratete di Mallo: I frammenti* (La Spezia).
Brooks, E., ed. (1970), *P. Rutilii Lupi De figuris sententiarum et elocutionis* (Leiden).
Brown, P. (1967), *Augustine of Hippo* (London).
Brugnoli, G. (1955a), *Studi sulle 'differentiae verborum'* (Rome).
Brugnoli, G. (1955b), "Una silloge inedita di differentiae in un manoscritto di S. Gallo." *Rend. Ist. Lomb.* 88: 189–216.
Brugnoli, G. (1961), "I Sinonima Ciceronis." *Atti del 1 Congresso internazionale di studi Ciceroniani* (Rome) 1: 283–99.
Brugnoli, G. (1964), "Il *Liber de differentiis rerum* di Isidoro di Siviglia." *Vetera Christianorum* 1: 65–82.
Brugnoli, G. (1988), *Identikit di Lattanzio Placido: Studi sulla scoliastica staziana* (Pisa).
Brugnoli, G. (1989), "Questioni biografiche II: La 'Vita Donati grammatici parisina.'" *GIF* 41: 291–5.
Brugnoli, G. and M. Buonocore, eds. (2002), *Hermeneumata Vaticana (cod. Vat. Lat. 6925)* (Vatican).
Brugnoli, G. and F. Stok, eds. (1997), *Vitae Vergilianae antiquae* (Rome).
Brugnoli, G. and F. Stok (2006), *Studi sulle Vitae Vergilianae* (Pisa).
Brummer, J., ed. (1912), *Vitae Virgilianae* (Leipzig).
Bruni, Sandra, ed. (1997), *Alcuino: De orthographia* (Florence).
Bruns, P., ed. (1811), *Terentii Afri comoediae sex* (Halle). [Hathi].
Buffa, M. F. (1977), "Emilio Aspro: I commentari sallustiano e terenziano." *Studi e Ricerche dell'Istituto di Latino* 1: 7–49.
Buffa Giolito, M. F., ed. (1990), *Expositio artis Donati (seu Incipit ars Donati quam Paulus Diaconus exposuit)* (Genoa).
Bürsgens, W., transl. (2003), *Cassiodor: Institutiones divinarum et saecularium litterarum/ Einführung in die geistlichen und weltlichen Wissenschaften* (Freiburg).
Bursill-Hall, G. L., S. Ebbesen, and K. Koerner, eds. (1990), *De ortu grammaticae: Studies in Medieval Grammar and Linguistic Theory in Memory of Jan Pinborg* (Amsterdam).
Butterfield, D. (2013), *The Early History of the Text of Lucretius* (Cambridge).
Butterfield, D., ed. (2015), *Varro Varius: The Polymath of the Roman World* (Cambridge).
Butzer, P. L. and D. Lohrmann, eds. (1993), *Science in Western and Eastern Civilization in Carolingian Times* (Basel).
Cadili, L. (2003a), "Gli *Scholia Bernensia* alle *Georgiche* di Virgilio." *Lexis* 21: 381–92.
Cadili, L., ed. (2003b), *Scholia Bernensia in Vergilii Bucolica et Georgica*, Vol. 2 Fasc. 1 (Amsterdam).
Cadili, L. (2008), "Scholia and Authorial Identity: The *Scholia Bernensia* on Vergil's *Georgics* as *Servius auctus*." In Casali and Stok 2008: 194–206.
Cadoni, E. (1987), *Studi sul* De compendiosa doctrina *del Nonio Marcello* (Sassari) [http://eprints.uniss.it/7689/].

Cameron, A. D. E. (1966), "The Date and Identity of Macrobius." *JRS* 56: 25–38.
Cameron, A. D. E. (1967), "The Treatise *De verbo* Ascribed to Macrobius." *BICS* 14: 91–2.
Cameron, A. D. E. (1974), "The Date of Priscian's *De laude Anastasii*." *GRBS* 15: 313–16.
Cameron, A. D. E. (1986), "Martianus and His First Editor." *CP* 81: 320–8.
Cameron, A. D. E. (2004), *Greek Mythography in the Roman World* (Oxford).
Cameron, A. D. E. (2010), "The Date of the Scholia Vetustiora on Juvenal." *CQ* 60: 569–76.
Cameron, A. D. E. (2011), *The Last Pagans of Rome* (Oxford).
Cameron, A. D. E. (2012), "Anician Myths." *JRS* 102: 133–71.
Canale, A. V. (2004), *Etimologie o origini di Isidoro di Siviglia* (Turin).
Capelli, A. (1961), *Dizionario di abbreviature latine ed italiane* (ed. 6, Milan).
Cardauns, B. (2001), *Marcus Terentius Varro: Einführung in sein Werk* (Heidelberg).
Cardinali, L. (2014) "A proposito della cronologia e dell'origine di Lattanzio Placido: Osservazioni sulla questione." In Longobardi et al. 2014: 287–304.
Carracedo Fraga, J. (2005), "Sobre la autoría del tratado gramatical atribuido a Julián de Toledo." *Euphrosyne* n.s. 33: 189–200.
Casaceli, F., ed. (1973), *Foca, "De nomine et verbo"* (Naples).
Casali, S. and F. Stok, eds. (2008), *Servio: Stratificazioni esegetiche e modelli culturali* (Brussels).
Casas Homs, J. M. (1964), "Una gramatica inedita d'Usuard." *Analecta Montserratensia* 10: 77–129.
Cavajoni, G., ed. (1979–90), *Supplementum Adnotationum super Lucanum* (Vols. 1 and 2, Milan; Vol. 3, Amsterdam).
Cavallo, G., P. Fedeli, and A. Giardina, eds. (1990), *Lo spazio letterario di Roma antica*, Vol. 3: *La ricezione del testo* (Rome).
Cavallo, G., C. Leonardi, and E. Menesto, eds. (1995), *Lo spazio letterario del medioevo*, Vol. 1: *Il medioevo latino*; Part 3: *La ricezione del testo* (Rome).
Cavazza, F. (1981), *Studio su Varrone etimologo e grammatico: La lingua latina come modello di struttura linguistica* (Florence).
CETEDOC (1982a), *Concordance to Ars Ambrosiana: Commentum anonymum in Donati partes maiores* (Turnhout).
——(1982b), *Concordance to Donatus ortigraphus, Ars grammatica* (Turnhout).
——(1992a), *Concordance to Smaragdus, Liber in partibus Donati* (Turnhout).
——(1992b), *Concordance to Anonymus ad Cuimnanum* (Turnhout).
Chahoud, A. (2007), "Antiquity and Authority in Nonius Marcellus." In *Texts and Culture in Late Antiquity: Inheritance, Authority, and Change*, ed. D. Scourfield (Swansea): 69–96.
Chase, W. J., transl. (1926), *The Ars Minor of Donatus, for One Thousand Years the Leading Textbook of Grammar* (Madison).
Chatelain, É. (1883), "Un Gradus ad Parnassum de l'extrême décadence." *Revue de philologie* 7: 65–76.
Chatelain, É. (1900), *Introduction à la lecture des notes tironiennes* (Paris).
Chiesa, P., ed. (2000), *Paolo Diacono: Uno scrittore fra tradizione longobarda e rinnovamento carolingio* (Udine).
Chin, C. (2008), *Grammar and Christianity in the Late Roman World* (Philadelphia).
Chittenden, J., ed. (1982), *Donatus Ortigraphus: Ars grammatica* (Turnhout).
Christes, J. (1979), *Sklaven und Freigelassene als Grammatiker und Philologen im antiken Rom* (Wiesbaden).
Ciaffi, V. (1963), *Fulgenzio e Petronio* (Turin).
Ciccolella, F. (2008), *Donati Graeci: Learning Greek in the Renaissance* (Leiden).
Ciccone, L. (2016), *Esegesi oraziana nel medioevo: Il commento "Communiter"* (Florence).

Cichorius, C. (1888), *Über Varros Libri de scaenicis originibus* (Leipzig). [Hathi].

Cignolo, C., ed. (2002), *Terentiani Mauri De litteris, de syllabis, de metris* (Hildesheim).

Cinato, F. and A. Grondeux, eds. (2015), *L'activité lexicographique dans le haut Moyen Âge latin: Rencontre autour du Liber glossarum (suite)*. Dossier HEL 8. [http://htl.linguist.univ-paris-diderot.fr/hel/dossiers/numero8].

Cioffi, C. (2012), "Ricerche sulla tradizione manoscritta del Commento di Donato a Terenzio." *MD* 69: 145–83.

Cioffi, C., ed. (2017), *Aeli Donati quod fertur commentum ad Andriam Terenti* (Berlin).

Citroni, M. (2013), "Horace's *Epistle* 2.1, Cicero, Varro, and the Ancient Debate about the Origins and the Development of Latin Poetry." In *Augustan Poetry and the Roman Republic*, ed. J. Farrell and D. P. Nelis (Oxford): 180–204.

Clackson, J. (2015), "Latinitas, Ἑλληνισμός and Standard Languages." *Studi e Saggi Linguistici* 53(2): 309–30.

Clark, A. C., ed. (1907), *Q. Asconii Pediani Orationum Ciceronis quinque enarratio* (Oxford). [Hathi].

Clark, A. C. (1918), *The Descent of Manuscripts* (Oxford). [Hathi].

Clausen, W. V., ed. (1948), *Erchanberti Frisingensis Tractatus super Donatum* (Chicago).

Clausen, W. V. and J. E. G. Zetzel, eds. (2004), *Commentum Cornuti in Persium* (Munich).

Codoñer, C. (1984–5), "Historia del texto del libro I de las *Differentiae* de Isidoro de Sevilla." *RHT* 14–15: 77–95.

Codoñer, C. (1985), "Les plus anciennes compilations de 'differentiae': Formation et évolution d'un genre littéraire grammaticale." *RPh* 59: 201–19.

Codoñer, C. (1986), "La conception de la 'differentia' dans le recueil 'Inter aptum' d'Isidore de Séville." *RPh* 60: 187–96.

Codoñer, C. ed. (1992), *Isidor de Sevilla, Diferencias Libro I* (Paris).

Codoñer, C. (1996), "Isidore de Séville: Différences et vocabulaires." In Hamesse 1996: 57–77.

Codoñer, C. (2012), "Los glosarios hispánicos y su posible relación con el *Liber glossarum*." In Alberto and Paniagua 2012: 11–39.

Codoñer, C. (2015), "Posibles sistemas de compilación en las notae iuris y el *Liber glossarum*." In Cinato and Grondeux 2015: 111–29.

Coleman, R. C. (2001), "Varro as an Etymologist." *Papers on Grammar* 6: 61–96.

Coletti, M. L. (1985), "Un'opera grammaticale di Remigio di Auxerre: Il commento al De Barbarismo di Donato." *Studi Medievali* 26: 951–67.

Collart, J. (1954a), *Varron grammarien latin* (Paris).

Collart, J., ed. (1954b), *Varro De lingua Latina, livre V* (Paris).

Collart, J. (1963), "Analogie et anomalie." In Reverdin 1963: 117–32.

Collart, J. (1965), "Varron grammarien et l'enseignement grammaticale dans l'antiquité romaine, 1934–1963." *Lustrum* 9: 213–41.

Collart, J. (1978), "L'oeuvre grammaticale de Varron." In Collart et al. 1978: 3–21.

Collart, J. et al. (1978), *Varron, grammaire antique, et stylistique latine par/pour Jean Collart* (Paris).

Collignon, A. (1883), "Note sur une grammaire latine manuscrite du VIIIe siècle appartenant à la bibliothèque de Nancy." *Revue de Philologie* 7: 13–22.

Comparetti, D. (1997), *Vergil in the Middle Ages*, transl. E. F. M. Benecke, introduction by J. M. Ziolkowski (Princeton).

Condorelli, S. (1989–90), "Un testo grammaticale tardo-antico: Il *De nominibus dubiis*." *Helikon* 29–30: 43–74.

Conte, S. (2005), "*Vita Donati grammatici*: Testo, trasmissione, e milieu culturale." *GIF* 57: 285–311.

Copeland, R. and I. Sluiter, eds. (2009), *Medieval Grammar and Rhetoric: Language Arts and Literary Theory, AD 300–1475* (Oxford).
Corazza, D. (2003), "Sulla tradizione artigrafica *de finalibus* con quattro inediti." In Gasti 2003: 93–129.
Corazza, D., ed. (2011), *[Maximi Victorini] Commentarium de ratione metrorum* (Hildesheim).
Courcelle, P. (1942), "Histoire d'un brouillon Cassiodorien." *REA* 44: 65–86.
Courcelle, P. (1957), "Les exégèses chrétiennes de la quatrième éclogue." *REA* 59: 294–319.
Courcelle, P. (1969), *Late Latin Writers and Their Greek Sources*, transl. H. Wedeck (Cambridge, MA).
Cristante, L., ed. (1987), *De nuptiis Philologiae et Mercurii liber IX* (Padua).
Cristante, L. (2003), "Grammatica di poeti e poesia di grammatici: Coronato." In Gasti 2003: 75–92.
Cristante, L. (2012), "Appunti su PseudoCensorino frg. 9–11 (con una proposta di edizione)." In Alberto and Paniagua 2012: 104–19.
Cristante, L. (2014), "*Haec musicae summa sunt* (Ps. Cens. *frg.* 12)." In Longobardi et al. 2014: 57–66.
Cruquius, J., ed. (1597), *Q. Horatius Flaccus: Cum commentariis et enarrationibus commentatoris veteris, Et Iacobi Cruquii Messenii, literarum apud Brugenses professoris* (Leiden). [MDZ].
Cugusi, P. (2003), "Lucio Anneo Cornuto esegeta di Virgilio." In Gualandri and Mazzoli 2003: 211–44.
Cupaiuolo, G. (1992), *Evanzio: De fabula* (ed. 2, Naples).
Dahlmann, H. (1932), *Varro und die hellenistische Sprachtheorie* (Berlin).
Dahlmann, H. (1953), *Varros Schrift* De poematis *und die hellenistisch-römische Poetik* (Wiesbaden).
Dahlmann, H. (1963a), *Studien zu Varro 'De poetis'* (Wiesbaden).
Dahlmann, H. (1963b), "Zu Varros Literaturforschung, besonders in *De poetis*." In Reverdin 1963: 1–20.
Dahlmann, H., ed. (1966), *Varro De lingua Latina Buch VIII* (ed. 2, Berlin).
Dahlmann, H. (1970), *Zur Ars grammatica des Marius Victorinus* (Wiesbaden).
Daintree, D. (1990), "The Virgil Commentary of Aelius Donatus—Black Hole or 'Éminence Grise'?" *Greece & Rome* 37: 65–79.
Daintree, D. (1999), "Virgil and Virgil Scholia in Early Medieval Ireland." *Romanobarbarica* 16: 347–61.
d'Alessandro, P. (2001–2), "Cesio Basso e il *De versuum generibus* di Diomede." *Incontri triestini di filologia classica* 1: 115–30.
d'Alessandro, P., ed. (2004), *Rufini Antiochensis Commentaria in metra Terentiana et de compositione et de numeris oratorum* (Hildesheim).
d'Alessandro, P. (2012), *Varrone e la tradizione metrica antica* (Hildesheim).
Daly, L. (1967), *Contributions to a History of Alphabetization in Antiquity and the Middle Ages* (Brussels).
Damaggio, J. (2011), "Un corpus des premiers fragments grammaticaux à Rome." *Eruditio Antiqua* 3: 23–55.
Dammer, R. (2001), *Diomedes Grammaticus* (Trier).
D'Angelo, R., ed. (2001), *Carmen de figuris vel schematibus* (Hildesheim).
Davies, P. V., transl. (1969), *Macrobius: The Saturnalia* (New York) [www.humanitiesebook.org].
De Angelis, V. (1997), "I commenti medievali alla *Tebaide* di Stazio: Anselmo di Laon, Goffredo Babione, Ilario d'Orléans." In Mann and Munk Olsen 1997: 75–136.

Del Castillo Herrera, M. (1990), *La metrica latina en el siglo IV: Diomedes y su entorno* (Granada).

Del Corso, L. and O. Pecere, eds. (2010), *Libri di scuola e pratiche didattiche: Dall'Antichità al Rinascimento* (Cassino).

Della Casa, A. (1969), *Il* Dubius sermo *di Plinio* (Genoa).

Della Casa, A., ed. (1977), *Arusianus Messius: Exempla elocutionum* (Milan).

Della Casa, A. (1978), "Giulio Romano nella storia della grammatica latina." In Collart et al. 1978: 217–24.

Della Casa, A. (1985), "Rassegna di studi sui grammatici latini (1934–1984)." *Bollettino di studi latini* 15: 85–113.

Della Casa, A. (1992), "Le 'differentiae verborum' e i loro autori." *Civiltà classica e cristiana* 13: 47–62.

Della Corte, F. (1954), *Varrone: Il terzo gran lume romano* (Genoa).

Della Corte, F. (1986), "La posizione di Cassiodoro nella storia dell'enciclopedia." In Leanza 1986: 29–48.

Dell'Era, A. (1979a), "Una miscellanea astronomica medievale: Gli 'Scholia Strozziana' a Germanico." *Atti della accademia nazionale dei Lincei, Memorie: Classe di Scienze morali, storiche e filologiche* 23: 147–267.

Dell'Era, A. (1979b), "Gli 'Scholia Basileensia' a Germanico." *Atti della accademia nazionale dei Lincei, Memorie: Classe di Scienze morali, storiche e filologiche* 23: 301–79.

Dell'Era, A. (1979c), "Una rielaborazione dell'Arato latino." *Studi Medievali* ser. 3, 20.1: 269–301.

Delvigo, M. L. (1987), *Testo virgiliano e tradizione indiretta: Le varianti probiane* (Pisa).

Delvigo, M. L. (1990), "L'emendatio del filologo, del critico, dell'autore: Tre modi di corrigere il testo? (I)." *MD* 24: 71–110.

Delvigo, M. L. (2011), *Servio e la poesia della scienza* (Pisa).

Delvigo, M. L. (2012), "*Secundum fabulam, secundum veritatem*: Servio e il mito." *Prometheus* n.s. 1: 179–93.

De Marco, M. (1952), "Remigii inedita." *Aevum* 26: 495–517.

De Marco, M., ed. (1968), *Tatuini opera omnia* (Turnhout).

De Nonno, M. (1982), *La Grammatica dell'Anonymus Bobiensis* (Rome).

De Nonno, M. (1983a), "La raccolta grammaticale del codice napoletano IV A 17 e il testo dell'*Anonymus Bobiensis*." *RFIC* 111: 314–29.

De Nonno, M. (1983b), "Frammenti misconosciuti di Plozio Sacerdote con osservazioni sul testo dei Catholica Probi." *RFIC* 111: 385–421.

De Nonno, M. (1988), "Tradizione e diffusione di Mario Vittorino grammatico, con edizione degli *Excerpta de orthographia*." *RFIC* 116: 5–59.

De Nonno, M. (1990a), "Un nuovo testo di Marziano Capella: La metrica." *RFIC* 118: 129–44.

De Nonno, M. (1990b), "L'*Auctor ad Caelestinum* (*GL* IV 219–264 Keil): Contributi al testo e alla caratterizzatione." In *Dicti Studiosus: Scritti di filologia offerti a Scevola Mariotti dai suoi allievi* [no editor] (Urbino): 223–58.

De Nonno, M. (1990c), "Le citazioni dei grammatici." In Cavallo et al. 1990: 597–646.

De Nonno, M. (1990d), "Ruolo e funzione della metrica nei grammatici latini." In *Metrica classica e linguistica*, ed. R. Danese, F. Gori, and C. Questa (Urbino): 453–94.

De Nonno, M. (1992), "Un esempio di dispersione della tradizione grammaticale latina: Gli inediti *Excerpta Andecavensia*." *AION* (*filol*) 14: 211–62.

De Nonno, M. (2000), "I codici grammaticali latini d'età tardoantica: osservazioni e considerazioni." In De Nonno et al. 2000: 133–72.

De Nonno, M. (2003), "Grammatici, eruditi, scoliasti: Testi, contesti, tradizioni." In Gasti 2003: 13–28.

De Nonno, M. (2007), "L'*Appendix Probi* e il suo manuscritto: Contributi tipologici e codicologici all'inquadramento del testo." In Lo Monaco and Molinelli 2007: 3–26.

De Nonno, M. (2009), "*Ars Prisciani Caesariensis*: Problemi di tipologia e di composizione." In Baratin et al. 2009: 249–78.

De Nonno, M. (2010), "*Et interrogavit Filocalus*. Pratiche dell'insegnamento 'in aula' del grammatico." In Del Corso and Pecere 2010: 169–205.

De Nonno, M. (2013), "Ancora 'libro e testo': Nuova descrizione del ms. Oxford, Bodl. Lib. Add. C 144 con osservazioni codicologiche e testuali." In *Libri e testi: Lavori in corso a Cassino*, ed. R. Casavecchia, P. De Paolis, M. Maniaci, and G. Orofino (Cassino): 63–109.

De Nonno, M. (2014), "'Manuali brevi' di metrica latina e caratteristiche d'autore. Con anticipazioni sul *De arte metrica* di Marziano Capella." In Longobardi et al. 2014: 67–92.

De Nonno, M., P. De Paolis, and L. Holtz, eds. (2000), *Manuscripts and Tradition of Grammatical Texts from Antiquity to the Renaissance* (Cassino).

De Paolis, P. (1986–7), "Macrobio 1934–1984." *Lustrum* 28–9: 107–254.

De Paolis, P. (1990a), "Per una nuova edizione critica del 'De differentiis' di Macrobio." In *Dicti studiosus: Scritti di filologia offerti a S. Mariotti dai suoi allievi* [no editor] (Urbino): 259–93.

De Paolis, P., ed. (1990b), *De verborum Graeci et Latini differentiis vel societatibus excerpta* (Urbino).

De Paolis, P. (1995), "Tradizioni carolinge e tradizioni umanistiche: Il *De orthographia* attribuito a Flavio Capro." In Pecere and Reeve 1995: 263–97.

De Paolis, P. (2000), "Le *Explanationes in Donatum* (*GL* IV 486–565) e il loro più antico testimone manoscritto." In De Nonno et al. 2000: 173–221.

De Paolis, P. (2003a), "Miscellanee grammaticali altomedievali." In Gasti 2003: 29–74.

De Paolis, P. (2003b), "I codici miscellanei grammaticali altomedievali. Caratteristiche, funzione, destinazione." *Segno e testo* 1: 185–211.

De Paolis, P. (2010), "L'insegnamento dell'ortografia latina fra Tardoantico e alto Medioevo: Teorie e manuali." In Del Corso and Pecere 2010: 229–91.

De Paolis, P. (2013–14), "Le croci di un editore: Alcuni problemi di critica testuale nel *De orthographia* dello Ps. Capro." *Incontri di filologia classica* 13: 21–47.

De Paolis, P. (2014), "*Sordidi sermonis viri*: Velio Longo, Flavio Capro e la lingua di Lucano." In G. Piras, ed., *Labor in studiis: scritti di filologia in onore di Piergiorgio Parroni* (Rome): 97–109.

De Paolis, P. (2015), "La parentela linguistica fra Greco e Latino nella tradizione grammaticale latina." In Haverling 2015: 611–25.

Desbordes, F. (1983), "Le schéma 'addition, soustraction, mutation, métathèse' dans les textes anciens." *Histoire, épistémologie, langage* 5(1): 23–30 (reprinted in Desbordes 2007: 55–63).

Desbordes, F. (1985), "Raison et dérision de la grammaire chez Virgile 'de Toulouse.'" In *La linguistique fantastique*, ed. S. Auroux et al. (Paris): 35–43.

Desbordes, F. (1995), "Les débuts de la grammaire à Rome." *LALIES* 15: 125–37 (reprinted in Desbordes 2007: 217–33).

Desbordes, F. (1996), *La rhétorique antique* (Paris).

Desbordes, F. (2007), *Idées grecques et romaines sur le langage: Travaux d'histoire et d'epistémologie* (Lyon).

Deufert, M. (2001), "Zur Datierung des Nonius Marcellus." *Philologus* 145: 137–49.

Diaz y Diaz, P. R. (1982), "La doctrina metrica de Mallio Tedororo." *Estudios de filologia latina* 2: 13–28.

Diaz y Diaz, P. R., transl. (1995), "Marciano Capela, Libro III: la gramática: (traducción y notas)." *Florentia Iliberritana* 6: 109–55.

Diaz y Diaz, P. R., transl. (1996), "Malio Teodoro, 'Los metros': Traducción y notas." *Florentia Iliberritana* 7: 343–68.

Di Benedetto, V. (1958), "Dionisio il Trace e la Techne a lui attribuita." *Annali della Scuola Normale Superiore di Pisa* 27: 169–210.

Dick, A., ed. (1925/1978), *Martianus Capella* (Leipzig, 1925; with corrections and additions by J. Préaux, Stuttgart, 1978).

Dickey, E. (2007), *Ancient Greek Scholarship* (Oxford).

Dickey, E. (2010), "The Creation of Latin Teaching Materials in Antiquity: A Re-interpretation of P. Sorb. inv. 2069." *ZPE* 175: 188–208.

Dickey, E. (2012, 2015), *The Colloquia of the Hermeneumata Pseudodositheana* (Cambridge).

Dickey, E. (2016a), *Learning Latin the Ancient Way: Latin Textbooks from the Ancient World* (Cambridge).

Dickey, E. (2016b), "The Authorship of the Greek Version of Dositheus' Grammar and What It Tells Us about the Grammar's Original Use." In Ferri and Zago 2016: 205–35.

Dickey, E. and R. Ferri (2010), "A New Edition of the Latin–Greek Glossary on P. Sorb. inv. 2069 (verso)." *ZPE* 175: 177–87.

Diederich, S. (1999), *Der Horazkommentar des Porphyrio im Rahmen der kaiserzeitlichen Schul- und Bildungstradition* (Berlin).

Dietz, D. (1995), "*Historia* in the Commentary of Servius." *TAPA* 125: 61–97.

Di Maria, G. (1989), "Pseudoboethiana." *Sileno* 15: 207–17.

Di Maria, G. (2001), "Per un'edizione critica di Boezio, Commentaria in Topica Ciceronis." *Pan* 18–19: 225–37.

Di Napoli, M., ed. (2011), *Velii Longi De orthographia* (Hildesheim).

Dionisotti, A. C. (1982a), "From Ausonius' Schooldays? A Schoolbook and Its Relatives." *JRS* 72: 83–125.

Dionisotti, A. C. (1982b), "On Bede, Grammars, and Greek." *Revue Bénédictine* 92: 111–41.

Dionisotti, A. C. (1984), "Latin Grammar for Greeks and Goths." *JRS* 74: 202–8.

Dionisotti, A. C. (1985), "From Stephanus to Du Cange: Glossary Stories." *RHT* 14–15: 303–36.

Dionisotti, A. C. (1988), "Greek Grammars and Dictionaries in Carolingian Europe." In Herren 1988: 1–56.

Dionisotti, A. C. (1996), "On the Nature and Transmission of Latin Glossaries." In Hamesse 1996: 205–52.

Di Sciacca, C. (2008), *Finding the Right Words: Isidore's* Synonyma *in Anglo-Saxon England* (Toronto).

Di Stefano, A., ed. (2011), *Arusiani Messi Exempla Elocutionum* (Hildesheim).

Dorfbauer, L. J. (2010), "Die Bucheinteilung der *Saturnalia* des Macrobius." *MH* 67: 43–63.

Dorfbauer, L. J. (2011), "Zwei wenig beachtete Aspecte eines wenig beachteten Texts: Überlieferung und historischer Kontext der *Disputatio de Somnio Scipionis* des Favonius Eulogius." *Latomus* 70: 493–512.

Dümmler, E., ed. (1899), *Ermenrici Elwangensis epistola ad Grimaldum abbatem* in *Epistolae Karolini Aevi* III (Berlin): 534–79. [www.dmgh.de].

Duso, A. (2006), "L'Analogia in Varrone." In *Atti della Giornata di linguistica latina, Venezia, 7 Maggio 2004*, ed. R. Oniga and L. Zennaro (Venice): 9–20.

Eckstein, F. A., ed. (1852), "Anecdota Parisina rhetorica." *Programm der Lateinischen Hauptschule zu Halle für das Schuljahr 1851–52* (Halle). [MDZ].

Ehrle, F., ed. (1906), *M Cornelii Frontonis aliorumque reliquiae, quae codice Vaticano 5750 rescripto continentur* (Milan).

Ehwald, R., ed. (1919), *Aldhelmi Opera* (Berlin). [www.dmgh.de].
Eichenfeld, J. von and S. Endlicher, eds. (1836–7), *Analecta grammatica maximam partem anecdota* (Vienna). [Hathi].
Elder, J. P. (1947), "The Missing Portions of the *Commentum Einsidlense* on Donatus' *Ars Grammatica*." *HSCP* 56–7: 129–60.
Elfassi, J., ed. (2009), *Isidori Hispalensis episcopi Synonyma* (Turnhout).
Elice, M., ed. (2007), *Romani Aquilae De figuris* (Hildesheim).
Elice, M. (2008–09), "Il *De centum metris* di Servio: Un 'manuale' di metrica tardoantico." *Incontri triestini di filologia classica* 8: 155–74.
Elice, M., ed. (2013), *Marii Servii Honorati Centimeter* (Hildesheim).
Endt, J. (1906), *Studien zum Commentator Cruquianus* (Leipzig). [Hathi].
Endt, J., ed. (1909), *Adnotationes super Lucanum* (Leipzig). [Hathi].
Esposito, P., ed. (2004), *Gli scolii a Lucano e altra scoliastica lucanea* (Pisa).
Esposito, P. (2011), "Early and Medieval *Scholia* and *Commentaria* on Lucan." In *Brill's Companion to Lucan*, ed. P. Asso (Leiden): 453–63.
Everett, N. (2006), "The *Interrogationes de littera et de singulis causis*: An Early Medieval School Text." *Journal of Medieval Latin* 16: 227–75.
Fehling, D. (1956–7), "Varro und die grammatische Lehre von der Analogie und der Flexion." *Glotta* 35: 214–70 and 36: 48–100.
Ferrari, M. (1970), "Le Scoperte a Bobbio nel 1493: Vicende di codici e fortuna di testi." *IMU* 13: 139–87.
Ferré, M. (2002), "La genèse du second livre des *Institutions* de Cassiodore." *Latomus* 61: 152–62.
Ferri, R., ed. (2011a), *The Latin of Roman Lexicography* (Pisa).
Ferri, R. (2011b), "*Hermeneumata Celtis*. The Making of a Late-Antique Bilingual Glossary." In Ferri 2011a: 141–69.
Ferri, R. (2014), "Alcuni aspetti della metologia e delle fonti del glossario priscianeo." In Martorelli 2014: 85–113.
Ferri, R. and A. Zago, eds. (2016), *The Latin of the Grammarians: Reflections about Language in the Roman World* (Turnhout).
Filiscus, S. (1518), *M. Tulli Ciceronis oratorum omnium principis Synonyma ad Lucium Veturium* (Hagenau). [MDZ].
Flamant, A. (1977), *Macrobe et le néo-platonisme latin à la fin du IV*[e] *siècle* (Leiden).
Flammini, G., ed. (2004), *Hermeneumata Pseudodositheana Leidensia* (Munich).
Fleischmann, P. (2006), "Die *praefatio* zum *Aeneis*kommentar des Servius und die Tradition der Auslegung." In *Suus cuique mos: Beiträge zur paganen Kultur des lateinischen Westens im 4. Jahrhundert n. Chr.*, ed. U. Schmitzer (Göttingen): 59–114.
Flobert, P., ed. (1985), *Varron: La langue latine*, Vol. 2 [all published] (Paris).
Flobert, P. (1994), "Les *differentiae* chez les grammariens latins ou le refus de la synonymie." In *Les problèmes de la synonymie en latin*, ed. C. Moussy (Paris): 11–23.
Fögen, T. (1997–8), "Der Grammatiker Consentius." *Glotta* 74: 164–92.
Fontaine, J. (1959–83), *Isidore de Séville et la culture classique dans l'Espagne wisigothique* (Paris).
Fontaine, J. (1986), "Cassiodore et Isidore: l'évolution de l'encyclopédisme latin du VIe au VIIe siècle." In Leanza 1986: 72–91.
Fontaine, J. (1988), *Tradition et actualité chez Isidore de Séville* (London).
Fowler, D. (1997), "The Virgil Commentary of Servius." In *Cambridge Companion to Virgil*, ed. C. Martindale (Cambridge): 73–87.
Fox, W., ed. (1902), *Remigii Autissiodorensis In Artem Donati minorem commentum* (Leipzig).
Fraenkel, E. (1964), *Kleine Beiträge zur klassischen Philologie* (Rome).
Franklin, C. V. (2000), "The Date of Composition of Bede's *De schematibus et tropis* and *De arte metrica*." *Revue Bénedictine* 110: 199–203.

Franklin, C. V. (2002), "Grammar and Exegesis in Bede's *Liber de schematibus et tropis*." In Lanham 2002: 63–91.

Frazel, T. D. (2009), *The Rhetoric of Cicero's "In Verrem"* (Göttingen).

Frenz, T. (2010), *Abkürzungen: Die Abbreviaturen der Lateinischen Schrift von der Antike bis zur Gegenwart* (Stuttgart).

Freyburger, G. (1994), "Le savoir philologique du grammairien Censorinus." In *Grammaire et rhétorique: notion de romanité*, ed. J. Dangel (Strasbourg): 13–18.

Frier, B. W. (1985), *The Rise of the Roman Jurists: Studies in Cicero's* Pro Caecina (Princeton).

Friis-Jensen, K. (1997), "Medieval Commentaries on Horace." In Mann and Munk Olsen 1997: 51–73.

Friis-Jensen, K. (2007), "The Reception of Horace in the Middle Ages." In *Cambridge Companion to Horace*, ed. S. Harrison (Cambridge): 291–304.

Friis-Jensen, K., B. Munk Olsen, and O. L. Smith (1997), "Bibliography of Classical Scholarship in the Middle Ages and the Early Renaissance (9th to 15th Centuries)." In Mann and Munk Olsen 1997: 197–251.

Froehde, O. (1892), "De C. Iulio Romano Charisii auctore." *Jahrbücher für class. Philol.* Suppl. 18: 567–672.

Froehde, O. (1893), "Valerii Probi de nomine libellum Plinii Secundi doctrinam continere demonstratur." *Jahrbücher für class. Philol.* Suppl. 19: 157–203.

Funaioli, G. (1930), *Esegesi virgiliana antica. Prolegomeni alla edizione del commento di Giunio Filargirio e di Tito Gallo* (Milan).

Fusi, A. (2013), "La *recensio* gennadiana e il testo di Marziale." *Segno e Testo* 11: 79–122.

Gamberini, R. (2014), "Divertirsi con la grammatica. Riflessioni sulla storia del testo delle *Epitomae* e delle *Epistolae* di Virgilio Marone Grammatico." *Filologia Mediolatina* 21: 23–52.

Ganz, D. (1990), "On the History of Tironian Notes." In P. Ganz 1990: 35–51.

Ganz, D. (1991), "Heiric d'Auxerre glossateur du *Liber glossarum*." In Iogna-Prat et al. 1991: 297–312.

Ganz, D. (1993), "The *Liber Glossarum*: A Carolingian Encyclopedia." In Butzer and Lohrmann 1993: 127–35.

Ganz, P. ed. (1990), *Tironische Noten* (Wiesbaden).

Garbarino, G. ed. (2003), *Philosophorum Romanorum fragmenta usque ad L. Annaei Senecae aetatem* (Bologna).

Garcea, A. (2008a), "*Consule ueritatem*: Cicéron, Varron et un chapitre de l'histoire de la vérité à Rome." *Revue de métaphysique et de morale* 57: 93–110.

Garcea, A. (2008b), "Varron et la constitution des paradigmes flexionnels du latin." *Histoire épistémologie langage* 30.1: 75–89.

Garcea, A. (2009), "Substance et accidents dans la grammaire de Priscien." In Baratin et al. 2009: 125–38.

Garcea, A. (2012), *Caesar's De Analogia: Edition, Translation, and Commentary* (Oxford).

Garcea, A. (2013), "Le traité *De figuris numerorum* de Priscien." In *Polyphonia Romana: Hommages à Frédérique Biville*, ed. A. Garcea et al. (Hildesheim) 2: 769–79.

Garcea, A. (2015), "Il criterio della definitezza nell'*Ars breviata* di Agostino." In *Parole, gesti, interpretazioni: Studi linguistici per Carla Bazzanella*, ed. E. Pistolesi, R. Pugliese, and B. G. Fivela (Rome): 349–61.

Garcea, A. (2016), "Gli *schemata dianoeas* di Carisio: Un'*unicum* tra grammatica, retorica, e letteratura." In Ferri and Zago 2016: 145–66.

Garcea, A., M.-K. Lhommé, and D. Vallat, eds. (2016), *Fragments d'érudition: Servius et le savoir antique* (Hildesheim).

Garcea, A. (forthcoming), "Nigidius Figulus' Naturalism: Between Grammar and Philosophy." In Pezzini and Taylor forthcoming.

García Román, C., M. A. Gutiérrez Galindo, and M. Díaz de Alda Carlos (1999), *Prisciani Institutionum grammaticalium librorum XVII et XVIII indices et concordantiae* (Hildesheim).

García Román, C. and M. A. Gutiérrez Galindo (2001), *Prisciani Institutionum grammaticalium librorum I–XVI indices et concordantiae* (Hildesheim).

García Román, C. and M. A. Gutiérrez Galindo (2003), *Prisciani operum minorum grammaticalium indices et concordantiae* (Hildesheim).

Gasti, F., ed. (2003), *Grammatica e grammatici latini: Teoria ed esegesi* (Pavia).

Gatti, P., ed. (1993), *Synonyma Ciceronis (Arba, humus)* (Genoa).

Gatti, P., ed. (1994), *Synonyma Ciceronis: La raccolta Accusat, lacescit* (Trento).

Gatti, P. (1996), "Nonio." In Hamesse (1996): 79–91.

Gatti, P., ed. (2001), *Un glossario Bernense (Bern, Burgerbibliothek, A. 91[18])* (Trento).

Gatti, P., ed. (2005), *Glossae Nonii Leidenses: La prima serie* (Trento).

Gatti, P. (2011), "Nonio Marcello e la *Compendiosa doctrina*" in Ferri 2011a: 49–62.

Gatti, P. and E. Salvadori, eds. (2014), *Nonio Marcello De conpendiosa doctrina*, Vol. 3 (Florence).

Gatti, P. L. (2014), *Ovid in Antike und Mittelalter: Geschichte der philologischen Rezeption* (Stuttgart).

Gebauer, G. and B. Löfstedt, eds. (1980), *Bonifatii (Vynfreth) Ars grammatica; accedit Ars metrica* (Turnhout).

Geerlings, W. and C. Schulze, eds. (2002–4), *Der Kommentar in Antike und Mittelalter: Beiträge zu seiner Erforschung* (Leiden).

Georgii, H. (1891), *Die antike Äneiskritik aus den Scholien und anderen Quellen* (Stuttgart). [Hathi].

Georgii, H. (1893), *Die antike Äneiskritik im Kommentar des Tiberius Claudius Donatus* (Stuttgart). [Hathi].

Georgii, H., ed. (1905–6), *Tiberi Claudi Donati Interpretationes Vergilianae* (Leipzig). [Hathi].

Gessner, A. (1888), *Servius und Pseudo-Asconius* (Zurich). [Hathi].

Giammona, C., ed. (2012), *[Prisciani] De accentibus* (Hildesheim).

Giammona, C., ed. (2016), *Ars Ambianensis: Le tre redazioni delle* Declinationes nominum (Hildesheim).

Gianotti, G. F. (2010), "Ventura e sventura dei custodi del linguaggio. Spigolature svetoniane." In *Linguaggi del potere, poteri del linguaggio*, ed. E. Bona and M. Cumis (Alessandria): 331–64.

Giarratano, C., ed. (1920), *Q. Asconii Pediani Commentarii* (Rome).

Gibson, R. and C. S. Kraus, eds. (2002), *The Classical Commentary: Histories, Practices, Theory* (Leiden).

Gioseffi, M. (1991), *Studi sul commento a Virgilio dello Pseudo-Probo* (Florence).

Gioseffi, M. (1995), "Problemi di fonti nel *Commento alle Bucoliche* dello Pseudo-Probo." In *Esegesi, parafrasi e compilazione in età tardoantica*, ed. C. Moreschini (Naples): 133–45.

Gioseffi, M. (2003), "*Ut sit integra locutio*: Esegesi e grammatica in Tiberio Claudio Donato." In Gatti 2003: 139–59.

Gioseffi, M. (2007–8), "Il commento del Ps.Probo al IV libro delle *Georgiche* di Virgilio." *Incontri triestini di filologia classica* 7: 145–76.

Gioseffi, M. (2011), "Per un lessico dei commenti tardoantichi a Virgilio: Il caso dello Pseudo Probo." In *Il calamo della memoria*, Vol. 4, ed. L. Cristante and S. Ravalico (Trieste): 301–38.

Gioseffi, M. (2012a), "Allegoria e ceremoniale negli scolii Serviani." In Zumbo 2012: 39–61 (reprinted from *Acme* 57 [2004] 45–68).

Gioseffi, M. (2012b), "'Introducing Virgil': Forme di presentazione dell'*Eneide* in età tardoantica." In Alberto and Paniagua 2012: 120–43.

Gioseffi, M. (2014), "A Very Long Engagement: Some Remarks about the Relationship between *Marginalia* and Commentaries in the Virgilian Tradition." *Trends in Classics* 6: 176–91.

Girard, P. (1907), "Un document sur l'édit anterieur à Julien: Valerius Probus, de litteris singularibus, 5, 1–24." In *Aus Römischem und Bürgerlichem Recht. Ernst Immanuel Bekker zum 16. August 1907 überreicht* [no editor] (Weimar): 21–56. [Hathi].

Girard, P. (1910), "Un second manuscrit des extraits alphabétiques de Probus (Paris Latin 4841)." *Nouvelle revue historique de droit français et étranger* 34: 479–520.

Girard, P. (1937), *Textes de droit romain* (ed. 6, Paris).

Gitner, Adam (2015), "Varro *Aeolicus*: Latin's Affiliation with Greek." In Butterfield 2015: 33–50.

Glinister, F. (2007), "Constructing the Past." In Glinister et al. 2007: 11–32.

Glinister, F., C. Woods, J. A. North, and M. H. Crawford, eds. (2007), *Verrius, Festus, & Paul* (London).

Glorie, F., ed. (1968), *Variae collectiones aenigmatum Merovingicae aetatis (Pars altera)* (Turnholt).

Glück, M. (1967), *Priscians Partitiones und ihre Stellung in der spätantiken Schule* (Hildesheim).

Goetz, G. (1891), "Zu dem Gronovscholiasten des Cicero." *Neue Jahrbücher für Philologie und Paedagogik* 143: 429–32.

Goetz, G. (1923), *De Glossariorum Latinorum origine et fatis* [= *CGlL* Vol. 1] (Leipzig).

Goetz, G. and F. Schoell, eds. (1910), *M. Terentius Varro De lingua Latina quae supersunt* (Leipzig).

Goldlust, Benjamin (2010), *Rhétorique et poétique de Macrobe dans les "Saturnales"* (Turnhout).

Gómez Heredia, A. (1999), "Julián de Toledo, su *Ars grammatica* y la doctrina métrica de su *Conlatio de generibus metrorum*." *Florentia Iliberritana* 10: 147–61.

Goold, G. P. (1970), "Servius and the Helen Episode." *HSCP* 74: 101–68.

Gorman, M. (1997), "Wigbod and Biblical Studies under Charlemagne." *Revue Bénédictine* 107: 40–76 (reprinted in M. Gorman, *Biblical Commentaries from the Early Middle Ages* [Florence, 2002]).

Gorman, M. (2000), "Peter of Pisa and the *Quaestiunculae* Copied for Charlemagne in Brussels II 2572." *Revue Bénédictine* 110: 238–60.

Gorman, M. (2002), "Alcuin before Migne," *Revue Bénédictine* 112: 101–130 (reprinted in M. Gorman, *The Study of the Bible in the Early Middle Ages* [Florence, 2007]).

Goulet-Cazé, M.-O., ed. (2000), *Le commentaire entre tradition et innovation* (Paris).

Goullet, M. (2009), "Priscien dans la lettre d'Ermenrich d'Ellwangen à Grimald, abbé de Saint-Gall." In Baratin et al. 2009: 481–6.

Gourinat, J.-B. (2008), "Cornutus: Grammairien, rhéteur et philosophe stoïcien." In Pérez and Griffe 2008: 53–92.

Gräfenhan, A. (1843–50), *Geschichte der klassischen Philologie im Alterthum* (Bonn).

Grafton, A. T. (1991), *Defenders of the Text* (Cambridge, MA).

Grazzini, S., ed. (2002), *Scholia in Iuuenalem recentiora* I (Pisa).

Grebe, S. (2000), "Kriterien für die *Latinitas* bei Varro und Quintilian." In *Hortus litterarum antiquarum (Festschrift für Hans Armin Gärtner zum 70. Geburtstag)*, ed. A. Haltenhoff and F.-H. Mutschler (Heidelberg): 191–210.

Grebe, S. (2005), "Martianus Min(n)e(i)us Felix Capella." In Ax 2005b: 133–63.

Grondeux, A. (2013), *À l'école de Cassiodore* (Turnhout)

Grondeux, A., ed. (2016), *Le Liber glossarum (s. VII–VIII). Sources, composition, réception*. Dossier HEL 10. [http://htl.linguist.univ-paris-diderot.fr/hel/dossiers/numero10]

Gualandri, I. and G. Mazzoli, eds. (2003), *Gli Annei: Una famiglia nella storia e nella cultura di Roma imperiale* (Como).

Guillaumin, J.-B., ed. (2011), *Martianus Capella: Les noces de Philologie et de Mercure, Livre IX: L'harmonie* (Paris).

Guittard, C., transl. (1997), *Macrobe: Les Saturnales, Livres I–III* (Paris).

Hadot, I. (2005), *Arts libéraux et philosophie dans la pensée antique* (Paris).

Hadot, P. (1971), *Marius Victorinus: Recherches sur sa vie et ses oeuvres* (Paris).

Hagen, H., ed. (1867), *Scholia Bernensia ad Vergili Bucolica atque Georgica* (Leipzig).

Hagen, H., ed. (1902), *Appendix Serviana* (Leipzig). [Hathi].

Halporn, J. W. (2002), "After the Schools: Grammar and Rhetoric in Cassiodorus." In Lanham 2002: 48–62.

Halporn, J. W., transl. (2004), *Cassiodorus: Institutions of Divine and Secular Learning and On the Soul* (Liverpool).

Hamesse, J., ed. (1996), *Les Manuscrits des lexiques et glossaires de l'antiquité tardive à la fin du moyen âge* (Leuven).

Hand, F. (1848), *Incerti auctoris Libellus de differentiis* (Jena).

Hardie, C., ed. (1966), *Vitae Vergilianae antiquae* (ed. 2, Oxford).

Haslam, M. (1988), "On the Sedulius commentary on Donatus' *Ars maior*." *RHT* 18: 243–56.

Haverling, G. V. M., ed. (2015), *Latin Linguistics in the Early 21st Century* (Uppsala).

Hays, G. (2002a), "Tales out of School: Grammatical Culture in Fulgentius the Mythographer." In Lanham 2002: 22–47.

Hays, G. (2002b), "The Pseudo-Fulgentian *Super Thebaiden*." In *Vertis in usum: Studies in Honor of Edward Courtney*, ed. C. Damon, J. Dillery, S. Myers (Leipzig): 200–18.

Hays, G. (2003), "The Date and Identity of the Mythographer Fulgentius." *Journal of Medieval Latin* 13: 163–252.

Hellmann, M. (2000), *Tironische Noten in der Karolingerzeit: am Beispiel eines Persius-Kommentars aus der Schule von Tours* (Hannover).

Helm, R. ed. (1898), *Planciadis Fulgentii V.C. opera* (Leipzig). [Hathi].

Henderson, John (2007), *The Medieval World of Isidore of Seville: Truth from Words* (Cambridge).

Hendrickson, G. L. (1906), "The *De Analogia* of Julius Caesar; Its Occasion, Nature, and Date, with Additional Fragments." *CP* 1: 97–120.

Herren, M. (1979), "Some New Light on the Life of Virgilius Maro Grammaticus." *Proceedings of the Royal Irish Academy* 79: 27–71 (reprinted in Herren 1996).

Herren, M. (1981), "Classical and Secular Learning among the Irish before the Carolingian Renaissance." *Florilegium* 3: 118–57 (reprinted in Herren 1996).

Herren, M., ed. (1988), *The Sacred Nectar of the Greeks: The Study of Greek in the West in the Early Middle Ages* (London).

Herren, M. (1992), "The Hiberno-Latin Poems in Virgil the Grammarian." In *De Tertullien aux Mozarabes: Mélanges offerts à Jacques Fontaine*, ed. L. Holtz (Paris): 141–55 (reprinted in Herren 1996).

Herren, M. (1996), *Latin Letters in Early Christian Ireland* (Aldershot).

Herren, M. (2012), "The Graeca in the Tituli of Lucretius: What They Tell Us about the Archetype." *Wiener Studien* 125: 107–24.

Herren, M. (2014), "The Authority of Authors and Schools in the Writings of Virgilius Maro Grammaticus." In *Auctor et Auctoritas in Latinis medii aevi litteris. Author and Authorship in Medieval Latin Literature*, ed. E. D'Angelo and J. Ziolkowski (Florence): 479–88.

Herren, M. and H. Sauer (2016), "Towards a New Edition of the Épinal–Erfurt Glossary: A Sample." *Journal of Medieval Latin* 26: 125–98.
Hexter, R. J. (1986), *Ovid and Medieval Schooling: Studies in Medieval School Commentaries on Ovid's Ars Amatoria, Epistulae ex Ponto, and Epistulae Heroidum* (Munich).
Hildebrandt, P. (1894), *De Scholiis Ciceronis Bobiensibus* (Berlin). [Hathi].
Hildebrandt, P., ed. (1907), *Scholia in Ciceronis Orationes Bobiensia* (Leipzig). [Hathi].
Hildebrandt, P. (1908), "Zur Abwehr." *Berliner philologische Wochenschrift* 28: 473–7.
Hillgarth, J. (1983), "The Position of Isidorian Studies: A Critical Review of the Literature, 1936–75." *Studi Medievali* 24: 817–905.
Hillgarth, J. (1990), "Isidorian Studies, 1976–1985." *Studi Medievali* 31: 925–73.
Hine, H. (2015), "Philosophy and *philosophi*: From Cicero to Apuleius." In *Roman Reflections: Studies in Latin Philosophy*, ed. G. Williams and K. Volk (Oxford): 13–29.
Hofman, R. (2000), "The Irish Tradition of Priscian." In De Nonno et al. 2000: 257–87.
Holder, A., ed. (1894), *Pomponi Porfyrionis Commentum in Horatium Flaccum* (Innsbruck). [Hathi].
Holder, A., ed. (1901), *Favonii Eulogii Disputatio de Somnio Ciceronis* (Leipzig). [Hathi].
Holford-Strevens, L. (2003), Review of Rosellini (2001). *BMCR* 2003.03.24.
Holford-Strevens, L. (2005), *Aulus Gellius: An Antonine Scholar and His Achievement* (ed. 2, Oxford).
Holford-Strevens, L. (2008), Review of Biddau (2008). *BMCR* 2008.11.34.
Holford-Strevens, L. and A. Vardi, eds. (2004), *The Worlds of Aulus Gellius* (Oxford).
Hollis, A. S. (1992), "'Apuleius' *de Orthographia*, Callimachus fr. [815] Pf. and Euphorion 166 Meineke." *ZPE* 92: 109–14.
Hollis, A. S., ed. (2007), *Fragments of Roman Poetry* (Oxford).
Holtz, L. (1971), "Tradition et diffusion de l'oeuvre grammaticale de Pompée, commentateur de Donat." *Revue de Philologie* 45: 48–83.
Holtz, L. (1972), "Sur trois commentaires irlandais de l'*Art Majeure* de Donat au IXe siècle." *RHT* 2: 45–72.
Holtz, L. (1974), "Édition et tradition des manuels grammaticaux antiques et médiévaux." *REL* 52: 75–82.
Holtz, L. (1975), "Le Parisinus Latinus 7530, synthèse cassinienne des arts libéraux." *Studi Medievali* 16: 97–152.
Holtz, L. (1977a), "La typologie des manuscrits grammaticaux latins." *RHT* 7: 247–69.
Holtz, L., ed. (1977b), *Murethach (Muridac): In Donati Artem maiorem* (Turnhout).
Holtz, L. (1977c), "A l'école de Donat, de saint Augustin à Bède." *Latomus* 36: 533–8.
Holtz, L. (1977d), "Grammairiens irlandais au temps de Jean Scot: Quelques aspects de leur pédagogie." In *Jean Scot Erigène et l'histoire de la philosophie* [no editor] (Paris): 69–78.
Holtz, L. (1978), "Sur les traces de Charisius." In Collart et al. 1978: 225–33.
Holtz, L. (1981), *Donat et la tradition de l'enseignement grammatical* (Paris).
Holtz, L. (1986a), "La tradition ancienne du *Liber in partibus Donati* de Smaragde de Saint-Mihiel." *RHT* 16: 171–200.
Holtz, L. (1986b), "Quelques aspects de la tradition e de la diffusion des Institutions." In Leanza 1986: 281–312.
Holtz, L. (1991), "Murethach et l'influence de la culture irlandaise à Auxerre." In Iogna-Prat et al. 1991: 147–56.
Holtz, L. (1992), "Una nuova fonte manoscritta dell'arte Bernese." *AION (filol).* 14: 5–29.
Holtz, L. (1995), "Glosse e commenti." In Cavallo et al. 1995: 59–111.
Holtz, L. (1996), "Glossaires et grammaire dans l'antiquité." In Hamesse 1996: 1–21.
Holtz, L. (2003), "Insediamenti monastici e diffusione del libro." In *Il monaco il libro la biblioteca*, ed. O. Pecere (Cassino): 65–83.

Holtz, L. (2005a), "Prolégomènes à une édition critique du commentaire de Pompée, grammairien africain." In Taifacos 2005: 109–19.
Holtz, L. (2005b), "Aelius Donatus." In Ax 2005a: 109–31.
Holtz, L. (2009), "L'émergence de l'oeuvre grammaticale de Priscien et la chronologie de sa diffusion." In Baratin et al. 2009: 37–55.
Holtz, L. (2011), "Servius et Donat." In Bouquet and Méniel 2011: 205–17.
Horster, M. and C. Reitz, eds. (2010), *Condensing Texts—Condensed Texts* (Stuttgart).
Howley, J. A. (2017), *Aulus Gellius and Roman Reading Culture: Text, Presence, and Imperial Knowledge in the* Noctes Atticae (Cambridge).
Hubert, M. (1971), "Isidore de Séville novateur? (*Origines* I, xviii–xix)." *REL* 49: 290–313.
Huemer, J., ed. (1883), *Cruindmeli sive Fulcharii Ars metrica* (Vienna).
Huemer, J. (1885), "Zu Walahfrid Strabo." *Neues Archiv der Gesellschaft für ältere deutsche Geschichtskunde* 10: 166–9.
Huemer, J., ed. (1886), *Virgilii Maronis grammatici opera* (Leipzig). [Hathi].
Huygens, R. (1954), "Remigiana I." *Aevum* 28: 330–42.
Ihm, M. (1890), "Die Scholien im Codex Mediceus des Vergilius." *RhMus* 45: 622–36.
Iogna-Prat, D., C. Jeudy, and G. Lobrichon, eds. (1991), *L'École carolingienne d'Auxerre de Murethach à Remi, 830–908* (Paris).
Ippolito, A., ed. (2006), *Marii Victorini Explanationes in Ciceronis Rhetoricam* (Turnhout).
Irvine, M. (1986), "Bede the Grammarian and the Scope of Grammatical Studies in Eighth-Century Northumbria." *Anglo-Saxon England* 15: 15–44.
Irvine, M. (1994), *The Making of Textual Culture: "Grammatica" and Literary Theory, 350–1100* (Cambridge).
Jahn, O. (1851), "Über die Subscriptionen in den Handschriften römischer Klassiker." *Berichte über die Verhandlungen der königlich sächsischen Gesellschaft der Wissenschaften zu Leipzig, Philologisch–Historische Klasse* 3: 327–72.
Jahnke, R., ed. (1898), *Lactantii Placidi qui dicitur Commentarios in Statii Thebaida et Commentarium in Achilleida* (Leipzig). [Hathi].
Jakobi, R. (1996), *Die Kunst der Exegese im Terenzkommentar des Donat* (Berlin).
Jakobi, R. (1997), "Notizen zu mittelalterlichen Klassikerkommentaren." *Studi Medievali* 38: 305–15.
Jakobi, R. (1999) "Beobachtungen zu der *Accusat lacescit*-Redaktion der *Synonyma Ciceronis*." *Glotta* 75: 226–8.
Jakobi, R., ed. (2002), *Grillius: Commentum in Ciceronis Rhetorica* (Leipzig).
Jakobi, R. (2004a), "Textgeschichte als Kulturgeschichte: Der sogenannte Lactantius Placidus-Kommmentar zur 'Thebais' des Statius." In Geerlings and Schulze 2002–4: 2: 1–16.
Jakobi, R. (2004b), "Die 'Thebais'-Erklärung des Ps.-Fulgentius." In Geerlings and Schulze 2002–4: 2: 17–20.
Jakobi, R. (2005), *Grillius: Überlieferung und Kommentar* (Berlin).
Jakobi, R. (2007), "Das Commentum Brunsianum." In Kruschwitz et al. 2007: 37–49.
Jakobi, R. (2009), "Zum 'Berner Glossar.'" *Philologus* 153: 187–9.
Jakobi, R. (2014), "Martianea." *Hermes* 142: 499–504.
Jakobi, R. (2015), "Coronatus Grammaticus." *Rheinisches Museum* 158: 419–31.
Jeauneau, E. (1985), "Pour le dossier d'Israel Scot." *Archives d'histoire doctrinale et littéraire du Moyen Age* 60: 7–72.
Jeep, L. (1893), *Zur Geschichte der Lehre von den Redetheilen bei den Lateinischen Grammatikern* (Leipzig). [Hathi].
Jenal, G. (2005), "(Flavius) Magnus Cassiodorus Senator." In Ax 2005b: 217–46.
Jeudy, C. (1971), "La tradition manuscrite des *Partitiones* de Priscien et la version longue du commentaire de Rémi d'Auxerre." *RHT* 1: 123–43.

Jeudy, C. (1972), "L'*Institutio de nomine, pronomine et verbo* de Priscien: Manuscrits et commentaires mediévaux." *RHT* 2: 73–144.

Jeudy, C. (1974a), "Les manuscrits de l'Ars de uerbo d'Eutychès et le commentaire de Rémi d'Auxerre." In *Études de civilisation médiévale, IXe–XIIe siècles: melanges offerts à Edmond-René Labande* [no editor] (Poitiers): 421–36.

Jeudy, C. (1974b), "L'*Ars de nomine et verbo* de Phocas: Manuscrits et commentaires médiévaux." *Viator* 5: 61–156.

Jeudy, C. (1975), "Le Commentaire de Rémi d'Auxerre au Livre III de l'*Ars maior* de Donat (ms. Vatican, Reg. lat. 1560)." In *La Cultura Antica nell'occidente latino dal VII all'XI secolo*, ed. Centro Italiano di studi sull'alto medioevo (Spoleto) 1: 213–35.

Jeudy, C. (1976), "La Tradition manuscrite du *De aspiratione* attribué au grammairien Phocas." In *Hommages à André Boutemy*, ed. G. Cambier (Brussels): 197–215.

Jeudy, C. (1977), "Israël le grammarien et la tradition manuscrite du commentaire de Remi d'Auxerre à l'*Ars minor* de Donat." *Studi Medievali* 18: 185–248.

Jeudy, C. (1978a), "Un manuscrit glosé d'Eutychès à Reims à l'époque de Rémi d'Auxerre." In Collart et al. 1978: 235–43.

Jeudy, C. (1978b), "Donat et commentateurs de Donat à l'abbaye de Ripoll au Xe siècle (ms. Barcelone, Archivo de la Corona de Aragón, Ripoll 46)." In *Lettres latines du moyen âge et de la renaissance*, ed. G. Cambier, C. Deroux, and J. Préaux (Brussels): 56–75.

Jeudy, C. (1982–83), "Le *Scalprum Prisciani* et sa tradition manuscrite." *RHT* 12–13: 181–93.

Jeudy, C. (1983), "Le florilège grammatical inedit du ms 8° 8 de la bibliothèque d'Erfurt." *ALMA* 1983: 91–128.

Jeudy, C. (1990), "Un commentaire anonyme de l'*Ars minor* de Donat." In Bursill-Hall et al. 1990: 133–46.

Jeudy, C. (1991a), "L'Oeuvre de Remi d'Auxerre." In Iogna-Prat et al. 1991: 373–96.

Jeudy, C. (1991b), "*Remigii Autissiodorensis opera (Clavis)*." In Iogna-Prat et al. 1991: 457–500.

Jeudy, C. (1993), "Fragments Carolingiens de la grammaire de Dynamius." In Law 1993a: 127–44.

Jeudy, C. (1996), "Glossaires Juvenaliens du haut moyen âge." In Hamesse 1996: 254–82.

Jeudy, C. (2003), "Rémi d'Auxerre et le livre II de l'*Ars maior* de Donat." In Lardet 2003: 131–41.

Jeudy, C. and Y.-F. Riou (1974), "L'*Achilléide* de Stace au moyen âge. Abrégés et arguments." *RHT* 4: 143–80.

Jeunet-Mancy, E., ed. (2012), *Servius: Commentaire sur l'Énéide de Virgile, Livre VI* (Paris).

Jocelyn, H. D. (1984–5), "The Annotations of M. Valerius Probus." *CQ* 34: 464–72, 35: 149–61, 35: 466–74.

Jones, C. and C. Kendall, eds. (1975), *Bedae Venerabilis Opera*, Vol. 6: *De orthographia, De arte metrica, De schematibus et tropis, De natura rerum liber, De temporum ratione liber* (Turnhout).

Jones, L. W., transl. (1946), *An Introduction to Divine and Human Readings, by Cassiodorus Senator* (New York).

Kalinina, A. (2007), *Der Horazkommentar des Pomponius Porphyrio: Untersuchungen zu seiner Terminologie und Textgeschichte* (Stuttgart).

Karsten, H. T., ed. (1912–13), *Commenti Donatiani ad Terenti fabulas scholia genuina et spuria* (Leiden)

Kaster, R. A. (1978), "Servius and *Idonei auctores*." *AJP* 99: 181–209.

Kaster, R. A. (1980a), "The Grammarian's Authority." *CP* 75: 216–41.

Kaster, R. A. (1980b), "Macrobius and Servius: *Verecundia* and the Grammarian's Function." *HSCP* 84: 219–62.
Kaster, R. A. (1983a), Review of Holtz (1981). *Speculum* 58: 478–84.
Kaster, R. A. (1983b), "Notes on 'Primary' and 'Secondary' Schools in Late Antiquity." *TAPA* 113: 323–46.
Kaster, R. A. (1988), *Guardians of Language: The Grammarian and Society in Late Antiquity* (Berkeley).
Kaster, R. A., ed. (1995), *Suetonius De grammaticis et rhetoribus* (Oxford).
Kaster, R. A. (2010), *Studies on the Text of Macrobius's "Saturnalia"* (New York).
Kaster, R. A., ed. (2011a), *Macrobius: Saturnalia* (Cambridge, MA).
Kaster, R. A., ed. (2011b), *Macrobii Ambrosii Theodosii Saturnalia* (Oxford).
Kauffmann, G. (1888), *De Hygini memoria scholiis in Ciceronis Aratum Harleianis servata* (Breslau).
Kaufmann, H. (2015), "*Papinius Noster*: Statius in Roman Late Antiquity." In *Brill's Companion to Statius*, ed. W. Dominik, C. Newlands, K. Gervais (Leiden): 481–96.
Keil, G. (1889), *De Flavio Capro Grammatico quaestionum capita II* (Halle).
Keil, H. (1868), *De grammaticis quibusdam Latinis infimae aetatis commentatio* (Erlangen).
Keil, H. (1872), *Quaestionum grammaticarum pars II: De Maximi Victorini libris De arte grammatica qui feruntur* (Halle). [Hathi].
Keil, H., ed. (1874), *Marii Victorini Excerpta de orthographia* (Halle). [Hathi].
Keller, O., ed. (1902–4), *Pseudoacronis scholia in Horatium vetustiora* (Leipzig). [Hathi].
Kendall, C. B., ed. (1991), *Bede: Libri II De arte metrica et De schematibus et tropis: The Art of Poetry and Rhetoric* (Saarbrücken).
Kent, R. G., ed. (1938), *M. Terentius Varro: On the Latin Language* (Cambridge, MA).
Keyser, P. (1994), "Late Authors in Nonius Marcellus and Other Evidence of His Date." *HSCP* 96: 369–89.
Kindermann, U. (2005), "Isidor von Sevilla." In Ax 2005a: 273–90.
Klotz, A. (1908), "Die Statiusscholien." *ALL* 15: 485–525.
Klotz, R. (1895), *De scholiis Statianis commentatio* I (Treptow). [Hathi].
Knappe, G. (1996), *Traditionen der klassischen Rhetorik im angelsächsischen England* (Heidelberg).
Kramer, J. (1980a), "Kommentar zum Kölner griechisch-lateinischen Glossar (Folium Wallraffianum)." *ZPE* 38: 229–43.
Kramer, J. (1980b), "Kommentar zum Göttinger lateinisch-griechischen Glossar (App. Dipl. 8 C und D)." *ZPE* 40: 161–79.
Kramer, J. (1983), *Glossaria bilinguia in papyris et membranis reperta* (Bonn).
Kramer, J. (1996), "I Glossari tardo-antichi di tradizione papiracea." In Hamesse 1996: 23–55.
Kramer, J. (2001), *Glossaria bilinguia altera* (Munich).
Kraus, C. S. and C. Stray, eds. (2015), *Classical Commentaries: Explorations in a Scholarly Genre* (Oxford).
Krotz, E. and M. Gorman, eds. (2014), *Grammatical works attributed to Peter of Pisa, Charlemagne's tutor* (Hildesheim).
Kruschwitz, P., W. Ehlers, and F. Felgentreu, eds. (2007), *Terentius poeta* (Munich).
Kulcsar, P., ed. (1987), *Mythographi Vaticani I et II* (Turnhout).
Lambot, C. (1932), "Opuscules grammaticaux de Gottschalk." *Revue bénédictine* 44: 120–4.
Lambot, C., ed. (1945), *Oeuvres théologiques et grammaticales de Godescalc d'Orbais* (Leuven).
Lammert, F. (1931), "Bericht über die Literatur zu den lateinischen Grammatikern, zur Scholienliteratur und Glossographie (1921–1925)." *Jahresbericht über die Fortschritte der klassischen Altertumswissenschaft* 231: 31–121.

Lammert, F. (1936), "Bericht über die Literatur zu den lateinischen Grammatikern, zur Scholienliteratur und Glossographie (1926–1933)." *Jahresbericht über die Fortschritte der klassischen Altertumswissenschaft* 252: 105–62.

Landgraf, G. (1896), "Über die Latinität des Horazscholiasten Porphyrion." *ALL* 9: 549–65.

Landgraf, G. (1902), "Das Alter der Martial-Lemmata in den Handschriften der Familie B." *ALL* 12: 455–63.

Lanham, C. ed. (2002), *Latin Grammar and Rhetoric: From Classical Theory to Mediaeval Practice* (London).

La Penna, A., ed. (1959), *Scholia in P. Ovidi Nasonis Ibin* (Florence).

Lapidge, M. (1986), "The School of Theodore and Hadrian." *Anglo-Saxon England* 15: 45–72.

Lapidge, M. (1996), "Foreword." In Lindsay 1996: ix–xviii.

Lapidge, M. (2003), "Rufinus at the School of Canterbury." In Lardet 2003: 119–29.

Lapidge, M. and J. Rosier, transl. (1985), *Aldhelm: The Poetic Works* (Cambridge).

Lardet, P., ed. (2003), *La tradition vive: Mélanges d'histoire des textes en l'honneur de Louis Holtz* (Paris).

Law, V. (1979), "The Transmission of the *Ars Bonifacii* and the *Ars Tatuini*." *RHT* 9: 281–8.

Law, V. (1981), "Malsachanus Reconsidered: A Fresh Look at a Hiberno-Latin Grammarian." *Cambridge Medieval Celtic Studies* 1: 83–93.

Law, V. (1982), *The Insular Latin Grammarians* (Woodbridge).

Law, V. (1984), "St Augustine's *De grammatica*: Lost or Found?" *Recherches Augustiniennes* 19: 155–83.

Law, V. (1987), "An Unnoticed Late Latin Grammar: The *Ars minor* of Scaurus?" *Rheinisches Museum* 130: 67–89.

Law, V. (1990), "*Auctoritas, Consuetudo* and *Ratio* in St. Augustine's *Ars grammatica*." In Bursill-Hall et al. 1990: 191–207.

Law, V., ed. (1993a), *History of Linguistic Thought in the Early Middle Ages* (Amsterdam).

Law, V. (1993b), "The Historiography of Grammar in the Early Middle Ages." In Law 1993a: 1–23 (reprinted in Law 1997: 4–27).

Law, V. (1993c), "Grammar in the Early Middle Ages: A Bibliography." In Law 1993a: 25–47 (reprinted in Law 1997: 273–97).

Law, V. (1993d), "Erchanbert and the Interpolator: A Christian *Ars minor* at Freising (Clm 6414)." In Law 1993a: 223–43.

Law, V. (1994a), "The Sources of the *Ars Donati quam Paulus Diaconus exposuit*." *Filologia Mediolatina* 1: 71–80.

Law, V. (1994b), "The Study of Grammar." In *Carolingian Culture: Emulation and Innovation*, ed. R. McKitterick (Cambridge): 88–110 (reprinted as "The Study of Grammar under the Carolingians" in Law 1997: 129–53).

Law, V. (1995a), "The Transmission of Early Medieval Elementary Grammars: A Case Study in Explanation." In Pecere and Reeve 1995: 239–61.

Law, V. (1995b), *Wisdom, Authority and Grammar in the Seventh Century* (Cambridge).

Law, V. (1997), *Grammar and Grammarians in the Early Middle Ages* (London).

Law, V. (2000), "Memory and the Structure of Grammars in Antiquity and the Middle Ages." In De Nonno, De Paolis, and Holtz 2000: 9–57.

Law, V. (2003), *The History of Linguistics in Europe from Plato to 1600* (Cambridge).

Law, V. and I. Sluiter, eds. (1995), *Dionysius Thrax and the Techne Grammatike* (Münster).

Leanza, S., ed. (1986), *Atti della settimana di studi su Flavio Magno Aurelio Cassiodoro* (Soveria Mannelli).

Lazzerini, F. (2017), "Romulus' *Adytum* or *Asylum*? A New Exegetical Proposal for Varro, *De lingua Latina* 5, 8." *Ciceroniana On Line* 1: 97–128.

Leclercq, J. (1948), "Smaragde et la grammaire chrétienne." *Revue du moyen âge latin* 4: 15–22.

Lecompte, S. (2009), *La chaîne d'or des poètes: Présence de Macrobe dans l'Europe humaniste* (Geneva).

Lehmann, Paul (1929), *Sammlungen und Erörterungen lateinischer Abkürzungen in Altertum und Mittelalter* (Munich).

Lendinara, P. (1996), "L'attività glossatoria del periodo anglosassone." In Hamesse 1996: 615–55.

Lenel, O. (1883), *Das Edictum Perpetuum: Ein Versuch zu dessen Wiederherstellung* (Leipzig).

Lenel, O. (1889), *Palingenesia Iuris Civilis* (Leipzig).

Lenoble, M., P. Swiggers, and A. Wouters (2000), "L'enseignement grammatical entre latin et grec: Le manuel de Dosithée." In *The History of Linguistic and Grammatical Praxis*, ed. P. Desmet, L. Jooken, P. Schmitter, and P. Swiggers (Leuven): 3–22.

Lentini, A. (1975), *Ilderico e la sua "Ars grammatica"* (Montecassino).

Leonhardt, J. (1989a), "Die Beiden metrischen Systeme des Altertums." *Hermes* 117: 43–62.

Leonhardt, J. (1989b), *Dimensio syllabarum: Studien zur lateinschen Prosodie- und Verslehre von der Spätantike bis zur frühen Renaissance* (Göttingen).

Lepschy, G., ed. (1994), *History of Linguistics* (London).

Lewis, R. G. (2006), *Asconius: Commentaries on Speeches by Cicero* (Oxford).

Lhommé, M.-K. (2001), "Le *De verborum significatione*, de Verrius Flaccus aux *Glossaria Latina* de Lindsay: Éditions de lacunes, lacunes des éditions." *Živa Antika* 51: 39–62.

Lhommé, M.-K. (2007), "Varron et Verrius au 2ème siècle après Jésus-Christ." In Glinister et al.: 33–47.

Lhommé, M.-K. (2011), "De l'encyclopédie au glossaire: Festus et son adaptation par Paul Diacre." In Ferri 2011a: 29–47.

Lindemann, F., ed. (1831–40), *Corpus grammaticorum Latinorum veterum*, Vols. 1–3, 4.1 (all publ.) (Leipzig). [Hathi].

Lindsay, W. M. (1901), *Nonius Marcellus' Dictionary of Republican Latin* (Oxford). [Hathi].

Lindsay, W. M., ed. (1903a), *Nonii Marcelli De compendiosa doctrina libri XX* (Leipzig). [Hathi].

Lindsay, W. M. (1903b), *Ancient Editions of Martial* (Oxford). [Hathi].

Lindsay, W. M., ed. (1911), *Isidori Episcopi Etymologiarum sive Originum libri XX* (Oxford). [Hathi].

Lindsay, W. M., ed. (1913), *Sextus Pompeius Festus De verborum significatu* (Leipzig). [Hathi].

Lindsay, W. M. (1921a), *The Corpus Glossary* (Cambridge). [Hathi].

Lindsay, W. M. (1921b), *The Corpus, Épinal, Erfurt and Leyden Glossaries* (Oxford) (reprinted in Lindsay 1996). [Hathi].

Lindsay, W. M., ed. (1922), *Julian of Toledo "De vitiis et figuris"* (Oxford). [Hathi].

Lindsay, W. M. (1927a), "The Primary MS of Probus Inst. Art." *AJP* 48: 231–4.

Lindsay, W. M. (1927b), Review of *Glossaria Latina* I–III. *Archivum Latinitatis Mediii Aevi* 3: 95–100 (reprinted in Lindsay 1996).

Lindsay, W. M. (1963), *Notae Latinae*, with a Supplement by D. Bains (Hildesheim).

Lindsay, W. M. (1996), *Studies in Early Mediaeval Latin Glossaries*, ed. M. Lapidge (Aldershot).

Llorente Pinto, A. L. (1996), "The Lemmatic Arrangement of the Fourth Book of the *Compendiosa Doctrina* of Nonius Marcellus According to Its Manuscript Tradition." In Hamesse (1996): 93–100.

Llorente Pinto, A. L. (2009), "La 'Compendiosa doctrina' de Nonio Marcelo." *Helmantica* 60: 15–72.

Löfstedt, B. (1965), *Der Hibernolateinische Grammatiker Malsachanus* (Uppsala).

Löfstedt, B. (1972a), "Zu Tatwines Grammatik." *Arctos* 7: 47–65.
Löfstedt, B. (1972b), "Weitere Bemerkungen zu Tatwines Grammatik." *Acta Classica* 15: 85–94.
Löfstedt, B. (1976), "Zur Grammatik des Asper minor." In *Latin Script and Letters A.D. 400–900*, ed. J. O'Meara and B. Naumann (Leiden): 132–40.
Löfstedt, B., ed. (1977a), *Ars Laureshamensis* (*Expositio in Donatum maiorem*) (Turnhout).
Löfstedt, B., ed. (1977b), *Sedulius Scottus in Donati Artem maiorem* (Turnhout).
Löfstedt, B., ed. (1977c), *Sedulius Scottus in Donati Artem minorem, In Priscianum, In Eutychem* (Turnhout).
Löfstedt, B. (1980), "Zu den Quellen des hibernolateinischen Donatkommentars im Cod. Ambrosianus L 22 sup." *Studi medievali* 21: 301–20.
Löfstedt, B., ed. (1982), *Ars Ambrosiana: Commentum Anonymi in Donati Partes maiores* (Turnhout).
Löfstedt, B. (1987), "Eine wenig beachtete hibernolateinische Grammatik." In *Irland und die Christenheit: Bibelstudien und Mission = Ireland and Christendom: the Bible and the missions*, ed. P. Ni Chathain and M. Richter (Stuttgart): 272–6.
Löfstedt, B. (1998), "Zur Grammatik in Paris Bibl. Nat. MS Lat. 7491." *Peritia* 12: 95–7.
Löfstedt, B., ed. (2003), *Virgilius Maro Grammaticus, Opera omnia* (Munich).
Löfstedt, B. (2005), "Nochmals zum Latein des Virgilius Maro Grammaticus." In Taifacos 2005: 131–6.
Löfstedt, B., L. Holtz, and A. Kibre, eds. (1986), *Smaragdus, Liber in partibus Donati* (Turnhout).
Loewe, G. (1876), *Prodromus Corporis glossariorum Latinorum* (Leipzig). [Hathi].
Loewe, G. (1884), *Glossae nominum* (Leipzig). [Hathi].
Lomanto, V. (1994), "Il sistema del *sermo Latinus* in Quintiliano." In *Voce di molte acque: Miscellanea di studi offerti a Eugenio Corsini*, ed. G. Bàrberi Squarotti (Turin): 237–56.
Lomanto, V. (2001), "Nomi a confronto." *Papers on Grammar* 6: 165–90.
Lomanto, V. and N. Marinone (1990), *Index grammaticus: An Index to Latin Grammar Texts* (Hildesheim).
Lo Monaco, F. (2007), "Tra paeleografia e storia della cultura. Alcune considerazioni su prolemi di datazione e localizzatione nella produzione manoscritta dell'Italia settentrionale Longobarda." In Lo Monaco and Molinelli 2007: 125–59.
Lo Monaco, F. and P. Molinelli, eds. (2007), *L'"Apppendix Probi". Nuove ricerche* (Florence).
Longobardi, C. (2014a), "Il *corpus* pseudoacroniano: Per una revisione dell'edizione Keller." In *Dalla civiltà classica all'umanesimo*, ed. F. Longo Auricchio (Florence): 186–96.
Longobardi, C. (2014b), "Il *corpus* pseudoacroniano: Lemmi, citazioni, tradizione indiretta." In Longobardi et al. 2014: 203–12.
Longobardi, C., C. Nicolas, and M. Squillante, eds. (2014), *Scholae discimus: Pratiques scolaires dans l'Antiquité tardive et le Haut Moyen Âge* (Lyon).
Lowe, E. A. (1972), *Palaeographical Papers* (Oxford).
Luhtala, A. (2000), "*Excerpta* di Pietro da Pisa da Prisciano, Diomede, e Pompeo." In De Nonno et al. 2000: 327–50.
Luhtala, A. (2002), "On Definitions in Ancient Grammar." In Swiggers and Wouters 2002a: 257–85.
Luhtala, A. (2005), *Grammar and Philosophy in Late Antiquity* (Amsterdam).
Luhtala, A. (2009), "Priscian's Philosophy." In Baratin et al. 2009: 109–24.
Luhtala, A. (2010), "Latin *Schulgrammatik* and the Emergence of Grammatical Commentaries." In Horster and Reitz 2010: 209–43.

Lunelli, A. (2001–3), "*Scholiorum in Vergilium Veronensium reliquiae*: Notizie degli scavi, edizione provvisoria." *Maia* 53: 65–141 and 55: 5–83.

Maass, E., ed. (1898), *Commentariorum in Aratum reliquiae* (Berlin). [Hathi].

Maestre Yenes, M., ed. (1973), *Ars Juliani Toletani episcopi: Una gramática latina de la España visigoda. Estudio y edición crítica* (Toledo).

Madvig, J. N. (1828), *De Q. Asconii Pediani et aliorum veterum interpretum in Ciceronis orationes commentariis disputatio critica* (Copenhagen). [Hathi].

Magallón García, A.-I. (1995–2006), *Concordantia in Isidori Hispaliensis Etymologias* (Hildesheim).

Magallón García, A.-I. (1996), *La tradición gramatical de* differentia *y* etymologia *hasta Isidoro de Sevilla* (Zaragoza).

Magallón García, A.-I. (2002), "El *Comentario a Terencio* de Donato: La lengua de Terencio y los *veteres*." *Revista de Estudios latinos* 2: 17–32.

Magnus, H., ed. (1914), *P. Ovidi Nasonis Metamorphoseon Libri XV* (Berlin). [Hathi].

Mai, A., ed. (1828–38), *Classicorum auctorum e vaticanis codicibus editorum*, Vols. 1–10 (Rome). [Hathi].

Mai, A., ed. (1852–1905), *Nova patrum bibliotheca* (Rome). [Hathi].

Maltby, R. (2007), "Donat über die Stegreifelemente in Terenz' Phormio." In Kruschwitz et al. 2007: 15–28.

Maltby, R. (2011), "Servius on Stylistic Register in His Virgil Commentaries." In Ferri 2011a: 63–73.

Maltby, R. (2012), "The *De barbarismis et metaplasmis* of Consentius as Evidence for Late and Vulgar Latin." In Biville et al. 2012: 727–37.

Manca, M., ed. (2003a), *Fulgenzio: Le età del mondo e dell'uomo* (Alessandria).

Manca, M. (2003b), *Concordantia Fulgentiana: A concordance of Fulgentius* (Hildesheim).

Manitius, M. (1911), *Geschichte der lateinischen Literatur des Mittelalters. Erster Teil* (Munich).

Manitius, M. (1912), "Micons von St. Riquier De primis syllabis." *Münchener Museum fur Philologie des Mittelalters* 1: 122–77.

Manitius, M. (1913a), "Zu Iohannes Scottus und Remigius." *Didaskaleion* 2: 43–88.

Manitius, M. (1913b), "Remigiusscholien." *Münchener Museum für Philologie des Mittelalters* 2: 79–113.

Mann, N. and B. Munk Olsen, eds. (1997), *Medieval and Renaissance Scholarship*: Proceedings of the Second European Science Foundation Workshop on the Classical Tradition in the Middle Ages and the Renaissance (London, Warburg Institute, 27–28 November 1992) (Leiden).

Mantelli, F. (2008), "Interpretazioni virgiliane a confronto: Cesellio Vindice e Sulpicio Apollinare in Gellio II 16 (a proposito di *Aen*. VI 760–766)." *Maia* 60: 80–86.

Mantelli, F. (2015), *Gaio Sulpicio Apollinare, grammatico latino del II secolo d.C.* (Rome).

Mantero, T. (1975), "La *Inscriptio* dei codici del *De compendiosa doctrina* e *Nonius Marcellus Peripateticus Thubursicensis*." *Studi Noniani* 3: 123–88.

Marcellino, G., ed. (2012), *Favonii Eulogii Disputatio de Somnio Scipionis* (Naples).

Marcos Casquero, M.-A., ed. (1990), *Varrón De lingua Latina: Edición bilingüe* (Barcelona).

Mari, T. (2016a), *Consentius'* De barbarismis et metaplasmis: *Critical edition, translation, and commentary* (Diss. Oxford).

Mari, T. (2016b), "I metaplasmi in Consenzio." In Ferri and Zago 2016: 277–89.

Mari, T., ed. (2017), *Pauca de barbarismo collecta de multis* (Pisa).

Marina Sáez, R. and J. Mesa Sanz (1997), *Concordantia Macrobiana* (Hildesheim).

Marinone, N. (1977), *I Saturnali di Macrobio Teodosio* (ed. 2, Turin).
Marinone, N. (1990), *Analecta graecolatina* (Bologna).
Mariotti, I., ed. (1967), *Marii Victorini Ars grammatica* (Florence).
Mariotti, S. (1984), "Il *Fragmentum Bobiense de nomine* (*Gramm. Lat.* VII 540–544 Keil)." In Questa and Raffaelli 1984: 37–68.
Marmorale, E., ed. (1939), *Arusiani Messii Exempla elocutionum* (Naples).
Marrou, H.-I. (1931), "Autour de la bibliothèque du Pape Agapit." *Mélanges d'archéologie et d'histoire* 48: 124–69.
Marrou, H.-I. (1976), *Patristique et humanisme* (Paris).
Marshall, B. A. (1985), *A Historical Commentary on Asconius* (Columbia, MO).
Marshall, P. K., ed. (1983), *Isidori Hispalensis Etymologiae II* (Paris).
Marshall, P. K. (1993), "Tiberius Claudius Donatus on Virgil *Aen.* 6.1–157." *Manuscripta* 37: 3–20.
Marshall, P. K. (1997), *Servius and Commentary on Virgil* (Asheville).
Marshall, P. K. (2000), "The Spangenberg *Bifolium* of Servius: the Manuscript and the Text." *RFIC* 128: 192–209.
Marshall, P. K. (2012), "DServius and Festus: Some Further Evidence of Indebtedness." In Zumbo 2012: 69–75.
Marshall, R. (2010), "Studies on the *Ars grammatica Sergi{li}i*." *Journal of Medieval Latin* 20: 167–231.
Marsili, A., ed. (1952), *Alcuini Orthographia* (Pisa).
Marti, B. (1950), "*Vacca in Lucanum*." *Speculum* 25: 198–214.
Marti, H. (1961, 1963), "Terenz 1909–1959." *Lustrum* 6: 114–238, 7: 5–101.
Martin, J. (1927), *Grillius: Ein Beitrag zur Geschichte der Rhetorik* (Paderborn).
Martorelli, L., ed. (2011), *Ps. Aurelii Augustini Regulae* (Hildesheim).
Martorelli, L., ed. (2014), *Greco antico nell'occidente carolingio: Frammenti di testi Attici nell'*Ars *di Prisciano* (Hildesheim).
Matthaios, S. (2005), "Das Wortartensystem der Alexandriner. Skizze seiner Entwicklungsgeschichte und Nachwirkung." In Taifacos 2005: 13–39.
Matthaios, S., F. Montanari, and A. Rengakos, eds. (2011), *Ancient Scholarship and Grammar: Archetypes, Concepts and Contexts* (Berlin).
Matthews, P. (1994), "Greek and Latin Linguistics." In Lepschy 1994: 2.1–133.
Mattingly, H. B. (1957), "The Date of Livius Andronicus." *CQ* 7: 159–63.
Mazhuga, V. I. (2003), "À quelle époque vivait le grammairien Phocas?" *Revue de Philologie* 77: 67–77.
Mazzacane, R., ed. (2014), *Nonio Marcello De conpendiosa doctrina*, Vol. 1 (Florence).
Mazzarino, A. (1948–9), "Una nuova pagina di Plinio il Vecchio." *Maia* 1: 200–22 and 2: 43–52.
McDonough, C., R. Prior, and M. Stansbury, transl. (2002), *Servius' Commentary on Book Four of Virgil's Aeneid: An Annotated Translation* (Wauconda).
McKitterick, R. (1976), "A Ninth-Century Schoolbook from the Loire Valley: Phillipps MS 16308." *Scriptorium* 30: 225–31.
McNamee, K. (1997), "An Innovation in Annotated Codices on Papyrus." *Archiv für Papyrusforschung, Beiheft* 3: 669–78.
McNamee, K. (2010), "Reading Outside the Library." In *Philology and Its Histories*, ed. S. Gurd (Columbus): 20–46.
Mentz, A. (1931), "Die Entstehungsgeschichte der römischen Stenographie." *Hermes* 66: 369–86.
Mentz, A. (1939), "Die tironischen Noten. Eine Geschichte der römischen Kurzschrift, I." *Archiv für Urkundenforschung* 16: 287–384.

Mentz, A. (1941), "Die tironischen Noten. Eine Geschichte der römischen Kurzschrift, II." *Archiv für Urkundenforschung* 17: 155–303.
Merrills, A. (2013), "Isidore's *Etymologies*: On Words and Things." In *Encyclopaedism from Antiquity to the Renaissance*, ed. J. König and G. Woolf (Cambridge): 301–24.
Mesa Sanz, J. F., transl. (2009), *Macrobio: Saturnales* (Madrid).
Mette, H. J. (1936), *Sphairopoiia: Untersuchungen zur Kosmologie des Krates von Pergamon* (Munich).
Mette, H. J. (1952), *Parateresis: Untersuchungen zur Sprachtheorie des Krates von Pergamon* (Halle).
Miller, J. M., M. H. Prosser, and T. W. Benson, eds. (1973), *Readings in Medieval Rhetoric* (Bloomington).
Moatti, C. (2015), *The Birth of Critical Thinking in Republican Rome* (Cambridge).
Möller, L., transl. (2008), *Die Enzyclopädie des Isidor von Sevilla* (Wiesbaden).
Mommsen, T. (1907), *Gesammelte Schriften*, Vol. 7 (Berlin).
Moreau, P. (2007), "Le Lexique de Festus témoin de la naissance d'une science de la parenté à Rome." In Glinister et al. 2007: 69–86.
Morelli, C. (1910), "I trattati di grammatica e retorica del cod. Casanatense 1086." *Rendiconti della Reale Accademia dei Lincei, Classe di scienze morali, storiche e filologiche* Series 5, 19: 287–328.
Morelli, C. (1916), "La fortuna dell'opuscolo *De finalibus metrorum*." *Athenaeum* 4: 321–34.
Morelli, G. (1989), "Le liste degli autori scoperti a Bobbio nel 1493." *RFIC* 117: 5–33.
Morelli, G. (2000), "Metricologi latini di tradizione Bobbiese." In De Nonno et al. 2000: 533–59.
Morelli, G. (2008), "Tra Atilio Fortunaziano e Servio." In *Amicitiae templa serena: Studi in onore di Giuseppe Aricò*, ed. L. Castagna and C. Riboldi (Milan) 2: 1155–7.
Morelli, G., ed. (2011–12), *Caesii Bassi De metris, Atilii Fortunatiani De metris Horatianis* (Hildesheim).
Most, G. W., ed. (1999), *Commentaries—Kommentare* (Göttingen).
Mountford, J., ed. (1934), *The Scholia Bembina* (London).
Mountford, J. and J. T. Schultz (1930), *Index rerum et nominum in scholiis Servii et Aelii Donati tractatorum* (Ithaca).
Müller, K. O., ed. (1880), *Sexti Pompei Festi* De verborum significatione *quae supersunt* (Leipzig). [Hathi].
Munk Olsen, B. (1982), *L'étude des auteurs classiques latins au XIe et XIIe siècles*. Vol. 1 (Paris).
Munk Olsen, B. (2009), *L'étude des auteurs classiques latins au XIe et XIIe siècles*. Vol. 4.1 (Paris).
Münzer, F. (2012), *Kleine Schriften*, ed. M. Haake and A.-C. Harders (Stuttgart).
Munzi, L. (1980–1), "Il 'De partibus orationis' di Giuliano di Toledo." *AION (filol)* 2–3: 154–231.
Munzi, L. (1990), "Una inedita Summa memorialis delle Metamorfosi ovidiane." In *Dicti Studiosus: Scritti di filologia offeri a Scevola Mariotti dai suoi allievi* [no editor] (Urbino): 329–385.
Munzi, L. (1992), "Il ruolo della prefazione nei testi grammaticali." *AION (filol.)* 14: 103–26.
Munzi, L. (2000), "Testi grammaticali e *renovatio studiorum* carolingia." In De Nonno et al. 2000: 351–88.
Munzi, L. (2003–4), "*Omnia et furibunde explicabat*: Per una nuova edizione della *Vita* parodica del grammatico Donato." *Incontri triestini di filologia classica* 3: 261–77.

Munzi, L. (2004), *Multiplex Latinitas: Testi grammaticali latini dell'Alto Medioevo* (AION, Quarderni 9) (Naples).
Munzi, L. (2007), *Littera legitera: Testi grammaticali latini dell'Alto Medioevo* (AION, Quarderni 11) (Naples).
Munzi, L. (2008), "Ancora sul 'Donato furioso.'" In *Amicitiae templa serena: Studi in onore di Giuseppe Aricò*, ed. L. Castagna and C. Riboldi (Milan): 2:1159–73.
Munzi, L. (2009), "Prisciano nell'Italia meridionale: La *Adbreviatio artis grammaticae* di Orso di Benevento." In Baratin et al. 2009: 463–79.
Munzi, L. (2010), "Due note su testi grammaticali latini dell'alto medioevo." *AION (filol.)* 32: 137–45.
Munzi, L. (2011), "Exégèse biblique et commentaire grammatical dans le haute moyen âge." In *Ancient Grammar and Its Posterior Tradition*, ed. N. Kazansky, V. Mazhuga, I. Medvedev, L. Stepanova, P. Swiggers, and A. Wouters (Leuven): 203–24.
Munzi, L. (2015), Review of Bonnet (2013). *Gnomon* 87: 608–14.
Munzi, L. (2016), "Littera fundamentum sapientiae." *Maia* 68: 46–62.
Murgia, C. E. (1975), *Prolegomena to Servius 5—The Manuscripts* (Berkeley).
Murgia, C. E. (2003), "The Dating of Servius Revisited." *CP* 98: 45–69.
Murgia, C. E. and R. A. Kaster, eds. (2018), *Serviani in Vergili Aeneidos libros IX–XII commentarii* (Oxford).
Mynors, R. A. B., ed. (1937), *Cassiodori Senatoris Institutiones* (Oxford).
Navarro Antolín, F., transl. (2006), *Macrobio: Comentario al "Sueño de Escipión" de Cicerón* (Madrid).
Navarro Antolín, F., transl. (2010), *Macrobio: Saturnales* (Madrid).
Neri, M., ed. (2007), *Macrobio: Commento al Sogno di Scipione* (Milan).
Netz, R., F. Acerbi, and N. G. Wilson (2004), "Towards a Reconstruction of Archimedes' Stomachion." *Sciamus* 5: 67–100.
Niedermann, M., ed. (1937), *Consentii Ars de barbarismis et metaplasmis. Victorini fragmentum de soloecismo et barbarismo* (Neuchâtel).
Norden, E. (1895), *De Stilone Cosconio Varrone grammaticis commentatio* (Greifswald). [Hathi].
North, J. A. (2007), "Why Does Festus Quote What He Quotes?" In Glinister et al.: 49–68.
North, J. A. (2008), "Restoring Festus from Paul's Epitome." *AAntHung* 48: 157–70.
Nosarti, L. (1992), "Questioni metriche. GL VI, 620–625 K.: Fragm. Bob. De uersibus; GL VI, 81,3,3 ss. K.: Apthon., De metris lib. II." *AION (filol)* 14: 65–101.
Noske, G. (1969), *Quaestiones Pseudoacroneae* (Munich).
Ó Cróinín D. (1993), "The Irish as Mediators of Antique Culture on the Continent." In Butzer and Lohrmann 1993: 41–51.
O'Donnell, J. J. (1979), *Cassiodorus* (Berkeley).
Omont, H. (1881), "Grammaire grecque du IXe siècle." *Bibliothèque de l'École des chartes* 42: 126–7.
Oniga, R. (2007), "La teoria delle *conexiones* nella grammatica agostiniana e la sua origine in Varrone." *Augustinianum* 47: 171–8.
Orelli, J. and J. Baiter, eds. (1833), *M. Tullii Ciceronis scholiastae* [= J. Orelli, ed., *M. Tullii Ciceronis Opera*, Vol. 5] (Zurich). [Hathi].
Orlandi, S. (2001), "Un grammatico tardoimperiale tra i senatori del Colosseo?" *RFIC* 129: 422–9.
Oroz Reta, J. and M.-A. Marcos Casquero (2000), *San Isidoro de Sevilla: Etimologías* (ed. 3, Madrid).
Osann, F., ed. (1826), *L. Caecilii Minutiani Apulei De orthographia fragmenta et Apulei minoris De nota aspirationis et De diphthongis libri duo* (Darmstadt). [Hathi].

Ottonello, A. (2008), "Il commento alle *Bucoliche* di Virgilio attribuito a Fulgenzio." *Maia* 60: 424–39.

Pagani, L. (2011), "Pioneers of Grammar: Hellenistic Scholarship and the Study of Language." In *From Scholars to Scholia*, ed. F. Montanari and L. Pagani (Berlin): 17–64.

Pàmias i Massana, J., ed. (2013), *Ératosthène de Cyrène: Catastérismes* (Paris).

Pascucci, G. (1979), "Le componenti linguistiche del latino secondo la dottrina varroniana." In *Studi su Varrone, sulla retorica, storiografica e poesia latina. Scritti in onore di Benedetto Riposati* [no editor] (Milan) 2: 339–63.

Passalacqua, M. (1978), *I codici di Prisciano* (Rome).

Passalacqua, M., ed. (1984), *Tre testi grammaticali Bobbiesi* (Rome).

Passalacqua, M., ed. (1987), *Prisciani Caesariensis Opuscula*, Vol. 1 (Rome).

Passalacqua, M. (1993), "Priscian's *Institutio de nomine et pronomine et verbo* in the Ninth Century." In Law 1993a: 193–204.

Passalacqua, M., ed. (1999), *Prisciani Caesariensis Opuscula*, Vol. 2 (Rome).

Passalacqua, M. (2007), "La nuova *Appendix Probi*." In Lo Monaco and Molinelli 2007: 27–39.

Pecere, O. (1982), "La *subscriptio* di Statilio Massimo." *IMU* 25: 73–123.

Pecere, O. (1984), "Esemplari con *subscriptiones* e tradizione dei testi latini: L'Apuleio Laur. 68,2." In Questa and Raffaelli 1984: 113–37.

Pecere, O. (1986), "La tradizione dei testi latini tra IV e V secolo attraverso I libri sottoscritti." In *Società romana e impero tardoantico* IV: *Tradizione dei classici, trasformazioni della cultura*, ed. A. Giardina (Bari–Rome): 19–81.

Pecere, O. and M. D. Reeve, eds. (1995), *Formative Stages of Classical Traditions: Latin Texts from Antiquity to the Renaissance* (Spoleto).

Pégolo, L. and J. Cardigni (2006), *La música de las esferas: Textos de Cicerón, Macrobio, Favonio* (Buenos Aires).

Pellizzari, A. (2003), *Servio: Storia, cultura e istituzioni nell'opera di un grammatico tardoantico* (Florence).

Pennisi, G. (1963), *Fulgenzio e la Expositio sermonum antiquorum* (Florence).

Pérez, B. and M. Griffe, eds. (2008), *Grammairiens et philosophes dans l'Antiquité gréco-romaine* (Montpellier).

Perutelli, A. (2004), *Prolegomeni a Sisenna* (Pisa).

Pesenti, G. (1917), "Anecdota Latina 1: Paperino." *RFIC* 45: 70–85.

Peterson, W. (1901), *Collations from the Codex Cluniacensis s. Holkhamicus, a Ninth-Century Manuscript of Cicero, now in Lord Leicester's Library at Holkham* (Oxford).

Pezzini, G. and B. Taylor, eds. (forthcoming), *Language and Nature in the Classical Roman World* (Cambridge).

Pfaffel, W. (1981), Quartus gradus etymologiae: *Untersuchungen zur Etymologie Varros in* De lingua Latina (Königstein).

Pfeiffer, R. (1968), *History of Classical Scholarship from the Origins to the End of the Hellenistic Age* (Oxford).

Pieroni, P. (2004), *Marcus Verrius Flaccus'* De significatu verborum *in den Auszügen von Sextus Pompeus Festus und Paulus Diaconus* (Frankfurt).

Pintus, G. M. (2006–7), "'Eucherio Agroecius.'" *Sandalion* 29–30: 145–61.

Piras, G. (1998). *Varrone e i poetica uerba: Studio sul settimo libro del de lingua Latina* (Bologna).

Piras, G. (2015), "*Cum poeticis multis verbis magis delecter quam utar*: Poetic Citations and Etymological Enquiry in Varro's *De lingua Latina*." In Butterfield 2015: 51–70.

Pirovano, L. (2006), *Le "Interpretationes Vergilianae" di Tiberio Claudio Donato: Problemi di retorica* (Rome).

Pisani, V. (1976), "*Non solum ad Aristophanis lucernam, sed etiam Cleanthis*: La teoria grammatica e quella filosofica nell'etimologia di Varrone." In *Atti del congresso internazionale di studi varroniani, Rieti Settembre 1974* [no editor] (Rieti): 1.197–207.
Pizzani, U., ed. (1968), *Fabio Planciade Fulgenzio: Definizione di parole antiche* (Rome).
Pizzani, U. (1985), "Gli scritti grammaticali attributi a S. Agostino." *Augustinianum* 25: 361–83.
Polara, G., ed. (1979), *Virgilio Marone grammatico* (transl. L. Caruso and G. Polara) (Naples).
Polara, G. (1992), "Per un'edizione di Terenziano Mauro." *AION (filol.)* 14: 39–59.
Polara, G. (1993), "Le Dottrine grammaticale di Virgilio Marone." In Law 1993a: 205–22.
Pollock, S. I. (2015), "Introduction." In Pollock et al. 2015: 1–24.
Pollock, S. I., B. Elman, and K. Chang, eds. (2015), *World Philology* (Cambridge, MA).
Popma, A., ed. (1788), *M. Ter. Varronis De lingua Latina libri qui supersunt cum fragmentis ejusdem* (Zweibrücken). [Hathi].
Porter, D., ed. (2002), *Excerptiones de Prisciano: The Source for Aelfric's Latin–Old English Grammar* (Cambridge).
Powell, J. G. F. (2007), "A New Text of the *Appendix Probi.*" *CQ* 57: 687–700.
Powell, J. G. F. (2011), "The *Appendix Probi* as Linguistic Evidence: A Reassessment." In Ferri 2011a: 75–119.
Prete, S. (1970), *Il codice di Terenzio Vaticano Latino 3226* (Vatican).
Pronay, A., ed. (1997), *C. Marius Victorinus, Liber de definitionibus: Eine spätantike Theorie der Definition und der Definierens* (Frankfurt).
Pronay, A., transl. (2014), *Cassiodorus Senator: Einführung in die geistlichen und weltlichen Wissenschaften (Institutiones divinarum et saecularium litterarum)* (Hildesheim).
Pugliarello, M. R., ed. (1978), *Agroecius: Ars de orthographia* (Milan).
Pugliarello, M. R. (1998), "Rassegna di studi sui grammatici latini (1985–1997)." *Bollettino di studi latini* 28: 506–47.
Pugliarello, M. R. (2003), "La Sintassi di Arusiano Messio." In Swiggers and Wouters 2003: 241–53.
Pugliarello, M. R. (2005), "Lingua scritta e lingua parlata nel trattato di Martirio *De b muta et v vocali.*" In Taifacos 2005: 121–9.
Pugliarello, M. R. (2009), "Teoria e prassi dell'*Ars grammatica*: Integrazioni di Servio alle *Artes* di Donato." In *Scuola e trasmissione del sapere tra tarda antichità e Rinascimento*, ed. S. Pittaluga (Genoa): 55–66.
Pugliarello, M. R. (2014), "Da Probo a Probo. Testi in cerca di autore." In *Il falso letterario dall'antichità al rinascimento*, ed. S. Pittaluga (Genoa): 47–66.
Putschen, H., ed. (1605), *Grammaticae Latinae auctores antiqui* (Hanau). [MDZ].
Questa, C. and R. Raffaelli, eds. (1984), *Il libro e il testo* (Urbino).
Quirk, R. (2006), *The "Appendix Probi": A Scholar's Guide to Text and Context* (Newark, DE).
Ramelli, I., ed. (2001), *Marziano Capella: Le nozze di Filologia e Mercurio* (Milan).
Ramelli, I., transl. (2006), *Tutti i commenti a Marziano Capella: Scoto Eriugena, Remigio di Auxerre, Bernardo Silvestre, e Anonimi* (Milan).
Ramires, G., ed. (1996), *Servio: Commento al libro IX dell'Eneide di Virgilio* (Bologna).
Ramires, G., ed. (2003), *Servio: Commento al libro VII dell'Eneide di Virgilio* (Bologna).
Rand, E. K. (1909), "Early Medieval Commentaries on Terence." *CP* 4: 359–89.
Rand, E. K., J. Savage et al., eds. (1946), *Servianorum in Vergilii carmina commentariorum editio Harvardiana*, Vol. 2 (Lancaster).
Rauner-Hafner, G. (1978), "Die Vergilinterpretation des Fulgentius. Bemerkungen zu Gliederung und Absicht der Expositio Vergilianae continentiae." *Mittellateinisches Jahrbuch* 13: 7–49.

Raventós, J., transl. (2003–6), *Macrobi: Les Saturnals* (Barcelona).
Rawson, E. (1985), *Intellectual Life in the Late Roman Republic* (London).
Regali, M., ed. (1983–1990), *Macrobio: Commento al Somnium Scipionis* (Pisa).
Reinhardt, T., ed. (2003), *Cicero's "Topica"* (Oxford).
Reinhardt, T. and M. Winterbottom, eds. (2006), *Quintilian: Institutio oratoria Book 2* (Oxford).
Reinikka, A. (2008), "On the Attribution of a Latin School Grammar Transmitted in Munich Clm 6281." *Arctos* 42: 147–57.
Reinikka, A. (2013), *Ars Pseudo-Scauri: A Critical Edition and Commentary* (Diss. Helsinki).
Reitzenstein, R. (1887), *Verrianische Forschungen* (Breslau).
Reitzenstein, R. (1901), *M. Terentius Varro und Johannes Mauropus von Euchaita: Eine Studie zur Geschichte der Sprachwissenschaft* (Leipzig). [Hathi].
Reppe, R. (1906), *De L. Annaeo Cornuto* (Leipzig). [Hathi].
Reverdin, O., ed. (1963), *Varron* (Geneva).
Ribbeck, O. (1866), *Prolegomena Critica ad P. Vergili Maronis opera maiora* (Leipzig). [Hathi].
Ribémont, B. (2001), *Les origines des encyclopédies mediévales: D'Isidore de Séville aux Carolingiens* (Paris).
Riché, P. (1976), *Education and Culture in the Barbarian West, Sixth through Eighth Centuries*, transl. J. Contreni (Columbia, SC).
Riesenweber, T. (2009), Review of Ippolito (2006). *Gnomon* 81: 25–32.
Riesenweber, T., ed. (2013), *C. Marius Victorinus: Commenta in Ciceronis Rhetorica* (Berlin).
Riesenweber, T. (2015), *C. Marius Victorinus: Commenta in Ciceronis Rhetorica* (Berlin).
Riganti, E., ed. (1978), *Varro De lingua Latina: Libro VI* (Bologna).
Riou, Y.-F. (1973), "Essai sur la tradition manuscrite du *Commentum Brunsianum* des Comédies de Terence." *RHT* 3: 79–113.
Riou, Y.-F. (1997), "Les Commentaires médiévaux de Térence." In Mann and Munk Olsen 1997: 33–49.
Riposati, B. and A. Marastoni (1974), *Bibliografia Varroniana* (Milan).
Ritschl, F. (1866–79), *Opuscula philologica* (Leipzig).
Rizzo, S. (1973), *Il lessico filologico degli umanisti* (Rome).
Robathan, D. and F. E. Cranz (1976), "A. Persius Flaccus." *Catalogus Translationum et Commentariorum* 3: 201–312.
Robert, C., ed. (1878), *Eratosthenis Catasterismorum reliquiae* (Berlin). [Hathi].
Roberts, C. H. (1935), "The Antinoë Fragment of Juvenal." *Journal of Egyptian Archaeology* 21: 199–209.
Rochette, B. (1997), *Le latin dans le monde grec* (Brussels).
Rochette, B. (2014), "*Vtriusque sermonis cognatio*: La lexicographie bilingue à la fin de l'Antiquité." In Martorelli 2014: 3–31.
Rochette, B. (2015), "L'enseignement du latin à Constantinople: Une mise au point." In Haverling 2015: 626–39.
Rodgers, R. H., ed. (1972), *Petri Diaconi: Ortus et vita iustorum cenobii Casinensis* (Berkeley).
Romanini, F., ed. (2007), *Malli Theodori De metris* (Hildesheim).
Rosellini, M. (1998), "Le *Regulae Palaemonis* e le *Regulae Augustini*: Ipotesi su una relazione ambigua." *Riv. Fil.* 126: 414–45.
Rosellini, M. (2000), "Sul testo delle *Regulae Palaemonis*." In De Nonno et al. 2000: 223–41.
Rosellini, M., ed. (2001), *Ps. Remmii Palaemonis Regulae* (Hildesheim).
Rosellini, M. (2006), "Tra linguistica e grammatica antica: Che fine ha fatto il futuro del congiuntivo?" *Atene e Roma* 51: 23–7.

Rosellini, M., ed. (2015), *Prisciani Caesariensis Ars, Liber XVIII, pars altera* (Hildesheim).
Rosenblum, M. (1960), *Luxorius: A Latin Poet among the Vandals* (New York).
Rostagni, A., ed. (1964), *Svetonio "De poetis" e biografi minori* (Turin).
Roth, C., ed. (1877), *C. Suetoni Tranquilli quae supersunt omnia* (Leipzig). [Hathi].
Rutella, F. (1977), "Chi fu Flavio Capro?" *Studi e Ricerche dell'Istituto di Latino* 1: 143–59.
Sabbadini, R. (1900), "L'Ortografia latina di Foca." *RFIC* 28: 529–44.
Sabbadini, R. (1967), *Le scoperte dei codici latini e greci ne' secoli XIV e XV*, ed. 2 by Eugenio Garin (Florence).
Sallmann, N., ed. (1983), *Censorini De die natali liber, accedit anonymi cuiusdam Epitoma disciplinarum (Fragmentum Censorini)* (Leipzig).
Salvadore, M. (1995), *Concordantia Varroniana* (Hildesheim).
Salvadore, M., ed. (1999–), *M. Terenti Varronis fragmenta omnia quae extant* (Hildesheim).
Sanford, E. M. (1960), "Juvenalis, Decimus Junius." *Catalogus Translationum et Commentariorum* 1: 175–238.
San Juan Manso, E. (2013a), "Glosas y comentarios medievales a Terencio: Una hipótesis acerca de la formación del *Commentum Monacense* y de la historia de la comentarística terenciana." *Cuadernos de Filología Clásica. Estudios latinos* 33: 303–27.
San Juan Manso, E. (2013b), "Acerca de los orígenes del *Commentum Monacense* a Terencio." *Euphrosyne* 41: 259–76.
San Juan Manso, E., ed. (2015), *El 'Commentum Monacense' a Terencio* (Vitoria-Gasteiz).
Santini, C. (2014), "Scoliastica staziana: Lattanzio Placido e le due ultime edizioni." In Longobardi et al. 2014: 305–21.
Santini, C. and F. Stok, eds. (2004), *Hinc Italae gentes: Geopolitica ed etnografia dell'Italia nel Commento di Servio all'Eneide* (Pisa).
Savage, J. J. (1925), "The Scholia in the Virgil of Tours, Bernensis 165." *HSCP* 36: 91–164.
Sbordone, F. (1974), "Sul De poematis di Varrone." In *Atti del congresso internazionale di studi varroniani, Rieti Settembre 1974* [no editor] (Rieti): 2.515–24.
Scappaticcio, M. C. (2013), *Papyri Vergilianae* (Liège).
Scappaticcio, M. C., ed. (2015), *"Artes grammaticae" in frammenti: I testi grammaticali latini e bilingui greco-latini su papiro* (Berlin).
Scarpa, L., ed. (1974), *Favonii Eulogii Disputatio de Somnio Scipionis* (Padua).
Scarpa, L., ed. (1981), *Macrobii Ambrosii Theodosii Commentariorum in Somnium Scipionis libri duo* (Padua).
Schad, S. (2007), *A Lexicon of Latin Grammatical Terminology* (Pisa).
Schenkeveld, D. (1990), "Studies in the History of Ancient Linguistics: III. The Stoic ΤΕΧΝΗ ΠΕΡΙ ΦΩΝΗΣ." *Mnemosyne* 43: 86–108.
Schenkeveld, D. (1996), "Charisius, *Ars grammatica* I.15: The Introduction." In Swiggers and Wouters 1996: 17–35.
Schenkeveld, D. (1998), "The Idea of Progress and the Art of Grammar: Charisius *Ars grammatica* 1.15." *AJP* 119: 443–59.
Schenkeveld, D. (2004), *A Rhetorical Grammar: C. Iulius Romanus, Introduction to the Liber de Adverbio* (Leiden).
Schiaparelli, L. (1915), "Segni tachigrafici nelle Notae iuris." *Arch. Stor. Ital.* 73/1: 245–322.
Schindel, U. (1968), "Die Quellen von Bedas Figurenlehre." *Classica et Mediaevalia* 29: 169–86.
Schindel, U. (1975), *Die lateinischen Figurenlehren des 5. bis 7. Jahrhunderts und Donats Vergilkommentar* (Göttingen).
Schindel, U. (1999), "Zur Datierung des Basler Figurentraktats (cod. lat. F III 15d)." *Göttinger Forum für Altertumswissenschaft* 2: 161–78.

Schindel, U. (2002a), "Wechselwirkungen zwischen Autoren-Kommentar und systematischem Lehrbuch." In Geerlings and Schulze 2002–4: 1.103–18.
Schindel, U. (2002b), "'Pompeius auctus' und die Tradition der christlichen Figurenlehre." *Göttinger Forum für Altertumswissenschaft* 5: 255–60.
Schironi, F. (2007), "Αναλογια, *Analogia, Proportio, Ratio*: Loanwords, Calques, and Reinterpretations of a Greek Technical Word." In *Bilinguisme et terminologie grammaticale gréco-latine*, ed. L. Basset, F. Biville, B. Colombat, F. Swiggers, and A. Wouters (Leuven): 321–38.
Schlee, F., ed. (1893), *Scholia Terentiana* (Leipzig). [Hathi].
Schlegelmilch, U. and S. Mayer (2004), "Persiuskommentierung im Ottonischen Köln—zu den Nürnberger Persiushandschriften aus der Bibliothek Ebner." *Würzburger Jahrbücher* 28: 141–73.
Schmidt, P. L. (2008), "(Macrobius) Theodosius und das Personal der *Saturnalia*." *RFIC* 136: 47–83.
Schmitz, W. (1893), *Commentarii notarum tironianarum cum prolegomenis* (Leipzig). [Hathi].
Schnetz, J. (1901), *Ein Kritiker des Valerius Maximus im 9. Jahrhundert* (Neuburg). [Hathi].
Scholz, U., C. Wiener, and U. Schlegelmilch, eds. (2009), *Persius-Scholien: Die lateinische Persius-Kommentierung der Traditionen A, D und E* (Wiesbaden).
Schönberger, A., ed. (2008), *Priscians Darstellung der lateinischen Präpositionen. Lateinischer Text und kommentierte deutsche Übersetzung des 14. Buches der Institutiones Grammaticae.* (Frankfurt)
Schönberger, A., ed. (2009), *Priscians Darstellung der lateinischen Pronomina. Lateinischer Text und kommentierte deutsche Übersetzung des 12. und 13. Buches der Institutiones Grammaticae.* (Frankfurt).
Schönberger, A., ed. (2010a), *Priscians Darstellung der lateinischen Konjunktionen. Lateinischer Text und kommentierte deutsche Übersetzung des 16. Buches der Institutiones Grammaticae.* (Frankfurt).
Schönberger, A., ed. (2010b), *Priscians Darstellung der lateinischen Syntax (I). Lateinischer Text und kommentierte deutsche Übersetzung des 17. Buches der Institutiones Grammaticae.* (Frankfurt).
Schönberger, A., ed. (2010c), *Priscians Darstellung des silbisch gebundenen Tonhöhenmorenakzents des Lateinischen. Lateinischer Text und kommentierte deutsche Übersetzung des Buches über den lateinischen Akzent.* (Frankfurt).
Schönberger, O. and E. Schönberger (2008), *Ambrosius Theodosius Macrobius: Tischgespräche am Saturnalienfest* (Würzburg).
Schorsch, F., ed. (2011), *Das 'Commentum Monacense' zu den Komödien des Terenz. Eine Erstedition des Kommentars zu 'Andria,' 'Heautontimoroumenos,' und 'Phormio'* (Tübingen).
Schröter, R. (1960), *Studien zur varronischen Etymologie, Erster Teil* (Wiesbaden).
Schröter, R. (1963), "Die varronische Etymologie." In Reverdin 1963: 79–100.
Schulz, F. (1946), *History of Roman Legal Science* (Oxford).
Scialuga, M. (1993), "La trattazione sistematica della sillaba nella tarda tradizione metrico-grammaticale latina." *Sileno* 19: 295–360.
Semi, F., ed. (1965), *M. Terentius Varro* (Venice).
Seppänen, M. (2014), *Defining the Art of Grammar: Ancient Perceptions of γραμματική and grammatica* (Turku).
Serbat, G. (1978), "Le 'futur antérieur' chez les grammariens latins." In Collart et al. 1978: 263–72.
Shanzer, D. (1986), *A Philosophical and Literary Commentary on Martianus Capella's* De Nuptiis Philologiae et Mercurii *Book 1* (Berkeley).

Siebenborn, E. (1976), *Die Lehre von der Sprachrichtigkeit und ihren Kriterien: Studien zur antiken normativen Grammatik* (Amsterdam).

Simoni, C. (1988), "Il secondo libro di Sacerdote e i Catholica Probi. Revisione dei testimoni manoscritti." *RFIC* 116: 129–53.

Simoni, C. (1990), "Il De metris di Plozio Sacerdote: una proposta di stemma codicum." In *Dicti Studiosus: Scritti di filologia offeri a Scevola Mariotti dai suoi allievi* [no editor] (Urbino): 209–19.

Slater, D. A. (1927), *Towards a Text of the Metamorphosis of Ovid* (Oxford).

Soraci, Giuseppe, ed. (1988), *Marii Servii Honorati grammatici De centum metris* (L'Aquila).

Squillante Saccone, M. (1985), *Le Interpretationes Vergilianae di Tiberio Claudio Donato* (Naples).

Stahl, W. H., transl. (1952), *Macrobius: Commentary on the Dream of Scipio* (New York). [www.humanitiesbook.org].

Stahl, W. H., R. Johnson, and E. L. Burge, transl. (1971–7), *Martianus Capella and the Seven Liberal Arts* (New York). [www.humanitiesbook.org].

Stangl, T. (1883), "Pseudoboethiana II." *Jahrbücher für class. Philol.* 127: 285–301.

Stangl, T. (1884), *Der sogenannte Gronovscholiast zu elf ciceronischen Reden* (Prague). [Hathi].

Stangl, T. (1888), *Tulliana et Mario-Victoriniana* (Munich). [Hathi].

Stangl, T. (1907), "Erklärung gegen Dr. Paul Hildebrandts Teubneriana der Bobienser Ciceroscholien." *Berliner philologische Wochenschrift* 27: 1501–4.

Stangl, T. (1908a), Review of Hildebrandt (1907). *Berliner philologische Wochenschrift* 28: 38–49.

Stangl, T. (1908b), "Erwiderung." *Berliner philologische Wochenschrift* 28: 477–80.

Stangl, T. (1909), *Pseudoasconiana* (Paderborn). [Hathi].

Stangl, T., ed. (1912), *Ciceronis Orationum scholiastae* (Vienna). [Hathi].

Starr, R. J. (1991), "Explaining Dido to Your Son: Tiberius Claudius Donatus on Vergil's Dido." *CJ* 87: 25–34.

Starr, R. J. (1992), "An Epic of Praise: Tiberius Claudius Donatus and Vergil's *Aeneid*." *Classical Antiquity* 11: 159–74.

Starr, R. J. (1995), "Vergil's Seventh *Eclogue* and Its Readers: Biographical Allegory as an Interpretative Strategy in Antiquity and Late Antiquity." *CP* 90: 129–38.

Steinová, E. (2014), "Carolingian Critters IV: Leiden, Universiteitsbibliotheek, BPL 67F. A Peep into the Workshop of a 'Text Engineer.'" In *Mittelalter. Interdisziplinäre Forschung und Rezeptionsgeschichte*, 30 January 2014, http://mittelalter.hypotheses.org/2929 (accessed 1/28/17).

Steinová, E. (2016), "The List of *Notae* in the *Liber Glossarum*." *Journal of Medieval Latin* 26: 315–62.

Stephanus, H. (1573), *Glossaria duo e situ vetustatis eruta* (Paris). [MDZ].

Steup, J. (1871), *De Probis grammaticis* (Jena). [Hathi].

Stock, B. (1971), "A Note on Thebaid Commentaries: Paris, B.N., lat. 3012." *Traditio* 27: 468–71.

Stock, C., ed. (2005), *Sergius (Ps.-Cassiodorus): Commentarium de oratione et de octo partibus orationis artis secundae Donati* (Munich).

Stocker, A. and A. Travis, eds. (1965), *Servianorum in Vergilii carmina commentariorum editio Harvardiana*, Vol. 3 (Oxford).

Stok, F. (1991), *Prolegomeni a una nuova edizione della* Vita Vergilii *di Svetonio–Donato* (Rome).

Stok, F., ed. (1997), *Appendix Probi IV* (Naples).

Stok, F. (1999), "La silloge differentiarum del Neap. lat. 2." *Vichiana* s.IV, 1: 89–104.

Stok, F. (2008), "Servio fra sinonimia e *differentiae verborum*." In Casali and Stok 2008: 132–58.

Stok, F. (2010), "The Life of Vergil before Donatus." In *Blackwell Companions to the Ancient World: Companion to Vergil's Aeneid and Its Tradition*, ed. J. Farrell and M. Putnam (Chichester): 107–20.

Stok, F. (2012a), "Commenting on Virgil, from Aelius Donatus to Servius." *Dead Sea Discoveries* 19: 464–84.

Stok, F. (2012b), "Servio e le *differentiae verborum*." In Zumbo 2012: 97–105.

Stok, F., ed. (2013), *Totus scientia plenus: Percorsi dell'esegesi virgiliana antica* (Pisa).

Stok, F. (2014), "Esegesi antiche della sesta egloga." In Longobardi et al. 2014: 151–76.

Stokes, L. C. (1972), "Fulgentius: *Expositio virgilianae continentiae.*" *CF* 26: 27–63.

Stoppacci, P., ed. (2010), *Cassiodoro De orthographia* (Florence).

Stoppacci, P. (2012), "Le Fonti del *De orthographia* di Cassiodoro: Modalità di ricezione e fruizione." In Biville et al. 2012: 739–51.

Strecker, K. (1922), "Studien zu karolingischen Dichtern." *Neues Archiv* 43: 479–511.

Strecker, K., ed. (1937), *Die lateinischen Dichter des deutschen Mittelalters*, Vol. 5 (Leipzig). [www.dmgh.de].

Strzelecki, W. (1932), *Quaestiones Verrianae* (Warsaw).

Strzelecki, W. (1932–3), "Zur Entstehung der *Compendiosa doctrina* des Nonius." *Eos* 34: 113–29.

Strzelecki, W. (1936), *De Flavio Capro Nonii auctore* (Cracow).

Strzelecki, W. (1938), "De Velii Longi auctoribus quaestiones." *Eos* 39: 11–27.

Strzelecki, W. (1949), *De Ps.-Capri "Orthographia"* (Bratislava).

Stump, E., transl. (1988), *Boethius's "In Ciceronis Topica"* (Ithaca).

Suringar, W. (1834–5), *Historia critica scholiastarum Latinorum* (Leiden). [Hathi].

Sweeney, R. D. (1969), *Prolegomena to an Edition of the Scholia to Statius* (Leiden).

Sweeney, R. D., ed. (1997), *Lactantii Placidi in Statii Thebaida commentum* (Stuttgart).

Swiggers, P. and A. Wouters, eds. (1996), *Ancient Grammar: Content and Context* (Leuven).

Swiggers, P. and A. Wouters, eds. (2002a), *Grammatical Theory and Philosophy of Language in Antiquity* (Leuven).

Swiggers, P. and A. Wouters (2002b), "*De adverbio*: Statut et significations de l'adverbe chez les grammairiens latins." In Swiggers and Wouters 2002a: 287–323.

Swiggers, P. and A. Wouters, eds. (2003), *Syntax in Antiquity* (Leuven).

Swiggers, P. and A. Wouters (2010), "Condensed Grammatical Knowledge in Antiquity: Doxographical Accounts of the Parts-of-Speech System." In Horster and Reitz 2010: 135–63.

Swoboda, A., ed., (1889), *P. Nigidii Figuli operum reliquiae* (Vienna). [Hathi].

Syska, E. (1993), *Studien zur Theologie im ersten Buch der Saturnalien des Ambrosius Theodosius Macrobius* (Stuttgart).

Szerwiniack, O. (2003), "L'Irlande médievale et la culture antique." In Lardet 2003: 85–105.

Taeger, B. (1978), "Exzerpte aus Martianus Capella in einer frühen hibernolateinischen Grammatik (Anonymus ad Cuimnanum)." *Beiträge zur Geschichte der deutschen Sprache und Literatur* 100: 388–420.

Taeger, B. (1991), "Multiplex enim ut lex Dei etiam Latinitas." *Studi Medievali* 32: 1–91.

Taifacos, I. G. (1983), "The Lexicographical Work of Caesellius Vindex and Its Arrangement." *Hermes* 111: 501–5.

Taifacos, I., ed. (2005), *The Origins of European Scholarship* (Stuttgart).

Takács, L. (2004), "The Story of a Fragment of L. Annaeus Cornutus." *AAntHung.* 44: 35–46.

Tannenhaus, G. H. (1962), "Bede's *De Schematibus et Tropis*: A Translation." *Quarterly Journal of Speech* 48: 237–53.

Tarrant, R. J. (1995), "The *Narrationes* of 'Lactantius' and the Transmission of Ovid's *Metamorphoses*." In Pecere and Reeve 1995: 83–115.

Tarver, T. (2007), "Varro and the Antiquarianism of Philosophy." In *Philosophia Togata II*, ed. J. Barnes and M. Griffin (Oxford): 130–64.
Taylor, D. J. (1974), *Declinatio: A Study of the Linguistic Theory of Marcus Terentius Varro* (Amsterdam).
Taylor, D. J. (1977), "Varro's Mathematical Models of Inflection." *TAPA* 107: 313–23.
Taylor, D. J. (1986), "Rethinking the History of Language Science in Classical Antiquity." *Historiographia Linguistica* 13: 175–90.
Taylor, D. J., ed. (1996), *Varro De lingua Latina X* (Philadelphia).
Taylor, D. J. (2015), "The New Varro and the Structure of His *De Lingua Latina*." In Butterfield 2015: 19–31.
Teeuwen, M. and S. O'Sullivan, eds. (2011), *Carolingian Scholarship and Martianus Capella: Ninth-Century Commentary Traditions on "De nuptiis" in Context* (Turnhout).
Tempesti, A. M. (1977), "Quinto Terenzio Scauro, grammatico adrianeo." *Studi e ricerche dell'Istituto di Latino* 1: 175–220.
Thilo, G., ed. (1881–7), *Servii Grammatici qui feruntur in Vergilii carmina commentarii* (Leipzig). [Vol. 1 Hathi].
Thomas, E. (1880), *Scholiastes de Virgile: Essai sur Servius et son Commentaire sur Virgil d'après les manuscrits de Paris et les publications les plus récentes* (Paris). [Hathi].
Timpanaro, S. (1978), *Contributi di filologia e di storia della lingua latina* (Rome).
Timpanaro, S. (1986), *Per la storia della filologia virgiliana antica* (Rome).
Timpanaro, S. (1994), *Nuovi contributi di filologia e di storia della lingua latina* (Bologna).
Timpanaro, S. (2001), *Virgilianisti antichi e tradizione indiretta* (Florence).
Tolkiehn, J. (1910), *Cominianus: Beiträge zur römischen Literaturgeschichte* (Leipzig). [Hathi].
Tolkiehn, J., ed. (1913), *Dosithei Ars grammatica* (Leipzig). [Hathi].
Tolkiehn, J. (1916), *Philologische Streifzüge* (Leipzig). [Hathi].
Tolkiehn, J., ed. (1928), *Clementis Ars grammatica* (Leipzig). [Gallica].
Tomsin, A. (1952), *Étude sur le Commentaire Virgilien d'Aemilius Asper* (Paris).
Torzi, I. (2000), *Ratio et usus: Dibattiti antichi sulla dottrina delle figure* (Milan).
Townend, G. (1972), "The Earliest Scholiast on Juvenal." *CQ* 22: 376–87.
Traglia, A. (1963), "Dottrine etimologiche ed etimologie varroniane con particolare riguardo al linguaggio poetico." In Reverdin 1963: 31–67.
Traglia, A., ed. (1974), *Opere di Marco Terenzio Varrone* (Turin).
Traube, L., ed. (1896), *Poetae Latini Aevi Carolini*, Vol. 3 (Berlin). [www.dmgh.de].
Traube, L. (1907), *Nomina Sacra* (Munich). [Hathi].
Traube, L. (1920), *Vorlesungen und Abhandlungen*, Vol. 3: *Kleine Schriften*, ed. S. Brandt (Munich). [Hathi].
Uhl, A. (1998), *Servius als Sprachlehrer: Zur Sprachrichtigkeit in der exegetischen Praxis des spätantiken Grammatikerunterrichts* (Göttingen).
Uhlfelder, M. L. (1954), *De Proprietate sermonum vel rerum: A Study and Critical Edition of a Set of Verbal Distinctions* (Rome).
Upson, H. (1943), "Medieval Lives of Virgil." *CP* 38: 103–11.
Uría Varela, J. (2005), "What Can We Learn from Place-Names in Charisius' *Ars grammatica*?" In Taifacos 2005: 99–107.
Uría Varela, J., transl. (2009), *Carisio: Arte gramática, Libro I* (Madrid).
Uría Varela, J. (2012), "Iulius Romanus and Statilius Maximus (Char. Gramm. 252, 14–31): A Reappraisal." *MD* 69: 225–38.
Uría Varela, J. (2016), "*Nomen an adverbium?* Latin Grammarians on the Adverb." In Ferri and Zago 2016: 123–44.
Usener, H., ed. (1869), *M. Annaei Lucani Commenta Bernensia* (Leipzig). [Hathi].

Usener, H. (1913), *Kleine Schriften*, Vol. 2: *Arbeiten zur Lateinischen Sprache und Literatur* (Leipzig). [Hathi].
van den Hout, M. (1999), *A Commentary on the Letters of M. Cornelius Fronto* (Leiden).
van de Vyver, A. (1935), "Dicuil et Micon de Saint-Riquier." *Revue Belge* 14: 25–47.
van de Vyver, A. (1941), "Les *Institutiones* de Cassiodore et sa fondation à Vivarium." *Revue Bénédictine* 53: 59–88.
van de Woestijne, P. (1950), "Les scolies à la 'Thébaïde' de Stace: Remarques et suggestions." *L'Antiquité Classique* 19: 149–63.
van Weddingen, R.-E., ed. (1957), *Favonii Eulogii Disputatio de Somnio Scipionis* (Brussels).
Vardi, A. (2001), "Gellius against the Professors." *ZPE* 137: 41–54.
Velaza, J., ed. (2005), *M. Valeri Probi Beryti fragmenta* (Barcelona).
Victor, B. (2013), "History of the Text and Scholia." In *Blackwell Companions to the Ancient World: Companion to Terence*, ed. A. Augoustakis and A. Traill (Somerset, NJ): 343–62.
Villa, C. (1984), *La "Lectura Terentii"* (Padua).
Villa, C. (1995), "La tradizione di Orazio e 'la biblioteca di Carlo Magno': Per l'elenco di opere nel codice Berlin Diez. B. 66." In Pecere and Reeve 1995: 299–322.
Villa, C. (2007), "Commenti medioevali alle commedie di Terenzio." In Kruschwitz et al.: 29–35.
Vineis, E. (1994), "Medieval Linguistics." In Lepschy 1994: 2.134–272.
Vitale, M. T. (1977), "Cesellio Vindice." *Studi e ricerche dell'Istituto di Latino* 1: 221–58.
Vitale, M. T. (1982), "Per una terminologia grammaticale: παρεπόμενα—accidentia." *Studi e ricerche* 5: 199–222.
Volk, K. (2017), "Varro and the Disorder of Things." *HSCP* 110 (forthcoming).
Volk, K. and J. E. G. Zetzel (2015), "Laurel, Tongue, and Glory (Cicero, De consulatu suo fr. 6 Soubiran)." *Classical Quarterly* 65: 204–23.
von Büren, V. (2010), "Le Juvénal des Carolingiens à la lumière du MS Cambridge Kings College 52." *Antiquité Tardive* 18: 115–37.
von Fritz, K. (1949), "Ancient Instruction in 'Grammar' According to Quintilian." *AJP* 70: 337–66.
Wallace-Hadrill, A. (2008), *Rome's Cultural Revolution* (Cambridge).
Waszink, J. H. (1948), "Varro, Livy and Tertullian on the History of Roman Dramatic Art." *VChr* 2: 224–42.
Watson, A. (1968), *The Law of Property in the Later Roman Republic* (Oxford).
Weber, C. F., ed. (1831), *Marci Annaei Lucani Pharsalia, Volumen tertium continens scholiastas* (Leipzig). [Hathi].
Weber, C. F., ed. (1861), *Aurelii Augustini Ars grammatica breviata* (Marburg). [Hathi].
Weijers, O. (1989), "Lexicography in the Middle Ages." *Viator* 20: 139–53.
Weiss, E. (1933), "Notae iuris." *Zeitschrift der Savigny-Stiftung für Rechtsgeschichte, Romanistische Abteilung* 53: 482–8.
Welsh, J., (2010), "The Grammarian C. Iulius Romanus and the *Fabula togata*." *HSCP* 105: 255–85.
Welsh, J. (2011a), "Accius, Porcius Licinus, and the Beginning of Latin Literature." *JRS* 101: 31–50.
Welsh, J. (2011b), "Evanthius *De fabula* 3.5 and Varro on ἤθη and πάθη." *Hermes* 139: 485–93.
Welsh, J. (2012), "The Methods of Nonius Marcellus' Sources 26, 27 and 28." *CQ* 62: 827–45.
Werner, S. (1994), "On the History of the *Commenta Bernensia* and the *Adnotationes super Lucanum*." *HSCP* 96: 343–68.
Werner, S. (1998), *The Tradition and Scholia to Lucan's* Bellum civile (Hamburg).

Wessner, P. (1893), *Quaestiones Porphyrioneae* (Leipzig). [Hathi].

Wessner, P., ed. (1899), *Fabii Planciadis Fulgentii Expositio sermonum antiquorum. Commentationes Philologae Ienenses* 6: 2.63–143. [Hathi].

Wessner, P. (1902), "Bericht über die Erscheinungen auf dem Gebiete der lateinischen Grammatiker mit Einschluss der Scholienliteratur und Glossographie für 1891–1901." *Jahresbericht über die Fortschritte der classischen Altertumswissenschaft* 113: 113–227.

Wessner, P., ed. (1902–8), *Aeli Donati Commentum Terenti. Accedunt Eugraphi commentum et scholia Bembina* (Leipzig). Note that the Bembine scholia were never published in this edition; all that exists is Vol. 1–2 (Donatus) and Vol. 3.1 (Eugraphius). [Hathi].

Wessner, P. (1905), *Aemilius Asper: Ein Beitrag zur römischen Literaturgeschichte* (Halle). [Hathi].

Wessner, P. (1907), "Der Terenzkommentar des Eugraphius." *RhM* 62: 203–28, 339–65.

Wessner, P. (1908), "Bericht über die Erscheinungen auf dem Gebiete der lateinischen Grammatiker mit Einschluß der Scholienliteratur und Glossographie für 1901–1907." *Jahresbericht über die Fortschritte der klassischen Altertumswissenschaft* 139: 81–210.

Wessner, P. (1921), "Bericht über die Erscheinungen auf dem Gebiete der lateinischen Grammatiker mit Einschluß der Scholienliteratur und Glossographie für 1908–1920." *Jahresbericht über die Fortschritte der klassischen Altertumswissenschaft* 188: 34–254.

Wessner, P. (1929), "Lucan, Statius und Juvenal bei den römischen Grammatikern." *Philol. Woch.* 49: 296–303, 328–35.

Wessner, P., ed. (1931), *Scholia in Iuvenalem vetustiora* (Leipzig).

Wessner, P., ed. (1968), *Ciceros Rede für T. Annius Milo mit dem Kommentar des Asconius und den Bobienser Scholien* (ed. 2, Berlin).

Whitbread, L. G., transl. (1971), *Fulgentius the Mythographer* (Columbus).

White, D. C. (1980), "The Method of Composition and the Sources of Nonius Marcellus." *Studi Noniani* 8: 111–211.

Widmann, S. (1883), "Differentiae sermonum." *Neue Jahrbücher für Philologie und Paedagogik* 127: 649–52.

Wieacker, F. (1960), *Textstufen klassischer Juristen* (Göttingen).

Wieacker, F. (2006), *Römische Rechtsgeschichte, Zweiter Abschnitt: Die Jurisprudenz vom frühen Prinzipat bus zum Ausgang der Antike* (Munich).

Wiener, C. (2002), "Persius-Kommentierung vom 10. bis 15. Jahrhundert: Beobachtungen zur handschriflichen Überlieferung der sog. Tradition A." *Würzburger Jahrbücher* 26: 171–83.

Willis, J., ed. (1970a), *Ambrosii Theodosii Macrobii Saturnalia* (ed. 2, Leipzig).

Willis, J., ed. (1970b), *Ambrosii Theodosii Macrobii Commentarii in Somnium Scipionis* (ed. 2, Leipzig).

Willis, J., ed. (1983), *Martianus Capella* (Leipzig).

Wilmanns, A. (1864), *De M. Terenti Varronis libris grammaticis* (Berlin). [Hathi].

Wolff, É. (2003), "Fulgence et l'*Expositio sermonum antiquorum*." In *Autour de Lactance: Hommages à Pierre Monat*, ed. Jean-Yves Guillaumin and Stéphane Ratti, (Franche-Comté), 197–203.

Wolff, É. (2008), "Vergil and Fulgentius." *Vergilius* 54: 59–69.

Wolff, É., ed. (2009), *Virgile dévoilé* (Villeneuve-d'Ascq).

Wolff, É. (2010), "Retour sur la datation et l'origine de Lactantius Placidus, commentateur de Stace." *Phoenix* 64: 423–9.

Wolff, É. and P. Dain, eds. (2013), *Fulgence: Mythologies* (Villeneuve-d'Ascq).

Wölfflin, E. (1908), "Die Interpretationes Vergilianae des Claudius Donatus." *ALL* 15: 253–60.

Woods, C. (2007), "A Contribution to the King's Library: Paul the Deacon's Epitome and Its Carolingian Context." In Glinister et al. 2007: 109–35.

Wouters, A. (1979), *The Grammatical Papyri from Graeco-Roman Egypt: Contributions to the Study of the 'Ars Grammatica' in Antiquity* (Brussels).

Yanes, E. S., ed. (2017), *Prisciani Caesariensis Ars, liber XVIII, Pars altera* (Hildesheim).

Zago, A. (2010), "Alla scuola del *grammaticus*: Maestri, allievi e testi nella tarda antichità." *Rassegna di pedagogia* 68: 201–18.

Zago, A., ed. (2017), *Pompeii Commentum in Artis Donati partem tertiam* (Hildesheim).

Zekl, H. G., transl. (2005), *Die Hochzeit der Philologia mit Merkur* (Würzburg).

Zelzer, M. (1995), "La tarda antichità." In Cavallo et al. 1995: 301–38.

Zetzel, J. E. G. (1973), "*Emendavi ad Tironem*: Some Notes on Scholarship in the Second Century A.D." *HSCP* 77: 225–43.

Zetzel, J. E. G. (1974). "Statilius Maximus and Ciceronian Studies in the Antonine Age." *BICS* 21: 107–23.

Zetzel, J. E. G. (1975), "On the History of Latin Scholia." *HSCP* 79: 335–54.

Zetzel, J. E. G. (1980), "The Subscriptions in the Manuscripts of Livy and Fronto and the Meaning of *Emendatio*." *CP* 75: 38–59.

Zetzel, J. E. G. (1981), *Latin Textual Criticism in Antiquity* (New York).

Zetzel, J. E. G. (1996), "Natural Law and Poetic Justice: A Carneadean Debate in Cicero and Virgil." *CP* 91: 297–319.

Zetzel, J. E. G. (2002), Review of Timpanaro (2001). *BMCR* 2002.02.09.

Zetzel, J. E. G. (2005), *Marginal Scholarship and Textual Deviance: The* Commentum Cornuti *and the Early Scholia on Persius* (London).

Zetzel, J. E. G. (2015), "The Bride of Mercury: Confessions of a 'Pataphilologist." In Pollock et al. 2015: 43–62, 339–43.

Zetzel, J. E. G. (forthcoming), "Natural Law and Natural Language in the First Century BCE." In Pezzini and Taylor forthcoming.

Ziolkowski, J. and M. C. J. Putnam, eds. (2008), *The Virgilian Tradition: The First Fifteen Hundred Years* (New Haven).

Zorzetti, N., ed. (1995), *Le premier mythographe du Vatican* (Paris).

Zumbo, A., ed. (2012), *Atti del Seminario internazionale di studi Il testo e i suoi commenti: tradizione ed esegesi nella scoliastica greca e latina: Messina, 21–22 settembre 2000* (Messina).

Index

Major bibliographic references are in **bold**; references to quotations are listed at the end of the relevant entries. Familiar names rather than formal Roman nomenclature are used for authors and important figures; thus "Cicero", not "Tullius Cicero, Marcus." For manuscript citations see 367–74.